Rethinking Development *and* Politics

Rethinking DEVELOPMENT *and* Politics

Essays on India, China and Global Change

MEGHNAD DESAI

Edited by Marika Vicziany

SPEAKING TIGER

in association with MONASH University Publishing

SPEAKING TIGER PUBLISHING PVT. LTD
4381/4, Ansari Road, Daryaganj
New Delhi – 110002

First published by Monash University Publishing
Published in India by Speaking Tiger 2019

ISBN: 978-93-88874-25-0
eISBN: 978-93-88874-26-7

10 9 8 7 6 5 4 3 2 1

Printed at Repro India

CONTENTS

PREFACE

Professor Lord Meghnad Jagdishchandra Desai has been an outstanding scholar, policy advisor and public intellectual in India, many other countries in Asia, the USA and Britain. Monash University Publishing is privileged to bring together this first volume of his unpublished and difficult-to-access publications spanning some four decades of thinking.

Lord Desai began life as a precocious child. Born in Vadodara (Gujarat) in 1940, he attended secondary school when he was only 7 years old and matriculated when he was 14. He began his Masters work at Bombay University where he met Professor Charles Whittlesey, Professor of Money and Banking at Pennsylvania University and Visiting Ford Foundation Fellow. He was encouraged to study in the US and in 1961 arrived in Pennsylvania with a Ford Foundation Scholarship. Throughout his early life, Professor Desai hated mathematics but ironically in the US he was assigned as a research assistant to Lawrence Klein who assumed that his new student was a maths buff. Thanks to Klein's personal tuition, Lord Desai quickly learned econometrics (i.e. mathematical economics and model building) and completed his doctoral thesis on the subject of 'An Econometric Model of the World Tin Economy' in 1963. He then found himself working as a Research Officer in the Department of Agricultural Economics, University of California building econometric models about the determination of milk prices.

Like many other young scholars at this time, the Vietnam War and America's involvement made Professor Desai critical of US foreign policy. This, together with the risks of being drafted into the US military in the event that he was allowed to stay, compelled him to leave the USA for a more neutral country, namely England, where he arrived to take up a lectureship at the London School of Economics (LSE) in 1965. His reading of Karl Marx, together with his left wing attraction to the Marxian inspired student movement, were also factors that convinced him to leave.

During his early years at the LSE Lord Desai was determined to shed his image of being a numbers man and authority on tin and milk. He began to familiarise himself with the lively debates that were taking place in the West about economics, Keynes, economic history, development economics and poverty. These interests were reflected in his establishing at the LSE the Centre for the Study of Global Governance in 1992. At the LSE he also befriended A. K. Sen, whose ideas on inequality influenced him as much as Marx. Despite his hatred of mathematics, Professor Desai came to love econometrics and published his study of *Applied Econometrics* in 1976 but only after publishing a book about his first love in 1973, namely *Marxian Economic Theory*. Professor Desai's introductory essay to this collection, explains in greater detail the evolution of his ideas since then.

Apart from Marx, Professor Desai's big love has been for Dilip Kumar, perhaps India's most famous film star. Born in 1922, Dilip Kumar's life spanned the turbulent years of India's independence movement – something that Professor Desai has sought to commemorate with his opening in Amritsar of the Partition Museum in 2017. In 2004 Professor Desai published *Nehru's Hero Dilip Kumar: In the Life of India*. The title of the book again reveals the close connection in Professor Desai's thinking between the world of art and politics. His great admiration for Dilip Kumar led him to Roli Books who appointed a personal editor for this work – Kishwar Desai. She subsequently became his second wife.

Lord Desai's life as a public intellectual in Europe, America and India has been reflected in his membership of many high-level policy committees, his work as a journalist for leading newspapers such as *Indian Express* amongst others and acting as a media commentator. A lesser known part of his life is his involvement with various entrepreneurial ventures as documented by Bloomberg: for example he has been a Non-Executive Independent Director of Elara Securities (India) Private Limited since 21 December 2011. By contrast, his contributions to the British Labour Party, Finsbury Constituency Labour Party and Islington South are well known and admired. In recognition of this work, he was made a life peer of St. Clement Danes in Westminster and was honoured as 'Baron Desai'. Since retiring from the LSE in 2003 he has continued there as Emeritus Professor in addition to serving in the House of Lords as a major participant in various policy debates including Brexit.

In India, his public life has focused on analysing the political and economic trends of the liberalisation of the economy that began in 1991. From about the same time, significant shifts were occurring in Indian politics with the rise of the Bharatiya Janata Party. The essays in this collection reflect his thoughts on these changes. As always, Professor Desai's personal political preferences play a secondary role to his defence of democracy. As he argued in his opinion piece in *Indian Express* on 26 June 2016 the vote in favour of Brexit was 'a strange idea for a country which is the oldest continuous polity in Europe. The notion that joining a multi-country union is a loss of independence is hard to credit. But ultimately that is the message the people have given'. In other words, whatever the electorate has decided that is what parliaments need to act on. In an age defined by strong ideological positions, Lord Desai's defence of democracy via the electoral process is unfashionable.

His many achievements have been admired with public recognition given in awards such as the prestigious Padmabhusan in 2007 by the Indian government. Numerous universities have also awarded him Honorary Doctorates, including Monash University in 2005. His long association with Monash University began in the 1980s and has included short-term lecturing and fellowship appointments, acting as keynote speaker at various Australian and international conferences, and supporting the work of scholars in the humanities and economics with suggestions about their work and that by their doctoral students. Professor Desai has been a dynamic and razor-sharp commentator on world affairs, but in a generous and humorous manner that wins friends despite the vigour of his arguments. Given the international interest in his work, it is a testament to Lord Desai's involvement with Australian public and academic life that he approached Monash University to bring out this volume.

In concluding this preface I would like to thank all the publishers who kindly agreed to allow Monash University Publishing to republish many of the chapters in this volume. The original publisher is fully acknowledged at the end of each chapter.

Professor Emerita Marika Vicziany
Editor
Director, National Centre for South Asian Studies,
Monash Asia Institute, Monash University

INTRODUCTION

This book brings together various essays I have written singly or jointly over the last thirty years. They were written for conferences, for edited collections, as single 'Working Papers' or in literary magazines (such as the *IIC Quarterly* – India International Centre Quarterly). They all relate to political economy but in a global context as well as against the background of the tensions between national strategies and globalisation.

The essays have been arranged thematically rather than chronologically. The first section relates to the theme of globalisation. Today we debate the threat to globalisation and the rise of nationalism. The election of Donald Trump has started a debate as to whether the long period of freer trade, liberal economic policy and sustained economic and political cooperation between the principal powers – G7 or G20 – is about to end. Will the Davos Man soon be a thing of the past?[1]

It is hard to remember that at the outset of the 1990s 'globalisation' was a new buzz word, a word that inspired fear and scepticism. But was there such a thing as globalisation? On the one hand there was the collapse of the Soviet Union and with it the salience of the alternative to capitalism. Suddenly we were in a unipolar world with the USA as the sole hyperpower. The world was going to be borderless; the Earth was flat; it was the End of History – titles given to oft-quoted books at the time.

I was lucky to have a perch from where to chart the progress of globalisation. At the London School of Economics, in 1991, I was able to establish a Centre for the Study of Global Governance thanks to some generous research grants. This led me to add global political economy to my extensive research portfolio. The first chapter in the present collection is a product of this Centre. It was the introductory chapter in the first edited collection of articles the Centre published.[2] This is a sort of general introduction to what globalisation means.

But very soon it became clear that globalisation was not to everyone's liking. Trade unions in richer countries could see that freer trade which had benefited them since the end of the Second World War was taking

---

1 In this respect see my recent book *Politicshock: Trump, Modi, Brexit and the Prospect for Liberal Democracy* (Delhi: Rupa Publications, 2017).

2 *Global, Governance: Ethics and Economics of the World Order*, edited by Meghnad Desai and Paul Redfern. (London: Pinter Publishers, 1995).

jobs away to Asia. Whereas earlier anti-capitalist movements were in the 'periphery' and not in the 'metropolis' (to use words from the 1960s), now the shoe was on the other foot. The Seattle meeting of the World Trade Organization (WTO) was disrupted by American trade unions and radical groups. Many misunderstood this as a progressive left wing movement but I could see that this was a defence of established privilege.[3]

What was clear (at least to me) was that the widespread enthusiasm for globalisation was fragile and depended on the perceived distribution of benefits from globalisation. This is where the essay on the 'The Possibility of Deglobalisation' comes from. It was 2003 and too early for deglobalisation to occur but the warnings were there.

The early Davos meetings also witnessed the arrival of a global protest movement, the Social Summit, which often met in parallel. The two essays co-authored with Yahia Said examine that phenomenon. The fear that rapid growth may affect sustainability is examined in the 1996 essay.

The happy saga of globalisation was interrupted by the financial crash of 2008. Paradoxically the progressive left movements were more worried than ever before. As it was, the almost two decades of globalisation along with the financial revolution, had spread benefits all around. The so-called Third World countries became Emerging Economies and the acronym BRICS[4] was invented by Jim (now Lord) O'Neill of Goldman Sachs. Welfare states had become smarter and more market friendly in the developed countries but as there was sustained growth, everyone – Left and Right – was happy. There was a convergence between Left and Right and politicians such as Bill Clinton and Tony Blair announced the emergence of the Radical Centre. The crisis brought the reality of open economies with a global capital market to the fore. Keynesian-style deficit spending was ruled as being against the dictates of the global capital markets. The crisis of 2008 forced austerity and hardships onto the developed countries. There was fear that social democratic movements would be threatened with an existential crisis. The Helsinki essay on the future of social democracy addresses that question.

I was lucky in spotting the distinct 'charm' of Donald Trump before he even won the Republican nomination. This was when he expounded his economic philosophy during the election campaign. In a world where

3 See my chapter 'Seattle: A Tragi-Comedy' in B. Gunell and D. Times (eds), *After Seattle: Globalisation and Its Discontents* (London: Catalyst Aldgate Press, 2000).

4 BRICS refers to the five new emerging economies: Brazil, Russia, India, China and South Africa.

austerity had become the orthodoxy and debt was a dirty word, he had a plan to repair the public infrastructure of the US. The essay on the political economy of Donald Trump is an attempt at taking Trump seriously and sees him as an unorthodox 'Keynesian' politician. As an unorthodox politician, Trump also recognises that for a developed country, globalisation has ceased to be an advantage. The economic baton has passed to Asia from the West. Few could have seen, in May 2016 when the essay was written, that he would be elected. I was glad to have sensed that here was someone unusual whatever his style.

The second section of this book traces the truly revolutionary result of the phase of globalisation. This was the rapid rise of Asia especially of China and, to a lesser extent, India. Henry Kissinger had said in the mid-1960s that if only China and India could feed themselves, the world would have no other problems. Few could have foreseen that China would achieve a double digit growth rate for over three decades and end up with the second largest GDP in the world. Asians no longer complain that they are victims of multinationals or of global capitalism. They have become competitive in the manufacturing sector and China has even taken on the IT giants at their own game with Huawei and Alibaba.

There has been a sort of informal race between China and India through the second half of the twentieth century. In the Cold War years, it was democracy versus communism. But as late as 1975 the two were equally poor despite following different political paths. In 1991, India changed its policy and became more open while China had already moved in that direction after 1979 thanks to Deng Xiaoping's initiatives.

The second section begins with an essay in the *longue durée* style comparing China and India. Another essay pursues the same theme of the possibility of catch up between India and China. As of now there is little doubt that China has marched way ahead of India. What the next few decades will show is anyone's guess.

One of the reasons for the slow progress of India has to do with the way development has been understood as a phenomenon. The theory of development itself is a product of the post-1945 years. Initially the urgent problem was seen to be South Eastern Europe. But decolonisation coincided with the rise of development economics. India was the largest open economy which posed a severe challenge for development theorists. India's problems occupied many economists, Indian and foreign. I survey fifty years of 'Development Thinking' in the essay here but it is very much India centred.

Indian debates on development even after all these years continue to bear the birthmarks of an ex-colony. There is suspicion of business, especially of foreign capital, distrust of the market and a love for government regulations and an eagerness to surrender to populist pressures for subsidies whatever the fiscal costs.

The third and last section of this collection is exclusively on the political economy of India over the last twenty-five years, i.e. since the reforms of 1991. Over the same period there has been as much change in the political situation of India as in its economic record. The rise of the BJP (Bharatiya Janata Party) was hardly on anyone's mind at the outset. The first victory of the BJP in 1996 was not sufficient for it to form the government but the arrival of the BJP was a shock to the Indian political system. Few had taken the party seriously except for its 'Hindu nationalist' ideology. I began to study its economic policy and the essay here is one of the first, if not *the* first to do so. I should acknowledge the generous hospitality of the National Centre for South Asian Studies in Melbourne which made it possible.

The BJP did finally form the government in 1998 and ruled till 2004. Its defeat in 2004 was a surprise. I discuss it here in my essay about the '*Hindutva's* March Halted?' (i.e. Hindu nationalism). The Congress-led coalition ruled for ten years but it was beginning to falter. This is the background to the essay 'Could Indian Economy Do Better?'[5] Now of course the BJP is back in power under the leadership of Narendra Modi who has tried to speed up the pace of development. But even so, the growth rate fluctuates and reforms face obstacles. The longer run outlook for India is hopeful but the short run shocks still abound.

The rest of the essays in the third section relate to India more generally. There is an essay on the perennially difficult subject of Kashmir. The last essay is an introductory attempt at my critique of the Bhagavad Gita about which I authored a book.[6] This detour from political economy was undertaken by me as a corrective to the revival of a somewhat unquestioning and irrational respect for the ancient texts. The return of the BJP has encouraged a literal interpretation of ancient 'holy' works. I want to propose a rational explanation for one such much revered text.

The book would not have been possible without the enterprise and heroic effort on the part of my friend Professor Marika Vicziany (assisted by Ifti

---

5 See my recent book *The Raisina Model: Indian Democracy at 70* (Delhi: Penguin, 2017).

6 *Who Wrote The Bhagavadgita?* (Delhi: Harper Collins, 2014).

Arman Rashid) and her colleague Nathan Hollier and his staff at Monash University Publishing. They chased the publishers of the books and magazines where the essays were first published and unearthed quite a few of the essays I had long forgotten I had written. I am grateful to Marika's team.

Lord Meghnad Desai

Part 1

Global Issues

Chapter 1

GLOBAL GOVERNANCE

Meghnad Desai[1]

(1995)

The need of a constantly expanding market for its products chases the bourgeoisie over the whole surface of the globe. It must nestle everywhere, settle everywhere, establish connexions everywhere.

The bourgeoisie has through its exploitation of the world-market given a cosmopolitan character to production and consumption in every country. To the great chagrin of Reactionists, it has drawn from under the feet of industry the national ground on which it stood. All old-established national industries have been destroyed or are daily being destroyed. They are dislodged by new industries, whose introduction becomes a life and death question for all civilised nations, by industries that no longer work up indigenous raw material, but raw material drawn from the remotest zones; industries whose products are consumed, not only at home, but in every quarter of the globe. In place of the old wants, satisfied by the productions of the country, we find new wants, requiring for their satisfaction the products of distant lands and climes. In place of the old local and national seclusion and self-sufficiency, we have intercourse in every direction, universal interdependence of nations. And as in material, so also in intellectual production. The intellectual creations of individual nations become common property. National one-sidedness and narrow-mindedness

1 I am grateful to Ian Rowlands and Paul Redfern for their comments though I admit I have not done full justice to them.

> become more and more impossible, and from the numerous national and local literatures, there arises a world literature.
>
> The bourgeoisie, by the rapid improvement of all instruments of production, by the immensely facilitated means of communication, draws all, even the most barbarian, nations into civilisation. The cheap prices of its commodities are the heavy artillery with which it batters down all Chinese walls, with which it forces the barbarians' intensely obstinate hatred of foreigners to capitulate. It compels all nations, on pain of extinction, to adopt the bourgeois mode of production; it compels them to introduce what it calls civilisation into their midst, ie, to become bourgeois themselves. In one word, it creates a world after its own image.
>
> (Marx and Engels, 1848, *Communist Manifesto*)

The collapse of the Soviet Union and the end of the Cold War without the much feared nuclear holocaust have opened out various possibilities for rethinking the international system. In one sense there is now an opportunity to get back to the ideals of the Atlantic Charter and fulfil the promise of the original United Nations concept. There has been much enthusiasm on some people's part about the end of communism, the triumph of the market economy, the emergence of the USA-led coalition as the sole surviving Great Power configuration – the package known as 'the end of history' (Fukuyama, 1992). This is the New International Order that President Bush talked about, or the New Imperialism that Douglas Hurd, the British Foreign Secretary, mentioned.

Other considerations which have led to a desire to rethink the international order are the realisation of the environmental constraints which are global rather than local, the challenge of population growth and/or world poverty, which seems incapable of any simple solution by individual countries, the growing sentiment in favour of a minimum level of human rights guarantee – against torture, starvation, discrimination. These issues have led to a search for a *global* rather than merely an international or multinational solution.

An added influence has been the globalisation of the world economy. The growing interdependence of the economies around the world through trade flows and capital flows, as well as the effects of currency and other financial speculation, is a phenomenon of the last ten years, if not even more recent.

Flows of drugs, armaments and 'hot' money, as well as the international spread of AIDS and terrorism, have been the dark side of the globalisation of the world economy. In areas of Africa and Latin America which experienced a severe decline in incomes as a result of the debt crisis of the early 1980s, this has meant flows of economic as well as political refugees; flows which have come nearer home to the Western world with the collapse of the socialist economies of Eastern Europe.

The world then presents dangers and opportunities to anyone who would reopen the question of global governance, though the term itself lacks in precision what it offers in its novelty. It is quite certain in most people's minds that *governance is not government*. It is not the ideal of one world government which is being revived (Tinbergen, 1994). But beyond that negative stance, the concept of global governance needs to be clarified, amplified and, if thought desirable, made operational. In this chapter, I hope to take a broad-ranging view of the manifold aspects of the concept of global governance, being fully aware that this will be the start and not the end of a long debate. (Many references to the existing literature are available. A good starting point is Rosenau and Czempiel, 1992.)

The Context

One way in which one can characterise the present situation is to highlight four aspects:

1. post-mural
2. post-imperial
3. post-Keynesian
4. post-industrial

These four aspects can be explained further as follows.[2]

Post-mural

This refers to the world after the fall of the Berlin Wall, the collapse of the Soviet Union, the end of the Leninist State and central planning in Eastern Europe, and the transition to market economy in all formerly central-planned economies except, at least at present, Cuba and North Korea.

2 It has been put to me that I have missed out the environmental revolution as an important aspect. I take this question up later but admit that I have not integrated it completely with what follows.

This is the prospect described somewhat grandly as 'the end of history' by Fukuyama. Even without accepting the pseudo-Hegelian echoes in his thesis, we must accept that the end of the Cold War as well as the defeat of Leninism as a serious political alternative for countries to follow, are events which have reshaped the world. The world is no longer bi-polar in the old way; there is only one economic system – capitalism (Fukuyama, 1992).

Post-imperial

In 1945 the world was still divided into imperial powers and colonies. By 1990, not only the British but the French, Portuguese and Spanish empires had been unwound, as had the great Russian empire. But by the same token the problems created by the dismantling of empires are still some of the most bloody and intractable ones. The Ottoman empire left a legacy in the Middle East and the problems of the former Yugoslavia, Georgia, Azerbaijan, Angola and Mozambique are all post-imperial.

The world is also post-imperial in other senses. First, in the sense that the Eurocentric bias of much of the Cold War politics – the claim, for example, that there was peace through nuclear stalemate despite the evidence of a loss of at least 20 million lives in the wars in the non-European periphery – can no longer be sustained. At the same time the 'Third World' is no longer homogeneous. There are newly industrialising countries (NICs) which are nearly part of the Organisation for Economic Co-operation and Development OECD group, the rapid growth of their industries being already seen as a threat by the developed West.

Post-Keynesian

A significant feature of post-war life has been the ability of the governments of developed capitalist countries to ensure a high and stable level of employment, a sustained growth rate of income and consumption, and a safety net for the poor and unemployed. This Keynesian Golden Age lasted until about the mid-1970s. The oil price crisis and the subsequent stagflation undermined the attractiveness of the Keynesian path. Through the 1980s the liberalisation of financial markets and the many innovations in telecommunications, transport and electronics created a global economy. In this new regime all economies are open economies and governments find it difficult to control them. Much macroeconomic policy-making has to do with preserving credibility *vis-à-vis* financial markets. Microeconomic, supply-side, structural policies are being increasingly adopted by governments since they know that their ability to control the macroeconomy is limited.

There is still the possibility that Keynesian demand management policies may work at the multinational level, for example at the European Community (EC) level, but this requires a much stronger governance mechanism than we have found so far. Old style Keynesianism working within one country is now obsolete.

Post-industrial

The term 'post-industrial' has been much used. I want to use it here in a specific sense. For the OECD countries, especially for the USA and the EC but notably not in the case of Japan, the industrial sector, particularly the manufacturing part of it, has been shrinking both in terms of the share of GDP but much more sharply in terms of employment. While there is still much hope in developed countries of a 'revival' of manufacturing, the only serious prospect is for these 'old industrialised countries' to seek new products and services to develop if they wish to preserve the level of their real incomes. This will demand a lot of investment in people as well as in ideas (Research and Development – [R&D]) and finally in hardware of some sort or another. The reshaping of the global economy with industry moving from north-west to east and south-east will be a major influence in the context of global governance.

Global governance as a concept and as a programme needs to be defined in the context of these four 'pillars'. The two political pillars, the post-mural and the post-imperial, define the constraints on the United Nations [UN] system as currently understood. The two economic pillars run across the political ones and are reconstituting the world in a way more radical than the political pillars. Each set of pillars needs to be further elaborated in terms of its implication for global governance.

The Political Pillars

The United Nations was born in 1945 as a creature of the victorious Allies. Its presumption in starting its charter with 'We the peoples …' was breathtaking since, at that time, imperialism of the European powers meant unequal relations between members of the UN (for example, between the UK and India who were both founding members). Soon this inequality was overlaid by the Cold War. The intersection of the metropolis/periphery divide with the East/West divide characterised much of the early troubles of the UN. As imperialism unwound itself, or was forced to unwind, the membership of the UN grew until it became a large collection of *nation states* which were unequal in size and power – economic and military – though formally equal as sovereign states. A basic inequality is that of the veto states – the permanent members of the Security Council – and the rest, though with the presence of China among the veto powers there is no one-to-one correspondence between economic power (as measured by GDP etc.) and political power. This lack of correspondence has been reinforced by the retention of its seat by Russia as the largest surviving member of the USSR and persists in a weaker form in the continued presence of the UK and France, two declining economic powers.

Thus in the growth of numbers of member states and the continued but unjustifiable retention of permanent membership status by the original allies, the UN suffers simultaneously from adapting to changing circumstances (admitting new members) and failing to adapt to changes (retention of permanent status). The unravelling of old empires during the three decades following the Second World War created the first anomaly: the collapse of communism and the relative decline of the erstwhile imperial powers creates the second anomaly. But at the end of this double decline we are left with a world in which there is no single hegemonic power, though formally the USA qualifies as the one (by and large) non-imperial, relatively non-declining economic and political power. Alone among the permanent members, it could claim to have won the battles of the Cold War without losing much. Thus, although it overreached itself and lost in Vietnam, this did not prove to be a prelude to long-term decline; or if it did, its rivals declined even further than the USA. By contrast, the UK won the Boer War but its economic decline is traced back to the same years. Despite the switch from a creditor nation to a debtor nation on foreign capital account and a stubborn deficit in its budget, the USA retains its primary status.

But precisely because of that debt and the deficit, the USA is less powerful than it used to be. Had it been the sole hegemon in, say, the 1950s, or if it had retained its economic strength of those days into the 1990s, the USA could have aspired to fulfil the role that Britain did in the nineteenth century. The vision of Franklin Delano Roosevelt in setting up the UN could have been implemented. As it was, the UN became distorted through the Cold War visions of Harry Truman and subsequent US presidents and so could not fulfil the original vision. By the time the Cold War had ended the USA was primus, but the extra height it has is marginal.

A more particular problem has been the growth of public opinion in the USA against foreign policy adventures which lead to loss of life. The 'body bag' issue – the return of the dead from wars abroad – has now meant that as a hegemon, the USA is reluctant to commit its own troops abroad. When it does do so, as in the Gulf War, it uses a military strategy that places a tremendous premium on minimising loss of human life *of its own citizens*. Previous hegemons, such as the UK, had Imperial armies – Indians, Irish, Australians, Africans – to fight alongside its own subjects/citizens and in overwhelming numbers in its foreign wars. Even then, given the less than fully democratic nature of UK politics, there was no premium on the lives of their own citizens – as the First World War showed. The new hegemon has no formal empire from which to recruit its mercenary army. This has been evident in the case of the conflict in Bosnia, where the USA has been reluctant to send troops to implement UN Security Council resolutions.

So we have the paradox of a world of unequally powerful nations, among which there is *too little inequality* to make one nation state dominant and *too much inequality* to establish a symmetrical framework of the Rule of Law. The world of nation states is neither ready for a Lockean contract for a democracy, nor for a Hobbesian Absolutist monarch. There are querulous barons of unequal size – too many for comfort – but with no one powerful enough to lay down the law.

Athwart this anomaly lies the democratic deficit, whereby the peoples or the nations are not represented directly in the UN but only the sovereign states. The only way for a nation to obtain representation is to become a nation state; hence the premium on secession and the profits of a civil war. (For the problems that this causes see Gottlieb, 1993.) It is as if the US Constitution had created only the Senate and not the House of Representatives as well (but had allowed the original thirteen states veto powers).

Along the way, in the course of the last fifty years, another important change has been the growth and spread of democracy based on universal adult franchise (UAF) and multi-party parliaments (MPP). In 1945 there were very few among the members of the UN which satisfied either requirement; over the years, both in the metropolis and the periphery and now in the East as well as the West, there is a growth of UAF/MPP democracies. Even within some of the oldest democracies there remained many inequities between one person and another. Thus women's suffrage was delayed in many countries (for example, France) till after 1945. Equal voting rights for Afro-Americans were achieved only in the late 1960s as a result of the movement for civil rights.

The success of the civil rights movement created in the USA a climate in which citizens' voluntary associations were fighting against the State for justice and their rights but, at the same time, were seeking codification of rights as an instrument for equity. Positive discrimination for blacks led to articulation of other dimensions of disadvantage due to status, gender, race, age and sexual orientation. Civil rights became an issue of human rights, not only in the USA but in other democracies. As a result, within these countries the civil society has been enriched by active intermediate associations – Non-governmental organisations (NGOs) of various description – and there is more political activity (lobbying, etc.) between elections as well as at the time of elections. This growth of NGOs has spilled over into the international arena.

The presence of these NGOs was seen very strongly at the United Nations Conference on Environment and Development (UNCED) in Rio as well as at the Human Rights Conference in Vienna, where they played a role in setting the agenda. One of the questions of global governance is the channel through which the contribution of the NGOs can be directed. There are questions about the accountability of these NGOs themselves but these questions will only be faced once these groups have some official standing.

The Economic Pillars

The combination of the decline of single-country Keynesianism and (for the present at least) the drift away from the north-western metropolitan core of the manufacturing industries towards the Far East is reconstituting the world in a different way. Thus if in politics the nation states are growing in number and in their ability to create serious problems of inter-ethnic rivalry, pan-national religious fundamentalism, regional blocs etc., the economics sphere is undermining the nation state. As political sovereignty is being reaffirmed for ever-smaller states, economic sovereignty is being undermined in even the most powerful countries.

The phenomenon which has accomplished this reconstitution is labelled globalisation. In one sense, globalisation – the increasing interdependence and integration of the separate economies of the globe – has been happening since the late fifteenth century and the beginnings of capitalism as a world system. But, over the years, there has been an ebb and flow in the pace of globalisation. The nineteenth century – say, 1815 to 1914 – saw a rapid growth of globalisation foreseen so brilliantly by Marx, as the quotation at the beginning of this chapter shows. There was the Gold Standard, as well as a single powerful capital market in London where money could be raised for projects in any part of the world, growth of trade, revolutions in transport and communications, etc. But the fifty-plus years following the end of the First World War, say from 1920 to 1975, saw a brake on globalisation. The Gold Standard ran into trouble and was abandoned by the 1930s. Tariff barriers went up. The notion of relatively autonomous national economies controllable by their governments, whether by central planning or Keynesian demand management, took hold. Trade declined, only to resume its growth in the 1960s.

It is the resumption of the pace of globalisation in the last quarter of the twentieth century that is the novel phenomenon. Its origins lie immediately in the Organization of the Petroleum Exporting Countries (OPEC) oil price rise of 1973, but the strains on the previous economic order were already apparent before that. The abandonment of the gold-dollar link in August 1971 by the USA saw the collapse of the dollar exchange standard which was a pillar of the Bretton Woods System. This in itself could be traced back to US trade deficits caused by the Vietnam War and its monetary consequences. The growth of international trade which had resumed in the 1960s and the restored state of the manufacturing economies of Japan and Western Europe, made the USA relatively less powerful as it made all the developed market economies more open. A world economy was about to reconstitute itself aside and away from the influence of national economies and their policy-makers. The Eurodollar market had already given a glimpse of what could happen. The petrodollar market brought the phenomenon to the fore.

The oil price rise of 1973 created trade surpluses in the oil exporting economies and corresponding deficits in the developed market economies of the OECD. (There were also problems for developing economies which were oil importers, but they are not germane to the issue here.) The task of recycling petrodollar surpluses fell, not to the International Monetary Fund (IMF) or World Bank or even the Bank of International Settlements (the club of central bankers), but to private commercial banks located in the financial centres of London, New York, Paris and Tokyo. Whereas during the two previous decades the flow of capital from the developed to the less developed world had been through official government-to-government channels, now there grew a flood of private commercial loans from the banks in the centre to, by and large, the governments in the periphery. The economies of Eastern Europe were brought within this nexus as much as the countries of the South.

In fact, for the first time since the beginning of the First World War, all parts of the world were being bound together in a financial network on a private commercial basis. As in the nineteenth century, some of the borrowers were governments but the lenders were private. Unusually, however, the primary 'savers' were not numerous *rentiers* but a few large holders of petrodollar surpluses.

At this juncture in the mid-1970s, the metropolitan countries were not major borrowers. They were still, by and large, Keynesians in their fiscal and monetary stance and they chose to 'print money' rather than to fund their deficits by borrowing. These policies failed to overcome the stagflation then endemic in the metropolitan countries. The failure of Keynesian policies exposed them to the monetarist critique. The stagflation was, however, only partly a macroeconomic phenomenon. Behind it lay the decline in profitability of metropolitan manufacturing industries and the search by capital for more profitable locations. Be it the north-east of the USA or the UK, deindustrialisation had arrived.

By 1979, the monetarists had won the battle. In the USA as well as the UK, monetarist policy was now official. West Germany had always been hardline monetarist anyway. The second OPEC oil rise of 1979 helped this process by making inflation a lively issue again. A deep recession during 1980–81, the deepest in the post-war period, coincided with anti-inflationary policies being put in place. The metropolitan countries emerged as borrowers of OPEC surpluses and the real interest rate, which had been negative in the mid-1970s, shot up to its highest level since records started being kept. Monetarists were also backed by a libertarian programme of deregulation and dismantling of the state sector. The deregulation of financial markets began at this time. The 1980s began with the creation of global financial markets. The Eurodollar market was now officially universalised.

Technological innovations in transport, telecommunications and information technology also allowed capital – financial as well as real – to become much more mobile. It was the same process that had started in the 1970s but it now accelerated. In the search for higher profitability, capital became footloose, as it had been in the previous century. This process was aided by the fact that in many sectors of the manufacturing industries, products had reached a mature stage in their life cycle and thus could be shifted away from the metropolitan countries for their production. The mid-1970s, which were stagflation-ridden for the metropolitan countries, were years of rapid industrialisation for a small number of Third World countries – in Asia and Latin America. These NICs or Asian tigers were the new base for the manufacturing industries which were leaving the metropolitan shores. Mobility of capital and flexible foreign exchanges undermined the ability of countries to pursue an autonomous economic policy. The academic theorising in macroeconomics reflected this by speaking of credibility as the main concern of macro policymakers – credibility *vis-à-vis* the financial markets which were now global. The fear of inflation or in other cases (for example, the enterprise risk management stance of the UK) the political infeasibility of the chosen policy stance caused a sudden efflux of funds and forced the reversal of policy. Thus France in the 1981–83 period witnessed the last attempt at 'go it alone' Keynesian reflation. After that experience, caution was urged constantly upon governments by the markets. Asset price inflations fingered into the late 1980s but the collapse of these booms in Japan and the UK in the late 1980s drove home the lesson about global interdependence.

It is now conventional wisdom that individual countries have limited economic sovereignty. Of course, the 'body' to which they have conceded this sovereignty is an abstract one – the market. Occasionally, the frustration of diminished sovereignty takes the form of railing against speculators or multinationals on the part of politicians of the metropolitan countries. But the fact of the loss of sovereignty is not denied.

The developing world has also suffered a similar loss. In their case, there was always a perception that political independence had not brought with it economic independence. The neo-colonialist spectre was always there. These countries felt more threatened by Western governments as well as by Western multinationals. But the 1970s again proved a watershed in their case. On the one hand the OPEC price rise strengthened not only the oil exporting countries but also gave hope to many other countries exporting primary products. The easy availability of commercial bank loans made many of them relatively independent of Western governments. The multinational capital was now seeking a base for manufacturing rather than merely extractive or raw material exporting activities in the Third World. The developed world was in stagflation and feeling worried about the rise of commodity exporting cartels.

In this atmosphere it was easy for the Third World to put the New International Economic Order on the agenda. The United Nations Conference on Trade and Development (UNCTAD) was able to embark on an ambitious scheme for commodity price stabilisation in the form of a common fund. The USA, for a while during the Carter presidency, took all this quite seriously and showed willingness to negotiate. There seemed to be a real possibility of reversing some of the asymmetries of the imperial order.

The 1980s proved a complete reversal of all trends. As the developed world went monetarist and real interest rates shot up, there emerged a severe debt crisis for the developing countries. Starting with Latin America, the middle-income, relatively industrialised countries – Mexico, Brazil, Chile and Argentina, as well as poorer countries such as Bolivia – got caught in the debt trap. Any hope that they would threaten the markets of the Western world with their products was postponed. Soon after, the countries of Sub-Saharan Africa were in the same trap although their debt was official rather than commercial. Their hope of enhanced primary commodity exports were dashed when primary commodity prices declined as the recession in the Western countries affected them.

With the debt trap came the IMF and the World Bank. These Bretton Woods institutions had survived the demise of the dollar-exchange standard. Although set up to be international banking institutions, they had failed to perform any such function for a long time. Thus the IMF did nothing to monitor the recycling of petrodollars or the emergence of the debt problem. Once the debt problem had created a severe liquidity crisis for the developing countries, stabilisation plans and structural adjustment programmes were imposed, respectively, by the IMF and the World Bank. These programmes advocated and got compliance with a package of exchange rate, fiscal and monetary policies, which the countries in trouble had to adopt if they were going to receive the various borrowing facilities available. Conditionality became the watchword for the developing countries as credibility was for the developed ones.

It is not the occasion to go through the details of these programmes or their appropriateness, but they led to a diminution of economic sovereignty without any doubt. The various iniquitous policies advocated by the IMF and pursued by these countries do nothing to correct the impression that the asymmetry, as between the rich and the poor, was being sanctified by the IMF, since neither the indebtedness nor the trade budget deficits of the USA came in for any strictures from the IMF. The countries of the North, with the sole exception perhaps of the UK in 1976, escaped the IMF's criticism. Thus, while the world of the 1950s and 1960s was full of inter-governmental inequalities with asymmetry of power mediated by the compulsions of the Cold War, now the relatively faceless Bretton Woods institutions, beyond even the formal debates of the UN General Assembly, had emerged as masters of the Third World. They, of course, said that they only represented economic rationality and prepared the Third World for the market order. Even so, the economic sovereignty conceded by the developing countries seemed to be less to the impersonal market than to the faceless bureaucracies of the Bretton Woods institutions.

Either way, the world has now got used to the idea that economic sovereignty is not absolute; that market forces require a certain fiscal and monetary discipline. While the role of the State remains important, having been transformed from an intervening to an enabling agent, the fact remains that this State is powerless in many ways.

Global Corporations: A New Phenomenon?

The other side of this coin is the emergence of global corporations, which are taking an active role in restructuring the world economy, and the shift of the centre of economic gravity to Asia – mainly Southeast and East Asia. The global corporation is the descendant of the multinational corporation. It is less dependent on its home base, either for its market or for tax and credit facilities. It recruits its top management globally and has multiple locations for its production.

The contrast between a multinational corporation and a global or a transnational corporation is well drawn by Henry Wendt in his book *Global Embrace*:

> In operation, multinationals tend to clone themselves in other countries, and, regardless of the degree of autonomy they grant to foreign subsidiaries, the centre of the companies remain [sic] at their headquarters in the home market. Thus companies often transplant managers and invariably alter the national identities of any foreign companies they acquire. Products are generally introduced in the home market and then later rolled into foreign markets. In organisation and outlook, the multinationals traditionally follow the colonial model.
>
> Transnationals, by contrast, locate various parts of their operation anywhere in the world it makes sense to do so. Production facilities may be located in many countries to gain proximity to local markets or in just a few locations to maximise efficiencies of scale. New products are introduced simultaneously in as many markets as possible. Design functions may be carried out in areas that are rich in human talent, or marketing may find a home in several strategic locations. Research and development, one of the most important activities of transnationals, may be located in countries with superior technologies, talented researchers and engineers, or desirable markets. (Wendt, 1993)

The reconstitution of the world economy by the transnational corporation is a recent event but one that is likely to be durable. After 75 years or more of thinking of the world economy as consisting of individual national economies, the time has come simultaneously to think of it as consisting of transnational corporations as well. Looked at in these two alternative ways, as a collection of national economies, or, as (largely) a collection of global/transnational corporations, the world economy can be seen either as a single trading area or as dominated by two or three large regional blocs – NAFTA, EU, APEC – if we adopt a nation-state perspective. Alternatively, it can be perceived as a system of conflict and strategic collaboration between large multi-product conglomerates. Technological progress shapes and reshapes the futures of these corporations as they compete in markets around the world. The rivalry and cooperation between the companies, as much as between the nations, are the warp and the woof of the global economy.

One effect of globalisation is to have shifted the centre of economic activity from the north-west (Europe and North America) to the Far East. The Asian economies are registering sustained high growth rates of income as well as exports. Japan was the pioneer in this respect in the 1960s and 1970s, but now it has been followed by what the World Bank calls the High Performing Asian Economies (World Bank, 1993). As yet, in terms of proportions of total output the numbers are small, but the trend towards 'Asianisation' of the world economy is unmistakable.

For our purposes, the interesting aspect of globalisation is the reduction of asymmetry as between countries in Asia and Europe/North America. After a century or more of economic domination by the latter, with imperial domination added on the part of some European countries, the tide seems to be turning in favour of the former colonies. History will be remembered as old inequities are recalled. The Malaysian episode in March 1994, with the Malaysian prime minister accusing the British press of moral decadence (*Financial Times*, 17.3.94), is an example of the challenge to Western values from a newly emerging economic power. The decision by the Clinton Administration to drop human rights conditionality before granting Most Favoured Nation status to China in May 1994 is another example of the shifting power balance. Many more such episodes could happen with India, Indonesia and Korea all flexing their economic muscles.

The second aspect of globalisation is that it is creating a set of powerful players in the world who are not regulated or regulatable (if there is such a word). Unlike nation states which are nominally supposed to abide by the

UN Charter and various conventions of Human Rights etc., the companies are subject to individual country regulations but no overall *global* regulation. Thus it was possible for Bank of Credit and Commerce International (BCCI) to locate in a country with weak banking supervision, and although it was caught out in the USA and the UK, the two sets of litigation were not coordinated and they took, and are taking, a considerable time to secure convictions and compensate the depositors. There is no regulation of international capital flows, although schemes have been put forward by the Nobel Laureate James Tobin to tax transactions in foreign exchange markets. The many emerging stock markets are attracting large quantities of funds from around the globe but there is no institution like the SEC in the USA to regulate these transactions.

A third and perhaps, for many people, the most important aspect of globalisation, is what Barbara Ward tried to inculcate so many years ago in the minds of the decision-makers – the realisation that the planet Earth is a unique but fragile system (Ward, 1966; Ward and Dubos, 1972; but see also Carson, 1962). Although she argued the case in the 1960s, it was only in the early 1970s that the Stockholm Conference on the environment (UN, 1972), as well as the Club of Rome report 'The Limits to Growth' (Meadows et al., 1972) reinforced her argument. The OPEC oil price rise strengthened the notion that there may be a finite limit to non-renewable resources. But again, there was a lull in the environmental policy debate until the mid-1980s. By then the hole in the ozone layer and the prospect of global warming were added to the finite resources argument. The report of the Brundtland Commission (1987), the UNCED conference in Rio and the formation of the UN Commission on Sustainable Development were the responses (Grubb et al., 1993).

The international community is aware of the problem but even now there is no global approach. The difference of perception between the North and the South about the nature, the urgency and the cure of the environmental problem remains. The asymmetry of power and the memories of historical wrongs block any convergence of interests. Besides the nations, the global corporations and the NGOs are also emerging as players in the environmental negotiations (McCormick, 1989). The Montreal protocol on the banning of CFCs and the adoption of targets on CO_2 emissions are encouraging signs that some consensual strategies can succeed. But the gap between international, that is, inter-state and global policymaking persists.

Globalisation may thus be generating a need (if not the demand) for some form of economic global governance by way of regulation.

A Global Civil Society?

The other, but more speculative, side of this coin is that globalisation may be creating a genuinely *global civil society*, albeit embryonic at present. Civil society, let us recall, in the works of Adam Smith, Adam Ferguson and Hegel, is the sphere of contract, of private interests. It is the sphere where the Invisible Hand may rule and if not, the State steps in to regulate the conflicts of private interest that the civil society cannot resolve. (The civil society is frequently taken to be the civilised society or the welfare state or the civic society. For my purposes it is the original Enlightenment connotation that is relevant.)

Within nations, indeed within kingdoms before they became nations much less nation states, the state existed prior to the civil society, in as much as the civil society presumes the right to private property and the enforcement of contractual obligations (Desai, 1986). This is the sense in which the Scottish philosophers conceived of the civil society. The State is thus prior to civil society but the growth of the private sphere modifies the State. The reason for discussing the issue here is whether the analogy of the modern state/civil society relationship can be extended to the global level. Can we, for example, draw a parallel between the UN as a proto-state and the global economy as a proto-global civil society?

The speculation can be continued further by asking whether the undermining of the nation state by the transnational corporations would weaken or strengthen the international institutions which will be involved in global governance – the UN, the Bretton Woods institutions, GATT/WTO, ILO, etc. If the globalising of the world economy is to undermine global as well as national governments, then the question of global governance will move on to a very different terrain of creating a new set of institutions analogous to the self-regulating organisations in financial markets. This will mean less than even a night-watchman state at the global level. If, on the other hand, globalisation will weaken nation states but create a need for a global governance framework (corresponding to the emergent global civil society), then again we are on a very different terrain. In this latter case, 'market forces' will strengthen global institutions and urge compliance by nation states with global rules – harmonisation of taxation, free trade, single currency, a proper global central bank, etc.

It is not possible, with the data at hand, to judge which way the balance will go. It is early days of globalisation, and the nation states are by no means powerless, either singly or in groups, when it comes to international economic issues. The completion of the Uruguay round of GATT showed how much the narrow national economic interests of the powerful can detract from the promotion of global welfare. In a truly globalised economy, trade would be market determined; we are far from that world, even now, if it is at all a realistic possibility and not just a pipe dream of neoclassical economists.

Governance

Governance, at the minimum, has to be about providing a framework of rule by which all the participating parties in the commonwealth agree to abide. It is the provision of a 'Rule of Law', a symmetric framework in which the weak as well as the strong are subject to the same rules. A second task the state has performed has been the issuance of currency and coins which are legal tender. A third, and much more recent, task has been the promotion of public well-being and, later yet, the maintenance of high employment or low inflation and the promotion of economic growth.

Can we at the present juncture envisage the possibility of even a minimal framework of law and order? The foregoing analysis has pointed out the asymmetries of power that arise from history. The political pillars sustain an unequal, undemocratic international order in which the powerful set rules for the rest but do not themselves obey the laws they promulgate. The economic pillars, however, give some hope that the asymmetries may be in the process of correction – Asianisation and globalisation being the economic forces which are the corrective ones. Economic rules and regulations, especially those that go with the grain of the market (after all, the nation state was established very much in parallel with the market economy in a mutually determining way), may be easier and early established forms of global governance. The political framework – respect for human rights, especially those of the citizens of the weaker states by the governments of the powerful ones (asylum, refugees, labour mobility, etc.) – may take longer to put into place. A United Nations with an entrenched Security Council with permanent powers armed with veto is hardly likely to be the best vehicle for a symmetric rule of law. An undemocratic General Assembly only adds to the weakness of the UN in this respect; no member government will allow the UN to champion its own citizens in defiance of the government. It may yet be that, paradoxically, globalisation may be the only hope for global governance.

References

Brundtland Commission (1987), 'World Commission on Environment and Development', *Our Common Future*, Oxford, OUP.

Carson, R. (1962), *Silent Spring*, New York, Fawcett Crest.

Desai, M. (1986), 'Men and Things', *Economics*, February.

Fukuyama, F. (1992), *The End of History and the Last Man*, London, Hamish Hamilton.

Gottlieb, G. (1993), *Nation Against State: A New Approach to Ethnic Conflicts and the Decline of Sovereignty*, New York, The Council of Foreign Relations Press.

Grubb, M. et al. (eds) (1993), *The 'Earth Summit' Agreements: A Guide and Assessment*, London, Earthscan for the RIIA.

McCormick, J. (1989), *The Global Environmental Movement: Reclaiming Paradise*, London, Belhaven Press.

Marx, K. and Engels, F. (1848), *Communist Manifesto*. Reprinted in K. Marx and F. Engels (1968), *Selected Works*, London, Lawrence & Wishart Ltd, pp. 38–9.

Meadows, D.H. et al. (1972), *The Limits to Growth*, New York, Universe Books.

Rosenau, J.N., and Czempiel E.-O. (eds) (1992), *Governance Without Government: Order and Change in World Politics*, Cambridge and New York, Cambridge University Press.

Tinbergen, J. (1994), *Global Governance for the 21st Century*, UNDP.

UN (1972), 'United Nations Conference on the Human Environment: Final Documents' (Stockholm, Sweden: 5–16 June 1972), reprinted in *International Legal Materials*, Vol. 11, No. 6, November 1972: 1416–69.

UNDP (1994), *Human Development Report*, Oxford, OUP.

Ward, B. (1966), *Spaceship Earth*, London, Hamish Hamilton.

Ward, B. and Dubos, R. (1972), *Only One Earth: The Care and Maintenance of a Small Planet*, New York, W. W. Norton and Co.

Wendt, H. (1993), *Global Embrace: Corporate Challenges in a Transnational World*, New York, Harper Business.

World Bank (1993), *The East Asian Miracle: Economic Growth and Public Policy*, Oxford, OUP.

Acknowledgement

First publication: Desai, Meghnad (1995) 'Global Governance' in *Global Governance: Ethics and Economics of the World Order*, edited by Meghnad Desai and Paul Redfern. London, Pinter Publishers, pp. 6–21. Used by kind permission of Bloomsbury Publishing Plc.

Chapter 2

THE POSSIBILITY OF DEGLOBALISATION

Lord Meghnad Desai

(2003)

Introduction

Globalisation and all that it entails has led to a large and continuing controversy. The many issues that have been raised can be listed here only briefly:

a) Is globalisation a new phenomenon or merely a repeat of the late-nineteenth-century pattern? Can we even say that globalisation is a fact or that inter-nationalisation is still the norm and globalisation is just an overhyped concept?[1]

b) Has globalisation made territorial borders irrelevant, has it made the territorial (nation) state powerless or has it enhanced national and religious conflicts (fundamentalism) and hardened state boundaries?[2]

c) Is globalisation a Western/MNC-run operation to reinforce the present inequitable divisions in the world or is it a self-organising process which no one controls and of which all are victims or beneficiaries at various times?[3]

---

1 Hirst and Thompson (1996/1999) and Weiss (1998), among others.

2 Ohmae (1990) and Weiss (1998); see Halliday (1995) on fundamentalism.

3 Many Third World authors take this view but see also the two books entitled *Globalization and Its Discontents* by Sassen (1998) and by Burbach et al. (1997).

d) Is globalisation an impossible utopian experiment to run the world on the basis of a free market system bound to be ruinous or is it a liberalising, freedom-enhancing affirmation of the merits of private property and the market?[4]

e) Has the impact of globalisation been positive or negative on work opportunities, income growth and environment and in terms of countries and ethnic groups – who has gained and who has lost?[5]

f) Is culture being homogenised and trivialised or is the full diversity of all cultures becoming available across the globe due to the diasporas spreading everywhere?

I could list many more issues on each of which the opinion is divided. My own position is that globalisation is capitalism, in a phase that is a repetition of the late-nineteenth-century pattern, but at a higher level of technology and with many more democratic state formations than we had the last time around. Thus it is a spiral, not a circle. The most important thing about globalisation is the unregulated movement of capital inaugurated by policy changes in the USA and UK in the 1970s followed by other developed capitalist countries in the 1980s and later. This free movement of capital had been stemmed by the Bretton Woods conventions and thus the Golden Age of Keynesianism is separated from the inauguration of globalisation. The new technologies of information processing, communication and transport were important ingredients in this but so was the changed climate of opinion in favour of liberal free market policies. Globalisation is a dialectical dynamic process whose good and bad effects are intertwined. It is a gale of creative destruction, to use Schumpeter's phrase. It is a process in which multinational corporations (MNCs) are as important players as states and the MNCs are beginning to behave as if they were truly global, with no national bias.[6]

We are in the early days of this new phase of globalisation and so in order to distinguish it from the earlier globalisation episode, I shall label

4 John Gray's *False Dawn* has argued the Polanyi thesis about the utopian nature of the globalisation experiment; the Hayekians and neoliberals have argued the libertarian case (Gray 1998).

5 Paradoxically, the complaints from the North have been as loud as those from the South: see, in no particular order of merit, Bauman (1998), Korten (1995), Greider (1997), Barnes (1999) and UNDP (1999).

6 I have argued the case of G20 as being shaped by MNCs in M. Desai 'Global governance' in Desai and Redfern (1995), *Global Governance*, London: Cassell.

it G20 (globalisation in the 20th century). At the earliest it started in the mid-1970s or at the latest after the fall of the Berlin Wall. Its nineteenth-century predecessor ('G19' hereafter) is dated loosely as starting sometime in the second half of the century and ending in 1914. It would do us no harm to take the period 1873–1914 as the length of G19. Now G19 came to an abrupt end in the First World War. The reasons for the war have been endlessly debated but I wish to pose a stark, somewhat naïve question. Was the war a way of ending G19, an endogenous response against the utopian market experiment a la Polanyi (though he himself dated the end of globalisation at the Second World War)? And what is more: could G20 come to an end due to endogenous systemic reasons and, if so, what would they be?

I am quite aware that this is a very naïve, mechanistic way of posing the question – does history repeat herself? I know she does not, not even as a farce having been a tragedy. Yet to pose the question of deglobalisation is at the same time to pose the question of the endogenous systemic limits to globalisation. What are the forces working for globalisation and what are the retarding, checking forces? Is there an endogenous dynamic to globalisation whereby it may self-destruct, much as many Marxists-Leninists thought (and still think) capitalism would?

The First Deglobalisation

The reasons for the First World War are many and there is no settled story of the causality. But there is no doubting the fact that the war put a stop to the globalised world of the nineteenth century – capital flows dried up, the gold standard broke up, trade progressively shrank, mobility became difficult due to passports etc. But what were the forces for and against globalisation in that case? What I want to do below is to mention five factors which are relevant to understanding both the First World War and its context, if not its causes, which may have resonance in this phase of globalisation.

Imperialism/Capitalism as a Cause of War

The growing international socialist movement debated and prepared for a war. It was convinced that an imperialist war would happen in Europe and in 1907 at the Stuttgart Conference the strategy to be adopted in case of a war was debated. Socialists, especially Marxists, wanted to use the First World War to further the collapse of capitalism which they thought was imminent. The new cartelised phase of capitalism with the domination of finance capital (though this was a German rather than an Anglo-Saxon concept) would, it was said, lead to territorial wars. Markets would be fought over and in that fight war would break out.[7]

Lenin articulated this thesis in 1916 in his *Imperialism*, but that was after the war had already happened. So it was not a predictive model. Hobson had thought imperialism to be irrational – a search for land rather than markets motivated by the land hunger of the aristocratic classes. Hobson was a radical Whig who had thought that free trade would bring universal peace but for the pre-capitalist elements in the ruling classes. His thesis was similar to that of Schumpeter. So, while for Lenin it was capitalism that was the cause of imperialism and war, for Hobson and Schumpeter it was imperialism as an atavistic pre-capitalist form that was responsible for the First World War. Kautsky, on the other hand, thought capitalism would see the advantages of collaboration among the imperial powers and they would form a supercartel of imperial powers (EU, anyone?).[8]

Thus imperialism led to war either as a phase of capitalism or as a form of atavistic pre-capitalist throwback. In the first case Marxism as practiced at that time led to two contradictory predictions of capitalism/imperialism as leading either to war or to a supercartel. The 1914 war seemed to vindicate Lenin (though, as I said, he had postdicted it) rather than Kautsky. But later events after the Second World War – EU, G7 etc. – seem to support Kautsky.

In as much as G20 is a new phase of capitalism (one after the highest phase which, according to Lenin, was imperialism), the question can be asked again – Is there anything about the nature of G20 that may lead to its violent end? I will come to this question below.

Nationalism as a Cause of War

The war did, after all, start with the assassination of Archduke Ferdinand by a Serb nationalist, Gavrilo Princip. The dynamics of the national movements in the Austro-Hungarian Empire as well as the Ottoman Empire on the mainland of Europe were definitely a force for instability in the pre-war period. This was imperialism as a political rather than an economic phenomenon. The Boer War had preceded the Great War as a rehearsal;

7 See Schorske (1955).

8 Lenin (1916), *Imperialism, the Highest Stage of Capitalism* was not published until later and Schumpeter's *Imperialism and Social Classes* was published in 1919, i.e., both after the war had finished. Hobson (1902), *Imperialism* (London: Macmillan). For Kautsky, see Massimo Salvadori (1979).

Hobson, after all, was writing in reaction to the Boer War. That too was a nationalist uprising against an imperial power. Japanese nationalism had defeated Russia in 1905 and was seen as a threat. There was an upsurge of nationalism in China and India in the first decade of the twentieth century. One of the end products of the war was the end of empires and the formation of new nation states in Europe. Nationalism put pressure on the metropolitan centre in each empire. Though the war was between these empires and no link-up took place among nationalisms across empires, nationalism was a more potent anti-imperialist force than socialism.

It could also be said that the territorial disputes which preceded the war – the two Morocco incidents of 1905 and 1911 – were not motivated by economic gain but by pure territorial atavistic aggrandisement on the part of Germany which felt left out of the imperial club.

The interest of nationalism for G20 is that it is very similar to the fundamentalism forces which are seen as a serious threat today. Also the detritus of the break-up of the Ottoman and the Hapsburg empires is still with us in the form of national and subnational conflicts – Yugoslavia, Israel/Arab wars, Greece/Turkey etc. Since 1991, the break-up of the Romanov/Bolshevik Empire has added new fragile 'nations'. They link up G19 and G20.

Trade Wars

Free trade was scrupulously practiced by the British and advocated by them. The liberal free traders believed that wars would be inconceivable in a world of free trade. But the USA and continental Europe were not fully committed to free trade and even in Britain the tariff debate was gathering pace (witness Joseph Chamberlain's defection to the Tory Party). The perception by the then richest country that it could be suffering the adverse effects of free trade has been echoed in more recent times by politicians of developed countries such as James Goldsmith, Pat Buchanan and Ross Perot. While there were no trade wars before 1914, free trade as a philosophy was eroding. The notion of empires as *zollvereins* – free trade within the Customs Union and protection against the outside – was gaining ground. Thus was Friedrich List, rather than David Ricardo, ruling the waves.

Diasporas

America had become a melting pot with many Central and East European nationalities well represented there. There was much pro-German and anti-British feeling in its politics. The Industrial Workers of the World (IWW) as a trade union owed much to the European background of many first-generation immigrants. If America did eventually enter the war albeit on the British/French side, it was as much due to diasporic pressure as not. It was the un-diasporic people, the English, who had migrated in the 1600s who finally triumphed in this choice. Elsewhere, the migration from Asia to Africa and to the Caribbean had also created large Indian and Chinese minorities in these regions.

The diasporas are again a force in G20 even more than they were in G19. They are more multi-racial and wider spread than in G19. Thanks to decolonisation and the immigration since, from the periphery to the core, diasporas are much more varied than before.

Long Waves

The theory of long waves has been popular with many who want to be able to predict long run. Kondratieff waves have long been popular. No one quite believes in regular fifty-year cycles but there may be some advantage in thinking in broad long waves terms. Thus the 1870s as well as the 1970s witnessed a change of gear for the world economy. No one believed in the 1960s that full employment could come to an end in the 1970s. The 1890s were a boom time when Eduard Bernstein was arguing that capitalism had changed its character and was no longer cyclical. In the 1990s we heard much talk of a new paradigm or eliminating boom and bust cycles. Kondratieff was wrong in locating a fifty-year cycle but the world has an uncanny habit of repeating itself, especially where it means committing errors. (For a discussion of long swings, see Mandel (1995).)

Now the Kondratieff wave started from its trough in 1873 and should have lasted until, say, the 1920s. The war interrupted the downswing of the Kondratieff wave from the mid-1890s to the 1920s. Before that the 1790–1820s period was also characterised by wars in Europe. Are we in for another interrupted downswing of the Kondratieff?

Deglobalising of G20

These issues listed above as the context of the deglobalisation of G19 will not come back exactly as before. It is a spiral, not a circle, as I said above. The context is different now and to begin with I wish to bring out the major differences in the context today.

Equity and Democracy

The big issue for G20 is the reconciliation of free movement of capital with equity. This is not merely the equity/efficiency choice of economics textbooks but has a special dimension in G20. The reasons lie in the major difference between G19 and G20.

The big difference between the two episodes of globalisation is democracy. We have not only many more states today which have parliamentary democracy and public accountability but the ethos of the late twentieth century was much more anti-elitist, much more suspicious of decisions coming down from the top, much more irreverent than was the case in the 1890s. At that time the growing population of Europe had made its presence felt as 'the mob' became an object of study. There was also an explosion of the print media, radio had just come on the scene and cable and telephones were making new forms of communications available. But now the mob has been enfranchised. The electoral process has empowered it much more than was the case a hundred years ago. The NGOs have become a parallel extra-governmental level of governance at both the national and international levels. We tend not to be impressed by these developments because they are too familiar for us. But mass democracy with universal franchise is a bigger problem for global capitalism than the growing socialist movement was in the late nineteenth century.

The consequence is that equity issues are much more prominent now than before. It is not enough to say nowadays that the market will in the long run promote welfare. It may be true and I believe it has more truth than many admit. But the twenty-five years of the Golden Age of Keynesianism gave a different version of capitalism much credibility. This version had full employment, a growing welfare state and the market was contained. Although that phase has passed and the passage away from it in the 1970s and 1980s was painful, the memory of a regulated capitalism at the national level is a very strong one. Equity-based NGO movements will seek to establish regulatory competence at the global level – Tobin taxes, world financial authority, global Keynesianism, environmental taxes or restrictions on pollution, fair trade issues before the WTO, etc. If they succeed it will lead to a globalised world which emulates the best properties of the Golden Age (although that was restricted to the OECD countries). The reconciliation of equity issues with the unregulated flow of capital is the biggest challenge to G20.

The reason why such a solution may yet be arrived at is that, unlike in G19, the costs of G20 are being felt in the North as much as in the South.

During G19, and indeed up to the early 1970s, there was asymmetry in the way the world economy operated. Crudely put, the North won every time and the South lost.[9] Now, while there is still a lot of inequality between the regions there is much less asymmetry as a result of the outflow of capital and consequentially jobs, especially blue-collar jobs, from the North to the South. Indeed for the first time since the birth of capitalism, the North is frightened of it as never before. Groups in the North – those losing from technological change – the Luddites, for example, have always protested but they have never been able to stem the tide of capitalism. Now the pain is more widespread as the free movement of capital seeks profits wherever it can, with no loyalty to the country where the MNC headquarters are. Right-wing politicians are becoming anti-globalisation as much as left-wing ones who have always been.

Equity issues centre around three considerations: job displacement, real wage erosion (both of these are North issues) and job insecurity (which is both a North and a South issue). The first reaction to job displacement was an alarmist one of 'end of work'. But in the 1990s, in the USA as well as the UK, the paradox is that rates of unemployment are lower than they have been for twenty years and yet there is a fear of job displacement. It is of course a class and a generation thing. Blue-collar jobs for men in their forties and above have been lost while jobs for women and the educated are growing. Since the blue-collar workers were the backbone of politically powerful trade unions and because they were employed in manufacturing which is also displacing itself to the South, both unions and subcontracting suppliers etc, are complaining about the impact of globalisation.

Real wage erosion is another factor where 'Are your wages determined in Beijing?' becomes the rhetorical cry. Real wages of manufacturing workers are growing less quickly than they used to and in the USA until very recently there was, if anything, decline rather than growth. This effect is well predicted by international trade theory as an effect of freer trade between labour scarce/capital rich countries with labour rich/capital scarce countries. The effect of trade is to lower the return to the relatively scarce factor. The debate is still raging amongst economists as to the effect of trade, as against technical change, in this respect. Yet again the growth of wage inequality in the developed countries has helped the educated and the young and hurt the less educated and older workers.

9 I use 'north' to refer to the dominance of the old European/American powers and developed countries, and 'south' to refer to the developing economies of Asia, Latin America and Africa.

But both real wage erosion and job displacement are mirror images of the positive effects of globalisation for the South, not all of it, but for those countries, which are industrialising and exporting manufacturers. Some North NGOs are countering this result by complaining about low wages in the South, but while these wages are low relative to those in the North, they are less so than they were before globalisation and they are higher than what these workers could earn in the non-tradeable or agricultural sector in their countries. So globalisation has shifted industrialisation to the South and any attempt to jack-up wages in the South will only benefit the North, which is well endowed as it is. This is one reason why many South countries are opposing the social clause discussion in the WTO.

Job insecurity is a pervasive worry. Flexible labour markets may create jobs but these jobs are not long-term ones and the anxiety about job insecurity pervades in the North and South. There is an admission that while some OECD countries can take the burden of a high level of unemployment and maintain their welfare states, this is a diminishing option. In any case, for most countries in the world this is not an option at all.

Equity issues are unlikely to lead to global coalitions but in many rich countries they could generate a backlash against freer trade (I say freer trade rather than free trade since free trade does not exist as of now) and against the larger corporations. Such a backlash would have trade union and industrial [SME] support. It will be a Right/Left alliance, which will reconstitute politics much as it did with the split in the Liberal Party in the UK when Chamberlain joined the Tories on a tariff platform. There could also be a reimposition of some controls on the flexible labour market but this conflicts with the pressure to be competitive which cannot be easily avoided by most economies. But the reaction will be country-specific rather than global. Global alliances are difficult to build up in this case because there is no commonalty of interest across countries or even within countries.

Environment and Sustainability

The environment was not an issue in G19 although the problem of greenhouse gas emission was first mooted in the 1890s. Since the publication of Rachel Carson's *Silent Spring* in 1962, and especially since the oil crisis of 1973, the questions of non-renewable resource exhaustion, biodiversity and endangered species, greenhouse gas emission and global warming and the ozone layer have come to the forefront. In the 1970s these problems failed to be addressed by governments in a global fashion. But in the 1990s, the Rio Conference, the Montreal Convention and the Kyoto Summit have attempted global solutions to these problems. This is not to say that problems have been solved but, as the Montreal Convention example shows, given the will, solutions can be found. While there is a North/South divide, especially about who will bear the costs, in terms of both economic restructuring and financial resources, there is here a potential for a global cross-national alliance which could, given sufficient strength, bring about a major regulation of economic activities worldwide. This is because these are genuinely global problems as employment and wage problems are not.

Of course there will be debate as to whether solutions cannot be found with a market approach rather than an institutional/regulatory one. Thus, tradable pollution permits may work better than any quantitative restriction on consumption of say gasoline, especially if the USA is a party to the deal. The Green Clause as proposed in WTO negotiations by the North has shown that in some matters the free market is preferable to the South, than a restriction when it is likely to be a non-tariff barrier. Thus when environmental issues interfere with trade, no global coalition is likely, at least between states. There could be a combination of some NGOs and some states which may become globally powerful but even NGOs are often split across North/South lines on issues, such as the Green Clause.

Thus neither employment/wage nor Green issues are likely to generate a global coalition powerful enough to 'stop', much less reverse globalisation; by 'stop' I mean bring about a global regime with serious restrictions on capital movements or back to a Bretton Woods regime. This is not surprising since it is difficult to find a commonalty of interest in any economic area. It is not that such topics are a zero sum game but that the drive to find positive sum solutions will dominate those that rely on a threat of zero sum or negative sum outcomes as a way of forging a global coalition. The only exception is the global warming problem and that too only if a market-based solution is rejected as politically or technically unfeasible. But at that stage deglobalisation is unlikely to come about without conflict and catastrophe.

Nationalism/Fundamentalism

This is very much a revisit to G19 but again with a difference. There are many more independent nations and many movements for nations to be recognised and given status as independent political entities, i.e. as nation states. The break-up of Yugoslavia is an instance. The Kurds, the Palestine people, the Tamil in Sri Lanka, the Kashmiris in India and Pakistan occupied Kashmir, the many struggles in Africa, are all examples of this tendency. As I said above, many of these nations are the leftovers of the dissolution of the empires at the end of the First and the Second World Wars. Some of these conflicts have been with us ever since. Greece versus Turkey and its consequent Cyprus problem is a prime example of this. When empires dissolved, the boundaries they first drew were arbitrary, as indeed the victorious nationalist movements themselves said, but now the same nationalist movements in power have to defend those imperial demarcations as legitimate. The India–China border dispute of 1962 is another example of this.

The 1990s decade has seen simultaneously a unipolar power structure at the top and an almost anarchic and uncontrollable set of conflicts at the bottom. These are mainly 'new wars' but there have also been some old wars – Iran–Iraq and Operation Desert Storm being two examples (Kaldor, 1999). NATO and G7 have tried to build up a fire-fighting capability, as was seen in Bosnia and Kosovo and East Timor, but it is of course always late and selective, as was seen in the appalling Great Lakes tragedy. The new order born at the end of the Cold War that George Bush hailed has not yet succeeded in preventing wars or mitigating their effects in time. But they have contained them geographically. Unlike in 1914, a Serbian atrocity is unlikely to cause a worldwide conflagration.

Associated with nationalism is fundamentalism, and in particular Islamic fundamentalism. It is not because there are not other kinds of fundamentalisms but the Islamic one runs across countries and has a wider global reach than, say, Christian fundamentalism (very much an American phenomenon) or Hindu fundamentalism (confined to India) or Jewish fundamentalism (an Israeli problem). Islamic fundamentalism has unsettled many countries in the Middle East and North Africa. Thus Algeria, Egypt, Iran and Afghanistan have all suffered from terrorism or domestic civil wars or worse during the 1990s. While Islamic fundamentalism has been demonised by some Western experts as a threat to the West, it is its destabilisation of Muslim countries which is remarkable. So far its capacity to cause a global crisis has been limited.

The one channel through which fundamentalism of any kind can spread is the diaspora. On the one hand the competing ethnic groups in the diaspora make a bias for one side or the other in any dispute difficult for the metropolitan countries – for instance Kashmir where the UK government is confronted by Indian and Pakistani diasporas. But the loyalty of a diaspora member is multiple and cannot be exclusively to the state where s/he has taken citizenship. This makes them suspects in any paranoia about international terrorism, howsoever unfairly. It is not just that they may strike against their new habitat but even conspiring against their birthplace can be seen to be a problem. In September 1998, the British Parliament was recalled in a special session to pass legislation, one purpose of which was to prohibit activities which might be hostile against distant countries of interest to the diaspora. This was a major restriction of civil liberties of all citizens and a retrogression from the freedoms available in the G19 days.

The tendency of nationalism/fundamentalism is to cause havoc in its backyard rather than disrupt the global flows of capital or trade. It raises the costs of doing business but more for the poor or middle-income countries than for the rich ones. It has the potential for disruption and wars in particular regions but these regions can be sealed off and the spillover of the violence prevented. This is what seems to have happened in Yugoslavia and FSU. So I do not think this force, though potent in causing local trouble, can be a force for deglobalisation.

Unipolarity

American domination of the world's international relations as well as its economy raises some anxiety. American politics can be very parochial and disregarding of the rest of the world's welfare. This happened with the League of Nations vote, with the ITO vote, and continues to be the case in most environmental disputes in which the Americans have been involved. It has been glaring in the unilateral trade war America can launch with Super 301 and its disputes with the EU regarding bananas, hormone-fed beef, genetically modified organisms etc. Congress cannot be trusted to abide by rules to which it wants all else to be subject if it perceives American interests (and these may be parochial in terms of regions within America) to be at stake. America's commitment to free trade in the post-1945 world has been maintained more by elite manipulation than by populist support. If the global regime of freer trade and unregulated capital movements is seen to conflict with American interests, a protectionist President and a similar-minded Congress can easily renege on the commitments. After all, one of the reasons for the withdrawal of the Multilateral Agreement on Investment (MAI) was the reluctance of the Congress to sign up to any deal which would impose a rule of law on America.

Conclusion

So the fragility of G20 is not from the grass roots equity movements which will no doubt fight against globalisation. Nor will it come from the ecological dangers, real though they are, which threaten the globe. The nationalist forces will cause local trouble but not coalesce to undo the global order. G20 can only be undone by the powerful and only if the powerful feel their interests threatened. It may come from the USA. This is a paradox. But recall that G19 was not destroyed from below by the forces of protest of the excluded. It was destroyed by the powerful when their interests did not agree with the global regime.

It is an elementary principle of dialectics that one must look for weakness in the strongest element of any structure.

A Post-Seattle Postscript

This paper was written and delivered on 5th November 1999, at a Conference of the European Association of Evolutionary Political Economy. Since then the WTO ministerial meeting at Seattle has ended in a shambles. As I imply above, some people in the US economy are beginning to doubt the gains from further free trade. Clinton thought more of the US Presidential election of 2000 and pressures of American Federation of Labor and Congress of Industrial Organizations (AFL-CIO) when he practically sabotaged the meeting by his aggressive insistence on labour standards. There were other anti-MNC groups at Seattle but the balance in my view was held by the powerful labour lobby defending its high-wage jobs at the cost of slowing down deglobalisation. The issue remains: will American and other multinationals buckle under such pressure or will they fight for freer trade?

References

Alexander, T. (1996), *Unravelling Global Apartheid: An Overview of World Politics*, Cambridge: Polity Press.

Amin, S. (1997), *Capitalism in the Age of Globalization: The Management of Contemporary Society*, London: Zed.

Barnes, J. (1999), *Capitalism's World Disorder: Working Class Politics at the Millennium*, New York: Pathfinder.

Bauman, Z. (1998), *Globalization: The Human Consequences*, Cambridge: Polity Press.

Burbach, R., O. Nunez and B. Kagarlitsky (1997), *Globalization and Its Discontents, The Rise of Postmodern Socialisms*, London: Pluto.

Desai, M. (1995), 'Global governance', in M. Desai and P. Redfern, *Global Governance: Ethics and Economics of the New World Order*, London: Cassell.
Gray, J. (1998), *False Dawn*, Cambridge: Polity Press.
Greider, W. (1997), *One World Ready or Not: The Manic Logic of Global Capitalism*, New York: Simon and Schuster.
Halliday, F. (1995), *Islam and the Myth of Confrontation*, London: IB Taurus.
Hirst, P. and G. Thompson (1999), *Globalisation in Question* (2nd edn), Cambridge: Polity Press.
Hobson, J.A. (1902), *Imperialism*, London: Macmillan.
Kaldor, M. (1999), *New and Old Wars*, Cambridge: Polity Press.
Korten, D.C. (1995), *When Corporations Rule the World*, San Francisco, CA: Bewett-Koehler.
Lenin, V.I. (1916), *Imperialism, the Highest Stage of Capitalism*, various printings.
Mandel, E. (1995), *Long Waves of Capitalist Development: A Marxist Interpretation*, London: Verso.
Ohmae, K. (1990), *The Borderless World*, New York: Collins.
Ohmae, K. (1995), *The End of the Nation State: The Rise of Regional Economies*, London: Harper Collins.
Richmond, A. (1994), *Global Apartheid: Refugees, Racism and the New World Order*, Oxford: Oxford University Press.
Salvadori, M. (1979), *Kautsky and the Socialist Revolution 1880–1938*, London: Verso.
Sassen, S. (1998), *Globalization and Its Discontents: Essays on the New Mobility of People and Money*, New York: The New Press.
Schorske, C. (1955), *German Social Democracy 1905–1917: The Development of the Great Schism*, Cambridge, MA: Harvard University Press.
Schumpeter, J. (1919), *Imperialism and Social Classes*, Oxford: Basil Blackwell.
Scott, A. (ed.) (1997), *The Limits of Globalization: Cases and Arguments*, London: Routledge.
UNDP (1999), *Human Development Report*, New York: Oxford University Press.
Weiss, L. (1998), *The Myth of the Powerless State: Governing the Economy in a Global Era*, Cambridge: Polity Press.

Acknowledgement

First publication: Desai, Meghnad (2003) 'The Possibility of Deglobalization' in *Globalization, Social Capital and Inequality: Contested Concepts, Contested Experiences,* edited by Wilfred Dolfsma and Charlie Dannreuther. Cheltenham, Edward Elgar, pp. 1–13. Republished with kind permission of Edward Elgar.

Chapter 3

THE NEW ANTI-CAPITALIST MOVEMENT

Money and Global Civil Society

Meghnad Desai and Yahia Said

(2001)

Washington DC, Prague, Seattle, Davos, and wherever 'the money men' meet have been the foci of protest which have mobilised a broad coalition of groups, activists and lay individuals. While they may differ on many things, they agree on one. They consider many of the recent developments in globalisation as harmful, disruptive of their communities, and destructive in the long run. Such protests have taken many by surprise both in their scope and in their intensity, and have contributed to the increased interest in civil society in recent years. The protesters rarely attack globalisation as such, targeting instead corporate globalisation, global capitalism, the neo-liberal order, multinational companies, international financial institutions (IFIs) and trade agreements. Whatever the target, however, these protests are often branded as anti-globalisation. The counter-argument is usually a defence of globalisation as helpful to the world at large in enhancing output growth by expanding trade, helping the developing countries industrialise, and affording an opportunity for the first time in human history to eradicate world poverty.

In a framework where globalisation is understood as a symbiotic relationship between global capitalism and global civil society, this chapter analyses the interactions between the two. These interactions make up what we define as global civil society irrespective of whether or not it includes the market.

Given the breadth of its subject, this chapter focuses on money and finance as a proxy for global capitalism. This simplification is permissible for three reasons:

1. Finance is the dominant force in global capitalism. Financial flows far exceed trade flows and play an ever-growing role in every market transaction. Any sizeable trade today will almost certainly include bank credits on both sides, hedges against exchange rates and commodity price fluctuations in the form of futures and derivatives, and other forms of insurance. The growth and spread of the financial services industry and the unprecedented liberalisation of financial markets can be explained by the investment needs of the new industrial paradigm. The shift to information and communication technologies requires the mobilisation of vast financial resources, and global finance is the fastest way to achieve that. Similar financial booms occurred during previous technological revolutions (Perez 2000).

2. The financial services industry is among the main promoters of global capitalism, pushing for the opening of new markets and ever deeper liberalisation. The financial services industry is more dependent than any other on the low inflation advocated by the neo-liberal orthodoxy. Currently, the industry is pushing hard for the expansion of the WTO into the area of finance and investment through the General Agreement on Trade in Services (GATS). This will significantly expand the organisation, giving it jurisdiction over two-thirds of world GDP and bringing it into areas that affect every aspect of human life.

3. As we explain below, the financial services industry has traditionally been singled out for moral condemnation. So it is today, when it represents an extreme version of global capitalism. Financial juggernauts several times larger than many countries, fat-cat investment bankers and International Monetary Fund (IMF) executives playing God, astronomical profits on both the upside and the downside of the economic cycle, and bizarre financial products seemingly useless for anything other than the enrichment of those who invent them make finance an inevitable and often convenient target for those seeking to confront global capitalism.

Money and Morality

Our analysis deals with the ways in which global civil society has responded to the many activities of the financial sector – domestic and international, private and public – as they have affected the lives of the people. Finance is organised, complicated and pervasive. It comprises bank loans and debts, bonds and share markets, central bank and IMF regulation, and new innovative services such as futures and derivatives. It operates around the globe for twenty-four hours a day from places like the City of London and New York's Wall Street.

Financial developments have been at the forefront of globalisation. But even so, the core of financial market activities is age-old: buying and selling, borrowing and lending. The world has been familiar with money, credit and exchange for millennia. There are deeply ingrained moral attitudes about money, exchange and credit which shape the response of global civil society to recent developments.

Money has long been regarded as morally questionable. It is thought to be barren, which in turn calls into question the morality of charging interest. Money is often alleged to break up established communities, leaving atomised rootless individualism in its wake. Money is said to devalue relationships by reducing them to a financial calculus; money-using societies are contrasted with 'primitive' or pre-modern societies, which are said to embody more genuine emotional relationships since they are based on barter or gifts rather than monetary exchange. The anti-money critique leads to a utopian vision in which monetary exchange is superseded and relations based on 'real' values are re-established.[1] Against this is the view that money is an enabling, liberating and helpful device which oils the wheels of commerce and brings prosperity all round.

There have always been religious and philosophical objections to monetary transactions. The ideal is the self-sufficient household, or even the self-sufficient community, based on barter. Aristotle believed that money should be limited to restoring self-sufficiency. 'Interchange of this kind is not contrary to nature and is not a form of moneymaking: it keeps to its original purpose – to re-establish nature's own equilibrium of self-sufficiency' The objection is thus more to profiting from the use of money than from money in itself. If money is barren, it should not be made to yield a return. This logic is at the heart of the medieval Christian ban on usury as well as the Koranic injunction against charging interest on credit.

It was in the eighteenth century with Bernard Mandeville, David Hume and Adam Smith that a new understanding of money emerged. Smith reversed the story about the naturalness of self-sufficiency by asserting that mankind had a 'propensity to truck, barter and exchange'. It was this

1 In some of this discussion we rely on Parry and Bloch (1989). The quotations from Aristotle and Simmel are taken from this source.

propensity, motivated by self-interest, that brought happiness. Smith was aggressively modernist and did not concede anything to the earlier moral discourse about the immorality of exchange. He argued that the 'system of natural liberty' guaranteed prosperity not only to some but to all: 'the Kings of primitive tribes could not have gained such wealth' (Smith in Desai 2001).

Against Smith, Marx argued that whereas in previous modes of production the purpose of money was to facilitate the exchange of commodities (C-M-C), under capitalism its purpose was to increase the quantity of capital (M-C-M).

The sociologist George Simmel saw money 'as an instrument of freedom, and a condition for the extension of individual personality and the expansion of the circle of trust; but, at the same time, as a threat to the moral order' (Parry and Bloch 1989: 3). That threat came from the transition that money facilitated from Gemeinschaft (community) to Gesellschaft (association) (Tönnies 1955), encouraging rational calculation and abstract relationships as opposed to the primacy of feelings and emotion in traditional society.

Marcel Mauss, the French anthropologist, argued that money not only dissolves bonds of community but also allows for a separation between persons and things (Mauss 1996). This is the one aspect of money which has been crucial in globalisation. According to Simmel:

> Money permits possession at a distance. Only in the form of money can profits be easily transferred from one place to another, allowing for a spatial separation between the owner and his property which 'enables his property to be managed exclusively according to objective demands while it gives its owner a chance of leading his life independently of his possessions' (quoted in Parry and Bloch 1989: 5).

The change from an Aristotelian to a Smithian view of money was not accidental. For about a thousand years before the Iberian maritime expansion of 1490s which inaugurated the modern world system, Europe was starved of precious metals. It ran an adverse balance of trade with Asia, mainly India and China, and exported gold and silver to pay for imports from Asia. Money, being scarce, was expensive and interest rates were high. But the arrival of bullion from the Iberian colonies of West Africa and South America changed that. It affected social relations, favouring Peruvian merchants at the expense of the old landed wealth. Things began to be bought and sold for money which were previously not subject to exchange. Commerce began to create more wealth than agriculture had done for millennia. Money became the gateway to modernity and capitalism.

That does not, however, mean that traditional societies did not use money or that money coincided with modernity or the frail identification of money and capitalism with the West. The use of money has been found to be very important in many traditional pre-capitalist economies. The reciprocal interdependence of non-monetary, caste-based exchange of the Hindu jajmani system – a classic example of village self-sufficiency – is a myth propagated by modern (Western) investigators who wanted to see non-monetary exchange as a feature of 'traditional' society. As Parry and Bloch say:

> What implicitly seems to underlie the misrepresentation is a deeply entrenched notion about the transformative potential of money such that its presence becomes an index of a 'modern' society, with the corollary that in a 'traditional' one it can only be of peripheral significance. (1989: 7; see especially also Fuller 1989)

Thus we can dismiss the notions that traditional societies were based on real relationships unmediated by money, and that money, like the serpent in the Garden of Eden, arrived and corrupted the innocent. Money, and our views of its good or bad effects, are therefore never context-free. Our culture – that is, the modern, post-colonial, post-imperial world as it has come to be shaped by two centuries of industrial capitalism – is shot through and through with money and its higher form, credit. Indeed, it is impossible to imagine our economy without money, though pockets of 'local money' networks survive which use labour time as units of account and even means of payment. (See Box 3.5.)

The major concerns we have, however, are not with such local pockets of resistance but with global finance and especially the ways in which global civil society has encountered the massive money flows which have become the distinguishing feature of globalisation. It is here that we encounter the contrasting views of money as barren or liberating, and it is these that we must consider in more detail. These two competing views of money and its usefulness represent the two extremes and the many possible positions between them.

At one extreme there is the libertarian view in which the market and all its works are benevolent and beyond criticism. An allied view is that, benevolent or not, the market is a self-organising process and its regulation self-defeating and counterproductive. There is the moderate view that the market is more or less self-regulating but needs an occasional correction. Then there is the view that the market is prone to failure and the state should be ever-ready to regulate it. This view easily slides into one which

Box 3.1: Civil Society and the International Financial Institutions

The message is abundantly clear. There is no confusion, dithering, or doubt:

> The IMF and the World Bank, far from bringing economic stability and reducing poverty, are destroying the environment and impoverishing people. Their calls for dialogue are just a public relations ploy and the announced reforms are cosmetic. The Bretton Woods institutions should be abolished and all Third World debt cancelled. Moreover, the entire political and economic system of global capitalism needs to be overhauled. This is to be achieved by a global movement of solidarity opposed to the neo-liberal model imposed by multinational companies, the rich countries, and their minions at the World Bank and the IMF.

This was, in short, the message delivered by Katerina Liskova, one of the leaders of the Movement Against Economic Globalisation (INPEG), the coalition of NGOs and activists which organised the anti IMF/World Bank protests in Prague in the autumn of 2000. Katerina was speaking at a panel debate organised by Czech President Vaclav Havel at Prague Castle. The 20-year-old activist delivered this defiant message flanked by World Bank President James Wolfenson and IMF Managing Director Horst Kohler. UN Human Rights Commissioner Mary Robinson was moderating this unique forum, which also included international financier and philanthropist George Soros, Jubilee 2000 founder Ann Pettifor, Filipino academic/activist Walden Bello, and South African Minister of Finance Trevor Manuel. Despite the predictability of the protesters' message, the global financial leaders seemed dumbfounded. Wolfenson just reiterated his readiness for dialogue while Kohler insisted that he also had a heart. Indeed, World Bank and IMF representatives always appear hurt and surprised when attacked by civic activists.

The International Bank for Reconstruction and Development (IBRD), also known as the World Bank, and the International Monetary Fund (IMF) emerged out of the Bretton Woods conference held in the US in 1944. They were designed as components of an international regime of fixed exchange rates which was meant to deliver growth and stability to the post-war world economy. British economist John Maynard Keynes, who believed that public intervention could improve on market outcomes, at least in the short run, was one of the founding fathers of the two institutions.

The organisations were shaped by their origins. First, they are proactive; they are supposed to combat 'market failures' on a global scale: poverty in the case of the World Bank and financial instability in the case of the IMF. Second, they tend to be elitist and undemocratic primarily because they are dominated by their founder and main donor, the United States, and because they are run by 'experts' who don't expect ordinary people to understand complex economic problems. Over time neo-liberal economists came to represent the overwhelming majority of these 'experts', reflecting both trends in the economic profession and political change in the major donor countries. US and Western domination in general meant that political considerations often prevailed over economic ones in determining World Bank and IMF policies, especially when it came to regimes which were deemed pro-Western or at least anti-communist. This continued even after the end of the cold war, as was the case with billions of IMF and World Bank dollars loaned to Russia with the aim of propping up President Yeltsin and his 'reformers'.

The combination of activism and elitism described above meant that the Bretton Woods institutions were, and continue to be, attacked from both right and left. Extreme neo-liberals who see no point in public intervention, especially at the international level, view the IMF and the World Bank as examples of 'big government'. The Meltzer Report commissioned by the Republican majority in the US Congress exemplifies this approach, albeit with some moderation (IFIAC 2000). The report is critical of the proactive 'mission creep' at the Bretton Woods institutions and stresses the potential for market distortions caused by their interventions, such as the displacement of private investment and moral hazard. Attacks from the right have increased since the two institutions, especially the World Bank, embarked on a number of reforms aimed at increasing transparency and dialogue and taking policies beyond the neo-liberal scriptures. It is because of the constant attacks from the right that IMF and World Bank officials feel hurt when they are attacked from the left.

The leaders of the IMF and the World Bank believe that they have gone out of their way to accommodate activists' concerns and point out that the institutions are constrained by the will of the member states. They blame both developed countries for holding the purse strings too tight and developing country governments for blaming the IMF and the World Bank for their own failures.

Ann Pettifor partially agrees with this opinion but she would not go as far as to blame the developing countries for the debt crisis. At the Prague Castle meeting she invited activists to direct their attention to the 'puppet masters' in the G7 countries instead of the Bretton Woods institutions. This opinion was seconded by George Soros, who believes that things would be a lot better if developed countries adhered to their commitment to allocate 0.7 per cent of their GDP to foreign aid.

The World Bank, the IMF and other international institutions are facing similar problems of content – guiding principles, mission, goals – and form – accountability and participation, checks and balances. Solving these issues in each institution separately seems inefficient if not impossible. There is a need to explore 'global' solutions such as a set of common principles, parameters, guidelines, or common structures such as an Ombudsman or appeals court. International institutions may even share an 'upper/second chamber', like the ones proposed by the Angela Wood of the Bretton Woods Project (Wood 2001), which would better represent poor countries or non-state actors. Speaking at the Prague Castle meeting, Mary Robinson congratulated Katerina on her courage and proceeded to outline such a global solution. She calls it the 'rights-based approach' and it entails cross-referencing trade and global finance rules with human rights principles and environmental norms.

Such 'global' solutions, however, require a political momentum which does not seem available at the moment. Quite the contrary: the new unilateralist US administration is likely to attempt to curtail the Bretton Woods institutions, reducing them to extensions of US foreign policy. While Walden Bello sees no problem in a tactical alliance with the extreme right against the Bretton Woods institutions, other activists would think twice before hopping into bed with the likes of Pat Buchanan. They may also heed the sombre observation raised by the South African Finance Minister Trevor Manuel, at the Prague Castle meeting. He pointed out that, without the IMF and the World Bank, only three countries in sub-Saharan Africa would have access to external financing. Time will show whether activists will be able to keep the heat on the IFIs without playing into the hands of the extreme right.

sees the market as chronically malfunctioning and hence in need of overarching control. The extreme view would be a rejection of the market and all its works and its replacement by a self-conscious democratic rule of 'Society' (Desai 2001). There is extremism at either end of the spectrum in which one celebrates the market while the other excoriates it. In between are nuanced objections, not to abstractions such as the 'market' or 'money' but to concentrations of economic power (transnational/global corporations) or to excessive income and wealth inequalities; not against 'market failures' in general but environmental degradation or racial or gender discrimination; not to flows of capital as such but to the uses to which they are put and the returns obtained and to inequalities of power in international trade. The theme common to all of these is the economic or the monetary link which unites them.

Given the Manichean division at the extremes and the multiplicity of nuanced attitudes in the middle, it is necessary to distinguish the types of money flows or trading arrangements which attract different degrees of protest. Capital flows are singled out because it is the unregulated, or at least freer, flow of capital in the last ten to fifteen years which, in our view, marks out the new phase of globalisation.

Capital Flows: Types, Impacts, Responses

The shock of globalisation and the flows of capital it sets up are not new phenomena in world history. Trade has taken place between the different continents by sea or land for millennia. Europe and Asia especially have a continuous history of trade and gold flow, which goes back to the Phoenicians. The dawn of capitalism in the 1500s introduced a new element of violence in the relationships of trade and gold flow between Europe and Africa and the Americas. Massive gold flows to Europe were forcibly extracted from the older civilisations of those continents. This sorry saga has been well mapped out by Immanuel Wallerstein in his many writings (see, for example, Wallerstein 2000).

With the industrial revolution, capital and commodity flows took very different forms and had a very different impact. Now labour could be harnessed at home and abroad without coercion; surplus could be extracted from labour made more productive by new machines. Capital began to flow outwards to the periphery as much as it flowed back in the form of repatriated profits. The periphery was transformed in the process of colonisation by the flow of industrial capital. Soon the colonies began to crave their emancipation, which to them implied their own industrialisation, and decided upon independence to pursue capital accumulation and industrial self-sufficiency. In this new context after 1945, private flows of capital from the core to the periphery dried up. Much of the capital flowed within the core. The flows from the core to the periphery took the form, for the first time in history, of massive government-to-government transfers and some smaller flows from the multilateral lending institutions set up at the Bretton Woods conference in 1944 – the World Bank and the International Monetary Fund – to the countries of what in the 1950s came to be called the Third World.

The founders of the Bretton Woods system believed that they had discovered the magic formula which would harness the creative forces of capitalism while mitigating its negative side effects. A fixed exchange-rate regime backed by the promise of IMF intervention was supposed to help everyone reap the fruits of free trade without worrying about instability. Aid facilitated by the World Bank was meant to help address issues of poverty and inequality.

The 1970s and the Petrodollar Debt

This new dispensation persisted until the early 1970s. At that juncture the first of many events occurred which began the transformation of the post-war world by what we now call 'globalisation'. The United States came off the dollar-exchange standard and the Bretton Woods system of fixed exchange rates collapsed. The quadrupling of oil prices generated a massive transfer, of up to about 5 per cent of their GDP, from the OECD countries to the oil-exporting countries. This was the largest flow in the 200 years since the industrial revolution of money from the developed countries to the (oil-exporting) developing countries. This in turn led to the recycling of petrodollars, which brought private bank loans from developed-country banks to the developing countries. This integration of the periphery into the global banking world heralded a new phase of the world economy.

The First Crisis of the 1980s

It was when international debt became a problem in the early 1980s that we may say global civil society encountered the financial world. As Marx saw 150 years ago, capitalist power relations are non-coercive in a crude physical sense. The distancing between the owner of capital and its effects on the ground further complicates the agency problem. When debt piles up and interest payments mount, the poor may starve but whose fault is it really? The borrowers – those in power in the developing countries – eagerly shift the blame to the lenders – the IMF or Western banks. The IMF and the banks accuse the borrowers of economic mismanagement. But the real reason for the debt crisis was that the developed world had decided to put its house in order, adopted monetarist policies, and began to borrow rather than print money. This led to the turnaround in the bond markets when interest rates rose from 5 per cent to 15 per cent in nominal terms and from around minus 10 per cent to plus 10 per cent in real terms.

Through the 1980s, as country after country with debt problems had to seek IMF loans and submit to structural adjustment, civil society everywhere began to realise the severe impact such flows could have on daily life. It was as if, until then, people had been insulated from the outside world of global finance whose rules were non-negotiable even to their sovereign governments. Governments tried to bear down on their people in order to repay their debts, however wisely or foolishly the money had been used, and in response to the protests of their people could only plead helplessness in the face of IMF or foreign banks. In the years since independence people had thought that their governments were on their side or could at least be brought round to their side, and had some power to better their lives, as they had been promised. Now there was a cleavage between them and their governments, which pointed a finger at a bigger external power.

It was in devising defensive responses to this new situation that civil societies began to form in many countries. Until then, there had been a unity between the state and the people, which had arisen from twentieth-century independence movements in Asia and Africa. Now the people had to articulate their voices against the state, even their own state. People began to build defensive, cross-class alliances to fight against the cutbacks in food subsidies, rises in taxes and prices, unemployment, shutdown of public facilities, pricing of previously freely available goods, and so forth (Cornia et al. 1987).

The resolution of the debt crisis of the 1980s was in one sense surprising and in another quite business-like. It took the intervention of the US government in the form of Brady Bonds (see the Glossary) to allow the banks to do what they normally do with bad debts: write them off. After much misery, much of the debt was written off, converted into equity, swapped for factories in debtor countries, or forgiven in recognition of some environmental good deed. It was painful and messy but once the write-off had been agreed by the developed country governments (which had to bear the tax burden of debt write-offs) the private commercial debt issue was resolved.

The 1990s: The Peso and the Asian Crises

The events of the 1990s were yet another phase of the movement that had started in the 1970s. Communist economies had by then collapsed and begun their transition to market economies. China had adopted market-oriented policies, albeit without renouncing socialism. Stock markets were springing up all over the emerging market economies. Developed countries had all by then deregulated capital movements. The financial markets and the foreign exchange markets were dealing in $1 trillion per day, helped by the revolution in telecommunications and information technology. The preferred form of capital flow was equity rather than debt. Foreign direct investment (FDI) flows to the Third World were soon outstripping foreign-aid flows by a factor of 4 to 1.

Two further shocks jolted the brave new world of global finance during the 1990s. First was the Mexican peso crisis in December 1994. Having followed an orthodox fiscal and monetary policy, much to the approval of the IMF, Mexico loosened the purse-strings in a pre-election year and made a risky dollar conversion of its debt. The uprising in Chiapas coincided with a transition to a new presidency, and the credibility of the peso collapsed. A massive rescue operation of $18 billion had to be organised by the IMF. A bad deflationary year followed in 1995 with much loss of output, but 1996 saw a recovery and a flow of funds back into Mexico.

The other shock was the Asian crisis of 1997 and 1998. This spread across nations previously hailed as miracle economies. Starting with the Thai baht, the currency depreciation and stock market collapse moved to Malaysia, then to Indonesia, and finally to South Korea. The Asian crisis was truly the first crisis of globalisation of the late twentieth century. It started on the periphery but spread to the metropolis via Russia. It originated in the financial sector, which is at the forefront of globalisation. Its resolution, partially at least, came when the US Federal Reserve cut interest rates three times in quick succession in recognition of the likely impact of the crisis on US stock markets.

The Asian crisis was special in that it was triggered by bank lending rather than by portfolio investments or FDI. It took place in countries with high growth rates, high savings rates and generally good macroeconomic policies. The IMF misdiagnosed the crisis as one of 1980s-style macroeconomic mismanagement. But it was a private lending crisis, not a public finance one. The policy of pegged exchange rates proved to be inconsistent with unrestricted bank lending from abroad. What seemed like risk-free lending became risky when the baht could no longer hold on to its peg to the US dollar. Since the bulk of the debt liability was in foreign currency, the domestic central bank could not help by performing its function as lender of last resort.

The Asian crisis was serious in terms of loss of output and currency depreciation. It also meant a substantial adverse impact on living standards of many people who had just recently emerged from poverty (see Box 3.2). In some countries, especially Indonesia but also Thailand and South Korea, the crisis became one of political authority. South Korea succeeded in making a transition to democracy and a peaceful change of regime, and Thailand reformed its constitution. Indonesia also went through a traumatic transition to democracy which remains fragile. The democratic deficit enhanced the need for civil society to organise resistance movements. By its clumsy intervention, the IMF seemed to be as much part of the problem as of any solution. The insistence of the Malaysian prime minister, Dr Mahathir, that controls on capital movements be revived in face of IMF opposition strengthened this impression, as in the event Malaysia did insulate itself against the worst effects of the crisis.

Calls for reform of the international financial institutions, for a new 'global financial architecture', were made in the wake of the Asian crisis during the summer of 1998. But the resolution of the immediate impact on US markets by the Federal Reserve cooled the ardour for any fundamental change among the G7 countries. No lender of last resort has been set up at the global level. The IMF escaped either bolstering of its powers or downsizing, as advocated by the Meltzer Report for the US Congress (IFIAC 2000). There were some changes in terms of greater transparency, greater accountability and wider consultation with developing countries.[2] But there was no radical reform.

Growth and Persistence of Foreign Direct Investment

Through the 1990s, despite the peso and the Asian crises, the movement of FDI to developing countries proved much less volatile than that of portfolio capital or bank lending. This has not excused FDI from criticism and its volume now exceeds that of foreign aid by between three and four times. While the large volume of turnover in the foreign exchange and bond markets – $1 trillion plus daily – attracts much attention, it is FDI which has effects at a local level and has longer-term effects on growth, employment and the environment than portfolio capital. Its spread is confined to a small

2 For an overview of the Financial Stability Forum and other IMF reforms, see IMF's website.

Box 3.2: The Cost of the Asian Crisis

> In East Asia, it was reckless lending by international banks and other financial institutions combined with reckless borrowing by domestic financial institutions – combined with fickle investor expectations – which may have precipitated the crisis; but the costs – in terms of soaring unemployment and plummeting wages – were borne by workers. Workers were asked to listen to sermons about bearing pain just a short while after hearing, from the same preachers, sermons about how globalisation and opening up capital markets would bring them unprecedented growth. (Stiglitz 2000: 1)

East Asia enjoyed an unprecedented 7 per cent GDP growth per year for the last two decades of the twentieth century. This enabled some countries in the region, namely, Hong Kong, South Korea, Singapore and Taiwan, to become the only ones to actually make the transition from Third World to First World. Following the 1997 crisis, the region's economies shrank by 4 per cent (United Nations 1999). Inflation and unemployment, hitherto virtually unknown in most of these countries, skyrocketed. Although most of the region's economies managed to recover by 1999, they remain below their potential level had pre-crisis trends persisted:

The crisis left these countries with a heavy public debt burden, forcing the governments to spend a greater proportion of GDP on interest payments.

GDP deviation from pre-crises growth trend in 1999 (%)

Indonesia	-16.6
Malaysia	-7.2
Korea	-12.9
Thailand	-14.5

Source: World Bank (2000)

The crisis left these countries with a heavy public debt burden, forcing the governments to spend a greater proportion of GDP on interest payments.

Increase in debt servicing costs as % of GDP after the crisis

Indonesia	3.9
Malaysia	2.2
Korea	0.5
Philippines	2.1
Thailand	10.3

Source: World Bank (2000)

While most of the region's economies are growing again, the social consequences of the crisis persist. In the aftermath of the crisis, the number of people in the region earning less than $1 day increased by 10 million (18 per cent).

South Korea, which had an unemployment rate of 2 per cent before the crisis, was still reporting a rate of 4 per cent at the end of 2000, despite the fact that the economy grew by 9.5 per cent in the same year. Real unemployment is even higher, as unemployment numbers do not reflect either the percentage of people who are nominally employed but receive no salary or the 117,000 migrant workers who had to leave South Korea after the crisis. South Korea also had no unemployment insurance until the crisis. The scheme since established does not cover most of the unemployed. Real wages declined by 14 per cent in the aftermath of the crises after growing by 7.3 per cent in 1996. This, combined with inflation, led consumer spending to decline by 12 per cent, the steepest drop in South Korean history. The result of all this is a persisting increase in poverty. Before the crisis 7.5 per cent of the urban population were poor. This number jumped to 23 per cent at the height of the crises and was standing at 14 per cent at the end of 1999, despite the recovery.

In Indonesia, unemployment rose from 4.9 per cent to 13.8 per cent after the crisis. Real wages dropped by between 40 per cent and 60 per cent. The percentage of people living in poverty jumped from 11 per cent in 1996 to 20 per cent at the end of 1999, an addition of 20 million people.

In Thailand, unemployment remains at three times the pre-crisis level, despite strong recovery. Combined with a 6 per cent decline in real wages, this translates into an increased incidence of poverty of 15 per cent.

Hong Kong and South Korea are the only East Asian countries who have an unemployment insurance system. In Hong Kong unemployment rose from 2.2 per cent in 1997 to 5 per cent in 1998. At the end of 2000 it stood at 5 per cent despite two consecutive years of growth.

The cost of the Asian crisis, 1996–1999

	1996	1997	1998	1999
GDP growth rates (%) (IMF)				
Hong Kong	4.5	5.0	-5.0	2.9
Indonesia	8.0	4.5	−13.0	0.3
Korea	6.8	5.0	−6.7	10.7
Malaysia	10.0	7.3	−7.4	5.7
Philippines	5.8	5.2	-0.6	3.3
Singapore	8.0	8.4	0.4	5.4
Taiwan	5.7	6.8	4.7	5.7
Thailand	5.9	-1.7	−10.0	4.2
Unemployment as a percentage of workforce (ILO)				
Hong Kong	2.8	2.2	4.7	6.3
Indonesia	4.0	4.68	5.46	N/A
Korea	2.0	2.6	6.8	6.3
Malaysia	2.5	2.5	3.2	3.4
Philippines	7.4	7.9	9.6	9.37
Singapore	3.0	2.4	3.2	4.6
Taiwan	N/A	N/A	N/A	N/A
Thailand	1.08	0.87	3.41	3.0

Sources: Stiglitz (2000); United Nations (1999); World Bank (2000).

number of countries with high savings rates, large pools of semi-skilled labour, good governance and high levels of literacy. There is, however, no IFI which monitors FDI or polices its accountability. Within the domestic jurisdiction of all OECD countries, there are tough regulations on corporations (for example, the US Justice Department's moves against Microsoft) and regulatory bodies such as the Securities and Exchange Commission in the US and the Financial Services Authority in the UK. There is, however, no move afoot today for a global regulator of FDI. The Multilateral Agreement on Investments (MAI) was an attempt to introduce a uniform structure of rules for both domestic and foreign capital, but it did not extend to a uniform and universal regulation regime such as exists in individual OECD countries. The demise of the MAI was due as much to protests by the NGOs as to the reluctance of the US Congress to contemplate symmetric treatment of foreign and domestic capital. (See Box 3.3.)

If there has been no global move towards regulation of FDI or any serious move for the reform of the IFIs, there has been a successful single-issue movement – Jubilee 2000 – for the reduction of Third World debt. While the petrodollar debt owed to commercial banks caused serious debt default problems in the 1980s and much misery, it was resolved, as noted above, by some cancellation of debt, some payment in lieu in the form of environmental policy changes, and even some capital sales. Public debt has proved to be a much tougher nut to crack. For one thing, the World Bank, as well as the governments of developing countries who are the lenders, do not believe in writing off bad debt. What is a sound commercial practice is forbidden to public agencies. This is a peculiar example of the inflexibility of government finance.

This Third World debt arises from a small amount of intergovernmental or IFI lending to some very poor countries in the late 1980s and early 1990s, including Uganda, Mozambique and Niger. The original principal has now mushroomed into a much larger sum due to the inability of many of the debtor countries to service it, as unpaid instalments have been added and compounded. The size of the debt now bears little relation to the original amount. Debtor countries have been weakened by the collapse of primary commodity prices since the late 1970s and many local and civil wars. Individual G7 countries have taken some initiatives; the UK has been in the lead since 1990, when John Major was briefly the Chancellor of the Exchequer, and has accelerated this lead under Chancellor Gordon Brown; but the World Bank's Highly Indebted Poor Countries (HIPC) initiative has been on the table since the mid-1990s. It has been mired in inaction.

The total amounts are smaller than those in the 1980s but the debtor countries are now much poorer. It is also more difficult to persuade countries, especially the G7 which dominate the voting in the IFIs, to agree to any debt forgiveness.

Paradoxically, Third World debt, which Jubilee 2000 focused on, has little to do with globalisation. Indeed, it is the countries which cannot access the private lenders in the form of either debt or equity because they are abysmally poor that are forced into the arms of governmental or multilateral institutional lenders. Their plight is an aspect of the unequal nature of the global power structure as enshrined by the UN constitution, which gives veto power to the permanent members of the Security Council, and in the decision-making structures of the Bretton Woods institutions. The Asian crisis was a crisis of countries that had become just rich enough to be attractive to private lenders. The public-debt crisis is that of countries that are too poor to be of interest to commercial lenders and too weak to be a threat to the powerful governments which have lent them money.

Box 3.3: The Demise of the MAI

At the end of 1998, negotiations within the framework of the Organisation for Economic Cooperation and Development (OECD) for a Multilateral Agreement on Investment (MAI) were abandoned. The collapse of the negotiations was precipitated by a number of factors including a broad international campaign coordinated by Friends of the Earth, 50 Years Is Enough, and other international and local groups.

The MAI was intended to promote cross-border investments by providing a unified set of rules governing interactions between governments and investors worldwide. The rules proposed were favourable to investors, prohibiting governments from discriminating among or against them and giving investors the right to prosecute offending governments in international courts. For example, the agreement would have eliminated a government's right to place certain industries or areas of activity out of reach for foreign investors. It would have prohibited the imposition of local content or other performance requirements committing foreign investors to purchase a certain proportion of their outlays from local suppliers or to create local jobs. It would have allowed investors the freedom to move money in and out of countries without restrictions and prohibited any form of expropriation.

The negotiations, which were taking place largely unnoticed since 1995, began to attract unwanted attention after the Asian crisis of 1997. The crisis left both governments and activists with little appetite for further financial-market liberalisation. Disagreements among G7 countries were also on the rise. The US wanted to maintain the right to persecute companies investing in Cuba or Iran. France wanted to protect its film industry from Hollywood. Hungary wanted to preserve employee and management-centred privatisation schemes. In the end it was France's withdrawal from the process which sealed the MAI's fate.

Activists succeeded in amplifying and leveraging government disagreements up to the point of defeating the MAI.

The critical method employed by anti-MAI campaigners was education and information. They provided in-depth analysis of the proposed agreements and their possible environmental, social and political implications. They published glossaries explaining obscure legal and trade terms and provided real-time coverage and analysis of the negotiating positions.

This was probably the first time such negotiations were conducted in the spotlight of public attention. It presented a radical break from the tradition of conducting negotiations among technocrats away from public scrutiny, providing only a doctored summary of concluded agreements to the public and parliaments at the ratification stage.

One may agree with the technocrats' contention that the popularised version of the MAI draft agreements and the analysis of their impact by NGOs are not scientifically accurate or that many of those involved in the debates were not qualified to pass judgement on such matters. This is changing rapidly, however, and many activists today have access to high-quality research on economic issues. The campaign against the MAI was, however, a breakthrough in terms of democratising international trade negotiations by providing the public with an alternative opinion; forcing politicians to scrutinise the proposed agreement; and requiring the technocrats to be more transparent and to defend their positions to a sceptical public.

The MAI negotiations also witnessed increased cooperation/coordination between NGOs and governments trying to alter or stop the agreement altogether. France used NGO arguments against the agreement in both domestic and international deliberations. The government-commissioned Lalumière Report, conducted in the summer of 1998, relied heavily on NGO testimony to justify France's reservations (Friends of the Earth 1998a).

The MAI defeat was a temporary and, some would say, a pyrrhic victory for civil society. Most groups involved in the campaign would have preferred to see an alternative agreement which would regulate foreign investments in ways that protect the environment, labour, human rights and indigenous cultures. Many wanted to see multinational corporations and financiers brought under national or international jurisdiction. An international agreement on investment is necessary to avoid a race to the bottom among governments in their quest for foreign investments. Faced with the choice between a dangerous treaty and an even more dangerous lack thereof, campaigners, unable to come up with a comprehensive alternative, opted for the latter. They leveraged the nationalism of individual governments to derail the whole process.

> Offering suggested changes to the MAI is a trickier issue. Whereas it is important to eliminate the MAI's worst features in case the agreement goes forward, but [sic!] eliminating those sections alone would not result in an acceptable agreement. Good rules on investment would include binding language on investors' responsibilities for the environment, workers and human rights. Therefore, signalling any support for the MAI in exchange for textual changes can be dangerous because the agreement as a whole is fundamentally unbalanced in favour of investors. (Friends of the Earth 1998b)

The issues covered under the MAI are back on the table again through the General Agreement on Trade in Services (GATS) in the framework of the WTO. GATS covers a much wider area of activities than investment alone and is already the target of intense opposition from activists worldwide (see for instance the World Development Movement URL). Will they be able to advance an internationalist alternative or will they ally themselves with protectionists to derail the whole process as they did with the MAI?

Anti-capitalism: An Overview

Throughout the forty or so years following 1945, there was a vibrant anti-capitalist movement, in the form either of orthodox Leninist communist parties or of democratic socialist parties. Feminist and civil rights movements were added to this worldwide. The focus everywhere was the state because the state was seen as an instrument of control over capital or over the unequal power structure. Political parties of the left were part of this broad protest movement even when they were in office, as were the trade unions which supported these parties. The 1960s saw a big explosion of these movements across Western Europe and in the USA at a time when 'capitalism in one country' was perhaps performing at its best in terms of full employment and growth. The 1970s saw a worsening of economic performance, with stagflation and a deepening of the crisis of the state, but also of resistance against it. But even in the 1970s the various national movements were separate; only the environmental movement forged global interconnections. It was the changes in the 1970s and in the 1980s discussed above which shattered the logic of capitalism or socialism in one country and began to shape the new global economy not as an ecological ideal but as an economic reality.

The anti-capitalist movement of the 1960s and 1970s was wounded if not defeated by the structural changes which capitalism underwent in the 1980s in the developing countries. The collapse of the Soviet Union demoralised the Leninist left and shut down many communist parties. There was instead a growth of NGOs, many of them concerned with development or ecological issues. Other movements, like the women's movement and human rights campaigns, survived the neo-liberal onslaught of the 1980s. They have now emerged as the opposition to globalisation in the 1990s and beyond. Their numbers are larger, both individually and in their memberships. They are more globally networked. They are also less connected with political parties. In the following sections these movements are analysed in terms of their stances on the financial effects of globalisation.

The last ten years have witnessed historic changes in the world system. The state socialist countries of Europe have transformed themselves into fledgling democracies and fragile market economies. Across OECD countries, social democratic parties in office or out of it have rethought their old philosophies and abandoned any desire for state ownership or control of capital. A system of countries each pursuing 'capitalism in one country' with weak articulation through trade has changed into one with strong articulation through international capital flows, inter-country, inter-corporate competition, flexible exchange rates and converging long-term interest rates through global bond markets. Governments have suffered a narrowing of their scope for fiscal discretion. Stock markets have grown in size and numbers across the world. The logic of globalisation is one of unregulated global flows and a single bond market, although that logic is as yet far from realised.

Civil Society and Global Finance: Four Responses

Interactions between civil society and global capitalism take place at two friction points. At one point, society is reacting to market encroachment on both personal and public spaces: consumerism, atomisation, the erosion of public services, and nation state models of democracy. At the other, society is reacting to socio-economic consequences of capitalism such as poverty, inequality and instability.

At these friction points the anti-capitalist movement raises two corresponding sets of questions:

1. What are the boundaries of the market? How are they determined and enforced?
2. Can the market be trusted to produce just and stable outcomes or does it require external intervention? How would such intervention be carried out?

These questions, although as old as capitalism itself, have gained in relevance over the past twenty years, providing an impetus to the anti-capitalist movement. The reasons for this renewed attention are set out below.

First, there is a perception that liberal democracy is lagging behind neo-liberal economics or even being threatened by it (Mittelman 2000). The neo-liberal reforms rammed through during the 1980s by right-of-centre governments in the West and by the IMF in the East and the South, the inexorable encroachment of the market into the public sphere, the unchecked reign of multinational corporations, and the apparent inability of national leaders to challenge any of the above has given the anti-capitalist movement a new angle of attack.

Second, the abandonment of nation state–based answers to the contradictions of capitalism, be they the welfare state in the North or state-sponsored development or superpower patronage in the South, is generating pockets of extreme poverty in both rich and poor countries. While overall levels of prosperity are increasing, the situation at the bottom of the socio-economic ladder has actually been deteriorating. The widening gap between rich and poor, both within and between countries, is increasingly difficult to conceal, justify or sustain.

The anti-capitalist movement has changed in tandem with its target. In the era of state capitalism the focus was on the state. Some wanted to capture it, others to reform it, and yet others just wanted it out of the way. Today, attention is shifting to the corporation as the main target of the anti-capitalist movement. Some strands of the movement against corporate globalisation would even call for protecting and strengthening the territorial state while others demand solutions that require the creation of a global welfare state. To be sure, the state, especially in the G7 countries, remains an important target for many movements. There is a growing awareness, however, of the limitations of state power under globalisation.

The movement against global capitalism falls into four groups: isolationists, supporters, reformists and alternatives. As with all such classifications, no movement, campaign or event can be allocated solely to any one of the categories. Many shift from one to the other depending on the issue, event or time frame in question.

Isolationists

In addition to remnants of communist and Stalinist groups, isolationists include some environmental groups such as Friends of the Earth, who tend to be more radical in their economic than in their ecological agenda; think tanks and groups promoting national solutions to Third World development issues, such as Focus on the Global South; anti-globalisation groups such as the International Forum on Globalisation, Global Exchange, and 50 Years Is Enough; local social movements such as the Landless Workers Movement in Brazil (MST); individuals such as Walden Bello and Noam Chomsky; and media outlets such as *Le Monde diplomatique*.

The isolationists represent the only global civil society response to global capitalism which openly claims to be anti-globalisation. The isolationists call directly or indirectly for the abolition of the existing global economic order. Walden Bello says:

> Indeed, I would contend that the focus of our efforts these days is not to try to reform the multilateral agencies but to deepen the crisis of legitimacy of the whole. I am talking about disabling not

> just the WTO, the IMF, and the World Bank but the transnational corporation itself. And I am not talking about a process of 're-regulating' the TNCs but of eventually disabling or dismantling them as fundamental hazards to people, society, the environment, to everything we hold dear. (Bello 2000)

Other isolationists are less categorical. Many call for 'economic diversity' (Friends of the Earth 2000), presumably allowing for certain elements of global capitalism to continue in some areas. The demands they advance, however, can hardly be compatible with a functioning market economy, particularly given their objection to such concepts as economic growth or comparative advantage.

Isolationists treat globalisation and global capitalism as synonyms. They oppose globalisation in most of its manifestations, promoting instead deglobalisation (Bello 2000) or localisation (Hines 2000) which entails:

- *economic subsidiarity*: trade should be minimised, goods should be produced as closely as possible to the site of consumption;
- *political subsidiarity*: states and local communities should be re-empowered at the expense of transnational corporations and international organisations, decisions should be taken as closely as possible to where they take effect; and
- *self-sufficiency*: resources for investment should be mobilised locally, reliance on foreign investment should be minimised.

In their blanket opposition to the IMF and the World Bank, left-wing isolationists find strange bed-fellows among their right-wing rivals and supporters of global capitalism. To quote Bello on this subject:

> The motivation of the incoming Republicans in criticising the IMF and World Bank lies in their belief in free-market solutions to development and growth. This may not coincide with that of progressives, who see the IMF and World Bank as a tool of US hegemony. But the two sides can unite behind one agenda at this point: the radical downsizing, if not dismantling, of the Bretton Woods twins. (Bello 2001)

On the specific issues of global finance, the isolationists hold the following positions.

Public debt. Third World debt is a direct consequence and responsibility of Western powers, banks and international lending institutions. Loans were knowingly made to corrupt and/or incompetent Third World leaders for political reasons, for example to ensure loyalty during the cold war or to perpetuate a relationship of dependence. Lending was also used as a beachhead to secure access for transnational corporations. Hence, all Third World debts should be written off. Moreover, given the real transfers[3] from the Third World to the rich countries caused by unfavourable terms of trade and interest payments and outright looting in colonial days, the debt relationship should be reversed. In the future, Third World countries should avoid borrowing altogether and rely on their own resources for investments.

Short-term capital flows. Equity investments, derivatives and foreign exchange transactions are all part of a global casino. On the upside, they only enrich Western speculators; on the downside, they cause widespread suffering to working people both in the North and in the South. Speculators often get bailed out by the IMF and other rescue programmes. They may even benefit from crises, as did George Soros, attacking the European Union's exchange rate mechanism and the Thai baht.

Short-term capital flows are inherently volatile and destabilising. The responsibility for financial crises such as those in 1997–98 lies squarely on the shoulders of Western speculators and their private-sector counterparts in the afflicted countries. It also lies with the IMF, which forced the emerging economies to liberalise their capital markets in the first place. Post-crisis IMF interventions bail out speculators while aggravating the effects on working people. Countries should have the option to introduce currency and exchange controls and opt out of the global capital market altogether.

Long-term foreign direct investments. Foreign investments benefit only the multinational corporations that make them. They serve to perpetuate the exploitation of the poor and destroy the environment. Consequently, structural adjustment programmes and other liberal reforms aimed at encouraging foreign investments are part of the same conspiracy:

DEBT ⟶ DEBT CRISIS ⟶ STRUCTURAL ADJUSTMENT ⟶ OPENING TO TRANSNATIONAL CORPORATIONS

Self-reliance and self-sufficiency are the only way forward. This is the unifying slogan which brings together the isolationists in the Third World

3 Adverse terms of trade meant that Third World countries over many years sold relatively cheap raw materials to industrialised countries in exchange for relatively expensive manufactured goods.

with protectionists in the North by shielding national favourites, such as state-sponsored manufacturing industries, in the developing countries and sunset industries, such as the car industry, in developed ones.

Supporters

Civil society responses to global finance in the 'supporters' category include no movements and very few NGOs. They consist mainly of organisations, groups, media outlets, think tanks and individuals lobbying on behalf of business, be it an individual company, an industry or private enterprise in general. Examples of supporters include the Centre for Civil Society in India, the Chamber of British Industry in the UK, the American Enterprise Institute in the US, the *Economist,* the *Wall Street Journal*, the Meltzer Commission and Thomas Friedman.

Although attention is usually devoted to instances when the interests of civil society collide with those of global capitalism, the interactions between the two are not always negative. Civil society may benefit when market expansion takes place at the expense of authoritarian regimes, fundamentalism or autarky. Capitalism can also be more just and efficient than such alternatives as feudalism or central planning. This is the main rationale behind civil society responses which are unequivocally supportive of global capitalism in its current form. Supporters are indeed the most influential of the civil society responses to global capitalism.

Since they occupy the two extreme ends of the spectrum, it should come as no surprise that supportive responses to global capitalism often coincide with isolationist positions. For diametrically different reasons both are dismissive of reforms and global governance proposals aimed at mitigating the negative consequences of global capitalism. The most important point of agreement among them is the equation of globalisation and global capitalism. As Thomas Friedman says:

> The driving idea behind globalization is free-market capitalism – the more you let market forces rule and the more you open your economy to free trade and competition, the more efficient and flourishing your economy will be. Globalization means the spread of free-market capitalism to virtually every country in the world. Globalization also has its own set of economic rules – rules that revolve around opening, deregulating and privatising your economy. (Friedman 2000)

Global capitalism, according to its supporters, is not only the best way to prosperity: it is the only way. 'There Is No Alternative' (TINA) is an often-repeated argument to this end. TINA does not only mean that anyone who refuses to open up to global capitalism will be left behind; it also points to the perils of rolling back global capitalism. Supporters claim that if governments and international organisations succumb to anti-capitalist sentiments and try to rein in global capitalism, then globalisation as a whole will be rolled back, leading inevitably to results similar to those encountered when the previous era of globalisation came to an end early in the twentieth century, namely, war, fascism and communism.

Supporters not only bristle at all forms of anti-capitalism but also reject most reform proposals. According to the supporters, all the injustices and inefficiencies attributed to global capitalism are not a result of too much market but of too little. Government interference of all kinds, including protectionism, welfare provisions, corruption and incompetence is, according to them, responsible for the plight of the poor. The *Economist* (2000) states:

> Governments are apologising for globalisation and promising to civilise it. Instead if they had any regard for the plight of the poor, they would be accelerating it, celebrating it, exalting it…

Supporters attack the World Bank and the IMF for even listening to NGOs, let alone engaging them in any serious deliberations. Many of them are actually opposed to these and other international institutions as examples of interventionist big government. On the specific issues of global finance, the supporters hold the following positions.

Public debt. Most of the burden of Third World debt is the responsibility of corrupt and incompetent governments. Cancelling it will not help these countries but may actually hurt them if it is seen as rewarding bad government. Government lending in the future should be kept to a minimum and used mostly as an instrument of foreign policy. Even international lending institutions should try to stay out of the debt market. The Meltzer Report (IFIAC 2000), for example, recommends that the World Bank use grants rather than loans, but these should be disbursed through private service providers instead of being handed to governments.

Short-term flows. Short-term flows, be they loans, portfolio investments, foreign-exchange transactions, derivatives or other exotic instruments are all part of the proper functioning of market mechanisms. Derivatives, for example, help distribute risk in a way that best reflects market realities and the preferences of individual market participants. Crises attributed to short-term flows, such as the Asian crisis, always have their roots in government interference, in this case Asian crony capitalism and subsequent IMF intervention. The answer is, therefore, always more liberalisation.

Long-term foreign direct investment. FDI is the best way to match savings and investments worldwide. It allocates financial resources to their most productive use, promotes the best technologies and produces the most-needed products and services. Moreover, FDI is the best way to transfer know-how and technology, business prowess and even democratic culture. FDI is the only way for the Third World to catch up.

Not only is it self-defeating for countries to place any restrictions on foreign investment; they should do their utmost to attract it. This is done through neo-liberal reforms including deregulation, privatisation, small government, balanced budgets and tight money. The pain and dislocation caused by these policies are all justified by the expected benefits.

Reformists

The majority of movements, organisations and campaigns active in the area of global finance are reformist. They include the bulk of the labour movement and associated think tanks such as the Institute for Policy Studies; development organisations such as Oxfam and World Vision; watchdogs such as the World Development Movement and the Bretton Woods Project; issue-specific campaigns such as Jubilee 2000 and Action pour une Taxe Tobin d'Aide aux Citoyens (ATTAC); and individuals such as George Soros and Ann Pettifor. Even James Wolfenson, the head of the World Bank, could be included in this category.

Reformists comprise a broad category ranging from NGOs dedicated to monitoring the IMF to those IMF employees who are serious about reform. The reformists aim 'at partial change to try to offset current injustices and inequalities' (Cohen and Rai 2000: 2). Unlike the isolationists, movements demanding cancellation of Third World debt or IMF reforms are not pursuing a radical new social order.

The reformists pursue variations on the 'social democratic' agenda for the global era. Their aim is to maintain the advantages of the capitalist model while mitigating its excesses through re-regulation and redistribution. As the largest US trades union states:

> We need a global New Deal that establishes new rules to temper the excesses of the market; promote sustainable egalitarian growth; and assure the rights of working people everywhere are respected. (AFL-CIO 1998)

The reformists view themselves as the only true defenders of globalisation. They believe that both isolationist calls to reverse the process and supporters' insistence on 'ultra-liberal' forms of global capitalism are bound to derail globalisation, with tragic consequences. According to reformists, globalisation can succeed only if it is civilised and made more democratic, equitable and stable.

Reformists propose a variety of global governance solutions to address this task. These proposals are usually built around reforming or augmenting existing international institutions or establishing new ones.

The reformists advance a set of global governance initiatives such as the Tobin tax (explained below) or regulations for multinational corporations, which may actually require a global state to implement. John Cavanagh says:

> Some scholars such as Walden Bello, argue that developing countries would be better-off with no international financial institution rather than the IMF because this would allow local and national governments and citizens groups more autonomy in pursuing alternative development strategies. However, in an era of global capital, we would ideally have international financial institutions that could help reduce volatility and contagion in ways that can not be accomplished through nation states. An International Bankruptcy Authority has already been discussed. In addition, a number of scholars have proposed the creation of a new Global Financial Authority or a Global Central Bank. (Anderson and Cavanagh 2000)

On the specific global finance issues the reformists hold the following positions, although given the wide range of groups in this category the positions listed here are not all encompassing:

Public debt. Both developed and developing countries share the responsibility for the debt overhang and should share the burden of its resolution. For example, countries should be compensated for failed structural adjustment programmes or World Bank projects, which would offset some of their outstanding obligations. Debt should be cancelled for the poorest countries. The burden for the rest should be reduced to a level where it does not jeopardise their ability to provide basic human services. An International Bankruptcy Mechanism should be established to deal with debt cancellation and restructuring in situations when countries are no longer capable of meeting their debt obligations (Anderson and Cavanagh 2000).

Both lenders and borrowers should ensure that lending proceeds through an open and transparent process to avoid misuse through corruption or incompetence. Civil society should be involved in all stages of the process.

Short-term flows. The position of the reformists on short-term flows is close to that of the isolationists. Instead of dismissing these flows out of hand, however, the reformists seek solutions which would reorient them from speculation to long-term investment. Countries should have the option to impose 'speed bumps' and other defensive measures based on internationally agreed criteria. The IMF should not pursue the opening up of the capital account in member countries but should leave that to the discretion of governments. In case of crises, rescue packages should be aimed at minimising the negative impact on the real economy as opposed to bailing out reckless investors.

At the global level, proposals to tame short-term flows range from strengthening existing regulations to the establishment of a global lender of last resort/central bank and a Tobin tax. Named after the Nobel Prize–winning economist James Tobin of Yale University, such a tax of anything between 0.05 and 0.25 per cent levied on all foreign-exchange transactions would act as a deterrent to speculative transactions. The ATTAC platform claims that:

> Even fixed at a particularly low rate of 0.05%, the Tobin tax would gather close to 100 billion dollars a year. Collected, primarily, by industrialised countries, where the largest financial centres are located, the sum could be redirected to international organisations for activities aimed at fighting inequality, promoting education and public health in poor countries and food security and sustainable development. This kind of mechanism would put sand in the gears of speculation. It would feed the logic of resistance, give citizens and nations back some room to manoeuvre and in particular it would show that politics can be restored to its proper place. (Platform of ATTAC 1998)

Long-term foreign direct investment. Few reformists would deny the benefits of foreign investment. Like the supporters, the reformists believe that foreign investment is the best way to allocate capital to its most productive uses. It is also the only way for poor countries to catch up with the rich given the difference in savings rates.

As discussed above, the reformists promote solutions which would redirect short-term flows to longer-term investments. The reformists, however, reject the link between neo-liberal structural adjustment policies and the flow of investments. Indeed, they reject neo-liberal structural adjustment policies because of the pain they cause to the poorest in society, their 'one-size-fits-all' approach, and the fact that they have not even been proved to promote growth or investment.

The reformists also emphasise the need to augment private investments by public funds to achieve development goals. According to the ICFTU (2000), for example, public investments by both national governments and IFIs should be targeted at social protection, primary education, health care and employment.

Alternatives

The anti-capitalist protests in Seattle 1999, Washington 2000 and Prague 2000 were driven by the alternatives. Alternatives exist both as organisations – for example, the Zapatistas, Adbusters and Reclaim the Streets – and as 'submerged net-works' which come to the fore only around certain campaigns or exercise resistance through a particular lifestyle, such as INPEG (see Box 3.1), which existed only for the purpose of organising the Prague protests, or alternative money (LETS) groups (see Box 3.1). Alternatives are wary of leaders but there are alternative spokespeople such as Naomi Klein and Subcomandante Marcos. (See Box 3.4.)

Instead of aiming to transform or reform global capitalism, the alternatives are concerned with reclaiming 'things' from the encroaching market and creating space for alternatives. They are concerned with the political and cultural consequences of capitalism as much as they are with its economic and environmental costs. They perceive the encroachment of the market into the public space as a threat to democracy, which takes the form of 'corporate censorship' in the North and human rights abuses in the South (Klein 1999).

The fact that the alternatives comprise broad coalitions means that it is difficult to pin down their agenda or even what they stand for. But instead of being a weakness, the lack of a 'little red book' is translated into an advantage, ensuring mass appeal, especially among the young.

> It's not the last gasp of the old left, or the resurgence of the new right. It's not protectionism, or even anarchism. It's something entirely different; something fresh being pieced together from the shards of old ideas, and glued with new solutions for a new age. (Kingsnorth 2000)

Box 3.4: The Zapatistas

The story of the Zapatistas' uprising is a textbook example of the relation between the local and the global in civil society today. The Zapatista Army for National Liberation burst on to the international stage when it seized several towns and villages in Mexico's poorest state of Chiapas on 1 January 1994. The insurgency coincided with the launch of the North American Free Trade Agreement and made a mockery of Mexico's planned celebration of joining the First World. The armed stage of the uprising lasted for only twelve days but it succeeded in drawing international attention to the plight of Mexico's indigenous population and forced the government to give serious consideration to their demands.

The desperate insurgency had every chance of being drowned in blood or joining the long list of forgotten ethnic conflicts. Instead the Zapatistas succeeded in tapping a vast transnational network of civic activists who provided it with visibility, protection, legitimacy and support. Naomi Klein says:

> The Zapatista uprising was a new way to protect land and culture: rather than locking out the world, the Zapatistas flung open the doors and invited the world inside. (Klein 2001)

The Zapatistas brought networking to a new level. Their ideas, which spread initially through word of mouth, dominate the Internet. According to Naomi Klein, there are at least 4,500 Zapatista websites based in 26 countries. There is a Zapatista cottage industry selling 40 kinds of T-shirts, baseball caps, posters and Mayan dolls. Zapatista gatherings – Encontros – both in Mexico and elsewhere are attended by thousands of activists from all over the world. Their latest event, the Zapatour, in which the movement's masked leaders toured the country promoting their cause, culminated with a 150,000-strong rally in Mexico City.

One of the secrets behind the Zapatistas' success is their ideas as formulated by the movement's eloquent non-leader Subcomandante Marcos. These ideas go far beyond the immediate demands of the Mayan communities to articulate an alternative global vision. Marcos is inviting the millions 'stoodup' by globalisation to unite behind the Chiapas Indians by defining the 'savage capitalism of the end of the 20th century' as the common enemy. Anyone who feels disenfranchised by global capitalism can join the Zapatistas by doing whatever they can wherever they are.

The Zapatistas are sceptical both of cosmetic reforms and of 'fascist' nationalist solutions. Indeed they are sceptical of any ready-made alternatives, promoting instead a 'revolution which makes the revolution possible'. Their main goal is to create the democratic space in which alternative social proposals can compete and coexist with each other as long as they are just. Marcos says, describing the revolution:

> It will be, primarily, a revolution which is the result of the struggle on different social fronts, with many methods, within different social forms, with different degrees of commitment and participation. And its results will be, not a party, organisation or alliance of victorious organisations with its specific social proposal, but a chance for a democratic space in order to resolve the confrontation among diverse political proposals. This democratic space for resolution will have three fundamental premises which are inseparable historically: democracy, in order to decide upon the dominant social proposal, liberty in order to subscribe to one or the other proposal and justice in which all proposals should be enclosed. (Don Durito 1995)

This ambiguity combined with the movement's aversion to hierarchy and classical concepts of leadership make it ideal for the alternatives. Indeed, these ideas are the closest thing to a 'manifesto' for the alternative stream of the anti-capitalist movement. Klein says:

> I may never have made the pilgrimage to Chiapas, but I have watched the Zapatistas' ideas spread through activist circles, passed along second- and third-hand: a phrase, a way to run a meeting, a metaphor that twists your brain around. Unlike classic revolutionaries, who preach through bullhorns and from pulpits, Marcos has spread the Zapatista word through riddles. Revolutionaries who don't want power. People who must hide their faces to be seen. A world with many worlds in it. A movement of one 'no' and many 'yesses'. (Klein 2001)

Many of those who made the 'pilgrimage' to Chiapas went on to play a critical role in the major anti-capitalist protests in Seattle, Prague and Davos. Zapatista slogans, ideas, non-hierarchical methods of organisation, irreverence, humour and romanticism are omnipresent in alternative anti-capitalist events. Indeed it is hard to say today who needs the other more, the Zapatistas or the alternatives.

Box 3.5: The Other Alternatives

Civil society responses to global capitalism extend beyond protests and lobbying to 'practical' alternatives. In the area of money and finance such alternatives include LETS schemes and other money alternatives, micro-lending and Grameen banking, and socially responsible investment. These alternatives can be isolationist, reformist, supporter or alternative in nature depending on their compatibility with global capitalism. They also vary in spread and success.

According to Project LETS (see website) there are around 500 LETS schemes and networks in 36 countries. The average size of these schemes is 50 to 60 participants although larger ones can have thousands of participants.

A typical example of LETS schemes is Ithaca Hours, based in the small university town of Ithaca, New York. One Hour is equivalent to $10 or one hour of work. The core of the system is a bi-monthly tabloid in which people and businesses that accept Ithaca Hours advertise their products and services. Each advertiser receives Four Hours so that s/he can purchase other peoples' products. The currency is limited to a 20-mile radius and payments can be made in both dollars and hours. The scheme involves about 2,000 participants (Lietaer 2001). Since LETS currencies are usually based on the exchange of labour hours, most LETS schemes are community-based, although this is changing with the advent of the Internet. Formalised LETS schemes are usually political rather than practical in nature. Environmental sustainability, anti-consumerism and efforts to promote community cohesion and culture are among their main motivations. Formalised LETS schemes are trying to carve out space away from the market and as such could be designated as alternative.

The most prevalent forms of alternative money, however, are neither political nor formalised. Money shortages due to state failure or neo-liberal reforms may force millions in developing and transition countries to seek alternatives to money. In the former Soviet Union people augmented barter arrangements originally developed to deal with the shortage economy to handle the tight money of shock therapy. Such arrangements involve the exchange of both goods and services, including labour hours. Rather than being an alternative to market relations such arrangements are part of the new market economy in these countries.

The Grameen Bank extends loans as small as $50 to the poorest people in rural Bangladesh. The loans are given without collateral. The main clients are women whom the bank deems more likely to spend the money wisely and to repay it on schedule. The bank relies on community and peer pressure to ensure repayment. As such it uses social capital in the form of community relations and gender as a substitute for collateral and as a way to reduce lending costs. Grameen banking and similar forms of micro-lending have been extremely successful, reaching 14 million people in December 1999, a growth of 82 per cent in two years (Empowering Women with Microcredit 2000). The success of Grameen banking has prompted aid agencies, international lending institutions and commercial banks to emulate it in other countries. Originally, Grameen banks were all NGOs. Micro-lenders today are divided between NGOs, who have predominantly a social/environmental agenda, and banks. Grameen banking and other forms of micro-lending are firmly anchored within market structures. They could be designated as reformist since they correct a market failure by extending lending to the poorest people who are usually shunned by commercial banks.

Socially responsible investing (SRI) is the most successful of the practical alternatives. Indeed, it is becoming so commonplace for pension funds – the largest portfolio investors – to demand SRI from their fund managers that it is gradually becoming the norm rather than the alternative. In 1999 over US$2 trillion was invested in socially responsible ways, accounting for 13 per cent of assets under management in the United States. This represented a growth of 45 per cent over the 9 per cent figure for 1997 (Social Investment Forum 1999). The numbers are expected to grow especially since SRI funds are proving to be as profitable as, if not more so than, traditional ones. SRI is also spreading into Europe, albeit at a slower pace. The introduction of regulation in the UK requiring pension funds to disclose SRI policies has provided a needed boost.

Socially responsible investing in the US in 1999

- Screening: $1,232 billion
- Community investing: $5.4 billion
- Shareholder advocacy: $657 billion
- Screening and advocacy: $265 billion
  (Social Investment Forum 1999)

British SRIs are estimated to have £45 billion under management. There are several varieties of SRI, from passive screening of companies according to certain criteria to the active use of corporate governance mechanisms to inject environmental sustainability and labour and human rights standards into corporate policies. SRI could be described as supportive because it takes place within the framework of global capitalism, using its existing tools and mechanisms. One could say that SRI proves that market mechanisms such as corporate governance are the most efficient way to produce desired public goods without government intervention.

The alternatives do not necessarily seek to overthrow capitalism and are definitely not interested in gaining power. They seek instead to defend a 'way of life' and thus, place a strong emphasis on cultural issues. It is not surprising that their protests look more like cultural happenings than political action. Indeed, the alternatives' grasp of popular culture is one of their main strengths.

The alternatives have a schizophrenic relationship to globalisation. On the one hand, by espousing many isolationist ideas they appear anti-globalisation; on the other hand they are fiercely global in placing a strong emphasis on solidarity or, as Reclaim the Streets puts it: 'The resistance will be as transnational as capital'. The alternatives are also the most technologically savvy of all the resistance movements, which further ties them to globalisation.

There are parallels between the alternatives of today and the radicals of the 1960s. For example, the radicals brought together emancipatory and rights politics of the 'old' and the life politics of the 'new' social movements. The alternatives reproduced this link in the form of the Longshoremen providing protection to the anti-sweatshop student demonstrators in Seattle. The radicals and the alternatives are also similar in their emphasis on popular culture and forms in general. But there are also differences between the two: chief among them is that the 'authority' being challenged today is the corporation, not the state.

Alternatives do not have a particular position on global finance issues. Instead they espouse a mixture of isolationist and, to a lesser degree, reformist ideas.

Table 3.1: Civil society responses to global finance

	Organisation					Activity					Position			
	Individual	NGO/Group	Movement/Network	Think tanks/Academia	Media/Website	Inform/Educate	Lobby	Mobilise	Serve	Riot/Celebrate	Rejectionist	Supportive	Reformative	Alternative
ATTAC			◑	●		●		◑					●	
Bank Information Center		●				●	○	◑			●		◑	
Bankwatch		●				○	◑	●			●		◑	
Bello, Waldon	●					●		◑			●			
Bretton Woods Project		◑		●		●	◑						●	
Centre for Civil Society				●		●		●				●		
Corporate Watch		●				◑		●			◑		●	
Don Durito (Subcomandante Marcos)	●						●	●			◑			●
Economist					●	●	◑					●	◑	
Fifty Years is Enough		●						●			●			
Financial Times					●	●	◑					◑	●	
Focus on Global South				●		●		◑			●			
Friedman, Thomas	●					●	◑					●	◑	
Friends of the Earth		◑	●				◑	●			●		◑	
Global Exchange			●	◑		◑		●			●			
Grameen Bank		●				◑			●				●	
INPEG			●					◑		●				●
Institute for Policy Studies				●		●	◑	○			◑		●	
International Forum on Globalization			◑	●		●		◑			●			
Ithaca Hours			●					◑	●		●			◑
Jubilee 2000			●			○	◑	●					●	
Klein, Naomi	●					●		◑						●
Landless Peasants Movement (MST)			●					◑	○	●	◑			●
Le Monde diplomatique					●	●		◑			●			◑
Meltzer Commission				●		●	◑					●		
Nader, Ralph	●							●			●			
OneWorld.net					●	●			◑		◑		●	○
Oxfam		●				○	◑		●				●	
Reclaim the Streets			●					◑		●	◑			●
Ruckus Society		●							●	●				●
Social Investment Forum		●				◑	○		●			●	◑	
Stiglitz, Joseph	●					●	◑						●	
Wall Street Journal					●	●	◑					●		
Wolfenson, James	●					○	◑		●			◑	●	
World Development Movement		●	◑			◑	○	●					●	
Zapatistas (EZLN)			●					●	○	●	◑			●

● PREDOMINANT ◑ SIGNIFICANT ○ TO SOME EXTENT

Conclusion: The Total Is More Than the Sum of the Parts

Civic responses to capitalism are as old as the system itself. Reactions to money are even older. Isolationists, supporters, reformists and alternatives existed previously in various forms. Most of the time, governments and markets confronted or ignored them when they could not co-opt them. Lately, the individual responses have been coming together, creating something larger than the sum of its components. In Seattle and Prague, myriad individuals, organisations, movements, ideas and methods came together to deliver a message so powerful that it took everyone by surprise.

Seattle and Prague, however, are only the most visible expression of global civic responses to capitalism. The various responses are actually working together all the time.

The alternatives lend mass appeal and visibility to what would otherwise be marginal isolationist and reformist movements. They also create the space where the various responses come together. The isolationists with their militancy and radical demands keep the issues alive and sharpen the debate. The ultimate winner from these synergies are the reformists, who eventually fill the gap between the supporters and the isolationists with constructive solutions.

Civic responses to global capitalism are also coming together across regions despite supporters' claims to the contrary. The Zapatistas not only were saved by global solidarity; they are also the inspiration for alternatives worldwide. IMF and World Bank reforms are influenced by demonstrations in Turkey, Nigeria and Argentina as much as they are by riots in Prague and Washington. The Jubilee 2000 campaign would not have achieved what it did had it not been a truly global movement.

What is it that brings Ann Pettifor, Katerina Liskova, George Soros and Walden Bello together to dress down the heads of the World Bank and the IMF?[4] Why would the leaders of the Bretton Woods institutions subject themselves to such public upbraiding? After all, activists were championing Third World issues before Katerina was born. Soros made his millions even earlier, totally unaware of Bello and his fellows in the national liberation

4 Katerina Liskova is one of the organisers of the Prague World Bank/IMFD protest. Ann Pettifor is the founder of Jubilee 2000 campaign to cancel Third World debt. Walden Bello is a radical Filipino academic and anti-capitalist activist. Gorge Soros is a financier and philanthropist. The four participated in a meeting held at Prague castle together with the heads of the IMF and World Bank hosted by Czech President Vaclav Havel (see Box 3.1).

movement. Twenty years ago most anti-capitalist activists did not even know who the leaders of the Bretton Woods institutions were, and if they did they wouldn't have dreamt of sitting with them at the same table.

It could be that for the first time in decades the bottom rung seems to have dropped from the global social ladder, that along with overall prosperity there are more and more pockets around the world where people seem to have nothing to lose. Regardless of where they are, people are terrified by widening disparities. Many are all too aware that the Zapatista insurrection and Landless Peasant Movement land occupations are comparatively benign outbursts by those left behind, that unless something is done we can expect more violent eruptions with unpredictable consequences.

It could be that even those enjoying the fruits of prosperity are feeling less and less in control of their lives. It is, after all, frustrating to get virtually identical economic policies no matter whom you vote for and to watch your elected representatives facilitate or at best stand by helplessly as markets devour precious public space.

Maybe the whole thing is just a successful public relations stunt by the alternatives who are deftly mixing pop culture and information technology to lend a sheen of novelty and broad appeal to tired slogans. The new anti-capitalist movement may just be giving a new form to an old idea. Like its predecessors, it is unlikely to succeed in terms of defeating global capitalism (after all, supporters are the most influential of the civic responses to global capitalism) but it may just transform it.

Given the cacophony of voices behind it, the message from Seattle and Prague may be neither coherent nor constructive. It is more like an alarm, a shout of protest and despair. But it is loud enough that corporations, international organisations and governments can ignore it only at their peril.

References

AFL-CIO (1998). 'US Workers Addressing the Global Crisis' (Executive Council Statement). Monterey, California (14 October).

Anderson, Sarah and Cavanagh, John (2000). *Bearing the Burden: The Impact of Global Financial Crisis on Workers and Alternative Agendas for the IMF and Other Institutions*. Washington DC: Institute for Policy Studies. http://www.ips.dc.org.

Bello, Walden (2000). Excerpt from a talk delivered at a series of engagements during the demonstrations against the World Economic Forum in Melbourne, Australia, 6–10 September. http://www.focusweb.org.

Bello, Walden (2001). 'Is Bush Bad for the World Bank?' January. http://www.corpwatch.org.

Cohen, Robin and Rai, Shirin (2000). *Global Social Movements*. London: Athlone.

Cornia, Giovanni Andrea, Jolly, Richard, and Stewart, Frances (1987). *Adjustment with a Human Face*. Oxford: Clarendon Press.

Desai, M (2001). *Marx's Revenge: The Resurgence of Capitalism and the Death of Statist Socialism*. London: Verso.

Don Durito of the Lacandon Errant Knight for whom Sup Marcos is shield-bearer (1995). *Durito IV: Neoliberalism and the Party-State System*. Mexico: Zapatista Army of National Liberation, 11 June. http://www.eco.utexas.edu/ faculty/Cleaver/ chiapas95.html.

Economist (2000). 'The Case for Globalization'. 21 September.

Emerging Markets Companion (1996–9). *Brady Bond Primer*. http://www.emgmkts.com/ research/bradydef.htm.

Empowering Women with Microcredit (2000). *Microcredit Summit Campaign Report*. http://www.microcreditsummit.org/ campaigns/report00.html.

Friedman, Thomas (2000). *The Lexus and the Olive Tree; Understanding Globalization*. New York: Anchor. http://www.lexusandtheolivetree.com/ globalization.htm.

Friends of the Earth (1998a). *MAI Update*, October. http://www.foe.org.

Friends of the Earth (2000). *Towards Sustainable Economies: Challenging Neoliberal Economic Globalisation*. 1 December. http://www.foei.org.

Friends of the Earth (1998b). *Licence to Loot: The MAI and How to Stop it*, http://www.foe.org/international/loot.html.

Fuller, C. J. (1989) 'Misconceiving the Grain Heap: a Critique of the Concept of the Indian Jajmani System', in Jonathan Parry and Bloch, Maurice (ed.), *Money and the Morality of Exchange*. Cambridge: Cambridge University Press.

Hines, Colin (2000). *Localisation: A Global Manifesto*. London: Earthscan.

ICFTU (International Confederation of Free Trades Unions) (2000). 'Securing the Conditions for Reducing Poverty and Achieving Sustainable Growth'. Statement by the ICFTU, TUAC, and ITS to the Spring 2000 meeting of the IMF and the World Bank in Washington DC.

IFIAC (International Financial Institution Advisory Commission, 'Meltzer Commission') (2000). *Report* (March). http://www.house.gov/jec/imf/ ifiac.htm.

IMF (International Monetary Fund). http://www.imf.org.

Jubilee 2000. http://www.jubileeplus.org.

Kingsnorth, Paul (2000). 'Seeds of the New in the Prague Autumn'. *The Ecologist*, 30/8: 44–5.

Klein, Naomi (1999). *No Logo: Taking Aim at the Brand Bullies*. New York: Picador.

Klein, Naomi (2001). 'The Unknown Icon'. *Guardian* (3 March).

Lietaer, Bernard (2001). *The Future of Money*. London: Century.

Mauss, Marcel (1996). *The Gift: Forms and Functions of Exchange in Archaic Society*. London: Cohen and West.

Mittelman, James (2000). *The Globalization Syndrome, Transformation and Resistance*. Princeton: Princeton University Press.

Parry, Jonathan and Bloch, Maurice (1989). 'Introduction: Money and the Morality of Exchange', in Jonathan Parry and Bloch Maurice (ed.), *Money and the Morality of Exchange*. Cambridge: Cambridge University Press.

Perez, Carlota (2000). 'Technological Revolutions and Financial Capital', paper presented at 'The Other Canon Conference', Oslo.

Platform of ATTAC (Action pour une Taxe Tobin d'Aide aux Citoyens), 3 June 1998. https://www.attac.org.

Project LETS. http://lentils.imagineis.com/letslist.

Reclaim the Streets. http://www.reclaimthe streets.net.

Social Investment Forum (1999). *1999 Report on Socially Responsible Investing Trends in the United States*, November. http://www. socialinvest.org/areas/research/ trends/1999-Trends.htm.

Stiglitz, Joseph (2000). 'Democratic Development as the Fruits of Labor', Keynote Address, Industrial Relations Research Association, Boston, January. Taken from Anderson and Cavanagh. http://www.ips.org.

Tönnies, Ferdinand (1955). *Gemeinschaft und Gesellschaft* (Community and Association) (trans. Charles P. Loomis). London: Routledge and Kegan Paul.

United Nations (1999). *World Economic and Social Survey*. New York: United Nations.

Wallerstein, Immanuel (2000). *The Essential Wallerstein*. New York: New Press.

Wood, Angela (2001). *Structural Adjustment for the IMF Options for Reforming the IMF's Governance Structure*. Brettonwoods Project (January). http://www.brettonwoods project.org/briefings/reform/sapimf.html.

World Bank (1998–1999). *World Development Report: Knowledge for Development*. New York: Oxford University Press.

World Bank (2000). *East Asia: Recovery and Beyond*. Washington, DC: World Bank.

World Development Movement. http:// www.wdm.org.uk/campaign/GATS.htm.

Acknowledgement

First publication: Desai, Meghnad and Said, Yahia (2001) 'The New Anti-Capitalist Movement: Money and Global Civil Society', in *Global Civil Society 2001* (Yearbook), edited by Anheier, Helmut K., and Glasius, Marlies. Oxford, Oxford University Press, pp. 51–78. Republished with kind permission of Oxford University Press.

Chapter 4

TRADE AND GLOBAL CIVIL SOCIETY

The Anti-capitalist Movement Revisited

Yahia Said and Meghnad Desai
(2003)

Introduction

Thousands of people attended the rally which marked the launch of the Third World Social Forum (WSF) in Porto Alegre, Brazil on 22 January 2003. It was the same crowd that has perfected the art of turning desperation into hope, fear into cheer, and chaos into purpose at anti-capitalist riots throughout the world. However, we suggest in this chapter that something was amiss in Porto Alegre, that the 'movement of movements' is in danger of losing its dynamism and taking a dogmatic and ultimately self-defeating turn.

The formidable-looking Brazilian paramilitary policemen and women were on the side of the demonstrators – eager to assist and protect at every step. There was no chance of tear-gas and clubs. Brazilian authorities and businesses, including the state-owned oil multinational Petrobras, did not limit their support to words. They also footed much of the estimated US$3.5 million bill (Osava 2003). Klaus Schwab, founder and President of the World Economic Forum, had 'just one word for Porto Alegre: We are the same' (Mekay 2003).

Why were there no signs of resistance from 'the system' to this event, which is meant to represent the climactic expression of a movement out to destroy it? Why is the political and business establishment so keen on supporting the 'rabble'? (Temel-Kuran 2003)

In this chapter we will argue that three developments have been taking place in the anti-capitalist movement, especially the part of it that focuses on the global trade regime: success, institutionalisation and radicalisation.

After a moment of hesitation following the September 11 attacks in the US, the Global Justice and Solidarity Movement, as some of its followers like to call it, continued its meteoric rise. Millions around the globe took part in anti-capitalist protests and social forums. National and coordinated international campaigns succeeded in reversing privatisation plans in Peru and El Salvador. The movement also claimed a success when South Africa won the battle with multinational pharmaceuticals over the compulsory licensing of AIDS drugs. Most importantly, however, the movement succeeded in undermining the legitimacy of the Washington consensus: the neo-liberal economic orthodoxy which captured national and multilateral policymaking throughout the 1980s and much of the 1990s.

Part of the movement's success stems from the adoption of some of its rhetoric, if not spirit, by nationalist leaders and business elites on both sides of the North-South divide. Chavez and Chirac, Mugabe and Mahathir[1] have tried to attach themselves to the movement, with various degrees of success. Their goal is to leverage the movement's power and legitimacy in their struggle with domestic and foreign opponents.

Some in the movement are ready to accept these new allies. The newly elected Brazilian President Luiz Inacio Lula da Silva and Hugo Chavez were leading attractions at the WSF, which also featured three ministers from Chirac's Gaullist government. Some Asian activists spoke warmly of Mahathir's tough rhetoric, downplaying his authoritarian tendencies. 'How on earth', wonders Naomi Klein (2003), commenting on the reception accorded to Chavez at the WSF, 'did a gathering that was supposed to be a showcase for new grassroots movements become a celebration of men with a penchant for three-hour speeches about smashing the oligarchy?'

The coming together of anti-capitalist activists and nationalist capital and politicians is in part a sign of the movement's radicalisation: a predictable reaction to the advent of the Bush administration in the US and its policies, especially since the September 11 attacks. Susan George (2003a), vice-president of ATTAC France, speaking at the WSF states that the 'rich and powerful have apparently concluded...that hundreds of millions of people in the world today are superfluous'. Samir Amin (2003), one of the

1 Hugo Chavez, President of Venezuela; Jacques Chirac, President of France; Robert Mugabe, President of Zimbabwe; and Mahathir Muhammed, Prime Minister of Malaysia.

main organisers of the WSF, speaks of 'Washington neo-Nazis' who need to be confronted before 'September 1939'.

Along with the acceptance/collusion with national capital/nationalism, there seems to be a general sense of resignation among activists to the impossibility of reform. As Argentina's Mothers of the May Plaza put it: 'Another world is possible, only with revolution and socialism' (Cockroft 2003). In Porto Alegre and elsewhere, activists repeatedly stated that they have given up hope of transforming the international trade regime and its main institution, the World Trade Organization (WTO). Efforts to make the WTO more transparent and accountable, work towards improving market access for Southern products, and campaigns aimed at injecting environmental, social and labour considerations into the trade regime are giving way to an agenda centred around rolling back international treaties and organisations and returning power to the nation-state.

By seeking to 'Derail the WTO', the activists seem to have misinterpreted the major changes in the international arena resulting from the ascent of the neo-conservatives in the US and the September 11 attacks. The activists seem still bent on fighting a Washington consensus which no longer exists. The US administration has no particular commitment to the WTO or any multilateral institution. Globalisation and global institutions are tolerated only if they serve the interests of US and mature industry corporations associated with the Republican Party. If it is impossible or difficult to agree on rules that benefit the US, then it is better for them not to have any.

A trade regime without rules is unlikely to be more just than one governed by the WTO. Indeed, in the absence of a global set of rules economic superpowers will seek to carve up captive markets by constructing regional trade blocs. Indeed, the US administration is already pursuing such a strategy in the Free Trade Area of the Americas (FTAA) and bilateral negotiations with Chile, Singapore, Jordan and Australia. Activists are aware of this strategy but do not seem to draw the logical conclusions from it regarding their WTO strategy. Most activists calling for the abolition of the WTO suggest that a new organisation should be built from the ground up to replace it. We have yet, however, to see a detailed proposal for such an alternative or a convincing explanation why that would be more effective than a reformed WTO. Advocates of the abolition of the WTO seem implicitly opposed to global trade in principle: a position few activists would care to embrace.

Civil society movements have not always taken an uncompromising stance on international trade, indeed historically many have been pro-trade.

The next section will address some theoretical and historical aspects of civil society movements on trade. It will be followed by an outline of the various positions on trade issues today. These positions will then be illustrated with the examples of the WTO and FTAA. We will also explore strategies and methods employed by the various strands in the movement in specific campaigns and activities. We will conclude by addressing the challenges and opportunities facing the movement today.

Trade and Civil Society: Theoretical and Historical Aspects

Trade has been a major plank of the global social justice movement. The WTO is seen by many as the driving force of globalisation, and free trade is blamed for many ills: environmental damage, commodification of subsistence crops and consequent food insecurity, falling commodity prices, inequality and inequity in the global distribution of income, and so forth. There are demands for fair trade, for special treatment of the least developed countries, especially in help with negotiations at WTO meetings. But, unlike in the case of money and finance, which we surveyed in Chapter 3 of this book, there are few religious objections to trade. While there are some 'anti-trade fundamentalists' (Hines 2000), even they are only against international trade, that is, trade across national boundaries.[2] This is because some sort of exchange, whether based on money or barter, is endemic to all societies. It is also more or less axiomatic that trade benefits all parties. The dispute arises about the distribution of the gains from trade; the inequality of gains from trade is often blamed for the inequalities of income and wealth in the world today.

Trade and Comparative Advantage

The counter-argument from the days of the classical economists has always been that, far from being a cause of inequality, trade is 'an engine of growth' and that economies which are open and trade in a free environment thrive, as demonstrated by the experience of the rich developed countries. At issue is the theory of comparative advantage, which was the linchpin for

2 There is an age-old objection to movement of food grains far from their place of origin. Famines were blamed in pre-modern and early modern days on inter-regional movements of food grains. The Physiocrats in the eighteenth century were the first to argue for the unimpeded, toll-free movement of food grain across France; hence the expression 'laisser-passer'. See for an insight into this Rothschild (2001). The idea of 'food miles' indicates that resistance persists in some to food trade even within countries.

Ricardo's argument for free trade and the reason for the triumph of classical economics in the nineteenth century.

Classical economics started as a reaction against the mercantilist system, in which politics dominated markets and national interest was supreme. Adam Smith in his *Wealth of Nations* (Smith 1776/1993) questioned the efficiency of the mercantilist system. Ricardo in his *Principles of Political Economy and Taxation* (Ricardo 1821/1992) made resource efficiency (though he did not call it that) an objective in place of the national interest. Here indeed is the first separation in economic theory between the interests of the state and those of its citizens, even of civil society.

This theory of comparative advantage holds that if two countries – England and Portugal, in Ricardo's much cited example – are capable of producing two commodities – wine and cloth – then each should specialise in producing, and exporting to the other country, that commodity which it can produce more cheaply, *even if it could produce both commodities more cheaply than the other country*. By that specialisation, both countries will benefit from the optimal use of resources. Later neoclassical economists added that consumer welfare will be enhanced in both countries as goods will be cheaper if countries specialised along the lines of comparative advantage.

A History of Trade Activism

What converted an abstract and unrealistic theory into practical politics was civil society agitation in the nineteenth century on behalf of free trade and against the corn laws, which imposed a tax on food grain imports into Britain. Ricardo's theory became a weapon in the hands of the Anti-Corn Law League, which succeeded in having the corn laws repealed and British agriculture 'globalised'. It was a classic redistributive struggle in which the workers and capitalists challenged the power of the landed aristocracy. In the particular English context of the 1840s, consumers were largely the urban workers and their families, so this movement also acquired a class character, which is why Marx supported free trade against protection (Desai 2002). The Anti-Corn Law League raised money and set up machinery across England and Wales to increase voter registration, which then enabled it to get MPs elected who would vote down the corn laws. Established in 1839, it succeeded within seven years and the corn laws were abolished in 1846. The Anti-Corn Law League represents the first civil society movement on a trade issue, though pro–free trade.

Despite its triumph in Britain, Ricardo's theory had several features which have made it controversial ever since it was first propounded. First, in theory, free trade operates between countries, but the politics of international relations is absent. Thus, many critics point out that when Ricardo wrote about trade between England and Portugal the Methuen Treaty between the two countries had already relegated Portugal to a subordinate status. Also, by specialising in an industrial commodity – cloth – England could reap the advantages of dynamic increasing returns to scale, while Portugal would be confined to a commodity in which there were diminishing returns and few innovations. Of course, in that case cloth would become cheap over time but not wine; thus, the terms of trade – the ratio of the price of wine to that of cloth would move against England and in favour of Portugal. But later, a terms-of-trade pessimism developed among economists, and the Singer-Prebisch thesis held that over time the country producing the agricultural commodity would see its terms of trade decline (Prebisch 1950). This was because the demand for the primary commodity was income-inelastic as well as price-inelastic (that is, the price of primary commodities and the level of income have little or no impact on the demand for that commodity). Thus, with growing world incomes the demand for primary commodities did not keep pace. Moreover, the markets for primary commodities were competitive; and so, as output increased due to the introduction of new land or better techniques, the price of the primary commodity declined; but this decline in price did not lead to higher demand. Manufactures, on the other hand, it was averred, were produced under oligopolistic conditions and their prices were determined on a cost-plus mark-up basis. Hence, the price of the manufacture would not fall but stay constant or rise while that of the primary commodity would fall. Thus trade would heighten the inequalities between the two rather than narrow them. (The Singer-Prebisch thesis did not go unchallenged. See Spraos 1983 for a response.)

Second, in theory goods move but factors do not. Trade imposes restructuring on the domestic economy – for example, complete as opposed to partial specialisation – but the theory takes no account of the short-run human costs while emphasising the long-run welfare gains. When one industry has to be shut down while another expands, then workers bear the burden of unemployment and the costs of re-skilling. Politicians are concerned with immediate or short-run losses and not willing to sacrifice their voters for the sake of long-run gains. Thus, tariffs and protection have always had much more political support than free trade. Even in England, the classic free trade country, there was a move against free trade in the early twentieth century after the franchise had been extended.

Free trade in fact operates through the inter-state (so-called international) system. Free markets filter through the power system. The theory of comparative advantage sets out the limits of specialisation on theoretical grounds, but power relations between states define the actual limits. In practice, the international trading system has been an uneasy compromise between mercantilism and free trade. When there has been a hegemon – Great Britain in the nineteenth century and the USA post-1945 – championing free trade, then the balance between mercantilism and free trade has edged towards the latter. But even here there has always been a gap between the hegemon's rhetoric and the practice. Thus, Great Britain's shipping acts in the nineteenth century stipulated that British exports should be transported exclusively in British ships, and the USA today protects its agriculture and other sectors.

Free trade theory was denounced as an English ideological plant to harm continental economies. Friedrich List (1837/1966) as well as many American economists of the mid-nineteenth century argued that free trade might be suitable for rich and developed England, but Germany and America needed protection. The *Zollverein*, established in 1833, was a customs union comprising Prussia and other German states. It combined free internal trade with tariff barriers against imports, rather like the European Union today. List began the anti–free trade movement by giving it a developmentalist edge.

This also helped to radicalise the anti-colonial struggles in India, where nationalists saw free trade as part of an imperialist strategy to keep India de-industrialised. A distinction was drawn between the interests of domestic capital/state and foreign capital/state, which turned the discourse against free trade. Classical economic theory had contrasted the interest of the civil society (consumer) with that of the state in attacking mercantilism. With List the contrast was between the rich/developed/metropolitan state and the poor/underdeveloped/colonial state. The interests of civil society in the poor/colonial state were to be identified with those of the state.

There are problems of trade in manufactured goods where production is determined by the status quo in comparative advantage. Until the middle of the twentieth century, most manufacturing industries were located in OECD countries and exported to developing countries. Developing countries as they started industrialising by import substitution methods encountered the criticism that they were ignoring comparative advantage. Nationalists in developing countries dealt with this criticism in Listian fashion by championing the interests of domestic against foreign capitalists regardless of any harm done to the interests of consumers (Box 4.1).

Box 4.1: Actors in International Trade: Classes and Interests

The conflict that trade generates within a country, as in the corn law agitation in nineteenth-century Britain, or across countries, as in contemporary movements, can be analysed in a schematic way by delineating the principal actors and how their interests may combine or clash. In the original Anti-Corn Law League debate, the 'actors' were:

(a) manufacturers/capitalists/shopkeepers;
(b) industrial/urban workers;
(c) landlords;
(d) farm/rural workers;
(e) consumers;
(f) civil society.

The story is that (a) and (b) combined to defeat (c). The (d) element was not enfranchised and played little part in the debate. The then government consisted of MPs elected by (a) and (c). Usually it is only (a) and (c) that feature in the argument but governments are also part of the action as signatories to treaties such as the WTO. In neoclassical economists' interpretations of the free trade argument, consumers (e) are the most important group as against industrial producers, (a) and (b) together with agricultural producers (c) and (d). In the neoclassical story free trade benefits (e) by providing cheaper goods and hurts (a) and (b) or (c) and (d) in the short run due to competition; but the long run effects are beneficial to all by improving resource allocation and allowing higher levels and perhaps a higher growth rate of output and income. Of course, consumers can also be seen as civil society, but to keep the notation clear we label civil society separately as (f).

Under Friedrich List's analysis we have to add the foreign counterparts to the six actors above. Label them (A) to (F). In what follows the rich country is denoted by lower-case letters and the poor country by upper-case letters. Thus (A) would be the local (poor country) manufacturer and (a) the English (rich country) manufacturer. List saw the battle as between (a) and (A). From the two sets of interest groups (a) to (e) and (A) to (E), we can map the location of various protest groups as identified with one or other cluster. Thus the anti-colonial struggle for tariffs took the interests of (A) and (B) to be pitted against those of (a) and perhaps (b). During his visit to England for the Round Table Conference of 1930, Gandhi tried to win over the Lancashire mill workers who had been adversely affected by his insistence that Indians bought only Indian cloth. Thus he was aware of the harm to the interests of (b) but sought international solidarity between (b) and (B).

Today we have to add a further dimension: capital is mobile and 'foreign' capital could be hiring domestic workers. In this case the interests of (a) and (B) combine to harm (b) as well as possibly (A). Thus, in attacking foreign direct investment for employing cheap labour and taking jobs away from the home country (as argued by some AFL-CIO groups in Seattle), the interests of (b) are pitted against (B) but blamed on the tendency of (a) to compete with or even align with (A). Farm subsidies by the US or the EU help (d) in these areas but hurt (e) and, via dumping, (D). In denouncing multinational corporations, protesters identify the villains as (a) foreign capital; but often (A) domestic/poor country capital is no better than foreign capital, say in health and safety risks, environmental damage, or gender discrimination.

Another new element resulting from globalisation is the capacity of civil society movements to forge international or indeed global alliances. In this respect alliances of rich-country and poor-country anti-trade groups do have some confusing clashes of interests which if not resolved can lead to contradictions between anti-trade movements in theory as well as in practice. If we characterise the Anti-Corn Law League as a combination of (a), (b), and (f) against (c) and (d), today we have the possibility of combinations of (f) and (F) championing individual or groups of countries against others i.e. aligning with any permutation of (a) to (e) and (A) to (E).

Thus from the simple alliances of (a) and (b) versus (c) and (d), or even (a) and (b) versus (A) and (B), we have (a) and some (B) versus (b) and some (A) and some (B). We have antagonism of (c) and (d) towards (C) and (D). The anti-trade movement may then represent an alliance of (f) and (F) or some sections thereof against workers in poor countries (B) and in favour of workers in rich countries (b) just because they don't like the rich-country capitalists (a). The movement against trade in food may hurt poor-country farmers (D); but silence on trade distortions such as EU and US farm subsidies benefits rich-country farmers (c) and workers (d) but hurts (C) and (D). Being anti-trade is no longer simply being anti-rich and pro-poor.

For many years the General Agreement on Tariffs and Trade (GATT), set up after the Second World War, tolerated this deviation from free trade as long as the offending countries were poor and not exporting their goods to rich country markets. But with the Uruguay Round concluded in 1993 things changed. Developing countries which had successfully acquired industries that could compete in export markets wanted greater access to rich country markets. Rich countries in their turn were eyeing the newly emerging markets where there were potential consumers of their products. Thus, the context of international trade negotiations began to change and a long series of negotiations resulted in the Marrakech Agreement and the upgrading of GATT to the WTO.

But with freer movement of capital the old comparative advantage is changing. New developments in Internet, transport, and communications technology are making the dispersal and fragmentation of the production process not only possible but profitable, and industries are relocating from North to South. This leads to the charge that capital is footloose and that it is employing/exploiting cheap labour, that American wages are being determined in Beijing, and so on. It is in this context that the WTO is suddenly emerging as the villain of the piece since these developments in global production relocation coincide with the establishment of the WTO. Of course, not all developing countries have experienced successful industrialisation or acquired an ability to export manufactures. Thus, within the old solid South there are divisions between those whose interests lie in greater access to foreign direct investment and OECD markets, and those who are left outside this process. The latter, mostly in Sub-Saharan Africa, are exporters of primary products and suffer from the inequities of agricultural export subsidies in OECD countries, which in turn dump their surplus primary products on the developing countries. These countries have a genuine complaint about the tardiness of the WTO in tackling this distortion in the world trading system. They also receive little foreign direct investment and hence do not benefit from the globalisation of world manufacturing.

Thus, there are several strands to the modern anti-trade movements and some of them are mutually contradictory. There is resentment of developed-country domination in industrial markets but also fear of footloose capital employing cheap foreign labour and hurting rich-country workers. There is concern about the falling prices of primary commodities of the Third World but also support for farm subsidies in rich countries. There is a sentiment against the environmental consequences of global growth led by free trade, which could deny the poor countries the capacity to export and enrich themselves in exactly the ways that rich countries have done until now. In some cases the interests of the different elements in the anti-capitalist coalition are inconsistent with one another.

Positions on Global Trade

In Desai and Said (2001) we divided civil society responses to global capitalism into Supporters, Reformers, Isolationists and Alternatives. Both Isolationists and Supporters believe that globalisation and global capitalism are one and the same and that they are reversible. They believe that globalisation entails the gradual erosion of the nation-state and the expansion of the rule of the market into every sphere of life. Isolationists think that globalisation should therefore be resisted and reversed. In its place they promote values of self-sufficiency and self-reliance and seek a return to the national liberation states. Supporters believe that globalisation and global capitalism are the only way to combat poverty and totalitarianism and should therefore be embraced wholeheartedly by all and sundry. Reformers believe that there is more to globalisation than capitalism. The state, according to Reformers, is not eroded but transformed, working under new constraints of 'overlapping sovereignties'. They do not believe that globalisation could or should be reversed; instead, they call for it to be humanised. Alternatives reject the entire conceptual framework and are more concerned with carving out spaces where alternative paradigms can co-exist. Over the past three years, due to the resurgence of the new group we call the Regressives (see below) and the weakening of Reformers, many activists are being pushed into Isolationist positions.

Today, in contrast to Seattle in 1999, there is a near (if not always declared) consensus within the movement on an agenda of abolishing the WTO and most other international trade initiatives. In this chapter we use a revised classification of civil society positions on trade to reflect these changes (see also Tables 4.1, 4.2 and 4.3).

Supporters advocate a strict interpretation of trade theories. This group, comprised mainly of academics and officials at international organisations, believe that even without equity or redistributive mechanisms trade liberalisation will benefit everyone by improving productivity. An example of the supporters' argument is a recent call by Nicholas Stern, the World Bank's chief economist, for developing countries to open their markets, even if this was not reciprocated by the developed countries, since liberalisation benefits the liberaliser (Luce 2002). What's good for business is good for everyone.

Supporters, who also include industrial lobbies, especially those associated with new industries, in addition to some of the main liberal media such as the *Economist* and the *Wall Street Journal*, are a declining minority today. 'Even the staunchest partisans of free trade suspect it is an idea whose time has not just come but gone' (Caldwell 2003).

The Supporters' ranks have been dwindling due to defections to the *Regressives*, who claim to adhere to the same orthodoxy but make an exception for their, usually rich-country, governments and corporations. According to this group, globalisation can work only under the leadership of hegemonic superpower(s). Since the well-being of the world community is dependent on the well-being of the superpower(s), they should be allowed to break the rules of free trade when those clash with their national interests. What is good for the superpower(s) is good for everyone.

Civil society Regressives are exemplified by some of the think tanks and mature industry lobbyists associated with the current US Administration. Some of them are ardent supporters of market liberalisation and free trade. As such, it would be hard for them to openly attack the WTO. Nonetheless they occasionally bemoan the organisation's unwieldy nature, which they attribute to its consensus mechanism and the resulting 'disproportionate'

Table 4.1: The new layout

	Globalisation is	Position on globalisation	Position on global trade
Supporters	Capitalism minus the state	Should be defended at all costs. The alternative is fascism.	Good even if unequal. The problem is in the inter-state system. Support the WTO.
Regressives	Capitalism plus the state	On our terms or deglobalisation	Good if on our terms. Same for WTO.
Isolationists	Capitalism minus the state	Deglobalisation	Inherently bad. Re-empower the state. Abolish the WTO.
Reformers	Capitalism plus transformed state	Should be humanised	Can and must be made more equitable. WTO reform, national and international redistributive policies.
Alternatives	Less capitalism and less state	Space for alternatives to compete and coexist	Neutral, the problem is with states and corporations

Table 4.2: Positions on trade agreements

	Isolationists	Reformers	Supporters	Regressives
	(e.g. Bello, Hines, Wallach)	(e.g. Oxfam, WDM, Greens, most Third World governments)	(e.g. academics, USTR Zoellick, European Commission)	(e.g. The Heritage Foundation, the rest of the US Administration, France, Italy)
Agreement on Agriculture (AoA)	Take food out of the WTO	Scrap Western subsidies and barriers. Allow poor countries to erect barriers when necessary.	Eliminate all barriers	Keep barriers when in the our national interest
New areas (investment, government procurement, competitions, trade facilitation)	No expansion to new areas	No expansion before addressing outstanding issues	Expand while dealing with outstanding issues	Expand with no restrictions as long as it is to the benefit of our companies
TRIPS (intellectual property and health)	Abolish	Should allow for preferential treatment of poor countries and national emergencies	Should have allowances only for emergencies such as health (both production and import)	Full global protection of intellectual property rights with the exception of our national emergencies
GATS (services)	Abolish	Should not extend to critical public services and public goods	Expand short of ill-defined areas necessary for the exercise of government	Expand as long as it is to our benefit
FTAA	Abolish	Abolish/amend	Support but not at the expense of WTO	Promote as alternative to WTO
Fair trade	Too little too late	At least something	May be trade-distorting	Trade is fair

Table 4.3: Civil society responses to global trade

	Organisation					Activity					Position				
	Individual	NGO/group	Movement/network	Think tank/academia	Media/website	Inform/educate	Lobby	Mobilise	Serve	Riot\celebrate	Supportive	Regressive	Isolationist	Reformative	Alternative
Action Aid		●				○	◑	●						●	
American Enterprise Institute				●		●		◑			●	◑			
ATTAC			●	◑		○	◑	●					◑	●	
Bello, Walden	●					●		◑					●		
Christian Aid		●				○	◑	◑	●					●	
Corporate Europe Observatory			●			●	◑	○					●	◑	
Economist					●	●	◑				●			◑	
Emergency Committee for American Trade		●					●	◑			●				
Financial Times					●	●	◑				●			◑	
Focus on Global South				●		●		◑					●	◑	
Food First		◑		●		●	○	◑					●	◑	
Friends of the Earth		◑	●				◑	●					●	◑	
GATS Watch					●	●		●					●	◑	
Global Trade Watch (at Public Citizen)					●	●		●					●		
Hemispheric Social Alliance			●					●					◑	●	○
Heritage Foundation				●		●	◑				●	◑			
Institute for Agriculture and Trade Policy				●		●							●	◑	
International Chamber of Commerce			●				●				●				
International Confederation of Trades Unions (ICFTU)			●			○	●	◑						●	
International Federation for Alternative Trade			●			○	◑	●						●	◑

	Organisation					Activity					Position				
	Individual	NGO/group	Movement/network	Think tank/academia	Media/website	Inform/educate	Lobby	Mobilise	Serve	Riot\celebrate	Supportive	Regressive	Isolationist	Reformative	Alternative
International Forum on Globalization			◑	●		●		◑					●	◑	
International Gender and Trade Network			●			●	○	◑					●	◑	
Klein, Naomi	●					●		◑							●
OneWorld.net					●	●			◑				◑	●	○
Our World Is Not For Sale			●				◑	●					●		
Oxfam		●				○	◑		●					●	
Peoples Global Action			●				●				●				
Polaris Institute				●		●		◑					◑	●	
Public Citizen		●				○	◑	●					●		
Rand Corporation				●		●	◑				●	◑			
SalAMI		●						◑		●			◑		●
Terraviva (of Inter Press Service)					●	●		◑					◑	●	○
Third World Network		●	◑			◑		●					◑	●	
Trade Justice Movement			●					●						●	
Trade Observatory (previously WTO Watch)					●	●		●	●				◑	●	
Trans Atlantic Business Dialogue			●				●				●				
Transnational Institute				●		●	◑	◑					◑	●	
Via Campesina			●				◑	●					◑	●	
Wall Street Journal					●	●	◑				●	◑			
World Development Movement		●				◑	○	●						●	

● PREDOMINANT ◑ SIGNIFICANT ○ TO SOME DEGREE

influence of Third World nations (Wolf 2002). Yet it is revealing that most of their strategic advice to the Administration is focused on bilateral treaties and negotiations. In the extreme case, the Heritage Foundation completely ignores the WTO in its trade strategy advice to the administration (O'Driscoll and Fitzgerald 2002).

Indeed, the US Administration's policy towards the WTO is similar to that towards other multilateral initiatives. While Trade Representative Robert Zoellick is pursuing a 'positive agenda' at the organisation, the rest of the Administration and Congress are busy sabotaging it.[3] The introduction of 30 per cent steel tariffs in 2001 and the US Farm Bill which substantially increases farm subsidies are recent examples of new trade barriers erected by the Administration. The US recently backtracked on commitments made during the WTO Ministerial Meeting in Doha in 2001 on allowing developing countries to import unlicensed medicines to protect public health. These commitments were critical in obtaining developing country governments' agreement for the launch of a new round of negotiations. Such acts significantly undermine the prospect for the new round. In recent years the EU has won five cases against the US at the WTO. The US is, however, refusing to implement the WTO judgments, thus further undermining the system (Lamy 2003). On the other side of the Atlantic, France and Germany are engaged in similar tactics of pushing for WTO expansion while stonewalling on the Common Agricultural Policy (CAP). CAP subsidies amount to US$50 billion annually. If they are left unchanged until 2016, as suggested by a recent Franco-German agreement, they will further undermine the prospect of success at the current Doha Round of trade negotiations. Regressive politics (on both sides of the Atlantic) have more to do with industrial lobbying than with demands by farming communities and labour to which they are sometimes attributed.

The implicit double standard of this approach and the fact that its proponents are now in power not only in the US but also in many European counties is behind the radicalisation of activists on the other side of the trade debate. Even reformers are beginning to embrace *Isolationist* positions. The critical plank of the Isolationists argument is that it is almost impossible to make global trade work for the poor. They view trade as a Trojan Horse through which multinationals and their political

3 US Trade Representative Robert Zoellick is one of few multilateralists within the current US Administration. He could be described as a Supporter under our framework. As such his positions are often at odds with the general policy thrust of the Administration and the Republican majority in Congress.

representatives spread their power. The results are a loss of jobs in the North, poverty and loss of sovereignty in the South, and environmental degradation all round. What is good for the corporation is bad for everyone.

> Once upon a time, empires were built through direct conquest. Armies plundered their way across continents, claiming lands and resources for king and country, justifying their acts as 'bringing the light of civilisation to the savages of dark continents'. These days such invasion has lost its primary appeal, but the equivalent gains are routinely achieved through different, and more efficient, means, which those in power prefer to call not open theft but 'open markets'. (Mittal 2003)

Many Isolationist groups are united in the Our World is Not For Sale (OWINFS) network, which brings together such groups as Public Citizen, Focus on the Global South, Friends Of the Earth (FOE) International, and Food First. Isolationists call explicitly or implicitly for the abolition of the WTO and other international trade initiatives. As Lori Wallach of Public Citizen explained at the WSF, the goal is to 'Derail the WTO'. Ronnie Hall, Trade Program Manager at FOE, says that it is her 'personal' opinion (though not that of the organisation) that the WTO should be abolished. Kevin Danaher of Global Exchange calls himself an abolitionist (WSF 2003). Aye Aye Win of Dignity International was critical of this approach, describing the mood at the WSF in these terms:

> If you want a big cheer from the crowd, it's clear what the speakers should do: smash neo-liberalism to pieces, condemn foreign debt, demonize the enemy, the TNCs, the IFIs, and to round it off call for their abolition. A deafening applause is guaranteed. That's exactly what we are witnessing at the big conferences and seminars here. (Win 2003)

The Isolationists promote two alternatives to the current trade regime: the re-empowerment of the nation-state and the development of an alternative global regime from the bottom up. The alternative regime they call for, however, is defined in quite broad terms for the time being. Examples include *Another World is Possible: Popular Alternatives to Globalization at the World Social Forum* (Fisher and Ponniah 2003) or the new International Forum on Globalization report *Alternatives to Economic Globalization: A Better World is Possible* (IFG 2002). Following is an excerpt from the editors' synopsis of the report:

> Written by a premier group of thinkers from around the world, Alternatives to Economic Globalization is the defining document of the antiglobalization movement. The culmination of a three-year project by the International Forum on Globalization, whose members include Ralph Nader, David Korten, John Cavanagh, Lori Wallach, and Jerry Mander, it presents both a sober critique of globalization as well as practical, thoughtful alternatives. The authors assert ten core requirements for democratic societies, including equality, basic human rights, local decision making, and ecological sustainability, and demonstrate how globalization undermines each. Offering specific strategies for reining in corporate domination, they address alternative systems for energy, agriculture, transportation, and manufacturing; ideas for weakening or dismantling the WTO, World Bank, and IMF; and rebuilding economies that are responsive to human needs.

The main themes of these proposals are state control over food, water and public services, localisation and subsidiarity, re-regulation and 'weakening or dismantling' of multi-lateral economic institutions, and establishment of new structures which put people before profits.

The *Reformers*, once the broadest camp, embracing not only activists but also many mainstream politicians and representatives of new industries, are in the retreat, squeezed between superpowers that would rather see no rules than any which may inhibit their freedom of action and activists who also seem to have given up on the reform/institution-building agenda at the global level. The main claim of the Reformers is that international trade can, as the theory predicts, bring broad benefits to everyone provided mechanisms and rules are put in place at regional, national and international levels to ensure optimal and equitable outcomes. Conversely the lack of such rules would not only entail deepening inequality but also may threaten globalisation as such.

The main reformist groups are represented in the Trade Justice Movement (TJM), a coalition which involves groups like Oxfam International, Action Aid, The World Development Movement (WDM) War on Want, and others. Box 4.2 illustrates the debate between reformers and isolationists. There is some overlap between the Isolationists and Reformers; they are united in their opposition to the expansion of the WTO into the new areas such as investment. However, even here Reformers see an opportunity to address outstanding issues at the WTO and other global forums while

Isolationists view it as part of a strategy to derail the WTO and return power to the nation-state.

> For the movement against corporate-driven globalization, derailing the 5th Ministerial or preventing agreement on the launching of a new comprehensive round would mean not only fighting the WTO and free trade to a standstill. It would mean creating momentum for a rollback of free trade and a reduction of the power of the WTO. This is well understood by, among others, the *Economist*, which warned its corporate readers 'globalization is reversible'. (Bello 2002)

Another plank of the Reformist framework is the incorporation of labour and environmental standards in the trade regime:

> The key issue we are addressing here is the worker's human rights, which are clearly defined, such as the right to organize and bargain, and freedom and protection from forced labor, child labor and discrimination…The problem we have had with the WTO in recent years, is that they are saying 'these issues have nothing to do with us', that workers' rights are not trade issues. (Seneviratne 2003)

Such demands are not only difficult to pursue at the WTO, but some Southern activists view them either as a way to legitimise the WTO or as another attempt to discriminate against Southern producers. Moreover, the radicalisation of the movement means that, instead of the painstaking work needed to bridge such differences, compromise is being achieved on the basis of the lowest common denominator of deglobalisation.

The polarisation of the debate and the retreat to comfortable old dogmas means that less space is available for the *Alternatives*. The Alternatives are the foot soldiers of the global justice and solidarity movement. Young and with a keen eye for popular culture and new technology they speak globalisation's language. In the tradition of the 1960s radicals, the Alternatives have a deep distrust of authority, be it political or economic. They are not likely to be found in traditional organisations and NGOs. At the WSF they did not even have the particular passes necessary to attend most of the 1,400 workshops. The Alternatives not only account for the bulk of the participants at riots, demonstrations and social forums but they are also responsible for the most creative ideas at these events: guerrilla gardening (digging up tarmac to plant trees), Marcus's mask (hiding one's face to identify with the faceless victims of global capitalism), white overalls

Box 4.2: The 'Rigged Rules and Double Standards' Debate

When Oxfam decided to discontinue its Fair Trade business on pro bono advice from management consultants McKenzie and Co., it replaced it with a two-pronged strategy. On the one hand it continued to provide technical assistance to small developing country exporters in accessing Northern markets. On the other it started an ambitious advocacy campaign on trade issues. The campaign is based at the MakeTradeFair.com website. It includes education, advocacy and lobbying. The campaign's flagship document, Oxfam's first major foray into the area of trade advocacy, met a maelstrom of criticism from the Isolationist camp.

The debate, which centred around Oxfam's 'Rigged Rules and Double Standards' report (Oxfam 2002a) began at the Second World Social Forum in Porto Alegre in 2002 between Oxfam on the one hand and a number of groups and individuals including Colin Hines, Focus on the Global South and Food First on the other. It highlights the differences between the Reformers and the Isolationists. The debate was quite animated and continued in the media and online long after the publication of Oxfam's report. By the time of the Third Forum, however, there was no debate at all, since the great majority of participants including many Oxfam people sided with the Isolationists on most points (WSF 2003).

The Oxfam report, which exemplifies Reformist thinking on the issue of trade, is centred on the proposition that international trade can be beneficial to the poor. Indeed, it argues that trade, as in the example of East Asia, has already lifted as many as 400 million people out of poverty. The problem, however, is that international trade rules today are 'rigged' for the benefit of rich countries and their corporations. Moreover, rich-country governments preach free trade to the developing countries but do not practise it themselves. Finally, even when developing countries are benefiting from trade, the benefits are skewed towards large suppliers and intermediaries at the expense of the poor as a result of inadequate policies pursued by these countries' governments and the multilateral organisations. The report proposes access for poor-country products into rich-country markets: agriculture and textiles in particular should be a major thrust of the campaign for a fairer international trade regime. The report does not promote market access as a panacea and stresses that it should be coupled with domestic policies to ensure an efficient and equitable distribution of the gains from trade. Oxfam also believes that focusing on market access is a useful strategy aimed at exposing the hypocrisy of developed-country leaders who do not practise what they preach.

> International trade can work for the poor or against the poor. Just as in any national economy, economic integration in the global economy can be a source of shared prosperity and poverty reduction, or a source of increasing inequality and exclusion. Managed well, the international trading system can lift millions out of poverty. Managed badly, it will leave whole economies even more marginalized. (Hobbes 2002)

Opponents of the report attack it on several fronts. First, they argue that market access, far from providing benefits to the poor in the South, aggravates commodity export dependency. According to this argument, underdeveloped countries get locked into a pattern of exporting low value added products to rich countries and importing expensive manufactured goods and services. Growing efficiency and productivity means that the relative value of poor country exports is constantly declining, thus condemning these countries to immiserisation in the long term no matter how much they succeed in expanding their exports (Prebisch 1950). Variations of this theory cover agricultural and natural commodity exports as well as exports of labour intensive products, a phenomenon known as the fallacy of composition (UNDP 2003).

Second, opponents of the report believe that by negotiating for market access Third World governments will be forced to make concessions in other areas. Finally, they argue that focusing on market access is a dangerous diversion from the efforts which should focus on derailing the WTO.

Box 4.3: The Fair Trade Movement

In the aftermath of the Second World War some church organisations marketed handicrafts made by refugees as a way of helping them gain economic independence. Many fair trade groups trace the beginnings of the movement to that period. Alternative Trade Organisations (ATO) spread in the 1960s to market handicrafts and agricultural commodities purchased in the Third World at 'fair' prices.

The ATOs' main argument is that many poor country producers and especially small farmers and cooperatives are not getting a fair price for their products due to the difficulties they face in gaining access to rich-country markets and to finance. The big difference between the retail price in the developed world and the income that these producers receive for the fruits of their labour is, ATOs argue, unfairly appropriated by various intermediaries in both rich and poor countries.

ATOs set out to correct this imbalance by direct trading: purchasing products at higher prices and selling them in rich-country markets, thus circumventing the traditional distribution channels. Many of these organisations combine direct trading with the provision of technical assistance to their suppliers in everything from management to production techniques and market access. They also campaign on all matters related to fair trade. As such ATOs are a unique hybrid of for-profit organisations and NGOs.

Oxfam was a pioneer of fair trade in the UK in the 1960s. In the US the first ATOs included 10,000 villages and Equal Exchange. Many ATOs are based in Third World countries working to protect the rights of disadvantaged producers.

With the growth of the fair trade movement and increased awareness of the issues involved, especially among rich-country consumers in the 1980s and 1990s, many of the twentieth-century fair trade groups began to coordinate efforts across borders and work towards establishing common and certifiable fair trade standards. In 1989 the International Federation of Alternative Trade (IFAT) was established, which claims to represent 160 groups in 50 countries of which two-thirds are based in the Third World. The various local groups also coalesced into national organisations which in turn established the Fairtrade Labelling Organization International (FLO) in 1997.

- The FLO is an umbrella organisation which issues the 'Fairtrade' label to qualifying products based on a set of standards applied to both producers and traders. Compliance is monitored by a network of inspectors and an auditing process. There are different sets of requirements for traders and producers. Traders must:
- pay a price to producers that covers the costs of sustainable production and living;
- pay a premium that producers can invest in development;
- partially pay in advance when producers ask for it;
- sign contracts that allow for long-term planning and sustainable production practices. (http://www.fairtrade.net.)

For producers, the requirements are different for small holders and cooperatives and for organisations dependent on hired labour. There are minimum progress requirements and specific standards for the various products. The requirements cover social, economic, organisational, labour and environmental issues.

Most products covered by FLO are food commodities such as coffee, sugar and cocoa; but the organisation is beginning to address manufactured products starting with footballs. The member organisations cover a much wider selection of products.

Coffee is one of the main fair trade commodities and shows both the success and limitations of the movement. Despite rapid growth since 1973, when the first batch of fair trade coffee was imported into the Netherlands, it accounts for only 2 per cent of the total coffee market (Oxfam 2002b). Even some of its most avid proponents admit that fair trade coffee can be targeted only at the top end of the market. Moreover, by paying a premium price the fair traders may be sending the wrong signal to a market which is already suffering from excess supply. On the other hand, fair trade buyers are lending a helping hand to some of the most disadvantaged communities in the world in a context where little effort is being made by national governments or multilateral organisations to address the issue of over-supply and the need to shift to other crops. Finally, the example of the fair trade movement is creating an incentive for large coffee buyers to address the issues at hand.

(heavily padded protesters who can withstand police truncheons), critical mass (cyclists who obstruct automobile traffic by riding in large numbers), the pink march (which succeeded in penetrating the heavily fortified World Bank/IMF meeting venue in Prague by looking unthreatening) and the controversial black block (anarchists who do not shy away from using stones and occasionally fire-bombs to attack riot police).

The Alternatives are also the driving force behind 'submerged networks' which surface around certain campaigns, such as SaIAMI, which organised the riots against the Summit of the Americas in Quebec in 2001. SaIAMI is a direct action network. Its first activities coincided with the Multilateral Agreement on Investments. It is also known for its non-violent blockade of the Montreal Conference on Economic Globalisation in May 1998.

Other submerged networks exercise resistance through the promotion of a particular lifestyle such as the Fair Trade movement (Box 4.3). The network in this case comprises of consumers who choose to pay premium prices for fair trade products (or boycott those viewed to be in violation of ethical trade norms) in addition to those who are involved in organising Fair Trade schemes.

Instead of aiming to transform or reform global capitalism, the Alternatives are concerned with reclaiming 'things' from the encroaching market and creating space for alternatives. They are concerned with the political and cultural consequences of capitalism as much as with its economic and environmental costs. They perceive the encroachment of the market into the public space as a threat to freedom, which takes the form of 'corporate censorship' in the North and human rights abuses in the South (Desai and Said 2001).

Alternatives do not represent a distinct set of positions on the issues of trade. They could thus be viewed as a particular form of global civil society, rather than a particular take on globalisation. That said, in a debate where one is expected to take sides between Western governments and corporations on the one hand and Third World leaders and industries on the other, the Alternatives have no favourite. This may explain why some of them felt so uncomfortable with certain aspects of the World Social Forum in Porto Alegre.

> For some, the hijacking of the World Social Forum by political parties and powerful men is proof that the movements against corporate globalization are finally maturing and 'getting serious'. But is it really so mature, amidst the graveyard of failed left political projects, to

believe that change will come by casting your ballot for the latest charismatic leader, then crossing your fingers and hoping for the best? Get serious. (Klein 2003)

In the following sections we address issues which illustrate the civil society position on trade described above.

The World Trade Organization (WTO)

The WTO is at the heart of most civil society campaigns on trade issues. Established in 1995, it is one of the youngest multilateral organisations. It is simultaneously one of the smallest in terms of staff and bureaucracy yet one of the most influential in terms of impact on peoples' lives worldwide.

For its staunchest opponents, the WTO embodies everything that is wrong with global capitalism and superpower hegemony: a one-size-fits-all tool aimed at prising open Third World markets for the benefit of rich-country-based corporations. One of the organisation's most loathed features is the finality of its mandate: once a market is open it cannot be closed again.

For its proponents, the WTO is the most democratic of the multilateral organisations, including the UN. It is, they argue, the only place where Costa Rica can lodge a complaint against the US and win, as was the case with underwear import restrictions (WTO Appellate Body 1997). WTO proponents view the irrevocable nature of market opening as a strength, imparting certainty to global markets by removing the threat of ad hoc government intervention.

The debate about the WTO focuses on two main issues: governance and mandate.

Governance

On governance, the WTO's opponents argue that, despite the 'one nation, one vote' and consensus systems, the so-called Quad countries (US, EU, Canada and Japan) and their corporations dominate the WTO agenda:

- The so called 'Green Room' negotiations involving the Quad countries and a selected group of others are where consensus is forged in secret, with the remaining countries left to join the consensus.
- Mini-Ministerials are often organised involving the Quad countries and a selected list of invitees. These meetings are unofficial and are therefore unreported.

- The Quad countries use their political and economic muscle to force concessions from Third World leaders. This was the case with the US using the 'war on terrorism' rhetoric at the Doha Fourth Ministerial meeting in November 2001 (TWN, http://www.twnside.org.sg).
- The negotiations are packaged in rounds: bundles of issues specifically for the purpose of horse-trading between the various issues. Some activists argue that this makes for further pressure on poorer nations (WDN, http://www.wdm.org.uk).
- The influence of corporations and the coordination between Quad governments and multinationals is seen by many, including the WTO's new director Dr Supachai, as problematic (WDM, http://www.wdm.org.uk).
- The WTO has built-in mechanisms which are aimed at rendering the process of market liberalisation irreversible. Once agreement is reached there is very little room for individual countries to revisit certain issues or reinstate barriers, regardless of circumstances. Even existing exemptions, on grounds of health and safety for example, are quite difficult to exercise, as was revealed during the dispute over generic AIDS drugs.
- The WTO's dispute-settlement mechanism, which adjudicates on violations of signed agreements, is specifically designed as an enforcement rather than an arbitration mechanism. The panel's decisions can be reversed only by consensus, rendering them virtually impossible to appeal. However, even detractors of the system admit that it is the right mechanism if the goal is the promotion of market liberalisation (US Senate Finance Committee 2000).

There are other, more prosaic reasons why Third World leaders cannot exercise their full rights within the WTO. Many cannot afford having a full-time representative in Geneva. Some lack the qualified staff and the resources to field representatives to several simultaneous meetings.

WTO proponents concede some of these charges and call for increased 'technical assistance and capacity building [for developing country governments] to be better equipped to participate in the multilateral trading system'. The WTO head considers this one of 'four pillars' which would help successfully conclude the current round of WTO negotiations

(Panitchpakdi 2002). Other shortcomings are attributed to the imbalances in the inter-state system rather than the organisation itself.

Developing-country governments, especially India, Brazil and South Africa, are displaying ever more skill in using WTO mechanisms to defend their interests. There are several Third World blocs within the organisation aimed at pooling resources and coordinating negotiating positions, including the thirty-country-strong African Bloc, the Like-Minded Group which includes almost all Third World countries, and the Cairns Group which includes both poor and rich agricultural commodity exporters. Third World governments are leveraging divisions in the Quad group as well as support and pressure from civil society to pursue their goals (see below). The Doha Fourth Ministerial (the first after the failed meeting in Seattle) was a demonstration of this new-found confidence, although it resulted in only limited achievements for developing countries in the shape of a commitment to address the issues deemed critical by these countries before embarking on a new round of negotiations at the upcoming Fifth Ministerial in Cancun. Although no progress has been made so far on any of these issues, governments and activists both seem to have identified elements in WTO procedure from which they can attack the organisation:

> If derailing the drive for free trade at the 5th Ministerial is indeed the goal, then the main tactical focus of the strategy becomes clear: Consensus decision-making is the Achilles heel of the WTO, and it is the emergence of consensus that we must prevent at all costs from emerging. (Bello 2002)

Mandate

Campaigns around the Agreement on Agriculture (AoA), the General Agreement on Trade in Services (GATS), Trade-Related Aspects of Intellectual Property Rights (TRIPS), and the new areas of investment, government procurement, trade facilitation and competition policy provide an illustration of the ongoing debate over the WTO's mandate.

According to activists, by limiting the nation-states 'policy space' the WTO denies developing countries essential tools of development. These countries claim to need preferential treatment to be able to catch up, while the WTO rules are not even equal. Trade in sectors where developing countries are most competitive – agriculture and textiles in particular – is not being liberalised by the rich. At the same time, developed countries press for liberalisation in sectors where trade mostly flows from North to

South, such as intellectual property, services and investment. The WTO also limits governments' freedom to protect small producers, to the benefit of large multinationals which are also predominantly based in the North. The activists use data showing poor countries losing anything from $100 billion to $300 billion a year due to imbalances in the global trade regime (Oxfam 2002a).

WTO defenders argue in response that, if developed countries are dragging out liberalisation in certain markets like agriculture and textiles, it is their consumers who will be the primary losers from such protectionism. They point out that discretionary policy tools such as import substitution and the promotion of infant industries, which were used by many developing countries under GATT, at best were ineffective and at worst promoted patronage and corruption. The main rejoinder from WTO proponents, however, is that the question is not whether the poor are losing out under the current trade regime but whether they would be losing more without the WTO (Bello and Legrain 2000–1). The debate over the impact of the WTO on development is ongoing and has fuelled demands to conduct an economic impact assessment before any further trade negotiations rounds are launched (Martin Khor speaking at WSF 2003).

The Fourth Doha Ministerial Meeting of the WTO in 2001 launched a new round of negotiations, dubbed the Doha Development Round, to replace the Millennium Round, which failed to materialise at the Seattle 1999 Ministerial. Doha is a compromise whereby developing countries agree to the expansion of the WTO mandate into new areas in exchange for redress of their concern over issues from previous rounds.

Outstanding Issues

Agreement on Agriculture

Developing countries are demanding the elimination of agricultural subsidies by developed countries, including the US$50 billion dispensed annually by the EU Common Agricultural Policy (CAP). They are specifically concerned with export subsidies which have direct bearing on their domestic markets as well as tariffs which prevent access for their products. The US supports this approach (in words if not in deeds, in view of the recent adoption of the Farm Bill) and is proposing across-the-board reductions in its own tariffs and subsidies. The EU, however, is baulking at compromise due especially to resistance from France. Recent agreement between the German and French governments to postpone any changes to CAP until

2016 has been met with indignation across the board. The deadline set at Doha for reaching an agreement on these issues was missed.

Isolationists dismiss the AoA and demand that agriculture and food in particular be taken out of the WTO remit. According to the isolationists, free trade in agriculture inevitably leads to the promotion of export crops at the expense of subsistence agriculture, which amounts to discrimination against small farmers and leads to environmental degradation and hunger (OWINFS, http://www.ourworldisnotforsale.org; Food First, http://www.foodfirst.org). Reformers are campaigning for the elimination of developed-country subsidies and other barriers while allowing developing countries some leeway to ensure food security and the protection for small farmers and indigenous people (see below).

Implementation

Rich countries which were supposed to eliminate tariffs and quotas on textiles over ten years by 2005 have left most of them in place until the last minute. Developing countries are demanding that the rich start reducing tariffs in this area immediately. The US, as part of its 'positive engagement' policy, is proposing drastic reductions not only in textiles but in industrial tariffs across the board. The deadline for reaching agreement on implementation issues has not been met. Reformers support the developing country position in this respect. The Isolationists dismiss this approach as a gimmick designed to allow the developed countries to present their fulfilment of their long-standing obligations as a concession and give the Reformers a sense of achievement (Bello 2002).

Special and Deferential Treatment

The WTO offers a number of avenues to take special consideration of the development needs of its poorer members. Those include longer implementation periods and technical assistance both during negotiations and at the implementation stage. Agreements usually have mechanisms whereby developing countries can negotiate certain exceptions to satisfy their policies. The developing countries are demanding more flexibility in designing policies which they deem essential for development. The US and the EU are willing to consider such flexibility provided developing countries agree on 'graduation' criteria (Korea, an OECD member, is still benefiting from developing-country exceptions). No agreement was reached on these issues within the deadline set at Doha.

Both Isolationists and Reformers agree that developing countries should be allowed freedom in choosing development strategies and certain forms of protectionism which were employed successfully by developed countries, including late developers in East Asia (Oxfam 2002a).

Trade Related Aspects of Intellectual Property Rights (TRIPS) and Public Health

One of the few tangible achievements of the Doha meeting for developing countries was the agreement in the final declaration 'that it is important to implement and interpret the TRIPS Agreement in a way that supports public health – by promoting both access to existing medicines and the creation of new medicines'. This is done either by allowing countries to manufacture needed drugs without having to obtain a licence (compulsory licensing) or by importing generic unlicensed drugs from third countries (parallel importing) (WTO 2001). Negotiations were supposed to take place to clarify the modalities for making use of this exception especially by countries that did not have their own pharmaceutical industry. The negotiations broke down when the US backtracked on the principles agreed at Doha and sought to limit the number of diseases to which the exception would apply. Pharmaceutical companies that are behind the US trade representative's change of heart claim, not without some justification, that a blanket exception could be open to abuse by manufacturers of generic drugs, including those based in South Africa and India (Alfeld and Hofheinz 2003). The deadline was missed in this case as well. Activists of all persuasions have no love for TRIPS, especially when it comes to medicine.

New Areas

While there are disagreements among activists on the outstanding issues, there is an almost unanimous rejection of proposals for WTO expansion into new areas. Apart from previously mentioned strategies of reforming or abolishing the WTO, opposition to expansion is based on the activists notion of the market limits and the optimal level of policy space which should reside at the nation-state level.

Market limits are based on an understanding of what is tradable. Can public goods be left to the market or should they remain fully under state control? Should these goods, in principle, also be tradable internationally? Even if there is no principled objection to either, should they be subject to international trade under the present system?

The tradability of utilities and public services is a thorny issue since these usually include social costs and benefits which are not reflected in their market value. Markets for such services have therefore a higher risk of failure, the consequences of which can be more devastating than in other sectors of the economy. A collapsing health-care system is more dangerous than a collapsing automotive industry.

Beyond the issue of market failures and externalities, however, public services and utilities tend to have emotional, cultural and political dimensions which sit uneasily with market relations, let alone foreign control. 'Services are the public tangible manifestation and expression of our shared values as citizens. How we choose to heal our sick, teach our kids, protect our water, connect to one another through transport and communication are expressions of our collective vision for society' (Klein 2000). 'Water', as a banner in Porto Alegre exclaimed, 'is Life. It cannot be bought and sold' (WSF 2003). Finally, poor countries and poor people depend on the free or nearly free provision of these services for their survival, much more than their more fortunate counterparts.

One of the main complaints about the WTO compared with its predecessor, the GATT, is its impact on domestic *policy space* – an issue which arises from its targeting of non-tariff barriers. Environmental and safety regulations and other domestic policies have often been successfully contested through the WTO as trade-restricting. The famous image of protesters dressed in turtle suits in Seattle is related to one example of the WTO reaching into environmental regulations. The activists were protesting a WTO ruling in favour of Asian shrimp exporters who successfully contested a US environmental regulation which prohibits the import of shrimp farmed in ways which harm sea turtles (WTO 1998). There are many other examples of such rulings, including the well-known case when Europe was penalised for banning the import of US hormone-treated beef (WTO 1997).

The expansion of the WTO remit into new areas of services, investment, government procurement competition policy, and trade facilitation will further limit the scope of domestic policy. This is one of the main reasons why many in the Third World view the WTO as a new form of colonialism (Romapu 2003). The New Areas are at the heart of most WTO campaigns. These are not strictly trade issues, but any coverage of the WTO that did not address these issues would be incomplete. The discussion of the Multilateral Investment Framework also provides an update on the Multilateral Agreement on Investment campaign covered in Chapter 3 in this book.

The Multilateral Investment Framework (MIF)

Objections to the MIF are not dissimilar to those raised against its defeated predecessor, the Multilateral Agreement on Investment (MAI; Desai and Said 2001). It reduces government's regulatory discretion and grants foreign investors unprecedented legal rights. Activists question the agreement's capacity to increase foreign direct investment. Some even question the link between investment and development (TWN, http://www.twnside.org.sg). Activists would like to see an agreement which improved regulatory control over multinationals, but believe that such an agreement is unlikely to emerge within the WTO framework. The agreement, according to its detractors, would establish a false equality between the developed and the underdeveloped, which is inconsistent with affirmative action principles. Finally, unlike trade, investment flows only from North to South, which means that the agreement will largely benefit the developed countries and their corporations.

A workshop on the 'WTO Investment Issue' was organised in Geneva on 18–21 March 2003 by the Third World Network, Oxfam International, WWF, Public Services International, Center for International Environmental Law and Institute for Agriculture and Trade Policy. The workshop issued a statement signed by fifty groups calling on governments to drop investment from the agenda for the upcoming WTO ministerial in Cancun (Khor and Yen 2003).

The defenders of the MIF argue that the agreement will not necessarily restrict regulatory space but make it more transparent. Rules and transparency will promote investment and lead to development (WTO, http://www.wto.org).

General Agreement on Trade in Services (GATS)

The GATS has been in effect since the establishment of the WTO in 1995. It is a rolling agreement which aims to open up ever more areas of services, a market estimated at US$5 trillion, to WTO rules. GATS in theory should cover 'everything that you cannot drop on your foot' (WDM 2002) with the exception of services associated with the direct exercise of government. This exception is, however, circumscribed by the proviso that these services are not offered on a commercial basis.[4] As Susan George (2003b) puts it in *Red Pepper*, 'All human activities are to become, in the fullness of time, profit-oriented commodities that can be invested in and traded'.

---

4 For example, a government's right to exclude government-owned postal services from the GATS remit is limited if those services are provided on a commercial basis.

Its proponents argue that GATS covers only sectors which governments agree to include; moreover, governments are entitled to place exemptions on sectors which they offer for opening. For example, India has opened its tourism sector but maintained certain restrictions including the requirement that foreign operators act through local subsidiaries. Malaysia opened up its insurance sectors but maintained a 51 per cent limit on foreign ownership (Lal Das 2003).

GATS is currently undergoing a request-offer round which was supposed to end in April 2003. Countries are exchanging lists of sectors which they want included in GATS. There are also demands to lift previously established restrictions such as the ones listed above. Once a country offers the opening of a sector or a lifting of restrictions to any WTO member, it is obliged to open it to all under most favoured nations (MFN) rules.

Unlike goods, services can cross borders in a variety of ways. GATS also covers four modes of delivery of services:

1. cross-border supply, such as banking via wire transfer;
2. consumption abroad, for example studying in a foreign country;
3. commercial presence, for example the establishment of a hotel as part of an international chain; and
4. presence of natural persons such as a construction crew travelling to another country to participate in a project.

Of most interest to many developing countries is Mode 4, which covers provision of services through the movement of physical persons. Developed countries have, however, diluted the potential of Mode 4 by invoking exceptions on grounds of security. Mode 3, on the other hand, is more interesting for developed countries. It covers the provision of services through movement of legal persons and could offer a back-door introduction of the MIF.

The sectors most targeted for inclusion into GATS or further liberalisation are utilities, transport, tourism and financial services. Thanks to an energetic bipartisan (reformist-isolationist) campaign against it, GATS expansion does not seem to be justifying the activists' worst fears. To judge from the sectors offered for opening by the EU, health, education and water will remain outside reach of GATS as far as Europe is concerned (OWINFS, http://www.ourworldisnotforsale.org).

Bypassing the WTO: From NAFTA to FTAA

Corporations and the neo-conservatives who serve them are not waiting for the WTO to pursue the opening of new markets. There is a cascade of multilateral, regional and bilateral arrangements through which liberalisation is being pursued in ways which are more radical than ever envisaged under the WTO.

While the GATS negotiators debate whether trade in water itself should be liberalised or whether it is 'environmental services' such as water treatment and supply which should be opened to competition, the World Bank has already succeeded in privatising water and utilities in several Third World countries. Trade officials who reject linking the liberalisation of services with privatisation of health and education (WTO, http://www.wto.org.) have been pre-empted with the introduction of fees for education and health care under the Bank's conditionality, a process which is correctly viewed as a first step towards privatisation.

The FTAA includes radical versions of GATS and the other new agreements on investment and government procurement.

> Our objective with FTAA is to guarantee North American companies the control of a territory that goes from the Arctic Pole all the way to Antarctica, free access to the whole hemisphere without difficulties or obstacles for our products, services, technology, and capital. (US Secretary of State Colin Powell, quoted in Mittal 2003)

Finally, bilateral treaties such as the one between the US and Chile or British Petroleum (BP) and Turkey go even further than the FTAA in placing multinational corporations above the law. These treaties lack even the few monitoring and control mechanisms that are available in a multilateral framework like the WTO. For example, the agreement between the Turkish government and the Baku-Tbilisi-Ceyhan Pipeline Consortium led by BP exempts the pipeline from obligations under any current or future Turkish law that may threaten the project's profits, including environmental, social and human rights legislation. The only Turkish law not superseded by the agreement is the Constitution (Baku Ceyhan Campaign 2002).

Negotiations for the establishment of FTAA were launched at the first Summit of the Americas in 1994. It was then conceived as a trade alliance encompassing all 'democratic' states in the hemisphere, that is, excluding Cuba. The FTAA seeks to expand to the entire continent the model of the North American Free Trade Agreement (NAFTA), which brought together the US, Canada and Mexico in 1993. The FTAA is seeking a mandate almost identical to that of the WTO, including the new areas of government procurement, competition policy, trade facilitation, and investment. FTAA by design is meant to 'improve upon these [WTO] rules and disciplines wherever possible and appropriate' (FTAA, http://www.ftaa-alca.org). FTAA, like NAFTA but unlike the WTO, is likely to incorporate some labour and environmental provisions.

> Essentially, what the FTAA negotiators have done, urged on by the big business community in every country, is to take the most ambitious elements of every global trade and investment agreement – existing or proposed – and put them all together in this openly ambitious hemispheric pact. (Barlow 2001)

Like the WTO Doha Round, FTAA negotiations are supposed to be completed by 2005. Like the WTO, they have been bogged down in the face of fierce resistance by civil society and, to a lesser degree, governments in most Latin American countries. Like the WTO, the FTAA requires consensus to be approved, which is inspiring optimism among its opponents about its chances of success.

The FTAA seems to attract more vociferous opposition and from a broader set of actors than the WTO. Few of the treaty's opponents seek to improve it, focusing instead on preventing it from ever coming into force. One reason may be the NAFTA track record and the damage attributed to the treaty in the US and Canada but especially in Mexico. Unlike the WTO, NAFTA is directly associated by its opponents with the loss of manufacturing jobs in the US and Canada and the devastation to small-scale agriculture and indigenous livelihoods in Mexico. Global Exchange attributes the loss of 766,000 jobs in the US to NAFTA (Global Exchange NAFTA FAQ, http://www.globalexchange.org/ftaa/faq.html) while Food First claims that 600 Mexican farmers are forced off their lands every day due to the treaty (Mittal 2003; see also Chapter 8). Moreover the maquiladora jobs[5] created by NAFTA along the US-Mexico border are notoriously unstable and underpaid. Flagrant labour and environmental abuses are attributed to the operators of factories established specifically to service the US and Canadian markets. Environmental degradation along the US-Mexico borders attributed to NAFTA has

5 'Maquiladora': these are foreign-owned factories in Mexico that import components and assemble them for export. Jobs created in such factories were supposed to stop migrant labour from leaving Mexico and moving into the US.

prompted the establishment of 'Border XXI', a binational border environmental plan to address air and water problems (US Trade Representative, http://www.ustr.gov/regions/whemisphere/ftaa.shtml). Another explanation for the vociferous opposition to the FTAA is fear of being overwhelmed by the USA. More than any of the other regional and international alliances, the FTAA will be dominated by the USA, which accounts for 75 per cent of the hemisphere's GDP.

The campaign against the FTAA has evolved since 1997 into the focal point of anti-capitalist and, over the past year, anti-war activities in the hemisphere. Hundreds of groups have joined forces in myriad activities, predominantly trades unions in the US and Canada and peasants organisations in Latin America. The organisation which best represents the movement is the Hemispheric Social Alliance (HSA). A network of networks, the HSA involves multi-sectoral national and regional networks such as the Common Frontiers (Canada), the Quebec Network on Hemispheric Integration, the Alliance for Responsible Trade (United States), the Mexican Action Network on Free Trade, the Chilean Alliance for Just and Responsible Trade, and the Brazilian Network for Peoples Integration. It also involves sectoral networks such as the hemispheric coordinators of the labour sector (ORIT) and the peasant sector (CLOC). The HSA claims to unite groups representing more than 45 million members.

The HSA organised among others the first Peoples' Summit in Santiago, Chile, in April 1998 parallel to the second official Summit of heads of state of the Americas. It has been a visible presence in almost every major activity targeted at NAFTA/FTAA and the WTO in the Americas. The HSA elaborates and updates its own alternative agenda to the FTAA in *Alternatives for the Americas*. The latest version of the document was drafted in December 2002. *Alternatives for the Americas* covers topics on the official agenda, such as investment, finance, intellectual property rights, agriculture, market access, services and dispute resolution. It also addresses issues of human rights, sustainability, environment, labour, immigration, the role of the state, and gender, which are either ignored or addressed inadequately at the negotiations. The main guiding principle of the document is set out in these terms:

> Trade and investment should not be ends in themselves, but rather the instruments for achieving just and sustainable development. Citizens must have the right to participate in the formulation, implementation, and evaluation of hemispheric social and economic policies. Central

goals of these policies should be to promote economic sovereignty, social welfare, and reduced inequality at all levels. (HSA 2002)

Strategy

Most civil society groups involved in trade issues pursue a mix of strategies in varying proportions. Most seek to multiply their impact by being involved in overlapping regional, thematic and international networks.

Inform and Educate

The movement on trade issues has developed by leaps and bounds since Seattle. The various groups have almost real-time access to the minutiae of trade negotiations: secret or public, within the WTO or the other treaties. Secret documents are regularly leaked by sympathetic government negotiators and trade bureaucrats. Information is extracted skilfully through parliaments and freedom of information tools. One recent leak in this context is an EU document listing the services which the EU would request for opening under GATS from various countries (WDM, http://www.wdm.org.uk).

Groups have their own experienced cadre of trade experts and lawyers. They also draw on resources from academia, the civil service, and international organisations, especially the UN. They provide almost real-time analysis of the available information, evaluate negotiating positions and scenarios, and recommend countermeasures.

Outcomes are passed on to the public, parliaments and friendly negotiators in digestible, actionable, and campaignable form through websites such as Global Trade Watch (Public Citizen), Trade Observatory (Institute for Agriculture and Trade Policy), The Third World Network Information Service on the WTO and MakeTradeFree.com (Oxfam).

Special tools and information packages are produced for the various audiences including briefs, step-by-step talking points, frequently asked question lists and guides for MPs, their constituents, trade negotiators and government officials. Some groups produce and commission in-depth research papers, reports and monographs and conduct workshops for activist policymakers and experts, and organise speaking tours.

Lobby

Groups target multiple levels in their lobbying including parliament, government, negotiators and international organisations. Groups have become adept at using fissures among the various establishment actors: MPs, trade officials in the capitals, trade negotiators, ambassadors and WTO employees. Activists are also quick to exploit tensions between the various actors: EU, US, Japan, Like Minded Group and Cairns Group.

Movement–Third World Government Cooperation

There are numerous examples of cooperation between NGOs, think tanks and UN agencies on the one hand and Southern governments on the other. Cooperation includes designing both negotiating strategies and domestic policies aimed at maximising benefits or reducing adverse effects of trade liberalisation, and improving the bargaining position of the South at the WTO.

One organisation active in this field is Martin Khor's Third World Network (TWN). An example of TWN's projects is the Asia Pacific regional consultation which was organised in Colombo, Sri Lanka, on 17–19 April 2003. The consultation dedicated to the WTO/TRIPS Agreement and Access to Medicines was attended by about seventy government officials, health-related NGO representatives, health professionals, and international trade and intellectual property rights experts. It was organised jointly by the Health Action International-Asia Pacific, Sri Lanka Ministry of Health, and the World Health Organization (South East Asia Regional Office). The main conclusion of the meeting was that TRIPS, despite its adverse impact, does provide flexibilities for governments to safeguard public health. Governments were advised on policies to utilise these flexibilities based on, among other things, the experience of the North.

TWN closely monitors WTO developments and issues regular research and strategy papers for the benefit of Southern delegations and NGOs. Most recently it issued a guide to Southern countries' delegations on handling GATS negotiations (Lal Das 2003). The guide author, Lal Das, is a former Indian representative at GATT.

The Southern and Eastern African Trade Negotiations Institute (SEATINI) is another organisation providing support to Southern governments at the WTO, with a specific focus on Africa. SEATINI is 'dedicated to strengthen Africa's capacity to take a more effective part in the emerging global trading system and to better manage the process of Globalization'. It is an affiliate of the International Southern Group Network (ISGN). It draws on academic, NGO, legal and trade negotiations resources from governments, UN agencies, academia and the WTO itself. SEATINI organises regular meetings and advises African policymakers on negotiating positions and trade policies. It conducts research on trade-related issues and runs an Advisory Clinic which provides ad hoc online assistance to African trade negotiators (SEATINI, http://www.seatini.org.).

Conclusions

The anti-capitalist movement has racked up some impressive advances over the past four years. No longer a ragtag army of romantic activists, the movement has evolved into a well-informed and organised political force to be reckoned with. It has chalked up impressive victories, reversing some privatisation and liberalisation policies in Latin America and restraining the fervour of free traders in Europe. Most importantly, it dealt a severe blow to its main target: the Washington consensus.

The movement may yet fall victim to its own success. Its meteoric rise has attracted some nasty fellow-travellers in the guise of nationalist leaders, Third World multinationals and old left gurus. They are threatening to hijack the movement and blot out its most attractive features – openness, cosmopolitanism, informality and popular appeal.

The movement is also at risk of falling into the old trap of investing too much stock in the ability of great national leaders to deliver the goods of justice and equality. Historically these leaders did not justify this trust. They turned into tyrants, or sold out, or provided convenient targets for the forces of global capitalism.

While boosting the positions of Southern leaders and multinationals may contribute to levelling the global economic playing field, these actors are no more committed to global justice than their opponents. Indian and South African pharmaceutical companies produce generic drugs for profit and not out of concern for those dying of AIDS and malaria. More ominously, however, the exclusivist nationalism which comes with some of the newly found allies is threatening to contaminate the movement: 'The Forum's place as a focus for what I would call the new global solidarity is being put in question by those who seek to not only give it national but nationalist character' (Waterman 2003).

A catastrophic success scenario may materialise if the nationalists succeed in using the movement to 'derail the WTO'. At a time when multilateralism is under siege, destroying the only international organisation which has the potential to hold superpower(s) to account is not what one would expect from a global justice and solidarity movement.

Dismantling the WTO won't solve the problems of injustice in the global trading system. Quite the opposite: it may lead to an even less equitable and more hegemonic globalisation. It will hand an easy victory to the movement's worst enemies: unilateralist neo-conservatives, rusty old industries, and politicians who are trying to go back in time. Without the constraints of the WTO they will be free to muscle their way into any market through bilateral and regional agreements like the much maligned NAFTA. It will be a pyrrhic victory like the one chalked up by the music industry when it shut down Napster, only to push music swapping into distributed networks with no single reference point.

Global justice needs global solutions which national leaders, no matter how enlightened, cannot deliver. Present tensions between the negotiators of North and South on how to safeguard the environment and protect labour without jeopardising development will be swept aside. If the painstaking work needed to build a just global trade system is abandoned as futile, unity can be based only on a lowest common denominator agenda of deglobalisation. The progressive answer to one-size-fits all, elitist institutions which serve corporate interests is democratic multilateral institutions that serve the causes of development and equity, in addition to a robust movement that holds governments, businesses and international organisations to account. Given the sophistication of the tools at the movement's disposal and its growing political clout, it is no longer sufficient for it be engaged in a purely negative purpose. Drawing up utopian plans to return to the anti-colonial state or, further back, to the state of nature does not amount to building an alternative future.

The movement has matured to the point where it has both the ability and the obligation to get down to the painstaking business of institution (re) building. Fixing GATS or the MIF so that they put people before profits, hold the rich and powerful to account, and protect nature is neither easy nor glamorous but it has to be done.

Delivering an hour-long litany of worn conspiracy theories at the end of the World Social Forum, Noam Chomsky almost managed the incredible feat of putting a full stadium of jubilant young people to sleep. Mercifully, he was followed by his exact opposite: Arundhati Roy was quiet, powerful, cryptic and accessible. She spoke of the twin evils of liberalisation and nationalism. She called on activists to lay siege to the empire, mocking it with their culture and joy instead of confrontation. By the end of the speech the crowd was ecstatic. Despite its young age this is a sophisticated movement, which we hope will not be content with tired old slogans and idols. Activists are seeking sophisticated answers to the issues of globalisation. They should be prepared to do the hard work necessary to find them.

References

Editor's note: URLs were correct at the time of first publishing but may no longer be correct.

Alfeld, Haiko and Hofheinz, Paul (2003). 'End the Squabble'. *Wall Street Journal*, 14 March.

Amin, Samir (2003). 'Confronting the Empire'. Contribution to WSF. 22–7 January http://www.forumsocialmundial.org.br/dinamic.asp?pagina=conf_samir_amin_ing.

Baku Ceyhan Campaign (2002). 'Oil Companies Colonise Turkey: MAI by the Back Door?' Press Release. 30 August.

Barlow, Maude (2001). 'The FTAA and the Threat to Social Programs, Environmental Sustainability and Social Justice in Canada and the Americas' http//www.stopftaa.org.

Bello, Walden (2002). *The Oxfam Debate: From Controversy to Common Strategy*. http//www.maketradefair.com.

Bello, Walden and Legrain, P. (2000–1). 'Should the WTO be Abolished?'. *The Ecologist*, 30/9.

Caldwell, Christopher (2003). 'Free Trade is Running Out of Time'. *Financial Times*, 1 April.

Cockroft, James (2003). 'Report on Porto Alegre 2003', 25 March. http://www. forumsocialmundial.org.br/ dinamic.asp?pagina=bal_cockcroft_ing.

Desai, Meghnad (2002). *Marx's Revenge: The Resurgence of Capitalism and the Death of Statist Socialism*. London, New York: Verso.

Desai, Meghnad and Said, Yahia (2001). 'The New Anti-Capitalist Movement: Money and Global Civil Society'. In Helmut Anheier, Marlies Glasius, and Mary Kaldor (eds), *Global Civil Society 2001*. Oxford: Oxford University Press.

Fisher, William F. and Thomas Ponniah (eds) (2003). *Another World is Possible: Alternatives to Globalization at the World Social Forum*. Basingstoke: Palgrave Macmillan.

FLO (Fairtrade Labelling Organization International) http://www.fairtrade.net.

Food First http://www.foodfirst.org.

FTAA (Free Trade Area of the Americas) http://www.ftaa-alca.org.

George, Susan (2003a). 'Corporations Domain and Crisis in the International Financial System'. Contribution to WSF. 22–27 January. http://www.forumsocialmundial.org. br/dinamic.asp?pagina=conf_susan_george_in.

George, Susan (2003b). 'How GATS Could Affect Your Life'. *Red Pepper*. January.

Global Exchange. NAFTA FAQ http://www.globalexchange.org/ftaa/faq.html.

Hines, Colin (2000). *Localization: A Global Manifesto*. London: Earthscan.

Hobbes, Jeremy (2002). Speech at WTO Symposium. April.

HSA (Hemispheric Social Alliance) (2002). *Alternative for the Americas*. Ottawa: HSA.

IFG (International Forum on Globalization) (2002). *Alternatives to Economic Globalization: A Better World is Possible*. San Francisco: Berrett-Koehler.

Khor, Martin and Yen, Goh Chien (2003). 'NGOs Call on Governments to Drop Investment Issues at WTO Cancun Meeting'. *TWN Information Service on WTO Issues*. March.

Klein, Naomi (2000). Speech at WDM's GATS campaign launch, November. http://www.wmd.org.uk.

Klein, Naomi (2003). 'Cut the Strings'. *The Guardian*, 1 February.

Lal Das, Bhagirath (2003). 'Services Negotiations in the WTO: Requests And Offers'. *TWN Information Service on WTO Issues*, 25 February.

Lamy, Pascal (2003). 'Come on America, Play by the Rules!'. *Wall Street Journal*, 3 March.

List, Friedrich (1837/1966). *The National System of Political Economy*. New York: Kelly.

Luce, Edward (2002). 'Poor Nations Urged to End Trade Barriers'. *Financial Times*, 29 November.

Mekay, Emad (2003). 'Interview with Klaus Schwab'. *TerraViva*, 27 January.

Mittal, Anuradha (2003). 'Open Markets or Open Plunder'. *TerraViva*, 27 January.

O'Driscoll, Jr, Gerald P. and Fitzgerald, Sara J. (2002). *Trade Promotes Prosperity and Security*. Washington, DC: Heritage Foundation.

Osava, Mario (2003). *TerraViva* (official newsletter of the WSF), 22 January.

OWINFS (Our World is Not For Sale) http://www.ourworldisnotforsale.org.

Oxfam (2002a). *Rigged Rules and Double Standards: Trade Globalization and the Fight Against Poverty*. London: Oxfam.

Oxfam (2002b). Coffee Report. http://www.maketradefair.com.

Panitchpakdi, Supachai (2002). 'From Doha to Cancun and Beyond'. Speech at the General Assembly of the Swiss Bankers Association, 22 September.

Prebisch, Rudiger (1950). *The Economic Development of Latin America and its Principal Problems*. New York: United Nations.

Ricardo, David (1821/1992). *The Principles of Political Economy and Taxation* (ed. Donald Winch). London: Dent.

Romapu, Mina (2003). TWN activist speaking at WSF.

Rothschild, Emma (2001). *Economic Sentiments: Adam Smith, Condorcet, and the Enlightenment*. Cambridge, MA: Harvard University Press.

SEATINI (Southern and Eastern African Trade Negotiations Institute) http://www.seatini.org.

Seneviratne, Kalinga (2003). 'Interview with Guy Ryder, Head of the International Confederation of Trades Unions (ICFTU)'. *TerraViva*, 24 January.

Smith, Adam (1776/1993). *An Inquiry into the Nature and Causes of the Wealth Of Nations*. Savage, MD: Rowman & Littlefield.

Spraos, John (1983). *Inequalising Trade? A Study of Traditional North/South Specialisation in the Context of Terms of Trade*. Oxford: Clarendon Press in cooperation with UNCTAD.

Temel-Kuran, E. (2003) 'Report from Porto Alegre'. *Milliet*, 24 January.

TWN (Third World Network) http://www.twnside.org.sg.

UNDP (United Nations Development Programme) (2003). *Making Global Trade Work for People*. London: Earthscan.

United States Senate Finance Committee, Subcommittee on International Trade (2000). *Testimony of Lori Wallach Regarding the WTO Dispute Settlement System: Powerful Enforcement of Unbalanced, Extensive Regulations Without Basic Due Process Protections*, 20 June.

United States Trade Representative FTAA http://www.ustr.gov/regions/whemisphere/ftaa.shtml.

Waterman, Peter (2003). 'Reflections' http://www.forumsocialmundial.org.br/dinamic.asp?pa gina=balan_waterman2003in.

WDM (World Development Movement) (2002). *Trade in Services: MP Briefing*. http://www.wdm.org.uk.

Win, Aye Aye (2003). 'Righting Global Wrongs: No Simple Solutions'. *TerraViva*, 27 January.

Wolf, Charles (2002). 'The WTO Controversy: Exaggerated Fears and Unrealistic Hopes'. *Straddling Economics and Politics: Cross-Cutting Issues in Asia, the United States, and the Global Economy*. Arlington, VA: Rand Corporation.

WSF (World Social Forum) (2003). Notes from WSF proceedings by Yahia Said who attended the Third WSF in Porto Alegre, Brazil, 22–7 January.

WTO (World Trade Organization) http://www.wto.org.
—— (1997). *EC Measures Concerning Meat and Meat Products (Hormones) Panel Report.*18 August. Geneva: WTO.
—— (1998). *United States – Import Prohibition of Certain Shrimp and Shrimp Products: Report of the Panel* (WT/DS58/R). Geneva: WTO.
—— (2001). *Final Declaration: Fourth Ministerial Meeting*. Doha. November.
WTO Appellate Body (1997). *United States – Restrictions on Imports of Cotton and Man-made Fibre Underwear.* 10 February. WTO.

Acknowledgement

First publication: Said, Yahia and Desai, Meghnad (2003) 'Trade and Global Civil Society: the Anti-capitalist Movement Revisited', in *Global Civil Society 2003* (Yearbook), edited by Kaldor, Mary; Anheier, Helmut & Glasius, Marlies. Oxford, Oxford University Press pp. 59–85. Republished with kind permission of Oxford University Press.

Chapter 5

GLOBALISATION AND POVERTY

Meghnad Desai

(2003)

Introduction

Broadly speaking my view is very positive on globalisation. I think that globalisation is the only way that mass poverty will be cured and no better way has been found yet. I recall my days as a graduate student in the '50s and early 1960s. I had just started practising economics and there was a great debate about the prospect of developing countries ever getting rid of poverty. It used to be said by Paul Baran and Andre Gunder Frank that if developing countries depended on capitalism they would never get rid of poverty because monopoly capital hinders development of the Third World. So the only way the Third World could develop was by rejecting capitalism and taking on socialism. The *Political Economy of Growth* that Paul Baran wrote is very good and people should read it if only to remind themselves of what that thesis was about. Baran's argument was based on pessimism about the possibility of growth in developed countries because he and others believed that developed countries would suffer from secular stagnation and if they suffered from secular stagnation the forces of monopoly capitalism would not allow rivals to exist and come into the world markets. Markets would be restricted, competition would be deleterious and so developed countries would keep developing countries out of that market.

When you think about this period you will also note that it was not only economists who were pessimistic. Politicians were also pessimistic about developing countries ever getting out of poverty. I remember Henry

Kissinger saying if only China and India could get rid of the problem of food supplies we could then proceed to tackle other problems. No one in the 1960s would have believed that China or India would have developed as they are today. My argument is that not only was the Baran thesis wrong, but that he was already wrong in his own day because by the late 1950s secular stagnation was not the story in the capitalist countries. Rather sustained growth was the story.

What really happened in the second half of the twentieth century was the defeat of the Leninist model as an alternative path of development for all developing countries. This model bit the dust, although the Leninist political programme survives in China, Cuba and North Korea. But the story of China is a quite remarkable example of first having tried the Leninist economic model and then abandoning it in the late 1970s and latching onto a different path and achieving spectacular success. Asia has had spectacular success. The fact that northeast Asia and Southeast Asia have achieved such remarkable growth is amazing. I am old enough to remember when people had not seen 5 per cent growth rates. Now growth rates can be 8 or 9 per cent. First Japan did it, then Korea in the 1970s. We were all in denial saying it was due to American defence aid and it would all collapse. But it did not collapse, it went on and on. What is remarkable about that is that Asia has shown that capitalism is a game that any country can play. There are no cultural restrictions. This is not a Max Weber model of Protestantism or anything like that. Anyone can do this. One of the merits of the capitalist model is that anyone can play the game and win. And therefore to think within cultural paradigms where capitalism is only a Western game is all gone now. The success of Asia has defied that Eurocentric logic – the first example being the astonishing development of Japan.

I need not go into all this in great detail because I have written a book about this – *Marx's Revenge*. The most remarkable thing about the twentieth century is that Italian and German fascisms were defeated. Remember that fascism was the first system to try planning. Unfortunately, they got bad press so we have forgotten all that. The Germans had five-year plans with private and state enterprises. Fascism was defeated first. Then after the Second World War communism was defeated. So by the end of the twentieth century there is only one mode of production left and that is capitalism. Even if you have different varieties of capitalism, still there is only the capitalist mode of production.

Asia's Achievements

Another remarkable thing about the history of Asia, especially from 1970 onwards, is the extraordinary reduction of mass poverty. The figures for China, Taiwan, Korea, Thailand, Malaysia all show real success stories. The stories in the Philippines, Indonesia and India are not that good, but Sri Lanka has a good story to tell. Given that much of the world lives in Asia the reduction of poverty in Asia in absolute numbers must be the largest reduction ever in human history. From the mid-1970s onwards, a number of Asian countries saw that they had to have an open economy policy. This does not have much to do with either free markets or free trade as such. What is relevant is that it was about pursuing policies that were profit friendly and not profit reducing. The contrast between India and Korea is not that the state did not intervene – they interfered in both countries, but in Korea the state was a smart state and went with the market and encouraged industries and firms that were competitive. They got subsidies but they were monitored to ensure competitive performance and the only point of competitive performance was to produce exports. In contrast, India was not export oriented. It only catered for the home market and foreign trade pessimism ruled.

Again, all of the eastern European economies that we used to read about all had massive amounts of investments. If you go back and read the Reports of the Economic Commission of Europe, every year eastern Europe was growing healthily and all the GDP calculations showed impressive growth. But what was actually happening in eastern Europe was that they produced output which they did not have to sell abroad. They did not have to satisfy what Marx called, the law of value. As a result, many economic activities such as producing concrete and steel buildings ignored the markets. No economic value was being generated. Economic value is not a matter of engineering. What you had in the German Democratic Republic was a system without economic value. As a result, when Germany was unified, the entire capital stock of the GDR could not be sold to anybody. It was a complete pile of junk. As this dramatic example shows, it is possible to pursue policies, as India has, to merely generate output and create nothing but junk.

The open economy context in East and Southeast Asia was very different. What happened was that the trigger of globalisation was released when capital movements became possible across countries in a reasonably unregulated fashion. Capitalist firms realised that if they were going to realise adequate profits they had to relocate their companies. The relocation of industries from the industrial North to the developing South started in the 1970s and accelerated in the '80s and '90s to the extent that we have now redrawn the map of manufacturing. The old developed countries are witnessing a decline in the share of manufacturing in terms of output and employment. Manufacturing is no longer the leading sector in many developed countries and manufacturing employment is growing, if anywhere, in the developing countries.

Globalisation and Industrialisation of the South

If you recall in the late 1960s there was a conference of the United Nations Industrial Development Organisation in Santiago, Chile. They had set a target that by 2000 the South's share of manufacturing export should be 25 per cent and very few people thought that that was possible. Even in the 1980s people were very pessimistic about this. But now there is a remarkable resurgence of manufacturing exports from the South and it happened not by South-South cooperation that also used to be fashionable. South-South cooperation is not useful. Beggars cannot sell things to each other, to put it bluntly. The key was developing countries getting access to the markets of developed countries. The way East Asia and Southeast Asia reduced their poverty was by having access to the markets of the West and selling things that the West could not make itself at prices that the people could afford. This has happened to many mature industrial products that have migrated to the South from the North. North capital and South labour are creating a whole new manufacturing industry in the South and that is very much a part of globalisation. This has been made possible by other aspects of globalisation such as the IT and communications revolution, satellite technologies, cheaper transport and the faster movement of money.

Globalisation has made possible the relocation of production processes. At the same time it has also made possible the fragmentation of the production process so that very frequently an entire product is not made in the same location. Much of the success of the 1950s and '60s, especially the Japanese success story, had much to do with recognising this principle. In the 1950s and '60s people used to believe in economies of scale. Steel factories were integrated and they would try to own their own mines and steel marketing. For example, there used to be something called US Steel – a very powerful corporation – it defeated President Kennedy in his attempt to regulate their price-fixing powers. Now there is no US steel in the US because the Japanese discovered that you do not have to locate everything in the same place. You can have just-in-time inventories and you can have completely displaced branches and assemble different manufacturing components. In no single location in Europe is a car made; cars are made in different locations and then put together. What that does is that it keeps the high value added, high knowledge intensive parts of the production process (design and engineering) in the West and the more routine part of the production processes in the South. So if you are wearing a pair of Nike shoes, only 10 per cent was made in a single country and much of what you pay for is design. You are paying for those little holes on the Nike shoe through which your feet can breathe etc. And you buy the Michael Jordan image because Michael Jordan is endorsing a product. You are buying a dream, an abstract commodity. What globalisation has made possible is the production of a tremendous amount of abstract commodities in which, to some extent, the North has an advantage but you still need the routine production of the kind that happens in the South.

Poverty and the Welfare State

It is very hard for me to understand people who go on about globalisation. There was nothing like this possible in the 1950s and '60s. There was no way we thought that this kind of industrialisation was possible then. And what is also interesting is that in the West poverty came down, in a substantial sense, only after WWII. If you look at what happened to living conditions in the inter war years, it is quite amazing how poor people were. In the North poverty was tackled under the Keynesian regime. You had relatively sustained full employment and good growth. But at that stage the participation in the labour force was quite limited. Core poverty was tackled through the State. What we find in the North is that State action was regarded as the way of dealing with poverty by creating a Welfare State. Through the State, people who were out of employment got part of the surplus via government taxation.

Two things have happened since then. That strategy cannot work in a developing country as they cannot afford to establish a Welfare State. Moreover, if you are poor you cannot afford to be unemployed. If you are unemployed, you starve to death. So in a developing country you need to have anti-poverty strategies that depend on creating work and creating skills for that work. Developed countries are also finding after the Keynesian boom that they also cannot afford the Welfare State that they used to have. They can't afford it partly because their own employment structures have been transformed by globalisation. Their unskilled workers no longer have the lifetime employment they used to have in manufacturing because those manufacturing jobs have moved away. Their workers are having episodic employment experiences, they are not having any continuity of employment. At the same time, they are living longer. What the Welfare State used to do is take your own income and redistribute it over your lifetime. What the Welfare State did not do, at least in Britain, is take from the rich and give to the poor. It took from the poor while they were young and working and gave it to them when they retired, or in between during unemployment episodes which were very infrequent. This is what British studies show.

Today, that model breaks down because people are living far too long after retirement and even the savings they are setting aside during their working lives will not be enough to finance their retirement. So suddenly ageing becomes a problem and all Welfare States are facing this crisis of how to tackle poverty and retirement. And they have found exactly the same answer that developing countries have found – it has to be a work related, poverty reduction strategy. You can no longer have poverty reduction done through the State unconnected with work. To say that the UK government is going to help them out of poverty means that they have find work and give them some subsidies and tax cuts, in order to enhance their take home pay. They will give back their tax payments in some form or another, as long as they stay in work. So suddenly, across the world the strategy for poverty reduction has become identical because of globalisation and increased longevity. Even in the heyday of Keynesian policy, people were complaining that poverty was not being tackled. There was a rediscovery of poverty in the 1960s in the US and UK. Even then they found that there was relative poverty. What we have found about poverty reduction is that it is very difficult to design massive redistributive programmes that can effectively tackle poverty in any meaningful sense. Again, we have been forced to rethink our alternative strategies even in developed countries because while they remain capitalist, the nature of capitalism has changed even within our lifetimes. So the developed countries are feeling much more subjected to global competition than ever before.

Migration and Stabilisation

What do we do from now on? It is a paramount duty for developed countries not to obstruct the process of globalisation; not to adopt restrictive trade policies. Ideally I would like to see the abolition of all agricultural subsidies in Europe and in the USA. Each cow in Europe per day gets a subsidy of US$2.25. This is above the poverty line that the World Bank applies to the poor in developing counties i.e. the poor are defined as those that live below US$2 per day per capita. According to this definition, even the European cow is above the global poverty index. The smallest American cotton farmer gets US$100,000 for an industry which should not exist at all – why does America need to grow cotton when there is perfectly good cotton grown in the Third World? But much more than that the European Common Agricultural Policy by dumping abroad is a serious cost to Third World agriculture. There is no point in Lionel Jospin, the former PM of France, talking about Tobin taxes when if he really does want to redistribute wealth he should stop his own agricultural subsidies. Many anti-globalising movements should really be marching in the streets against agricultural subsidies. I have been quoted as saying that the Common Agricultural Policy is a crime against humanity and I stick by that.

The same applies to industrial products. There has to be continuous liberalisation of trade. Some of the things that happened at Seattle at the WTO meeting were a protectionist backlash against the growth of trade. The American Trade Union Movement was very much against the admission of China into the WTO because they could see that this would mean the displacement of their jobs. What developed countries have to be ready for is the restructuring of manufacturing towards more R&D intensive, more knowledge intensive manufacturing and more service activities that are more value adding.

These are the two primary problems that developed countries need to face. But in addition to removing agricultural subsidies and expanding markets for manufacturing, there is a third thing which is increasingly important. This is the more controversial question of the movement of people. With globalisation we have accepted that one of the distinguishing marks of globalisation is the freer movement of capital across the world. It is not a complete freedom of movement for capital; many restrictions remain but by and large all the OECD countries have completely liberalised capital markets. And there are more and more countries of the Second and Third World that have capital liberalisation policies. I have nothing against that and I am very sure that the volatility that goes with such capital movements can be lived with.

But the movement of capital is not the only movement we need. It is quite remarkable that in the nineteenth century when we had the phenomenon of globalisation, there was also a lot of movement of people. Today we have forgotten that between 1914 and 1945 the world became deglobalised and we started thinking within the boundaries of the territorial state. Today we think of economics within the territorial state; we think of welfare as taking place within the territorial state. We have forgotten that that was not the way the world normally functioned. The territorial state was a very short, peculiar period in European history. During the nineteenth century people moved across international boundaries quite a lot; one-third of the population of Europe moved to north America and Australia. When you think of one-third being displaced, you realise that that fundamentally changed the prospects for poverty reduction. People who moved across state boundaries clearly moved because they knew their conditions would improve. They suffered a horrible passage across; when they got there they had no entitlements; they had no welfare payments; they had to work their way up; practically nothing was given except admission to the US. But if not to them, by the second generation they had achieved a remarkable living standard that they could not have enjoyed had they stayed in Europe. And we forget how much poverty reduction occurred by people moving away from where they are stuck.

In the post-1945 period we think of poverty as those people over there. Whereas in the nineteenth century it is quite possible for the poor to say this place is a hopeless place I am going to get up and go somewhere with better job prospects. We know that there is a lot of movement within countries but in the nineteenth century there was a lot of movement across countries. A lot of people from the Indian subcontinent moved to Malaysia and to the Caribbean and to Florida. A lot of Chinese moved to Southeast Asia, to the west coast of America and a lot to Australia until in the beginning of the twentieth century Australia stopped Asian immigration.

In the new phase of globalisation, migration is going to be the biggest topic in the next ten to fifteen years. We have already noticed that people have taken the initiative on their own to travel across state boundaries; they are taking enormous risks to move to where there is prosperity. And country after country has to deal with immigration problems. By and large developed countries are making a total hash of it. We have all decided that we are not going to admit economic refugees because they are dirty people who want to make themselves better off. How absurd it is to try to make yourself better off – you should stay where you are! We don't necessarily want to give them foreign aid but we certainly don't want them here. This is what is happening today in countries already full of economic refugees.

We are also trying to deal with another consequence of globalisation – the asylum seekers. We have decided to have some asylum seekers; we will take some but not all. We have decided to put restrictions on the number. There is a simple reason for it. As Nigel Harris points out in *The New Untouchables* when we created the Welfare State during the First World War it guaranteed it would look after the welfare of its citizens. The emergence of the Welfare State coincided with the emergence of the territorial state. By creating a category of citizen, it also created a category of foreigners that did not exist in the nineteenth century. Today's State will look after its citizens but not after foreigners. The nation-state was invented to stop the movement of people. The nation-state also had aspirations to stop people leaving – hence the debate about the brain drain. The problem is that welfare does not come packaged with the territorial state; it travels with people. We have to understand that there is going to be a need to match the free movement of capital with the free movement of labour. There is no reason in logic why people who accept the free movement of capital cannot accept the free movement of people.

Lots of arguments have been used to think of welfare in terms of territorial states. The 'good people' or progressives in the territorial state (NGOs, bishops etc) have a view that they should only admit people to whom they can give the full welfare entitlements. But because we can't afford too many like that we don't want too many foreigners to come in. There is great resistance to diluting the conditions of citizenship – they just don't want the people to be there. Lots of countries are trying to restrict the access of asylum seekers that they are by treaty bound to admit. They are using a whole range of arguments to do this – you are not a genuine asylum seeker, you are an economic refugee and so on.

The nineteenth century approach was very different. The nineteenth century said you can come in if you want to but you need to go through an intermediate passage until you get full citizenship. It was a bit like the 'Green Card' today: you are welcome to come and live in America but you are not a citizen; you pay the tax but you do not get a full entitlement to welfare. You only get a full welfare entitlement when you become a citizen.

I would like to propose that countries should adopt 'Green Card' strategies. Some people would argue that the conditions are very harsh but they are actually kinder than the strategies we are adopting now. What we want to say to people who want to come in is, yes you can come but you get no welfare benefits at all. I would only make an exception for the children of new arrivals. There should be full child benefits but adults should not get any. Adults know what is good for them; they have chosen to come here. After perhaps five or ten years they would get full citizenship rights. It is actually a cruel strategy to adopt but in terms of redistribution, it is much kinder than saying don't come, stay out there because we can't afford you. Even with this strategy, there are all sorts of cultural problems, but the economic problems are also interesting.

The major economic problem is that if these people are going to work and we want them to work, our labour market structures are very exclusionary and they will be undermined by an influx of people. Most particularly our minimum wage legislation will be affected. This is the dilemma. Ronald Dworkin, a distinguished advocate of human rights, gave an example of a case in a New York bakery with someone working sixteen hours a day. He asked the audience what people thought about this. They were all horrified. But it turned out that the immigrant could not get a job in most regulated industries; he could only get a job in an unregulated industry. He could only get a job where he had to work for sixteen hours. For him this was the only humane passage out of poverty into work for an immigrant because everywhere there was regulation and restrictions on people coming in and getting jobs.

We do have to think very seriously about the nature of the labour market structures we have adopted for a certain era of capitalism when we thought only about the territorial state in which there was a privileged membership for citizens and no membership for outsiders. We clearly want to make many more people better off and one way we can do this is to have an intergenerational shift in benefits by saying you can come into this country to work and your children will be better off but you won't be entitled to benefits.

This is a very cruel way of putting it but I think that short of that we will have considerable problems with labour migration in the world. A lot of the developed world, having come through a development process, is now essentially taking away the ladder for other people who have come later. And I don't think it is going to benefit the developed world. One reason is that the age structures in developed countries are already such that they either cannot afford their pension system or their welfare state, and the clear demographic projections in Britain and Europe (I am sure Australia as well) show a dependency ratio of aged people that is already of such proportions that all the needed welfare cannot be financed by the welfare state.

There are obviously some other solutions whereby you can extend the working life of the workforce or dilute their pension entitlements, but another solution is to import people. And calculations have been made about this for the European Union. It has been estimated that the EU needs to import some 100 million people over the next fifteen years in order to keep up its current economic output. The EU was so shocked by this study conducted by the UN Department of Social and Economic Affairs that the EU refused to have the report circulated. They were worried about the impending demographic crisis. It can be shown that there are certain cruel but kind ways of dealing with immigration that are mutually beneficial – not in the immediate short run but in the intermediate and long run. But there has been no political leadership that has been able to explain this to the citizens of the developed countries; nor have the people who have argued for mass poverty reduction in the World Bank and UNDP taken this option. Because everyone is thinking of countries as separate little blocs and they can only deal with poverty by getting the money out there but not moving the people.

The argument that people have been the most immobile factor of production and everything else can move is a complete fallacy. All world history shows that people do move. And different countries will solve this problem in different ways. The Americans have an interesting strategy of getting skilled people into the country in generous quantities. They also get unskilled workers illegally across the Mexican border. If you look at the American population figures she has a growing population both in terms of internal reproduction rates and net migration unlike Europe that has a stagnant or declining population and severe restrictions on immigration. Sooner or later Europe will have to do something about this, perhaps adopting a strategy similar to the Americans. But strategies will be different according to the relative economic strengths and weaknesses of the economies.

My own view is that this is something that needs a global examination of some kind through the WTO or ILO; the world will have to reach a decision of some sort over the next fifty years to deal with the mass movement of people. In principle asylum seekers are temporary stayers. There is some evidence in the UK with Kosovo and Afghanistan that asylum seekers have been temporary and many have returned home. One can be generous to these, knowing that they want to go back and one might only admit them on the basis of temporary migration. But so far as economic refugees are concerned, we do not need to be more generous to them. Let them bear the costs of migration and have no costs bearing on the citizens. Of course citizens will carry the indirect cost of such economic refugees but in return they will also have some benefits from that migration in terms of a more youthful age profile and increased economic productivity.

Globalisation has provided a remarkably great opportunity for tackling mass poverty. There is one exception to this – Africa as a continent has not benefited as much as Asia. Partly this has to do with commodity prices. Another feature of modern industry is that commodities have become 'weightless' – they use less raw material and are lighter and artificially manufactured materials are used. So primary commodity prices have been on a secular decline through the last twenty-five years. Another problem has been the failure to create the nation-state and coherent political societies or governance. This is a major contrast between Asia and Africa. It is not a problem to do with corruption or authoritarian vs. democratic systems. It is really a question of the difference between a responsive state and an unresponsive state. The Asian state in a variety of forms has always responded and paid back to its citizens some of the fruits of development. That connection between the state and the people has been there in the case of Malaysia and China for instance. In both Malaysia and China the ruling parties have been in touch with the grassroots and have been able to deliver some development. But that has not been the case in Africa. Except for the first few years after independence there has been an extraordinary failure of the rulers to respond to the citizens. Why this is true is very complex but one thing is certain – this has nothing to do with globalisation. Globalisation has ignored Africa rather than ruined it whereas globalisation helped Asia because Asia was able to create a successful polity. We will have to think about how Africa can be brought into globalisation.

Bibliography

Baran, Paul (1960) *The Political Economy of the South*, New York: Monthly Review Press.

Desai, Meghnad (2002) *Marx's Revenge: The Resurgence of Capitalism and the Death of Statist Socialism*, London: Verso.

Frank, Andre Gunder (1965) *Capitalism and Underdevelopment*, New York: Monthly Review Press.

Harris, Nigel (1997) *The New Untouchables*, London: I B Taurus.

Acknowledgement

This is the text of a speech delivered by Lord Desai to a public lecture in Melbourne, Australia, on 11 December 2003. The lecture was hosted by the Monash Asia Institute, the Monash Institute for the Study of Global Movements and the Productivity Commission. Lord Desai's visit to Australia was made possible by the Australia South Asia Research Centre at the Australian National University, Canberra.

Chapter 6

THE POLITICAL ECONOMY OF DONALD TRUMP

Meghnad Desai

(2016)

Trump the Unorthodox: A Figure Who Surprises

Donald Trump will be the Republican nominee for the 2016 US presidential election. He has come this far fighting, or perhaps disregarding, widespread disbelief, as well as undisguised contempt on the part of the elite of both main US parties and almost the entire liberal community. But he won the primaries and has caught the imagination of millions of people, garnering their votes.

Let us move a step on and imagine that Trump wins the election and takes over from Barack Obama in 2017. What sort of president would he make? More particularly, what will his economic policy be? How will he be able to fulfil the many promises he has made? Here again, dire predictions are being made about the economic consequences of a Trump presidency. Most commentators see him going on a fruitless journey, promising the moon and not even delivering cheese.

This report explores the possible outcomes of the unorthodoxy of Trump's economic thinking and asks whether he may surprise us. After all, odious political views have coexisted with successful unorthodox economics in the past. During the Great Depression of the 1920s and 1930s, European fascist parties in Germany and Italy were the first and very successful Keynesians.

Trump has been careful not to articulate a complete and consistent economic philosophy. Tactically this is shrewd – he is a moving target and difficult for his critics to shoot at. He is not a fool as many say he is. Nor is he confused or self-contradictory. His is a studied stance intended to sow confusion in the minds of his opponents. Trump has made promises to create jobs, restrict immigration, build a wall along the US-Mexico border, and reverse the 'drain' caused by trade, particularly in respect of China.

The Republican nominee is a mercantilist and a protectionist. (This is a hallowed American tradition: until the end of the Second World War the US was a protectionist nation.) He has said things financial market experts view as beyond the pale, such as reneging on debt and talking down the dollar. But memories are short. Most people believe a strong dollar has been a permanent feature of US economic policy. But they forget the volatility in the dollar's value in the two decades after the US exit from the dollar exchange standard in August 1971, which ended the Bretton Woods system and inaugurated flexible exchange rate markets. As John Connally, Richard Nixon's Treasury secretary, told European leaders, 'The dollar is our currency and your problem'.

Trump's Cavalier Stance on Public Debt

Trump has been cavalier in his statements about debt – as to its size, buying back and/or reneging on it; about trade – US repudiation of its international obligations; about immigration and the expulsion of illegal immigrants; and about renouncing Obama's policy on the environment. He has been rude about Muslims, Mexicans, Hispanics more broadly, and women.

This sort of right-wing populism is not new. But it has rarely had popular resonance to the extent that Trump has provided it with. Previous right-wing presidential candidates such as George Wallace in 1968 were anti-black Americans, given that Hispanics and Mexicans then had a negligible presence in the US. Easy contradictions can be pointed out in Trump's rhetoric. But there is much agreement about the malaise that has given him a willing audience.

The American middle classes have suffered in relative terms in the four decades since the first oil shock of 1973. These are the people who feel they have lost out from globalisation (which can be used as a portmanteau term for freer trade, liberal immigration policies, fiscal discipline in the matter of obeying the message of the bond markets, independent central banks, and the pursuit of inflation targeting as a central policy).

But here is the first contradiction. Since the deprived sections of the American middle class span white, black and Hispanic households, can Trump gain by focusing on white grievances and alienating black and Hispanic voters?

Normally one could summarise the Republicans' stance by saying that they favour lower income and corporation taxes, especially for the better-off; constantly worry about the size of the public debt and the budget deficit; and express anxiety over growth in public spending, especially entitlements for the less well-off.

Trump, however, has based his campaign on appealing to blue-collar manual workers and the growing number of unemployed in those regions dominated by failing manufacturing industries. He has railed against 'the system', including the large banks and international corporations, which has advocated and benefited from globalisation at the expense of American workers. He has shown hostility to international free trade and has advocated boosting public spending to counteract some of the impact on American workers.

This blurs the traditional distinction with the Democrats, who would like, but have been unable, to increase taxes on the rich and spend more on benefits. With Democratic primary contender Bernie Sanders' message having gained significant traction, the policy of the Democratic nominee (which, almost certainly, will be Hillary Clinton) may swing more to the left, against Wall Street (using that as a portmanteau term for corporate tax deductions, lax regulation, shunting the tax liability to tax havens abroad, high corporate salaries and bonuses).

British Referendum Benefits for Candidate Trump

The British decision to leave the European Union will help Trump in a number of ways. The right-wing populist and xenophobic thrust that was a feature of the UK Leave campaign is very much in his style.

He may enjoy the tough attitude towards globalisation and trade treaties. The idea that a nation should not be bound by previous commitments is his message too.

There is also confirmation of the Trump style of campaigning and presenting serious issues in simplified binary form. Liberal critics have sought to contrast his somewhat boorish approach to international relations with Europe's more subdued style of politics.

Now one of the oldest European polities has gone his way.

The shock of 'Brexit' has weakened sterling relative to the dollar. The uncertainty created by the UK decision is one of the factors dissuading the Federal Reserve from an immediate increase in interest rates. Bond yields have dropped to their lowest level in recent years.

Trump should benefit from this as his stance would be fiscally unorthodox, taking on debt and spending on infrastructure.

Even if the pound rallies moderately after the arrival of a new British prime minister, nervousness in sterling and bond markets may continue. Trump can use this to his advantage.

Theresa May, the new British prime minister who took office on 13 July, has appointed Boris Johnson, the larger-than-life former mayor of London, as foreign secretary. Johnson has frequently been compared to Trump in his demeanour, appeal to a cross-party spectrum and approach to national issues (including hostility to the EU). Like Trump, Johnson has ascended the political firmament in unlikely fashion – and is capable of springing surprises from a variety of directions.

Businessman as President

The first thing to remember about Donald Trump is that he is a businessman, and a very successful one. He has a hand in real estate, television, casinos and other entertainment products. He is the first business person (and seasoned television performer) to run for president and be a nominee of a major political party since the emergence of Ross Perot in 1992, a Texas businessman who ran as an independent and garnered 19 per cent of the popular vote.

Other nominees and contestants may have made their money in business, but usually entered politics and competed for the presidency only some years after being successful in the business world. Mitt Romney, who contested the 2012 presidential election, worked in the management consultancy and private equity industries before entering politics in 1994. George H. W. Bush was an oil industry executive. Barry Goldwater, the Republican nominee in 1964, had a background in business, as did Wendell Wilkie, who ran against Franklin D. Roosevelt in 1940.

Trump has had no schooling in politics. He has been in the public eye for decades as a businessman and a public personality. The implication is that his economics may derive more from his daily experience and knowledge than other candidates, who require expert advice on economic issues. This has been clear in his very unorthodox attitude to debt. As a businessman who has amassed a fortune, he views debt not as a burden but as a tool for doing business.

Thus, while the economic programme of Paul Ryan, the speaker of the House of Representatives, has focused on tackling the size of the public debt above all else, Trump does not see debt in the same light. He knows that you have to end up richer than when you started. If debt is necessary to achieve that goal, so be it. It is easy to deplore this attitude towards debt. Yet we have to remember that, since September 2008, many rules of orthodox finance have been broken.

Bankrupt banks and financial institutions have been bailed out using taxpayers' money while the ruling politicians have eschewed a sufficient fiscal boost to the economy to benefit the excluded middle. Federal actions such as the 2008 Troubled Asset Relief Program (to acquire 'toxic' assets and equity from beleaguered financial institutions) have channelled money to the few but denied it to the many. The deprived middle classes have seen rules being broken and the guilty being rewarded rather than punished.

Quantitative easing may now be sold as merely an enhanced version of open market operations, but it has broken all the previous rules in its extent and scope. Monetarists told us that monetising public borrowing was unsound and could lead to inflation.

In the US and the UK, not to mention Japan, central bankers have been printing money with scant regard to previous rules and orthodoxies. There has been little response in terms of inflation. The Federal Reserve and Bank of England have taken interest rates to near zero, while the European Central Bank and Bank of Japan have driven them into negative territory. The main beneficiaries of these policies have been asset owners and large borrowers, including big companies, who still refuse to invest but profit from the availability of cheap credit to increase their asset values. 'Joe public' has got nothing out of this departure from orthodoxy, hailed as innovation.

If Trump takes the view that he wants to borrow to create jobs with infrastructure investment, it would be hard to mount too strong or moralistic a protest. The long recession has heightened income inequalities. Bank and corporate bonuses have soared; wage income has not. Trump could argue that orthodoxy has much to answer for. His critics have also displayed amnesia about American history. We are told how, ever since Alexander Hamilton was Treasury secretary in the late eighteenth century, financial probity has been the rule for the US. This is fanciful history.

Critics need to revisit the period between the destruction of the Second Bank of the United States by Andrew Jackson, then president, in September 1833, and the creation of the Fed eighty years later.

Box 6.1: The Men behind Trump's Economic Policy

Sam Clovis – Policy Director

Professor of economics at Morningside College, activist for the Tea Party movement. Holds a Ph.D. in public administration from the University of Alabama. Responsible for shaping many campaign policies, involved in most of its domestic and foreign policy proposals. In 2014, he ran for Republican nomination for Senate in Iowa and then as state treasurer.

Larry Kudlow – Economic Adviser

Working with Trump on tax plan with Moore (see below). Syndicated television talk show, long history as a political commentator, first as a liberal and then a conservative. Columnist for a range of newspapers, and a distinguished scholar at the Mercatus Center of George Mason University, Virginia. Former Reagan administration official, chief economist at Bear Stearns.

Arthur Laffer – Economic Adviser

In campaign background, may re-emerge. Policy co-chairman, with Kudlow, of the Free Enterprise Fund: 'the pre-eminent lobbying force in Washington for the passage of legislation that will promote economic growth, lower taxes, and limited government'. Member of Reagan's Economic Policy Advisory Board in 1981–89.

Paul Manafort – Campaign Chairman and Chief Strategist

Senior partner in consulting firm Davis, Manafort, and Freedman. Largely responsible for messaging and communications. Gained control in April over expanded $20 million campaign budget, hiring decisions, advertising and media strategy. Track record of advising Republican presidential contenders: Ford, Reagan, Bush senior and junior.

Steven Mnuchin – Fundraiser

Heads campaign's fundraising as national finance chairman. Yale-educated banker, film producer and political fundraiser, former partner at Goldman Sachs. Set up hedge fund Dune Capital Management. Former chair of OneWest Group, formed from failed housing lender Indy Mac in 2009, sold to CIT Group in 2015.

Stephen Moore – Economic Adviser

Economics writer and political analyst. Working on Trump tax plan. Founded Club for Growth, a conservative organisation with a tax-cutting agenda, in 1999, president until 2004. Former member of *Wall Street Journal* editorial board, and a distinguished visiting fellow at the Heritage foundation, a conservative American think tank.

Other advisers with an economics, business or financial background include Carter Page, foreign policy adviser, who is founder and a managing partner of Global Energy Capital, and George Papadopoulos, senior policy and economic adviser to former Republican presidential contender Ben Carson. John Mashburn, campaign policy director, has worked on budget and appropriations bills in Congress. Kent Gray, Illinois state director, is a former executive assistant to the Illinois Comptroller.

The Politics of American Credit

Throughout the nineteenth century, American credit abroad was not sound. The battle over joining the gold standard after the American civil war, particularly the struggle of farmers who suffered from the resulting deflation as against the East Coast corporations, has planted a permanent distrust of banks and bankers in the American political psyche.

More recently, in 1971, the US unilaterally reneged on a promise to buy gold at $35 an ounce, destroying the Bretton Woods system of monetary management. The US has a dubious record in terms of financial responsibility and Trump has many precedents to cite.

Trump is pragmatic about trade. Like any businessman, he would like a captive market, even though he may mouth platitudes about competition. He wants to capture as many of the gains from trade as possible. If this requires trade restrictions or exchange rate devaluation, then he would not be against using these instruments.

Again, what matters to him is not dogma but success – the bottom line. Trump does not agree with the argument that free trade leads to mutual advantage for both parties and is optimal for each. More to the point his core supporters do not agree with this view either. It has not been part of their life experience.

This may be for cogent economic reasons – the 1973 oil price shock, the migration of manufacturing abroad in search of cheap labour, a strong dollar. But Trump and his core support cannot accept that they should be helpless as a result of external factors. Their instinct is to use the levers of political power to regain control.

Again, while free trade is 'first best' and freer trade is better than protection, practice has always departed from theory. US and European Union protection of their respective agricultural sectors generates much resentment in emerging economies. The Doha Round of World Trade Organization talks aimed at lowering trade barriers has been stuck for years because of developed country resistance to developing countries demanding similar protection for their farmers.

At least this is what Xi Jinping, China's president, and Narendra Modi, the Indian prime minister, tell the US. Now Trump complains about China not playing by the rules. But this is just a sign that the US is no longer as dominant in international trade – in manufacturing at least – as it was in the 1960s and 1970s. Even the EU has complained about the US in the Transatlantic Trade and Investment Partnership negotiations.

The Politics of American Deficits

Despite the homilies about budget deficits, in practice both Democrats and Republicans have presided over deficits. Ronald Reagan, viewed as a paragon of Republican virtue, in the 1980s spent money in an almost Keynesian fashion, running a deficit in each of his eight years in office.

The country's debt to GDP ratio, which had fallen to 31 per cent by 1974, had reached 50 per cent by the end of Reagan's presidency and rose above 60 per cent in 1992. With further deficits under George H. Bush and Bill Clinton, it peaked at 65 per cent in 1996, subsequently declining to 55 per cent in Clinton's second term.

George W. Bush ran a budget deficit in each of his eight years as president. The debt to GDP ratio was 67 per cent in 2008. Then, as has happened in other countries, output growth reversed and debt continued to rise. The debt to GDP ratio rose steadily from 67 per cent in 2008 to 101 per cent in 2013 after the 2008–09 recession, and was around 102 per cent in 2014 and 2015.

Table 6.1: US is the world's largest debtor economy
Net international investment position of the largest debtor countries, 2014–15

	Largest debtor economies			
	NIIP ($bn)		NIIP (% of GDP)	
	2015	2014	2015	2014
US	-7,357	-7,020	-41	-40.5
Spain	-1,065	-1,208	-88.8	-87.3
Brazil	-799	-723	-26.6	-50.1
Australia	-689	-553	-56.3	-25.9
Italy	-475	-799	-26.2	-33.1
France	-416	-508	-17.2	-17.9

Source: IMF, Eurostat, OMFIF calculations

The Long Tradition of Raising Public Debt

The US budget has been in surplus in only twelve years since 1946 – four years under Harry S. Truman (1947–49, 1951); three years under Eisenhower (1956–57, 1960), and four years under Clinton (1998–2001). The only other year in which the country ran a surplus was 1969, Nixon's first year in office.

Trump would not be the first US president to run a deficit and increase debt. All he would need is a pliant Congress. Republicans attribute the deficit during the Reagan years to winning the Cold War, and the Bush deficit to the September 2001 attacks on New York and Washington (and the subsequent war on terror). Trump has to find a headline-grabbing theme for his deficits. He will then be in good and safe company.

The US has run a persistent current account deficit for more than twenty years, rapidly increasing its net foreign debt. At end-2015 US liabilities were almost $7.36 trillion, equal to 41 per cent of GDP. This has risen from under $800 billion, or 9 per cent of GDP, in 1997. Countries with large external debts and/or current account deficits should, in theory, face downward pressure on their currencies and rising costs of borrowing, encouraging them to adapt their monetary, fiscal and regulatory policies and ultimately rebalance domestic and foreign demand.

America's stable and attractive domestic financial and political environment and deep liquid markets, however, have meant the US has been able to draw in reserves, investments and other sources of long- and short-term capital from around the world. Along with its role as the main reserve currency-issuing country, these factors make the US a special case, allowing it to borrow heavily, at cheaper rates, while maintaining a strong currency.

Trump's Choices

If Trump ran serial budget deficits or increased the debt, this would be the norm rather than the exception.

Of course, the key to keeping the debt to GDP ratio under control is to work on the denominator as much as restricting the numerator.

But it could be argued that the US has under-borrowed, if anything. The country's infrastructure is badly in need of repair, while its total infrastructure investment needs have been calculated at $3.63 trillion. These needs include surface transport (almost $2 trillion), waterways and port ($131 billion), electricity ($736 billion) and airports ($134 billion).

US infrastructure is old. There is some urgency here. The 2014 dirty water crisis in Michigan state, where high levels of lead were found in the drinking water, provides a painful reminder of infrastructure neglect.

US Wage Stagnation

The other problem is flatness of wages (average hourly compensation of production/non-supervisory workers in the private sector) over the last forty years.

Between 1973 and 2014, productivity grew by 72.2 per cent and wages by 9.2 per cent, according to the Washington-based Economic Policy Institute. Only 15 per cent of the additional growth generated since the 1970s has accrued to workers. The rest has contributed to corporate income.

This has been as much a redistribution induced by policies that have deregulated financial markets, lowered taxes and increased deductions for corporations as a result of competition from cheaper labour in emerging economies.

The Secret of Trump's Appeal

Trump's core supporters want an unorthodox economic policy because the orthodox policy has not brought benefits to many middle-class voters who now feel alienated and disenfranchised. These supporters blame Washington because they see the malaise as the result of a deliberate policy choice, justified on the grounds of 'sound economics' or 'benefiting the wealth generators'. Sanders has concentrated on corporate privileges (Wall Street), while Trump has focused on creating jobs and shutting down foreign trade to help American workers.

Changing the climate of free and open trade may not be as easy as Trump thinks. International treaties cannot be changed or reneged on that easily. (The Paris climate agreement, which Trump has denounced, has built-in safeguards against unilateral withdrawal by any country.) But there may be a synergy in his desire for large infrastructure projects (such as the wall along the border with Mexico) and further tackling the US infrastructure deficit, a long neglected priority.

Members of Congress like spending the money that comes to their constituencies. 'Shovel-ready' projects could generate demand for workers lacking the education levels to take jobs in the services sector but who could take on manual jobs.

Of course, sentiment against the liberal globalisation orthodoxy has been rising around the world. We see the rise of right-wing nationalist parties in Europe, as well as anti-capitalist leftist extremist parties. It may be that, as in the past, the boom cycle of globalisation may yield to a rise of 'deglobalisation' as a result of the 2008–09 crisis and persistent low growth and deflation. If so, Trump will face less hostility internationally than many orthodox observers expect.

Reviving Infrastructure: Lessons from Eisenhower

A model for Trump to follow is Eisenhower's approach to infrastructure investment. The Interstate Highway System – the network of highways, turnpikes and motorways that still covers America – was built during the 1950s. Eisenhower initiated these projects in a sustained fashion. Arthur F. Burns was his chief economic adviser between 1953 and 1956, and went on to serve as chair of the Federal Reserve in the 1970s.

Burns was a conservative and a compassionate person as far as his economic beliefs were concerned. He was not a Keynesian in respect of his economics, but his advice led to the best public capital spending years the US has enjoyed. Gross public investment peaked at around 7 per cent per annum during the Eisenhower administration and has not reached those proportions since.

Eisenhower did this while pursuing a prudent fiscal policy, bringing the debt to GDP ratio down to 53 per cent in 1960 from 72.7 per cent in 1952 (the last year of the Truman administration). Public works spending in these years exceeded that during Roosevelt's 1933–38 New Deal. These were also years of full employment (with a mild recession in 1957) and sustained growth, keeping tax revenues buoyant.

The 'baby boom' had given the US a young and growing population that placed few demands on health infrastructure. Welfare spending was modest and would remain so until Lyndon Johnson's 'Great Society', a series of programmes aimed at eliminating poverty and racial injustice. Income growth prevented the debt to GDP ratio from rising.

As an icon of prudent public finance, Eisenhower beats Reagan, Bush and the rest of Republican presidents hands down. He pioneered a public-private initiative in the way the Saint Lawrence Seaway – a network of locks, canals and channels linking the US and Canada – was financed.

Attracting Sovereign Funds to Finance US Infrastructure

Trump could initiate a second large-scale public capital spending programme by taking advantage of low interest rates and borrowing to meet the need. Following the Saint Lawrence Seaway example, he could even tap sovereign funds to finance his proposals. After all, the total infrastructure deficit, estimated at $3.63 trillion, is just 19.6 per cent of GDP.

A capital spending programme at 5 per cent of GDP would amount to around $900 billion. This much could be borrowed as a sound principle of public finance. Sovereign funds as well as pension funds would be attracted if the US borrowed with long maturity, fixed coupon bonds. If sustained over four years, the borrowing would address the entire US infrastructure gap. It is difficult to estimate the number of jobs it would create, but it cannot be negligible.

If Trump undertook such a bold investment programme, he could meet most of the promises he has made without provoking a trade war with China. He may yet want to adopt an aggressive stance for the sake of popularity. But he may equally choose to live with a Congress that would not let him effect a major protectionist move.

What Trump May Achieve

Trump is an unorthodox person in respect of his politics and is promising to be one in terms of his economics too.

There has been paralysis in the G7 and G20 international forums in terms of bold fiscal policy. There may have been a time to hold back on fiscal spending (as in the UK) immediately after the steep rise in the deficit and debt in the first few years following the financial crisis. Borrowing is defensible for investment purposes at all times.

Monetary policy – quantitative easing – took up the task of easing the pain of the recession and helped 'zombie households' and 'zombie companies' survive.

But following years of QE monetary policy has reached its limits. Negative interest rates have become the latest problem. Companies are using cheap money for share buybacks or other ways of pursuing asset bubbles. Little of the money has been channelled into reviving the economy, raising wages or driving inflation back to the target level of 2 per cent.

In this climate, rather than seem helpless in the face of insurmountable problems, a bold unorthodox policy would remove obstacles to growth.

Technical progress – for example, artificial intelligence or driverless cars or robots – will only take care of the skilled when it comes to jobs. The many unskilled manual workers who used to enjoy a high and rising standard of living have lost out over the last forty years. American unemployment rates remain low, but there is still much dissatisfaction over wages. Household debts have risen.

Capital Spending will Boost Job Growth

A bold policy of capital spending on infrastructure projects will increase the job opportunities precisely for those workers who need it and revive the economy. A policy of sustained capital spending will raise income and its growth rate.

These indirect/multiplier effects are difficult to estimate, but they can only be positive. This itself may reduce the debt to GDP ratio to a level lower than it would have been were the debt incurred because of a shortfall of tax revenues below current spending. If Trump adopts such a policy, he may yet turn out to be a Keynesian, despite himself.

Ultimately, an American president with an economic plan to enact requires a compliant Congress that accommodates budget proposals and provides the sought-after extension of the debt ceiling.

This depends on whether Trump has coat tails that will carry Republicans into the two houses and maintain the party's majority – and whether the Republicans themselves have an appetite for Trump's unorthodox policies. None of this is guaranteed. If Trump wins in November, those who fear his actions should pray for four years of legislative gridlock. This would not be a propitious outcome, for the US and the world – and we must hope that it is not the best on offer.

Acknowledgement

First publication: Desai, Meghnad (2016) 'The Political Economy of Donald Trump', Report, Official Monetary and Financial Institutions Forum, 20 July 2016, pp. 7–22. Republished with kind permission of the OMFIF.

Chapter 7

IS THERE A FUTURE FOR SOCIAL DEMOCRACY AFTER THE CRISIS?

Meghnad Desai

(2009)

The deepest financial crisis in the last eighty years has come and almost gone. But in the midst of this crisis of global capitalism, socialist and social democratic parties have not been at the forefront of the efforts for the rescue and reform of the system. In France and Germany, the Left is in retreat. In the UK, while the Labour Party is in power, it is widely expected to lose the election when it is held next year. It is the case that Gordon Brown can rightly claim to have initiated the recapitalisation of banks in the UK which was then copied by other countries. The recent victory of PASOK in Greece apart, the European Left does not have much good news. Obama could be said to be as far 'left' as US Presidents go, though even he in the context of his own party is a centrist.

In rescuing the system from its double crisis of financial system dysfunction and real economy recession, the answers have been uniform across the European Left and Right. Merkel and Sarkozy, as well as Brown, have adopted the policy of restoration first and reform later. Obama has done the same.[1] The prospect is of better regulation of the financial system, perhaps greater competition or even the return to the old structures – Glass-Steagall

---

1 For a comment on how mild the Obama reforms are see Jeff Madrick 'They Did Not Regulate Enough and Still Don't', *New York Review of Books*, November 5–18, 2009, Vol LVI, number 17, pp. 54–7.

Even mildly radical reform such as the restructuring of the auto industry to make it more 'green' or adapt electrical or hydro powered cars has not been pursued even as a lot of money has been given to the car industry by Obama.

as they are labelled – of separation of retail banking from investment banking. The European Commission has put its emphasis on greater competition and enforcement of its code against state aid. In industrial restructuring the approach is again of restoration and handing back ownership to the original owners as and when the time comes. Capitalism has come to stay, bloody and battered but bandaged with tender care by governments of the Right and Left.

Thus it is clear that even more so than the prospect of electoral victory or holding of office, there is a singular lack of a viable alternative vision around which the Progressive parties could coalesce. Even after reminding the world 'we said so', radical debates have not proposed a viable scheme which would deliver a better future.

What Then is the Future of the Left?

My contention is that the Left has lost because of a failure to comprehend the working of capitalism. The twentieth century was the century of the Left, both of the Leninist anti-democratic Left and the social democratic Left. The Leninists were very influential in arguing that capitalism was in one of its terminal crises and would disappear soon ushering in the possibility of socialism. As we celebrate the twentieth anniversary of the destruction of the Berlin Wall, we note that, North Korea and perhaps Cuba apart, there are no regimes still subscribing to that idea. In my book *Marx's Revenge* (MR) I have labelled this as Socialism Outside Capitalism (SOC).

Social democracy began with a critique of capitalism, but, rather than rejecting it, tried to humanise it. In much of the developed world, in Western Europe especially, it succeeded beyond its expectations. The last great crisis of capitalism in the 1930s gave social democracy its opportunity, and the war solidified its democratic mandate. Social democracy delivered socialism within capitalism (SwC) successfully – welfare state, trade union rights, guaranteed incomes if unable to work, as well as, more recently, human rights, gender rights and the freedom to pursue a lifestyle of your choice. As many of the OECD countries become multiracial, it is the social democrats who have led the attempt at welcoming the newcomers and allowing them to settle in their new countries with dignity. Status equality has now been guaranteed in the developed economies although income equality remains elusive.

But SwC was always predicated upon the nation-state captured by social democracy being able to direct the economy. This in turn required that the national economy be not strongly integrated with the rest of the world. This was a capitalism where we had an archipelago of national economies loosely articulated. But by the 1990s we arrived at a new phase of globalisation with much greater integration of the economies and consequently much less control of the nation-state over the domestic economy. The global flows of capital both direct and via portfolio movements across many stock markets, the explosion in global trade and the much slower yet significant upsurge in global movement of people created a situation in which the ship of the economy had to be steered at high seas, with much less control in the hands of the State.

Although social democracy always claims to be internationalist, its structures and even more so its ideology did not get out of the archipelagic world of many national economies run by the separate nation-states. There was no global social democratic vision to match the global phase of capitalism. Where has the Socialist International been in the recent crisis? The market moved globally and the politics did not catch up. The failure of the Left is not accidental; it is systemic. It is a failure of theory – the worst failure imaginable for anyone on the Left.

There is also a somewhat academic point to be made *inter alia*. This is that the Left never developed its own economics/political economy. It did not quite embrace Marxian economics (such as it was). It adopted neoclassical economics with the emphasis on market failure at the micro level and Keynesian economics at the macro level. (Scandinavian countries had an older tradition of macroeconomics thanks to Wicksell and the Stockholm School of economics.) The ideas about state intervention and capturing the 'commanding heights' of the economy were derived from the war time experience during 1914–18 and corporatism and planning in a mixed economy from the fascist economies – Italy and Germany – during the 1930s. Thus market failure at the microeconomic level, Keynesian underemployment analysis at the macro level plus State ownership of the commanding heights defined the distinctive social democratic approach to economic policy. All three aspects required State intervention and the Left was confident that it could deliver its promises if it controlled the State.

During the 1980s, state intervention in the industrial economy lost its appeal. State-owned companies became loss making and were a burden of the budget while other more urgent needs were claiming priority. In any case, thanks to the new technologies of transport and communication, it became more profitable to relocate the manufacturing industries to Asia and Latin America. The industrial working class shrank across the developed economies. Trade unions representing workers in manufacturing and mines and transport declined in numbers and strength. They had been the bedrock on which social democratic parties had been built. Without the 'commanding heights', social democracy was left with administering the public sector services with white collar unions, and began to face questions of consumers' choice in public services which had already been the fact in private sector. This led back to orthodox neoclassical economics. The issue was no longer the correction of market failure but to mirror the market in publicly provided services.

Globalisation also imposed constraints on the conduct of macroeconomic policies which made them more orthodox. This move started with anti-inflation policies with the dominance of central bank rather than treasury, and, after much debate among economists, a consensus developed that governments had to inspire credibility in their conduct of macroeconomic policies by making medium term commitments and avoiding surprises and sudden changes. The distinctive political economy the Left had fashioned for itself out of neoclassical economics – market interventions with taxes and subsidies and an aggressive fiscal stance to guarantee full employment – began to lose out to the compelling logic of the ideology of liberal markets.

The best social democracy could do was, *faute de mieux,* to adapt to global capitalism and combine a progressive social policy with a liberal economic policy. The label 'New Labour' or 'Third Way' may have been British but European social democratic parties had converged on this message in their own separate trajectories, with Sweden in the vanguard decades before UK. In doing so, social democracy lost its previous critical reservations about how the system had in-built failures; it did not update its theory to match the new phase of globalisation. When the system did break down, it had no remedy of its own. The electorate knew this. The Right could do the job of restoring the system just as well as the Left. Merkel and Sarkozy were singing a similar tune to Brown.

Perhaps it is worth mentioning that while social democracy prided itself on a vibrant culture of ideas, it thought that the Right was unthinking and blinkered and only represented 'old money'. But there was a thinking revolution on the Right during the 1960s and '70s. The dividing line was no longer 'Free Market' versus the State as between the Right and the Left. The Right used state power to restructure the industrial economy and privatised much state capital. It also gave power to central banks to control inflation. More crucially the Right facilitated the change from state ownership to state regulation of industries and public utilities. The Left was caught napping and had to scramble to get even in the battle of ideas.

What Is to Be Done?

The most serious challenge to the Left is to understand yet again how capitalism works. Why even as it fails, it revives itself, albeit with a lot of help from the nation-state. The State is the lender of last resort when the financial system is in difficulty. This however assumes that the liabilities are in terms of the domestic currency which the State can print in any amount. But as the case of Iceland shows, when the liabilities of the financial system are in terms of foreign currencies and its assets have gone toxic, even the State may not have the (foreign exchange) resources to bail the system out. The State can go bankrupt. This is a lesson familiar to Third World countries and was indeed learned bitterly in 1997 during the Asian crisis, but developed countries did not know it till now. As some EU and EEA countries faced bankruptcy, the IMF had to come to their rescue. The IMF, which in the 1980s and '90s was left with only the Third World to look after, has now become important for developed countries as well. In the phase of global capitalism, the individual nation-state is not powerful enough to stand on its own without outside help. In the latest crisis, the G7/G20 has shown that intergovernmental coordination has been for the time being both necessary and sufficient along with national intervention to manage the crisis. This however may not be the case the next time around.

The Crucial Question for the Left

Is capitalism a fully self-adjusting system which has cycles and crises but no end-point?

Or

Is capitalism a hopelessly crisis-ridden system where the system cannot be trusted to run itself without extensive state control?

Or

Is capitalism a system which most of the time works with cycles and crises and but only occasionally needs extensive, though internationally coordinated intervention?

The first way is that of laissez faire politics, the second of the old social democracy. If the present crisis has shown the validity of the third way of looking at capitalism how should the Left think about it?

Rethinking Economics

Academic economics has been in a bad repute recently. The models of mainstream macroeconomics about market rationality have been much mocked and quite rightly. But the issue is why did 'practical' men and women take such ideas so seriously. Academic economists often, if not always, only talk among themselves and know all the unstated qualifications to what they say to each other. But policymakers and politicians did swallow such ideas and did not know the unstated qualifications being made. What is more is that while many people rightly criticise academic economics for neglecting economic history and the history of economic ideas, why did the practical people fall into this trap as well?

Thus while recent macroeconomics may have ruled out crises (though the actual case is more nuanced as Robert Lucas argued in his essay in the *Economist,* 6 August, 2009), there are a number of well-known ideas in economics which predict cycles and crisis. Marx, Wicksell, Schumpeter and Hayek are four names which come to mind besides Keynes whose ideas are enjoying a revival. [Keynes in fact never went away. It is his policy nostrums which have helped to contain the present crisis thanks to 'built-in' stabilisers; the extra fiscal stimulus provided by governments of the Right and the Left was also thanks to his ideas. Keynes had no remedy for bank failures. Here it was Milton Friedman and Anna Schwartz's study of the Great Depression which told us that the Fed then had failed to provide sufficient liquidity to keep the banks going. This time around Ben Bernanke and Mervyn King were not going to repeat that mistake.]

The idea that capitalism is never, fully permanently stable but subject to recurrent cycles and crises used to be common knowledge, not just on the Left but among the business people as well. There was until the mid-1970s a flourishing subject area about business cycles taught in economics departments. We need to revive that part of economics. Even where economists knew the theory of markets working perfectly on their own, as in the case of Wicksell, Hayek and Schumpeter they asked as to why in that case there were cycles. In more recent times, Richard Goodwin of the University of Cambridge and the University of Sienna devoted himself to that topic. Charles Kindleberger wrote lucidly about crashes in his book *Manias, Panics and Crashes* and Hyman Minsky provided a theory of financial meltdowns. All this literature should be known to practical people and even more so to those who want to reform capitalism.

No one should be carried away with the claims of modern economists that they can provide the tools to 'eliminate boom and bust'; the best that economists can do is to moderate the effects of wrong policy which exacerbates such booms and busts.

It is not a mystery why the crisis happened. We have to lay aside ideas about greedy bankers and newfangled financial instruments having 'caused' the crisis. Every crisis had greedy bankers, and financial innovations have happened ever since cheque clearing was first mooted. These new elements may cause surprise but should not obscure the real reasons.

It was Knut Wicksell who first theorised about rises caused by bank lending. [Marx had a theory of cycles based on the movements in wages and profits. But there were few banks in his day. I have dealt with his theory in *Marx's Revenge*]. Wicksell said that if the rate at which investors can borrow (the market rate) is below the rate which they can earn from their investment (the natural rate), then there will be a cumulative upward movement in the economy. If the natural rate is below the market rate then there will be a cumulative downturn. To this Hayek added the caveat that at some stage the banks panic that they have over-lent and suddenly jack up the market rate. At this point the boom collapses and the long downturn begins.

What is Wealth?

But there are some other old fashioned ideas which need reviving. Since the housing bubble has been at the centre of the crisis and indeed house ownership has been a major political selling point, we need to ask why people are led to believe that a house represents wealth. Most houses are bought on a mortgage and for a number of years the house mortgagee owns a small part of the equity in the house. But even if that were not the case why is the house an asset? What is the *value* of a house?

Note that I say value not the price of a house. We have had people surprised that the price of their house has plummeted and they face negative equity. But the house stands as usable as it was before the price fell. How does a house lose wealth without any physical change? If I buy a car or a refrigerator I know that its second-hand price will be much less than the price I paid at purchase time. But with a house we all expect that the longer we hold on to it the higher its price would be. Houses are like pensions; they come in handy in old age.

None of the above discussion is predicated upon ignoring the many problems capitalism creates and with which we are familiar. But somehow the world seems to have voted for capitalism rather than any of the alternatives which were on offer during the twentieth century. The instincts of democratic politics are to rank the welfare of our own nation's citizens above that of others. Is there a cosmopolitan vision which we can cultivate to match the global phase of capitalism and if we can, how do we implement it?

Acknowledgement

This chapter was presented as a speech at The Foundation for European Progressive Studies and The Kalevi Sorsa Foundation Conference, Helsinki, on 6–7 November, 2009.

Chapter 8

GLOBALISATION AND SUSTAINABLE DEVELOPMENT

Meghnad Desai
(1997)

Globalisation is a new buzz word, a cliché, a new term to frighten the children. Its champions say that it has altered all economic relations, marginalised the nation-state, given unregulated and highly mobile capital the upper hand over labour and over governments, and that it is ushering in a borderless world. Its detractors say that it is globaloney or gobbledegook to say these things. Globalisation is not new: it is merely a throwback to the nineteenth century or, indeed, merely another chapter in the saga of the world systems built up by capitalism since the fifteenth century. Economists point out that, despite all the hype about globalisation, interest rates diverge even between OECD markets, and that domestic savings still correlate highly with domestic investment which they should not if there was a global market and that national policies still have a significant role to play. Political economists on the Left especially discount globalisation by saying that it is merely internationalisation, that there is no truly global firm but only multinationals, based in a few advanced countries, parading falsely as global.

There has been, however, a fundamental change in the world economy as I shall explain below (see also Desai 1995). First, capitalism is alive and well and pervading all over the globe except for a very small number of countries – Cuba and North Korea – which still retain fully a Leninist character with central planning and a command economy. Leninism, as a variant of socialism, is dead and gone, after occupying a pivotal position as an alternative to capitalism (Desai 1992). Capitalism has a variety of formations across the world, from Anglo Saxon to Scandinavian, to Asian/ Confucian to European social corporatist. But even as debate continues about the role of the State one thing is clear: successful State intervention, as in the Asian case, has to be capitalist friendly, i.e. profit enhancing. Call it managing the market, but it is a market friendly way of intervening that we have all come to accept as the limit of intervention, as against the Fabian or the Leninist versions which were market hostile and sought to control and divert the market from its uncontrolled dynamic flow.

The defeat of socialism at the level of a single country, and indeed even the demise of Keynesianism in one country, has led to a search for new limits to global capitalism on the Left. There is no global state nor a global working class ready to take on global capital. May not the ecological crisis define the limits to global capitalism? people ask, half in hope and half in desperation. What with global warming and exhaustible non-renewable resources and the hole in the ozone layer, could it not be that global capitalism will run into its contradictions with the ecosphere? Sustainable development becomes the new cry.

The purpose of this paper is to damp down this speculation. I shall argue that the globalisation process is more robust than people think and that markets remain powerful instruments even in the face of the environmental problem. At the same time I argue that globalisation, for the first time in 200 years, challenges the hegemony of the North *vis-a-vis* the South and that only a structural adjustment in the North, as drastic as the South has experienced during the last twenty-five years, will save the North.

I argue these points in the context of the now widely accepted, but loosely defined, notion of sustainable development. The following section questions the precision of the concept of sustainable development and gives examples of where the market has worked in an eco-friendly way. It then goes on to describe globalisation as a process with some asymmetric effects on the North and the South and shows that the North will have to alter its ways drastically to survive global competition.

Can Sustainable Economic Growth be Measured?

Sustainable economic growth (SEG) has not been defined rigorously and, given the fuzziness of the concept, it is difficult to see how it can be defined in a satisfactory operational way. The Brundtland Commission definition, which mentions leaving the world for our grandchildren as we would like to find it, essentially evokes the Hicksian definition of income (Brundtland 1987; Hicks 1939). Income is the maximum sustainable level of consumption, given a set of interest rates and price expectations such that the value of the stock of assets is the same at the beginning of the period as at the end. (Hicks's definition is discussed in further detail in the Appendix to this chapter.)

Thus income is an *ex ante* forward-looking concept. It depends crucially on expectations of prices and interest rates over the period where you are desiring to measure income. It starts with an initial valuation of the stock of assets (given their existing prices) and it relies on the possibility of computing the expected value of the stock at the end of the period. In addition, it must be borne in mind that this concept of income pertains to the individual. Aggregating it over individuals is not just a technical problem: it is a general equilibrium problem.

Hicks, when discussing this concept, confessed that he did not think income thus defined was measurable. This is so even if all the commodities – consumption goods as well as assets – are marketable and have deep markets which can determine prices. The principal reason is uncertainty. Even if we take a conventional (not Keynesian) view of uncertainty, the longer the period over which projections have to be made, the more unreliable the measure would be. Thus at the minimum, there would be multiple values of income over the same future period. There is no unique value of income that could be sustainable.

Since SEG is the ratio of income over the value of assets, i.e. a growth rate, there will be multiple rates of SEG. If we compound this problem with variables for which there are no markets and no prices, for which there are not even estimates of current levels of physical stocks, the multiplicity will obviously increase. Also implicit in the notion of value of assets are prices of each type of commodity which goes into the total capital stock. Now for conventional marketed commodities, prices purport to measure relative substitutability under conditions of competitive equilibrium. If we deviate from competitive equilibrium conditions, even in this case of conventional commodities, prices fail to signal relative substitutability.

When we come to components of the ecosystem, the notion of substitutability, say, among the species or of one non-renewable resource for another, is itself in dispute. Are we willing to trade an endangered species for more clean air or less global warming? (Desai 1995).

Thus even excluding the ecosystem, to compute income over the next fifty years will not give us a unique answer. If we add the ecosystem, the concept is impossible even to define.

Of course, gross national product (GNP) is nothing like this Hicksian concept. It is an *ex-post* measure of marketed outputs (or incurred expenditures or money incomes) with marginal adjustment for non-marketed (but in principle *marketable*) outputs (Desai 1993).

Thus it is premature, if not dishonest, to speak of SEG as if we knew what it is or should be – whether, in terms of gross domestic product (GDP) growth, the rate should be high, low, positive, zero or negative. GDP is such an imperfect measure (as indeed the Greens always remind us) that any amount of environmental damage could be associated with the same growth rate of GDP. Negative GDP growth can often be more damaging than a positive rate. The total amount of environmental deterioration is determined by the particular mix of production processes and products as well as consumption patterns (including residential location) and working habits. Thus it may be enough to change processes or products rather than reduce GNP or its growth rate in some sense.

Given the pervasive uncertainty about the future as well as the indeterminate nature of our knowledge of the present levels of natural capital of all types, what is to be done? One strategy would be to exercise caution just in case our worst fears were justified. Since, if they are, in the event, not justified, we (or our grandchildren) are alive to adjust to the higher consumption path. If they are true, then the cautious strategy may prolong human life on the planet a bit longer.

But being cautious is not an operational recipe. Cautious in what – in targeting high growth or in taxing energy? Although market prices are myopic, there is no guarantee that not following market prices will lead us to correct prices (or price paths) since no unique correct prices exist, *even in principle*. The longer the time period over which we project, the less unique such prices (or price paths) will be. Thus over the very short run, market prices may be the *least unsatisfactory alternative* available because the only guarantee of market prices is that they will change in the light of changes in the immediate circumstances. In a dense fog with very low visibility, the only thing you can do is to take one extra step at a time. (By market prices, I mean the prices corrected for such externalities as are perceivable at present.)

Market Prices as Appropriate Green Signals

Thus it may be interesting to examine the role of market prices, knowing full well that these prices are not perfect competition prices and that they have to be supplemented by taxes and subsidies. Let me outline five examples when market pricing led to desirable outcomes, whether intended or not, as well as examples when taking a decision in defiance of the market led to ecologically undesirable outcomes. These are:

1. *Nuclear Energy*: Only when the UK government decided to privatise the electricity industry, nuclear energy was subjected to the market test and revealed to be expensive as well as dangerous. Only in countries with state subsidies (e.g., France) does nuclear energy survive. The ecological danger posed by nuclear power stations in the former USSR is grave and a lot of money (US$100 billion) may have to be expended to decommission these power stations. These costs have to be made more public.
2. *Oil Shock*: The 1973 quadrupling of oil prices led to a steady diminution of the use of energy per unit of GDP in the OECD countries. Of course, this adjustment took time and the short-run reactions took the form of a recession, but in the medium term, energy economy did occur. I doubt whether such economising could have occurred via a conference declaration or an intergovernmental coordination effort.

   I should also mention that the forecasts made in 1972 by The Club of Rome and many others, underestimated the scope for substitution of scarce material as well as the augmentation of supplies of such scarce material. Thus the oil price today is lower in relative terms than it was before 1973.
3. *The Debt Rescheduling Problem*: At the beginning of the 1980s, the problem of the Third World debt burden became prominent. But by the end of the 1980s, Latin American countries, which had contracted their debt with private commercial banks, had successfully tackled their debt burden by securitising the debt. The debt was floated on the market, and some of it was settled for as little as 10 cents on the dollar.

   The official debt of Sub-Saharan African countries has been more difficult to reduce. Despite the Trinidad conditions announced by the UK prime minister three years ago, there is still no debt forgiveness on the part of governments. Thus the market found it easier to tackle debt than governments do.

4. *The DM/OM Exchange Rate*: The fixing of the exchange rate, as between the Deutschmark and the Ostmark on the reunification of Germany, is an example of the market defying political decisions which imposed enormous extra burdens on the reunification process. A market based approach would have been much easier. The problem of poverty in East Germany could have been tackled separately.
5. *The US Gasoline Price*: The US is a high energy consumer, in large part due to its failure to price gasoline in the way it is set in Western Europe. The lack of courage to tax gasoline in the US is doubly damaging – it fails to tackle the budget deficit and is environmentally damaging.

I do not mean to imply that markets are perfect, but that often they are quicker to act, although not without side effects, to accomplish certain environmental economies or produce developmental outcome. There will be a need to intervene in the market to correct externalities, but it would be better to take care to pursue incentive compatible market intervention rather than one that goes against market signals. In any case neither governments nor markets can overcome the problem of uncertainty and the impossibility of correct forecasts.

Globalisation

What has happened in the last few years to alter the balance in favour of the market has been the renewed dynamic growth of capitalism. Confounding the prophecies of its imminent or eventual demise through much of the twentieth century – by Lenin, by Schumpeter, and many others – capitalism is still a vibrant dynamic system. It has also globalised in recent years. While capitalism has always been international, indeed 'a world system' in the words of Immanuel Wallerstein,' it is only recently that technological innovation and institutional deregulation has made the system truly global. Manuel Castells has defined globalisation 'as an ability to act in real time on a planetary scale'. Financial markets are truly global in this sense. Direct foreign investment is also globally mobile, but it is by sourcing and sub-contracting using electronic devices (email, fax) that instant changes in plans can be implemented. Thus a Western airline can have its global reservation plans carried out in India due to the availability of good software. A New York corporation can get its accounts processed every day in Galway in Ireland, exploiting the time difference and availability of cheaper skilled labour.

The process which led to globalisation began as early as 1973 after the oil shock, but could be said to have accelerated during the 1980s. The most important aspects of it today are that on the one hand it has made the world more symmetric as between North and South. It has also led to a fragmentation of the South into rapidly developing regions and those still left behind.

The picture of the world economy in the 1960s and 1970s was one where the North and its trans-national corporations (TNCs) dominated/exploited/robbed the South. The South was thought of as passive, dependent and exploited. There was much pessimism, for example in the works of Baran, Frank and others, about the possibility of rapid economic growth in the South (Baran 1960; Frank 1967). Although this image persists in some people's discourse, even to the extent of a refusal to believe that growth has occurred, the reality is very different today. Today, for example, there is a lot of worry in the North about competition in the manufacturing sector from the Asian countries and pessimism about the possibility of generating full employment or about financing the welfare state (Reich 1992; Goldsmith 1995). Fifteen years ago, no one anticipated that the manufacturing industry of South Korea, Taiwan, Malaysia, Indonesia, China or India, would be seen as posing a threat to the industrialised North. Some of these fears have crystallised around the Uruguay Round of GATT and the ratification of the GATT treaty. There is now suddenly an attempt to impose a social clause or an environmental labelling as part of GATT. The rapidly industrialising countries of the South view this as a cynical ploy to impose non-tariff barriers to their exports.

At the same time, the South is no longer homogenous. East and Southeast Asia are industrialising rapidly and South Korea will soon join Japan in the OECD. South Asia is also undergoing an economic liberalisation process and becoming fully integrated with the global economy. Latin America has come out of its debt-ridden state and is resuming its industrialisation. It is a middle income region, and Mexico has already entered OECD. (None of this is meant to ignore the inequalities of income distribution in these countries but these were present as much during the phase of relative autonomy pursued by the South as is the case now. In some cases, inequalities may even improve, as is the case in South Korea and Taiwan.)

Sub-Saharan Africa is still left in the classic category of South, though even here, Southern Africa as a region may grow rapidly now that apartheid has been removed.

Against this background, I wish to argue that globalisation is a process that is not necessarily hostile to sustainable growth and that indeed it should be harnessed for the purpose. Policies which further globalisation should be supported and those blocking it (e.g., protectionism) should be resisted (Goldsmith 1995). Especially important here is the near certainty that globalisation will force certain harsh structural adjustments on the North that will have the welcome effect of cutting consumption levels and increasing savings. Let me explain.

One major problem that confronts the developed countries of the North is that of restoring full employment levels. The rate of unemployment has trebled during the 1980s relative to the 1950s and 1960s (Layard, Jackman and Nickell 1993). Since the 1970s, although per capita GDP has risen, unemployment has also gone up – hence the jobless growth, as it was called by the Human Development Report, 1993 (UNDP 1993). The only exception to the experience of jobless growth is Japan, which managed to increase employment as well as income, so that its unemployment rate stayed low (it did go up, however, in the recent recession).

One reason for jobless growth and for the frustration of the governments in tackling the problem of employment is the globalisation of the world economy. This has meant the loss of autonomy on the part of nation-states to determine their economic policy. In this sense 'Keynesianism in one country' is dead. This is not because governments are no longer able to affect employment but because the determinants of employment are no longer what they used to be. It is no longer lack of effective demand which determines the level of employment. Globalisation has shifted both the demand curve and the supply curve of tradeable goods and services. Thus any amount of exports can be sold as long as the economy is competitive. The competitiveness of the economy is determined by the rate of productivity growth which itself depends on the rate of investment and the speed of innovation.

The example of Japan is instructive in this respect. The Japanese economy invests more than 30 per cent, maintains a high speed of innovation by fostering domestic competition among its large conglomerates and thus, productivity growth is high. But Japan also practices the creation of a large number of jobs in the non-tradeable sector. These are low productivity/low wage jobs.

The tradeable sector is now increasingly the wealth-creating sector but not a job-creating sector. The challenge facing the developed West is to raise its investment rate by saving and investing more. It has also to maintain a high rate of productivity growth in its tradeable sector to go on creating wealth. But, at the same time, job creation in the non-tradeable sector poses a challenge not only in terms of the number of jobs which have to be created, but also because of the difficulty of the inequality of wages as between the tradeable and the non-tradeable sectors. To some extent this requires a transfer of surplus from the tradeable to the non-tradeable sector. This can be done either by differential pricing of the non-tradeable goods and services (to the extent that they can be priced) – I have discussed some of these problems in Desai (1994). Now one conclusion to which this analysis leads is that countries of the North, facing these problems of persistent unemployment, will have to:

1. raise their savings rate and to do this reduce the level and change the pattern of their consumption;
2. shift taxation from employment (payroll taxes of various kinds) to consumption, especially of natural resources;
3. and increase investment in non-material capital such as education, health and training.

It is not too much then to say that the impact of this effect of globalisation will be positive on the environment. This may be one of those dialectical contradictions, the unintended effect of human actions.

Conclusion

Globalisation has often been demonised. My purpose here is to point out that by forcing structural adjustment in the North, it may yet lead to benevolent effects on the environment.

Appendix

Hicks's definition was given in his 1939 classic *Value and Capital.* It may be useful to quote it here for future reference:

> The purpose of income calculations in practical affairs is to give people an indication of the amount they can consume without impoverishing themselves. Following out this idea, it would seem that we ought to define a man's income as the maximum value which he can consume during a week, and still expect to be as well off at the end of the week as he was at the beginning. (*Value and Capital*, p. 172)

Hicks goes on to explain that this forward looking definition of income has to be supplemented, adding that this measure of income depends upon the expectations concerning future prices and interest rates. Having considered these problems, he argues 'By considering the approximations (ie, for interest rates and prices (MD)) to this criterion (the definition quoted above (MD)), we have come to see how very complex it is, how unattractive it looks when subjected to detailed analysis. We may now allow a doubt to escape us whether it does, in the last resort, stand up to analysis at all, whether we have been chasing a will-o'-the-wisp' (op. cit., p. 178).

Even if these problems were overcome, this only pertains to the income of a single individual. At this level, income is equivalent to the *sustainable level of consumption*, assuming zero growth in the stock of wealth. But this income is subjective as it is conditional on expectations. It is also easy to take interest rates and prices as given when speaking of a single individual. But when we speak of many individuals or the economy as a whole (national or global), this assumption is no longer tenable. What is sustainable for an individual is not necessarily so for the economy.

Related to this issue of endogeneity of interest rates and prices is the problem of reconciling the subjective expectations of different individuals since, by the definition above, the sustainable level of consumption (i.e., income) is conditional on expectations, and there is no simple way of aggregating over the subjective expectations of different individuals. In the SEG context, think of either the present and the future generations or even the rich and the poor.

The answer, of course, has been to ignore all these complications in national income accounting and pretend that the *ex-post* measure of goods and services produced (which is what GNP is) is the same as the *ex-ante* welfare theoretic measure of income. This is often more a hindrance than a help. Thus the problem of properly measuring the depreciation of capital in order to derive a net national product from gross national product is important, even for the *ex-post* measurement of income, regardless of welfare implications. In this way the proper accounting of used up 'natural capital' is important. What it does not do is deal with the issue of future generations and sustainability.

References

Baran, Paul A. *Political History of Growth.* New York: Monthly Review Press, 1960.
Baranzini M. and A. Cencini (eds). *Marxs, Hayek and the Demise of Official Keynesianism.* 1996.
Brundtland G. H. *Our Common Future.* Oxford: Oxford University Press, 1987.
Desai, Meghnad. 'Greening the HDI?' in A. MacGillivray, ed. *Accounting for Change.* 1995.
Desai, Meghnad. 'No Easy Jobs', *New Statesman and Society*, 22 July, 1994.
Desai, Meghnad. 'Income and Alternative Measures of Well Being', in D. G. Westendorf and D. Ghai,
Monitoring Social Progress in the 1990s. Aldershot: Avebury, 1993.
Desai, Meghnad. 'Is Socialism Dead?' *Contention*, Winter 1992, 1.2, pp. 143–58.
Desai, Meghnad and Redfern P. (eds). *Global Governance: Ethics and Economics of the World Order.* London: Frances Pinter, 1995, pp. 6–22.
Frank. A. G. *Capitalism and Underdevelopment in Latin America.* New York: Monthly Review Press, 1967.
Goldsmith. J. *The Trap.* London: Macmillan, 1995.
Hicks. J. R. *Value and Capital.* Oxford: Clarendon Press, 1939.
Layard R., Jackman R. and Nickell S. *Unemployment*, Oxford: Blackwell, 1993.
Reich. R. *The Work of Nations.* New York: Alfred Knopf, 1991.
UNDP. *Human Development Report.* New York: Oxford University Press, 1993.
Westendorf. D. G. and Ghai. D. (eds.) *Monitoring Social Progress in the 1990s.* Aldershot: Avebury, 1993.

Acknowledgement

First publication: Desai, Meghnad (1997) 'Globalization and Sustainable Development', in Gupta S.D., Choudhry N.K. (eds) *Globalization, Growth and Sustainability.* Recent Economic Thought Series, vol. 58. Springer, Boston, MA; pp. 231–242. Reproduced with kind permission of SNCSC.

Part 2

India and China

Chapter 9

INDIA AND CHINA

An Essay in Comparative Political Economy

Meghnad Desai

(2005)

Introduction

India and China are two of the oldest and still extant civilisations. For Europeans, they were legendary seats of immense wealth and wisdom right up to the eighteenth century. Somewhere between the mid-eighteenth century and early nineteenth centuries, both of these countries became, in the European eyes, bywords for stagnant, archaic and weak nations. For China, this happened between the adulation of Voltaire and the cooler judgment of Montesquieu; in India's case, it was the contrast between Sir William Jones's desire to learn things Indian and James Mill's dismissal of Indian history as nothing but darkness.

The twentieth century brought nothing but a deepening of the perception of the two countries as bywords for misery and the perceptions were not too far behind actual conditions of the two countries. For one thing they were, and remain, the two most populous countries. In 1820, they had a combined population in excess of half a billion and by 1900, it reached 700 million. Within the twentieth century, their population had trebled. But they were also two of the poorest countries, typically thought of as locations of famine, disease, backwardness and superstition, of women with bound feet and men with long pony-tails in China, untouchables beyond the pale and myriad gods with many heads and limbs in India.

In the mid-twentieth century, particularly in the 1960s, the fortunes of these two countries seemed to have reached their nadir. They were independent republics supposedly launched on their path of development, but both suffered devastating famines. China's famine was hidden, perhaps more from China's own ruling classes than from its people or the world, but it had followed swiftly upon the debacle of the Great Leap Forward, a memorable piece of policymaking by fantasy. A double harvest failure in 1965 and 1966 brought India to its proverbial knees in terms of foreign policy and dependence on US food aid. These two countries were 'basket cases' in the then fashionable terms of international diplomacy.

In the span of less than forty years, we are discussing China and India not as failures nor for their ancient wisdoms, but as dynamic modern economies. The *Economist* has to write editorials to tell the world not to be afraid of China's economic power. American legislators pass laws to prevent their businesses from outsourcing work to India's software and telecommunication services. China ranks as the second largest economy in terms of gross domestic product (GDP) in purchasing power parity (PPP) dollars. Together the two countries account for 19.2 per cent of gross world product – China 11.5 per cent and India 7.7 per cent. This is still below their share of world population 37.5 per cent – with China 21 per cent and India 16.5 per cent.

National income estimates covering a long period are, by their nature, broadly indicative rather than precise.[1] Angus Maddison, to whom the profession is indebted for making these calculations his lifetime work, gives the shares of gross world product and population of China and India for two earlier dates in the twentieth century as follows.

Table 9.1 succinctly describes the course of the two economies over the twentieth century. They start with the share of income below that of population. Over the previous century they had slightly different trajectories. India's per capita income is estimated to have grown from M$533 in 1820 (Maddison dollars [M$] or 1990 international dollars) to M$673 in 1913 while China's per capita income declined from M$600 in 1820 to M$552 in 1913. But during the first half of the twentieth century, both countries saw a decline in their per capita incomes – India from M$673 in 1913 to M$619 in 1950 and China from M$552 in 1913 to M$439 in 1950.[2]

---

1 Beyond this vague assertion I do not intend to go into statistical measurement problems.

2 Dharma Kumar (1998), who independently made comparative estimates of India and China over the early twentieth century, arrives at not dissimilar estimates. She puts India's per capita income as US$60 in 1952 and China's as US$50 (at current prices).

Table 9.1 says two things: India and China both suffered a declining per capita income and a rising population during the first half of the twentieth century, but India was slightly better off than China between 20 per cent[3] and 40 per cent.[4] By 1998 this was reversed. Both countries were better off, but China was much better off than India. China's per capita income was M$3117 while India's was M$1760. Thus, while India roughly trebled its income, China increased it sevenfold. In earlier periods, China, while more populous than India, was not noticeably richer. In terms of GDP, the two economies were of roughly similar size. The ratio of China's GDP to India's was 1.18 in 1918; 1.08 in 1950; but in 1998, it was 2.28.

Table 9.1 Share of world output and population

	Share of world product (%)		Share of gross world population (%)	
Year	China	India	China	India
1913	8.9	7.5	26.4	17.0
1950	4.5	4.2	21.1	14.2
1998	11.5	7.7	21.0	16.5

Source: Maddison (2001).

Therefore, one theme of this chapter is the contrast between the economic performance of China and India and its proximate causes. But there are also a lot of similarities between the two, both in the path to modernisation and, as we shall see later, the future prospects for their economies. There are also political similarities and contrasts between the two, both as to their twentieth-century history and twenty-first century challenges.

Historical Legacies

Political Legacy

While both India and China have a long history, their histories are very different. China has been by and large a stable, centrally run state throughout its history with limited periods of instability and lack of a single authority. India's history has been exactly the reverse. The periods when a single king or political authority ruled over even the major part of India's territory

3 Kumar (1998).

4 Maddison (2001).

can be counted on the fingers of one hand. In China's case there was a deep desire for unification of the country as a driving force of nationalism in the twentieth century. But it was called reunification. Thus at the onset of the Second World War, China was divided, and Jonathan Spence (1999) expresses the drive for nationalists as follows:

> The solidification of such a group of new states, that is, war lords, KMT [Kuomintang], communists and Japanese enclaves, would return China to the situation that had prevailed before the Qin conquests of 221 B.C., during the so-called Warring States period when ten major regimes controlled the country among them; or it might bring a recurrence of the shifting patterns of authority and alliances that typified China's history from the third to sixth century A.D., and again from tenth to the thirteenth.[5]

In India's case, there never was any authority which has ruled over all of India; indeed, not even the British or even the present Indian government. India has been an idea in world culture for millennia, but its borders had been fixed only in the late nineteenth century sometime after the British gave up on Afghanistan and drew the Durand line. Kings have ruled over much of North India – the Maurya and Gupta dynasties just before and after the BC/AD division. The Mughals could be said to have ruled over much of India between the years of Akbar's maturity in 1570 and Aurangzeb's death in 1707. Their empire extended to Kabul but did not take in all of South India. The British could be said to have ruled over two-thirds of India between 1857 and 1947, with the remaining third being ruled by native princes under their paramountcy but not direct rule. In 1947, India was partitioned and thus even what is now called India is not what Nehru in 1946 wrote about in *The Discovery of India*.[6] Indian system of kingly power was not so much like a pyramid, but like a multi-tiered cake. It was flatter and while there was a top and a bottom plus layers in between, the power of the top king over his vassals below was not absolute. Loyalty, though owed by the lower tiers to the top, was always negotiable and there had to be some give and take.[7] The British were perhaps the first rulers to try a more absolute and hierarchical structure of power under the limitation of oversight by a democratic Parliament back in London.

5 Spence *et al.* (1999, p. 426).

6 Nehru (1946) and Keay (2001).

7 Inden (2000).

Yet in one sense it was British rule which gave India its definitive territorial extent, fixed its boundaries and gave it a structure of provinces and central government with an administrative 'steel frame'. The British gave India their language, which facilitates even today India's access to global markets, as do the legal system of property rights and Western orientation of its elite. India's independence movement was critical of the economic ruin the British had caused – deindustrialisation, drain of treasure, deskilling and diversion of agriculture into commercial crops away from food crops, and so on. But India began to acquire railroads and modern industry in the 1850s – a quarter of a century earlier than China. More foreign capital per capita was poured into India than in China; in 1913 India had US$6.9 per capita foreign capital while China had US$3.7.[8]

There is, however, another much less mentioned benefit that India derived from British rule. Of course, it might have been better for India to have never suffered foreign rule, but to have been united under a native king or republic. But between 1500 and 1800, India had several foreign trading companies vying for control – the Portuguese, the Dutch, the French, the Danes, and of course, the English. As a counterfactual of history, it is possible to imagine what we call India today and take it for granted as a single country being made up of several different 'countries' in the west, south, east and north with different foreign languages being spoken along with local languages. Thus the Tamils could have been French speaking and the Maharashtrians Portuguese speaking and so on. Thanks to the religious wars of Europe in the seventeenth century and British victories in European wars in the eighteenth century, India ended up with a single foreign power, and thus the idea of India as a single country developed with its modern nationalism. This is not entirely fanciful since Southeast Asia with a population and extent not dissimilar to India's was ruled by the Dutch (Indonesia), the French (Indochina) and the British (Burma, Malaysia and Singapore) with Thailand being independent. What is more, the hegemonic political ideology of the nationalist movement – liberal democracy – was also borrowed from the foreign rulers. The India we talk of today is a nineteenth-century product in more than one sense.

China, by contrast, never suffered foreign rule over majority of its territory. There were foreign concessions in ports and later in interior towns extracted by several foreign powers in circumstances that the Chinese found humiliating. But it had not suffered classic imperial rule until 1931 when

8 Maddison (2001, p. 99).

the Japanese invaded Manchuria and later in 1937 when they occupied large chunks of eastern and central China.[9] Yet China's attitude to foreigners was and is much more hostile than India's. The removal of foreigners, especially the reversal of concessions, became a driving force for China. For India, the hostility to things foreign, except perhaps for foreign private capital, melted like snow in spring soon after independence. If anything, India in its early days after independence sought foreign capital from public rather than private sources and from a variety of countries rather than merely its old colonial masters. China after 1949 relied on one country, the USSR, and soon came to regret its connection. China's problem, unlike that of India, was the multiplicity of foreign powers gnawing at its sides with no single hegemonic ruling ideology as India had had with liberal democracy from Britain. It had the Germans, Japanese, Americans, French and British jostling not so much for rule over Chinese minds as over their cash boxes. There was some missionary input, more than in India, but eventually China had to forge its own ideology of modernity. It had to struggle to confront Confucianism against Western ideologies – liberalism, fascism and communism.

These historical legacies shaped both the politics and economics of the two countries. For India, the problem was in achieving unity in diversity and in accommodating various languages and religions in a political structure, so as to give its centre enough power to maintain its territorial integrity but its regions enough room to develop their diversities. India had a problem of articulating a single vision of Indian nationhood since it had been a nation only since the mid-nineteenth century and even this was asserted against by the foreign rulers who saw India not as a single nation but a motley collection of races and religions.[10] India thus chose a federal polity with a strong centre able to alter state boundaries, split up states or create new ones. India even so is a soft state in Myrdal's famous description where the government has to work consensually and exert control sparingly and, that too, only against serious threats to national integrity.[11] India's fear is a break up of its territorial unity as had happened in the Partition.[12]

9 I am treating the Manchus as not being foreign, though many Chinese at the beginning of the twentieth century emphasised that they wanted to remove the Manchu empire and establish a Chinese republic.

10 Desai (2000).

11 I have learned a lot about federal structures and federalism in India while co-supervising Katherine Adeney (see Adeney, 2003).

12 Myrdal (1968).

China has always had a vision of itself as a nation. Through much of its history, there has been a strong central power, and China has been run as a unitary polity. Indeed, Sun Yat Sen and his Communist supporters viewed the prospect of federalism as akin to feudalism.[13] The theme of reunification in early-twentieth-century China meant recentralisation of authority. China has its minorities, but it is viewed and indeed views itself as a country of the Han people – a solid homogenous mass. While there are differences between Mandarin and Cantonese, the language is the same for an overwhelming majority of the Chinese. China is thus a unitary hard state which can pursue a single goal with determination and mobilise maximal resources in its achievement. It has ever been thus, be it in building the Great Wall or the system of grand canals, or in recent times in the Great Leap Forward.

There was a further advantage of being a unitary state which has often not been recognised. As Kent Deng has said in a recent survey of Chinese economic history:

> a basic structural factor – namely, that for most of the time most of China had a nationwide market, a single government (which was active in maintaining food supply, famine relief, and price control), a standardized written language, a uniform calendar and a system of weights and measures, a dominant Confucian code of conduct, a nationwide transport network, and the mechanisms for social mobility and inter-regional migration ... China could claim to have been a proto industrialized country by the 13th century and indeed has been considered by many scholars to have been a prime candidate for a capitalist revolution which it missed.[14]

But anticipating somewhat later themes, strong states can also be brittle states, while soft states are difficult to smash and break since they are pliable. India has through its history been ruled by many authorities and sometimes none, but it has had a social stability which is remarkable. In India's case the enveloping unity was provided by the Hindu social structure, especially the caste system, which determined the basis on which interregional mobility could be conducted. Indeed the caste system proved to be so powerful that even among the Muslims and Christians a caste hierarchy took root and

13 Spence *et al.* (1999).

14 Deng (2000, p. 6) surveys this literature. There has been a similar though less extensive discussion among Indian historians as to whether India could have had its own capitalist revolution (see Habib, 1971).

developed. While the concept of the Asiatic Mode of Production (AMP) is much derided nowadays, its essence was about a society in which the state was epiphenomenal and the peasant society went on impervious to changing rulers. India was throughout its history like that.[15] China, on the other hand strong as it was, became subject to spasmodic breakdowns which lasted several years. Within the modern period, we have had the Taiping Rebellion (1851–64), the Boxer Uprising (1900) which eventually led to end of empire (1911) and four decades of warlordism, and more recently the Cultural Revolution (1966–76). Even the Tiananmen incidents of 1989 are more a sign of brittleness than of strength.

Economic Legacy

Both India and China were a highly urban civilisation by the eighteenth century, though of course the bulk of the population lived in rural areas. China was much advanced in science and technology, with gunpowder, printing, paper and paper currency as its inventions. China's scientific and technological achievements are known to us thanks to the monumental efforts of Joseph Needham.[16] India was known for its mathematics and its philosophy. The Chinese gave the world the wheelbarrow and bureaucracy; India gave the world the zero, decimals and Buddhism. Both were major exporters of fine textiles, silks and muslins; their ships sailed around the world and indeed dominated the seas till 1500. After that the Chinese withdrew from the seas and while the Indians continued, the powers that be in Delhi or Agra had no need for a navy. It was the kingdoms in South India which were maritime adventurers. As they declined in power under the Mughals, Indian shipping began to be conducted increasingly on a private basis rather than a state sponsored one. The control of the seas passed to a series of Western European countries. Yet China and India remained economically vibrant till the late eighteenth century.

China had a higher productivity in its agriculture, the iron tipped plough having been in use at least half a millennium before it made its appearance in India. Thus Needham attributes the animal drawn plough to the period of the Warring states, while Habib says that the iron plough came to India in the first century AD.[17] Chinese irrigation systems were bigger and better

15 See O'Leary (1989) for a critique of the Asiatic Mode of Production (AMP). Also see Habib (1983) for a sympathetic account of Marx's views on India, and Deng (2000), who sees the AMP as a useful concept.

16 Needham *et al.* (1954).

17 Needham *et al.* (1954) and Habib (1995).

than any in India.[18] Thus Maddison's estimate of M$600 per capita income for China and M$533 for India in 1820 is roughly the right sort of relative difference.

The difference was made up in the next 130 years. By 1950, India had caught up with China, as we saw earlier, in the per capita as well as total income estimates. In output per person employed, Maddison shows India at M$1377 in 1950 and China at M$1297. The story is that in the nineteenth century India did enjoy a rising per capita income. This is not uncontroversial, as everything else about British impact on India. But it is consistent with much data.[19] India was a land surplus rather than a labour surplus country in the nineteenth century with a population of about 200–230 million, that is, one-fifth of the current level, and much the same amount of land. It became for a while an agricultural exporter rather than industrial exporter, but still managed a trade surplus. By the late nineteenth century, India began to acquire modern infrastructure and industry, not large relative to its population, but large relative to other countries. India is in this sense an early industrialising country. In 1945, it was the seventh largest industrial country by volume of output.

But their history drove both China and India to define industrialisation rather than economic development as their prime goal. Even within industrialisation, the strategy was one of concentrating on basic goods such as steel and machinery – 'Department I goods' in Marxian terminology – rather than consumer and low-tech goods. Both countries were inspired by the example of the USSR and its planning achievements. They both sought independence of foreign capital and self-sufficiency.

The contrast between the two was most stark in agriculture. Being vast territories there is a similar diversity in the eco-agricultural make up of regions in both countries. But China's central rule meant that a uniform revenue collection system and land ownership pattern prevailed especially while the central power was effective. India by contrast had different legal patterns of revenue collection and different land tenures as a result of a lack of central authority reinforced by British experimentation with Ryotwari, Zamindari, Mahalwari and the like. Land reform was a straightforward issue of changing ownership of large landholdings across China as far as

18 Oriental Despotism, a notion begotten by Wittfogel from Marx and Engels's AMP, was supposed to be good at hydraulic projects. Be that as it may, the abandoned city of Fatehpur Sikri is a monument to how a Mughal king built a city where he failed to provide water supplies.

19 See Heston in Kumar and Desai (1983).

the Communists were concerned. They were also committed to it as soon as they could become the sole powers. In India land reform was a maze of regional complexity and the Congress Party was not a revolutionary organisation. Land reform thus became a state/provincial subject rather than a union/central policy issue. Thus India added legal and economic variation to the eco-agricultural one.

Development Paths

Differences between China and India appear much greater from the current vantage point than they would have in 1973 or even 1983. Each has gone through two broad phases, which I characterise in this section.

Taking Nationalism Seriously – Mistakes and Learning

Both countries feared foreign domination and considered development as synonymous with industrialisation. Both considered the State as the engine and the driver of growth and suspected the private sector's initiatives. The ideology forged during the long march to independence – Marxism, Leninism, Maoism in China and Gandhism in India, plus an amalgam of social and liberal democracy in India shaped the response more than economic realities warranted. One man ruled the roost though his closest associates did not share his beliefs as much as they said they did while he was still around. Mao for China and Nehru for India laid down the path from which each country had to deviate, if only because the path led to a blind alley.

For China the first period lasted from 1949 to 1978; for India from 1947 to 1980. China learned quickly thanks to Deng Xiaoping. India did not have a Deng. Blood proved much thicker than pragmatism in matters of economic ideology. India began a half-hearted change in 1980 when Mrs Gandhi abandoned self-sufficiency as an ideal and took a big loan from the international monetary fund (IMF). But that loan and subsequent hard currency borrowing were frittered away. India could be said to have wasted ten years in a half-hearted liberalisation, which hit the buffers in 1991 when the country nearly went bankrupt.

Living in the Modern World and Adapting to It

In the second phase, each country forgot the lessons it had thought it had learned from its history, xenophobia, fear of foreign trade and foreign capital, distrust of private initiative and decentralisation. Each adapted to the rhythm of the world economy rather than sail against the wind. Being large vessels, they have a bit more freedom of manoeuvre than small countries. They misused the freedom in the first phase and corrected themselves in the second phase. Their comparators would be two smaller countries both with a colonial past – South Korea and Taiwan who did not go through a two-phase path. After 1960, South Korea single-mindedly pursued growth with spectacular results. Taiwan had a similar colonial background to Korea's but it also had the influx of the Guomindang elite, which transformed property rights in Taiwan and achieved what it could not on the mainland – a successful growth strategy.

The comparison between the two pairs of countries is revealing. In 1950 China and India had per capita incomes of M$439 and M$619, while South Korea and Taiwan had M$770 and M$936. By 1999, the numbers were: China M$3259, India M$1818, South Korea M$13,317 and Taiwan M$15,720. Let me examine the two phases in some detail.

The First Phase

Both China and India saw a development of Department I goods – steel, cement, machine-making equipment – as pivotal to their growth strategies. India had at this time a viable world-class textile industry which it chose to stifle in its search for an employment-intensive growth strategy meant to favour small-scale and low-tech firms over large-scale industrialised firms. India diverted resources from the production of domestic consumption goods, especially of the machine-produced variety, to the production of investment goods by the industrial sector and consumer goods by small-scale industries. However, its savings rate was not significantly raised and the growth rate remained modest. China seems to have concentrated its industrial efforts also on the basic goods sector initially, but after the first three or four years switched to an all-round emphasis on heavy as well as light industries. Apart from the aberration of backyard steel furnaces in the Great Leap Forward phase, it was not saddled with a small-scale industry strategy. But China had a more successful resource mobilisation strategy than India did. India's Second Five-Year Plan (1956–61) ran into a resource constraint by 1958. China on the other hand ran into the evils of overweening ambition in launching the Great Leap Forward. There seems to have been a slowdown in China in the 1960–65 period, whereas in India it came in the second half of the 1960s after the Third Five-Year Plan (1961–66).

China managed its agrarian reform better than India. Starting from a higher level of productivity, China went on to transform not only the tenurial relations in agriculture but also the production conditions. Thus abolishing of landlords and forming cooperatives and then communes changed not only the distribution of surplus, but also its size. India concentrated on changing the tenurial relations by abolishing zamindari and intermediaries and redistributing the surplus. Reform was of course different across regions as the polity dictated. But India did little to change production conditions – land pooling, technology used or labour deployed. These changed in India in the 1960s with the advent of the Green Revolution, where a combination of foreign knowledge, domestic subsidies and rural private initiative brought a capitalist revolution to the Indian countryside. Despite this, China's lead in agricultural productivity remained to the end of the first phase and indeed increased, when in the second phase, China moved to a more private initiative system.

But above all, China did very well by human development. Long-run calculations of Human Development Index (HDI) have been made by Nicholas Crafts. For China and India he has estimates for 1950, 1973 and 1992 (Table 9.2). The World Bank's Human Development Report (HDR) has over the various years published trends in countries' HDIs from 1960 onward. Its methodology has evolved over the years and so the estimates have also been revised even for earlier years. Using the 1997 HDR and the 2002 HDR we can see the trend up to 2002. The HDR estimates start in 1960 and are not strictly comparable to Crafts' estimates, but they are close enough.

Table 9.2 Human development indices, 1950–2000

	1950	1960	1973	1980a	1980b	1992	2000
China	0.163	0.248	0.407	0.475	0.554	0.594	0.726
India	0.160	0.206	0.289	0.296	0.434	0.439	0.577

Sources: Crafts (1997) for 1950, 1973 and 1992; United Nations Development Programme, *Human Development Report (HDR)* (1997) for 1960 and 1980a; and *HDR* (2002) for 1980b and 2000.

Thus we see that despite having similar HDIs in 1950, China had left India behind by 1973, even with similar per capita incomes. Over the fifty-year period, while the HDIs are not strictly comparable, China enhanced its HDI four-and-a-half times while India did so only three-and-a-half times. Taking the estimates for 1950, 1980b and 2000, we see that in the first thirty years, China advanced much faster – by three-and-a-half times – than in the last twenty years – only by a third more. India on the other hand took its HDI up two-and-three-quarter times between 1950 and 1980 and again by a third in the next twenty years. Some writers have argued that the slowing down of China's advance in human development was due to the disbanding of the communes and with it the downgrading of the health care facilities available to all.[20] On the other hand, the closer a country's HDI comes to the limit of 1.0, the harder each step becomes. Whichever way we look at it, China has done much better in human development than India.

While there may be an argument about the state of health care facilities in China after the Deng reforms were launched, it is in other dimensions that China kept on doing well. Its emphasis on education for all from early on paid handsome dividends, while education remains a blot on India's record. Here again the centralist versus federal polity makes a lot of difference. Social conditions differ immensely across India in terms of caste structures, religious influence and superstitions. Hinduism is not an egalitarian religion even in theory and Islam, at least in India, is not so in practice.[21] It is only when you go south where the influence of Christian missions was felt and social movements against the caste system were successful in the early twentieth century that you witness an improvement in human development statistics. India continues to pay a heavy price for its neglect of education, especially as it concerns women.[22]

The first phase, despite the differences in approach to agrarian transformation and human development, altered the relative positions of China and India from what they were in 1950, but not by much. By 1978, per capita income of China was M$979 and of India M$966. China had caught up with India over the thirty years, but not dramatically surpassed it. Agricultural productivity per worker was almost identical in 1975 in the two countries – China 2.3 and India 1.9 (relative to the United States =

---

20 Dreze and Sen (1989).

21 The distinguished French anthropologist Louis Dumont has celebrated India's inegalitarianism in his *Homo Hierarchicus* as well as other books (see Dumont, 1980).

22 The usual exception in India is of course Kerala, which shows what can be achieved even in a democratic society by committed public action. Kerala has had the benefit of a democratically elected Communist government ever since the mid-1950s. But historically Travancore Cochin, which was the native state in what became Kerala, had higher literacy rates even by the 1940s than its surrounding British India districts. Matriarchy and Christianity plus an enlightened ruler played their role here.

100).[23] One may ask why this was so. Why is it that China did not do much better than India despite its revolutionary effort in industry and agriculture and its immense achievements in education and poverty reduction. There are two responses to that question.

One, of course, is that it did. China's income doubled while India's only went up by 50 per cent. Of course, China had suffered from the ravages of foreign and civil war through the fifteen years since Japan's invasion of Manchuria in 1933. So its per capita income in 1950 was below its potential. But even then we must acknowledge that China's growth was not smooth. While it was rapid, China's growth suffered from the tendency of Mao to take immense risks and plunge the economy into catastrophes. I am personalising the problem because Mao was a dominant influence in China to an extent that Nehru never was. This is where a totalitarian system can differ from a democratic one. It can accelerate growth and mobilise immense resources, but if the direction is wrong it can also crash and waste an awful lot of resources in a short period of time. But added to that, the political culture of China has been long used to such imperial power, while India has been a much less commandable polity. Thus Mao plunged China into the Great Leap Forward as well as the Great Proletarian Cultural Revolution (GPCR), with the structure of centralised and personalised power which led to the catastrophic famine of 1962. China paid a price for this in terms of death, starvation and wasted resources in abandoned projects. Much human capital, of both university teachers and students, was revalorised during the GPCR.

India, by comparison, had its muddle and mess but no great discontinuities in its development experience. It had a multiparty system and even within the Congress Party had antagonistic factions, which could mobilise opposition to Nehru. Even before his death, Nehru was forced to abandon his preferred policy of cooperatives in agriculture by the farmers' leader Charan Singh, but then besides Nehru no one else in the Congress took cooperative agriculture seriously and had done nothing about it since the Agrarian Reforms Committee of the Congress proposed it in 1949. The Second Five-Year Plan had to be modified due to resource shortages, but the Third Five-Year Plan kept to the same basic strategy. During the 1960s, India went through what was known (in a Maoist parody) as the Three Twos – death of two prime ministers, two harvest failures and two wars. There was a policy reversal in agriculture when the High Yield

23 Maddison *et al.* (2002).

Variety programme was adopted. In addition, rural and regional political bosses asserted their hold over the Congress Party and displaced the urban Westernised elite after Nehru's death, but they in turn were displaced after 1969 when Mrs Gandhi regained control of the Congress. India also had to devalue its currency and felt the heat of the US and World Bank disapproval. Yet the economic strategy did not (sadly) change. The crisis of slow growth came in 1975 when in face of popular unrest, Mrs Gandhi was driven to suspend democracy and declare the Emergency. But that did not last long, proving yet again that India cannot be commanded by centralised and personalised power.[24]

The Second Phase

It was China, after 1978 under the influence of Deng, that accelerated, leaving India far behind. In the next thirty-five years China's per capita income more than trebled while that of India merely doubled. The logic of compound growth rates is pitiless, and China's per capita income is now almost double that of India. How did China do this?

China did this paradoxically by adopting a much more 'capitalist road' or Bukharinist strategy[25] than any other communist regime (the former Yugoslavia included). What is more, China adopted a road that India could always have adopted; indeed, this was possible right after independence except that no one, not even the Indian capitalists, were advocating greater import of foreign capital, opening up the economy to an export orientation, with Special Export Zones (SEZs).[26] While India went on restricting its large native capitalist class after independence, China had to practically reinvent its own bourgeoisie after 1978. Indeed according to a newspaper story cited by Dharma Kumar,[27] China, which had invented an examination system for the selection of bureaucrats in the mists of time, approached India in the 1980s to seek its guidance about conducting examinations for its civil servants on the lines of the Union Public Service Commission (UPSC) exams in India.

Of course, China's policy revolution was not seamless and Deng had to struggle to establish his hegemony. There is a debate among China scholars about the fang/shou (stop-go) cycle in Deng's reforms between 1978 and

24 Desai (1975).

25 For those old enough to recall these arcane labels.

26 In China's case, the SEZs are not all that different from the foreign concessions in ports which were so much resented before 1949.

27 Kumar (1998).

1989.[28] But once established, his control over policy was absolute; the political culture's habit of obedience to emperors helped.[29] Deng transformed agriculture by introducing the Family Responsibility System – privatisation Chinese Communist style. He then took on the industrial sector and opened it up to foreign capital while making room for the growth of village and local enterprises. He left the public sector enterprises untouched but slowly brought modern methods of fiscal and financial control to China. China had to introduce property rights and contract laws which India has had since Macaulay in British times.

India meanwhile also started to jettison some of its own orthodoxies, but the personality in power was still the same. Mrs Gandhi abandoned the fetish of national self-sufficiency and began to borrow abroad, from the IMF to begin with. She, however, changed little else in the dirigiste logic of Indian economic policy. The collapse of India's textile industry was symptomatic of the malaise. Within thirty-five years of independence, India had managed to bankrupt its once globally competitive industry. Freed from the constraint of food grain availability thanks to the Green Revolution, India did not manage to apply to its industrial sector the lessons learnt in its agricultural revolution – that is, to use foreign knowledge, rely on the dynamic private sector and deploy subsidies selectively. Instead, foreign borrowing was used to ease the consumption constraint in the public sector and to cushion lossmaking public enterprises. Ian Little and Vijay Joshi (1994) argue in their book on Indian economic reforms that Indian policymaking alternates between five-year spurts of radicalism then quiescence, flaring up under political or economic pressures.[30]

India really changed course only after the shock of 1991 when it was nearly bankrupt and had foreign reserves which would cover only two weeks' imports. But in changing the same personalities were involved as in the old dirigiste regime. Manmohan Singh as Finance Minister was crucial to the reform, but he was no Deng and neither was Narasimha Rao, who was prime minister 1991–96. Indeed, by 1994, India began to reveal its reluctance about economic liberalisation. Ever since, India has been reforming its economy, but in a much more embattled way than China. Given the nature of the political culture, reform can only be introduced by broad

28 See Baum (1994) and Shirk (1993).

29 After all, the establishment of Imperial authority had to go through such transition periods throughout Chinese history, but to support that claim will take me too far away from my theme as well as my competence.

30 Joshi and Little (1994).

consent, and all the potential losers (many of whom are in power) have to be bribed (sometimes literally so) to advance matters.

Thus, while China has received a lot of foreign capital, India has not. By 1998, Maddison's calculations show that foreign direct investment (FDI) per capita in China was US$183 and in India US$14. Even if a lot of China's FDI was due to the Chinese diaspora, it only shows the failure of India to attract its own diaspora to invest, in spite of a lot of trying. Indeed, India has sought portfolio capital more than FDI since suspicion of foreigners remains strong, not only among India's politicians but even more among its capitalists. There has been some change for the better in the five years under the government of the Bharatiya Janata Party (BJP) and its National Democratic Alliance, but there is a long way to go.[31] There are other more usual reasons for the difference in economic performance. For one, China's savings rate is almost 50 per cent of GDP, nearly twice that of India. Indeed given the higher savings rate in China plus the FDI influx, the growth rates are less far apart than should be the case. India averaged 5.5 per cent in the 1980s and around 6.5 per cent in the 1990s. Even at 7–9 per cent, China's growth rate implies inefficient use of capital barring gross measurement errors. Or it could indicate sharply diminishing returns to capital, but I doubt that given that a lot of FDI embodies the latest knowledge.

The reason may be that in both countries there is a large public sector where enterprises are seriously loss making. Both countries are wedded to Soviet-style emphasis on inputs rather than outputs and accumulation for its own sake. India had begun to shed some of these traits and has always had a smaller public sector than China. So the waste of resources by malinvestment[32] is larger in China. In both countries, there is also a budget deficit which is out of control; perhaps more so in India due to the exigencies of democratic and coalitional politics, as well as weak central control over provincial budgets.

The two countries have mobilised savings through their financial structures, but the mobilisation has left the financial sectors in fragile states. Nonperforming assets in the banking systems as well as the nonbank financial sector (international trade and investment corporations in China) indicate a problem ahead. India has failed to impose arm's-length regulatory regimes free of politics and the result has been fraud and corruption in

31 For recent restructuring efforts in the organised private sector in India, see Forbes, N. (2002) in *Doing Business in India: What Has Liberalisation Changed?* (ed. by Krueger, 2002).

32 An old fashioned Hayekian word.

equity market-related activities – Unit Trust of India (UTI), stock market scams of Harshad Mehta, and so on.

It is difficult to predict whether a combination of budget deficits, domestic debt and financial sector weakness will cause a major crisis in either country. Both have managed to run their external accounts fairly well. Their reserve positions are healthy, exchange rate policy – pegged to the dollar in China and a dirty float in India – are prudent. India has moved faster to full capital convertibility in recent years while financial sector reforms have yet to be fully undertaken. China has not moved as far with convertibility but its peg to the dollar may cause problems if the dollar weakens to any significant extent. India's foreign liabilities are more weighted toward the short run and portfolio end, while China has a larger FDI flow. The Asian crisis reminded us that even sound macroeconomic performance is no guarantee against a run on the currency if the markets suspect a mismatch between internal and external balance. Here it is India which is more fragile than China.

Speculations and Counterfactuals

I now turn to some very broad and highly speculative considerations. Having looked at China and India over the years since 1820 against a longer background, it is worth exploring a longer future. What follows is even more my own view than what has been said so far. In a *longue durée* perspective, the present strong relative position of China can be attributed to the radical changes there since 1978, thanks to Deng. Of course the foundations laid in the first phase wherein China doubled its per capita income obviously helped. But the similarities in their respective per capita incomes in 1980 merely reflects the longer history of the two countries. *A priori*, there is no reason why China should have opened such a large distance in such a short period of time. This is especially so because as I have already remarked earlier, China adopted a policy which it was always possible for India to adopt. Indeed anyone looking at the two countries at any time between 1950 and 1975 could have thought that India had a better capitalist infrastructure as well as commercial culture than China had. The diasporas of both China and India have always been adept at commercial activity so there is nothing in Chinese or Indian culture as such which could make a difference. The difference arises out of the political and institutional differences inside the country and these are very much short run and changeable.

Can China Combine Capitalism with One Party Rule?

China appears to have been able to separate the political institutions of a Leninist state with single party dominance from its economic imperative of state ownership of all means of production. This is unique in the political economy of modern times. The transition is not yet fully complete as there is still a lot of central control over economic life and a large state-owned sector. It would be a bold person who could predict how far China could go in this separation. Thus could one have a fully capitalist or even a largely capitalist economy with a Leninist state? This is not the same as market socialism but more like state capitalism, although the word has now been much maligned in the polemics on the left. When Lenin spoke of state capitalism, he had the German war economy during the First World War in mind – a private ownership economy run in a centralised fashion.[33] The Chinese version of state capitalism could in the limit amount to private diffuse ownership with single party monopoly of political power. Is this feasible or likely?

Normally we associate rise of democracy with a prosperous middle class with plenty of 'bourgeois' elements. A private ownership economy is bound to require a lot of economic freedom and as we are all crude materialists in this matter, we associate economic freedom with political liberties. While there is some opening out in the direction of separation of powers in some local jurisdictions,[34] it is difficult to envisage separation of powers in the absence of multiparty democracy with free elections and a possibility of change of the party in power. China's experiment is thus one of the most interesting episodes in modern political economy. Will China be able to sustain one-party rule with a private enterprise economy? Is state capitalism feasible in peaceful post-revolutionary times?

The implicit Chinese answer seems to be that if the Chinese Communist Party (CCP) delivers on fast and sustained economic growth while restructuring the economy continuously in a capitalist direction, then the CCP monopoly on political power will become feasible with limited concessions such as separation of powers but no party competition. Marxian and every other political economy says that this is not easy, even not possible.[35] Economic freedom will spill over into demands for political freedom. Even authoritarian governments – that is, noncommunist dictatorships – have been

33 Desai (2002a).

34 For example, SEZs in China such as Shenzen.

35 See Moore (1971) and Desai (2002a).

unable to sustain a monopoly on political power with developed capitalism. Leninist state formations in Europe collapsed along with their economic forms. Apart from China, only North Korea and Cuba remain as major non-capitalist economies and non-liberal democratic polities. Can China defy the so-called laws of historical materialism (or even cross section growth regressions of new political economy) and avoid the transition to democracy?

One particular problem in this respect relates to the legal framework. While civil and political liberties can be curtailed, once you grant property rights certain liberalising consequences inevitably follow, as any eighteenth-century political economist will tell you. Thus, the Communist Party *qua* contractor or buyer and seller of property cannot be above the law. There has to be accountability and auditing, legal sanctions and punishments for non-delivery or non-performance. From this requirement follows the need to have law courts and a legal profession which enjoy a certain degree of immunity from the perennial habits of communist parties to bully if not liquidate all those who disagree with them. An independent legal profession needs further freedoms of speech and association and so on. It is this compulsion to establish a rule of law which will be crucial for China. In a fascinating and detailed study of the growth of the rule of law in China, Peerenboom makes the following observation:

> In the end, however, a transition to democracy is likely to be necessary to overcome the [Communist] Party's legitimacy deficiencies, to address accountability issues, and to reduce growing social cleavages. It is possible that over time the Party could stave off extinction by transforming itself into a Social Democratic party. The Party could well gain support of its citizenry if in the next decade it is able to reduce corruption to a tolerable level and to sustain economic growth while dealing with such pressing problems as SOE [state-owned enterprise] reforms, reform of the banking and financial sectors, and the need to establish a social security system and to clean up the environment. It could further broaden its appeal by gradually relaxing its grip on society and allowing citizens greater, albeit still limited, freedom of speech, assembly, and association. In short, it could adopt a more communitarian approach. If it does not, and elections are held, it could very well lose out to the party that does adopt such an approach, all else being equal.[36]

36 Peerenboom (2002, p. 572–3).

This is a tall order for any country much less China. Indeed India itself has not eliminated corruption nor reformed its banking and financial sectors. But people will tolerate corruption if they can throw the corrupt out of office, even if this exit is only through a revolving door. Democracies coexist with all sorts of imperfections and can indeed even withstand a lot of misery unlike authoritarian regimes, as the fate of the USSR in face of the stagflation crisis of the 1970s showed in contrast to Western economies. What Mrs Thatcher could do to the British economy, Brezhnev, Chernenko or Gorbachev could not. So China does not have to make things perfect if it can only grant bourgeois freedoms to its people. If not it has to be better than the most perfect democracy. Can China find its way out of this paradox?

My interim answer to this is that the odds are stacked against China being able to do this. Not that it is impossible or even unlikely but the odds are not favourable. There is one major reason for this, for which I appeal to Chinese history. This is China's inability to handle dissent and defiance of central rule without a lot of damage. The episodes of the Taiping and Boxer Rebellions in the Imperial era and GPCR, as well as the 1989 troubles which were not confined just to Tiananmen, show that China is fragile if not brittle when it comes to dissent. In the next ten years, China will be adjusting to economic restructuring in response to the demands of the World Trade Organization (WTO), as well as facing up to global media exposure due to the 2008 Olympic Games. It will be an open invitation to human rights movements and Falun Gong to expose the regime to international scrutiny. Moscow's experience of the 1980 Olympic Games proved crucial in the way the Soviet Union collapsed. What about China?

I expect China to survive as a powerful economy, but after a short period of political turbulence on the lines of the Taiping Rebellion or GPCR. China will be forced to make a political transition as profound as the Eastern European states did with their economies. The final shape will be a more democratic China, but it may not necessarily be a liberal democratic Western-type regime. There are after all living examples of 'less-than-liberal' democracies – Singapore, Taiwan, Malaysia – which China can follow. You can have a multiparty democracy with a single party dominance as in Mexico and Japan, and India till 1989. One can also have dual power as in Iran, with the Ayatollahs vying for control with a democratically elected power. There are many choices on the way to a full transition to liberal democracy.

Can India Catch Up with China?

India has problems about delivering strong, focused government pursuing a single objective with total commitment. Its great achievement is to have constructed the world's most populous democracy against all the odds – illiteracy, multiple languages and religions, racial and social heterogeneity. There have been spurts of committed action – in the mid-1950s when the Second Five-Year Plan was formulated, in the early 1970s when Mrs Gandhi pursued her anti-poverty programme, in the mid-1980s when Rajiv Gandhi pushed the import liberalisation policy harder, the early 1990s with Narasimha Rao and Manmohan Singh liberalising the economy, and finally in the last five years when the reform process has been kept up rather than reversed as many had feared. The average growth rate has gone up from 3.5 per cent in the 1970s to 5.5 per cent in the 1980s and now to 6.5 per cent in the past decade.

India has also achieved another miracle relative to many post-colonial societies. It has maintained its territorial integrity, unlike for example Pakistan. It has not had a civil war, unlike Nigeria or Sri Lanka, and while multiethnic federations such as the former Yugoslavia and the USSR have broken up, India has not. This has absorbed resources as India has had to fight subnationalisms in the northeast Nagaland, in Panjab with Khalistan, and in Kashmir with international subversion added to internal dissension. It has had communal strife between Hindus and Muslims, Hindus and Sikhs, between caste Hindus and Untouchables/dalits and so on. It has also faced class-based revolts in Telangana in the 1940s, in West Bengal, Andhra Pradesh and Bihar with the Naxalites. Through all this it has survived as a democratic open society based on consensus and debate. Life is about more than per capita income and its growth.

For India any hope of growing faster depends on less government rather than more, on harnessing the private sector entrepreneurial talent which has always been there but was stifled for a long time. This requires a less interventionist government but also a better regulatory regime. India's bane is the politicisation of all aspects of economic life and the difficulty of constructing an arm's-length regulatory regime free of political interference. This is because of and despite its democratic politics.[37] Thus even after a major stock market fraud or the mishandling of Unit Trust of India (UTI) customers' investments, there has been little by way of punishment.

37 Desai (2002b).

Indeed, a large number of financial scandals have thousands of victims but no culprits convicted.[38] One cannot expect a flourishing private enterprise culture in the absence of trust and effective regulation. Thus a black economy, smuggling and criminalisation of financial markets flourish. Depoliticisation of the economy, therefore, remains a challenge. This is the same challenge as the more frequent complaint about control of the budget deficit, because the deficit is due to the compulsions of consensual politics with a coalition government and weak powers over regions.

What then are the chances for India that we may see a strong effective government emerge at the centre with effective fiscal control over its own budget as well as the budgets of states and an ability to depoliticise regulatory structures? Herein lies the deep dilemma of the Indian polity. India was set up after independence as a federal polity because of the awareness of the first generation of leaders of the difficulty of holding the various linguistic and religious groups together. Indian nationhood was defined as unity in diversity. But lately a new, more Unitarian construction of Indian nationhood has been advanced by the forces of *Hindutva* nationalism. Thus far, it has been muted in its approach, but is also quite successful. If in the forthcoming months and years the Unitarian approach were to be pursued harder and if it was to be electorally successful, then India may emerge simultaneously as a nonsecular, majority Hindu polity with single party dominance by the BJP and its parivar. The advocates of *Hindutva* often cite Israel as their ideal example.

Historically, modernity in India was supposed to come with a secular and perhaps even socialist society. This was certainly Nehru's ideal, as well as practice, and at least the rhetoric if not practice for the two Gandhis. But the events of the last ten years or so raise the serious possibility that modernity in India will come with a Hindu or religious rather than secular as well as a capitalist dispensation. It is conceivable that such a Unitarian nationalism may accelerate growth by following a more liberal policy. But it is also likely to lead to greater social disharmony. Of course a majoritarian rule of the largest religious group is possible with non-discrimination of the minorities, but in the Indian context and given the history, it is not very likely.

38 See *India Today* (2003) for a recent list.

Conclusion

My own view is that India will remain a soft state, a consensual polity, and it will not be capable of sustained growth at the sort of rates which China has attained. To stay a stable, peaceful society, India has to be a muddle and a mess. It is a miracle that proceeding in the way it has done, it has come as far as it has done, trebling its per capita income. But there will not be growth convergence between China and India.[39] India and China will both remove poverty in their midst and cease to be bywords for misery that they had become for 150 years after 1820. China will again become a viable Great Power; India may become just a Great Democracy.

References

Adeney, Katherine, 2003, 'Federal Formations and Consociational Stabilisation: The Politics of Identity Articulation and Ethnic Conflict Regulation in India and Pakistan' (Ph.D. dissertation; London: University of London).

Baum, Richard, 1994, *Burying Mao* (Princeton, NJ: Princeton University Press).

Crafts, Nicholas, 1997, 'The Human Development Index and Changes in Standards of Living: Some Historical Comparisons', *European Review of Economic History*, Vol. 1, pp. 299–322.

Deng, Kent G., 2000, 'A Critical Survey of Recent Research in Chinese Economic History', *Economic History Review*, Vol. LIII, No. 1 (February).

Desai, Meghnad, 2002a, *Marx's Revenge: The Resurgence of Capitalism and the Death of State Socialism* (London: Verso).

Desai, Meghnad, 2002b, 'Democracy and Development: India 1947–2002', presented at the K. R. Narayanan Lecture (Canberra: Australia South Asia Research Centre, The Australian National University).

Desai, Meghnad, 2000, 'Communalism, Secularism and the Dilemma of Indian Nationhood', in *Asian Nationalism*, ed. by Michael Leifer (London: Routledge).

Desai, Meghnad, 1975, 'Contradictions of Slow Capitalist Development', in *Explosion in a Sub-Continent*, ed. by Robin Blackburn (London: Viking Penguin).

Dreze, Jean, and Amartya Kumar Sen, 1989, *Hunger and Public Action* (Oxford: Oxford University Press).

Dumont, Louis, 1980, *Homo Hierarchicus* (Chicago: University of Chicago Press).

Forbes, Naushad, 2002, 'Doing Business in India: What Has Liberalization Changed?' in *Economic Policy Reforms and the Indian Economy*, ed. by Anne O. Krueger (Chicago: The University of Chicago Press).

Habib, Irfan, 1995, *Essays in Indian History: Towards a Marxist Perception* (New Delhi: Tulika).

Habib, Irfan, 1983, 'Marx's Perception of India', *The Marxist*, Vol. 1, No. 1 (July–September) and reprinted in Irfan Habib, 1995, *Essays in Indian History: Towards a Marxist Perception* (New Delhi: Tulika).

Habib, Irfan, 1971, 'Potentialities of Capitalist Development in the Economy of Mughal India', *Enquiry*, New Series (Winter).

39 Except unless China has a long breakdown in its transition to democracy.

Heston, Alan, 1983, 'National Income', in *The Cambridge Economic History of India, Volume 2, c.1757–c.1970*, ed. by Dharma Kumar and Meghnad Desai (Cambridge: Cambridge University Press).

Inden, Ronald B., 2000, *Imagining India* (London: Hurst, 2nd edn).

Joshi, Vijay, and I. M. D. Little, 1994, *India: Macroeconomics and Political Economy, 1964–1991* (New Delhi: Oxford University Press).

Keay, John, 2001, *India: A History* (London: HarperCollins).

Krueger, Anne O., ed., 2002, *Economic Policy Reforms and the Indian Economy* (Chicago: The University of Chicago Press).

Kumar, Dharma, 1998, 'The Chinese and Indian Economies, 1914–1949', in *Colonialism, Property and the State*, ed. by Dharma Kumar (New Delhi: Oxford University Press).

Kumar, Dharma, and Meghnad Desai, eds, 1983, *The Cambridge Economic History of India, Volume 2: c.1757–c.1970* (Cambridge: Cambridge University Press).

Maddison, Angus, 2001, *The World Economy: A Millennial Perspective* (Paris: Development Centre Studies, Organization for Economic Cooperation and Development).

Maddison, Angus, D. S. Prasada Rao, and W. F. Shepherd, eds, 2002, *The Asian Economies in the Twentieth Century* (Cheltenham, UK: Edward Elgar Publishing).

Moore, Barrington Jr, 1971, *Social Origins of Dictatorship and Democracy* (London: Allen Lane).

Myrdal, Gunnar, 1968, *Asian Drama: An Inquiry into the Poverty of Nations* (New York: Pantheon).

Needham, Joseph *et al.*, 1954, *Science and Civilisation in China* (various volumes) (Cambridge: Cambridge University Press).

Nehru, Jawaharlal, 1946, *The Discovery of India* (Calcutta: Signet Press, 1st edn).

O'Leary, Brendan, 1989, *The Asiatic Mode of Production: Oriental Despotism, Historical Materialism, and Indian History* (Oxford and New York: Basil Blackwell).

Peerenboom, Randall, 2002, *China's Long March Toward Rule of Law* (Cambridge: Cambridge University Press).

Shirk, Susan L., 1993, *The Political Logic of Economic Reform in China* (Berkeley: University of California Press).

Spence, Jonathan *et al.*, 1999, *The Search for Modern China: A Documentary Collection* (New York: W.W. Norton and Company, 2nd edn).

United Nations Development Programme, *Human Development Report* (various years) (New York and Oxford: Oxford University Press).

Wittfogel, Karl A., 1957, *Oriental Despotism: A Comparative Study of Total Power* (New Haven, CT: Yale University Press).

Acknowledgement

First publication: Desai, Meghnad (2005) 'India and China: An Essay in Comparative Political Economy' in *India's and China's Recent Experience with Reform and Growth*, edited by W. Tseng and D. Cowen, Procyclicality of Financial Systems in Asia. London, Palgrave Macmillan, pp. 1–22. Republished with kind permission of Palgrave Macmillan.

Chapter 10

THE VASE AND THE MUDPIE

Meghnad Desai

(2009/2010)

Forty years or so ago, Henry Kissinger observed wryly that if only India and China could feed themselves, all the world's problems would be solved. As usual, he was wrong. India and China have solved the problem of growing enough food grains, even if India has not quite managed to feed everyone. However, most of the world's problems are still to be solved. Ironically, the basket cases of Kissinger's time in the 1960s are the new hope for a world mired in the aftermath of a severe recession and financial crisis. In Copenhagen, the possibility of a global compact depended on whether China and India would play ball with G1 – the USA. Every other country just disappeared off the scene, almost like children frightened when they see their parents quarrel.

China and India are two of the world's oldest civilisations and have been in roughly the same form for the last 4000 years or so. China has also been a single state for most of that time while India became a nation-state for the first time in 1947.[1] However, they began their journey towards becoming modern nations simultaneously in the late 1940s. For the first twenty-five years after that, each had a strong ideological bias in their development strategy. China had Mao's version of the Bolshevik developmental state with drastic land reforms and forced industrialisation that plunged the economy into the worst famine it had faced, when 20 million Chinese people died. Yet, despite that, China in 1975 was more pro-poor in its development and had become a significant military power as well. India had a milder social

1 I have discussed this in greater detail in *The Rediscovery of India* (Penguin India, 2009).

democratic version of the Soviet disease, thanks to Jawaharlal Nehru. It, too, began to industrialise but the land reforms it undertook were mild. Nehru's major achievement was making India a democracy. His economic legacy was a low-growth rate, which his ideologically tougher daughter took still lower. The poor were sorely neglected. However, India too, like China, emerged as a nation with nuclear capability. In short, if the choice was guns or butter, both India and China were in no doubt: the choice was guns over butter.

* * *

Mao's death in 1975 gave his old associate Deng Xiaoping the chance to make a 180-degree turn in development strategy. Marxist/Maoist ideologue that he was, Deng soon became a pragmatic realist. He foresaw the sclerosis of the Soviet Union and the vibrancy of Taiwan and Hong Kong in achieving a high level of income. So he reversed the commune system and inaugurated private land leases. He also opened the economy to foreign investment and later gave the domestic private sector its head by establishing Special Economic Zones where capitalism could flourish.

The result was spectacular: three decades of double-digit growth. China – potentially, if not actually – has now come to be regarded as the world's second-largest economy. This goal has been achieved by following a path well laid down by Japan and then South Korea – the Standard East Asian Developmental model, as it were. This involves over-saving and under-consumption, export orientation and directed industrialisation, a model first perfected by Japan in the 1960s and 1970s when it was regarded as a miracle economy. In the 1970s and 1980s, South Korea followed the same path.

In 1975, India and China had a roughly equal per capita income.[2] Now, thirty-five years later, China's GDP stands at US$4.33 trillion while India's is US$1.22 trillion. With similar populations, China's per capita income is three-and-a-half-times that of India. The gap is only partially explained by the contrast between a democratic and a totalitarian polity. India did not change its path drastically till 1991, though some hesitant steps were taken by Rajiv Gandhi during his early years as prime minister. Like Deng, it was Dr Manmohan Singh, steeped in the orthodoxy of the muddled

2 I have surveyed the 500-year-old parallel history of the two economies in my 'China and India' in the IMF collection, *China and India Growth and Reform Processes*.

Nehru-Gandhi ideology of state-led development, who was able to escape the old mould. This was perhaps also due to the accident that, for the first time in twenty-five years, India had as prime minister someone who was not also a member of the Nehru-Gandhi dynasty.[3]

For India, moving to a more liberal market-oriented regime was not as much of a shock as a return to the earlier days of development. In the ninety years between 1857–1947, India had acquired a modern industrial structure and a lively entrepreneurial community, the largest in any colonial country. However, the nationalist movement was in an anti-capitalist phase in the 1930s, thanks to the Great Depression. After independence, Nehru neglected – if not distrusted – the private sector while his daughter was positively hostile to it. India, thus, wasted forty years after independence reinventing the wheel. The result was the low 'Hindu' rate of growth until 1980, which only marginally improved in the 1980s.

* * *

As we examine the economic and political dimensions of their growth, the question often asked now is about the future trajectory of the two countries. Let us first take a look at the economy. Most analysts simply project the recent trends into the indefinite future and this makes China speed ahead of India, as well as every other nation in the world. But history, one must remember, is not linear. If nothing else, the latest crisis, as well as the trajectory of these two nations over the last sixty years, should warn us against this fallacy. Again, the experience of Japan shows us that growth engines can slow down and stagnate. Thus we need to take care in projecting future growth scenarios.

In political futurology, many analysts see China as making a necessary transition to a Western-style liberal democracy.[4] This is based on the same crude version of economic determinism that used to be capsulated as Windmills – Feudalism, Watermills – Capitalism. The idea is that economic growth leads to the growth of a middle class that demands democracy. Or

3 I have argued that had Lal Bahadur Shastri lived and been prime minister for longer, India may have transited to a better model of development sooner. *The Rediscovery of India*, op. cit.

4 See my debate with Will Hutton, 'Does the Future Really Belong to China', in *Prospect Magazine*, no. 130, January 14 2007, https://www.prospectmagazine.co.uk/magazine/doesthefuturereallybelongtochina.

an assumption that, without democracy, China cannot progress much further. Again, if anyone wants to doubt such crude determinism, one only has to look at India, which adopted democracy before growth.

Let us set both these simple models aside. In a sense, both India and China will face severe challenges at home and abroad and each will require leadership of a high calibre to meet them. The three issues that need to be addressed, therefore, are: Is there a capacity for reform within the system? Is the economic growth sustainable? Can we take political stability for granted?

* * *

Since it has to be consensual, a persistent problem that plagues India is the slow pace of economic reform. Even if we grant that the latest election results indicate the end of the era of political fragmentation and the possibility that a stable Congress-dominated coalition will rule for the next ten years, the high hopes entertained by many – especially abroad – that sans the Left, the UPA will charge ahead with liberal reforms has been belied. The fact is that in India, the entire political system – not just the Congress – has a moderate left bias and a fear of the market. Few leaders are willing to openly admit that the growth experience of the last eighteen years has been good for the country as a whole, even for the poor. This is why, even though liberal reform is urgently needed, it has to take place by stealth in the guise of technical improvements, or in a halting manner.

India's rural economy has 60 per cent of the population but produces only 20 per cent of output. Low productivity translates into endemic poverty. The need is to industrialise faster with large factories that can employ 10,000 or 20,000 workers, as in Malaysia and China. Only then will the rural under-employed get round-the-year jobs that can use their unskilled or semi-skilled manual labour. This requires land to be freed for building large factories and a reform of the labour laws that makes hiring and firing more flexible in large establishments. Presently, the difficulty of these issues in factories of 100 employees and above has led to a proliferation of small high and medium-tech industrial establishments outside the organised sector. India's manufacturing sector has stagnated at around 25 per cent in its share of the GDP.

Vitally needed reforms of labour law and land markets, needed to speed up industrialisation and growth, will not be easy to deliver. Tata's experience in

Singur, West Bengal, illustrated this vividly: the Left-Right labels do not work any longer. Parties in power want change, but opposition parties are against change. With coalition politics still the norm at State and central levels, obstruction is easier to accomplish than change. This will remain a challenge for India until a clear mandate for change is won by some political party.

China's problem, on the other hand, is a combination of timidity and the overbearing power of its leadership. Even where the system needs change and the leadership can see the need, it is too cautious to make it lest it leads to yet another Tiananmen. The issue of some sort of pluralism – let alone democracy – haunts the leadership. It is not that China needs to move fast forward to liberal democracy. Its need is for pluralism and tolerance of dissent. Even inner party democracy remains a tough nut to crack.[5] China has many paths for greater pluralism – Singapore, Malaysia, Korea and Japan themselves offer many models of limited pluralism. Even Iran, with the control of the theologians over the parliamentary democracy, would be an apt model for the Chinese Communist Party to study. With increasing episodes of dissidence and the ever-present threat of the internet, Chinese leadership is showing less than its usual command over its polity.

* * *

Both India and China managed to weather the recession very well with only a slight slowdown in growth rate of GDP. Between the two, China's reflationary package was larger than any other country's and concentrated mainly on infrastructure. China had to redirect its economy away from exports since its markets in the OECD countries were in recession. It needs to shift away from an over-saving/under-consumption model to a better balance between domestic consumption and exports. Yet, when devising its reflation strategy, China chose the easy way out of concentrating on infrastructure since the pace can be dictated from above. This has led to excess capacity in the steel, cement and other capital goods sectors. Along with China's insistence that it will not revalue its currency, this also shows that there is a great deal of conservatism in China's economic management.

5 See 'Democracy in China: Control Freaks', *The Economist*, 19 December 2009–January 2010.

Again, China's growth strategy is excessively capital intensive. With around 50 per cent of saving and another 5 per cent in FDI, China achieves 10–11 per cent GDP growth. India saves around 35 per cent plus a small amount of FDI 2–3 per cent achieves 8–9 per cent growth. Thus China's Incremental Capital Output ratio is nearer five while India's is four. In this respect, China is reminiscent of the USSR, which had an input-driven model of growth and which collapsed. China's growth will not collapse, but unless it becomes more efficient in the use of resources, it may find it difficult to keep the growth rate up.

India has a domestic market-led growth model and it is also driven, by and large, by its private sector (though few in Delhi will admit this.) [China's capitalist class to a significant extent comprises the cronies of the Communist Party who have been sold public property at throwaway prices.] India is also equipped with a better macroeconomic policy since it is not excessively risk averse. India's problem is that the government is still a large borrower and a burden on the domestic savings. This leads to high interest rates and corporations find it difficult to raise money cheaply. However, divestment is proceeding far too slowly and it will again be some time before the budget deficit is back under control.

By and large, the Indian state does many things it should not (own banks and industrial enterprises) while not doing what it should. Thus its investment in primary and secondary education and public health lags behind even Third World averages. This is due to an elite preference for state enterprises where jobs are well paid and secure and also a weakness in governance as education is split between the centre and the states, and excessively politicised at each level. India has a demographic dividend relative to China but it may yet dissipate it due to its failure to get the state out of what it should not and into plugging urgent gaps in the human resource infrastructure.

* * *

India has survived twenty years of a fragmented political party system, which led to short-lived unstable governments mixed with some episodes of stability. Now with the UPA back into power, although still in a coalition, India has learnt to live with this somewhat costly but inclusive model of democracy. The slow growth of the first forty years after independence has built up massive demands from the many excluded non-elite groups. The more numerous of these groups – OBCs and dalits – have taken to the electoral path to get their share of the public resources. The result has been Mandal and further demands for positive discrimination in entry to higher education and government jobs. Yet there are still the numerically small but excluded communities, mainly in tribal areas where arid or hilly regions make agriculture unsustainable. It is in these areas that the Naxalite movement has gained strength. The challenge to the Indian democratic system is that its inclusive model has to reach beyond the electoral mode and find ways of re-enfranchising communities numerically too weak to work the electoral system for a defence of their own interests. They have been deprived of access to collective common property by the established system even sometimes under the excuse of development, not to say, socialism.

India is not faced with any threat of a Balkanisation. There are movements for the new states to be created, new identities to get recognition. But all this is routine democratic politics. At its birth, the founding fathers of India had a rigid Unitarian model in mind for the country and although that mould has been broken many times, India refashions itself again and again like a clay pot that can be smashed and moulded again after being made into a mud pie.

China, on the other hand, has the appearance of super-stability. The Communist Party's authority seems unchallenged and there is no organised domestic opposition, except perhaps among the minorities of Tibetans and Uyghurs and the Falun Gong. Yet the system is fragile in its own perception. The 1989 Tiananmen Square uprising has not been forgotten and the preparations for the 2008 Olympics involved excessive repression of the Falun Gong and many others.

Yet one must point out that in the last quarter of the past century, we have seen excessively stable regimes fall apart – in Iran, and Romania and indeed the entire Eastern European system. When these super-stable states face a crisis they have no internal mechanisms for affecting a change of direction. China's system has shown itself to be excessively cautious and conservative. It is in this respect, somewhat like a Ming vase, strong but brittle. Once smashed the system may take some time to remould. While this may not be very likely, its possibility cannot be dismissed in any attempt at a prospective analysis. After all, Mao destabilised the system during the Cultural Revolution, which cost China ten years of political chaos. Previous episodes, such as the Taiping and the Boxer Rebellions are also reminders that China goes through phases of chaos before returning to equilibrium. India, by contrast, is always in a state of perpetual, though mild, dis-equilibrium.

The chances are that China and India will still be around a hundred years from now, richer and better in terms of the well-being of their people. They may also be similar to what they are now as unified polities – one democratic and other led by a single party. But that may not be as certain as we think today.

Acknowledgement

First publication: Desai, Meghnad, 'The Vase and the Mudpie' in *India China Neighbours Strangers*, *India International Centre Quarterly*, vol. 36, no. 3/4, Winter 2009 / Spring 2010, pp. 172–179. Republished with kind permission of *India International Centre Quarterly*.

Chapter 11

FIFTY YEARS OF DEVELOPMENT THINKING

Lord Meghnad Desai
(2011)

When remembering how the Institute of Social Sciences [New Delhi] began in the mid-1980s, I thought of the famous Eleven Theses on Feuerbach: philosophers have hitherto only interpreted the world in various ways, the task, however, is how to change it. Of course the man who wrote it, the only way he could change the world was by writing another interpretation of the world. And the world must never neglect ideas. Ideas are very powerful instruments to change the world. What I'm going to do is I'm going to tell you my life story.

In 1958 I began to study development when I started doing my MA. And of course Professor D. T. Lakdawala was one of my teachers and I always associate the Institute with the name of Dr Lakdawala who was its first chairman. I'm just going to take you very rapidly through the way our whole thinking on development has changed in these last fifty years. In a broad way, it has gone from thinking about *things* to thinking about *people*. One very core idea of development is a very simple one: it says people are poor; they are really meant to be rich, or people are poor today but they were rich in a previous era or some golden age because there was large surplus which somebody has robbed them of. Now, in a sense, development is a creature of colonialism and independence from colonialism. Because the people who thought about development articulately were not so much the classical economists who were thinking about growth in a different way in the eighteenth and nineteenth centuries but people who are, as it were, living with a contrast between the poor countries and their rich masters. So one of the first ideas (in fact lots of ideas or a clutch of ideas) is the very basic idea that people are poor because there is a pot of gold sitting somewhere and if you could only get that pot of gold and distribute it, everybody would be rich. I think it's wrong but a very powerful idea and that is where the idea of 'drain' comes from. One of the first ideas of development that Dadabhai Naoroji developed was the idea of drain; there is a drain of surplus from India and because of that drain [taking wealth or resources] away it's not helping in development. Of course there were lots of drains going on even within India. I think that the Maharajas were probably draining away more surplus than the British were. Anyway there is an idea that people are poor because some people are rich and the only way for the poor people to become better off is to take surplus from the rich people. That idea I think will never ever leave us because emotionally it is a very powerful idea. Bangladesh was set up on the proposition that East Pakistan was poor because West Pakistan was robbing it and if East Pakistan would get rid of West Pakistan, Bangladesh would become Sonar Bangla. But it doesn't happen that quickly, it takes a few decades before you can realise that growth comes by raising productivity of the present generation of workers and not by living off past accumulations.

I'm going to tell you why this powerful idea is not correct. It is very popular in Africa – that Africa has been robbed and plundered. Let me go back roughly to around about the Second World War, longer than fifty years ago. There was, after the Great Depression, a real pressure on colonial powers to do something about their people, the people they were ruling over. They were really frightened. The Soviet Union had happened; they were worried about rebellion and revolution. Radicalism was in the air. A number of colonial powers adopted ameliorative policies. Now they have been completely forgotten but the first thinking on development was done by colonial officers. Furnivall who was an officer in Burma wrote a book on plural societies and Birken in Indonesia, called the Dutch/Netherlands East Indies, first argued that there is a dualism among the poor countries. There are some urban, Westernised, organised centres and there is also a large rural impoverished society. The idea was basically that poor countries were fragmented and rich countries were integrated.

Then there was an idea, which again became unfashionable because it came from colonial powers, that basically people were poor because their culture encourages laziness. A very, very strong idea, and to put it in a more sophisticated way, it says the supply curve of labour in poor countries is backward sloping; if you pay these guys two square meals a day, they will stop working. When a certain break happened in the Second World War and independence came, surprisingly the thinking in development was very much generated by Western economists. By 'Western' I don't mean just capitalist Western but communist Western as well because they both were Western thoughts. One was of course influenced by Keynes. Keynesian economics had triumphed and people thought that Keynesian economics could be used to solve the world's problems. In Keynesian economics the idea of growth had not at all been part of economics; it was only in the post-war period that growth became a subject of academic study. Roy Harrod, who was a student and biographer of Keynes, gave lectures in the London School of Economics (LSE) in 1949 titled 'Towards a Dynamic Economics' in which he put forward the first growth theory. His theory in that respect was extremely mechanical and very macroeconomic. It says, what is the percentage savings rate of a country? Look at the capital output ratio and divide the savings rate with the capital output ratio and that will give you the rate of growth of the economy. That is one formula, you can write it in various ways. In a sense there is absolutely no behaviour there, the idea is that there is a constant savings rate and there is technological capital output ratio and, Voila! You divide one by the other and you get the growth rate. If you go back and read the draft frame of India's First Five-Year Plan, which actually is the first official development document written down in the world, it is very much imbued by that spirit.

The story goes that K. N. Raj, fresh from the London School of Economics, went to work for the Planning Commission. Of course the ambition of the Planning Commission was great; the National Planning Committee had been established by Subash Chandra Bose and Nehru was the chairman of that and it had decided that in the first decade after independence they wanted to increase income or wealth by six times – just in one decade. Then they themselves realised it to be a little bit ambitious, they decided, maybe two to three times will do. Even to double income in a decade requires a 7 per cent growth rate per annum. K. N. Raj had to hesitantly tell the prime minister that even 5 per cent would be rather hard to achieve and perhaps they should plan for a slightly lower growth rate. Prime Minister Nehru got very angry and said, 'Young man, why are you so pessimistic? You've been imbued by Western economic thinking, you don't realise that people have great possibilities', and all that. Luckily, Nehru was not Mao Tse Tung. Mao Tse Tung was seriously mad and wrecked the Chinese economy spectacularly in trying to surpass Britain in one decade.

It caused a huge famine in which 30 to 40 million people died. Nehru afterwards calmed down and decided that the young man's words may have some truth in the matter and the growth rate was going to be much less. But in a way what the First Five-Year Plan was in India was a collection of the late colonial projects and schemes which had not yet been finished, plus a bit of Keynesian economics. It was drafted by the brother of C. D. Deshmukh, I'm told. He may have been an ICS officer, I don't remember. It is a very coherent document.

In any book on development thinking that anybody wants to write, India itself will play a part, both as an exemplar and as a contributor of ideas. India became a laboratory of development thinking both by Indians and by non-Indians. Anyway, it began to be really clear to the people that the capital output ratio was a given technological constant and that was that. Another version of this idea was developed in the Second Five-Year Plan, and that was the Mahalanobis model. Mahalanobis on his own, without reading any economics, discovered a planning model which was written for the Soviet Union. It is a two or four sector growth model with capital output ratios and all that. Then it became possible to describe the economy in certain input-output tables. Input-output tables got larger and larger. It is very interesting that everybody thought that economy is something like a machine which could be described fully by a set of numbers or a set of formulae. And to get growth you just have to get those numbers right. It was thought to be very left wing to believe in input-output analysis and very right wing (when I was young) to believe that Indian agriculture needed more resources. It was thought to be seriously right wing to say that in the Third Five-Year Plan the allocation for agriculture should be higher than in the Second Five-Year Plan. One was thought to be an American agent if you said that. Anyway, slowly it began to be clear that development is a slightly more complex idea. At least a multi-sectoral approach was needed. In India a notion of surplus labour was developed and the idea that surplus labour was a resource, it was a kind of hidden savings in the economy. If you could only mobilise surplus labour and put it to work then growth will occur. But surplus labour was out there in the villages and growth was happening in the cities through industries because industries were always in the cities and people were always in the countryside. So how do you move people from the countryside to the cities and how do you feed them and so on? W. Arthur Lewis, the first non-white professor of economics in UK and later on a Nobel prize winner had this article in 1954 'Economic development with unlimited supplies of labour' which became a classic. The idea was we have these people sitting in the countryside, eating but not producing anything matching how much they eat because they are surplus. So you take them, you transfer them somehow to the cities and they will get into factories, but they had to carry the lunch pack with them, i.e. the food they were eating had to follow them. Of course the problem was, once they have left, the people remaining would have more food to eat. Would they actually increase the consumption or could you tax them to keep their consumption constant? There were lots of debates about that.

One of the most interesting ideas which was never adopted very sadly, as an alternative to the Mahalanobis Plan, was by my own teacher Brahmanand, that basically development should proceed first with producing consumption goods and consumption goods will then generate labour mobilisation and that labour mobilisation will lead to production of other consumption goods and so on. But that was thought to be too right wing; the Left idea was first produce machines to produce machines to produce machines. Anyway, this whole body of ideas – and I'm sticking mainly to the Indian experience – was unfortunately rewarded with early success. I'm saying 'unfortunately' because the real difficulty with development in India did not become clear till the second decade or 1960s. The First Five-Year Plan was marvellous, 18 per cent growth rate over five years, sort of 3.5 per cent on an average. Second was even better, 23 per cent growth rate over five years and so between 3.5 per cent to 4 per cent growth rate for ten years and India had not had a growth rate like that for at least a century. So everybody was happy. Then the difficulty started mounting up because by and large what was happening was that dormant resources were being better utilised to begin with.

The Second Five-Year Plan ran into a resource crunch. Foreign exchange ran out but still it went through all right. The second decade was characterised by the Three Twos: death of two prime ministers, two wars and two famines. Resource shortage became a very serious problem and then it became obvious to people that putting resources into agriculture was not just a matter of transferring surplus. Real people actually live there and they had to think about development in terms of different sections of people living in different regions. Even so, the idea was very much on the production side, how did you raise agricultural production. There was a great belief in state farms, collective farms and all that. If you ever want to read books on agriculture written by people who have never seen a plough, read Lenin on agriculture. Lenin had never seen a plough. It's a brilliant book but nothing whatsoever to do with agriculture. Kautsky had written a book on agriculture as well and he had this mad idea that there are only two ways of developing agriculture, one was the American way and the other the English way. It was mind boggling but people took that sort of stuff seriously. So the idea was that only large farms were productive and for that therefore land had to be pooled. Panditji believed very much in cooperative land pooling because the land holdings had become very small and the fragments had to be pooled. That idea was put to rest by the Research Programmes Committee of the Planning Commission producing a report in the mid-1950s with one of the most powerful empirical results there has been that show that small farms were more productive than large farms. The agony of the left was spewed across the pages of the *Economic Weekly* and later the *Economic and Political Weekly* for the next fifteen years. Lots of people were more or less saying this cannot be true because theory tells me it cannot be true, there must be some empirical trap here because large farms must be more productive than small farms. Anyway, it went on and on but the empirical result was robust.

So the idea of the Green Revolution and all that starts from there. Don't worry about land pooling; find out where farms are more productive and give those farmers more money. Put more resources into agriculture and that will increase the food surplus. So development theory begins to ask questions about how do people invest, where does investment have real results and so on. Of course Indian development thinking, not now but so much in those days, was influenced by the Soviet Union which was very powerful. It was argued by the Left based on Russian history that if you are only going to regions where agriculture is successful and giving more money to them then you are doing what Stolypin did under the Czar's regime (I'm not going to tell you who Stolypin is, find out, you can Google). All this *a priori* thinking was thought to be contributing to development, but luckily for India, what happened was the discovery of high yielding seed varieties; technology plus the political compulsions of doing something about a failed agricultural policy compelled C. Subramaniam and other people to see that you had to make India self-sufficient in food. At that time India was relying on PL-480 shipments from America and it was pretty humiliating. But what nobody said at the time was that the Green Revolution was the *largest private sector success story* in India. Because the participants were all small self-employed firms. They were called farmers, they were small firms and they were self-employed and they were reacting to incentives which had been created through either input price subsidisation or output price subsidisation. The most remarkable story of that is that lessons learned in agriculture were not transferred to industry because people actually do not think of agriculture as an industry. Agriculture in the 1950s was not considered to be productive at all. It was supposed to be suffering from the surplus labour. Some argued that agriculture was productive but the zamindars were taking away all the surplus. Abolish zamindari and it will be all right. We abolished zamindari but productivity was still not very high. Productivity had to be raised. Now, the idea that productivity had to be raised began to then engage itself with behaviour. How do you raise productivity? You have to give people incentives and how do you give incentives? There began to be an exploration away from formulae and input-output tables to looking at where are the sectors of low productivity and high productivity. How could you get the high productivity people to give even higher productivity and then worry about the low productivity people.

Yet, not only in India but across the so-called developing world the first few decades of development [after independence] were actually better than before but they were not actually a success. This is when the world became aware that there is something called 'poverty'. That poverty is actually a problem of development. It's quite astonishing, if my memory serves me correctly, that the first and the second Five-Year Plans do not mention 'poverty eradication' as a goal. Poverty reduction was not formally a goal in either the first or the second or the third Five-Year Plan. Because the idea of development was to build the nation and at least in India Nehru had said explicitly to Marie Seton that he wanted this big public sector investment to make India militarily strong. He wanted to have domestic arms production and not foreign. That's why he was having this Mahalanobis Plan. Of course building up military strength is a perfectly legitimate objective of national policy. I'm not saying he shouldn't have done that, what I'm saying is that the idea that poverty had to be reduced doesn't actually figure in a lot of the literature on development till the late 1960s and early 1970s. By which time the developed countries had started talking about poverty. Poverty in America and poverty in Britain became the subject of books in the 1960s. In 1970s when McNamara became president of the World Bank (he was absolutely a hateful creature because of Vietnam) he was the first president of World Bank who said the objective of the Bank was to do something about reduction of poverty. And it is quite interesting how the whole development thinking shifts all sorts of gears after that.

From the 1970s onwards you begin to have the idea that the central problem is not about growth rate as such but about reducing poverty. If you can show that high growth rate is related to abolishing poverty that's fine. What it also did was that it removed the illusion that somehow poverty would be reduced by pure redistribution. Developed countries' experience of poverty showed that despite continuously high growth rate because of Keynesian policies, a welfare state and a progressive taxation policy, poverty persisted in rich countries. Of course poverty was ubiquitous in poor countries. What could you do to reduce poverty? Then began this very interesting deflation of hopes, which was really very healthy. The idea was that poverty elimination was actually a very difficult task. Poverty levels were measured in terms of a certain number of calories per day per person and you convert these calories into money expenditure – and you are familiar with this – into 32 rupees per day. The amount of calories required to sustain a person was measured only for the prison population. Just like Dadabhai Naoroji said in 'Poverty and Un-British Rule in India' that people have inadequate housing standards and adequate housing standards are defined by how much a prisoner is to be allocated in a British jail in India. President Roosevelt decided that whatever the calories were required for prisoners Americans have to have 500 more. So the calories required to sustain a poor person were decided by Roosevelt arbitrarily by adding 500 to the calories required by prisoners.

Even by that crude measure elimination of poverty anytime soon became starkly unrealisable and so we developed the idea of 'Basic Needs'. That development planning had to do something about basic needs. People have big quarrels about what they were, how basic were the basic needs. What is happening here across the way is that from things-oriented thinking it becomes a people-oriented thinking. People are still an abstraction because people are thought of in the large. They are thought of in terms of consumption levels.

A very big change occurs during 1970s because, say from 1945 to 1975, the story was that if poor countries don't have enough resources they needed foreign aid. This foreign aid was all part of the Cold War strategy. It had to be government to government, there is no other way to get in any capital. You had to calculate how much foreign aid was needed and so on. The oil crisis by which oil prices quadrupled completely changed the situation whereby 5 per cent of GDP of the developed countries was transferred to oil exporting countries. And those oil exporting countries were sparsely populated, most of them didn't know what to do with the money so they left it in the banks of some Western countries. And Western banks decided the only way they could pay any interest on its deposits was by lending it out and the most wild lending of money to developing countries followed in the

1970s. The whole situation completely changes the ideas about capital availability and it is very interesting that in banks you had loan desks in which people were told just make loans as large as possible and just get rid of this money! There was amazing inflation, negative interest rates and developing countries were getting money like there was no tomorrow. All sorts of completely unviable public sector industries were started because government has the money and they have to do something about it. And then the whole thing crashed when monetarism came and interest rates went up everybody was left with debt. One thing became clear, that there was a possibility of moving money from one side of the world to another side of the world through kind of private sector operations. This was still private loans to public governments. Then of course the debt crisis happens, especially in the developing countries, raising the question, is development just a problem of resources in some kind of abstract way – money, finance, debt and interest etc. But the importance of international linkages was established.

Another very important event happened due to the oil crisis – the oil crisis of 1973 is a crucial event for development thinking and development facts. In causing the Oil crisis of 1973, the immediate event was the Arab-Israeli war. But by then the developed countries had had nearly two decades of full employment and in those countries, especially the European countries and also in America, powerful trade unions had emerged and basically the real wages of industrial workers was going up year on year and of course government was guaranteeing full employment but limits had been reached. What was inflation was really a hidden war between the workers and their employers in terms of the fight over income shares. As workers' share got larger and larger and as employers' share got smaller and smaller, profit rates begin to suffer, a classic Marxian kind of cycle. The pressure on profitability became inflation, because employers want to sack workers and of course because full employment was to be maintained government had to spend money to hire them but not by setting up industry somewhere else. It was at that time in the early 1970s that Western capitalists decided that they would quit the shores of North East America or western Europe and travel eastwards. So the whole phenomenon of newly industrialised countries of Asia, the Asian Tigers and next batch of Asian Tigers, arises because it is classic Marx and Engels Communist Manifesto prediction – capital has no nation, no morality, and so forth.

Western countries, led by USA and UK, decided to relax the rules about capital mobility. They went for deregulation and more free market policies. Capital left Western countries and went to China, Indonesia, Malaysia,

Taiwan, wherever it was more profitable to go. So you begin to redraw the geography of where the manufacturing is. In the 1960s and 1970s everybody thought the North is not going to be very helpful and monopoly capitalism would obstruct the development of the Third World. This was the argument of Paul Baran in his book *The Political Economy of Growth*. South-South cooperation is what people hoped will solve the problems. In 1968 in a Santiago conference of United Nations Industrial Development Organization (UNIDO), it was thought that if a 25 per cent share of world manufacturing trade could be from southern countries that could be a great objective in twenty years time. Nowadays nobody would take it seriously. Nowadays you would say if 25 per cent is exported by developed countries they would be lucky and that has happened because of a combination of factors and that again changed the thinking in development. In the 1950s or 1960s big countries like Mexico, Brazil, India had distrusted foreign trade. They wanted tariffs, protection, import substitution industrialisation and all that. Because of the experience of colonialism, foreign capital was distrusted as much as foreign trade. Latin Americans also had their own sort of compulsions. There was a very influential thesis advanced by Raúl Prebisch, a great Latin American economist and Hans Singer, a British economist, which argued that terms of trade of primary products producers have a secular decline and therefore if you are in primary producing things, you will never have enough money to be able to buy industrial goods, you will have to manufacture them at home. That whole strategy collapsed with the emergence of South Korea and Taiwan and Hong Kong and so on. Because they had a very different strategy, they had suddenly grown by relying on export markets. They got the money and they exported manufactures aggressively. They didn't have sufficiently large domestic markets. What domestic market could Taiwan have? Suddenly development thinking begins to change; that the way out of poverty lies in getting capital from abroad, using your domestic labour in manufacturing sectors with fairly conventional technologies where there is not very much learning to do, there is no R&D required and you take cost advantage of cheap labour and go for it. Suddenly what you have is developing countries become interested in reform of the GATT (General Agreement on Trade and Tariffs) and they want greater access to developed country markets, *they* want free trade. You know the Uruguay round of GATT changed the equation because for a long time developing countries were saying to developed countries, we want to have nothing to do with your free trade, you go and cut tariffs if you want. In the Kennedy Round, Tokyo Round, we just want protection. Suddenly the whole dynamic changes and you have a group of emerging Asian countries which are fast growing. It was not either a State versus market question. The State was as important in Korea as it was in India or Mexico but the State was smarter in Korea than it was in India or Mexico. The State said we will give you a subsidy, we will give you money but you've got to prove yourself efficient if we give you a subsidy. And how do you prove your efficiency? Well, you get someone else to buy your products other than your own domestic consumers. That proves your efficiency, if a foreigner buys your goods. You can always appeal to patriotism and sell domestic consumers dubious products but will a foreigner buy it? That is a real test of efficiency and that's what the Koreans and Taiwanese were doing.

By the time the end of the 1970s comes the whole context of development thinking is very different. Suddenly possibilities open up. So-called developing countries can do anything. I remember that when South Korea start having double-digit growth rates people were suspicious; most people of a progressive tendency distrusted South Korea because it was part of the Cold War American empire. Of course the progressive people were Mexican, Brazilian and so on. First the Progressive people couldn't believe the numbers, they said they were cheating. And then China changed and that was the most significant event in development thinking. My own private theory is that Deng Xiaoping, when he finally got his chance, looked at Taiwan and more or less said this cannot be happening in my lifetime. These guys were failures, they ran away, renegades, terrible people. They were supposed to kind of collapse and come back to us on bended knees, and how come Taiwan is one of the fastest growing countries in the world? And not being stupid he actually jettisoned all his life's thinking and decided what I have been taught is wrong and what my enemies have been telling me is right and therefore I switch. One of the greatest examples of creative thinking in the world's history, quite astonishing. Why should a veteran Marxist, hardliner, been on the long march and gone through several purges, in his blue overalls, suddenly cut loose? That is what I think created a whole new firmament. At the same time, in developed countries macroeconomics Keynesianism was losing out, monetarism was rising. Keynesian economics lost all reputation because it had no cure for inflation and income policy did not work. I can't even begin to tell you how hard it was for us Keynesians in the West.

The next assault was the shift to free market thinking in the West, ideas of incentives and so on. In a sense what was happening in Korea and Taiwan was not actually a free market economy working but a different model of development which was more reliant on consumer goods markets in developed countries. Not that they believed in free markets, they believed in regulated market with government intervention but the success was selling in a market private consumer goods, cars or whatever. Development thinking at that stage was also beginning to move towards the idea that maybe development strategy was about how to do things by getting inputs from anywhere. The Japanese were actually very successful in this, they were the first people to prove that the kind of input-output thinking that was there until then was no longer necessary. Thus if you want a steel mill, it was thought that it is not very good to just have your own steel mill but you have to have your own iron ore and your own coal and have integrated large scale industry. US Steel is one of those examples. The Japanese had no coal or iron ore and they made a successful steel industry by basically getting things from elsewhere. It is called just-in-time inventory. Certainly it had become possible because technology had advanced through container shipping and communication satellites, computer aided design and management. Same thing with Asian countries. Asian countries decided they could borrow capital, they have the labour and off they went and so national self-sufficiency oriented idea of development also lost out. When the Chinese started importing foreign capital, who could defend national self-sufficiency?

The other aspect of what was happening is that the aftermath of debt crisis in Latin America was very hard, with the IMF battening down on them saying, you can't do this, you can't do that, adopt free markets. The fact that these nations were indebted compelled them really to adapt themselves to a very harsh fiscal policy and they were looking for how to think about development in a different way. And this is where the human development idea came from. I was part of the team, along with two of the speakers in this Institute of Social Sciences, Amartya Sen and Mahbub ul Haq. That's how the whole idea of human development was born. That you should forget about growth rate, forget about capital output ratio, forget about input-output tables, development is not any of that. It has got to do with life expectancy, health, education and later on what Amartya said, with human capabilities. Poverty not in terms of calories, poverty in terms of capabilities. What should people be expected to be able to do and why don't they have resources to do it and how can you organise it so that they do? So it is partly through the adversity of Latin American countries and partly through the adversity of developed countries when capital was leaving them, that thinking in development changes. And the human development story has now become so routine in India that every state and every district and maybe every *mohalla* [hamlet] has its own human development index. Yet the interesting thing is that it shifts the focus of development from nation state and macro to the quality of people's lives. What was interesting in the Indian case was that through the halcyon days of socialist pattern of society nobody talked about primary education or literacy at all. Steel production was the most important thing to do. Steel production, heavy machinery, heavy electricals, all sort of things, but not a single person talked about health or primary education or the gender issue. All those issues suddenly came to life in the 1990s. It was all about governance and accountability and transparency, life expectancy, morbidity, maternal mortality rate, infant mortality rate. I mean they were always there but you go back to the first, second, third and fourth Five-Year Plans, there is absolutely no mention of these. Somehow, through various actions and of course some brilliant thinking it finally comes to the idea that development has really got to do with the quality of people's life and basically of the Bahujan Samaj, the majority of the people. That is what has to be looked at. And very surprisingly the first person to talk about 'aam aadmi' (the common man) in Lok Sabha was Lal Bahadur Shastri. In a brilliant speech; he says what I see are all these plans and models. Are we actually improving the lives of the ordinary people who live in a small room in an urban area or of the peasants? Well, he was not there for a very long time and we had to wait another thirty years before this *aam aadmi* again emerges on the scene.

The interesting thing is that the way thinking about development changes is partly through the role of the material forces, changes in the outside world like the developed economies lost their industries and had to find some other solutions. Developing countries got into debt. Some of them used the State action imaginatively to get into export-oriented markets and you know India was one of the last countries to change in that respect. But it also changes due to new ideas such as human development or capabilities. It is now almost accepted universally that the measure of development in a country is the quality of life of its people. The disagreement is, or the alternative vision is, what will bring about that outcome.

Is there a conflict between growth and development which is a hot topic nowadays? I would argue not; have liberal economic reforms, high growth rate and then you can manage redistribution if you have revenues to redistribute. You can't have static economy and then insist on redistribution; that kind of redistribution never happens. We have a very peculiar notion in our mind of the economy being like a harvest – you harvest, then you thresh out the grain, then you divide the grain between different people's shares. That is not the way an economy functions; output is produced and distributed simultaneously. Then you have to tax people to raise surplus and then you have all these incentive problems. Even in developed countries with progressive taxation they have managed redistribution more by tilting the public spending towards the poorer classes than progressive taxation. So it is a combination of taxation and spending with spending having more importance. One of the disagreements is how much you need to sustain high growth rate. Secondly, to sustain high growth rate how much should the State take away. For example, I believe that high deficits are not a good thing, taking away money from the people for irresponsible fiscal policy is self-defeating. There are differences on how much foreign capital is required and so on. But there is no doubt that at the end of fifty years of development thinking, we are absolutely sure that there is no other measure of development except the people whose development you are pursuing. And for those people there are issues like gender which would now be unthinkable of obliterating from development indices. I recall that gender had become a big issue of development in 1995 when there was a UN conference on gender. I remember sitting in New York, myself, Amartya Sen, Mahbub ul Haq and various other people and inventing the gender equality measure and then all the human development measures were filtered through a gender perspective. That kind of change has come about through a variety of experiences. We will probably get more nuanced, more focused on diverse individual experiences and then ask ourselves, okay, even the human development index is not good enough because it is too general, can we calibrate it more, for example, to take care of disability or take account of old age, because old age is very important. Can we do something to specifically measure how well a society is doing by way of the disabled or by the elderly and things like that. There cannot be a single poverty measure, it is silly to have a single poverty measure. Not every person needs the same number of calories. Again and again development thinking becomes much more oriented towards outcomes. Outcomes are measured basically through quality of people's lives. In the next fifty years, which some of you will have to suffer, I think development thinking will get better. Thank you.

* * *

Question and Answer Session

Question: *Since the FDI proposal was turned down in Parliament the newspapers have been writing editorials saying this is the end of the world. If only FDI came in, if only the insurance sector was opened up, the economy would grow. I don't see the economics of this, in terms of the kind of money that is going to come in or the kind of employment that is going to be generated. I do not understand why such a huge fuss is being made about economic reforms because I believe that the problem in India today is that we are not doing things with the money we have. I think the fundamental problem is wastage, it's not about reforms. If we could run government properly and do things in a proper way, these so-called reforms can play a role on another plane. Would you agree with that?*

Lord Desai: No, of course not. I have been arguing for the last twenty years against that, partly because these are not two exclusive things. I entirely agree with you that there is a lot of wastage. But we passionately believe that governments are better than markets and we go on giving more and more money to the government who is wasting it and then in crisis we give *more* money to the government. So one problem is: there is wastage. Even today when the Food Security Bill is being discussed, the friends of the public distribution system (PDS) say we must support the PDS, the loss has come down from 54 per cent to 41 per cent – this is Jean Dreze in *The Hindu* a couple of months ago. Where would you see the madness of somebody saying I must insist on using a system which has only 41 per cent waste? I pay 40 per cent tax, in the UK that is, because I'm supposed to be a better-paid person. You are imposing tax relative to a high rate of income tax on the poorest people of India and that is supposed to be socialism. Thank you very much!

Secondly, when you say money comes, it is not just money which comes but new technology and new organising principles that come. For example there are large multinationals in the US, UK and so on which supply the corner stores, which are the equivalent of our Kirana stores. There is no reason why there should be apartheid, these multinationals are only supplying their own people and not a Kirana store. If they organise the supply chain properly they could supply the corner stores. The fear is that if they organise themselves in India, India will be ruined, it will be in a foreign trap, the East India Company will come back again – read Somnath Chatterjee's speech in Parliament in 1991. Through the forty years before 1991, the growth rate was 3.5 per cent. And not only that, health and education were neglected, poverty had not come down as rapidly as since 1991.

Yes, we should reduce wastage, that's quite right. But who is going to bell the cat? The system gains from wastage. The political system is financed through wastage of the public sector. This debatable black money, the whole political system lives on domestic black money. We know that. You know, the Election Commission in the Tamil Nadu election found something like 87 crores in cash in one truck of [a contestant]. I mean, how does the system not be actually shocked about this? And they debate black money in Parliament! My view is that, yes, we should reduce wastage. Wastage is always bad, in any economy. I don't think you've gone shopping in a large wholesale or vegetable market. I occasionally go to one. Look at the rats, rats sitting around with the fish being sold, mangy cats and dogs all over, puddles of dirty water, dog shit as well, what an unhealthy thing we suffer. We don't need to suffer. I don't need foreign capital to get rats out of markets. I also feel there is a more technical issue of the gap between the farmers' plight, what the farmers get and the price that consumers pay. If your middle bits are insufficient you end up paying the price for that.

* * *

Question: *I'm surprised at the omission of the ecological question in your speech and the question of the 'limits to growth'.*

Lord Desai: I consider the ecological question not to be a development question because it spans the whole world. The ecological question is a global question. There are a variety of ways of looking at the ecological question. Partly whether it is the stock of emissions which is the problem, which is mainly generated by the rich countries or the flow of the emission which is going to be done by the developing countries. All the battles from Copenhagen on are about this. Over the fifty years of development thinking very little was devoted to that aspect. Even today it is not an integral part. It ought to be, perhaps. And when it is done some of the issues are going to be similar but equally capable of diversity. One idea is that the whole world should come together and write down a beautiful global compact. Very technical areas of economics which I will not bore you with have shown that you cannot construct a social welfare function even for a homogeneous economy because people have diverse tastes. And if you try to do that you can only do it by assuming that people are completely identical and have identical tastes. But people value things diversely. The difficulty of Copenhagen and Cancun and Durban is that the issue is not global warming. If we talk about global warming you look at that single global number and environment is not a single global problem. It is a differentiated local problem, in different areas. Very often, what are needed are different local solutions for particular problems which may not be relevant to a global level solution. I'm very pessimistic about a global compact of the Kyoto-Durban kind. I'm very hopeful that people will do things, particularly locally. If you have flooding in Mississippi or in Queensland, or you have local famine, you've got to devise local solutions. As much as there is a relationship between ecology and development it can be furthered by local thinking at a fairly specific level and not get involved in a global discussion.

* * *

Question: *One issue that is disturbing me is the issue of patents. In the pattern of economics is the production again going to shift back and will there then be a reorientation in which we will be mere supplicants of their products?*

Lord Desai: What is interesting is that in London or the West they are terrified that the tectonic plates have shifted and development has gone away from them. The best prospect is that the European Union will have, maybe, between 0 to 1 per cent growth rate for the next fifteen years; they'll be lucky if it is not negative. I'm very serious. Obama is going around saying I'm really worried about the Indian educational competition or the Chinese competition. When I come to India I realise that people are seriously worried about the West still – but the West is very worried about India and China. It is not an unrealistic position. Just as in the 1970s the manufacturing moved out, what happened in the big crisis of 2008–10 is that developed countries had thought that they could not rely on manufacturing but started relying on services, financial and other services. In America the average wage of a manufacturing worker has not gone up for thirty-five years and families sustain themselves because two members of the family work. What in 1950s and 1960s a person working in a car company in Detroit could afford, a TV, a fridge, a car and so on, now two members work for and because they are working in the service sector which is lower paid they have to borrow money. This whole borrowing collapsed. So the sustainability of this Western standard of living is in serious danger.

The way I put it, is that capitalism in the West is geriatric and the dynamism in capitalism is out here. This is where things are happening. You know, people always say in Britain, we have lots of patents but no development. The real development, the 7, 8 and 9 per cent growth rate will happen here. Look at growth rates in Africa – in the last ten years they are fantastic and a place like Myanmar is going to explode in development. Look at Vietnam – who would have thought about it when I was marching on the streets about Vietnam in the 1960s that Vietnam would be one of the most rapidly growing economies. That is a perspective too much weighed down by the past. And I should add, a lot of people filing patents in the West are not actually Western-born. Because their education system is universalistic and admits everybody, you know, the Chinese, the Indians. A lot of the people in Silicon Valley are Indians. Another way to put it, I think, is that nation states don't develop, people develop. I always say about human development that if somebody moves from, say, poor India to US, his life expectancy doesn't go up by twenty years. His life expectancy is the same, more or less, so even the human development numbers can be misleading because it can be too macro. If that is the case let us do something about it. Response should be, let us beat them. Who would have thought that India would be an IT hub? Why is India an IT hub? Because IT was never part of the Planning Commission strategy of industrial development *(laughter)*. Why is Bollywood a success story? Because films were not even thought to be an industry, they never gave any money for films, and that's why they are a global success.

* * *

Question: *Is there a distinct form of Indian development thinking? You mentioned so many models, and the debate over these different ideas on development thinking.*

Lord Desai: The answer is somewhat mixed. I think what is true, partly because of Amartya Sen, we are argumentative, we write too much and talk too much. There has been more explicit thinking about development by Indians and by foreign experts given Indian data than for almost any other country. Some day someone will write the book which I absolutely have no time to write, about how India is unique to the development experience not because India developed fast but because India became a laboratory of people trying out their theories. For example, the whole notion of surplus labour – whether it exists or not, all that, which is what I started learning my development economics with, was very much fashioned with India in mind. Partly because China was not open to such thinking and experimentation for the first forty years, and partly because India was the only other large poor ex-colonial country where there was a sufficient number of very, very bright people in civil services, politics, academia – the number of people Nehru was receiving in the 1950s reads like a galaxy of international names. They wrote things, were heard, because Indians are very receptive. I'm not sure it actually helped because my picture of India is, after the first decade of 1950s, it floundered for the next three decades. Really badly floundered. Surjit Bhalla said its only because India has extremely clever people that these disastrous policies did not ruin the country. Somehow we made this totally impossible policy work. Or at least they did not break up the country.

It is quite remarkable that between roughly 1965 and 1990 India is not an example of good development policy strategy in terms of both overall growth rate or poverty removal. Mrs Gandhi picked up the slogan 'Garibi Hatao' (Remove Poverty) and all that and I hesitate to say this, but when Mahbub ul Haq wrote *The Poverty Curtain*, this idea, I'm sorry to say, originated in the World Bank. The first estimates of Indian poverty were not done by the Planning Commission or by the Government of India. It was Dandekar and Rath, two economists in the Gokhale Institute of Politics and Economics in Pune who were the first to give estimates on poverty. I remember the storm that broke out. Nobody could believe that so much poverty exists in India. Fifteen rupees per month or something like that. India doesn't really have the example that other people should follow. India is still stumbling around, partly because of the consensus building in our political system and partly because of its diversity – there is no single solution for all of India anyway, and its development experience is very diverse. For example, in the last ten years I would say, India is the test for the idea that governance matters. Governance matters more than anything else in the world. We didn't think about governance in the first fifty years of development thinking. So India is still a very good place to study, both for what to do and for what not to do. But it is not actually an example for a successful development strategy.

* * *

Question: *Your main argument, that we have moved over the last fifty years from things-oriented development to people-oriented development, that, I think, is not right, because this is a process which has been there even before 1961, the period which you are covering. For example, when Marx writes in Economic and Philosophical Manuscripts or even in China, in 1949, it was a 'People's Democratic Revolution'. They spoke in a different language, the language of contradictions between working class and peasantry, between mental and manual labour, and so on, but the concern for people was there. After the Second World War, the golden age of capitalism was possible because of the existence of a socialist block. And also because of the successful anti-colonial struggles. I think this Human Development Index in India is merely trying to lend a human face to the inhumane neo-liberal policies. It's nothing more than that.*

Lord Desai: I'm glad there's disagreement – I like disagreement.

* * *

Questions and Comments:

1. *I want to know whether the Lok Pal bill will give us anything sustainable regarding our economic system.*
2. *I agree with your view. Development thinking is changing and changing for the better. The change in progressive thinking in terms of development should be captured by changes in the way we govern ourselves. I believe only the decentralised form of governance can capture such thinking.*
3. *The quality of leadership is also very important because if the leadership is not interested in development, development won't take place. If leaders are co-opted into the (prevailing) system how can the system be changed?*

Lord Desai: No, it's peoples fault that there's no development!

* * *

Questions and Comments:

1. *Do you think that India can be poverty-free? And if yes, at which rate of development can that happen?*
2. *A simple layperson's question – America, Europe have (high) human development indices but why do they have all these bailout packages in the last so many years?*
3. *The government failure theories in 1990 built a case for liberalisation but despite this we had large-scale massive corporate fraud and corporate scams. But when the discourse of governance was being put forward fingers are pointed against the non-governance in/by governments. Fingers are never pointed at the misgovernance in the corporate sector.*
4. *We had a 'Hindu rate of growth' and then went for liberalisation. We had 8 to 9 per cent growth rate and even now it stands at 6 to 7 per cent. These large flagship programmes – Bharat Nirman and MNREGA show that government have not left people on their own. But despite this, we see the inefficiency where 83 per cent of our countrymen are living at merely Rs. 20 per day.*
5. *We seem to push a particular idea of development thinking that everything has to open up, economic reforms, open market and so on. On the other hand we seem to show that we don't really believe in it because we have huge funds invested in NREGA and the Food Security Bill. Isn't there a contradiction between these two? Doesn't this need attention? What does this finally display in terms of our own development thinking?*

Lord Desai: I am going to cluster the questions here – one was the question, will India be poverty-free? Another question, which Jaya Jaitly put, was in the contradictions in development thinking and practice with MNREGA, etc. Another was, does the old model not still have the maximum wisdom, i.e., the Left model of development? There's a very strong belief that somehow the true model is still a Left model and somehow the liberalisation model is full of scams and contradictions and corruption and so on. Then the question on the Lokpal bill.

On Poverty

On poverty, let me put it this way, and I am not just making it up on the spot. The definition of poverty in India ranges over such large numbers that you either have poverty of 24 per cent or of 80 per cent. It's not that anyone's being dishonest, but there are genuinely different views of development, like the 'calorific view'. The calorific view of development says, here are the calories, this is the food basket, translate the food basket into money, then add a little bit for shoes and clothes, and that is the poverty level. There's a long tradition of doing that.

Then, either you say like Tendulkar, no, let's have a little bit more added. All people can, say, live at $1 per day. Then there is [Arjun] Sengupta. The thing is that the notion of development is both absolute and relative; it always has been in the literature. Absolute notions are food-based notions, period. That you are poor if you can't have that many calories. There is no ambiguity about any other thing. If you have uncertainty in poverty measures you've got to be crude. Then there is a view that that's a very bad view of poverty, that the notion of poverty is, what in the view of the society, everybody should have something of. Make that list and see who cannot afford the things on that list. The famous economist Peter Townsend wrote a big fat book on poverty in the UK; he asked fifteen questions to everybody – one of the questions was: what do you have for breakfast, do you have eggs and beacon for breakfast or do you have one big meat meal in a week or 'Sunday roast' as it is called, and so on? And then he said, people who can't have that, or one or more of those things are poor, because they are not fully participant in the community life. Now that is a very different notion of poverty.

Then there is Amartya Sen's version of poverty, which arose from a debate with Peter Townsend, and Amartya said, don't be commodity minded, don't get stuck in commodities, think of what you would like people to be able to do. What are the set of capabilities people ought to have? And do they have the resources to use those capabilities? For example, everybody cannot be of the same calorific standards; or, if I'm disabled, I'm paraplegic, it may require four times as much money to make me mobile compared to you. If I get four times as much money, I'm not richer than you, I'm just as poor as you are, but my poverty level is different from yours.

In India there is this very interesting debate about Rs. 32 per day and these people couldn't explain where that Rs. 32 came from, but it came from the whole Dandekar-Rath tradition. I think the best way to define this is for the majority of people in the society to say we consider these sorts of things, it may be dal-roti every day, twice a day, whatever it is, what is the community's thinking of not being poor? (In India this has not happened yet). What does it cost? And how many people cannot afford this? It may be different by regions. It will be definitely different by gender, and it may also have elements like disability, area where you live and so on. If you live in Kashmir you may have a very different notion of poverty than you would have if you lived in Kerala.

Poverty is a very politicised subject. The idea is that if I can prove that 99 per cent of India is poor I'm more progressive, more left-wing than you are. If you go down on the percentage, you are a capitalist agent. Exactly as I used to say at the beginning of the 3rd Five-Year Plan especially, everybody who said there should be more money in agriculture was thought to be either a fascist or a capitalist agent, because agriculture was right wing and industry was left wing. Those are silly kinds of notions. I mean, India has sufficient resources for someone to say, let's get this poverty question very differently. If you are genuinely interested, you would say that people ought to have adequate livelihoods. And what does it take to get people adequate livelihoods? There was a man called Charles Booth in London, a businessman, in the 1870s. He was walking around in East End of London and he found lots of children wandering around. He asked why aren't you in school? (England didn't have free primary education till the twentieth century). And, they said, our families can't afford the money to send us to school. It was 4 pence a term or something then. So he started enquiring into the standard of life, the incomes of their families. How much did they spend on food, clothes, etc. His question was motivated not by calories but by children's access to education. So, for example, in your poverty level you must have whether children are getting an adequate education or not. About health access, etc. things like that. A lot of poverty is not about whether families can more or less meet everyday needs but if there is an accident, if somebody falls sick and can't go to work, they are wiped out.

From that point of view, I would say that no society should ever claim to be poverty-free. Because there is actually no limit to how much you can make people better off.

I do not believe that there will ever be a completely equal society. Okay, I am 71 years old and I have given up all hope of egalitarianism. But I do strongly believe that every society should try and reduce poverty as much as possible and not actually accept a limit, that this is good enough for the poor, but I would not live on that.

On MNREGA

Now, this MNREGA and so on. It's very interesting, there is a very basic contradiction in Congress thinking. It comes from the past. The liberalisers have discovered that there are ways of getting high growth rates. Basically, the corporates are growing very fast, exports are growing, all sorts of nice things are happening. That fills up the government's coffers. Government's revenue collection has been nothing like this in the past. They have got permanent account number (PAN) cards[1] and all that. But, the other people in the same party, they hate all this. They think all this high growth is terrible, high growth does nothing for the poor people. I don't know if they believe that only low growth does better for the poor people – because they are the guardians of the Low Growth Rate Society. That is where their dynasty had invested their energy in, the dynasty that was involved in the Hindu rate of growth.

They basically believe that the ideal government should subsidise everything and distribute money to the poor as quickly as possible. But it must be done in a way which doesn't enable the poor to get out of poverty. You must keep the people in poverty, and preferably, where they live. They will be allowed to live where they live, partly because then, they'll vote for you. The whole MNREGA in my view (I mean who am I to complain about people getting work 30 days, 100 days, a year or whatever it is, it would be cruel not to sympathise with that), but it is designed to keep people in that place doing work which more or less, has no value added but it prevents migration.

On Migration

I think migration is a good thing, partly because I migrated myself (*laughter*). I believe in full liberal migration all over the world and I think if people want to get out of poverty, very often one of the biggest weapons people have used is to up and go somewhere else. Why do you think the 'people of Indian origin' so-called, are in the Caribbean? Why are they in South Africa, in East Africa, in Malaysia? Why are there poor begging UP-walas in Maharashtra that Rahul Gandhi just discovered? Why, because they were miserable in UP, that's why they went there.

One-third of the European population in the nineteenth century migrated to North America. So migration is a way of getting out of poverty. It is a self-help strategy. But no, we can't allow that. That is, I think, the central contradiction.

1 Cards issued by the Indian Tax Office that are needed by non-resident Indians if they are investing in India or submitting tax returns in India.

On the Food Security Bill

And then this Food Security Bill is the next contradiction. If you allow public distribution system there is 41 per cent wastage. Now, I have been arguing for direct cash transfers. You want to remove poverty? Figure out what it requires and give the cash to whoever you think is poor. And you know what people say? 'You can't trust how they will spend the money'. Poor people don't know the value of money and you know the value of money? What kind of nonsense is this? The poor person understands the value of every penny and they spend it very carefully. They may be poor but they are not stupid. But cash transfer is thought to be not possible. I thought of this idea when I first asked a question in Parliament – there was US$50 billion in total foreign aid in those days, there were also a billion poor in those days. That's $50 per poor person with one dollar a week, why don't you just give people one dollar a week? If their income is less than one dollar a day, that very person will get at least 14 per cent addition to their daily income. And everybody can get larger than that.

Anyway, cash transfers I think has radical possibilities. It will not be done because you will lose control. Those six paises they get – where did the 94 paises go? It won't happen, because you would lose control over the money.

So, I still believe that high growth rate generates public revenue and if the public revenue was efficiently used, you'd get a much better bang for the buck in curing poverty, heath and all those things. Because the implementation, both the purchasing and the providing of public services is done by the public sector, we get an inefficient outcome. Public sector should purchase these services but not necessarily provide them. Either though decentralisation – that's one way – or through some other way. They ought to give up control, which they can't give up. So that is my long answer.

On the question on bailouts, basically, what was happening, in building an economy, manufacturing used to be 26 to 27 per cent of the GDP, and now it is 10 per cent in UK, for example. Manufacturing no longer employs many people, it has become high-tech and so an ordinary unskilled or semi-skilled worker has to have long terms of unemployment or work in the low-paid services sector. And, that has led to the crisis of living standards. That's led to borrowing, and the financial revolution has made possible construction of a huge credit mountain on a small cash base.

Now, that whole thing collapsed in 2008. For the Western countries right now, for the last three years, no way out has been found, of restoring the growth rate. There's lots of debate about it and because both governments and households are in debt, governments don't have the money to spend, and if you have the money to spend, households will not spend it because they have to pay back their debts.

In a sense, the Western model of living standards is becoming untenable and people are looking for a new model. The West doesn't feel mighty and powerful, like, in somewhere like India. There is a real, real scare right now going on. Certainly in the Euro zone countries. At least 15 out of the 17 Euro zone countries are not going to get back to their pre-crisis living standards of 2007 till 2025, if they're lucky. It's a deep, deep crisis in the Western economies. And it's not a crisis of capitalism because capital is alive and well, in Asia, Latin America and Africa. The great transformation in the world, the shifting of tectonic plates which started in the 1970s and continued, and its entirely a Marxist phenomenon, entirely predictable by Marxists because it's in the Communist Manifesto. Capital moves where it finds its highest profitability. That's the nature of capitalism.

Everybody has been saying, the great socialist revolution will come back. It won't, you should read my book on this. I'll tell you why – because it was premature socialism from a Marxian perspective. The Preface to *A Contribution to the Critique of Political Economy* says that 'No social order is ever destroyed before all the productive forces for which it is sufficient have been developed, and new superior relations of production never replace older ones before the material conditions for their existence have matured within the framework of the old society. Mankind thus inevitably sets itself only such tasks as it is able to solve, since closer examination will always show that the problem itself arises only when the material conditions for its solution are already present, or, at least in the course of formation.'[2]

Capitalism has not lost its energy. And the premature socialism of the Soviet Union collapsed in ignominy, without a single gun being fired. It collapsed because of economic inefficiency. In 1960 Khrushchev had said, we will bury you under a mountain of commodities. We'll produce more steel, more cement in the next twenty-five years. And you know, he was right. But it was the same steel, and more innovative steel had been developed in the West. It was the same cement, but better building materials had been found in the West. They went on doing the same thing again and again and again. It was a complete waste of time, because economics is not about production, it is about productivity.

---

2 Karl Marx, *A Contribution to the Critique of Political Economy* (Lawrence and Wishart, London; 1971) p. 21.

How much more productivity can you get one day to the next, by using better techniques, by skilling people better, by using better management, and things like that. And that's why capitalism has survived. And what's more, it's not a matter of being Christian or of Western values, nothing like that. Anybody can do capitalism. It's the easiest thing to do. Save hard, work hard and re-invest profits. That's why China is such a giant success. In 1965 the great man Henry Kissinger once said, if India and China could feed themselves there would be no problems left in the world. Less than fifty years ago this was said, and look where the world is now. And why is China so developed? Not because of the great People's Democratic Revolution. That was a disaster, and led to the largest famine ever in the world in which 40 million people died. Seriously, the biggest famine certainly in the twentieth century, perhaps ever, and all because of the Great Leap Forward. The 'People's Democratic Revolution' wasn't actually about people at all. People's name was used and misused, and people were traduced. I get very angry when I'm reminded of this because India, bourgeois, petty bourgeois, weak India, managed to get along without having such a famine of that sort at all. We did have two harvest failures in 1964–65 and 1966–67, but India didn't have the kind of deaths that China has had. Why? Because it was a miserable petty bourgeois democracy. It was not a 'people's democratic revolution'.

I think we have got to give up these illusions. I absolutely have no compunctions about saying, thank heavens, the world has cured itself of that socialism. We may get another socialism yet. But *that* socialism is, thank god, gone. Except in North Korea. I'm not at all apologetic about liberal economic reforms. I am old enough to remember what it was like – corruption was not invented in 1991 in India. Let me hasten to add, in 1946, Nehru said to, I forget to whom, maybe Sardar Patel, that the Congress fellows in UP were so corrupt that they have violated every article of IPC already and they have just been elected! I'm not making it up. This is 1946, before India became independent.

It's in the very interesting biography of Chaudhary Charan Singh by Paul Brass. You read that and you will see how Charan Singh was fighting against corruption.

The point about the misgovernance of corporations is entirely correct, but there are two things – regulatory structures are to be better and there is good Western example of better regulatory structures, and they have to be administered without political interference. Just take a British example – we have just had a report published on Monday on the failures of the Royal

Bank of Scotland on which the British tax payer had to give £84 billion or something like that. They wanted to prove they are pro-business. There is now written evidence that both Gordon Brown and his office were saying to the FSA, please don't be so hard on the banks. So it's one thing to have regulatory structures but you also need to have non-interference by political classes of all parties. What that does is that you have to review regulations again and again. Secondly, you really have to have very watertight ring fencing of the way those regulatory structures operate to keep them immune from political interference.

What is very interesting now is what the Security and Exchange Commission in the US is doing. In the last year there are a number of examples of heavy fines being imposed on Goldman Sachs, on Citibank, etc. Four years ago you sold this fraudulent package of mortgage securities to so-and-so; now pay US$200 million – for example, the trial of Rajaratnam. That is the kind of system you need. Americans hate being cheated and when their legal system gets going, it is merciless. Had the Royal Bank of Scotland thing happened in America, they would all have ended up in jail. All these guys need to end up in jail because they have defrauded the public.

Also if there is a real capitalism no bank would be saved, nobody needs to be saved in capitalism. These are deluded beliefs that people's welfare lies in saving banks. Banks do nothing for people's welfare. They may exist to make profits, if they don't make profits they should shut down.

About the Lokpal Bill. I think I'm surprised about the Bill. India has not lacked laws against corruption. There is a belief and you have to respect that there is some kind of overarching ombudsman sort of facility and then there is a debate whether the Central Bureau of Investigation (CBI) should be under it or not. Whether CBI should be under or not under, my opinion is that it has to be autonomous and free of political interference. In India there is confusion that because India is a democracy it entitles elected people to have infinite power to intervene in anything. That is not true. Mrs Gandhi started this very false doctorate of mandate, that because I have the mandate I can do anything I like including getting the Judiciary hassled. In a democracy there are strict limits on what the elected legitimate government can do and there have to be areas which are ring fenced because I think it is later on today or tomorrow that there is a judgement coming out against Jacques Chirac, who was president of France. He's been tried for fraud he committed when he was mayor of Paris and probably he may not go to jail but he will be convicted. That is a kind of thing you need, you need to have regulatory structures which are independent of political influence. I don't know whether the Indian parliamentary system is capable of giving up that much of power. Ok, we've got a good electoral commission which is alright but CBI is not independent and we have to see whether an independent Lokpal can be constructed. I should also say, actually it doesn't have to be done by 27th December 2011. There is no sacrosanct rule about the date that Anna Hazare wants it to be done. Law making is very, very difficult. I know something about this. Every comma, full stop and every sub phrase counts because lawyers will take you to court to get out of jail. So, formulating law is a very complex matter. Unfortunately, the Indian parliamentary system has got its own set of practices which is to 'avoid vote taking'. In the British political system, government would have a bill, there will be a clause, opposition would make an amendment, it would be debated and be voted upon. Indian parliamentary system is afraid of voting. So, everything has to be decided before the bill comes before parliament. This is a new trend. There's a nice paper by Liberty Institute as to why this has happened. That's a structural problem of the parliamentary system. There is paralysis of decision making unless everybody is in the same room and everybody has agreed to the package and then the package is voted through at a nod.

Acknowledgement

This chapter was originally delivered as the Closing Ceremony Address at the Silver Jubilee Celebrations for the Institute of Social Sciences, which was followed by a Q&A session, in New Delhi on 15 December 2011. Reproduced with kind permission of the Institute of Social Sciences.

Part 3

Indian Economy, Politics and Culture

Chapter 12

THE ECONOMIC POLICY OF THE BJP

Meghnad Desai

(1994)

The Bharatiya Janata Party (BJP) is the opposition party in the Indian Parliament and as such forms the shadow government of India. Its number of seats in the Lok Sabha rose from two in 1984 to eighty-six in 1989 and finally 119 in 1991. The BJP had also formed governments in four states – Uttar Pradesh, Madhya Pradesh, Himachal Pradesh and Rajasthan. These governments were dismissed by the President of India in December 1992 following the destruction of the Babri Masjid in Ayodhya and on evidence of the implication of BJP in that destruction. In the recent mid-term elections in these four states plus Delhi, the BJP has been returned to power in Rajasthan and Delhi though it lost Himachal Pradesh and Madhya Pradesh to the Congress and Uttar Pradesh to a conjunction of BSP and SP, two left parties representing backward castes.

Despite this reversal, the BJP remains the only credible alternative as a national government. Thus its economic policies are of interest to anyone interested in the prospects of the Indian economy. As is well known, the Indian economy is undergoing a process of structural reforms with liberalisation and integration into the world economy as prominent themes. Although the pace of economic reform has been uneven, it is clear that as long as the present government stays in power, economic reforms are irreversible. One of the questions at issue in examining the BJP's policy is its attitude to economic reform. As an ostensibly right wing but nationalistic party, the BJP combines (as any political party does) contradictory elements of liberalisation and dirigisme. The policy of the BJP is however neither a seamless cloth nor is it frozen in aspic. Factions within the party have differing views and the policy emphasis shifts over time. In this paper, I shall attempt to examine the economic policy of the BJP, discernible from its own documents.

Much of the literature on the BJP concentrates on its political stance, especially its Hindu nationalism as reflected in its slogan of Hindutva. There has been an upsurge in the study of the BJP and of the Sangh Parivar in general since the Babri Masjid's demolition. Important though the issues raised in this literature are – secularism, communalism, nationalism – they are not my concern. In its economic policy, the BJP allows no role for any specific Hindu or Hindutva element. Thus for example it does not espouse any notion of Hindu economics, as some of its followers, for example champion Vedic Mathematics (Jayaraman 1993). It is possible therefore to discuss the economic policy of the BJP without reference to its Hindu 'fundamentalism'.

Sources

Before going into the subject of this paper, it is appropriate to say that there seems to be no available treatment of the economic policy of the BJP to my knowledge. The BJP itself has published a pamphlet, 'Humanistic Approach to Economic Development (A Swadeshi Alternative)'. I have also referred to economic policy resolutions at various National Executive Meetings and the Election Manifesto for 1991 'Towards Ram Rajya'. Besides these, the BJP regards as a fundamental document, a set of lectures by its past president Deen Dayal Upadhyaya entitled 'Integral Humanism' (Upadhyaya 1965). [I have not yet however as of now consulted the 1986 Policy Statement].

The Economics of Economic Nationalism

The BJP is a right-wing nationalistic party. Until recently, it tried to maintain an image of a secular rather than a religious party. In the last three years, there has been a real tension within the party among elements which want to emphasise the Hindu face and those who want to maintain a secular nationalistic face. Be that as it may, the BJP is also often labelled a fascist party. It seems however that as far as economic thinking is concerned, there is no parallel between the corporatism of Italian fascism or the totalitarianism of German fascism and the economics of the BJP. Thus it would be fruitless to drag in the European literature on the economics of fascism. The economic thinking of the BJP has to be analysed within its Indian context.

In the broader context of Indian economic nationalism, there has always been the Nehruvian left-wing version and the Gandhian right-wing version. The contrast between the two runs across the role of the state, the importance of large versus small industries, the degree of centralisation, the reliance on Western as against indigenous models, the modern machine oriented versus the traditional handicraft production etc. These two strands coexisted uneasily within the Congress – and to some extent permeated official economic policy [eg in the restriction on machine textile sector to the advantage of handspinning/weaving sector]. During the brief regime of the Janata coalition 1977–79, it was the right-wing Gandhian economic nationalism which was much on display.

There is also another strand of right-wing economic nationalism. This could be labelled the big business economic nationalism. The Swatantra Party represented this strand with an acceptance of large scale industrialisation, foreign (Western capitalist) model but with an emphasis on the private sector rather than government. The Bombay Plan of 1946 was a preliminary version of this strand of nationalism.

It used to be thought that the Jan Sangh, the forerunner of the BJP, represented neither big business nor the Gandhians but the small shopkeepers. It was normal to characterise it as a petty bourgeois party. I am not aware of any hard documentation for this but do remember it being frequently asserted as obvious. It was also very protectionist and used to believe in the virtues of low imports.

What this brief outline of different economic tendencies points to is that a 'right-wing nationalist party' has no precise economic profile. Indeed being right wing may mean market oriented and internationalist which will conflict with being nationalist. Right-wing thinkers sometimes are anti-market and conservative, wishing to uphold the traditional social order. There is, in British terms, a difference between a Whig and a Tory though both are right wing. Socialists pride themselves in being internationalist but in economic matters are anti-market, protectionist and nationalist. In their aversion to the entry of foreign capital, a Nehruvian socialist will ride in tandem with a BJP follower.

A separate set of dividers will be along the centralist/decentralist orientation in which again the conventional Right/Left divide does not fit neatly.

Gandhians are right-wing decentralists but European fascists were right-wing centralists though recently on the European Left, a fashion has broken out for decentralist communitarian economics. Right and Left divide best along property ownership/redistribution lines with Leftists more keen to abridge private property ownership and use taxation/confiscation to redistribute income and wealth progressively. Right-wing thinkers treat private property as sacrosanct and even if they may deplore inequalities, they would rather rely on voluntary agency to effect redistribution. Gandhi with his idea of private property as trust is very much in the right-wing mould.

The BJP is in this sense an eclectic combination of right wing and nationalist elements. By the 1991 election, it had acquired an inclusive set of right-wing beliefs and once the economic reforms process was embraced by the Congress Government, it also moved decisively into the anti-internationalist camp. Reading the Humanistic Approach, we sense that by 1992, the BJP had staked a claim for the Nehruvian self-reliance, anti-foreign capital ground. While criticising the Licence-Permit-Quota Raj, the BJP emerges not as a free market, competitive libertarian party but a conservative nationalist dirigiste party. The best way to substantiate these claims is to follow the published sources.

The key document is the Humanistic Approach (HA hereafter) pamphlet. It brings together arguments put forward in earlier National Executive Economic Resolutions as well as the 1991 Election Manifesto. It is fifty-four pages long and has fifteen sections. It is a document that lays out a general philosophy as well as particular policy options on individual sectors agriculture, industry, infrastructure etc. As in all political documents written especially by opposition parties, there is more promise than is likely to be fulfilled, more criticism of the government than spelling out the hard choices that the party may have to face if and when it is in power. But this is the normal course of political rhetoric.

Significantly, the BJP starts off by claiming that its economic approach flows 'from our national heritage and from the concepts of Mahatma Gandhi's *Ram Rajya* and Pandit Deen Dayal Upadhyaya's *Integral Humanism*' (p. 7, emphasis in the original). Given the attitude of the RSS (Rashtriya Swayamsevak Sangh) towards Gandhi about other matters, it is remarkable that the BJP now claims the Gandhian mantle. The influence of Upadhyaya is much more direct. Perusing 'Integral Humanism' a pamphlet embodying four lectures delivered by Upadhyaya, one senses that his ideas are at the origin of the BJP's economics when it says it 'believes in a new social and economic order which is non exploitative, competitive and harmonious and which provides full play to the individual initiative and dignity' (ibid.).

The Upadhyaya pamphlet reveals an interesting and not wholly consistent jumble of ideas. The Indian ideal is said to be holistic and the Hindu way of fourfold goals which form Purushartha Dharma is said to define individual aspirations. There is an awareness of Marxism and of Western liberalism but a determination to reject both as too partial. There is an aversion to the market-oriented system prevailing in USA and a conservative critique of capitalism is attempted. In this respect, there is a parallel between Gandhi's *Hind Swaraj* and Upadhyaya's *Integral Humanism*. There is a vague desire for a third way but without any hard economic reasoning to back it up. It may be helpful to quote extensively from the last and fourth chapter of the pamphlet to give a flavour of the ideas.

> Both these systems, capitalist as well as communist, have failed to take account of the Integral Man, his true and complete personality and his aspirations. One considers him a mere selfish being lingering after money, having only one law, the law of fierce competition, in essence the law of the jungle; whereas the other has viewed him as a feeble lifeless cog in the whole scheme of things, regulated by rigid rules and incapable of any good unless directed. The centralisation of economic power is implied in both.
>
> ...
>
> Both therefore result in de-humanisation of man...
>
> We want neither capitalism nor communism. We aim at the progress and happiness of "man", the integral man. (pp. 76–77)

The sentiments expressed in the paragraph above are not untypical of many green, 'new economics', small is beautiful followers. Of course lacking any economic theory of how people behave or how things can be produced, allocated and distributed, much of this kind of thinking remains on the plane of the rhetoric. As happened with Gandhism, in the practical realm of economic affairs, these schools of thought live with the existing system and are thus conservative though they sound radical.

But such idealistic dressing up can be ignored. Its significance for our purposes is that there is no invocation of any old Hindu philosophy of economics as the correct one, no Vedic production system to worship.

Upadhyaya's thought is in line with many conservative and (in my view) muddled thinkers who are terrified by the market as well by planning.

Once we are past the idealist packaging, the BJP's economic policy is said to be based on '(t)he spirit of the Swadeshi and self reliance'. Right at the onset 'the growing resentment and resistance of many socially conscious groups and citizens of the country to operations of multinational companies in the country' is recorded sympathetically. Integration into a global economy, we are told, 'should not mean obliteration of national identity and predominant sway of powerful economic forces from outside'. Thus 'India must liberalise, industrialise and modernise – but it must do so the Indian way'.

This message of Swadeshi and the Indian Way looks politically attractive. Indeed, one doubts if the 'left forces' in India would disagree with this outline. However, what is lacking in the document is any appreciation of the economic consequences of following a severe Swadeshi path. Given India's indebtedness as well as the globalisation of the world economy during the recent years, it is necessary to understand that a strategy rejecting and restricting the entry of foreign capital imposes a severe burden on a domestic economy. [I have outlined some of these problems before. See Desai 1993]. The BJP's economic programme doesn't face up to this set of constraints and indeed in many ways makes inconsistent demands.

Indebtedness, both domestic and foreign, is clearly a major problem for the Indian economy. The BJP makes great play of criticising the government for getting into these debts. In a special pamphlet issued, presumably in 1992 (but like some other BJP documents, carrying no date), 'Towards a Debt Free India' (TDFI), the BJP blames the Nehru-Mahalanobis (NM) model. In fact, it is the 1980s dash for rapid economic growth with foreign borrowing, a tacit departure from the NM model that caused the indebtedness. This is not a rhetorical point since the NM model is as much based on self-reliance as the BJP advocates.

The BJP is acutely alarmed about the internal debt as much as the foreign debt. It was the growth of revenue deficit during the 1980s which allowed internal debt to go up from Rs. 310 billion in 1980–81 to Rs. 1700 billion in 1991–92, or 52 per cent of GDP. Foreign debt has grown from 10 per cent of GDP in 1980–81 to nearly 40 per cent by 1991–92.

The BJP asserts 'if we decide on a steadfast approach of reduction in foreign loans over the next 5 years, it is not a difficult job' (TDFI p. 9). Of course a *reduction* in foreign loans still *increases* the foreign debt. If anything can be said about the BJP's policy on debt, it is that it fails to understand that while there is some connection between internal and foreign debt, they require different policies.

Most of BJP's policies are directed towards reducing internal debt. There are general exhortations to convert deficits into surpluses, to liquidate existing debts by selling the holding of private sector equity in the hands of government financial institutions, leasing out surplus land, privatising of public sector undertakings etc.[1] But correct as these policies are, how do they reduce foreign debt? The 'Debt Free' pamphlet says:

> Instead of writing demeaning letters to the IMF and the World Bank begging for loans, let the Finance Minister draw up a programme for reducing the debt in a phased manner, cutting down on budget deficits and doing away totally with revenue deficits. Even the American Congress, which represents the richest society in the world, is asking for constitutional ceilings on budget deficits, after being burdened with huge debts. The BJP has also called for similar ceilings… (TDFI p. 10)

It is quite obvious from the quotation that the BJP confuses ceilings on internal debt with those on foreign debt. The reference to the American Congress is rather piquant and it is clear that the deterioration of the US capital account has escaped the BJP's notice. The reduction of internal debt by cutting budget deficits is alright; indeed, the IMF, much reviled by the BJP, insists on it. But the reduction of foreign debt requires cutting of the trade deficit by increasing exports above imports and/or by acting on capital account. It is here that the inflow of foreign equity investment whether direct or portfolio is a crucial step. Since much of India's foreign debt was incurred in the form of bonds or short run commercial paper, inflow of equity investment may help relieve the payments problem. A foreign debt denoted in equities has its risk shared between the lender and the borrower. The present Indian debt concentrates all the risk on the borrower. This was, however, the result of the mistaken belief that the Indian government would be better able to control the influx of foreign money if it borrowed abroad rather than let in foreign multinationals. National autonomy has costs attached to it and neither the Congress in the 1980s nor the BJP in the 1990s is willing to be able to face up to this hard fact.

1 However, as we shall see below, the BJP is opposed to any cut in agricultural subsidies on water and electricity which they consider to be the 'natural rights of farmers'.

It is in the question of entry of foreign capital that the BJP is most in line with the previous Nehru-Mahalanobis type policies. Thus, on foreign capital, HA says:

> Opening up of the country to external competition should be on selective basis and strictly keeping in view interests of the domestic economy – industry, materials, local talent and labour force. However the party realises that there is scope to welcome foreign investment and technology in areas where domestic efforts have been weak – energy conservation, pollution control, coal washery technology to name a few. The BJP's attitude is guided by the following principles:
>
> - Foreign investment should be allowed in high-tech, export-oriented and import substitution areas
>
> - Consumer goods should not be open for foreign investment
>
> - Existing multinational companies in the area of consumer goods industries will have to dilute their control within time frame to be evolved. In such cases, preference will be given to existing Indian employees in transfer of equities. (HA p. 23)[2]

This set of policy guidelines is of course precisely what was the official Congress policy. The problem with them as in many discussions of the issue of foreign capital in India is that the BJP sees India in a powerful position to be able to choose what type of foreign capital it would like. In the globalised world of the 1990s, countries are competing to attract foreign capital to their shores and this competition includes developed countries like the UK as well as developing countries – China, Vietnam, Malaysia etc. It is a peculiar mark of insularity of such nationalist thinking in India which will not accept this competition as a fact or as applicable to India. Then, of course, Indians complain that foreign capital refuses to come to India!

The solutions proposed to the external debt problem in the chapter on Balance of Payments in HA make this confusion obvious. Thus, despite the fact that the external debt problem is liable to be exacerbated by continuing borrowing from commercial banks or Non-Resident Indians (NRIs) on a no risk sharing basis (ie as debt rather than equity), the BJP promises that

2 I should say that in the copy of HA that I was given, the last paragraph has been cancelled out but is still readable. I compared this against other copies with the NCSAS and the paragraph is retained. I am not sure whether this is a recent modification in BJP which is being signalled exclusively to me.

'the scheme would be drawn to attract substantial portions of (NRI) savings' which it estimates at US$100 billion. It also advocates discriminating in favour of industrial units set up by NRIs which can only discourage direct investment by companies which are not NRI yet foreign.

The trade policy of the BJP is vague and exhortatory. Export promotion boards are promised for each export commodity: 'Corporate sector would have to fulfil its export obligation especially if its production is import intensive'. It advocates import restrictions for non-essential imports and thinks this is a rational import policy. The current climate of free trade in which other developing economies are hoping to gain by GATT provisions (Uruguay Round) is clearly not to the BJP's liking. Of course, any trade restrictions actually adopted may violate GATT principles and lead to a denial of MFN treatment for Indian exports. The damage caused by such denial of MFN treatment would be serious and worsen the debt problem.

There is a similar lack of consistency in the internal debt reduction policy. Thus while in the chapter on fiscal policy in HA and in TDFI, much is said about reducing the revenue deficit, the proposals scattered throughout HA are to raise government expenditure. A particularly dramatic example of this is also available in the Economic Resolution of September 1991 at the Thiruvananthapuram meeting of the National Executive of the BJP. It is worth quoting extensively from this document to show how the BJP straddles both sides of the issue:

> The Government resorted to slogan mongering of liberalisation with an ulterior motive to attract foreign loans. It played cruelly with economy of Agriculture Sector by slashing the subsidy and further trying to differentiate between functionally non-differentiable farmer community by restoring the subsidy partially. The Executive Committee not only demand full restoration of subsidy to the farmers and early finalisation of agricultural policy which should include among others availability of good seeds in sufficient quantity at reasonable rate, providing water resources, electricity and like at reasonable rate, loans at concessional rates of interest are facilities akin to industries be provided. (BJP September 1991)

The Election Manifesto for May 1991 'Towards Ram Rajya' (TRR) says in its Charter of Rights of Kisan:

> Ensure abundant supply of water and energy, *the farmers have a natural right on these basic inputs* (emphasis in the original, TRR, p. 12)

There obviously seems to be no realisation that subsidies on fertilisers, water and power add to the burden of the large deficit since they amount to selling these inputs at commercially loss-making prices and the losses of the public sector agencies selling them will be part of the internal debt. The additional fact that undirected subsidies encourage excess input use as well as having adverse distributional effects is another blind spot.

In the section on taxation measures in HA, the BJP is for raising the income tax exemption limit, corporate tax exemption to employment-oriented industries in non-municipal areas, abolition of octroi duty (with an exhortation to 'persuade state governments to make good the loss to municipalities'). There is not a single revenue raising proposal but only revenue reducing ones.

Markets or Intervention

The BJP combines a rhetoric of attack on the Licence-Permit-Quota Raj with a large list of measures which involve setting up government boards, subsidies, legal restrictions on corporations etc. Indeed, the balance in the party's thinking is interventionist of the 1960s and 1970s type rather than towards internal liberalisation. In no particular order of importance, I list the interventionist policy items from HA's section on the Industrial Sector:

- A separate Ministry for Handicrafts and Village Industries
- National Artisans Development Bank to be set up
- An agency to provide marketing assistance and intelligence for small industries
- A Board for revival of sick small scale units on the lines of the Board for Industrial and Financial Reconstruction
- Certain areas of industrial production to be reserved for the small scale sector; entry of large industry and multinationals not to be permitted
- Differential rates of interest for small scale sector as well as extra tax benefits and credit facilities

This is combined with pleas for the relaxation of licensing for the sugar industry, simplifying the procedure for setting up of new units in the large scale sector, disinvestment from public sector enterprises and sale of their equity to the public (but one presumes not foreign public). Having taken a pro-privatisation stance on public sector units in its section on the industrial sector, when it comes to exit policy in the subsequent section on Full Employment and Industrial Relations the BJP is very close to the left parties:

> Factories may be closed down only with a golden handshake and that too only when sickness is terminally manifested and so decided by the appropriate authority. (HA p. 25)

Conclusion

The BJP is an opposition party and as such it follows the normal practice of such parties to be strong on promises and short on costing of the delivery of such promises. It promises full employment, price stability, poverty removal, the uplift and levelling up of each individual and section of society etc. It is wedded to modernisation, liberalisation, industrialisation but in a self-reliant Indian way. It would like to lower internal and foreign debt, restrict the inflow of foreign (but not NRI) capital, protect agricultural subsidies, cut income taxes etc.

There are questions to be asked. Is this a coherent strategy? Is it feasible given India's indebtedness? Will it actually solve the problem it sets out to tackle? Before answering these questions, let me add once more that party political documents are by their nature designed not to be intellectually coherent or internally consistent. They are propaganda documents. They are also not infallible guides to what the party would do if by chance it were to be elected to office. These things are true of all political parties not just the BJP. Thus relying on political programmes and pamphlets is a somewhat treacherous exercise.

With those caveats, let me say that the BJP has no realistic idea of what a Swadeshi policy may imply in terms of a fiscal burden if India's internal and foreign debts were to be paid back. The party seems to understand internal debt better than the foreign debt problem. But even its policies of cutting internal debt are inconsistent with its reluctance to cut subsidies or increase taxes. It doesn't see the connection between the inflow of foreign capital and India's ability to pay back foreign debt. It does not face up to the fact that restricting the influx of foreign capital will increase the burden of debt repayment. An export surplus will have to be created over and above the amount necessary to cover imports. A budget surplus may help in this process though the connection is not one to one. It would be realistic to predict that when and if the BJP were to come to power, it would not be able to restrict the inflow of foreign capital since the budgetary consequences of this choice would be severe. (It was the unacceptability of cuts in domestic consumption designed to pay back foreign debt that finally brought the Polish communist system down). Nor would it be desirable for the flow of foreign capital to be so restricted.

But there is also the clear indication that the BJP has adopted the standard Government of India rhetoric on intervention and dirigisme as its own preferred model. Now it can be argued that India's problems arose precisely because suitable though the NM model was for the 1950s and 1960s, it was not abandoned in the late 1970s in favour of an open economy approach. This was the choice made by the Asian Tigers. Even if the NM model had been appropriate in the late 1970s, it is definitely outdated by the 1990s, as much due to globalisation as due to an increasing sophistication of the Indian economy. The partial abandonment of the NM model in the 1980s led to the influx of foreign borrowing and a rise in the growth rate of GDP from 3.5 per cent to 5.5 per cent. It was, however, due to only a partial rather than a total abandonment that the debt crisis hit the Indian economy in the 1990s. Other developing economies, especially the Asian Tigers – China, Indonesia, Malaysia, Thailand – have all abandoned protectionist, dirigiste economic policy. It leads neither to growth nor to economic justice. The BJP clearly has not appreciated this fact. (See Desai 1993 for a critique of Indian economic policy.)

The BJP emerges from this examination as a conservative, interventionist party, high on populist rhetoric but unable to form a coherent strategy to implement its chosen strategy or indeed to see its undesirability. But then in that it is probably not much different from the left parties in India.

References

Bharatiya Janata Party (1991a) 'Towards Ram Rajya: MidTerm Poll to Lok Sabha: Our Commitments'. (Pamphlet) (May).

Bharatiya Janata Party (1991b) 'National Executive Meeting in Thimvanthapuram (Kerala): Report'. (Pamphlet) (September).

Bharatiya Janata Party (1992a) 'National Executive Meeting in Bhopal (Madhya Pradesh)': Report. (Pamphlet) (August).

Bharatiya Janata Party (1992b) 'Towards a Debt Free India'. (Pamphlet).

Bharatiya Janata Party (1992c) 'Humanistic Approach to Economic Development (A Swadeshi Alternative): Economic Policy Statement, 1992: Our Commitment to Antyodaya'. (Pamphlet).

Desai, Meghnad (1993) *Capitalism, Socialism and the Indian Economy* (EXIM Bank, Bombay).

Gandhi, M. K. (1908) *Hind Swaraj*.

Jayaraman, T. (1993) *Science and Secularism* (Madras, Tamilnadu Science Forum/ Frontline).
Upadhyaya, Deen Dayal (1965) *Integral Humanism* (New Delhi, BJP).

Acknowledgement

First publication: Desai, Meghnad (1994) 'The Economic Policy of the BJP', Discussion Paper 1, Melbourne, National Centre for South Asian Studies, January, pp. 1–11. Republished with kind permission of the National Centre for South Asian Studies.

Chapter 13

INDIA'S TRIPLE BYPASS

Economic Liberalisation, the BJP and the 1996 Elections

Meghnad Desai

(1996)

I have been asked to deal with three things: what has happened to economic reform in India since 1991, where does the Bharatiya Janata Party (hereafter BJP) stand on liberalisation and what do the economic policies look like in the lead-up to the April 1996 elections.

The major thrust of liberal economic reform in India has now spent itself and while the reforms are irreversible the analogy is that of a bullock cart stuck in the mud: it is irreversible but that doesn't help very much. It's not going anywhere. It's not going anywhere because, as a lot of us have said, there are clearly tremendous democratic pressures in India. India is a federal polity with regular elections – and we are going to have national elections very soon in April 1996. In the current pre-election climate I see no political party, and no faction within any political party, which will take a positive view on liberalisation. I think this is unfortunate.

I think it is wrong. But it is my view. A consensus view has emerged in India that yes a lot of reform has happened, the economy has liberalised and it is not likely to go back to the pre-1991 or the pre-1980 Indian economy (people forget that a lot of reforms happened in the 1980s and of course, there was another set of reforms in the 1990s). I don't think there is any danger of going back to the 1970s but by the same token there is going to be a great difficulty in pushing forward reforms in the one or two major areas in which it has not fully realised itself.

The reason is that the popular political perception is that the reforms have, by and large, not helped the poor. They have not generated extra jobs and they have basically benefited a very small minority. Therefore, it is a task of a political party which wants to win political elections to go on a different platform which would say reforms are all right, but we must modify them, we must moderate them, we must qualify them and look after this other dimension. It is significant that in the national Cabinet, except for Dr Manmohan Singh (Finance Minister) and now the Commerce Minister Mr Chidambaram, there is no minister who is positively for economic reform and willing to argue its case up and down the country.

The case for reform, a case which I argued back in 1993 (Desai 1993), is that fast and radical integration into a globalising economy is India's best imaginable anti-poverty programme. Everything India did before 1991 failed to attack poverty. It is not true that before liberalisation happened, India was a socialist heaven. Indeed in all the statistics one can think of such as literacy and life expectancy, India was behind the average of all developing economies and therefore, despite the claim to be a democratic socialist republic, it was not actually doing very well compared to merely capitalist countries like Indonesia and Malaysia in terms of the anti-poverty programme or health or well-being of its people. So I think that nobody has been able to say that all that rhetoric is convincing.

The reform process has been slower than one would like to see partly because the old vested interests have been very hard to keep down. So all those subsidies continue and all those old burdens on the fiscal budget continue and state chief ministers are not stopped from getting into fiscal adventurism of the most gross nature (such as giving away rice at Rs. 2 per kilo). I don't care if they do it provided they raise enough taxation to pay for it. The point of saying that the deficits are bad is not to say that deficits are inflationary – I am not saying that – but by and large the burden of taxation in India falls on the poor. And to the extent that government expenditure is not retrenched, the poor go on paying the extra burden of taxation. Taxation in India is not progressive. Taxation is not progressive almost anywhere in the world but if you examine it carefully in India it certainly isn't.

The reform process has indeed helped the economy, much more than the sceptics said it would. Exports are growing very rapidly but the overall economic growth rate is stuck at 5 per cent, perhaps it is 6 per cent in 1995 as the government claims. But by and large India has not been taken even into a high, single digit growth rate of 8 or 9 per cent let alone Chinese type growth rates of 11 or 12 per cent. And because India is a democracy one has to understand that this in some sense is a choice which the people have made. And that if people make that choice one has got to respect it. If the perceptions of the political parties who are in touch with the people are that this is what is happening that is indeed what will happen. I expect that between now and six months after the elections of 1996 are over, there is not going to be any great dramatic gesture in terms of reform. A lot of small technical things which can escape the scrutiny of the Lok Sabha will go on. Technical reforms which the Finance Ministry, the Reserve Bank of India or various other bodies like the stock exchanges can put through, will go through. And a lot of those things are going through. Those reforms which have already been implemented have generated a dynamic in terms of what the businesses are doing. These will go on and that will create further opportunities in India. But the analogy I would give is that of a person who has followed a very unhealthy lifestyle in terms of eating, drinking and smoking and has a triple bypass. For the first six months or so he does what the doctor tells him. You know India had a triple bypass in 1991 and the doctor came and said you must do such and such. Of course the doctor said it not because the doctor happens to be evil but because doctors say this in the interest of the patient. But after a while the patient thinks 'ah…who is the doctor? What does he know. I am alright'. And you go back to the old habits. This is basically what is now happening. Now basically it looks to India as if it is all the IMF's fault that we had to liberalise – no fault of our own at all and the fact that the place practically went bankrupt is all somebody else's fault.

But I think that none of this is a new thing. You can study previous episodes of radical economic policymaking in India. I have recently published a paper in *India Briefing* by the US Asia Society in which I analyse this history (Desai 1995). You go through the last thirty or so years and see that each radical experiment has had a shelf life of about three to four years. After that it loses momentum. You can look at the Nehru-Mahalanobis experiment of the Second Five-Year Plan in 1955, then the Green Revolution, on to what happened to Mrs Gandhi's 'garibi hatao'[1] followed by the Janata government experiment and so on. This happens to radical policy reform because eventually if you cannot create a sufficient coalition of interests which see themselves benefiting from economic reform (I mean a numerically large coalition of interests), then eventually a combination of old interests which have been hurt by the reform plus those people who are not

1 Garibi hatao – literally 'poverty out' or abolish poverty.

benefiting and those whose hopes have been dashed, will eventually stop the reform. So what we will see in the forthcoming elections is that nobody will actually come out strongly against economic liberalisation as such. Liberalisation has joined ice cream and motherhood as something everybody has to swear by, but everyone will qualify economic liberalisation in two respects: exit policy and entry policy.

The exit policy, by which we mean the reform of public sector enterprises, is necessary. Whilst there are some profitable public enterprises there is an unacceptably large number which are loss-making. But the workforce in the public sector companies are the protected sector of the Indian working class. They represent about 8 per cent of the labour force, they enjoy special favours and they are especially well organised. I don't think there exists a political party in India which will touch it this side of the election and perhaps not the other side of the election. But what am I saying – after all I am standing here in Melbourne and all the local newspapers are full of battles between the ACTU and CRA. Who am I to talk about the justice of trade union claims in Australia? China has a very similar sort of problem even without trade unions. China has also for a long time, despite its rapid economic growth, carried a large State sector which is considerably less efficient than its village and town enterprises or its private sector. Thus I think it is unlikely that a dynamic exit policy will be pursued by any government that is likely to emerge after the next election.

Let me briefly indulge in an election forecast. Needless to say a lot of other people will have other forecasts. I don't expect any single party to emerge with a majority sufficient to form a government in the next election. I don't think anyone will disagree on that. What people will have differences on will be the identity of the largest single party. I will stick my neck out and say it is going to be the BJP. And I would say that despite what has happened in the Gujurat recently, which considerably tarnished the BJP's reputation as a clean party. The BJP has about 120 seats now and it will possibly get between 180 to 200 seats. Other people say this is madness and we have been taking bets ever since I arrived in Melbourne. I am going to be inundated with champagne bottles, I can tell you. Congress will be the next largest party – I imagine it will get between 140 and 160 seats and then there will be a variety of other parties. It is conceivable that the BJP will form the next government of India if it can string together a coalition with lots of small regional parties. Its tactic in Uttar Pradesh of supporting the BSP, a backward caste party which is normally anti-BJP, is a sign that at least the most sober part of the BJP (which is not always necessarily in control) wants to project itself as a minority-friendly, certainly not a minority-hostile, political party. I believe that no political party can come to power in India without having some sort of pro-minority stand. There are far too many minorities – it pays groups to define themselves as minorities in Indian democratic politics and people have to come to terms with the backward castes, dalits and Muslims and the regional influences. Therefore I think that the BJP has been trying to give signals, not entirely with the full approval of its membership because there are differences amongst them, but the BJP certainly has been down-peddling the Hindu bits of its image since earlier events. It may not be possible for them to find sufficient strength to form a government, but I believe that they will do that in 1996.

There is another possibility that the Congress will form the next government with the National Left Front (hereafter NLF) coalition of parties. Such a coalition will have to take a much more cool view of liberalisation because the NLF parties are not very pro-liberalisation. Certainly on the exit policy, nothing will happen.

Regarding the entry of foreign capital a lot has already happened – there has been a lot of legislation and there is not going to be any reversal in that. India is by and large a very law abiding place and if people want to change something they have to get a new law passed so I don't think that they are going to do anything sudden. The Enron case, in which the newly elected BJP–Shiv Sena government in Maharashtra tried to cancel the power contract, was shocking to a lot of people not because the stance was right or wrong but because it was done in such an arbitrary and extra-legal way. This is what shocked. Now you can see the Enron thing unravelling itself and the Maharashtrian government finally found out that there is money to pay for this sort of indulgence. And so now they are renegotiating the Enron deal. Apparently nobody had told them that these things are binding commercial agreements.

A Congress-NLF coalition will definitely be cool on the exit policy and it will be unenthusiastic but not obstructionist on entry policy. Much will depend on who stays on as Finance Minister. If Manmohan Singh stays we may have some guarantee that sanity will continue. Otherwise I do not give any such guarantee. If the BJP forms a government there is likely to be a modification on the entry policy. Those of you who have been following the BJP's policy will know that it has been all over the place since liberalisation started. Historically it was a very anti-dirigiste party. It was against all this permit-licence raj. It argued the case for the private sector. But the BJP is not a free market party. While it is against planning it is always going on about how pure capitalism is no good; pure socialism is no good either, they want something in the middle. Whatever that is. More important than that, since liberalisation started the BJP has moved itself into the arena vacated by the Congress. By and large it stands for an autonomous, self-sufficient, foreign capital-free development of the Indian economy. What I would call the Nehru-Mahalanobis model. The fact that that model has planning and restrictions is conveniently forgotten by the BJP. But that's what they now say they want – liberalisation but with an Indian image. Yes we will globalise but not at any cost; we will continue to have an Indian stamp. If you look at the BJP's various statements it is quite clear that they have not actually thought through very carefully what are the possible consequences of following a self-sufficient path in terms of taxation and other sacrifices. I do not think it's a feasible path. And I don't think that the BJP realises what is going on. But I believe that when in power they will more or less do what has been done so far with one important caveat. For a long time they have been backtracking on the foreign capital issue except for the matter of foreign capital in consumer goods industries. The BJP takes the view that we only want foreign capital in high technology areas and in areas where we 'need' foreign capital. We do not need foreign capital in the consumer goods industries they say. This is taking us back to the Janata Dal government of 1978–79 when, if you remember, we had problems with Coca-Cola. This is an interesting variant of the Gandhian-small-industries-local-industries stream of right-wing economic nationalism in India in which there is not so much interventionism in a planning sense but it is very much a protectionist position against foreign capital.

Now two things have happened which gives credence to this idea. One is, of course, the agitation against Kentucky Fried Chicken (hereafter KFC) in Bangalore. This was very much on a *Swadeshi*[2] platform. The same forces which opposed the Cargill Seeds office also have put obstacles in the way of KFC. In Delhi the local government is BJP run and when KFC opened recently, they had their licence revoked on health grounds. I don't want to go into the merits of whether KFC is actually worth eating or not – I've never eaten KFC so I don't know. The argument that there are health hazards in KFC, if it were true, should be systemically applied to non-foreign consumer goods being sold. If all the kitchens in all Delhi restaurants were examined (and not all the tandoors are always empty either) one would not

2 *Swadeshi*, literally 'of one's own nation', was originally based on an anti-British tactic by Tilak and then later Gandhi to boycott British imports and encourage Indian products.

find that KFC was the most unhealthy product available. But because it is foreign, it will be opposed. What I am saying is that this is the reality. You can't get on your high horse and say how can they do this? If these are the perceptions nothing can be done.[3] Nobody from the central Cabinet has got up and said how dare you do this – they didn't say anything about Enron and they didn't say anything about KFC. For small partisan advantage the Rao government is substantially compromising India's ability to obtain foreign capital in the future. What will happen is that the BJP will try to discourage the entry of foreign capital in the consumer goods industries – they cannot actually stop it because the legal situation is what it is. What I hope will not happen, and I can give no guarantee that it will not happen, is that they will not actually try to throw someone out. Even what has been done in Delhi is clearly not an action that a party aspiring to national office should lightly undertake. But then the BJP has a problem in that the national high command cannot always control its state units and so this thing has been allowed to happen. When Mr Advani[4] was recently in London he tried to say that the BJP was absolutely for foreign capital and how dare you say anything else. By and large he is trying to project a pro-foreign capital image. I think there are problems within his own party. There are people there who actually do have very strong feelings against foreign capital and the Indian Left is not likely to differ from the BJP on that question.

And so the pro-liberalisation enclave is surrounded from all sides. What I think will happened, because legal changes have already occurred, is this – there will be no change in the law but the climate may change. I'm not speaking on behalf of the government of India so I don't have to be upbeat on this. I'm merely making an analysis and my analysis is that to the extent that the BJP can keep the RSS[5] under control and under the *Swadeshi* banner, they will be able to have just a change of climate but not a change of policy. But clearly there is going to be a modification of the terms under which foreign capital will be admitted. This is extremely bad news. I do not think that there is a great nationalist path that India can follow that

---

3 In the event, the Delhi magistrates ruled the action against KFC as illegal.

4 Lal Krishna Advani was the leader of the BJP in the Lok Sabha and thus leader of the opposition. In January 1996 he resigned while facing corruption charges.

5 Rashtriya Swayamsevak Sangh (National Volunteer Corps) is a para-military pro-Hindu movement started before independence by the leaders of the Hindu Mahasabha. A member of the RSS, Nathuram Vinayak Godse was convicted for the assassination of Gandhi. The RSS has flourished in the last twenty-five years and is a fellow traveller of the BJP.

will do better for the people than the path of globalisation. If it were possible they had forty years to do it and they failed to do it. Therefore I don't see that the nationalist path will suddenly become the solution. But even in India's large scale private sector boardrooms there is not yet a complete willingness for liberalisation – and why should there be? Who likes competition? Who doesn't enjoy protection and high tariffs and subsidised industries which the large private sector has been enjoying? There are very few, positive, pro-globalisation forces which are pushing India forward. I don't see much further happening except for one, perhaps technically very important change – this would be complete liberalisation of the rupee on capital account, something which I have been urging for some time. I think that the Reserve Bank of India dipped its toe into the water and the rupee slipped down and I think the rupee will go down a little further. Not like a peso crisis but it will go down in the next year. So it will be some time before liberalisation of the rupee on capital account happens. But it will be necessary. That will happen if the Congress is part of the next government. It will not happen if the BJP is part of the next government.

* * *

Question and Answer Session

Question: *Why are you so pessimistic about economic liberalisation when India has this huge middle class of 300 million people?*

Lord Desai: I am wildly for liberalisation. I'm very interested in how the size of the middle class is very elastic. If you're selling India it is 300 million, otherwise it is 100 million. None of the statistics are accurate within 50 million. My view is that if India can only grow at 5 per cent and historically it has not grown at more than that, the promise of liberalisation will not have been fulfilled, since the fruits should be that India should grow at 8, 9 or 10 per cent. While export growth has been very high and manufacturing growth this year has been very high, the hesitancy and the slowness with which this liberalisation has taken place has meant that the fruits of liberalisation have not come as rapidly as they should come. Growth will generate the best anti-poverty programme possible. I'm happy to hear that 9 million jobs have been created but amongst the politicians out there no political party is going to come out and say that the reforms are fantastic, let's have more of them rather than less of them. All they are going to say is reforms are there, but our poor have not been helped, we need a third way. We must preserve India's independence. The ground which the BJP was occupying is again crowded in. I have a quotation from Mr Advani last week – he attacked Rao's economic reforms saying that they had opened the country to foreign investment but had brought in little for the great majority of Indians. That is where the consensus is going to form. I think it happens to be false but we're into perceptions, we're not into facts. If the political culture of all Indian parties is going to take that stance and reform is going to be technical, IMF led and not Indian, then there are problems. I wish it wasn't the case. I hope I could be more optimistic but I go around the world spreading gloom and despondency. That's my bag. I'm not a salesman. I'm an economist.

Question: *How do we explain that the middle class which has benefited most from the recent economic reforms in India is also the backbone of the BJP and it is the middle class which is voicing concern about economic imperialism? How do we explain this and do you think that the growing middle class will ultimately persuade these parties to change their agenda?*

Lord Desai: I think that the middle class is the backbone of every party in India – not just the backbone of the BJP. But I don't think that the middle class is going to be very politically articulate in pushing for reform. I've seen no sign of it. For a short time when Rajiv Gandhi was prime minister we saw some genuine interest amongst the middle managers and the technocrats for reform but right now there is no political personality on the Indian scene whose leadership and career reflect that dynamic of the x million Indian middle class. The middle classes, if they have their videos and TV, are very happy and don't feel like going out into the streets and doing anything further. There is this very strong view that somehow India will be able to combine liberalisation and national self-sufficiency in a great magic potion which nobody else has done so far. I think this is a delusion because foreign capital doesn't have to come to India – there are lots of other places for it to go to. We've now signed GATT so we can't restrict imports. They can't restrict manufacturers – if they don't manufacture in India they'll manufacture in Vietnam and export to India. And in having signed GATT Indian politicians are fooling themselves if they think people are lining up on India's doors just because of 300 million consumers. They can't just write their own ticket. There is no such thing.

References

Desai, M (1993) *Capitalism, Socialism and the Indian Economy*, Exim Bank Lecture, Bombay, January.

Desai, M (1994) *The Economic Policy of the BJP*, Discussion Paper No. 1, National Centre for South Asian Studies, Melbourne, January.

Desai, M (1995) 'Economic Reform: Stalled by Politics?', in Philip Oldenburgh (ed.) *India Briefing: Staying the Course*, New York, The Asia Society & M E Sharpe, Inc.

Acknowledgement

First publication: Desai, Meghnad (1996) 'India's Triple Bypass: Economic Liberalisation, the BJP and the 1996 Elections', Discussion Paper 2, Melbourne, National Centre for South Asian Studies, March, pp. 1–10. Republished with kind permission of the National Centre for South Asian Studies.

Chapter 14

COULD THE INDIAN ECONOMY DO BETTER?

Meghnad Desai

(2012)

Governor M. Narasimham, Dr. S. K. Rao, the family of Mr. K. L. N. Prasad and distinguished guests:

Thank you all very much for inviting me to come to Hyderabad and give this lecture. This is only my second visit to Hyderabad. My very good friend Prof. K. Krishnamurty was teaching here. And this is my first visit since his sad demise a few months ago. So for me, it is also a visit to pay my tributes to him. And of course, I should take advantage of this occasion to say something about the topic at hand.

I think as Governor Narasimham has said in his opening remarks, it is a rhetórical question to which the answer is obvious. I doubt that any such optimists are left who could say, well, India cannot do any better than this. There was a debate not all that long ago, when people were saying that, India could actually have a double-digit growth. But 9.5 per cent was as well as one could do, and therefore we must not aspire to anything higher. Now, as we are struggling to not slide down much below 7 per cent, clearly questions have arisen about India's growth path.

I think there are two kinds of issues involved. One is a very short-run issue, which is exercising all of us. And that is the current malaise in governance and in government. While it is no surprise to us that there is corruption, I think what people much more regret is the lack of decisiveness in policy. And how even when many people in the government and the majority outside are convinced that certain steps ought to be taken, the government seems to belatedly take them and then withdraw from those decisions.

Indeed, Finance Minister Pranab Mukherjee has openly talked about what he would like to do but he cannot do because they (the Congress Party) do not have the numbers. It is quite an astonishing thing! This is the first time, as far as I can remember in the history of Independent India, that in a coalition government, the leading party has a strength of 200 plus (208) – higher than the number of seats any party in a coalition has won since Prime Minister Narasimha Rao's government ended. And the largest party in the coalition actually says that they are helpless. Even Prime Minister Deve Gowda's coalition government did not get to this sorry state whatever else they may have done. I think, partly, this is a self-imposed paralysis. The paralysis of caution, the paralysis of a people who are risk-averse – the Congress Party specially is very risk-averse. All they want to do is to get to the finishing line first in the 2014 elections and, I presume, to pray for a miracle; but something may turn up before that.

But at another level, it is a structural problem. A structural problem which has been brewing for a while and has now come to a head. That is, despite twenty years plus of coalition governments in India, the rules by which a coalition government should be conducted have not been finalised or understood. Currently, the UK has for the first time in peacetime a coalition government since God knows how many years. When the Conservatives and the Liberal Democrats met to decide whether or not they should form a coalition government, there were intensive discussions for three days. Both sides had already read each other's manifestos and mapped out what areas they would be willing to concede and not willing to concede because a coalition was being considered between two parties that are unlikely to be in a coalition from what the people expected and required. The Liberal Democrats were quite surprised that the Conservatives had read their manifesto from day one. They had anticipated a coalition and prepared for it. The intensive discussions resulted in a formal detailed document, setting out where there are agreements and where there are disagreements. And that document is an official policy document of the coalition, to which both the opposition and the government can refer.

UPA-II has taught us a lot. In their case, there is no such document; there is not even an implicit agreement as to what are the common areas of policy. Not only that, another structural problem in a coalition government is that the cabinet government rules are suspended because above the cabinet, there is a higher circle of the coalition in which the leaders of the parties in the coalition sit. They conduct negotiations among themselves as to who shall be the ministers delegated by each party leader. If the UPA coalition leader had been the prime minister, we would not have had this diarchy or duality of power that we currently have. So that when Telecom Minister A. Raja had to be suspended, Mr. M. Karunanidhi was not talking to Dr. Manmohan Singh; he only talked to Sonia Gandhi, and similarly with Mamata Banerjee.

The NDA was a better-run coalition. During the NDA government, the coalition Convener was George Fernandes. Prime Minister Atal Behari Vajpayee was above the coalition leader. In the UPA, the coalition leader is above the prime minister.

These short-term problems are in some sense structural. India is not going to see in the reasonably distant future, a strong one-party majority government. In my view, it is not likely to see in 2014 even a dominant party, by which I mean a party with more than 100 seats in a coalition government. I very much suspect that we are going to have a third-front coalition government, which will not have a majority but which will have outside support from one or the other national parties. We will have a government reminiscent of the V. P. Singh/Deve Gowda type of regimes, but probably with a bigger coalition. Since those days, we have political leaders who have been state chief ministers with considerable success and India's polity has become more federal. So we will get a government that will not be a majoritarian, decisive government, but it will be functional, unlike the present government, which is not functioning.

Some of these issues are a matter of politics, party strength and so on. But, there is a serious lack of consensus in the country about India's record of globalisation, the balance to be struck in terms of the gains and losses, and the way we ought to go forward from here on.

My own beliefs have not been in doubt. I will very quickly summarise them. I think the economic changes since 1990–91 have been a good thing for the country. It raised our growth rate considerably and in a sustainable way. The growth rate before that was 3.5 to 4 per cent, the 'Hindu rate of growth'. The growth rate in FY 2010–11 was 8.5 per cent. Doubling of the growth rate in just over a decade is not an insignificant achievement. I also happen to believe that although inequality may have grown, poverty has come down. I know this is a contentious statement, but whether you take the National Sample Survey standard or the Tendulkar standard, or the dollar a day standard, on whichever standard, if you compare 1990–91 to 2011–12, the percentage of people below the poverty line, however it is defined, has come down.

In my book, *The Rediscovery of India*, I summarised the data until about 2008. Every time somebody mentions a poverty level of 'x' rupees, everybody goes into a tizzy. I feel very angry because India has a very long and strong tradition of measurement of standards of living, of doing the National Sample Survey work, of calibrating living standards, and debating about the poverty level. This work is not something that has recently been undertaken by the Office of Dr Montek Singh Ahluwalia, Deputy Chairman of the Planning Commission. This has been going on for forty years. And MPs at least ought to know that the tradition of poverty measurement in India is a glorious and very good tradition. I do not think people falsify data or cut corners. You may not like the result because you may not like the reality. There is also a tendency to award a prize to whoever says India is poorer than before. This tendency has been encouraged by the Congress Party of all people. The Congress Party has been around for sixty years, there have been fifty years of intense poverty, and to say that India's poverty level is higher now than ever before sounds crazy!

But, I want to say that India can do better. I would like to concentrate entirely on what to do about poverty. Because I think that is the central issue. Eventually, any growth programme is not about the rates of growth, per capita income or catching up with China. It is really about: Does human life get better in the growth process or not? Otherwise, you are wasting your time. During the first thirty years after independence, we were much prouder of our dams, factories and machine tools, the amount of steel output, and so on. That's okay; it gave us great pride. But eventually, it is about whether people are better off than before. Are they getting a better education, are they becoming healthier, are they getting more to eat? That is the question.

The central question of poverty can be related to a central failure of the development strategy, both before and after liberalisation. And that is the failure to industrialise at a rapid enough rate so that the surplus population in agriculture can have gainful employment. What we have seen since 1991 is an amazing growth of the services sector, which now contributes something like 56 to 57 per cent of the total national income. There is stagnation or some decline in the share of manufacturing in GDP, which is around 16 per cent right now; it used to be about 20 per cent. Manufacturing employs only about 13 to 15 per cent of the labour force. And then there is a vast section of the people in the rural sector. The agricultural sector's contribution to GDP is around 20 to 25 per cent. The percentage of Indian people living in rural areas is about 60 per cent. So, roughly speaking, the contrast between productivity in the services sector and productivity in the agricultural sector is 9 to 1. That is basically why there is poverty: it is because people are in low-productive occupations. Eventually, a country cannot pay its people higher than its average productivity. You can cut costs here and there, but that rule holds.

In ancient India, there were very rich rajas, and of course we are in Nizam's Hyderabad. Their wealth was fabulous, but ordinary living standards were not anywhere near close. So, the disparity was always there. The real challenge of development is how do you raise average productivity. Historically, the only way found has been to move people from agriculture to industry, or from rural areas to industry. Manufacturing is a remarkable thing in which people can get year-round employment, even for people who are unskilled manual workers or semi-skilled manual workers; and of course, you can train them for other things. India's manufacturing is predominantly medium to hi-tech products. It is hardly absorbing unskilled or semi-skilled workers; it is mostly absorbing skilled workers. Historically, all the Five-Year Plans have left behind the largely unskilled manual, semi-skilled manual people with limited literacy. A large part of the labour force in the informal sector is unemployed or under-employed. This has been going on since the first plan period. I think, it is astonishing that this persisting under-employment has not been seen to be the major reason for poverty. People have been giving all kinds of other reasons for poverty; they do not understand that, eventually, India has failed to industrialise. And you do not have to be China to do it; Indonesia has done it, Malaysia has done it. So, it is not rocket science.

India's response lately has been of two kinds. One is to set up special economic zones (SEZs), following the Chinese example. And more recently, there is the new manufacturing strategy. I want to argue that both these policies are misguided; they are not serious attempts to industrialise. The reason for that is very simple. Currently, the one asset you can own or capture which has the highest rate of return, apart from politics, is land. Basically, SEZs are land scams. People are keen on SEZs. They submit an application, get an allocation, hang on to the land, and after four years say, Sorry Sir, my project failed. They can make more money just holding on to the land than by doing anything else that I can think of. The idea is that land is a binding constraint to manufacturing. That is why you need SEZs. Setting up SEZs is a slightly dishonest idea. In these zones, companies are allowed to break the labour laws, they are allowed to deviate from the labour laws. Of course, the government completely denies that labour laws have been an obstacle to industrialisation. At the same time, they offer incentives to companies to go to SEZs or to a national manufacturing activity area. The problem with our labour laws is not so much that they do not permit hire and fire, but that India has very peculiar laws which do not allow a company to go bankrupt. If you cannot go bankrupt, you cannot be in business. You have got to have a rule that permits speedy bankruptcy, so that people can come in and go out. If you do not allow companies to go bankrupt, then people will be reluctant to set up companies. There are the tragic stories of Delhi Cloth Mills, which Dr Vinay Bharat Ram has narrated in his book, *From the Brink of Bankruptcy: The DCM Story*, about how long it took them to unwind. Or, in Bombay, the financial nerve centre of the country, the unwinding and shutting down of the textile mills and finally releasing the land for alternative work processes took something like twenty-five years.

I think the nation needs a serious debate about this. We need to industrialise rapidly. Industrialisation is a sure-fire way, much better than the National Rural Employment Guarantee Scheme (NREGS), to give people full-time employment. It is not for 100 days a year. It would be for 250 days per year of employment, which is full-time. And, it will transform the economics of the rural areas. If we want to industrialise, we have to have an open discussion as to whether land is a substantial obstacle. I do not think land is a substantial obstacle. Land is wrongly perceived to be a constraint. I do not think India needs industry in the middle of nowhere. Industries should be set up in small and medium-sized towns, on the edge of small and medium-sized towns. Industry ought to be set up so that people do not have to move too far away from their roots. Their housing is a problem. How do you create a community for workers in a SEZ? It is alright for the owners, but what about the workers? How are you going to create communities for them? There is considerable discussion about setting up infrastructure in SEZs. I have not come across any discussion of how you are going to create communities for the people who work in SEZs. If you want to create communities for workers, do what every country in the world has always done. I know they are called slums, but everybody has started by having slums on the edge of the city. Later on, the housing and amenities have improved, things are more right.

Rather than establishing SEZs or new manufacturing areas, the government should offer incentives to people even with respect to labour laws to set up industry in small and medium-sized towns and not in metros. They do not have to be clustered together, with 100 factories in the same compound. The factories can be scattered, which would be much better for all sorts of pollution. India can opt for a decentralised multiple location solution of setting up low-tech manufacturing industry, such as the one adopted by Indonesia, Malaysia and China, be it textiles or leather products. It can employ people who are currently either idle or in low productivity jobs in rural areas. This will enable India to enhance its rate of industrialisation, increase its share of manufacturing from 16 to 25 per cent, which is a key economic objective. Such a strategy can also generate a substantially great amount of employment; and that employment will come from rural areas. Capital is not a constraint; capital will be available. There is no dearth of capital, either from domestic sources, or from foreign sources. It is a misperception that land is a constraint. The so-called land constraint is due to the under-selling of land in SEZs and basically setting up a land scam. If India is to continue to set up SEZs, the land should not be sold; it should be put on rent or leased out. Then, nobody can make capital gain out of hanging on to the land. Because the government will never be able to tax it efficiently. So, we need to aim for a manufacturing growth rate of 15 to 20 per cent; it is not unthinkable. It is going to require an investment-GDP ratio in terms of manufacturing investment of not more than 10 to 12 per cent. There is infrastructure investment to be done by the government, which would be another 10 per cent or so; this is a ballpark figure.

The constraint is not so much of policy as of economic determination and political will, of having decided upon what the solution to the problem is; that it is an implementable solution and that the implementation is going to benefit not the people who are going to get concessions for setting up industry in SEZs, none of them deserve any concessions, but will benefit ordinary people who are going to find employment. So the national manufacturing strategy has got to be employment-oriented; it has got to be locationally diverse, and not concentrated. There ought to be an incremental growth in industrialisation in a variety of areas around the country, which will deliver sustained high economic growth. Then, the idea of a double-digit growth rate will not be beyond India's capacity. This will also lead to a reduction of the labour force in agriculture and non-agricultural rural activities, and an increase of the labour force in manufacturing. The services sector is doing quite well. So, this is the kind of scenario that I would strongly advocate.

Domestic Indian investors can borrow money abroad. It is not a question of a drastic change in taxation policy or anything like that. In a new climate of federalism where many States want to do things, you could say that the national manufacturing strategy is what the States do. Any State should be allowed to set up industries wherever they like, as long as they are located in small or medium-sized towns. If we can do these things, then a variety of constraints are relaxed and we may be able to do better. Obviously, there are several other things I could say about India doing better. But the other things which need to be done, like health or education, will be easier to do if at the centre of our strategy, there is productive employment for the majority of workers in India. Unless you generate sustainable livelihoods, things will not improve substantially.

I do not want to complain about poor people getting 100 days of work a year. But I do not think that is a sustainable way of generating livelihoods. Because you are not doing anything productive by engaging in those 100 days of work. You are just digging a hole and filling it up again for all practical purposes. It is a Keynesian way of income generation. Distributing income is a good thing, but India's problem is not a Keynesian one. India has a very different kind of problem. In a sense, you could even embark on the national manufacturing policy without necessarily having to rescind the NREGS.

That having been said, I want to take just a few more minutes to talk about whether or not it will happen. The difficulty in convincing people of this policy is a very strong misconception that promoting industrialisation by in any way moderating or changing the rules about hiring and firing and bankruptcy is the wrong way. All these years, because we have been much more interested in protecting jobs, we have not created sufficient employment. A very famous kind of paradox is that the more jobs you protect, the less employment you create. Eventually, you are defending existing jobs and not allowing the creation of new ones. And protection of existing jobs creates certain barriers to anybody prospectively thinking of starting a factory.

In Western countries, within my lifetime in the UK, we have been through this. We learned to abandon trying to protect jobs and have tried to create employment because we had a severe employment crash in the 1970s and 1980s. And, we are now back at fairly high levels of employment, apart from the recession, but with a flexible labour market and labour force activity of 75 per cent. This level of labour market activity is possible because flexible labour markets have been allowed to exist without in any sense creating exploitative labour practices. So, this can be done. The debate has to be much more open and much more political about whether that is the right way to go. Or, currently, what is called progressive policy is to leave the composition of the output frozen as it is, and pass on subsidies only to the rural sector. So, the anomaly of the rural sector not getting anything out of growth is corrected.

From approximately 2006–07 onwards, the policies of UPA-II have very systematically directed large sums of money to the rural areas through NREGS and other programmes. The idea being that rural areas have not gained much from liberalisation; therefore, money ought to go there. Roughly speaking, urban growth creates income and generates revenue; and the revenue has to be spent in rural areas, which have far less growth. Therefore, the fruits of growth are spent to keep people in the rural areas, where they are poor. But, this discourages mobility. NREGS discourages mobility. In a sense, the policy is to keep the poor poor, but make poverty tolerable.

Poverty can be tolerable because there is the *kamadhenu* (the sacred cow in Hindu mythology that grants all wishes and desires) of liberal economic growth. I think, this *kamadhenu* has stopped yielding as of the last quarter of 2011–12. If the growth rate is not seriously raised again, this way of tackling poverty, or at least alleviating the poverty problem, will not be open to India. Things are urgent. And an effective government will have to not only start a public debate about this, but actually change policy so that we use the revenue generated by growth in an economically efficient way – not so much to alleviate poverty but to get the poor out of poverty, which is a very different kind of goal. You can only get the poor out of poverty by giving them work which will generate enough income to get them out of poverty. Redistribution is not a permanent sustainable answer.

I will stop there. Thank you.

Acknowledgement

This speech by Lord Desai was the K. L. N. Prasad Memorial Lecture delivered at the Administrative Staff College of India (ASCI), Hyderabad, on 7 April 2012. First publication: Desai, Meghnad, 'Could the Indian Economy Do Better?' *ASCI Journal of Management*, vol. 42, no. 1, 2012, pp. 113–121. Republished with kind permission of *ASCI Journal of Management*.

Chapter 15

HINDUTVA'S MARCH HALTED?[1]

Choices for the BJP after the 2004 Defeat

Meghnad Desai

(2005)

Introduction

Two things are true about the 2004 general election in India. First, that they attracted worldwide attention, perhaps for the first time spontaneously and not because of some violent incidents that could have occurred. Second, because just about no one anticipated the results.[2] The day before the results were announced, the *New York Times* summed up the feelings of many forecasting that the National Democratic Alliance (NDA) would come in but with a reduced majority (Wildman 2004). This was the way most newspapers in India interpreted the successive rounds. As the exit polls came out, they were greeted with scepticism when they showed a large shortfall in the NDA's strength. Many had written off the Indian National Congress Party (INC), and 'India Shining' looked like the winning formula it was meant to be. A range of pre-budget sweeteners had been announced by the

1 Editor's note: this chapter was originally published as Chapter 13 in *Coalition Politics and Hindu Nationalism*, edited by Katharine Adeney and Lawrence Sáez, Routledge Advances in South Asian Studies. New York, Routledge, 2005. All references to other chapters here refer to chapters in *Coalition Politics and Hindu Nationalism*.

2 During the conference on 'Coalition Politics and Hindu Nationalism' held at the Institute of Commonwealth Studies, James Manor cautioned against automatically assuming that the NDA would win the 2004 general election.

Finance Minister Jaswant Singh from early January onwards. When the INC denounced them as doing nothing for the common man, few thought it had landed a blow.

The NDA's surprise defeat and the INC's return to power raise a number of questions. One of them is about the nature of social science and its usefulness. If everyone gets the forecast wrong, why should we trust social scientists / India's experts? In what follows, I shall first address that question. The second, much larger question, concerns the choices facing the Bharatiya Janata Party (BJP) in light of its defeat. In the title to this chapter I deliberately echo the question that Eric Hobsbawm asked of the British Labour Party after its election defeat in 1979 – rephrasing thus – '*Hindutva*'s march halted?' Had the BJP/NDA coalition won, there was little doubt that the BJP would have become the natural party of power, much like the INC used to be in the first ten years after independence. It would have moved into a hegemonic position in a Gramscian sense and controlled the discourse along its own ideological tramlines. School textbooks would have forever changed children's views of Indian history and minorities would have had to come to terms with a precarious state of existence, henceforth under suspicion of their loyalty. When this did not happen the question about BJP's future choices becomes urgent as much for the party activists as for students of Indian politics. The latter part of this chapter addresses that issue.

Uses of Social Science

What use are all the articles written about India, all the polls and surveys conducted, if virtually no one could predict the 2004 election outcome? Here I would like to make an econometrician's distinction between predictions and forecasts. Forecasts concern what would happen tomorrow or at some specific date in the future. The model at hand is cranked out, relevant values of the exogenous variables are fed in, and out comes the forecast values of the endogenous variables. An exit poll or an opinion poll tells us such a tale. Prediction is about questions of 'What if?'. If you alter some particular exogenous variable, what are the likely effects on the endogenous variables of interest? Prediction uses the structural information in the model to lay out the various likely effects, only some of which may actually come about. This is said not to evade the problem of failure of forecast. There still remains the question do experts know anything useful?

To answer that question I shall review the essays included in this volume [*Coalition Politics and Hindu Nationalism*]. The initial drafts were written in early 2004, before the results of the elections were announced. Their objective analysis of the NDA's performance did not concern itself with the issue of its re-electability. However, the analyses yielded insights about the NDA's policymaking challenges, largely at national level. Likewise, the post-election discussions of the results interpreted them at first as people's protest about the limited rewards of economic reform for the poor, of the need to manage globalisation more equitably. After more reflection some people instead interpreted the results as revealing no national message, but as an outcome of state-level forces which led to a surprise national outcome. This emerged clearly in articles written by Yogendra Yadav and colleagues from the Centre for the Study of Developing Societies (CSDS) which appeared on one of India's leading newspapers, *The Hindu*, on 20 May 2004. There, the defeat was attributed to a fatal choice of dropping DMK, siding with AIADMK in Tamil Nadu and the reversal in the fortunes of TDP in Andhra Pradesh that accounted for a substantial part of the loss of the NDA's fortunes. The Trinamul Congress was humiliated as the Left's fortunes brightened in West Bengal and then losses in Gujarat were a severe blow to the BJP.

Now this set of events tell us that the nature of the NDA coalition was itself a force in the election, over and above the individual electoral fortunes of the parties. This is discussed in Alistair McMillan's analysis of coalitions, both at a theoretical and at an applied level.[3] As he remarks '[r]ather than simply analysing coalition formation, coalition theory must also address the strategic incentives in maintaining or terminating coalitions in the light of the developing political context'. Quite so, since the BJP made a mistake in breaking with a local opposition party in Tamil Nadu and aligning with a governing party late in the life of the coalition. Given the strong anti-incumbency tendency of Indian electorates – some things are constant in Indian politics – this was a predictable own goal. Nevertheless, McMillan, as well as Jenkins, Zavos and Adeney bring out the federal nature of India's polity whereby people primarily choose a state government, but coalition politics determines what the national ruling coalition will be like. This interplay of state and federal politics, at both the executive and the party

3 Alistair McMillan, 'The BJP Coalition: Partisanship and Power-sharing in Government', Chapter 1 in *Coalition Politics and Hindu Nationalism*, edited by Katharine Adeney and Lawrence Sáez, Routledge Advances in South Asian Studies. New York, Routledge, 2005.

levels, is similar to a nested game, which McMillan cites as a possible analytical tool for studying coalitions.[4]

There are also insights in this volume about the BJP's conduct prior to the 2004 general election. While it relied on sophisticated TV commercials and Short Message Service (SMS) text messaging, the BJP appears to have ignored the rural and the poorer urban voter. James Manor's chapter[5] shows how the BJP's organisation is not at all strong, but quite thin, especially in rural areas. The INC was able to exploit this weakness by directing its leader, Sonia Gandhi, to large rural meetings. After the election, it was reported by many papers that the BJP had been sanguine about its chances and had failed to get its troops out for election work. In addition, there had been a reluctance of the Rashtriya Swayamsevak Sangh (RSS) cadres to come out. Manor warns us against assuming that RSS[6] always does the BJP's bidding or vice versa. This is an insight that will be useful in asking questions about the choices facing the BJP.

Nevertheless, between the RSS and the BJP, there are also differences about ideology. As Zavos[7] and Manor[8] point out, for the RSS *Hindutva* matters and its agenda is one of Hindu nationalism. The BJP, on the other hand, wants to win power and hold on to it. This requires coming out of the ghetto and making alliances. Thus, it was the alliance of the Jana Sangh with Jaya Prakash Narayan's *andolan* (movement) in Gujarat in 1974 that made the party respectable for the first time since the assassination of Mahatma Gandhi (for which the RSS and vaguely Hindu nationalist forces were blamed). Efforts of this type, as Jaffrelot points out,[9] were the

4 Alistair McMillan, 'The BJP Coalition: Partisanship and Power-sharing in Government', Chapter 1 in *Coalition Politics and Hindu Nationalism*, edited by Katharine Adeney and Lawrence Sáez. Routledge, New York.

5 James Manor, 'In Part, a Myth: The BJP's Organisational Strength', Chapter 3 in *Coalition Politics and Hindu Nationalism*, edited by Katharine Adeney and Lawrence Sáez, Routledge Advances in South Asian Studies. New York, Routledge, 2005.

6 The RSS cadres (and the youth cadres of the Bajrang Dal) have been a critical support base for the BJP for they work inside the crucial rural and urban electorates which the BJP has identified as crucial for winning elections.

7 John Zavos, 'The Shapes of Hindu Nationalism', Chapter 2 in *Coalition Politics and Hindu Nationalism*, edited by Katharine Adeney and Lawrence Sáez, Routledge Advances in South Asian Studies. New York, Routledge, 2005.

8 James Manor, Chapter 3 in *Coalition Politics and Hindu Nationalism*.

9 Christophe Jaffrelot, 'The BJP and the 2004 General Election: Dimensions, Causes and Implications of an Unexpected Defeat', Chapter 12 in *Coalition Politics and Hindu Nationalism*, edited by Katharine Adeney and Lawrence Sáez. Routledge, New York.

incipient attempts by the Jana Sangh at coalition building. It means tackling bread and butter issues, not just the ideological ones. In the statewide elections held in late 2003, the BJP tried a *roti/kapda/makan* (food/clothing/shelter) strategy, and reaped dividends. This encouraged it to play the same card in the 2004 general election. This not only kept its coalition partners happy, but it was a way of casting its appeal wider. Indeed by attracting many ex-INC members to its fold on the eve of the election, including Muslim members (Najma Heptulla, for instance), the BJP was launching itself as the true successor of Nehru's Congress Party. But this action alienated its core ideological support, which wanted a commitment on *mandir* (temple) issues. It is no surprise that the post-election reactions by the Vishwa Hindu Parishad (VHP) have been not entirely sympathetic. But this is precisely where the party lost its ideologically minded cadres. The British Labour Party, for instance, is undergoing a very similar experience. If and when an ideological party widens its appeal to garner more votes, it stands to lose the support of its more fanatical supporters. This is a classic democratic compulsion. The BJP has tried to become an inclusive party, like the INC, and thus weakened its hold over the Hindu nationalist core.

Governing also involves dealing with day-to-day challenges. Since the balance of payments crisis of 1991 successive governments have had to rethink what they said about the economic reforms while in opposition, mostly since reforms are no longer a matter of choice. The only choice is the pace of reforms and an occasional twist one way or another. India needs to display a willingness to attract foreign direct investment (FDI) and for that end demonstrate good governance. Thus, privatisation is urgent and reforms of the labour market necessary. This is a story, which again meshes in with the federalist theme as Rob Jenkins[10] points out. Of course, reforms do not please the ideologues of the RSS and the BJP; hence the dilemma of governing and keeping faithful to one's beliefs raises its head again. The success of the BJP/NDA in managing the economy (by the end of its tenure the growth rate of GDP was over 8 per cent) alienated its core support, since it was soft on liberalisation and the entry of foreign capital.[11] By pointing out in its 'India Shining' commercials what it had done, the NDA Government also reminded its supporters of facts which were not to their liking. Hence, the 'India Shining' campaign did not only alienate rural voters.

10 Rob Jenkins, 'The NDA and the Politics of Economic Reform', Chapter 9 in *Coalition Politics and Hindu Nationalism*, edited by Katharine Adeney and Lawrence Sáez. Routledge, New York.

11 Rob Jenkins, Chapter 9 in *Coalition Politics and Hindu Nationalism*.

The story of the BJP/NDA Government, as it unfolds in the various essays in this volume, is that of continuity rather than change. Whatever its rhetoric, the BJP is as much of a centralist political party as the INC. It wants a militarily strong India with a high status on the world stage. Thus Kundu,[12] as well as Chiriyakandath and Wyatt,[13] point out that the nuclear decision and the alliances with the US and Israel are driven by the *realpolitik* of India's ambitions to be taken seriously as a regional power. But at the same time, no 'national' party can ignore regional and caste forces in its policies. In a coalition with such parties that rely on caste, region and religion for their appeal, this is doubly so. Therefore, while an analysis of foreign policy and national security reveals continuity, it is in the domestic policy arena where we would expect local and contemporaneous pressures to differentiate the NDA's government's policy from other governments.

However, here again the brute facts of coalition building point to the limits of what any dominant party in a coalition can do. The facts of life in India compel any coalition to accommodate regional and caste parties. These parties are, by and large, non-ideological, their principal focus being rent seeking for sharing with their clientele. So provisions for minorities and for particular states, the need to direct more revenues to the states with each successive Finance Commission are the common concerns of every coalition. Now that the INC is in power, it will have to play to the same tune as BJP had to as head of the NDA coalition. Subrata Mitra deals with the issue of minorities,[14] while Katharine Adeney discusses in detail the BJP's attitude about the federal constitution.[15] They each show how the BJP had to come to terms with minorities and states, despite its centralist and monist view of Hindu society.

The reality is that neither of the two largest national parties – INC or BJP – can by itself come to power. Indeed in the 2004 general election, their combined strength in the Lok Sabha fell from 293 seats in 1999

12 Apurba Kundu, 'The NDA and National Security', Chapter 11 in *Coalition Politics and Hindu Nationalism*, edited by Katharine Adeney and Lawrence Sáez. Routledge, New York.

13 James Chiriyankandath and Andrew Wyatt, 'The NDA and Indian Foreign Policy', Chapter 10 in *Coalition Politics and Hindu Nationalism*, edited by Katharine Adeney and Lawrence Sáez. Routledge, New York.

14 Subrata Mitra, 'The NDA and Politics of "Minorities" in India', Chapter 4 in *Coalition Politics and Hindu Nationalism*, edited by Katharine Adeney and Lawrence Sáez. Routledge, New York.

15 Katharine Adeney, 'Hindu Nationalists and Federal Structures in an Era of Regionalism', Chapter 5 in *Coalition Politics and Hindu Nationalism*, edited by Katharine Adeney and Lawrence Sáez. Routledge, New York.

– 182 for the BJP plus 111 for the INC – to 283 seats in 2004 – 138 for the BJP and 145 seats for the INC – as did their vote share. India's politics is becoming more fragmented, more devolved and less majoritarian. This requires living with federalism. Katharine Adeney shows that, despite the BJP's ambivalence about linguistic states and its preference for a strong unitary India, the BJP has had to come to terms with regionalism and cope with the challenges of adapting and reforming the structure of the federation.[16] One strategy to strengthen the centre against the regions is to break up the larger states into smaller units. Nevertheless, as big states are divided into smaller states, the number of small parties with a strictly local focus is going to rise, and the fragmentation of politics will increase. But, if this is the case, then a larger question is raised. Can the BJP ever realise its dream of a *Hindutva*-based government in India?

The Halted March of *Hindutva*?

The defeat in 2004 is not just sad for the BJP; it is tragic for the party. Through the 1980s and 1990s, it has struggled to acquire a national status. Far from being a minority, extremist pariah party, it has commanded national attention and international respect. From the irresponsible behaviour of some of its leaders as part of a howling mob bringing down the Babri mosque in 1992, it rose to come to power (briefly) in 1996 and again in 1998 and 1999. Its strength was confirmed at 182 parliamentary seats in two general elections (1996 and 1998). This was a contrast from the Jana Sangh polling approximately 50 seats (much as the CPI/CPM used to). In 2004, it had the chance to move up 182 seats to the sunlit uplands of 200 seats and above. Had the BJP broken through to 225 seats, then it could have dominated the next coalition, or even ruled alone with outside support (much as Narasimha Rao managed to do between 1991 and 1996). Winning another five-year term would have been an immensely significant step for the BJP's programme of gaining cultural hegemony. What Murli Manohar Joshi wanted to do, as Marie Lall has argued in her piece[17], was to change the Indian view of history so as to demonise Muslim rule forever more. Five more years would have given the BJP ideologues a real stranglehold on history and social science disciplines.

---

16 Katharine Adeney, Chapter 5 in *Coalition Politics and Hindu Nationalism.*

17 Marie Lall, 'Indian Education Policy under the NDA Government', Chapter 8 in *Coalition Politics and Hindu Nationalism*, edited by Katharine Adeney and Lawrence Sáez. Routledge, New York.

The new Congress-led government has shown the importance of this by moving on the school history textbooks issue immediately.

However, the setback from 182 to 138 parliamentary seats is serious, despite the fact that in terms of share of the vote the BJP did better than the INC. The question is, 'Will this mean the end of the road for BJP's dream of ruling India as a single party and of installing a *Hindutva* Raj forever or is this just a blip, *reculer pour mieux sauter* (to back up so as to better leap over), and the BJP will bounce back next time?'

Through the 1990s, the BJP had a difficult trapeze act to perform. It wanted to be known as the party for Hindus and this required them to be strongly anti-Muslim, not simply anti-Pakistani. It also had to convince the voters that it could be a responsible party capable of competently ruling India. For the latter it needed to not only manage the economic reforms but also to build a coalition with disparate forces. Its Hindu phase led to Advani's *Rath Yatra* (chariot procession) of 1992 and the demolition of the Masjid at Ayodhya. Its more extreme supporters have moved from anti-Muslimism to sheer xenophobia, so that all non-Hindu religions are demonised. Attacks on Christian missionaries were the latest expression and weapon in the struggle. While Narendra Modi did not foment the post-Godhra riots in 2002, he did nothing to curb them and was re-elected later that year. This told one section of the BJP that coming to power via mob riot was, if unattractive, at least an effective option. There was much talk of a 'Modi strategy' for winning mid-term state elections in Himachal Pradesh and elsewhere after Modi's triumphal re-election. This section of the party is the traditionalist core of the BJP whose favourite ideologue is Hedgewar and whose custodian is Advani.

The other face of the BJP is not as a Hindu party, but as a nationalist party, believing in India emerging as a strong nuclear power able to strut on the world stage with its weapons rather than any message of *ahimsa* (non-violence). It wants to show competence in government. This BJP wants a high status in world politics for India; it wants rapid economic growth with the latest technological gizmos. It wants India to rival China and contain Pakistan. Its favourite ideologue is Savarkar and Vajpayee is its face.

In possessing this Janus face, the BJP is not unusual. Ideological parties of the Left or the Right also face such a perpetual problem. The core supporters want to change the world, the pragmatic office seekers merely want to manage the world better than other parties have done. The ideologues want to take to the streets, mobilise the masses, bring down the old order, and usher in a new era. The pragmatists want to move in the corridors of power, raise real resources and achieve set targets. The very success of the pragmatists ruins the chances of the ideologues since the world is not ruined but improved.

Thus far, the BJP has managed to keep the two factions together since it wanted to achieve power. Having tasted power and made inroads in the cultural sphere, it badly wanted to continue in power. Indeed, the ideologues let the pragmatists have the front line roles in the election in the hope that their strategy would win another term to sharpen the ideological struggle. Now with a defeat, recriminations are breaking out as to who was responsible. There has already been a skirmish around the issue of Narendra Modi. Vajpayee was quoted as having said that Modi needed to be removed if the BJP was to win national confidence. The ideologues shot this down pretty quickly. Instead, they were quick to blame Arun Shourie who as the minister for (under another name) privatisation was outstandingly successful. However, Shourie was not ideological enough for the RSS. On the other hand, the ideologues overreacted to the prospect of Sonia Gandhi becoming prime minister. BJP leaders, such as Uma Bharti and Sushma Swaraj, took this almost as a personal affront and instead of behaving like rulers of states; they behaved like the mob that destroyed the Masjid twelve years ago. In the event they were wrong-footed by Sonia Gandhi who stepped back from taking the position of prime minister.

In opposition, the BJP will have difficulty keeping the ideologues down, unless there is a real prospect of a return to power soon. The party faces a problem of competing generations. The 'old guard', composed of Vajpayee, Advani and Joshi is moving on, and the 'new generation' of Pramod Mahajan, Arun Jaitley, Narendra Modi and Uma Bharti are waiting to take over. The ideology/pragmatism divide stretches across the generations. Unlike the INC, the BJP does not currently rule in many states, though it gained a few in the 2003 state assembly elections. Narendra Modi and Uma Bharti are ideologues, rather than pragmatics. However, the pragmatists were not totally marginalised since they were able to secure Arun Shourie a seat in the Rajya Sabha.

The BJP and Its Choices

The critical problem, however, will not be solely one of managing factions or the transition from one generation to the next. The structural problem facing the BJP is whether a party based on *Hindutva* can command a large enough vote share to come to power on its own.

The choice is between a sharp ideological and Hindu focus, which will test the hypothesis that since the majority of the voters are Hindus then a party based on Hinduism should eventually command majority support. The example, often cited by BJP ideologues, is that of Israel which bases itself on the strong racial/religious identity of Jews. Hinduism is, however, nothing like Judaism. It is pantheistic, lacks a single church or even a single book. It has no priesthood that is universally accepted. Hindus worship different gods and have various practices all of which pass as correct. There is no confession and no necessity to go to the temple every day or even once a week.

Hinduism is not a single religion. It is neither unitary nor indeed unifying. Intra-faith rivalries between devotees of Vishnu as against Shiva are frequent, though not lethal like Shia-Sunni battles. During an attempt in 2003 by the Shankaracharya of Kanchi to settle the Ayodhya *mandir/masjid* (temple/mosque) dispute, the secretary of the VHP questioned his bona fides saying that the Shankaracharya was a Shivaite and the temple was dedicated to an avatar of Vishnu! If the VHP itself takes such a fragmented view of Hinduism what hope is there for ordinary citizens of uniting under the banner of Hinduism?

The founders of the RSS were aware of this problem. Indeed every effort at reforming Hinduism in the wake of the ideological challenge of British and indeed Western Imperialism has been at recasting the old religion in the image of a monotheistic creed such as Christianity. The movements of Brahmo Samaj, Arya Samaj and indeed Vivekanand, were efforts at sanitising if not semitising Hinduism, so that it would have one God, one Book. The exalted status that the nationalist leaders, such as Aurobindo, Tilak and Gandhi conferred on the *Bhagavad Gita* by writing commentaries was one such effort. Nevertheless, that approach proved too highbrow for the masses. Initially the RSS eschewed religion and emphasised social regeneration of Hindu society.

But Hindu society is also not a unity. Even in its idealistic conception, it is a structured hierarchy that rejects egalitarianism. The caste structure has evolved from a four-fold *varnashrama* (castes) to multifarious *jatis* (subcastes) but it still retains not only the distinction between the upper (twice born) castes and the lower castes, but also the untouchables-*harijans* or *dalits* who are outside the pale and yet part of Hindu society. What would be regeneration of Hindu society for an upper caste RSS man would not be the same for a lower caste or a *dalit*. For the *dalit*, it would be the abolition of the hierarchy, which would constitute reform or regeneration. Hence,

Ambedkar's decision to leave the Hindu fold altogether after a lifetime of fighting for reform and embracing Buddhism.

The upper castes are not numerous enough to hold power in a democracy by themselves. As Westernised urban elites, they had a head start soon after independence, but they were also members of the INC which meant that they were able to retain power. The pressures of democratic elections soon valorised the caste divisions and made jatis into vote banks. A party hoping to come to power had to recruit lower castes and dalits as well as Muslims. The INC did this effectively until the late 1980s. Then the Mandal Commission (1980–2008) split the Hindu vote along upper and lower caste lines. The BJP's moment came then.

The agitation for the Ram temple in Ayodhya was a stroke of genius. Instead of the abstruse philosophy of the *Bhagavad Gita* the unifying symbol of Ram was upheld; known from the epic mythologies as an ideal person and popularised by Gandhi no less in his favourite *bhajan* (prayer), Raghupati Raghav Raja Ram. Here was a unifying symbol for Hindus, of upper as well as lower castes. If the *Hindutva* programme could be recast along the Ram bhakti lines, there was indeed a rainbow at the end of that dream.

The destruction of the *masjid* damaged the BJP's reputation, but it recovered by putting Vajpayee forward as its sober face and it was able to come to power as the leading member of a coalition. However, the provocative act of destroying a mosque had antagonised many smaller parties and thus the temple issue had to be put on ice. Had its ideologues displayed patience until single party rule by BJP became a reality, it may have been possible for the BJP to build a temple at Ayodhya. As it was, the BJP could not deliver what its impatient ideologues wanted and there was a distinct cooling between the various parts of the *Sangh Parivar*. In light of this history, both the VHP and the RSS were less than enthusiastic when the general elections were held in April 2004.

The structural question is, thus, as urgent as ever. Can *Hindutva* be Hindu based and still win a majority or does it have to be reshaped as nationalism first with less of an emphasis on Hinduism? Of course, there have been attempts to say that *Hindutva* is not about Hinduism, but about India and Indianness. The destruction of the Babri Masjid devalued that defence forever. As all can see, *Hindutva* is anti-Muslim even before it is pro-Hindu. So while the temple issue excites the ideologues of BJP, there is no hope of convincing the electorate that *Hindutva* is an inclusive philosophy.

Thus, Hinduism is a risky gambit for majority power. At best it can make BJP the largest party in a coalition, but not strong enough to meet the ideologues' demands. That was the lesson of the last government. Mere competence in governing and raising the growth rate of GDP – policies which would be almost 'secular' also did not help. How can BJP then shape its strategy so that it can win a majority on its own?

Hindutva or Hindu Democracy?

In choosing Israel as their ideal country, the ideologues of *Hindutva* have missed a vital ingredient. Judaism is a non-proselytising religion, like Hinduism, but it is also exclusive and guards its frontiers fiercely. It has also the recent experience of the worst tragedy of modern times in the Holocaust. Its need for a protective approach to its identity is well understood. Hinduism is inclusive but, by and large, it has suffered no grave tragedy. The Partition of India was a traumatic event, but it was an Indian tragedy not a solely Hindu one despite efforts on the part of RSS and others to claim so. Muslims remain in India as do Sikhs, Christians and others, India is not so much a secular society as a multi-religious one. The Indian state in colonial times ran a regime that did not interfere in religious practices and discouraged, much to its chagrin, the Anglican Church from proselytising. The Indian state continued that after independence, though secularism was added in the title of the Republic only in the mid-1970s by Indira Gandhi.[18]

The Partition of India, as well as Nehru's own attitudes, made religious affiliations in political parties a disadvantage. Speculations about the possibility of a Hindu socialism, which flourished in the 1940s and early 1950s, were soon laughed off the court. Yet at the same time as India's independence, the recovery in Europe was aided by the revival of Christian democratic parties. In Germany and Italy, Christian democracy played a crucial role in stabilising and consolidating democracy after years of fascism. Christian socialism is a hardy plant in British politics (Stafford Cripps was a Christian socialist, for example). Zionism at its origin was a socialist movement. The idea that religion and politics cannot or should not mix is a very peculiarly Indian idea shared by 'progressive' elements. The BJP has not countered this idea by pointing to the European experience with Christian democracy. It has not even shown any awareness of Christian democracy.

---

18 Article 25 of the Indian Constitution provides for the free profession, practice and propagation of religion.

This is not the occasion to give a full account of Christian democracy, but suffice it to say that it has adapted Christian ideals for the Cold War era of liberal democracy. Christian democracy was always anti-communist, but also very much in favour of business treating workers fairly and in a spirit of communal harmony rather than class struggle. Christian democracy was a social as well as a political movement. It adapted itself to the secularising forces in European life by underplaying the formal religious elements in its make-up and bringing out the social relevance of religious values. It was a conservative but socially inclusive movement. For around forty years after 1945, it was the bulwark of Italian democracy and it is still alive as a powerful force in German politics.

It may be that the BJP may yet learn from the Christian democratic experience or it may fall foul to its own contradictions. It is not my purpose to solve the BJP's problems. The only point of discussing Christian democracy is to expose a successful model of combining religion with politics. If Christian democracy can flourish in a secular Europe there is no reason, in theory at least, why a Hindu democracy cannot flourish in India.

Conclusion

The defeat in the 2004 general election puts the BJP at a crossroads. It has to reconcile itself to never coming to power as a single party and hence implementing its *Hindutva* dream by stealth or not at all. In either case, a *Hindutva-based* India remains a distant prospect. It could, however, build a vote winning strategy by following the example of Christian democratic parties that downplayed religion as such but took its ethical message into the social sphere. Will it be *Hindutva* or Hindu-Lite for the BJP?

References

The Hindu (2004) 'How India voted: Supplement', *The Hindu*, 20 May. Online. Available at: http://www.hindu.com (accessed 21 May 2004).

Wildman, A. (2004) The New York Times, 13 May.

Acknowledgement

First publication: Desai, Meghnad (2005) '*Hindutva*'s March Halted? Choices for the BJP after the 2004 Defeat' in *Coalition Politics and Hindu Nationalism*, edited by Katharine Adeney and Lawrence Sáez, Routledge Advances in South Asian Studies. New York, Routledge, pp. 254–263. Republished with kind permission of Routledge.

Chapter 16

TWIN TROUBLES

Meghnad Desai
(2008/2009)

India and Pakistan are twins separated at birth. What was once a large and single economy until 1947 was split into two when the division of spoils took place at the time of Partition. Later, in 1971, it was split into three when a third country – Bangladesh – was born. Twins that become triplets are a rare medical occurrence, but an equally interesting economic development is the fact that South Asia has gone the opposite way from the path followed by the European Union, where a single market was created out of many (often mutually hostile) nations.

The two countries can also be contrasted in terms of the mode of governance each adopted after 1947: democracy for India and a mixture of democracy and dictatorship for Pakistan, secularism for India and a religious state for Pakistan. India also claims to be a socialist republic, something that Pakistan has never pretended to be. Finally, the two have fought many bitter battles and both have nuclear capability.

Yet for two countries that were once one and are neighbours, the extent of ignorance about each other that India and Pakistan share is unique. Most Indians think – indeed some openly say – that Pakistan's economy is a failure and the country is a basket case. Granted that today India's success as an economic power house is undeniable yet, as recently as ten years ago, the Pakistanis were equally snooty about India's economy. As it happens, there is and never has been much difference between the two countries if one studies their respective economic records.[1]

1 See my *South Asia: Economic Stagnation and Economic Change* written in 1997 on occasion of the fifty-year anniversary of independence of both countries, reprinted

* * *

In 1947, India was the larger, the more industrialised, the better educated and more 'bourgeois' society.[2] Pakistan, especially its western part, was better endowed in terms of land, and had a better agricultural and irrigation system. In terms of population, India is seven times (West) Pakistan but in area terms, India has only four times as much land. In 1947, India had a well-developed entrepreneurial class that had successfully launched many industries, such as steel and textiles. Pakistan, in contrast, had no industrial development and no industrialists. In the civil service as well, since India inherited the bulk of civil servants, Pakistan still needed British civil servants to stay on for a few years after independence.

Even so, there was not much difference between the two in economic terms. In terms of per capita income, India was ranked 55th and Pakistan 57th in a United Nations (UN) study of national income published in 1949, which also ranked Indonesia 67th, South Korea 68th and China 69th. Since both India and Pakistan started with a huge problem of resettling refugees, there was little growth in the first few years. However, India devalued the Rupee along with the Sterling in 1949 while Pakistan did not: a fact that was later to prove a costly mistake. Initially, India made a good start with economic development in the 1950s. Pakistan, on the other hand, had a difficult start since it had to set up industries from scratch. Both countries followed an Import Substitution Industrialization (ISI) strategy, but India neglected its private sector and boosted its public sector development instead. Conversely, Pakistan used State aid to build up private sector industrialists, but this ended up by creating a virtual monopoly where about twenty families owned most of Pakistan's industries. The 1960s were better for Pakistan during Ayub Khan's rule, which brought generous US aid. In India, on the other hand, industrial progress became slower in the 1960s.

We must remember that for the first twenty-four years of its existence Pakistan had an eastern wing – East Pakistan – which became Bangladesh after 1971. West Pakistan had a higher growth rate than East Pakistan. In the 1950s, West Pakistan grew at around 3.5 per cent, which was twice

---

in *Development and Nationhood: Essays in the Political Economy of South Asia* (Oxford, Delhi, 2005).

2 See Aitzaz Ahsan: *Indus Saga* (Roli Books, Delhi) for a cogent argument that what became Pakistan and India were two different social formations, one feudal and other commercial-bourgeois. He cites this rather than religion as the basis for the division.

the rate of East Pakistan's growth. Per capita growth was negative in the East and around 1 per cent in the West. In the first half of the 1960s, West Pakistan grew at 7.2 per cent (4.4 per cent per capita) and East Pakistan at 5.2 per cent (2.6 per cent). Pakistan's economic performance improved once it shed East Pakistan, even though the argument of Bangladeshis was that West Pakistan was exploiting East Pakistan. Between 1965 and 1980, Pakistan grew at 5.2 per cent, while India plodded at a slow 3.6 per cent. This lead continued during the 1980s as Pakistan grew at 6.3 per cent and India followed at 5.5 per cent.

By 1997 – that is fifty years after independence – Pakistan was ahead of India in terms of per capita income. Pakistan was placed at 120 while India at 143 was just one place ahead of Bangladesh ranked at 144. During the same period, South Korea was ranked 37, Indonesia 92 and China 111. It was in the sixth decade after Partition, that India began to outstrip Pakistan in economic growth. The table that follows shows how far ahead of Pakistan India has reached in the last five years. The reason for this extraordinary growth is not just that Pakistan's economy has stagnated in this period, but that India has enjoyed a remarkable rate of GDP growth.

Table 16.1. Comparative Growth Rates
GDP Growth Rates 2003–2008

Year	India	Pakistan
03/04	8.5	4.8
04/05	7.5	7.4
05/06	9.4	7.7
06/07	9.6	6.9
07/08	9.0	6.4

By 2007, the relative positions of India and Pakistan had become reversed. India was ranked 122 in World Bank per capita income (US$) ranking with an income of $1,012 and Pakistan was 131 with $884. China ranked 99 with $2,485, Indonesia 108 with $1,918 and South Korea 28 with $19,983.

The economic structure of the two countries is also remarkably alike. India splits its national income between agriculture at 18 per cent, industries at 29 per cent and services at 53 per cent. Pakistan's numbers are 20 per cent, 27 per cent and 54 per cent respectively. The two countries have always received similar ranking in the Human Development Index as both are placed in the 'Low' Human Development category. In the rankings for 2008, India was placed at 132 and Pakistan at 139 with China at 94, Indonesia at 109 and South Korea at 25. Life expectancy is almost the same in both India and Pakistan: 64 years in India and 65 in Pakistan. According to the 2008 Human Development Report, Pakistan scores in terms of access to safe water with 91 per cent of households compared to India's 86 per cent but as recently as the first half of the 1990s, India was ahead with 81 per cent to 60 per cent for Pakistan. Pakistanis have better access to sanitation facilities than their Indian cousins – 59 per cent to India's dismal 33 per cent. India is better in contraceptive care and in prenatal care with 47 per cent to 28 per cent and 60 per cent to 43 per cent, respectively. However, there are more doctors per capita in Pakistan than in India: 68 doctors per 100,000 while India has just 51 doctors per 100,000.

Where the statistics for poverty are concerned, Pakistan does better than India with only 23 per cent of its population below the mandatory US$1.25 level, compared to India's 41 per cent. Again, Pakistan has 60 per cent and India 76 per cent (all figures rounded) where the statistics for those below US$2 are concerned. In comparison to these, China has 16 per cent and 36 per cent in the two categories and Indonesia 21 per cent and 54 per cent, respectively. India also has a higher degree of income inequality than Pakistan. The Gini coefficient, which measures inequality, has a value of 37 per cent for India and 31 per cent for Pakistan (Human Development Report 2008).

What makes the big difference in our perceptions is the absolute size of India's economy. Since India's population is around seven times that of Pakistan, in terms of total GDP, India with US$1.17 trillion ranks as a giant in the global arena (Pakistan: US$143.6 billion). India is 12th and Pakistan 46th in world GDP rankings. Together, the two countries would move up two ranks above Brazil and be placed just under Canada. Indeed, throughout its history people have been beguiled into thinking of India as a rich and prosperous country because the area was so large, and because her rulers, whoever they were, had immense wealth. The truth is that India's ordinary people were always poor. And, after sixty years of independence, this continues to be the case in both countries.

* * *

There are several conclusions to be drawn from these bald comparisons. As a region, South Asia has not been an economic success story compared to other Asian countries. The countries of South Asia are laggards rather than leaders. Moreover, in the long run of fifty to sixty years, the relative performance of the two countries is very similar with the ratio of their per capita incomes being not much different from unity. Now one then another goes ahead, but they are similar in being behind the rest than being much ahead of each other.

The question that stares at us then is why has economic development in South Asia been so slow in tackling poverty? One reason is the top-down elitist nature of the development strategy adopted. In both countries, capital intensive organised industries were given large subsidies, but these did not generate much employment. The military-industrial sector developed faster than the consumer-civilian sector. While both countries have a nuclear weapon and can launch missiles at each other, 47 per cent of Indian children under five years are underweight as are 38 per cent of Pakistani children. The formal or organised labour market absorbs only around a sixth of the labour force; the rest survive in the informal sector. The formal sector has health and tenure protection, guaranteed inflation indexed wages while the informal labour sector has none of these cushions. The real burden of this duality falls on the rural sector which is the largest in terms of the proportion of population that depends on it but the lowest in terms of its contribution to income. This means that the agricultural worker has low productivity and hence low wages/income. Both countries have failed to generate a manufacturing transformation of their economies; services have a similar 50 per cent plus share in total income.

The second reason is a shocking neglect of education. South Asia (apart from Sri Lanka) lags behind Sub-Saharan Africa in literacy and educational enrolment. India may have improved its primary and secondary school enrolment, yet it has still not guaranteed universal primary education. It is these dismal literacy statistics that reveal the real secret of the slow rate of progress in improving mass welfare. The adult literacy rate is in the mid-60s for both countries while female literacy is merely 48 per cent (66 per cent of the male literacy rate) in India and 35 per cent (53 per cent of the male rate) in Pakistan. This represents a gross waste of human resources for which the governing elites of the two countries are solely responsible. China, Indonesia and South Korea have female literacy in the high 70s low 80s. South Korea adult literacy stands at 98 per cent, while China and Indonesia register 86 to 87 per cent on this score.

* * *

This essay has many more numbers than it has text. But the message is stark. There is not much difference between India and Pakistan when it comes to economic performance except that in the last few years India has at last gone ahead of Pakistan in terms of its per capita income. Both countries neglect their human resources by failing to provide education or sanitation or health. Life expectancy is in the mid-sixties and the extent of child malnutrition is shocking. Yet both India and Pakistan boast of nuclear bombs and sophisticated defence arsenals. The sad truth is that societies choose what they want to spend their scarce resources on. In the case of India and Pakistan there is a remarkable consensus on this: both have chosen weapons over human welfare.

It is as if these fraternal twins were identical after all.

Acknowledgement

First publication: Desai, Meghnad, 'Twin Troubles' in *The Great Divide*, *India International Centre Quarterly*, vol. 35, no. 3/4, Winter 2008 / Spring 2009, pp. 96–105. Republished with kind permission of *India International Centre Quarterly*.

Chapter 17

BHAGAVAD GITA

Outlines of a Secular Critique

Meghnad Desai

(2013)

The *Bhagavad Gita* is a central text of Brahmanism.[1] The German philosopher William von Humboldt called it 'the most beautiful, perhaps the only true philosophical song existing in any known language'. When the Atom bomb was first tested in the deserts of New Mexico, J. Robert Oppenheimer who led the project recited the first line of the verse 11.32[2] from the *Gita* to invoke the terrifying sight unfolding before him.

The *Gita* is perhaps the best known book of India and as S. Radhakrishnan puts it 'the most influential work in Indian thought'.[3] Unlike the *Vedas* and the *Upanishads*, the *Gita* is short and concise, a book of just 700 verses that one can compactly carry in one's pocket and even memorise in its entirety as many have done.

---

1 I use the word Brahmanism rather than Hinduism because I think it better represents the nature of the religion both because of the centrality of the notion of Brahman and the apex position of the Brahmins. Max Weber the famous German Sociologist in his book *The Religion of India* says 'Only in recent literature have the Indians themselves begun to designate their religious affiliation as Hinduism. It is the official designation of the English census for the religious complex also described in Germany as "Brahmanism"'. (Weber, *The Religion of India*, p. 4)

2 *Kalo'smi lokakshayakmt'pravruddho lokan samaharmmihah pravruttah* (The Blessed Lord said: I am the Time-Spirit, destroyer of the world, arisen huge-statured for the destruction of the nations). Aurobindo's translation of verse 32 first line of the 11th *Adhyaya* of the *Gita*.

3 S. Radhakrishnan. *Indian Philosophy*, vol. 1 (Oxford India), p. 510. Humboldt quote is also on the same page.

Of course what makes the *Gita* sacred is that presumably the Supreme Lord himself in his avatar as Krishna recited it for the benefit of his friend Arjun. It is because of this unique characteristic of having divine authorship that the *Gita* has become the best known and the most commented upon text over the centuries. Its status was confirmed by Shankara's commentary in the ninth century CE. While Shankara refers to commentaries before his own,[4] his is the first and most authoritative commentary. Indeed Swami Vivekananda thought Shankara may even have written the *Gita* himself. Thus, he says in his *Thoughts on the Gita* '(T)he book, *Gita*, had not been much known to the generality of people before Shankaracharya made it famous by writing his great commentary on it... Some infer that Shankaracharya was the author of the *Gita* and that it was he who foisted it in the body of the *Mahabharata*' (*Complete Works*, vol. 4: 102–3).

The Modern Life of the *Gita*

The modern life of the *Gita* begins with the enterprise of Warren Hastings to have it translated into English. Sir Charles Wilkins (1750–1833) who did the translation made it possible for those who could not read Sanskrit to access the message. Soon after, the fashion of translating the *Gita* into European languages grew till Max Weber was able to say that the *Gita* had been 'Translated into almost all the languages of the earth.' (Weber, 361), Wilkins opened the door to the global popularity of the *Gita*.[5]

Yet the best read version of the *Gita* was by Sir Edwin Arnold. 'The Song Celestial' published in 1885 was to influence the young Mohandas Karamchand Gandhi when he reached London three years later. The *Gita* became a weapon in the independence struggle when after the partition of Bengal in 1905, a militant movement broke out across India, most especially in Bengal, Maharashtra and Punjab. Young people formed a society called 'Anushilan' which was dedicated to a violent overthrow of British Rule. Khudiram Bose who was hanged for the killing of two English ladies died with the *Gita* slung across his neck on the gallows.[6] When the offices

4 Shankara mentions critics as Vrittika but not by name. Baudhayan is often cited as a possible earlier commentator but his manuscript has not been recovered as yet.

5 Malinar, op. cit., gives a detailed account of the many translations in German and the debates which followed.

6 This and other details on the use of the *Gita* by 'terrorists' is from Bhiku Parekh (1989/99) *Colonialism, Tradition and Reform: An Analysis of Gandhi's Political Discourse* (Sage Publications. Delhi).

of the Dacca (now Dhaka) Anushilan Samiti were searched, a dozen copies of the *Gita* were found. Members of secret societies dedicated to a violent overthrow swore on the *Gita*.

Questioning the *Gita*

Most people who take part in listening to lectures on the *Gita* or sometimes even read the *Gita*, do so uncritically. Just to recite or listen as many do is, by itself, supposed to give you *punya* – good marks with God. One need not question or even try to understand the contents of the work. Suffice it to know that at the beginning of the Mahabharat war, Krishna the God-charioteer told Arjun what the *Gita* now contains. The divine association is a guarantee of the truth and the sanctity of the text. As it is, it is a difficult, often confusing book which suddenly launches into new topics in the midst of other matters, has largely redundant Manichean sections attacking lower castes and non-Aryan people and at times is baffling. If you take it all as the saying of a single Divine persona, then you have to perform intellectual acrobatics to make it sound consistent. This is why commentators have disagreed among themselves and found whatever they wish to find. Tilak found in it a message for militant action while Gandhi, an apostle of nonviolence, accepted a text which is a long persuasion to go out there and kill all.

Yet, there are a few critics who differ from the majority of readers about the merits of the *Bhagavad Gita*. Kosambi and Ambedkar are two worth quoting. Kosambi in his essay 'Social and Economic Aspects of the *Gita*', fires an opening salvo:

> The *Gita* has attracted minds of bents entirely different from each other and from that of Arjuna. Each has interpreted the supposedly divine words so differently from all the others that the original seems far more suited to raise doubts and to split a personality than to heal an inner division. Any moral philosophy which managed to receive so many variant interpretations from minds in widely different types of society must be highly equivocal. No question remains of its basic validity if the meaning is so flexible (12).[7]

---

7 D. D. Kosambi (1962) 'Social and Economic Aspects of the *Bhagavad-Gita*', in *Myth and Reality: Studies in the Formation of Indian Culture* (Popular Prakashan, Bombay), 'Myth' hereafter.

Ambedkar starts with the same question as Kosambi does.

> One is forced to ask why there is such divergence of opinion among scholars? My answer to this question is that scholars have gone on a false errand. They have gone on a search for the message of the *Bhagvat Gita* on the assumption that it is a gospel as the *Koran*, the *Bible*, or the *Dhammapada* is. In my opinion this assumption is quite a false assumption. The *Bhagvat Gita* is not a gospel and it can therefore have no message and it is futile to search for one. (T)he *Bhagvat Gita* is neither a book of religion nor a treatise on philosophy. What the *Bhagvat Gita* does is to defend certain dogmas of religion on philosophic grounds… It uses philosophy to defend religion.
>
> …
>
> (T)he dogmas which the *Gita* defends are the dogmas of counter-revolution as put forth in the Bible of counter-revolution, namely Jaimini's *Purva-Mimansa*. There ought to be no difficulty in accepting this proposition. If there is any it is largely due to wrong meaning attached to the word *Karma yoga*. Most writers on the *Bhagvat Gita* translate the word *Karma yoga* as 'action' and the word *Jnana yoga* as 'knowledge' and proceed to discuss the *Bhagvat Gita* as though it was engaged in comparing and contrasting knowledge versus action in a generalized form. This is quite wrong. The *Bhagvat Gita* is not concerned with any general, philosophical discussion of action versus knowledge. As a matter of fact, the *Bhagvat Gita* is concerned with the particular and not with the general. By *Karma yoga* or action, the *Gita* means the dogmas contained in Jaimini's *Karma Kanda* and by *Jnana yoga* or knowledge it means the dogmas contained in Badarayan's *Brahma Sutras*…It is to lift the *Gita* from the position of a party pamphlet engaged in a controversy on small petty points and make it appear as though it was a general treatise on matters of high philosophy that this attempt is made to inflate the meaning of the words Karma and Jnana and make them words of general import. Mr. Tilak is largely to be blamed for this trick of patriotic Indians.[8]

Dr Ambedkar raises several issues in this critique. Of course by counter-revolution, he means the fight waged against Buddhism by Brahmanism

8 'Krishna and His *Gita*', in Valerian Rodrigues (ed.), *The Essential Writings of B.R. Ambedkar* (Oxford India, 2002), 193–204.

in which the *Bhagavad Gita* becomes a weapon. This fight was waged over more than 1000 years between the sixth century BCE and the ninth century CE when Shankara wrote his commentary. Not much has been written about this war between Buddhism and Brahmanism, and the traditional version of ancient Indian history erases all mention of Buddhism and pretends that Brahmanism was the most tolerant of all religions. There was a philosophical as well often a physical battle between the champions of Brahmanism and Buddhism.

The Place of the *Gita* in the *Mahabharat*

The *Gita* is read as a separate, standalone text. But, within the *Mahabharat*, it is a part of the *Bhishma Parvan*. When reading the *Gita* on its own, we get the impression that on the first day of the *Mahabharat* war, as the armies are assembled, there is Arjun depressed and shaken. Then, in front of the waiting armies, Krishna launches into his long exposition of philosophy of the paths to attain moksha. At the end of the 700 verses, Arjun is convinced and decides to fight.

The *Bhishma Parvan* however presents a very different picture. After all attempts at preventing war fail, as described in the *Udyog Parvan*, the *Bhishma Parvan* starts on the tenth day of the war, not the first one. Sanjaya who has magical powers to see into the past, present and the future *(pratyakshadarshi sarvasya bhutabhavyabhavisyavit)* comes to Dhritarashtra the blind King to report that Bhishma is dead.

In the sixteenth *Adhyaya* of the *Bhishma Parvan*, Sanjaya begins to describe in great detail the armies arranged on either side on the morning of the first day. The eighteen armies, eleven of Duryodhana and seven of Yudhishthira are ready once again. In the seventeenth *Adhyaya*, Bhishma is reported by Sanjaya to have said:

> *Adharmah ksatriyasyaisa yad vyadhimaranam grhe*
>
> *Yad ajau nidhanam yati so'sya dharmah sanatanah. (Bhishma, 17.11)*
>
> It is a breach of the Law (*Dharma*) for a baron (*ksatriya*) to die of sickness at home, and his everlasting Law is it to find death on the battlefield. (Van Buitenen, 50–1; bracketed insertions are mine)

In the twentieth *Adhyaya* we begin again with Dhritarashtra asking as to which were the troops to greet the sunrise – his son's led by Bhishma or those led by Bhīma. Sanjaya gives a long description of the armies.

> The warriors in both armies exulted, and in both rose a fragrance of flowers and incense. The first clash of the massed, marshalled troops that slowly and proudly advanced was magnificent, and the sound of music mixed with peals of conches and drums and the noise of roaring elephants and churning troops was deafening. (Van Buitenen, 68–9)

It is at this stage that Dhritarashtra asks once again the famous question with which the *Bhagavad Gita* proper starts

> *Dharmakshetre Kurukshetre samaveta yuyutsava*
>
> *Mamaka pandavaschaiva kim kurvat vada Sanjaya. (Bhishma 23.1. Bhagavad Gita 1.1.)*
>
> When in the Field of the Kurus, the Field of the Law, my troops and the Pandavas had massed belligerently, what did they do, Samjaya? (Van Buitenen, 68–9)

There are several things to notice about this famous opening *sloka* (verse). This is the first and the only time the expression *Dharmakshetre* is used, thus elevating a war over a fraternal property dispute into a sacred encounter. Why would Dhritarashtra call it a *dharmakshetra*, thus admitting the justness of the claim of his nephews? Then again the question that the blind King asks has been asked by him twice in the previous *Adhyayas* already and answered by Sanjaya. Why do we now need the blind King to ask again what Sanjaya has already told him?

The answer has to be that whatever was the original course of the narrative, someone wanted to make a standalone text of the eighteen *Adhyayas* which form the *Gita*. The introductory question and Sanjaya's reply which then takes up the next twenty verses allow us to ignore all that has gone before in the *Bhishma Parva* and focus on Arjun's problem. This is no proof but a strong indication that the *Gita*, if not inserted into the *Bhishma Parva* as Vivekananda suspected, at some later stage was so rearranged that it could be extruded so as to be read separately.

Sanjaya repeats much of what he has already said to Dhritarashtra in 23.2–20 (*Bhagavad Gita* 1.2–20) but then in 23.21 (*Bhagavad Gita* 1.21) Arjun requests Krishna to place his chariot in the middle of the two armies *(senayorubhayor madhye)*.

But then once the chariot is moved to the middle of the two armies, Arjun begins to have what can only be called a nervous breakdown: his body begins to shake, his mouth is parched, his limbs collapse and his favourite bow Gandiva slips from his hands as his skin burns. In short, he is in a funk. Thus he raises the fundamental issue: What is the point of war? I don't want victory, nor kingdom nor pleasures.

Krishna begins very much as one would expect any coach or mentor to do. He rebukes him and tries to shame him into action. Yet Arjun is unmoved and in distress submits to Krishna seeking instruction from him *(shadhi maam tvam prapannam),* Krishna replies to him laughing at first *(prahasan).* Then from 2.11 onward begins the *Gita* proper as many have come to see it. This is the beginning of Krishna's exposition of his response to Arjun's grief. The response can be described as twofold to begin with. The first response is what I would call Irrelevance of Agency. This occupies 2.11 to 2.30. Then there is a sudden change in the response and Krishna tries Humiliation of the Ego (2.31–38). This latter response is much more in line with what any good coach would do while the first is at a higher philosophical level.

When these two responses are done, I believe the *Gita* proper should have ended. What follows from 2.39 is another switch in theme. The text catches up with 2.30 and goes down philosophical byways and highways for the next sixteen more *Adhyayas*. Why should this be so?

Radhakrishnan gets to the heart of the matter when he says, 'It is possible that Arjuna might have had pointed advice from his friend Krishna which the poet (i.e. the author of the *Gita*) worked up into the poem of seven hundred verses.'[9] What is implied is that there was an author other than Krishna who found the original short text and then elongated it into a 700 verse poem. We shall see later why this is a very plausible idea.

Irrelevance of Agency

This is the first and what may be called Vedantic response. Krishna tells Arjun that in fact he will not be the author of his actions if he does fight and kill his relatives. Life and death are delusions that Arjun suffers from. He neither kills nor is he killed. Those he thinks are going to die have had their destiny already determined independently of what Arjun might or might not do. He has to wise up since the Wise know what is not what.

This is then a 'get-out-of-jail free' card from the Lord himself. You don't kill and are not killed. The body is transient and the soul cannot kill or be killed. So there are no consequences of human action. One can regard this

9 S. Radhakrishnan (1923/1999), *Indian Philosophy*, vol. 1, (Oxford India), 523.

as a deep doctrine as many do or as a fantastic escapism. Dr Ambedkar, being a lawyer, was unconvinced:

> To say that killing is no killing because what is killed is the body and not the soul is an unheard of defence of murder. This is one of the doctrines which make some people say that the doctrines make one's hair stand on their end. If Krishna were to appear as a lawyer acting for a client who is being tried for murder and pleaded the defence set out by him in the *Bhagvad Gita* there is not the slightest doubt that he would be sent to the lunatic asylum (Ambedkar, 197).

Humiliation of the Ego

But starting with 2.31, Krishna changes tack. The next argument is what I label Humiliation of the Ego. This is a conventional argument in which Krishna uses the logic that Bhishma has already been quoted above as using. Arjun had objected that killing and destruction of the kin group could be *adharma* (1.39). This could lead to sin (1.36). Krishna now changes tack and talks of *svadharma* which overrides any general concern for *dharma*. Svadharma for a Kshatriya is to fight and not brood over consequences of killing.

I reckon this short passage of eight verses 2.31–38 is much more likely to appeal to Arjun's own sentiments. He has been brought up as a Kshatriya (warrior), aware of his duties and his obligations. In the earlier *Adhyayas* of *Bhishma Parvan* the discourse of the blind King and of the Grand Sire Bhishma, is very much embedded in the culture of the family in *Kshatradharma*, a trap out of which Dhritarashtra knows neither his sons nor his nephews can escape. This is Arjun's duty explained in terms of the here and now rather than from the point of view of higher philosophy of the nature of the soul.

It is quite likely that the 'pointed advice' that Radhakrishnan thought Krishna may have given to Arjun is contained in 2.31–38. Nothing more would be needed to make Arjun fight. To be told that if he does not fight, his rivals would not credit him with higher wisdom but cowardice would be enough to rouse him. To be told even more pointedly that he could not lose either way would reinforce the message. To be told that it was sinful not to fight and no sin to fight clinches the moral argument as far as a Kshatriya like Arjun is concerned.

I would therefore suggest that Arjun's *Gita* is 1.21–46 and 2.1–10 and 2.31–38; forty-four *slokas* in all. It would make a perfect 23rd *Adhyaya* in Bhishma Parva. It is my argument that the *Gita* as it finally came to us is a result of many additions to what could have been a small original fragment, if there was one at all.

Gita as a Multi-authored Text

The idea that the *Gita* may be a multiple authored book is not new. Indeed it began with the first translation of Charles Wilkins' *Gita.*[10] Von Humboldt in reviewing Schlegel's Latin translation was 'aware of the possibility that the text had been composed by more than one author over a considerable period of time…(H)e regards the first eleven chapters as the "original" ones' (Malinar, 16). Deussen another distinguished Sankritist divided the text into three thematic units, (1) ethics (Chs 1–6) (2) metaphysics (7–12) and (3) psychology (13–18). The French scholar Charpentier believed that what follows 2.38 'can in no wise have belonged to the original epic text' (23–25).

The most cogent argument for multiple authorship was made by the Maharashtrian scholar Dr Gajanan Shripat Khair. His book *Quest for the Original Gita* was published in 1969 and a revised edition was issued in 1997.[11] Khair does not seem to be aware of any of the literature from which I cited earlier. He has arrived at his contention entirely on his own analysis which makes the coincidence of his ideas with those of previous scholars all the more remarkable.[12]

He divides the *Bhagavad Gita* into three parts – *Trikala Gita* as he calls it. According to him:

> The First Author wrote most of *Adhyayas* 1 to 6. The period of writing was of the Older Upanishads and pre-Buddhist, around 600 BCE. The principal philosophical issue is Sannyasa and the solution is *Karma yoga* (126 verses or 18 per cent).

The Second Author wrote portions of *Adhyaya* 8, *Adhyayas* 13 to 15, 17 and portions of 18. The period was contemporaneous with the Buddha and the philosophical authority is Old Upanishads as before. The problem is

10 Malinar, op. cit., is a good source of the debates about the text of the *Bhagavad Gita* in Germany.

11 G. S. Khair (1969/97), *Quest for the Original Gita* (Somaiya Publications, Mumbai).

12 Malinar does mention Khair but does not give his ideas any more room than she does those of the others (27–28).

karma – choice (as Khair describes it) and the solution is *sattvikatva* (119 verses or 17 per cent).

The Third Author is the editor and the final arbiter of the document. He wrote the entire *Adhyayas* 7, 9–12, 16 plus interpolated in the *Adhyayas* the two others wrote. The problem is 'diverse creeds' and the answer is bhakti. His authority is the New Upanishads and his period is 300 to 200 BCE. (455 verses or 65 per cent). Note that while Khair has a tripartite division of the *Bhagavad Gita*, his analysis is more subtle than that of Deussen as he argues that the third author mixed up the different parts which disguises the divisions.

If we are to take this classification as a working hypothesis, it would seem that the *Gita* gets settled into its final shape at the time when the battle between the Buddhists and the Brahmanists is at its most ferocious. Of course, Kosambi puts the final rendition of the *Gita* much later to the Gupta period rather than the highpoint of the Buddhist period as Khair does. The ideas common to Kosambi and Khair are that (a) there are multiple authors and (b) that the text evolves over time as it responds to different circumstances prevailing as per the struggle between Buddhism and Brahmanism while Khair alone contributes the idea that (c) the Third Author adds to and edits the text to give it a sort of unity.

This makes sense if we see that the First Author is not joining a battle against Buddhism but expounding the Upanshadic doctrine in a concise way. It is like a catechism for young students. Once we are beyond 2.38 Arjun becomes only a vehicle for expounding what has to be taught. Hence, we begin with a mention of Sankhya in 2.39 and other philosophical issues follow.

The Second Author is a contemporary of Buddha if we are to take Khair's dating seriously. He is also a didactic writer expositing what has to be learnt. His style is dispassionate. He uses words such as *jnanin*, *munih*, *yatih*, *yogin* but sparsely. This is also a teaching text, meant for select audiences.

It is the Third Author who addresses the ordinary people who have little time and inclination for philosophical subtleties. As Khair says, 'His main audience is the common people and the neglected persons, who were deprived of opportunities of spiritual and moral salvation. Traders, merchants, atheists, worshippers of ancestral and popular gods – this was his audience' (51) since by this time the need to spread Brahmanism as widely as possible to counter Buddhism's popularity is urgent. The second or third century BCE which Khair gives as the likely date is the high point of the spread of Buddhism with Ashoka having given royal patronage to

Buddhism. The champions of Brahmanism had to fight back. The *Gita* with a popularised section moulded along with the earlier parts was to be the weapon. The date suggested by Kosambi of 150–350 CE would be even more suitable because under the Guptas, the Brahminical fightback had Royal patronage.

Khair's virtue is that he proposes a plausible hypothesis of how the different layers were integrated into a seamless whole which gives the impression of an integral text which most readers of the *Bhagavad Gita* take it to be. The idea that there was an author who was also the last one in and who edited the entire text by his interpolations to weave the separate texts into one is the missing link in the discussions of the experts who wrestled with the problem before he came along. Above all, his virtue is that he arrives at his conclusion unprompted and uninfluenced by the previous literature. He is a homespun amateur reader of the *Bhagavad Gita* who stumbles upon his discovery all by himself and proceeds to construct a theory of why the *Bhagavad Gita* should be as it is – choppy and seamless at the same time.

We can conclude, however, that apart from Arjun's *Gita*, there may have been three other *Gitas*. Ignoring the interpolation attributed by Khair to the Third Author, we can say that the three *Gitas* were:

1. The Veda-Vedanta *Gita* or *Karma Yoga Gita* of the First Author mainly across *Adhyayas* 2 to 6
2. The Samkhya *Gita* or *Jnana Yoga Gita* of the Second Author *Adhyayas* 8 (part), 13, 14, 15, 17, 18 (part)
3. The *Bhakti Yoga Gita* of the Third Author *Adhyayas* 7, 9–12.

Indeed, the role of the *Bhagavad Gita* as a weapon in battle between Brahmanism and Buddhism is well explained by Pande (1994):

> The *Bhagavad Gita* is an evolving response which deals with the conflicts between Veda and Vedanta and then with the challenge posed to Vedanta by Buddhism. Its shift to Bhakti is thus the climax of the battle between Brahmanism and Buddhism.

Indeed, as Pande further has observed, 'The *Bhagvad Gita* represents a progressive adaptation of the Vedanta to the challenges of the *Mahajanapada* Age'.

Conclusion

What seems to be a cautious conclusion from the discussion above is that:

a) There are probably multiple authors of the *Bhagavad Gita* as shown by stylistic changes and the frequent shift of subject matter.

b) There was probably an original short sharp lesson for Arjun by Krishna assuming that these were historical characters as described in the *Mahabharat*.

c) The periodisation of the three other segments follows the pattern of pre-Buddhist, contemporary with Buddhism's early days and lastly in the period when Brahmanism was reviving.

The purpose of essaying such a secular or humanist critique of the *Gita* is not to delve into the religious ideas of Buddhism as against Brahmanism. The important point is that the battle between the two was waged on the social terrain as much as the religious one. Buddhism rejected *varna* distinctions, challenged the hegemony of Brahmins and the necessity of ritual performance. It doubted the existence of a God and of the soul. Its challenge to the Brahmanical social order was the most profound revolutionary challenge to the old order. Urban groups mainly Vaishyas and Shudras joined Buddhism in large numbers. For around 500 years between the death of Buddha and the advent of the Common Era Buddhism shaped the social order in parts of India north and south.

The recapture of the initiative by Brahmanism which took place during the first 700 years of the Common Era, was achieved as much by the religious and philosophical debates as by the contest for patronage from one or the other King (Verardi op.cit.).

When Buddhism was defeated and left India for other Asian regions, the caste society was re-established firmly in India. Buddhism was wiped out from the historical memory of India till James Prinsep inaugurated the rediscovery of Buddhism by his decipherment of the Brahmi script. We now know much more about Buddhism and its place in Indian history but that is no thanks to Brahmanism which suppressed all memory of the challenge. When Ambedkar chose to reject Brahmanism for himself and his followers he chose Buddhism. This as much as anything else demonstrates the radical challenge of Buddhism.

The *Bhagavad Gita* was the most effective instrument in this struggle. It offered a simple, easy to read or recite, source of philosophical ideas of Brahmanism. It lent authority to these verses by attributing them to Krishna whose *bhakti* became a powerful instrument for winning over the masses to the cause of Brahmanism.

All this happened over a thousand years and more. We still lack a proper history of the rise and fall of Buddhism and the decline and renaissance of Brahmanism. Further analysis of the *Bhagavad Gita* may yet help in this task.

References

Khair, G. S. *Quest for the Original Gita.* 2nd edn. Mumbai: Somaiya Publications, 1997.

Kosambi, D. D. Myth and Reality: Studies in the Formation of Indian Culture. 2nd edn. Mumbai: Popular Prakashan, 2005.

Malinar, A. *The Bhagavad Gita: Doctrines and Context.* Cambridge: Cambridge University Press, 2007.

Minor, Robert. *Modern Indian Interpreters of Bhagavad Gita.* Albany, New York: State University of New York Press, 1986.

Pande, G. C. *Life and Thought of Sankaracharya* Delhi: Motilal Banarasidass, 1994.

Radhakrishnan, S. *Indian Philosophy*, 2nd edn. New Delhi: Oxford, 1999.

Radhakrishnan, S. *The Bhagavad Gita.* New Delhi: Harper Collins Publishers, 2010.

Rodrigues, Valerian ed. 'Krishna and His *Gita*', *The Essential Writings of B.R. Ambedkar*, (Oxford India, 2002), 193–204 (2010)

Verardi, Giovanni. Hardships and Downfall of Buddhism in India. New Delhi: Manohar, 2011.

Vivekananda, Swami. *The Complete Works of Swami Vivekananda.* 29th impression. Kolkata: Advaita Ashrama, 2009.

Weber, Max. *The Religion of India: The Sociology of Hinduism and Buddhism*, 2nd edn, translated by Gerth, Hans and Don Martindale. New Delhi: Munshiram Manoharlal, 2007.

Acknowledgement

First publication: Desai, Meghnad (2013) '*Bhagavad Gita*: Outlines of a Secular Critique' in *Civilizational Dialogue: Asian Inter-connections and Cross-cultural Exchanges*, edited by Sharma, Anjana. New Delhi, Manohar, pp. 165–175. Republished with kind permission of Manohar.

GLOSSARY

ACTU – The Australian Council of Trade Unions, the largest affiliation of trade unions and workers in Australia.

AFL-CIO – American Federation of Labor and Congress of Industrial Organizations.

AIADMK – The All India Anna Dravida Munnetra Kazhagam is a Dravidian party founded in 1972 and based largely in Tamil Nadu and the Union Territory of Puducherry.

AoA – Agreement on Agriculture. The Agreement is an International Treaty signed during the Uruguay round of GATT discussions in 1994 and focuses on the reform of international agricultural trade and domestic agricultural policies of the member countries.

APEC – Asia Pacific Economic Cooperation came into effect in 1989 amongst the major Pacific Rim Countries.

ATO – Alternative Trade Organisations.

ATTAC France – Association for the Taxation of Financial Transactions and for Citizens' Action is a global anti-globalisation movement that focuses on questions of financial equity at the level of citizens, states and regions.

BCCI – Bank of Credit and Commerce International.

Bharat Nirman – A program to promote rural infrastucture by the business sector; it gives awards in recognition of achievements.

BJP – Bharatiya Janata Party is the political arm of the Sangh Parivar, a group of Hindu nationalist organisations that promote India as the land of Hindus (i.e. Hindu Rashtra). Its origin dates back to the early years of Indian independence when the same kind of Hindu nationalist interests called themselves the Bharatiya Jana Sangh (est. 1951).

Boer War – Was fought from October 11, 1899, to May 31, 1902, between Great Britain and the two Boer (Afrikaner) republics – the South African Republic (Transvaal) and the Orange Free State. The Boers or Afrikaners were the descendants of Dutch settlers.

Brady Bonds – 'Named after US Treasury Secretary Nicholas Brady, who in association with the IMF and World Bank sponsored the effort to permanently restructure outstanding sovereign loans and interest arrears into liquid debt instruments… Principal and certain interest is collateralized by U.S. Treasury zero coupon bonds and other high grade instruments. Creditor banks exchanged sovereign loans for Brady bonds incorporating principal and interest guarantees and cash payments. Debtor governments had their principal, interest and interest arrears reduced. Countries involved in the Brady Plan restructuring: Argentina, Brazil, Bulgaria, Costa Rica, Dominican Republic, Ecuador, Mexico, Morocco, Nigeria, Philippines, Poland, Uruguay. Potential future candidates for Brady Plan restructuring: Ex-Soviet Union (Vnesheconobank), Nicaragua, Panama, Peru' (Emerging Markets Companion 1996–9).

BSP – Founded in 1984, the Bahujan Samaj Party or the Majority People's Party was formed by the dalit movement in India. It traces its origins to the work of Ambedkar in the 1930s and stands for the interests of the *dalits* or former 'untouchables'.

BRICS – Refers to five new emerging economies: Brazil, Russia, India, China and South Africa.

CAP – Common Agricultural Policy. The CAP was the first major step taken by the European nations after World War Two in 1962 to move towards mutually beneficial economic policies. Such policies were designed to prevent future European wars. The CAP, above all other concerns, subsidises the income of European farmers. Given its large farm sector, the CAP was essential as a way of securing France's involvement in the development of the European Union.

CBI – Central Bureau of Investigation, the chief anti-crime investigative body in India.

The Club of Rome – traces its history to 1968 when it was set up as a 30 member discussion group so that international scientists, industrialists, economists and others could better inform themselves about global events and their impact on humanity. It describes itself as an organisation of individuals who share a common concern for the future of humanity and strive to make a difference. Their Secretariat is based in Switzerland and it has national associations in some 30 countries.

CRA – One of the largest mining companies in Australia now called Rio Tinto.

CSDS – Centre for the Study of Developing Societies (New Delhi).

Dalits – Former 'untouchables' castes, also known as 'scheduled' castes, because the Indian Constitution sets aside 'reservation' for them in parliament, schools, colleges and government services in general.

Derivatives – Futures, puts, options and other financial instruments which are derived from others, such as commodity prices, shares and bonds. Derivatives are often used as insurance against unfavourable movements in the underlying instruments. In portfolio investments derivatives are used to achieve a specific risk/return profile.

DMK – Founded in 1949 as part of the Dravidian movement, the Dravida Munnetra Kazhagam is an Indian political party based in the state of Tamil Nadu and Union Territory of Puducherry.

EC – European Community.

Enlightenment – Refers to the Age of Enlightenment and the ideas of this eighteenth century philosophical and intellectual movement which promoted reason, progress, liberty, tolerance, the separation of church and state and constitutional government.

ERM – enterprise risk management.

EU – European Union.

FDI – Foreign Direct Investment describes the investment by private individuals and firms in the domestic enterprises of foreign countries. FDI can take the form of either financial investments, the transfer of technology and or the transfer of expertise. The foreign individual or firm receives a partial share of the total equity value of the entity in which it invests.

FLO – Fairtrade Labelling Organization International.

FSA – The Financial Services Authority in Britain. It was a quasi-judicial body responsible for the regulation of the financial services industry in the United Kingdom between 2001 and 2013. It was founded as the Securities and Investments Board in 1985.

FSU – Former Soviet Union.

FTAA – Free Trade Area of the Americas. Negotiations to set up FTAA occurred over four years (1998–2002) to create a free trade zone between north America, south America, the Caribbean nations except Cuba. In the end it was not set up.

Futures – Financial instruments constituting a hedge against the uncertain fluctuations in the price of a commodity, or currency or exchange rate.
G7 – The seven largest, advanced economies of the world consisting of Canada, France, Germany, Italy, Japan, the United Kingdom, and the United States.
G19 – Globalisation in the 19th century.
G20 – Globalisation in the 20th century.
GATS – General Agreement on Trade in Services.
GATT – General Agreement on Tariffs and Trade.
GDP – Gross Domestic Product, one measure of the total output of a country.
GMO – Genetically modified organism.
GNP – gross national product.
HA – Humanistic Approach to economic development.
HDR – Human Development Report.
HIPC – Highly Indebted Poor Countries.
HSA – Hemispheric Social Alliance.
IFAT – International Federation of Alternative Trade.
ILO – International Labour Organization.
IMF – International Monetary Fund.
INC – Founded in 1885 as part of the Indian nationalist movement, the Indian National Congress Party claims to stand for secularism and tolerance in India.
INPEG – Initiative Against Economic Globalisation.
IPC – The Indian Penal Code, which is a comprehensive law first codified in British India in 1860.
ISGN – International Southern Group Network. Set up in 1984 in Cameroon as the Southern Networks for Environment and Development (SONED). Renamed in South Africa in 1994. It promotes cooperation and mutual aid between movements, alternative development centres and NGOs in the Third World countries.
ITO – International Trade Organisation; although it never came into existence, it was a precursor to the WTO.
IWW – Industrial Workers of the World.
Lokpal bill – The bill sought to establish an ombudsman to investigate cases of corruption. The bill was finally passed in 2013, more than 40 years after it was introduced to the Indian Parliament.
Luddites – Luddites were part of a 19th century movement that opposed machines and factory production; they often wrecked machines. In today's usage 'Luddites' refers to anti-industrial and anti-technology movements.
MAI – Multilateral Agreement on Investment.
MIF – Multilateral Investment Framework.
MFN – most favoured nations.
MFN rules – These rules mean that all countries belonging to the same agreement or group benefit equally from special arrangements made between two member partners: e.g. if one country grants a special favour to another, the same special favour applies to all members of the group.
MNC – Multinational corporation.
MNREGA – Mahatma Gandhi National Rural Employment Guarantee Act.
MPP – multi-party parliaments.
MST – Landless Workers Movement in Brazil.
NAFTA – The North American Free Trade Agreement, which came into effect in 1994 betweeen Canada, Mexico, and the United States.

NATO – North Atlantic Treaty Organization.
NDA – Founded in 1998 by the BJP, the National Democratic Allianceis a centre-right coalition of 13 Indian parties.
NGO – Non-governmental organisation.
NIC – newly industrialised country.
NLF – National Left Front.
NM model – Nehru-Mahalanobis model.
NREGS – National Rural Employment Guarantee Scheme. The history of legislative intervention in generating rural employment in India dates from the 1980s and focuses on various kinds of local public works programs. In 2005 the Government of India introduced the NREGS which was subsequently revised and extended as the MGNREGS.
NRIs – Non-Resident Indians.
OBC – other backward classes. This refers to castes that are 'backward' as measured by eleven socio-economic factors but not part of the Scheduled Castes and Scheduled Tribes of India. The benefits of reservation were extended to OBCs by the Mandal Commission set up in 1979. In 1980, the Mandal Commission recommended the extension of affirmed action to the OBCs, including the reservation of 27 per cent of jobs with the central government and public sector undertakings.
OECD – Organisation for Economic Co-operation and Development.
OPEC – Organization of the Petroleum Exporting Countries, founded in Baghdad in 1960.
OWINFS – Our World is Not For Sale. Describes itself as a loose grouping of organisations, activists and social movements which grew out of international campaigns against the WTO and MAI.
PAN cards – Permanent Account Number cards are cards issued by the Indian Tax Office which non-resident Indians need to have if they are investing in India and submitting tax returns in India.
PDS – Public Distribution System.
Portfolio investment – The purchase of debt, equity and other financial instruments. Equity portfolio investments usually stop short of obtaining management control in a particular enterprise. The goals of portfolio investments vary from growth to income to value preservation against adverse shocks.
QUAD – Refers to the Quadrilateral Security Dialogue which is an ongoing, informal strategic dialogue between the United States, Japan, India and Australia.
Quad countries – United States, Japan, India and Australia.
RD – Research and Development.
RSS – The Rashtriya Swayamsevak Sangh or National Volunteer Association serves as the ideological base of the Sangh Parivar, which is politically led by the BJP. The RSS was formed in 1925 by Keshav Baliram Hedgewar, in Maharashtra.
SEATINI – The Southern and Eastern African Trade Negotiations Institute.
Shiv Sena – A right wing, Hindu nationalist party which was formed in Mumbai in 1966 by a political cartoonist called Bal Thackeray. At first it was a local chauvinist formation that promoted the interests of Maharashtrians but later it adopted Hindu nationalist ideas in competition with the BJP.
SME – small and medium-sized enterprises.
SRI – Socially responsible investing.

Swadeshi – *Swadeshi*, literally 'of one's own nation', was originally based on an anti-British tactic by Tilak and then later Gandhi to boycott British imports and encourage Indian products.

TDP – Telugu Desam Party, set up in 1982 by N. T. Rama Rao and based in Andhra Pradesh and Telangan states.

TINA – 'There Is No Alternative'.

TJM – Trade Justice Movement. Set up in 2000, it is a British coalition of more than 80 organisations that campaigns for fair and just trade.

TNCs – trans-national corporations.

TRIPS – the Agreement on Trade-Related Aspects of Intellectual Property Rights; it was signed in 1995 by the members of the WTO.

TWN – Third World Network. This is is an independent non-profit international research and advocacy organisation involved in issues relating to development, developing countries and North-South affairs. It was set up in Penang, Malaysia in November 1984 during the International Conference on 'The Third World: Development or Crisis?', organised by the Consumers' Association of Penang and attended by over a hundred participants from 21 countries.

UAF – universal adult franchise.

UN – United Nations.

UNCED – United Nations Conference on Environment and Development.

UNCTAD – United Nations Conference on Trade and Development.

UNIDO – United Nations Industrial Development Organization.

UP – Uttar Pradesh, the largest and most popularist state in India. Not to be confused with UPA, etc.

UPA / UPA-II – The United Progressive Alliance, a coalition of centre-left political parties in India formed after the 2004 general election. It is chaired by Sonia Gandhi because the largest member party of the UPA is the Indian National Congress. UPA-II refers to the second ministry led by Manmohan Singh after the general elections of 2009.

VHP – Vishwa Hindu Parishad, a critical branch of the Sangh Parivar that helps the BJP to recruit members, especially international supporters. Its recruitment campaigns include devising and introducing new school text books.

WSF – Third World Social Forum.

WTO – World Trade Organization.

INDEX

Universal's

LAW RELATING TO ELECTRICITY WITH SPECIAL REFERENCE TO CONSUMER PROTECTION LAW

R.M. Vats

Formerly of the Indian Administrative Service

Universal
Law Publishing Co. Pvt. Ltd.

2002 Edition

ISBN 81-7534-312-8

Published by
UNIVERSAL LAW PUBLISHING CO. PVT. LTD.
C-FF-1A, Ansal's Dilkhush Industrial Estate,
G.T. Karnal Road, Delhi-110 033
Tel : 7215334, 7438103, 7458529
Fax : 91-11-7459023
e-mail : unilaw@vsnl.com
Website : www.unilawbooks.com

Computer Set at ULPC (Typesetting Division) & *Printed at* Taj Press, New Delhi

To

Rahul and Andrea

- my grandchildren

MAY THEY GET "LIGHT"

ABOUT THE AUTHOR

Formerly of the Indian Administrative Service, Shri R.M.Vats combines in himself several years of judicial experience with more than thirty years of administrative experience. He has been Secretary of various departments in Delhi Administration, Housing Commissioner in Delhi Development Authority and also on the Board of Directors of all the Public Sector Undertakings of Delhi Administration which provide services to the citizens and a member of the Delhi State Consumer Council.

He has also authored some well known books – "Consumer and the Law", "Law Relating to Insurance with special reference to Consumer Protection Act" and "Law Relating to Telephones with special reference to Consumer Protection Act".

Universal's

LAW RELATING TO
ELECTRICITY
WITH SPECIAL REFERENCE TO CONSUMER PROTECTION LAW

By The Same Author

- Consumer and the Law
- Law Relating to Telephones with special reference to Consumer Protection Law
- Law Relating to Insurance with special reference to Consumer Protection Law

INTRODUCTION

Popularly perceived as a good servant but a bad master, electricity has achieved thunderous results in the economics of modern life. It has now become one of the main necessities of man. Artificial light – for that is what we are actually using – has made night life more interesting and more popular, has illuminated homes and streets and has made factories more productive. Due to the rapid growth of trade and commerce, industry and urbanization, a large number of people are presently concerned with producing electric energy and the means of transmitting and using it. Surprisingly, however, very little is known of the precise nature of electricity despite mighty efforts of scientists and technologists all over the world.

Ages have passed, yet the origin and nature of light remains shrouded in mystery. In such a dark scenario even the most die hard atheist is apt to throw his arms up and turn to the Bible which says God's first command was "Let there be Light".

It is common knowledge that courts everywhere take judicial notice of the laws of nature and also of the forces which operate them, including electricity and its properties, though not of the methods of its production, transmission and use. Such matters are best left to the technocrats. The common man, too, has hardly anything to do with these aspects of electricity. He is ordinarily more interested in knowing how the courts, particularly the consumer courts, would look at and redress his grievances if he is wronged by the suppliers of electric energy.

The book in your hands also does not touch upon technical matters. Instead, it focuses attention on the rights and obligations of the consumer and the suppliers of electricity under the law. An attempt has been made to identify the areas where the Redressal Agencies set up under the Consumer Protection Act, 1986, would provide relief to the consumer and, to avoid wasteful litigation, where they would decline to interfere.

The book is divided into two parts : Besides the basics, Part I touches upon the important provisions of the Indian Electricity Act, 1910 and, with that as backdrop, Part II explains with the help of cases decided by the courts and the consumer Fora how the law has been applied by them.

CONTENTS

13

Model Forms under Consumer Protection Act

Appendix

TABLE OF CASES

A

B

I

J

1 Background

Electric energy is one of the most potent and dangerous agencies of nature. Its effect is sudden and can be totally destructive. Even with the most sophisticated appliances placed at our disposal by modern day technology, its high tension currents can spell disaster. Obviously, it is in public interest to control its generation, transmission and day-to-day use. The first legislation for this purpose – The Electricity Act – was placed on the Statute Book in 1887. It provided for the protection of person and property from injury and risks on account of supply and use of electricity for lighting and allied purposes.

The above Act was replaced by the Indian Electricity Act, 1903 (3 of 1903). Many practical difficulties were experienced soon after the passing of the previous law; it gave rise to a dual administration *viz.* the Governor-General-in-Council whose previous sanction was required in many matters, and the local Governments which were competent to grant licenses under the Act. The result was that on numerous occasions separate licenses were issued for the same purpose, for the same place and to the same person. It also involved unnecessary delay. It was impossible for the applicant to obtain a license within a period of two, or even three, years. Often, the financial position of the applicant company would change in the meanwhile. This discouraged investment of capital so essential for the development of the resources of the country. Keeping these and some other difficulties in view, a new bill was drafted.

The new law envisaged that, subject to the control of the Governor-General-in-Council, the general administration of the law and the grant of licences should remain with the local Governments but the rule-making power would be retained by the Governor-General-in-Council. This law was passed by the Legislative Council in March, 1910. It was christened as the Indian Electricity Act, 1910 (9 of 1910). It came into force with effect from 1st January, 1911. This Act provides for grant of licenses for supply of energy, laying of electric supply lines and overhead lines, obligations of licensees, disconnection of supply to consumers who fail to pay their bills, theft of energy, etc. Since the passing of this Act there has been phenomenal increase in the number of disputes relating to electricity and the law has been amended from time to time not only to resolve such disputes but also to meet fresh needs. However, the amending laws are not very relevant for the purpose of this study though a reference will be made to such enactments whenever necessary. It is understood that the Government of India proposes to introduce another law in the Parliament to replace the above Act which will obviate the necessity of the State Governments enacting their own laws on the subject.

2 Supply of Electricity – A Monopoly

For the reasons briefly stated a short while ago, the supply of electric energy cannot be left uncontrolled in the hands of the people. Section 28 of the Indian Electricity Act, 1910, therefore, lays down that –

> "no person, ,other than a licensee shall engage in the business of supplying energy to the general public except with the previous sanction of the State Government and in accordance with such conditions as the State Government may fix in this behalf".

Presently, electricity is being supplied to the consumers either through Electricity Boards/Undertakings or Local Bodies though some Boards/Undertakings are toying with the idea of entrusting it to private enterprises because of the heavy losses suffered by them which are mounting up further. Anyway, the fact remains that the supply of electric energy to the public for all purposes – domestic, commercial and industrial – is a monopoly[1] with all its attendant evils. A vast majority of consumers, one could say without fear of contradiction, are totally discontented with this service. The supply remains off for inexplicably long periods at a time. The usual explanation for the longest black out spread over vast areas often is that "it is a local fault". Complaints are not attended to despite people crying hoarse. Patients, particularly in summer, become impatient, children cry, the sleuths of the Department concerned are indifferent, if not discourteous too. Hefty bills for electricity which he has not even consumed land on the hapless consumer and, sad to say, his electricity can sometimes be disconnected without any notice.

---

1. I (1998) CPT 214; *Assistant Executive Engineer O&M, Rural Sub-Division, KEB* v. *Millind Dolli*, AIR 2002 Karn 120.

The functionaries of the Department do not fully realize that in providing this service on a monopoly basis they are running a public utility concern where the satisfaction of the consumer ought to be considered as a matter of prime importance.

Implicit in the above situation is another unsavoury fact : the consumer has to make use of this service on the terms unilaterally fixed by the Government. If, for example, the tariff is unreasonably hiked by the Government, the consumer can do precious little. He cannot look for this service elsewhere. He has, in fact, little choice and less bargaining power. In other words, he faces a "take it or leave it" situation. Regrettably, even the law cannot help him here, such matters being within the domain of public policy.[1]

The average citizen is, however, not so much concerned with questions of high policy. He is more interested in such day-to-day matters as inflated billing, arbitrary disconnection of his electric supply etc., and finding out whether he has a remedy and, if so, how he has to proceed to get relief. But before we discuss these matters, let us look at the rights and duties of the suppliers of electricity and also of the consumer.

---

1. *S. Narayanan Iyer* v. *Union of India*, AIR 1976 SC 1986.

3 Rights and Obligations of the Supplier and of the Consumer

THE SUPPLIER – HIS RIGHTS AND OBLIGATIONS

To supply electric energy to the people, the licensee – be it an Electricity Board or a Local Authority or the State Government – has to carry out certain works which involve laying of supply lines, installation of machinery, plants etc. This may also need alterations or replacement of certain existing works. For carrying out these functions, the Legislature has conferred necessary powers on the licensee and has cast certain obligations on him which the consumer must know so that if a dispute arises he may approach the appropriate Forum or authority for redressal of his grievances. We briefly describe below the powers and responsibilities of the licensee which fall under the following two heads :–

1. Works, and
2. Supply of Electricity

Works

Provision as to breaking of streets etc.

Section 12(1) of the Electricity Act, 1910 lays down that :–

Any licensee may from time to time but subject to the terms and conditions of his license, within the area of supply, or when permitted by the terms of his license to lay down or place electric supply lines without the area of supply, without that area–

(a) open and break up the soil and pavement of street, railway or tramway;

(b) open and break up any sewer, drain or tunnel in or under any street, railway or tramway;

(c) lay down and place electric supply lines and other works;

(d) repair, alter or remove the same; and

(e) do all other acts necessary for the supply of energy.

Sub-section (2) of this section prohibits the licensee from laying down or placing without the consent of the local authority any electric supply line or other work where any electric supply line or work has not already been lawfully laid down or placed by such licensee without the consent of the local authority or of the owner or occupier concerned as the case may be.

This sub-section has two provisos. The first proviso authorises the licensee to alter any support of an overhead line or any stay or strut required for the sole purpose of securing in position any support of an overhead line notwithstanding the objection of the owner or occupier of such building or land if the District Magistrate or, in a Presidency town, the Commissioner of Police by order in writing so directs.

The second proviso authorizes the District Magistrate or, in a Presidency-town, the Commissioner of Police, to direct that such support or strut may be removed or altered if the owner or occupier of such building shows sufficient cause for its removal or alteration.

Sub-section (3) empowers the District Magistrate or the Commissioner of Police, as the case may be, to fix the amount of compensation or of annual rent, or of both, which in his opinion, should be paid by the licensee to the owner or occupier.

Sub-section (4) provides that any such order shall be subject to revision by the State Government.

The consumer is not directly concerned with the provisions of sub-section (5).

Sub-section (6) – and this is important – lays down that "occupier" of any building or land means a person in lawful occupation of that building or land.

Section 13 of the Act requires the licensee to give a notice in writing of not less than one month to the authorities mentioned in that section before commencement of new work.

Section 14 deals with the powers of a licensee to alter the position of a pipe (which does not form part of a local authority's main sewer) or of any wire.

The provisions of section 15 which deals with the laying of electric supply lines or other works near sewers, pipes or other electric supply lines are not of much interest to the consumer.

Section 16(1) casts the following duties on the person who opens or breaks up the soil etc. Such person shall –

(a) immediately cause the part opened or broken up to be fenced and guarded;

(b) before sunset cause a light or lights sufficient for the warning of passengers, to be set up and maintained until sunrise against or near the part opened or broken up;

(c) with all reasonable speed fill in the ground and reinstate and make good the soil or pavement, or the sewer, drain or tunnel, opened or broken up, and carry away the rubbish occasioned by such openings or breaking up; and

(d) after reinstating and making good the soil or pavement, or the sewer, drain, or tunnel, broken or opened up, keep the same in good repair for three months and for any further period, not exceeding nine months, during which subsidence continues.

Where any person fails to comply with any of the provisions of sub-section (1), the person having the control or management of the street, railway, etc., in respect of which the default has occurred, may cause to be executed the work which the defaulter has delayed or omitted to execute, and recover from him the expenses incurred in such execution.

Where any difference or dispute arises as to the amount of the expenses incurred under sub-section (2), the matter shall be determined by arbitration.

Another duty cast on the licensee under section 17 of the Act is that before laying down or placing, within ten yards of any part of any telegraph line, any electric supply line or other works not being either service lines, electric or supply lines for the repair, renewal or amendment of existing works of which the character or position is not to be altered, give not less than ten days' notice in writing to the Telegraph authority, specifying –

(a) the course of the works or alternations proposed,

(b) the manner in which the works are to be utilised,

(c) the amount and nature of the energy to be transmitted, and

(d) the extent to, and manner in which, (if at all) earth returns are to be used,

and the licensee shall conform with such reasonable requirements, either general or special as may be, laid down by the Telegraph authority within that period for preventing any telegraph line from being injuriously affected by such works or alterations :

Provided that in case of emergency which shall be stated by the licensee in writing to the Telegraph authority arising from defects in any of the electric supply lines or other works of the licensee, the licensee shall be required to give only such notice as may be possible after the necessity for the proposed new works or alterations has arisen.

Where the works to be executed are of the laying or placing of any service lines, the licensee shall, not less than forty-eight hours before commencing the work, serve upon the Telegraph authority a notice in writing of his intention to execute such works.

Section 18(1) prohibits the licensee, except in case of emergency, from placing any overhead line along or across any street, railway, tramway land or waterway unless and until the State Government has communicated to him a general approval in writing of the methods of construction which he proposes to adopt :

Provided that the communication of such approval shall in no way relieve the licensee of his obligation with respect to any consent required by or under this Act.

(2) Where any overhead line has been placed or maintained by a licensee in breach of the provisions of sub-section (1), the State Government may require the licensee forthwith to remove the same, or may cause the same to be removed, and recover from the licensee the expenses incurred in such removal.

(3) Where any tree standing or laying near an overhead line or where any structure, or other object which has been placed or has fallen near an overhead line subsequently to the placing of such line, interrupts or interferes with, or is likely to interrupt or interfere with, the conveyance or transmission of energy or the accessibility of any works, a Magistrate of the First Class or, in a Presidency Town, the Commissioner of Police may, on the application of the licensee, cause the tree, structure or object to be removed or otherwise dealt with as he thinks fit.

(4) When disposing of an application under sub-section (3), the Magistrate or Commissioner of Police, as the case may be, shall in the case of any tree in existence before the placing of the overhead line, award to the person interested in the tree such compensation as he thinks reasonable and such person may recover the same from the licensee.

Explanation.—For the purpose of this section the expression "tree" shall be deemed to include any shrub, hedge, jungle-growth or other plant.

Under section 19(1), a licensee shall, in exercise of any of the powers conferred by or under this Act, cause as little damage, detriment and inconvenience as máy be, and shall make full compensation for any damage, detriment or inconvenience, caused by him or by any one employed by him.

Where any dispute or difference arises as to the amount or the application of such compensation, the matter shall be determined by arbitration.

Supply

Point where supply is delivered

For the purposes of the Electricity Act, 1910, the point at which the supply of energy by a licensee to a consumer shall be deemed to commence shall be determined in such manner as may be prescribed (Section 19A).

Power for licensee to enter premises and to remove fittings or other apparatus of licensee

(1) A licensee or any person duly authorized by a licensee may, at any reasonable time, and on informing the occupier of his intention, enter any premises to which energy is or has been supplied by him or any premises or land, under, over, along, across, in or upon which the electric supply lines or other works have been lawfully placed by him for the purpose of :–

(a) inspecting, testing, repairing or altering the electric supply lines, meters, fittings, works and apparatus for the supply of energy belonging to the licensee; or

(b) ascertaining the amount of energy supplied or the electrical quantity contained in the supply; or

(c) removing where a supply of energy is no longer required, or where the licensee is authorised to take away and cut off such supply, any electric supply lines, meters, fittings, works or apparatus belonging to the licensee.

(2) A licensee or any person authorised as aforesaid may also, in pursuance of a special order in this behalf made by a Magistrate of the First Class or in a Presidency Town by a Presidency Magistrate and after giving not less than twenty-four hours' notice in writing to the occupier –

(a) enter any premises or land referred to in sub-section (1) for any of the purposes mentioned therein;

(b) enter any premises to which energy is to be supplied by him, for the purpose of examining and testing the electric wires, fittings and apparatus for the use of energy, belonging to the consumer.

(3) Where a consumer refuses to allow a licensee or any person authorised as aforesaid to enter his premises or land in

pursuance of the provisions of sub-section (1), or sub-section (2), when such licensee or person has so entered, refuses to allow him to perform any act which he is authorised by those sub-sections to perform, or fails to give reasonable facilities of such entry or performance, the licensee may, after the expiry of twenty-four hours from the service of a notice in writing on the consumer, cut off the supply to the consumer for so long as such refusal or failure continues, but for no longer (Section 20).

Restriction on licensees controlling or interfering with use of energy

(1) A licensee shall not be entitled to prescribe any special form of appliance for utilizing energy supplied by him, or save as provided in any conditions made under sub-section (2) or by section 23, sub-section (2), or by section 26, sub-section (7) in any way to control or interfere with the use of such energy :

Provided that no person may adopt any form of appliance, or use the energy supplied to him, so as unduly or improperly to interfere with –

(a) the safety or efficient working of a licensee's electric supply lines or other works, or

(b) the supply of energy by the licensee to any other person.

(2) A licensee may, with the previous sanction of the State Government, given after consulting the State Electricity Board and also, the local authority, where the licensee is not the local authority, make conditions not inconsistent with this Act, with his license or with any rules made under this Act, to regulate his relations with persons who are or intend to become consumers and may, with the like sanction given after the like consultation, add to or alter or amend any such conditions, and any conditions made by a licensee without such sanction shall be null and void.

The proviso to this section is only of academic interest and need not be reproduced.

Sub-section (3) of this section empowers the State Government after like consultation as mentioned in sub-section (2) to add any new condition or cancel or amend any condition after giving the licensee not less than one month's notice in writing.

(4) Where any difference or dispute arises as to whether a licensee has prescribed any appliance or controlled or interfered with the use of energy in contravention of sub-section (1), the matter shall be referred to an Electrical Inspector and decided by him or, if the licensee or consumer so desires, be determined by arbitration (Section 21).

Obligation on licensee to supply energy

Where energy is supplied by a licensee, every person within the area of supply shall, except in so far as is otherwise provided by the terms and conditions of the license, be entitled, on application, to a supply on the same terms as those on which any other person in the same area is entitled in similar circumstances to a corresponding supply :

Provided that no person shall be entitled to demand, or to continue to receive, from a licensee a supply of energy for any premises having a separate supply unless he has agreed with the licensee to pay to him such minimum annual sum as will give him a reasonable return on the capital expenditure, and cover other standing charges incurred by him in order to meet the possible maximum demand for those premises, the sum payable to be determined in case of difference or dispute by arbitration (Section 22).

Powers of State Government to give direction to a licensee in regard to the supply of energy to certain class of consumers

(1) The State Government may, if in its opinion it is necessary in the public interest so to do, direct any licensee to supply in preference to any other consumer, energy required by any establishment which being in the opinion of the State Government an establishment used or intended to be used for maintaining supplies and services essential to the community, is notified by that Government in the Official Gazette in this behalf.

(2) Where any direction is issued under sub-section (1) requiring a licensee to supply energy to any establishment and any difference or dispute arises as to the price or other terms and conditions relating to the supply of energy, the licensee shall not by reason only of such difference or dispute be entitled to refuse

to supply energy but such difference or dispute shall be determined by arbitration.

(3) Where any agreement by a licensee, whether made before or after the commencement of the Indian Electricity (Amendment) Act, 1959, for the supply of energy with any establishment referred to in sub-section (1) expires, the licensee shall continue to supply energy to such establishment on the same terms and conditions as are specified in the agreement until he receives a notice in writing from the establishment requiring him to discontinue the supply.

(4) Notwithstanding anything contained in the Electricity Act, 1910, or in the Electricity (Supply) Act, 1948 (54 of 1948) or in his license or in any agreement entered into by him for the supply of energy, a licensee shall be bound to comply with any direction given to him under sub-section (1) and any action taken by him in pursuance of any such direction shall not be deemed to be in contravention of section 23 (Section 22A).

Power to control the distribution and consumption of energy

(1) If the State Government is of the opinion that it is necessary or expedient so to do, for maintaining the supply and securing the equitable distribution of energy, it may by order provide for regulating the supply, distribution, consumption or use thereof.

(2) Without prejudice to the generality of the powers conferred by sub-section (1) an order made thereunder may direct the licensee not to comply, except with the permission of the State Government, with —

(i) the provisions of any contract, agreement, or requisition whether made before or after the commencement of the Indian Electricity (Amendment) Act, 1959 for the supply (other than the resumption of a supply) or an increase in the supply of energy to any person, or

(ii) any requisition for the resumption of supply of energy to a consumer after a period of six months, from the date of its discontinuance, or

(iii) any requisition for the resumption of supply of energy made within six months of its discontinuance, where the requisitioning consumer was not himself the consumer of the supply at the time of its discontinuance (Section 22B).

Charges for energy to be made without undue preference

(1) A licensee shall not, in making any agreement for the supply of energy, show undue preference to any person.

(2) No consumer shall, except with the consent in writing of the licensee, use energy supplied to him under one method of charging in a manner for which a higher method of charging is in force.

(3) In the absence of an agreement to the contrary, a licensee may charge for energy supplied by him to any consumer –

(a) by the actual amount of energy so supplied, or

(b) by the electrical quantity contained in the supply, or

(c) by such other method as may be approved by the State Government.

(4) Any charges made by a licensee under clause (c) of sub-section (3) may be based upon, and vary in accordance with, one or more of the following considerations, namely –

(a) the consumer's load factor, or

(b) the power factor of his load, or

(c) his total consumption of energy during any stated period, or

(d) the hours at which the supply of energy is required (Section 23).

Discontinuance of supply to consumer neglecting to pay charge

(1) Where any person neglects to pay any charge for energy or any sum other than a charge for energy due from him to a licensee in respect of the supply of energy to him, the licensee may, after giving not less than seven clear days' notice in writing to such person and without prejudice to his right to recover such charge or other sum by suit, cut off the supply and for that

purpose cut or disconnect any electric supply-line or other works, being the property of the licensee, through which energy may be supplied, and may discontinue the supply until such charge or other sum, together with any expenses incurred by him in cutting off and reconnecting the supply, are paid, but no longer.

(2) Where any difference or dispute which by or under this Act is required to be determined by an Electrical Inspector, has been referred to the Inspector before notice as aforesaid has been given by the licensee, the licensee shall not exercise the powers conferred by this section until the Inspector has given his decision:

Provided that the prohibition contained in this sub-section shall not apply in any case in which the licensee has made a request in writing to the consumer for a deposit with the Electrical Inspector of the amount of the licensee's charges or other sums in dispute or for the deposit of the licensee's further charges for energy as they accrue, and the consumer has failed to comply with such request (Section 24).

Exemption of electric supply-lines or other apparatus from attachment in certain cases

Section 25 exempts electric supply-lines and other apparatus belonging to licensee placed in or upon any premises to be taken in execution under any process of any civil court or in any proceedings in insolvency.

Meters

Section 26 is one of the most important sections in the Electricity Act, 1910 as it provides for –

(i) assessment of electric energy to the consumer and, if he so desires, supply of a meter to him by the licensee;

(ii) duty of a licensee when the meter is hired (which is normally the case) by the consumer to keep it correct and maintain it;

(iii) duties of the consumer where the meter belongs to him and the procedure for settling the differences, if any;

(iv) reference of disputes to the Electrical Inspector by either party;

(v) placement of maximum demand indicator or other apparatus upon the premises of the consumer;

(vi) duty of the licensee to keep the meter, indicator or apparatus correct.

We have referred to, and reproduced, section 28 of the Act at the beginning of Chapter 2, sections 27, 29 and 29-A need not be discussed as their provisions do not relate to the consumer.

Control of transmission and use of energy

Section 30 provides that –

no person other than a licensee or a person to whom sanction is granted under section 28, duly authorised under the terms of his license or sanction, as the case may be, shall transmit or use energy at a rate exceeding two hundred and fifty watts and one hundred volts –

(a) in any street, or

(b) in any place –

(i) in which one hundred or more persons are likely ordinarily assembled, or

(ii) which is a factory within the meaning of the Factories Act, 1948 (63 of 1948) or a mine within the meaning of the Mines Act, 1952 (35 of 1952), or

(iii) to which the State Government, by general or special order, declares the provision of this sub-section to apply,

without giving, before the commencement of transmission or use of energy, not less than seven days' notice in writing of his intention to the Electrical Inspector and to the District Magistrate, or in a Presidency Town to the Commissioner of Police, containing particulars of the electrical installation and plant, if any, the nature and the purpose of supply and complying with such of the provisions of Part IV, and of the rules made thereunder, as may be applicable.

The first proviso to this section is not of much significance and need not be discussed here. The second proviso empowers the Government to exempt from the application of this section any person or class of persons using energy on premises upon or in connection with which it is generated.

The provisions of this section are binding on the Government. [Sub-section (3)].

Part IV of the Act contains general clauses to provide protection to railways, aerodromes, tramways, canals or waterways from any injury or interference in the execution of any works relating to generation, transmission, supply or use of energy. A similar protection is provided to telegraphic, telephonic and electric signaling lines.

Notice of accidents and Inquiries

Section 33 of the Act provides that if any accident occurs in the generation, transmission, supply or use of energy or in or in connection with any part of the electric supply lines or other works of any person and the accident results or is likely to have resulted in loss of human or animal life or in any injury to a human being or an animal, such person shall give a notice of the occurrence to the Electrical Inspector in such form and to such other authority as may be prescribed by the appropriate Government. The appropriate Government may cause an enquiry to be made by such Electrical Inspector as to the course or manner of such accident. The Electrical Inspector shall have the powers of a civil court for the purpose of enforcing attendance of witnesses for making such enquiry.

Prohibition of connection with earth

Under section 34, no person shall in the generation, transmission, supply or use of energy, permit any part of his electric supply-lines to be connected with earth except so far as may be prescribed in this behalf or may be specially sanctioned by the appropriate Government.

Sub-section (2) of this section lays down that if any part of an electric supply-line is connected with earth contrary to the provisions of the above sub-section or any electric supply-lines or other works are attended with danger to the public safety or to human life, or injuriously affect any telegraphic line, the appropriate Government may, by order in writing, direct the owner or user thereof to remedy in such manner as may be specified and may also forbid the use and supply of energy for such time as may be specified.

Advisory Board

Section 35 provides for the constitution of an Advisory Board by the Central Government for the whole or any part of the territories to which this Act extends and by the State Government for the whole or any part of it.

Electrical Inspector

Section 36 empowers the appropriate Government to appoint duly qualified persons as Electrical Inspectors to perform the duties and exercise the powers of such functionaries within such areas and in respect of such class of work and installations as it may direct.

An appeal shall lie from the decision of the Electrical Inspector to the appropriate Government or, if it so directs, to the Advisory Board.

Sections 36A, 36B, 37 and 38 relate to the constitution of Central Electricity Board and its rule making powers.

It might have been noted that the rights and obligations of the Consumer are not mentioned at one or the other places but are scattered all over the Act.

Crimes and Punishment

Sections 39 to 49A of the Act deal with the offences relating to electricity.

Theft of Energy

Section 39 deals with theft of electricity and lays down that whoever dishonestly abstracts, consumes or uses any energy shall be punishable with imprisonment for a term which may extend to three years, or with fine which shall not be less than one thousand rupees, or with both, and if it is proved that any artificial means or means not authorised by the licensee exist for the abstraction, consumption or use of energy by the consumer, it shall be presumed, until the contrary is proved, that any abstraction, consumption or use of energy has been dishonestly caused by such consumer.

Abetment

Section 39A makes abetment of theft of electricity punishable with the punishment provided for the offence.

Maliciously Wasting Energy

Whoever maliciously causes energy to be wasted or diverted, or with intent to cut off the supply of energy, cuts or injures, or attempts to cut or injure; any electric supply-line or works, shall be punishable with imprisonment for a term which may extend to two years, or with fine which may extend to one thousand rupees, or with both.

Penalty for unauthorised supply of energy by non-licensees

Whoever, in contravention of the provisions of section 28 engages in the business of supplying energy shall be punishable with fine which may extend to three thousand rupees, and in the case of a continuing contravention with a daily fine which may extend to three hundred rupees.

Penalty for illegal or defective supply or for non-compliance with order

Whoever –

(a) being a licensee or a person who has obtained the sanction of the State Government under section 28 to engage in the business of supplying energy to the public save as permitted under section 27 or section 51 or by his license or, as the case may be, by the conditions of sanction, supplies energy or lays down or places any electric supply-line or works outside the area of supply; or

(b) being a licensee or a person who has obtained the sanction of the State Government as aforesaid, in contravention of the provisions of this Act, or of the rules thereunder, or in breach of the conditions of license or of the sanction, as the case may be, and without reasonable excuse, the burden of proving which shall lie on him, discontinues the supply of energy or fails to supply energy; or

(c) makes default in complying with any of the provisions of an order or of any notice or requisition issued under section 5 or section 6; or

(d) makes default in complying with any directions issued to him under section 22A; or

(e) makes default in complying with any order issued to him under section 22B or sub-section (2) of section 34,

shall be punishable with fine which may extend to one thousand rupees, and, in the case of a continuing offence or default, with a daily fine which may extend to one hundred rupees.

Penalty for illegal use or transmission of energy

Whoever, in contravention of the provisions of section 30, transmits or uses energy without giving the notice required thereby, shall be punishable with fine which may extend to five hundred rupees, and, in the case of a continuing offence, with a daily fine which may extend to fifty rupees.

Penalty for interference with meters or licensee's works and for improper use of energy

Whoever –

(a) connects any meter referred to in section 26, sub-section (1) or any meter, indicator or apparatus referred to in section 26, sub-section (7), with any electric supply-line through which energy is supplied by a licensee, or disconnects the same from any such electric supply-line; or

(aa) unauthorisedly reconnects any meter referred to in sub-section (1) of section 26, or any meter, indicator or apparatus referred to in sub-section (7) of section 26, with any electric supply-line, or other works, being the property of the licensee, through which energy may be supplied, when the said electric supply-line or other works has or have been cut or disconnected under sub-section (1) of section 24; or

(b) lays, or causes to be laid, or connects up any works for the purpose of communicating with any other works belonging to a licensee; or

(c) maliciously injures any meter referred to in section 26, sub-section (1), or any meter, indicator or apparatus referred to in section 26, sub-section (7), or willfully or fraudulently alters the index of any such meter, indicator or apparatus from duly registering; or

(d) improperly uses the energy of a licensee,

shall be punishable with imprisonment for a term which may extend to three years, or with fine which may extend to five thousand rupees or with both, and in the case of a continuing offence, with a daily fine which may extend to fifty rupees and if it is proved that any artificial means exist for making such connection, there is a presumption, unless the contrary is proved, that such connection or reconnection was knowingly or willfully caused by such consumer.

Penalty for extinguishing public lamps

Whoever maliciously extinguishes any public lamp shall be punishable with imprisonment for a term which may extend to six months or with fine which may extend to three hundred rupees, or with both.

Penalty for negligently wasting energy or injuring works

Whoever negligently causes energy to be wasted or diverted, or negligently breaks, throws down or damages any electric supply-line, post, pole or lamp or other apparatus connected with the supply of energy shall be punishable with fine which may extend to two hundred rupees.

Penalty for offences not otherwise provided for

Whoever, in any case not already provided for by sections 39, 39A or sections 40 to 46 (both inclusive) makes default in complying with any of the provisions of this Act or with any order issued under it, or, in the case of a licensee, with any of the conditions of his license, or in the case of a person who has obtained the sanction of the State Government under section 28, with any of the conditions of the sanction shall be punishable with fine which may extend to one hundred rupees, and, in the case of a continuing default, with a daily fine which may extend to twenty rupees :

Provided that, where a person has made default in complying with any of the provisions of sections 13, 14, 15, 17 and 32, as the case may be, he shall not be so punishable if the court is of opinion that the case was one of emergency and that the offender complied with the said provisions as far as was reasonable in the circumstances.

Penalties not to affect other liabilities

The penalties imposed by section 39, section 39A or sections 40 to 47 (both inclusive) shall be in addition to, and not in derogation of, any liability in respect of the payment of compensation or in case of a licensee the revocation of his license, which the offender may have incurred.

Provisions where works belong to Government

The provisions of sections 39, 39A, 40, 44, 45 and 46 shall, so far as they are applicable, be deemed to apply also when the acts made punishable thereunder are committed in the case of energy supplied by or of works belonging to the Central or any State Government.

Offences by companies

(1) If the person committing an offence under this Act is a company, every person who at the time the offence was committed was in charge of, and was responsible to the company for the conduct of the business of the company as well as the company shall be deemed to be guilty of the offence and shall be liable to be proceeded against and punished accordingly :

Provided that nothing contained in this sub-section shall render any such person liable to any punishment, if he proves that the offence was committed without his knowledge or that he exercised all due diligence to prevent the commission of such offence.

(2) Notwithstanding anything contained in sub-section (1) where an offence under this Act has been committed with the consent or connivance of, or is attributable to any neglect on the part of, any director or manager, secretary or other officer of the company, such director, manager, secretary or other officer shall also be deemed to be guilty of that offence and shall be liable to be proceeded against and punished accordingly.

Explanation.– For the purpose of this section, –

(a) "company" means any body corporate and includes a firm or other association of individuals; and

(b) "director", in relation to a firm, means a partner in the firm.

Institution of prosecutions

No prosecution shall be instituted against any person for any offence against this Act or any rule, license or order thereunder, except at the instance of the Government or a State Electricity Board or an Electrical Inspector, or of a person aggrieved by the same.

Supplementary

Exercise in certain cases of powers of telegraph authority

This section empowers the State Government for coordination of works to confer upon any public officer, licensee or any other person engaged in the business of supplying energy to the public subject to such conditions and restrictions which it may think fit to impose and to the provisions of the Indian Telegraph Act any of the powers under that Act with respect to the placing of telegraph lines and posts.

State Government to have powers and obligations of a licensee under this Act

Where the State Government engages in the business of supplying energy to the public, it shall have all the powers and obligations of a licensee under this Act.

The proviso to this section exempts the State Government from certain obligations and duties of a licensee.

Arbitration

Where any matter is, by or under this Act, directed to be determined by arbitration, the matter shall, unless it is otherwise expressly provided in the license of a licensee, be determined by such person or persons as the State Government may nominate in that behalf on the application of either party, but in all other respects the arbitration shall be subject to the provisions of the Arbitration and Conciliation Act, 1996 (26 of 1996):

Provided that where the Government or a State Electricity Board is a party to a dispute, the dispute shall be referred to two arbitrators, one to be appointed by each party to the dispute.

Service of notices, orders or documents

Section 53 relates to service of notices, orders, documents etc. Section 54 relates to recovery of sums recoverable under certain provisions of this Act. Section 55 empowers the State Government to delegate some of its functions to the Electrical Inspector. Section 56(1) provides protection to public officers for acts done in good faith. Sub-section (2) of section 56 lays down that no court shall take cognizance of an offence without the sanction of the Central Government if the officer concerned is employed in connection with the affairs of the Union and, in any other case, of the State Government.

4 Applicability of the Consumer Protection Act

The Consumer Protection Act (hereinafter called the Act) is relatively a recent legislation. It came into force with effect from 24th December, 1986. It was brought on the Statute book with the avowed purpose of providing cheaper and expeditious remedy to the consumers for settlement of their disputes and for better protection of their interests. Hitherto, the interests of the consumers were protected through remedies available in such laws as the Civil Procedure Code, Law of Contracts, Sale of Goods Act, Law of Torts etc. The enactment of this Act is largely a recognition of the fact that settlement of disputes under the aforementioned laws was unduly delayed, cases moved with geological leisureliness and were inherited by one generation from another. Prolonged litigation was also financially ruinous.

The new Act provides a more expeditious and less expensive remedy for settlement of consumer disputes in as much as a Redressal Authority is ordinarily expected to decide the complaint within three months from the date of receipt of notice by the opposite party. There is no fee for filing a complaint. It is not necessary that the complainant should engage a counsel. Barring certain cases, the appeals before the State or National Commission are expected to be disposed of within ninety days from the first date of hearing. No fee is payable for preferring an appeal either before the State or the National Commission.

Disputes Relating to Electricity – Applicability of the Act

For the reasons stated above, more and more people would naturally consider it prudent to approach the Consumer Disputes Redressal Agencies to seek relief. However, before we describe the procedure prescribed under the law for initiating action, we might as well consider whether the provisions of the aforesaid Act are applicable to disputes relating to electricity. This question first arose before the Haryana State Commission *in Haryana State Electricity Board* v. *Dinesh Kumar*[1]. Upholding the decision of the District Forum that the complainant had a *locus standi* to file the complaint and the Forum had jurisdiction to entertain it, the Commission observed that the supply of electrical energy is hiring of service and not sale of goods as contended on behalf of the appellants. For proper appreciation of the law laid down in this case the relevant observations of the Commission are reproduced below in extenso :

"The supply of electrical energy has in express terms been included in the definition of "service" in clause (o) ... when the statute expressly labels the same as "service", then it is obviously difficult and, indeed, impossible, to label it as a "sale of goods" instead by an interpretative exercise. It is a well known principle of construction that the special overrides the general. Even if generally under other statutes, the supply of electric energy may tantamount to sale of goods, still when the Act specially places the same within the definition of "service", the same would have an overriding effect. General considerations under other provisions would, thus, be of little relevance. Therefore, on the larger principle, it has to be held that even though ordinarily or under other statutes the supply of electrical energy may come within the ambit of "sale of goods", yet for the special purpose of the Act, it would be excluded therefrom. If the Act has classified the same as a "service", then mandate of the Legislature must be given its full effect."

Elaborating the point further, the Commission added :

"Again, on the larger scheme of the Act, it deserves notice that the same draws a clear distinction between a consumer who purchases goods for consideration and the one who hires any service for the same. Whilst a person purchasing the goods for a commercial purpose is ousted from the definition of a "consumer", a person who hires services for consideration even for commercial purposes, remains, squarely within its ambit. The definition of a "defect" pertaining to goods in clause (f) of sub-section (1) of section 2 of the Act is distinct and different from a

1. II (1991) CPJ 38.

"deficiency" in service which is defined in clause (g) thereof. Both a defect in goods or a deficiency in service will give a cause of action to a consumer, but different consideration would necessarily apply because of the aforesaid definitions. Baring exceptional cases of composite nature, where to a sale of goods a further after-sales service may be annexed, the defect in goods and deficiency in services are things apart. Supply of electric energy, therefore, cannot possibly be both "sale of goods" or "hiring of services". It has to be either. When the Parliament in its wisdom has expressly placed the supply of electrical energy squarely within the definition of "service" in clause (o) then by no interpretative casuistry can this subject be taken out of the definition in clause (o) and thrust or inserted in clause (i). In essence when the Act labels the supply of electrical energy as a "service" one cannot possibly read it as a "sale of goods" by a strained process of interpretation. Holding so would not only be doing violence to the language of this statute, but would be contrary to all sound cannons of construction."

It follows from the judgment just cited that the consumers of electricity who hire this service even for commercial purpose are entitled to such redress by invoking the provisions of this Act. Should, therefore, a dispute arise, the consumer would do well if he understands how he should proceed. To set the redressal machinery in motion, he has, first of all, to file a complaint before the Agency having jurisdiction in his case.

Jurisdiction

The jurisdiction of the three-tier Redressal Agencies set up under section 9 of the Act is as under :

District Forum

(1) Subject to the other provisions of this Act, the District Forum shall have jurisdiction to entertain complaints where the value of the services and the compensation, if any, claimed does not exceed rupees five lakhs.

(2) The complaint shall be instituted in a District Forum within the local limits of whose jurisdiction, –

(i) the opposite party or each of the opposite parties, where there are more than one, at the time of the institution of the complaint, actually and voluntarily resides or carries on business or has a branch office, or personally works for gain; or

(ii) any of the opposite parties, where there are more than one, at the time of the institution of the complaint, actually and voluntarily resides, or carries on business or has a branch office, or personally works for gain, provided that in such case either the permission of the District Forum is given, or opposite parties who do not reside or carry on business or have a branch office, or personally work for gain, as the case may be, acquiesce in such institution; or

(iii) the cause of action, wholly or in part, arises.

(Section 11)

State Commission

Subject to the other provisions of this Act, the State Commission has jurisdiction to entertain complaints where the value of services and compensation, if any, claimed exceeds rupees five lakhs but does not exceed rupees twenty lakhs.

(Section 17)

National Commission

Subject to the other provisions of this Act, the National Commission has jurisdiction to entertain complaints where the value of services and compensation, if any, claimed exceeds rupees twenty lakhs.

(Section 21)

Barring exceptional cases, complaints against the suppliers of electric energy are likely be filed by the consumers before the District Forum as the amount of compensation claimed may not exceed rupees five lakhs.

Complaint

A complaint in relation to services as defined in section 2(1)(c) of the Act means:

an allegation in writing made by a complainant that the services mentioned in the complaint suffer from a deficiency in any respect ... with a view to obtaining any relief provided by, or under, this Act.

The complaint must be clear and concise, it should be free from acrimony and should not be couched in intemperate language. It should clearly identify the parties involved if there are more than one and should also spell out in unambiguous terms the relief sought and, if possible, state the amount of compensation to which the complainant believes he is entitled.

Procedure

The party which makes the complaint is called the "complainant" and the party or the parties against whom the complaint is made is/are called the opposite party. The complaint may be made on a plain paper. The complainant may make three copies of the complaint for members of the Forum or the Commission, as the case may be, one for himself and as many copies for the opposite party as there are respondents.

The complaint shall be presented to the District Forum (or the State Commission, as the case may be) by the complainant or his authorised representative on any working day or be sent by post. The District Forum on receipt of the complaint, if it relates to any service, shall –

(a) refer a copy of such complaint to the opposite party directing him to give his version of the case within a period of thirty days or such extended period, not exceeding fifteen days, as may be granted by the District Forum;

(b) where the opposite party, on receipt of a copy of the complaint, referred to him under clause (a) denies or disputes the allegations contained in the complaint, or omits or fails to take any action to represent his case within the time given by the District Forum, the Forum shall proceed to settle the consumer dispute –

(i) on the basis of evidence brought to its notice by the complainant and the opposite party where the opposite party denies or disputes the allegations contained in the complaint, or

(ii) on the basis of evidence brought to its notice by complainant where the opposite party omits or fails to take any action to represent his case within the time given by the Forum. [Section 13(2)].

The District Forum has the same powers as are vested in a Civil Court under the Code of Civil Procedure, 1908 while trying a suit in respect of the following matters, namely :–

(i) the summoning and enforcing attendance of any defendant or witness and examining the witness on oath;

(ii) the discovery and production of any document or other material object producible as evidence;

(iii) the reception of evidence on affidavits;

* * * *

(iv) issuing of any commission for examination of any witness; and

(v) any other matter which may be prescribed.

The complaint, it should be noted, is usually decided on the basis of affidavits filed by the parties in evidence. The complainant should, therefore, convert his complaint into an affidavit besides, wherever necessary, filing affidavits of his witnesses to prove his case.

Who can file a complaint

The complaint would ordinarily be filed by the consumer. However, under section 12(b), a recognised consumer association may also file a complaint whether the consumer to whom service is provided is a member of the association or not. Similarly, where there are numerous consumers having the same interest (e.g. defective service in a locality), one or more of them may file a complaint, with the permission of the District Forum, on behalf or for the benefit, of all consumers so interested.

Deficiency in Service

To succeed in a complaint against services, including supply of electrical energy, to which we are, as already stated, addressing ourselves specifically and exclusively in this study, the complainant must allege and establish that there was deficiency in the service provided to him. "Deficiency in service", as defined in this Act, means –

> "any fault, imperfection, shortcoming or inadequacy in the quality, nature and manner of performance which is required to be maintained by, or under, any law for the time being in force or has been undertaken to be performed by a person in pursuance of a contract or otherwise in relation to any service".

We shall shortly see with the help of decided cases how this expression has been interpreted by the Redressal Agencies in relation to the service we are presently studying.

Relief

The Redressal Forum does not have unlimited powers to grant relief to an aggrieved party. Section 14 of the Act lays down that if any of the allegations contained in the complaint about the services is proved, the Redressal Agency shall issue an order to the opposite party directing him to do one or more of the following things :-

* * * *

(c) to return to the complainant the price or, as the case may be, the charges paid by the complainant;

(d) to pay such amount as may be awarded by it as compensation to the consumer for any loss or injury suffered by the consumer due to the negligence of the opposite party;

(e) to remove the defects, or deficiency in the services in question;

* * * *

Since in this study we are dealing only with the service relating to supply of electrical energy, the reliefs under clauses (a), (b) and (f) to (i) would be irrelevant for our purpose.

The relief under clause (c) can be allowed if, for example, the Forum in a case of excess billing comes to the conclusion that the complainant has been charged an excess amount by the supplier which should be referred to or adjusted in future bills.

Clause (d) empowers the Redressal Forum to award compensation to the aggrieved party for any loss or injury suffered by him due to the negligence of the opposite party.

As held in *Gujarat Travels* v. *Ukabhai Lavaji Bhat*[1] compensation shall not be awarded if it is not claimed. Similar view was taken in *Sarvaran Steel Furniture* v. *Shabbudeen*[2] and a number of other cases decided by the State Commissions.

It also needs to be noted that compensation would, as held in *Tulicorn Plastice Pvt. Ltd.* v. *Ebemezer*,[3] be restricted to the amount claimed.

The complainant, as held in *Rani Narain Parmeshwar Major* v. *Larsen and Torbro Ltd*,[4] should prove damage or loss in a claim for compensation.

The claim for compensation should not be unrealistic. The nature and extent of the injury, loss, pain – physical and mental – suffered by the complainant by the action of the opposite party will have a bearing on the amount of compensation which might be awarded. If there is no evidence of the loss caused, the amount of compensation would be nominal.

The complainant has, in addition, to prove that the loss or injury for which he claims compensation was caused by the negligence of the opposite party.[5] It is only then, and not until then, that compensation would be warranted under this clause.

The complainants also need to be disabused of the impression that they can get any relief. The reliefs which a District Forum can grant are laid down in section 14(1) of the Act. The Redressal Forums cannot travel beyond the provisions of this section while granting relief. The District Forum, and for that matter any Redressal Agency, cannot, as held by the National Commission in *A.P. State Electricity* v. *A.P. State Electricity Consumer Association*,[6] *Union of India* v. *Chairman Madras*

1. 1992 CPR 599 (Guj SCDRC).
2. 1991(2) CPR 382 (TNSCDRC).
3. 1993(1) CPR 338 (TNSCDRC).
4. 1993(1) CPR 106 (NCDRC) : 1993 CPJ 215.
5. (1991) CPJ 97.
6. 1(1992) CPJ 148 (NC).

Provincial Consumer Association[1] and in *District Manager, Telephones* v. *Munilal Brijmohan*[2] grant an ad-interim injunction. The National Commission has also held in *National Dairy Development Board* v. *Consumer Protection Council*[3] that no interlocutory order can be passed by the Consumer Forum.

Before the insertion of clause (e) in section 14 of the Act, the Redressal Agencies could not pass a "do or desist" order. This clause has made the Consumer Forum more effective in granting relief to the aggrieved parties.

Appeals

If the decision of the District Forum is unfavourable, the person aggrieved may prefer an appeal against such order to the State Commission within a period of thirty days from the date of that order. The State Commission may, however, entertain an appeal after the expiry of this period if it is satisfied that there was sufficient cause for not filing it within that period. The State Commission has also jurisdiction to call for the record and pass appropriate order in any consumer dispute which is pending before, or has been decided by, any District Forum within the State where it appears to it that such District Forum has exercised a jurisdiction not vested in it by law, or has failed to exercise a jurisdiction so vested or acted in exercise of its jurisdiction illegally or with material irregularity.

An appeal against an order passed by the State Commission in its appellate jurisdiction, lies to the National Commission. The limitation for filing such appeal is also thirty days from the date of the order – not from the date of its communication[4] – passed by the State Commission.

The National Commission may, like the State Commission, entertain an appeal after the expiry of the period of thirty days if it is satisfied that there was sufficient cause for not filing it within the period of limitation.

1. 1992(2) CPR 710 (NCDRC).
2. 1991(2) CPR 118 (NCDRC).
3. 1(1993) CPJ 41 (NC).
4. (1992) CPJ 359.

An appeal against an order made by the National Commission lies to the Supreme Court. It has to be filed within a period of thirty days from the date of the order passed by the National Commission.

Like the State Commission and the National Commission, the Supreme Court also has the power to waive the period for filing the appeal if it is satisfied that there was sufficient reason for not filing it within the period of limitation.

The Act provides a comparatively shorter period of limitation for filing appeals to provide more expeditious relief to the aggrieved persons.

Finality of Orders

Every order passed by a District Forum, the State Commission or the National Commission shall, if no appeal has been filed against such order, be final.

Limitation for Filing Complaint

The Act lays down for the first time that the period of limitation for filing a complaint before any of the Redressal Agencies shall be two years from the date the cause of action arises, though a complaint may be entertained if, for reasons to be recorded in writing, the Redressal Agency concerned is satisfied that the complainant had sufficient cause for not filing it within the prescribed period.

Frivolous or Vexatious Complaints

A complainant need to be warned that a frivolous or vexatious complaint can recoil. For, section 26 of the Act provides that not only such a complaint shall be dismissed but the complainant shall also be required to pay to the opposite party an amount by way of costs which may extend upto ten thousand rupees. Failure to comply with an order made under this section is punishable with imprisonment for a term which shall not be less than one month but may extend to three years or with fine, which shall not be less than two thousand rupees but which may extend to ten thousand rupees or with both.

Penalties

The same punishment can be awarded to the opposite party for failure or omission to comply with any order made by the District Forum, the State Commission or the National Commission.

5 Disconnection of Electricity

Nothing is more irritating to the consumer than disconnection of his electricity. More so, if the supply is disconnected without any fault attributable to him or without even a semblance of justification. We state below the case of one of the harassed consumers who first approached the State Commission for relief and later the National Commission for further redress:

Three bills for three electric connections in the house of Shri Y.N. Gupta were delivered to him by the Delhi Electric Supply Undertaking (now D.V.B) on Sunday, the 25th March, 1990. The last date for payment was 28th March - the total amount of the bills being a whopping Rs.1,06,566/-. The current demand was Rs.3,110/-. The amount of previous arrears was Rs.1,03,456/-. The period to which the arrears related was not mentioned in the bills. On the next working day the complainant requested the Executive Engineer concerned for details of the arrears and the period to which they related. Instead of furnishing the requisite information, the electricity connection was disconnected on the 26th March itself without assigning any reason or serving any notice on him. The supply was, however, restored on the 29th March on the intervention of the General Manager.

The case of the complainant was that he had paid the entire amount due from him for electricity consumption till 6th December, 1988 after which the bills of 25th March, 1990 was received by him. Luckily for him the Electric Supply Undertaking discovered during the proceedings before the State Commission that the meters installed were defective as they showed the consumption in five digits instead of four. The bills were accordingly revised and the amount due came only to Rs.13,649/- for the period 21st December, 1988 to December, 1990 as against Rs.1,06,566/- and Rs.50,583/- from December, 1988 to September, 1990 on the basis of actual recording taken in September, 1990. Shri Gupta was, however, in for further trouble. For, D.E.S.U, discovered in the meanwhile that charges for consumption of another 10,000 units of energy for the period 1-1-1986 to 6-12-1988 were not included in the bills due to oversight. The complainant was also asked to pay late fee, though, according to him, bills were paid by him before the due dates.

The State Commission held that:

1. D.E.S.U. had been negligent in preparing bills of the complainant. As a result, he suffered unnecessary harassment and that it acted irresponsibly in raising the bills of more than Rs.50,000/-, that the amount due from him for a much longer period was only Rs.13,600/- It did not rectify the bills inspite of requests from the complainant.
2. The action of the officials of D.E.S.U. in disconnecting the electric supply was *mala fide* and was taken to harass him as a result of which he must have suffered mental torture.
3. D.E.S.U. was not entitled to charge late fee from the complainant and the same was liable to be returned.
4. The complainant was liable to pay charges for 10,000 units of energy because it was a genuine mistake on the part of the officials and was detected only when the meters were minutely examined.

Against the claim for damages for harassment and mental torture amounting to Rs.1.44 lakhs, the State Commission allowed only Rs.7,000/- as exemplary damages.[1]

Not fully satisfied with the decision of the State Commission, the complainant, *inter alia*, contended before the National Commission that the State Commission erred in:

1. allowing the claim of D.E.S.U. for 10,000 units of energy stated to have remained unbilled through oversight; and
2. awarding grossly inadequate compensation to him.

---

1. *Y.N. Gupta* v. *D.E.S.U*, 1(1993) CPJ 27 (NC).

Allowing his appeal, the National Commission held the following deficiencies in service to have been established[1] :–

(1) It was deficiency in service that the bills for electrical consumption were not prepared and served at the appointed time in accordance with the billing cycle and thereafter harassing the consumer with heavy arrears bill (the bill for the period from 21st December, 1988 to 25th March, 1990 was raised on 25th March, 1990).

(2) It was deficiency in service to have revised the bills without actual meter reading.

(3) It was deficiency in service to raise the arrears bill without details of the period to which the arrears pertained.

(4) It was deficiency in service to serve the bills on the consumer on Sunday, the 25th of March, 1990, and expect him to pay a sum of Rs.1,06,566/- by 28th March, 1990. We cannot imagine as to how the respondent D.E.S.U. expects consumer to find funds of such magnitude at short notice even if the bill is correct.

(5) The meters belong to D.E.S.U. and meter rent has been claimed in the bills. It is, therefore, the responsibility of the D.E.S.U. to maintain them in good condition. A mere scrutiny of the meter readings would have shown that the bills reflected consumption in five digits instead of four. Evidently, the bills were prepared most casually and indifferently and even elementary care was not exercised to see that the meters were malfunctioning. This constitutes deficiency in service as it inevitably leads to wrong billing against the consumer.

(6) Charging of late fee wrongfully, however, small it might be, also constitutes deficiency in service towards the consumers.

(7) Above all, the disconnection of power supply was arbitrary, high-handed and, as observed by the State Commission, *mala fide* with a view to harass the consumer.

The Commission expressed its distress over the manner in which the complainant and the members of his family were

---

1. *Y.N.Gupta* v. *D.E.S.U.*, 1 (1993) CPJ 27 (NC).

tortured by D.E.S.U. by arbitrarily and *mala fidely* disconnecting his power supply. It enhanced the compensation from Rs.7,000/- awarded by the State Commission to Rs.30,000/- and also awarded Rs.5,000/- as costs. The claim of D.E.S.U. for 10,000 units of electricity for the period 1986 to 1988 was also disallowed.

Further the Commission drew the attention of D.E.S.U. to the judgments of the Delhi High Court in AIR 1987 Del 218, *H.D.Shourie* v. *Municipal Corporation of Delhi*, and also to another case, *Major Zorawar Singh* v. *M.C.D.*, 1991 RLR 312 – in which the High Court pointed out that the maximum period for which a bill can be raised in respect of defective meter under section 26(6) of the Indian Electricity Act, 1910, is six months, and no more. It expressed the hope that in future D.E.S.U. would prefer bills in accordance with the judicial pronouncements to avoid harassment of the consumers and eliminate avoidable litigations.

The above case clearly shows that the days of arbitrary exercise of power by sleuths of Public Sector Undertakings are not yet over.

We give below the facts of another case which shows that arbitrariness in public dealings can be stretched to any extent :

The complainant-appellant was the owner of a brick-kiln. He applied for an electric connection therefor which was sanctioned. He was allotted meter No. 856. He continuously availed the electric energy and diligently paid the bills. Two other persons by the name of Narain Prasad and Bikhi Chand had separately been granted distinct electric connections against Meter Nos. 857 and 858 in the same premises. These two persons fell into arrears to the tune of Rs.24,868/-. However, to the appellant's surprise even though he had made no default whatsoever in the payment of electricity charges, his supply was disconnected and the respondent's official unauthorisedly removed his meter without any notice. Aggrieved thereby, he filed a complaint seeking compensation to the tune of Rs.60,000.

The respondent Board in their reply admitted that two other electric connections had been given to distinct persons with separate meter numbers 857 and 858. However, the suggestion was that the said persons were employees of the appellant and the three connections had been obtained for ulterior purposes.

The stand was that the arrears of Narain Prasad and Bikhi Chand against meter Nos. 857 and 858 had risen to Rs.24,868/- , the electricity connection of the appellant was disconnected being in the same premises.

The complainant filed detailed affidavit to establish his claim which were not even remotely challenged by way of cross-examination. The respondent Board did not lead any evidence worth the name. The District Forum summarily rejected the reliance of the appellant on the law laid down in AIR 1990 AP 131 and while holding that the meter numbers 857 and 858 were distinct and separate in different names surprisingly came to the following conclusion :

"In the present case, the complainant himself is paying the bills but he has consumed heavy electricity of the remaining two electric connections which are in his own premises. These connections have been disconnected but the complainant can make use of his own connections, as the connections were installed in his own premises and so he is liable to pay the arrears of these connections also. As he has not paid the arrears of these connections so his own meter No. 856 was rightly disconnected and the complainant is not entitled to the relief unless he clears the arrears of all the three connections installed on his own brick-kiln. The complaint is, therefore, dismissed as having no merit."

Setting aside this order of the District Forum and allowing the appeal of the appellant, the Haryana State Commission[1] observed that the core question in this case is whether the respondent Board can hold another recipient of electricity for the defendants or arrears of separate consumers holding independent electricity connections in their names and respective account numbers. On the principle itself, it is somewhat manifest that this cannot be so. The Commission further observed that the appellant is obviously entitled to compensation for the unwarranted action of the respondent Board and a patent deficiency in the supply of electricity services which they had undertaken. The Commission awarded an amount of Rs.5,000/- as compensation and Rs.500/- as costs.

1. II (1994) CPJ 566.

It must be observed that this action of the Haryana Electricity Board, while being patently unjust and unconscionable also borders on the ridiculous.

Disconnection without notice

Anticipating, perhaps, that the consumers could be harassed by the officials responsible for implementation of the Act by arbitrary disconnection of supply, the Legislature enacted a provision (section 24) that the electric supply of a consumer would not be disconnected or discontinued if he neglects to pay any charge for energy without giving him a notice of less than seven clear days. Section 24 of the 1910 Act is reproduced below :

Discontinuance of supply to consumer neglecting to pay charge

(1) Where any person neglects to pay any charge for energy or any sum other than a charge for energy due from him to a licensee in respect of the supply of energy to him, the licensee may, after giving not less than seven clear days' notice in writing to such person and without prejudice to his right to recover such charge or other sum by suit, cut off the supply and for that purpose cut or disconnect any electricity supply-line or other works, being the property of the licensee, through which energy may be supplied, and may discontinue the supply until such charge or other sum together with any expenses incurred by him in cutting off and reconnecting the supply, are paid but no longer.

(2) Where any difference or dispute which by or under this Act is required to be determined by an Electrical Inspector, has been referred to the Inspector before notice as aforesaid has been given by the licensee, the licensee shall not exercise the powers conferred by this section until the Inspector has given his decision :

Provided that the prohibition contained in this sub-section shall not apply in any case in which the licensee has made a request in writing to the consumer for a deposit with the Electrical Inspector of the amount of licensee's charges or other sums in dispute or for the deposit of the licensee's further charges for energy as they accrue, and the consumer has failed to comply with such request."

We refer now to a case decided by the Rajasthan State Commission where a consumer received a bill for Rs.164.68 on account of electricity consumption charges in respect of the month for which the bill was sent. However, another amount of Rs.2,364.05 was further shown in the bill as arrears of past electricity consumption. The complainant requested for details of the bill for arrears and the reasons for charging this amount in respect of past consumption. However, the opposite party did not furnish this information to the complainant and, instead, disconnected his electricity connection. Aggrieved by this action, he filed a complaint before the District Forum which was dismissed.

Setting aside the decision of the District Forum, the State Commission held that :

"Electric supply-line cannot be discontinued or disconnected in relation to a consumer if he neglects to pay any charge of energy without giving him a notice of less than seven clear days. It may be mentioned that in the electricity bill which had been sent to the complainant by the opposite parties, it is printed in the bill that in case payment of the amount is not made within a week of the last date of payment, the electricity connection will be disconnected. The very wording of section 24 of the Indian Electricity Act, 1910 goes to show that notice under this section mentioning that if the consumer neglected to pay any charge of energy in respect of the supply of energy to him and that notice will be given of clear seven days in writing. It is only after such a clear notice of seven days is served that the electricity connection can be disconnected if the charges are not paid."[1]

A compensation of Rs.4,000/- was awarded to the complainant in this case on account of wrongful disconnection of electricity supply.

A similar view was taken by the Tamil Nadu State Commission in *Chairman, Tamil Nadu Electricity Board* v. *T. Ravi Kumar*.[2] The plea of the complainant in assailing the action of the Board was that, his electricity was disconnected without

1. 1(1995) CPJ 136.
2. III (1996) CPJ 107.

giving him seven days notice. As against this, the opposite party contended that in the white meter card it has been clearly mentioned that if the electricity charges are not paid within seven days from the last date of payment, the electricity will be disconnected, and this amounts to seven days clear notice as contemplated under section 24 of the Indian Electricity Act. This plea was not accepted as the Commission remarked :

"A reading of section 24 clearly shows that the question of giving notice arises only when the electricity charges are not paid and not before and this being the case, the said statement mentioned in the white meter card cannot be considered or regarded as such a notice."

The Delhi State Commission has also held in *Vikas and Co.* v. *Delhi Electric Supply Undertaking*[1] and *Mahinder Pal Jain* v. *D.E.S.U.* that disconnection of supply of the appellant was illegal because no notice under section 24 of the Indian Electricity Act was served prior to disconnection. We may now refer to another case – *Additional Asstt. Engineer A.P.State Electricity Board* v. *Saldalen Chekrapani*[2] - in which the Andhra Pradesh State Commission after examining the relevant provisions of the Indian Electricity Act, 1910 has held, "in as much as the mandatory requirement of seven days' notice under section 24(1) of the 1910 Act was violated, disconnection of the complainant's service connection ... was, therefore, illegal and void..." The illegal connection effected by the appellants would mean that there was deficiency in service on the part of the appellants for the period from 25-8-1983 to 3-7-1994 when the supply of energy to the complainant's rice mill was cut off.

The Commission then referred to the provisions of section 22 of the 1910 Act under which the Board as licencee is bound, and the consumer is entitled, to supply of electrical energy on the same terms as those on which any other person in the same area is entitled in similar circumstances to a corresponding supply, and observed that "thus unauthorized or illegal or improper cut off... of supply to a consumer will constitute deficiency in service on the part of the Board and the consumer would be entitled to claim damages for such stoppage of supply of energy". The

1. III (1997) CPJ 119.
2. II (1998) CPJ 574.

Commission further referred to two decisions of the Supreme Court, *Punjab State Electricity Board* v. *Bassi Cold Storage, Kharar*[1] and *Punjab State Electricity Board, Mahilpur* v. *Guru Nanak Cold Storage and Ice Factory, Mahilpur*[2] in which it was held regarding damages that "the remedy of approach to the Civil Court would definitely be available to a consumer if he would seek to recover damages for disconnection due to wrongful manner".

The Commission awarded Rs.7,500/- as damages to the respondent as against Rs.10,000/- awarded by the District Forum, after as precise a calculation of loss suffered by him as was possible.

Theft of electricity

We have mentioned in the foregoing paragraphs a few cases in which the Consumer Courts have held that disconnection of electricity or its discontinuance without serving a notice of clear seven days is illegal.

But is that so in every case. No. Let us see the decision of the National Commission in *Calcutta Electric Supply Co. Ltd. (C.E.S. Co. Ltd., for short)* v. *Sunita Pal.*[3] The latter was a consumer of electricity supplied and serviced by C.E.S.Co. Ltd. Her electricity supply was disconnected by the suppliers on 9-5-1995. Aggrieved, she filed a complaint under section 12 of the Consumer Protection Act. In their written objections to the complaint, the C.E.S.Co. Ltd. stated that acting upon a credible information, the officers of C.E.S.Co. Ltd. paid a surprise visit to the premises of the consumer and upon inspection found that the consumer was drawing electricity directly from the service controls thereby bypassing the meter which was installed for registering consumption. It was stated that this was in gross violation of the statutory provisions and conditions of supply and that the officers of C.E.S.Co. Ltd. acting in exercise of the powers conferred on them under, *inter alia,* the 2nd proviso of Paragraph VI of the Schedule to the Indian Electricity Act, 1910 disconnected the electric supply immediately. A complaint was lodged with the police against the complainant herein for tampering with the meter and thereby committing an offence under the

1. 1994 Supplement (2) SCC 124.
2. (1996) 5 SCC 411.
3. III (1997) CPJ 116.

aforementioned Act. The complainant was also informed of this action, including that of lodging of F.I.R. The complainant also filed a complaint in the District Forum. The District Forum observed that theft of electricity is not deficiency in service of the licensee and that the matter need to be adjudicated in a separate proceeding. However, it ordered that the electricity of the complainant be restored within three days of the date of payment of charges on *ad hoc* basis. She cannot be expected to wait till the criminal case is decided.

The State Commission on appeal set aside the order of the District Forum and directed the C.E.S.Co. Ltd. to restore the supply of complainant within seven days of the communication of the order.

On a detailed consideration of the case, the National Commission held in revision :

> "Power is conferred upon the C.E.S.Co Ltd. under the provisions of the said Act, particularly paragraph V of the Schedule thereto, to disconnect the electric supply and it does not provide for any notice being given to the consumer where on inspection it was found that the metering equipment had been tampered with and the meter was being bypassed in consumption of electricity as artificial means within the meaning of section 39 of the said Act are *prima facie* evidence of theft."

The Commission recalled its earlier decision in *M.P. Electricity Board* v. *Badiu Lal*[1] on this point and observed :

"Where there was a tampering with the metering connection by the consumer it cannot be said that there was any deficiency in service on the part of the Electricity Board so as to warrant the grant of any relief to the consumer in proceedings under the Consumer Protection Act, 1986. In *M.P. Electricity Board* case, JT 1996(5) SC 443, the Supreme Court considered the provisions of section 24 of the said Act and held that the Board when it detects that any consumer had committed any malpractice with reference to his use of electric energy, including unauthorized alterations, installation, unauthorized extension and use of devices to commit theft of electric energy the Board may, without prejudice to other rights disconnect the supply of

1. II (1995) CPJ 132.

electricity forthwith and may call upon the consumer to make payment for compensation for the unauthorized use of the electricity. It was further held that section 24 does not apply to demand on detection of pilferage." Allowing the revision petition, the Commission observed that in this case,

"a *prima facie* conclusion of pilferage of electric energy has been reached, that the meters were tampered with by artificial means and thus the electric supply could be disconnected without any notice. The exercise of the power of disconnection is in accordance with the statutory powers and cannot be construed as any deficiency in service."

The law is thus well settled that if there is theft or pilferage of electricity by the consumer, he is not entitled to a notice of seven clear days under section 24 of the Act before disconnection or discontinuance of his supply.

What constitutes theft or pilferage

Theft of electric energy or its pilferage by the consumer is a serious offence and, like other offences, need to be proved beyond a shadow of doubt. Let us see with the help of decided cases whether theft or pilferage in a given case can be considered to be proved. In *S.D.O., A.E.E., City Division, Hissar* v. *Hotel Palki, Hissar*,[1] for instance, where theft was sought to be proved by a mere allegation that the seal of the meter was broken it was held that a mere broken seal of the meter is not a conclusive proof of theft of electrical energy. A host of other factors, like the fact that investigation was conducted at the back of the complainant and the fact that his meter has been regularly checked by the meter reader bi-monthly while the imposition of penalty was for a six months period, were also factors to be taken into account. The appeal against the order of District Forum was accordingly dismissed. Similarly, a mere allegation of theft in the written statement is no proof of theft. In *Patel Kanta Lal Devaldass* v. *The Deputy Engineer, Gujarat Electricity Board*,[2] the Gujarat State Commission observed that "the Board had not produced any evidence either by way of affidavit or oral evidence to prove that the complainant was engaged in theft. That a person was engaged in theft was a serious charge and one cannot

1. (1992) CPJ 127.
2. III (1992) CPJ 213.

jump to a conclusion merely because there is an allegation." Again, a relatively low consumption of electricity cannot be a foundation for assuming that there was necessarily theft of electricity.[1] Once again, the Haryana State Commission in *H.S.E.B.* v. *Krishan Dev*[2] held that a broken seal of a meter is not a conclusive proof of theft of electrical energy. The Commission further observed that the impugned report did not bear the signatures of either the consumer or any of his representatives, nor is it the appellant's case that the said report was at any time served upon the consumer or any opportunity afforded to him. That being so, the whole action seems to be in violation of statutory condition No. 24 A(vi)3 and 24A(1) duly notified by the Board itself.

The Andhra Pradesh State Commission has held in *A.P.S.E.B.* v. *Uday Kumar Jaiswal*[3] that if the Electricity Board detects pilferage and, as a result, disconnects the supply, no consumer dispute can arise because of this action. It will be open to the complainant to agitate the same in a Civil Court or before the High Court invoking Article 226 of the Constitution, if he is so advised.

---

1. III (1992) CPJ 214.
2. 1 (1994) CPJ 74.
3. III (1999) CPJ 521.

6 Excess Billing

Rarely, if ever, excess billing is by mistake of the officials concerned. More often, it is a ploy to harass the consumer who generally ends up by paying the amount demanded to avoid disconnection. We give below a few cases decided by the National Commission and some by the State Commissions to illustrate this point.

The complainant, Shri G.D. Khandsha, complained to the District Forum that inspite of his paying his electricity bills regularly, he received three excessive bills from the respondents, Maharashtra State Electricity Board – the last being for Rs.2,393.95. According to him, he was not required to pay this bill as the electricity supply was made not to him, but to the police quarters. However, due to threat of disconnection of his own supply he paid the bills, including the bill for Rs.2,393.95. Feeling aggrieved, he approached the District Forum for the redressal of his grievances of excess billing. The District Forum allowed the complaint and upheld his contention. The appeal filed by the Executive Engineer concerned against this order was also dismissed by the Maharashtra State Commission.[1]

We have already referred to the case of *Y.N. Gupta*[2] who received three bills for three connections on Sunday, the 25th March, 1990 – the total amount of the bills was Rs.1,06,566/- The current demand was just Rs.3,110/- the rest being arrears of past bills. The period to which the arrears related was not mentioned in the bills. When, on the next working day, he asked the Executive Engineer concerned for details, his electricity connection was disconnected on the 26th March. One of the findings of the State Commission, which was also upheld by the

1. III (1992) CPJ 555.
2. 1 (1993) CPJ 27 (NC).

National Commission in appeal, was that the action of D.E.S.U. in disconnecting the electric supply was *mala fide* and was taken to harass him.

Allowing his further appeal against the decision of the State Commission, the National Commission awarded an amount of Rs.30,000/- as compensation as against the amount of Rs.7,000/- awarded by the State Commission and held, as already stated earlier, a number of deficiencies in service to have been established, including an additional charge for 10,000 units which allegedly remained unbilled due to oversight.

Let us now see another case of high handedness: the complainant Chamanlal Madhavji was a hawker and earned his living by moving his hand cart from place to place. The Gujarat Electricity Board gave him his last electricity bill for Rs.21,284.98 for electricity consumption charges though his average consumption for two months came between Rs.80/- and Rs.90/- and he paid the bill for Rs.69.92 for December, 1991 to March, 1992. He had only one fan, one tubelight and two lamps in his house. He had no other activity which may require use of electricity. The bill was for the last seven years. The complainant did not pay. His electricity was disconnected. The complaint filed by him before the District Forum was not allowed. The contention of the Board was that the bill for 7,300 units was correct according to meter reading. The meter reader in his affidavit had, however, stated that he prepared the bill on *ad hoc* basis as the complainant and other people in the locality would not allow meter reading because of the threat given by them. Another justification given by the officials of the Board was that if average consumption of 190 units bi-monthly is taken for 97 months, consumption would come to 9,215 units.[1]

The Gujarat State Commission rejected outright the contention that the appellant and others threatened the meter-reader and prevented them from taking readings. In that case, the Commission held, they could seek and get police protection. The Commission further held that there is a great difference between the last bill and this disputed bill. The Commission directed the Electricity Board to prepare a new bill on an average

1. II (1994) CPJ 54.

consumption and the rates that were prevailing at the relevant time should be applied and charged from the complainant.[1]

Let us now look at a case decided by the Kerala State Commission[2] in which, following the National Commission, it has held that the Electricity Board has a statutory duty to take meter reading every six months and they cannot issue any bill for excess consumption for a period prior to six months. The Electricity Board in this case had issued a bill for excess consumption for three years.

We now turn to a decision of the National Commission in which one of the main questions for consideration was whether the word "due" used in section 2 of the Indian Electricity Act is to be interpreted in the narrower sense *viz.* as only restricted to the amounts within the period of limitation or which could be successfully claimed by a suit, or it could be interpreted in a wider sense for recovering even such amounts as may have become time-barred under the Limitation Act. Agreeing with the decision of the Bombay High Court in *Bharat Barrel and Drum Manufacturing Co. Pvt. Ltd.* v. *The Municipal Corporation of Greater Bombay*,[3] the Commission also felt that the wider meaning would be more in accordance with the scheme of the statutory provisions as also with commercial honesty.

This case which has the effect of overriding the relevant provisions of the Limitation Act arose out of the following facts :–

> "On an inspection of the electric meter of the respondent, the Maharashtra State Electricity Board found in January, 1985 that K.W and K.W.A.M.D were faulty and K.W.H unit recording was also faulty. It was accordingly decided by the appellant Board that reassessment of units consumed should be made on "average basis" for the period August, 1984 to December, 1984. No action was, however, taken by the Board on the report of January, 1985 till 5-2-1993. It was on that date that the appellant informed the respondent about the low recording of electricity consumption on his meter and enclosed a supplementary bill for Rs.3,17,659/-

1. II (1994) CPJ 548.
2. III (1995) CPJ 124.
3. AIR 1978 Bom 369.

for the period August, 1984 to December, 1984 indicating the details of the average units required to be charged, what was actually charged and the difference between the two. The respondent requested for payment of the supplementary bill by instalments of Rs.52,906/- each which was allowed. The respondent thereafter filed a complaint before the Consumer Disputes Redressal Commission, Maharashtra alleging that they were made to make payment under threat of disconnection. They also stated that recovery of a due after a long period of 9 years is time-barred and that the Electricity Board cannot take recourse to section 24 of the Act and that too when there was no negligence on their part to pay the dues on time."

The Maharashtra State Commission decided that the appellant after giving a notice under section 24 of the Act and by threatening the customer cannot make its claim alive after such a long period and, therefore, the recovery made by the Board from the respondent was illegal. They accordingly directed the Board to pay back the amount along with interest and costs. The Maharashtra State Commission noted that the judgment of the Bombay High Court cited above was brought to their notice but it did not discuss the implications of this judgment and its relevance in the case under decision.

Agreeing with the interpretation of the Bombay High Court of section 24 of the Act, the National Commission held in appeal that the Maharashtra State Commission had erred in not considering the legal aspects of the case, particularly noting that the judgment of the Bombay High Court was brought to their notice, and in allowing the complaint of the respondents only on the ground that such an old claim cannot be made alive by giving a notice or by threatening a consumer of disconnection of power supply. It is true that the appellants woke up after a period of 9 years to discover this report. This does not speak very well of the efficiency with which the appellants are functioning. But the inefficiency of the functionaries shall not be made a ground to cause loss to a public utility concern. Another view, it is most respectfully submitted, could, perhaps, have been that the public utility concern should have compensated itself by recovering the amount of loss from its employee – there is such a provision in the Government Servants Conduct Rules which are applicable to the employees of the Corporation – rather than attempt or pray for subversion of the provisions of the Limitation Act which are applicable in all situations.

In the foregoing case, the Maharashtra Board at least notified the complainant of the brief position of his case to afford him an opportunity to give his version of the matter. But what if after coming to know that the meter was not recording correctly electricity being consumed by the customer, the electricity authority itself overhauls the bill and to save his connection he pays the amount? Here are the facts of this case :

The complainant, Daljit Singh, had an electric meter installed in his industrial premises at Hoshiarpur. His meter was checked by the S.D.O., Punjab Electricity Board, on 4-10-1991 which was found to be defective. The meter was changed by him. Once again, the Flying Squad of the Board checked the meter on 15-10-1991 and reported that the meter was dead on two faces and C.T.C. was broken out. A bill dated 21-10-1991 was then issued to him. It was for Rs.46,111/-. To save his electric connection, he deposited the bill. He challenged the bill before the District Forum as arbitrary. The Board contested the claim and justified the bill asserting, *inter alia*, that the meter checked by the Flying Squad on 15-10-1991 was found dead on two faces due to improper joints in the leads of the meter C.T.C. and the same was set right at the spot and, as such, the account of the complainant was rightly overhauled from May, 1991 to September, 1991. On the basis of the report of S.D.O. the complainant was found liable to pay an additional amount of Rs.46,111/-

After hearing the complainant and also the Board, the District Forum dismissed the complaint.

Reversing the decision of the District Forum, the Punjab State Commission held that on the subsequent checking of the meter by the Flying Squad when earlier also the meter was found to be defective by the officers, the Board was not entitled to overhaul the accounts from May, 1991 to September, 1991 and to issue an arbitrary bill for Rs.46,111/. The Commission observed that if the officials of the Board were of the view that the meter was not correctly recording the electricity consumed, then, in our view, "remedy available with the Board was sub-section (6) of section 26 of the Electricity Act and to refer the case to the Electrical Inspector to get the difference or dispute settled from him." In the matter of supply of electricity, the Commission further observed, "the Board enjoyed the status of a monopoly concern. In the issuance of the bills to the consumers, the Board cannot be permitted to behave at its mere whims and caprice. In the facts and circumstances of the case, we are of the view that the issuance of the bill in dispute amounting to Rs.46,111/- is absolutely arbitrary and thereby the Board has rendered deficient service to the consumer and hence cannot be permitted to recover the amount in pursuance of the said bills."[1]

Rejecting the appeal of the State Electricity Board and upholding the decision of the District Forum, the Haryana State Commission took more or less the same view in *Suman Ice Factory* v. *Sub-Divisional Officer, H.S.E.B.*[2] The Commission observed that "if the H.S.E.B. was to revise or detect some mistake in the billing or some metering defect in the electricity meter, as it has been alleged to be running slow or sticky proper notice should have been served upon the respondent and after associating him with the investigation, the revision of the amount or even overhauling could be undertaken. Moreover, reference could also be made to the Electrical Inspector under section 26(6) of the Act but unilateral revision of the bill raising an additional demand on the basis of average consumption and disconnecting the electricity connection cannot be countenanced."

Much the same trend is noticed in another case decided by the Punjab State Commission (*Punjab State Electricity Board* v. *G.M.P. Finishing Mills*[3]) in which it was held that "the complainant was to be charged for the electricity under the Sales Manual or the instructions issued by the Electricity Board, and it was the duty of the Electricity Board to provide and maintain a correct electricity meter and to issue bills periodically as per meter readings recorded. If after a few years it was found that there was some defect in the meter and they wanted to raise a demand, straightaway issuing of bill was not contemplated. The complainant was to be associated in the process and if any such

1. III (1997) CPJ 217.
2. II (1998) CPJ 37.
3. III (1997) CPJ 76.

dispute was being raised, the same could be decided in view of the provisions of section 26(6) of the Indian Electricity Act. If arbitrarily the Electricity Board wanted to raise bills and under threat of disconnection consumers are made to pay the same, deficiency in rendering service would be writ large."

Billing on average basis

Every Board or Undertaking supplying electric energy has a Sales Manual or Terms and conditions of supply which are applicable when meter made available to the consumer is not functioning or has become non-functional for some time. The instructions contained therein are undoubtedly binding on the Board. Obviously, the officials of the Board cannot depart from the mandate of their own provisions and go by a formula whimsically devised by them. Yet, this has been happening as we shall see presently.

The complainant Gram Panchayat, Dahina, had bored a tube well which was energised by the Haryana State Electricity Board (the Board, for short) in 1988. It is common ground that the meter of the tubewell stopped functioning in September, 1990 and an amount of Rs.510/- was paid to the Board. The burnt meter of the tubewell was never replaced. It is the case of the complainant that before the meter was burnt, the electricity bills were for a small amount of Rs.7,606.60p which were duly paid but after September, 1990 highly inflated bills on an arbitrary average of 5,000 units per month were raised against him. The total amount of these bills by the end of 1991 was the astronomical figure of Rs.3,26,485/- which, on a representation, was reduced to Rs.1,81,701/-. In essence, the case was that the Board could not levy charge on an arbitrary average of 5,000 units per month for the tubewell or take advantage of its own wrong in refusing or failing to replace the burnt meter, the cost of which had been duly deposited and admitted to have been received. The relief claimed was that the demand of Rs.1,81,701/- may be set aside.

The case of the respondent Board was that the figure of 5,000 units was arrived at on the ground that the motor installed at the tubewell was 30 H.P., which consumed 25 units per hour and the further assumption was that the tubewell was run at an average of 8 hours per day through out the year (not even excluding the rainy days!)

Before allowing the complaint and setting aside the demand of Rs.1,81,000/- the Commission referred to the statutory and contractual provisions applicable when the meter becomes dead or goes out of order. These provisions are briefly stated below:—

Instruction No. 115

So far as charging the customer for the period the meter remained inoperative is concerned, some *ad hoc* charges based on the average consumption of the last 3 to 6 months or the average of the same months of the preceding year, whichever seems to be reasonable, should be levied.

Clause 14

(a) Should the Board at anytime detect the meter at the consumer's premises to be out of order (or the consumer so informs the Board) it should be replaced with a correct meter. The electricity supplied to the consumer during the period in which the said meter did not function should be determined by taking average consumption of 3 to 6 months preceding the period in which the meter had ceased to function, or the average of the corresponding months of the preceding year, whichever seems to be comparable.

The Commission also struck down the charges for 5,000 units per month as a patent deficiency in service.[1]

A peculiarly isolated case, though not the only one, came up for decision before the Karnataka State Commission.[2] It was not the case of a dead meter nor the one which became non-functional for some time but of a newly installed one which did not record consumption of even one full billing month. The regulation applicable of the Karnataka Electricity Board reads as under :—

---

1. III (1992) CPJ 483.
2. *G.S. Bhagwat* v. *Asstt. Executive Engineer,* II (1994) CPJ 37.

"*29.03* – When the recorded consumption of even one full billing month is not available, the installation shall be billed on the basis of the computed demand consumption as indicated in :

(i) Table	:	Low Tension Supply
(ii) Non commercial combine lighting and heating	:	100 units per K.W. or part thereof sanctioned load.

The complainant was billed an amount of Rs.3,140/-. The District Forum dismissed his complaint, upholding the stand of the respondent.

Setting aside the decision of the District Forum and recalling its earlier decision in an identical case (*K.E.B.* v. *K.P. Bhat*, Appeal No.148/1991) decided on 3-3-1992, the Commission observed that the rule relied upon by the respondents pre-supposes the installation of a working meter and that the meter should have recorded at least for a few days. In the present case, the meter has not worked from the date of its inception. It is very difficult to say that this rule is applicable to the facts in question. The Commission laid down the following guidelines for billing in such a case :–

> "As regards computation of the electricity charges for billing for the period of non-recording of consumption in the meter, the District Forum has directed that the 3 months average of the consumption recorded immediately after the working meter is installed should be taken into consideration. But in our opinion, it will be just and proper if 12 months average of the consumption recorded immediately after the working meter is installed should be taken to avoid the possibility of any manipulation by the consumer."

The Rajasthan State Commission has firmly held that no "averaging" is permissible under the law and any condition framed in contravention of section 26 of the Indian Electricity Act, 1910, (which lays down that the quality of electricity supplied to a consumer has to be measured by means of a correct meter) is invalid. It is the statutory duty of the Electricity Board to keep the meter correct. In the case of *Rajasthan State Electricity Board*

v. *Kishan Chand*[1] the meter remained defective from 25-5-1990 to November, 1990 and it was only in February, 1992 that the complainant was required to pay Rs.1,565.16 for the above six months on average basis under Condition No. 19(d)(VII) of the General Conditions of Supply issued by the Rajasthan Board. The Commission observed that despite finding that the meter had entirely stopped or was totally defective, it neither took any steps to replace the meter at once by a correct meter nor to send the bi-monthly electricity bills on the basis of average consumption in accordance with the above condition. It was only after two years when the departmental audit pointed out this short recovery that they conveniently shifted their own deficiency to the complainant by seeking to charge from him the amount mentioned above and by not describing the same as average charges but by mentioning it as audit charges. Admittedly, the Commission further observed, the meter was completely out of order for more than six months. The complainant was accordingly not liable to pay meter rent either for the period it remained out of order.

We now consider another case decided, once again, by the Rajasthan State Commission where the Electricity Board decided to recover energy charges from the agriculturists of Nagaut village not on average basis but on the basis of a flat rate which was introduced on the basis of an order issued by the Chief Engineer and which became effective from 1-3-1991. The Chief Engineer (Commercial) of the Board mentioned in this order that under the General Conditions of Supply, there was an option to supply electricity to agriculturists either on the basis of flat rate or on the basis of reading in meter. It was also mentioned that the Vigilance Branch of the Board was noticing on surprise inspections that theft of electricity was being committed. Therefore, the Chief Engineer mentioned, it was decided that if an agriculturist consumer is found to be committing theft of electrical energy then in future their option for being charged on the basis of meter reading will end and they will be charged on the basis of flat rate.

The 12 complainants in this case were earlier sanctioned electricity meters and were also paying meter rent of Rs.12/- each. Their meters were, however, re-issued in pursuance of the

---

1. I (1996) CPJ 110.

above decision and they were being billed at a flat rate. The complaint filed by them before the District Forum was dismissed mainly on the ground that any person aggrieved by such an order can file an appeal before the competent authority.

Commenting briefly on the decision of the District Forum, the Commission observed that it did not examine the real controversy between the parties. The complainants, it noted, had not challenged any particular bill. Their case was that they had been sanctioned electricity connections under the stipulation that they would be charged on the basis of meter reading and the meter had also been installed for each complainant and they were paying meter rent. They have also been paying electricity consumption charges on the basis of meter reading and it was only on 1-3-1991 that the meter was removed by the opposite party. These facts were not disputed by the opposite party in their version filed before the District Forum. The case of the opposite party in this version was that the complainants tamper with the meter and do not permit it to record correct reading and that was why electricity bills on the basis of flat rate were being issued.

The Commission noted that in relation to the complainants no inspection note was prepared by the competent officer mentioning the commission of any thefts or an act of malpractice. Even no disconnection was made. The Commission further observed that, that only shows that the opposite party wanted to get out of the agreement with the complainants for being charged on the basis of meter and wanted to charge them at flat rates under colourable exercise of power. The opposite party cannot be permitted to practice fraud on their own agreement. The District Forum was, therefore, wrong in dismissing these complaints. The Commission further directed the Board to fix working meters of each of the complainant and ordered it to pay Rs.2,000/- to each of them for removing their meters and not replacing the same right from 1-3-1991 till now.

In another case, the Rajasthan Electricity Board adopted a totally unprecedented and illegal method to prepare a bill for the past recovery. The District Forum dismissed the complaint of the aggrieved party but the State Commission on the basis of evidence found that it was not a case of the meter being out of order – stopped, burnt or having ceased to function. Admittedly, no action was taken against the complainant for either theft or any other malpractice. No reference was made to the Electrical Inspector either under section 26(6) of the Act. An arrear bill for Rs.3,922/- was, however, sent to the complainant for payment. It was sent on the basis of average charging for 54 months and, surprisingly, not of the preceding three or twelve months, whichever was the higher, as permissible under condition No. 19(d) VII Note 1, but on the basis of average of succeeding period which was totally illegal. The Commission, while quashing this bill, observed that it was misconceived and, if we may say so, it was a "misadventure."[1]

In *M.P. Electrical Board* v. *Shiv Kant Dubey*,[2] the Madhya Pradesh Commission found on the basis of evidence that no meter reader recorded the meter reading for a continuous period of six months. Accordingly, average bills were sent. Referring to the case of *Y.N. Gupta*[3] decided by the National Commission, the State Commission held that not preparing or sending the bills for electrical consumption in accordance with the billing cycle was deficiency in service as the consumer had to pay heavy arrears which amounted to his harassment.

Like the Rajasthan State Commission in *Rajasthan Electricity Board* v. *Kishan Chand*,[4] the Punjab State Commission also held in *Punjab State Electricity Board* v. *Ram Processor Merrakat Road*,[5] that the Electricity Board was not entitled to recover meter rent from the consumer for the period the meter remained inoperative. Referring to a decision of the Supreme Court *(M.P.E.B.* v. *Imanta Bhai,* AIR 1998 SC 71), the same State Commission also held in the same case that a dispute between the parties whether the meter was giving correct reading or not had to be decided by the Electrical Inspector on an application made by either of the two parties and it was the duty of the Inspector to estimate the amount due and to calculate the quantity of energy consumed by the consumer not exceeding six months.

---

1. *State of Rajasthan* v. *M.P. Pandya*.
2. II (1997) CPJ 472.
3. I (1993) CPJ 27 (NC).
4. I (1996) CPJ 110.
5. I (2001) CPJ 178.

The Punjab State Commission in the above case has further referred to a decision of the Madhya Pradesh State Commission in *Baboo Lal* v. *M.S. Yadav*[1] that the demand of additional amount for slow running of electrical energy is not justified without getting the dispute settled from the Electrical Inspector of the Board on the ground of defective meter. It has also been held that where the Board fails to refer the dispute first to the Electrical Inspector, it amounts to deficiency in service.

The Karnataka High Court has also held that :

> "in case of faulty meter, the Electrical Inspector is to determine the dispute and in case of under recording, the Board to raise the dispute before Electrical Inspector and in case of over-recording, consumer, being the affected party should raise the dispute – once dispute is raised the modification of the bill should await the decision of the Inspector."

The State Commission concluded in the above case that the action of the opposite party in preparing and issuing the impugned bills to the complainant is not in accordance with law. To that extent the Commission upheld the order of the District Forum but instead of quashing the bills, it modified the direction of the Forum to the opposite party that the dispute should be referred to the Electrical Inspector. After complying with the provisions of law, it may recover anything due from the complainant in accordance with law.

1. II (1994) CPJ 97.

7 Electrical Inspector

Most of us may, perhaps, be not aware of the existence of such a functionary or the duties he is expected to discharge under the law. He is not that universally reprobated functionary so common in Indian administration. Section 36 of the Indian Electricity Act, 1910, envisages the appointment of duly qualified persons to be Electrical Inspectors to exercise the powers and perform the functions assigned to them under the aforesaid Act.

By now it must be clear that, unless there is an agreement to the contrary, the amount of electrical energy supplied to a consumer or the electrical quantity contained in it shall be ascertained by means of a correct meter. The licensee if required by the consumer, has to supply such a meter on furnishing a security for its price and entering into an agreement for payment of hire thereof. The licensee in that case is responsible to keep the meter correct. However, the meter, being just a mechanical device may sometime go wrong either because of some manipulation by the consumer or due to some other reason, it may not record the energy passing through it correctly. It may run slow which is to the disadvantage of the licensee or run faster which adversely affects the consumer. Either way it would give rise to a controversy. The law has made a provision for resolving such disputes. Section 26(6) of the Indian Electricity Act, 1910 lays down that :

> "Where any difference or dispute arises as to whether any meter referred to in sub-section (1) is or is not correct, the matter shall be decided, upon the application of either party, by an Electrical Inspector, and where the meter has, in the opinion of such Inspector ceased to be correct, such Inspector shall estimate the amount of the energy supplied to the consumer or the electrical quantity contained in the supply, during such time, not exceeding six months, as the meter shall not, in the opinion of such Inspector, have been

correct; but save as aforesaid, the register of the meter shall, in the absence of fraud, be conclusive proof of such amount or quantity :

Provided that before either a licensee or a consumer applies to the Electrical Inspector under this sub section, he shall give to the other party not less than seven days' notice of his intention so to do."

As stated above, it is open to both the parties to make an application to the Electrical Inspector when any difference or dispute arises as to the correctness of the meter. Subject to any provision to the contrary, an appeal shall lie to the appropriate government from the decision of the Electrical Inspector, or if the appropriate government so directs, to an Advisory Board and when the Courts or the Redressal Agencies would give a direction that the matter may be referred to the Electrical Inspector for a decision under section 26(6) of the Indian Electricity Act, 1910. Following are the decisions of the courts–

In the case of *Asstt. Executive Engineer O&M, Rural Sub-Division, KEB* v. *Millind Dolli*, AIR 2002 Karn 120, it was held that it is incumbent on the part of the consumer to deposit the disputed amount before the Electrical Inspector to avoid disconnection.

In *Madhya Pradesh Electricity Board* v. *Basantibai,*[1] the Supreme Court observed :

"In the instant case, the dispute relates to whether the meter is correct one or it is faulty not recording the actual energy consumed in running the oil mill of the respondent. So this dispute squarely falls within the provisions of the said Act and as such it has been rightly found by the High Court that it is the Electrical Inspector who alone is empowered to decide the dispute. If the Electrical Inspector comes to the finding that the meter is faulty and due to some defect it has not registered the actual consumption of electrical energy, then the Inspector will estimate the amount of energy consumed and will fix the amount to be paid in respect of such energy consumed within a period not exceeding six months."

In this case the appellant Board had also sent a supplementary bill and had threatened disconnection of supply for its non-payment. On this point the court further observed :

---

1. AIR 1988 SC 71.

"The appellant 1 is not competent pending the determination of this dispute by the Electrical Inspector to issue the impugned notice threatening disconnection of supply of electricity for non-payment of supplementary bill prepared and sent by it. The Board is also not competent to prepare and send a supplementary bill in respect of energy consumed by the respondent."

Similar was the decision of the Madhya Pradesh High Court in the same case reported as AIR 1985 MP 70 at 72 Indore Bench. "The respondent Board," observed the Court, "or its authorities cannot prepare such revised or supplementary bill and call upon the consumer to pay in accordance with such bill, by whatever name it is called, either revised or supplementary. The very fact that the respondent board or its authorities are required to prepare such supplementary bill goes to show that they are satisfied with the correctness of the meter recording which is not disputed by the petitioner. The insistence to pay such a supplementary bill is, therefore, not supportable and the authorities would not be justified in insisting on such a payment before re-connecting or re-storing the electric supply by installing a meter. It is beyond the scope of their authority and such insistence has no foundation in law."

In *H.D. Shourie v. Delhi Municipal Corporation*,[1] the Delhi High Court has pointed out the illegalities committed by the respondents in dealing with the matter. The case was never referred to the Electrical Inspector for adjudication. The respondents took a unilateral decision and that also without notice to the petitioner and behind his back that the meter was defective. They themselves estimated the quantity of electricity consumed during the period and that also without notice to the petitioner. Another illegality committed was that the bill sent by them was for a period in excess of six months which was contrary to the provisions of section 26(6) of the Indian Electricity Act, 1910. In view of the fact that the mandatory provisions of section 26(6) of the Act were not complied, the Court quashed the demand raised by the respondents and left it to them to revise the bill only after complying with the provisions of section 26(6).

1. AIR 1987 Del 219.

The law is well-established that a dispute, whether correct or incorrect, can be resolved only by the Electrical Inspector who can be moved in the matter either by the consumer or by the Board. A revised bill sent for a period of five years is clearly illegal, for even when the matter is referred to the Electrical Inspector, the revised amount can be recovered for a period of six months only.[1]

It is equally well-settled that the power of disconnection vested in the licensee under section 24(1) cannot be exercised ignoring section 26(6) of the Indian Electricity Act, 1910.[2] In other words, if the dispute is pending with the Electrical Inspector the licensee cannot stop supplying electricity to the consumer for "neglecting" to make payment of dues. Non-payment of the amount in such a case cannot be termed as neglect but the result of a *bona fide* dispute.

Let us now see how the Redressal Agencies set up under the Consumer Disputes Act, 1986 have looked at the disputes or differences between the consumers and the licensee where the meter is alleged to be defective or non-functioning and where they have decided to refer the matter to the Electrical Inspector because the consumer, as we are aware, prefers to take up the matter with the Consumer Fora as he believes that redressal there is more expeditious and less expensive. Another good reason for approaching the Redressal Agencies is that they have the jurisdiction and power to declare that the act of commission or omission attributable to the opposite party constitutes deficiency in service and are competent to award compensation for such negligence. In *J.P. Khangare* v. *Executive Engineer, Maharashtra State Electricity Board*, the Maharashtra State Commission observed that in a dispute between the consumer and electrical undertaking a reference has to be made to the Electrical Inspector.[3] The Commission further observed that not adopting legal procedure as per rules and regulations which are required to be observed in case of disputed electric dues amounts to deficiency in service.

---

1. *Hamidullah Khan* v. *Chairman, M.P. Electricity Board,* AIR 1983 MP 3.
2. *Bharat Board and Drum Mfg Co. Ltd.* v. *Bombay Municipal Corp.*, AIR 1985 Bom 415 at 426.
3. II (1992) CPJ 963.

Relying on a decision of the Supreme Court in *M.P.E.B.* v. *Basantibai*[1] and of the Madhya Pradesh High Court itself in *Hamidullah Khan* v. *The Chairman, M.P.E.B.*,[2] the Madhya Pradesh State Commission held that the M.P. Electricity Board is not entitled to recover any amount from the appellant on the basis that the meter was defective and was not giving the correct reading unless it refers the matter to the Electrical Inspector and gets it decided through him. Demand and insistence on compliance with it on the part of the M.P. Electricity Board especially in the face of the decisions of the High Court and the Supreme Court against it is no doubt a deficiency in service.[3]

In *Ramrakh Vyas* v. *Rajasthan Electricity Board*,[4] the Rajasthan State Commission, while striking down condition No. 19(d)(vii) Note 1 as *ultra vires* of section 26(6) of the Indian Electricity Act, 1910, observed that in the case under decision, it was not the consumer who was questioning the correctness of the meter, it was the case of the Board that the meter glass had broken and the meter had stopped since November, 1986 and therefore, they sent the bill for past arrears amounting to Rs.2,364.05. It is clear that the opposite party is disputing the correctness of the meter and not the complainant. In such circumstances, it was for the opposite party to raise the dispute and refer the matter to the Electrical Inspector and it was for the Electrical Inspector to give opinion whether the meter had ceased to be correct and if he was of such opinion then it was the Electrical Inspector who had to estimate the amount of energy supplied to the consumer and that also he could do so for a period not exceeding six months. No such procedure was followed by the opposite party in the present case. The Commission held that no such bill as aforesaid could be sent to the consumer and his electricity could not be disconnected for its non-payment.

1. AIR 1988 SC 71.
2. AIR 1983 MP 3.
3. II (1994) CPJ 97, *Baboolal* v. *M.S. Yadav*.
4. 1(1995) CPJ 136.

In *Gita Rani Chakraborty* v. *Electric Superintendent Bankara,*[1] decided by the West Bengal State Commission the majority view that the meter was defective since July, 1991 to the knowledge of the respondents and they did not take any steps to replace it is serious negligence and deficiency in service. The minority view, however, was that the complainant himself could have referred the matter to the Electrical Inspector as the licensee did not take any such step. It will be improper to direct the licensee to pay any compensation until the meter is tested by the Electrical Inspector. This process may be undertaken immediately and the consumption may be assessed as per law for a period of six months.

Where the Electricity Board issued a fresh bill for the last six months on the ground that the meter of the complainant was running slow without referring the matter to the Electrical Inspector, the Haryana State Commission held that the Board was not competent in law to issue a fresh bill without complying with the provisions of section 26(6) of the Indian Electricity Act, 1910 – *Executive Engineer, Haryana State Electricity Board* v. *Madhu Suman Gupta.*[2]

We now refer to a case in which it was held that the protection of section 26(6) shall not be available to a consumer if the meter was not functioning but no reference was made by him to the Electrical Inspector. In support of this view, the Maharashtra State Commission held in *Bombay Suburban Electric Supply Ltd.* v. *The Secretary, Deepali Coop. Housing Society Ltd.*[3] that sub-section (6) of section 26 does not cast any duty on the licensee to refer any difference or dispute in respect of any meter for determination of the Electrical Inspector on behalf of the consumer. If any difference or dispute was raised by the consumer, it was for him to make a reference to the Electrical Inspector for determination. When no such application was made by him, it cannot be said that the licensee was not entitled to demand the arrears due from the consumer. The Commission

1. 1(1997) CPJ 450.
2. II (1998) CPJ 24.
3. III (1999) CPJ 416.

cited a decision of the Allahabad High Court[1] in support of this view.

In *Punjab State Electricity Board* v. *Sub-Divisional Engineer, Public Health P.J.J. Sub-Division,*[2] the Punjab State Commission following the decision of the National Commission in *Y.N. Gupta* v. *D.E.S.U.*[3] and of the Supreme Court in *Balwal Spinning Mills Ltd.* v. *U.P. State Electricity Board*[4] held that the Electricity Board was required to refer the dispute of defective meter to the Electrical Inspector which was not done. The opposite party cannot assume the statutory powers and functions of the Electrical Inspector. The action of the opposite party, the Commission observed, is not sustainable in law.

Where the electricity meter was alleged to be running slow and bills were issued to the consumer on average basis, the Punjab State Commission, following the decision of the Supreme Court in *Madhya Pradesh Electricity Board* v. *Imam Bhai*[5] and agreeing with the decision of the Madhya Pradesh State Commission in *Baboo Lal* v. *M.S. Yadav*[6] and of the Karnataka High Court in *Karnataka Electricity Board* v. *Topasra,*[7] held in *Punjab State Electricity Board* v. *Ram Processor Merrakat Road*[8] that the opposite party could not have issued the impugned bills to the respondents in violation of section 26(6) of the Indian Electricity Act, 1910. The Commission accordingly decided to direct the opposite party to take action in accordance with law *i.e.* the dispute should be referred to the Chief Electrical Inspector and after complying with the relevant provisions of law may recover anything due from the complainant.

After this survey of the law laid down by the Courts and the Redressal Agencies, we may say that the law is well-established that if there is any difference or dispute as to the correctness of

---

1. AIR 1998 All 8, *Premier Ice Factory* v. *Commercial Manager, Kanpur Electricity Supply Administration.*
2. I (2000) CPJ 9.
3. 1(1993) CPJ 27 (NC).
4. AIR 1997 SC 2393.
5. AIR 1998 SC 71.
6. II (1994) CPJ 97.
7. 1(1991) Civil Court Cases 472.
8. 1(2001) CPJ 178.

any meter, the matter shall be decided upon the application of either party, by an Electrical Inspector and where the meter has, in the opinion of such Inspector, ceased to be correct, such Inspector shall estimate the amount of energy supplied to the consumer or the electrical quantity contained therein, during such time, not exceeding six months, as the meter in the opinion cf such Inspector, have been correct.

8 Recovery of Arrears

Before we discuss this topic with the help of cases decided by the Courts, especially the Consumer Courts, we may state the law on the subject. Sub-section (1) of section 26 of the Indian Electricity Act, 1910 provides that in the absence of an agreement to the contrary, the amount of energy supplied to a consumer or the electrical quantity contained therein shall be ascertained by a correct meter, and the licensee shall, if required by the consumer, cause the consumer to be supplied with such a meter. Ordinarily, if not invariably, the meter is supplied by the licensee and it is he who is responsible to maintain it and keep it correct (Sub-section 3). But what if the meter goes wrong or is burnt or otherwise ceases to function? Sub-section (6) of this section takes care of such a contingency. It provides that, in that case, the matter shall be decided upon the application of either party by an Electrical Inspector, and where the meter has, in the opinion of such Inspector ceased to be correct, such Inspector shall estimate the amount of the energy supplied to the consumer or the electrical energy contained therein during such time, not exceeding six months, as the meter shall not, in the opinion of such Inspector, have been correct ...

Let us now see how the Courts and the Consumer Courts have interpreted and applied this provision. In *H.D. Shourie* v. *Municipal Corporation of Delhi*,[1] the Delhi High Court has held that :

> "...... the maximum period for which a bill can be raised in respect of a defective meter is six months and no more. Therefore, even if a meter has been defective for, say a period of five years, the revised charge can be for a period not exceeding six months. The reason for this is obvious. It

1. AIR 1987 Del 219.

is the duty and obligation of the licensee to maintain and check the meter. If there is a default committed in this behalf by the licensee and the defective meter is not replaced, then it is obvious that the consumer should not be unduly penalised at a later point of time and a large bill raised. The provision for a bill not to exceed six months would possibly ensure better checking and maintenance by the licensee."

The same view was reiterated in another case by the same High Court ; *Major Zorawer Singh* v. *Municipal Corporation of Delhi.*[1]

Following these two decisions, the Delhi State Commission also held in *Northern India Tiles Corporation* v. *D.E.S.U.*[2] that the opposite party cannot charge the amount of arrears, if any, for a period of more than six months.

There are more cases on the point decided by other State Commissions. The Haryana State Commission, for instance, held in *S.D.O. H.S.E.B, Jind* v. *Raj Kumar*[3] where a bill for the meter which was defective for 23 months was raised and was superadded with a surcharge penalty, that :

"The argument of the opposite party has only to be noticed and rejected because it is against the very teeth of the relevant statutory provisions and the settled interpretation thereof. The Commission referred to one of its earlier decisions where this question had come up for pointed consideration; *S.D.O.(O), H.S.E.B. Karnal* v. *Isher Dass Jain of Karnal*[4] and stated that it was concluded therein that "the Haryana State Electricity Board cannot recover the arrears of electricity charges for the defective meter from the consumer beyond this period of six months".

The Commission took a serious view of the lapse in this case and remarked after referring again to its earlier decision–

"Despite all this it would appear that the Appellate Board somewhat non-challantly, if not contumaciously, persists in

1. 1991 RLR 312.
2. I (1994) CPJ 255.
3. 1(1994) CPJ 255.
4. Appeal No. 246 of 1993 decided on 19-8-1993.

continuing to levy or impose arrears of electricity charges in this context on the helpless consumers far beyond the spelt out period of six months. This is typified by the present case and it appears to us that the respondent consumer herein is entitled to penal costs of Rs.1000/-."

In the case that follows[1] an arrears bill for a period of 7 years was issued to the complainant. Despite his representation that a bill for such heavy arrears could not be issued, his electricity was disconnected. He was paying his electricity bills initially on the basis of a slab fixed at Rs.10/- per month, which was raised to Rs.15/- and thereafter to Rs.18/- per month. He was paying his bills regularly for which he produced receipts issued by the opposite party. He, however, received a bill on 4-5-1991 for a sum of Rs.4,527.50p said to be an adjustment for the period March, 1982 to May, 1989. Inspite of his representations, as mentioned above, his electricity was disconnected.

On a complaint, the District Forum found that there were laches on the part of the opposite parties in not issuing the adjustment bill regularly once in a year during the slab system as stipulated and that the complainant has been paying the bills as and when they were issued. It was also noticed that arrears prior to 4-5-1989 were barred by limitation being over three years old. The last date for payment of the bill was 18-5-1991 whereas the electricity was disconnected on 25-4-1991. The Forum accordingly held that there was deficiency in service and the complainant was entitled to re-connection.

Upholding the decision of the District Forum, the Andhra Pradesh State Commission also referred to a decision of the National Commission in *Bombay Electric Supply and Transport Undertaking,* III (1993) CPJ 381, in which also it was held that recovery of arrears for more than 3 years was barred by limitation. The State Commission further held that even according to the opposite parties the adjustment bill had to be issued once in the year but in the present case it has been issued after 7 years. Following the ratio in *Y.N. Gupta's* case decided by the National Commission [1(1993) CPJ 27 NC], it was held to be deficiency in service. The State Commission also pointed out that a notice of not less than seven days, as held by the National Commission in *Haryana State Electricity Board* v. *Naresh*

---

1. *Assistant Accounts Officer* v. *N. Timarisheshar Rao*, 1(1998) CPJ 463.

Kumar, 1(1996) CPJ 306 should have been given before disconnection. Failure to give such a notice renders the disconnection illegal and further constitutes a deficiency in service. The appeal filed by the appellants was accordingly dismissed.

In *Balkrishna Patider* v. *Junior Engineer M.P. Electricity Board*, the complainant was charged the higher revised rate for misuse *i.e.* the appropriate commercial rate. The District Forum dismissed the complaint but, on appeal, the M.P.State Commission modified the order and held that a bare reading of clause (d) of condition No. 31 would make it clear that the bill so raised ought to have been for a period of six months from the date of detection of misuse. The excess amount charged for the additional period of six months, the Commission decided, was illegal.

Lest the consumer feels lulled to sleep if the Electricity authority has neglected to recover its dues for period of three years or more and remains under the impression that there is no liability to pay, it is clarified that under section 24 of the Indian Electricity Act, 1910, the electricity supplier can stop supplying the electricity till these dues are paid. We illustrate this point from a case decided by the Tamil Nadu State Commission. Shri Ramaswamy Naidu had an electric connection. There were arrears due from him. The service connection was disconnected. His legal representative applied for re-connection which the Electricity Board turned down as there were arrears due from the deceased. They were, however, allowed to clear the arrears by instalments. After paying the first instalment, they again defaulted. The service connection was once again disconnected.

On complaint the District Forum held that the payment of arrears was already time-barred, the amount had become a bad debt and the refusal of the Electricity Board to allow re-connection was deficiency in service.

Allowing the appeal of the Board, the State Commission held that there was no dispute that there were arrears due. There is also no dispute that no suit has been filed for recovery within the period of limitation. But that does not mean that the liability of the complainant stands extinguished.[1] If there are unpaid arrears of electricity, the complainant is not entitled to re-connection.

1. *The Divisional Engineer* v. *R.Somairaj*, II (1996) CPJ 96.

9 Fluctuation of Voltage

People file actions against the electricity supply agencies for compensation due to sudden high voltage surge causing damage to their electrical equipments. In all such cases the consumer has to prove before the Redressal Agencies that:

(a) he suffered loss or injury by the action of the other party,

(b) such loss or damage was due to the negligence of the opposite party, and

(c) there was deficiency in service rendered to him by the opposite party.

The case for compensation will not even take off the ground unless all these ingredients are proved. Let us now see where the Redressal Agencies have granted relief and where they have dismissed the complaints and the reasons therefor.

In *the Secretary, Karnataka Electricity Board* v. *The Secretary, Bellery Citizens Forum*,[1] the complaint was on behalf of nine consumers of Bellery. It was alleged therein that on 9-1-1990 at about 5.50 P.M. due to sudden high voltage surge, the electric equipments and fittings of the consumers got damaged. They claimed damages amounting to Rs.3,880/- in respect of the consumers together.

The complaint was resisted by the respondent Board on the ground, *inter alia*, that there was no surge as alleged by the complainants and that the allegation that their equipment and fittings were damaged is false. The Board denied that they were entitled to any compensation.

1. (1991) CPJ 97.

On evidence the District Forum held that there was deficiency in service in as much as there was surge in voltage and awarded compensation of Rs.1,515/- to each of the nine complainants.

The State Commission on appeal by the Board held that mere fluctuation in the voltage will not by itself give rise to cause of action to the complainant as according to Regulation 22 of the Board, it shall not be liable for any claim for loss or damage arising out of voltage variation. So the complainant has to prove that it was due to the negligence of the officials of the Board that they suffered loss resulting in damage to their electrical equipments. The Commission, however, decided to remand the case to the District Forum to give a fair opportunity, as suggested by the Counsel for the Board, to both the sides to prove their case as it would not prejudice the interests of either.

In another case, the Delhi State Commission in *New Delhi Municipal Corporation (Committee)* v. *S.P. Singha*[1] held that the alleged high voltage was not caused due to the negligence of any of the respondents. In this case the V.C.R. of the complainant was damaged due allegedly to the high voltage supply of electricity caused by the negligence of N.D.M.C. or C.P.W.D. The District Forum allowed the claim of Rs.900/- of the complainant against the N.D.M.C. On facts the State Commission held in appeal that there was no negligence either on the part of the N.D.M.C. or on the part of C.P.W.D. which was impleaded as a party by the State Commission. The order of the District Forum was accordingly set aside.

We now take up a case filed by an industrial concern against a State Electricity Board[2] reported in 1(1997) CPJ 17 (NC) wherein it was alleged by the complainants that due to irregular supply and mercurial fluctuation in the voltage of electricity, given to them by the opposite party for the past several years, their plant had to be switched off during the low voltage period resulting in production loss.

The case of the respondent Board in a nutshell was that although they were making every effort to maintain the required voltage level, low voltage is being experienced in some areas due

---

1. (1991) CPJ 560.
2. *Travancore Oxygen Ltd.* v. *Kerala State Electricity Board.*

to reasons beyond its control and that this phenomenon is not confined to the petitioner alone, but is experienced in different parts of the State. The Board had pleaded that they have not shown willful negligence for not keeping satisfactory voltage in the case of the petitioner.

After considering various clauses of the agreement and various other relevant factors, the Commission concluded :–

> "The main dispute between the parties revolves round the permissible range of fluctuations, clause 1(b) of the agreement specifies the permissible range of fluctuations only in terms of percentage and not in absolute terms. It is the agreement which is binding on both the parties and hence the entire dispute about the absolute values of the permissible range of fluctuation, *i.e.* whether it should be around 433 volts or 415 volts does not flow from the agreement. Further clause 2(a) has referred to the force *majeura* condition under which the opposite party cannot be held responsible for any defective supply of electricity. There is nothing in the complaint which goes to show that there was any willful action on the part of the opposite party – Board resulting in the alleged voltage fluctuation to the petitioner. It is also not established by the petitioner that the alleged losses in production are solely due to power constraints. In the facts and circumstances of the case, the Commission did not find any deficiency in the service of the opposite party – Board."

Thus, like the previous two cases, the two points on which the finding rests, in this case also are that there was no negligence on the part of the Board and there was no deficiency in its service to the complainant – petitioner. We have seen the foregoing cases in which the claims of the complainant for compensation for damage to their equipments on ground of surge in voltage were turned down by the Redressal Agencies concerned as they did not find any negligence or deficiency in service on their part. We now turn to a few cases where the complainants succeeded in their claims.

In *A.P.S.E. Board* v. *C. H. Appa Rao*,[1] the Andhra Pradesh State Commission upheld the order of the District Forum

1. III (1998) CPJ 171.

Vishakhapatnam directing the aforesaid Board to pay an amount of Rs.2,495/- as compensation for causing damage to his colour T.V. on account of sudden shooting up of the voltage of electricity. The District Forum had held that the Board did not produce any reliable evidence and convincing material to establish that there was no high voltage fluctuations during the period in question nor in support of the motive attributed to the complainant. Declining to interfere with the order of the District Forum, the State Commission held that when the Electricity Board undertakes to supply electrical energy at a particular voltage, the fluctuations in voltage should be restricted to certain acceptable parameters, and unless the authorities of the Board come up with good reasons for the wide fluctuations as a fact found in the voltage of the electrical energy supplied, the Board would be held to be deficient in service. The Commission looked at the question from another angle as well : if electrical energy is treated as goods then the voltage at which it has to be supplied by the Board to the domestic consumers has to be maintained at the agreed level failing which the goods supplied will not be of specified quality. On that basis also, the Commission observed, the Board will be liable.

The next case in which compensation for damage to electrical equipment was awarded was decided by the Tamil Nadu State Commission.[1] The 3 complainants in that case alleged that on account of surge voltage their T.V. sets, fans and jet motors were damaged as a result of which they suffered loss. The District Forum awarded compensation to each of them. The opposite party filed an appeal.

The case of the opposite party, both before the Forum and the State Commission, was that due to various safety devices provided by them there was no chance of higher voltage than the one prescribed. They denied the allegation of the complainant.

Upholding the decision of the District Forum, the State Commission held that there is no tangible material in the shape of any evidence, oral or documentary, to point out that the lines in question were three phase lines or simple phase lines – the latter according to the respondent preclude the possibility of higher

1. *Assistant Engineer (Urban) Tamil Nadu Electricity Board* v. *Apparwoo Thakur*, 1(1999) CPJ 70.

voltage passing through them. The burden of proof of such a special knowledge cast on the respondents under section 106 of the Evidence Act had not been discharged. The appeal was dismissed.

In a case in which due to a sudden surge in power supply, a number of T.Vs were damaged, the plea taken by the Electricity Board was that since the high voltage was on account of a tree falling on 3 phase-4 phase wire system, it was purely a case of accident for which it cannot shoulder any responsibility. The District Forum held that there was deficiency of service on the part of the opposite party and awarded compensation.

On appeal, the Karnataka State Commission upheld the decision of the District Forum and observed that under Rule 29(1) of the Indian Electricity Rules, a duty is cast on the supplier of electricity to protect the consumer presumably from any source which may hamper, fluctuate or cut off power supply. Tree branches crowding the power line is a constant source of hazard which requires constant trimming to avoid any mishap. The rule envisages that all such damages to the power lines are to be anticipated and removed timely so as to ensure safety of not only human beings and animals but also safety of property. Rule 30(1), in particular, enjoins a duty on the supplier to identify any source of danger to the installations in the premises of the consumer and take necessary steps to prevent mishap to the wires and supply-lines. The Commission held that there was definite shortcoming and inadequacy in the manner of performance of the opposite party and accordingly dismissed the appeal.[1]

In the last case being taken up here,[2] the complainant claimed what appears to be a rather large amount by way of damages to his electric equipment on account of high voltage flowing through the electric line installed in his house in Chandigarh.

The respondents denied the averments made in the complaint and took the plea that the wiring in the houses in Chandigarh,

---

1. *Karnataka State Electricity Board* v. *H.S. Sita Ram*, 1 (2000) CPJ 508.
2. *SDO Electricity (Operational) Anil Kumar* v. *R. C. Gupta*, 1 (2001) CPJ 564.

was insulated and bearable to weather conditions. The complainant, according to them, was putting up a concocted and false story with an exaggerated version.

A Local Commissioner was appointed by the District Forum, who *inter alia*, reported that :

> "The exposed and uninsulated main power line wires connecting power connection to the house ....had every likelihood of the two wires touching each other causing heavy sparking and possibly leading a short circuit."

The District Forum awarded compensation to the complainant and, in appeal, the State Commission held, referring to the report of the Local Commissioner, that negligence was writ large on the part of the Sub-Divisional Engineer and another.

10 Electrocution

We have said in the very beginning that electricity is a good servant but a bad master. More than anything else, electrocution illustrates this point better and also imparts some poignancy to the occurrence. However, when a claim for compensation is filed, the Courts, including the Consumer Courts, have to apply the relevant provisions of law before deciding it. For example, the Consumer Disputes Redressal Agencies have to consider and decide whether the complainant is a consumer or is otherwise entitled to the compensation. If the answer to these questions is in the negative, the Consumer Fora have no jurisdiction to go into the matter. We take up some cases decided by the Redressal Agencies on this subject because they are considered to be more liberal and less technical in their approach. These cases would also show where it will be fruitful to file a claim and where it will be a wasteful effort.

In *Malati Devi* v. *Orissa Electricity Board*,[1] the case arose out of the death of the complainant's husband who was electrocuted in a public place. The complaint was dismissed for the following reasons :–

(a) Where an electric connection is taken in a public place, no one hires that service. The complainant is thus not a consumer.

(b) A complaint case can be filed by a consumer or a registered voluntary organization or the State Government or the Central Government. The complainant does not come within any such category. Accordingly, the complaint is unauthorized and is not maintainable. The Commission observed that the complainant, if so advised, may approach the appropriate Fora for compensation.

1. III (1992) CPJ 123.

Reversing the decision of the District Forum in *Haryana State Electricity Board* v. *Ganga Devi*,[1] the National Commission held that order passed by the Forum was not clearly sustainable in law. In this case a cow belonging to the complainant had been electrocuted by coming into contact with an electric post. The plea of the petitioner claimant was that the State Electricity Board which was responsible for supply of electricity in the area should make good her loss. The National Commission referred to another similar case decided by the Haryana State Commission (R.P.No. 632/93 on 17-8-1994) and observed that in the aforesaid case it was held that the grievance put forward by the complainant did not constitute a consumer dispute as defined in the Act and it was not a case of deficiency in service on the part of the Board in relation to the performance of any service to a consumer of electricity. The said dictum holds good in this case also. The District Forum was in error in allowing compensation to the complainant.

The Punjab State Commission in a similar case where the buffalo owned by the complainant died on account of electrocution and the electricity was supplied by the appellant Electricity Board also held that the grievance put forward by the complainant – petitioner does not constitute a consumer dispute as defined in the Consumer Protection Act. Even if, the State Commission observed, the allegation of the complainant are accepted in toto, a finding cannot be recorded that the Board is deficient in supplying electricity to the complainant. The complainant cannot, therefore, seek redress before the Consumer Forum in respect of any matter arising out of such an accident.

In another case of death by electrocution, the facts were that the electrical wire broke down on account of a severe storm the previous evening and fell into a pond. The water got electrified. On the next morning a person went to the pond for fishing, but died instantly on account of electrocution. On hearing the shouts, the husband of the complainant jumped into the pond where he also died of electrocution. Hence the claim. The West Bengal State Commission held that the complainant was not entitled to any compensation as the deceased was not a consumer and the

1. III (1996) CPJ182(NC).

Consumer Protection Act was not applicable to the facts of the case; *West Bengal State Electricity Board* v. *Champa Bai.*[1]

We now come to a case – perhaps the only one reported so far – in which compensation was awarded to the complainant by the Redressal Agencies and in which it was held that he was a consumer. The facts of this case briefly are that the complainant lived in Village Rundh, District Dholpur, Rajasthan. Apart from carrying on cultivation, he had a cattle farm. His complaint was that the electric wire passing over his field and the fields of some neigbbours had become so loose that they were hardly 7 to 8 feet high from the ground. Whenever there would be storm they could be broken and fall to the ground. Written complaints were made requesting the Rajasthan State Electricity Board to pull up the wires, followed by personal representations but the grievance was not redressed. A letter was written to the Collector, Dholpur also on the subject who marked it to the State Electricity Board and another letter was sent by him to the Executive Engineer concerned.

On 29-6-1994 when the buffalo of the complainant was grazing in the field, the wire broke down resulting in the electrocution of the buffalo. After having the post-mortem of the buffalo done, he lodged a claim before the District Forum, Dholpur.

The complainant produced in evidence the bills of electricity paid by him to prove that he was a consumer, a copy of the complaint which he had made to the Collector three months before the incident and which, in turn, was marked by him to the Rajasthan State Electricity Board, record of the respondents themselves containing entry about the broken wire and the electrocution of the buffalo and all other relevant documents which proved his case to the hilt.

The respondents filed a very casual reply stating that the complainant was not a consumer, no service was rendered to him and the Board was not liable to pay any damages.

The District Forum after considering the facts and discussing the law on the subject granted compensation and costs to the complainant.

1. 1(2001) CPJ 51.

Aggrieved by the above decision, the Board filed an appeal. In appeal, the Rajasthan State Commission observed that "it is all the more unfortunate that an officer of the Rajasthan State Electricity Board of the rank of Assistant Engineer who has filed an affidavit before the District Forum which is far from the truth and is rather full of false facts, there is overwhelming evidence in the case to indicate that the complainant was the consumer as is borne out from the bills in his name. It appears that no body has cared to go through the record of the case while contesting the case at the District Forum." Dealing with the allegations of corruption amongst the staff of the Board, the Commission passed severe strictures on the officials and observed that "we cannot enhance the compensation in the case as there is no appeal before us but it is a fit case where the amount awarded should be realized by the Board from the defaulting persons, more particularly, the Executive and the Assistant Engineer, who ignored the Collector's letter and filed deliberately false replies before the District Forum."[1]

The responsibilities to supply electric energy in a particular locality is statutorily conferred on the Electricity Board. If the energy so transmitted causes injury or death of a human being, who gets unknowingly trapped into it, the primary liability to compensate the sufferer is that of the supplier of the electric energy. So long as the voltage of electricity transmitted through wires is potentially of dangerous dimension, the managers of its supply have the added duty to take all safety measures to prevent escape of such energy.[2]

1. *Rajasthan State Electricity Board* v. *Charan Singh*, 1(1999) CPJ 162.

2. *M.P.Electricity Board* v. *Shail Kumar*, AIR 2002 SC 551.

11 Deficiency in Service and Negligence

By and large people now prefer to approach the Redressal Agencies set up under the Consumer Protection Act for settlement of their disputes as, unlike the Courts, they do not look at their grievances mainly from technical view point. Besides, and this is unique – unlike the Courts – they are competent to grant relief when they find "deficiency in service", provided to the aggrieved consumer. Roughly speaking, "deficiency in service" means a sub-standard or an incomplete service. The definition of this expression needs to be reproduced even at the cost of repetition. "Deficiency", as defined in clause (g) of sub-section (1) of section 2 of the Consumer Protection Act, 1986, means:–

> "any fault, imperfection, short coming or inadequacy in the quality, nature and manner of performance which is required to be maintained by or under any law for the time being in force or has been undertaken to be performed by a person in pursuance of a contract or otherwise in relation to any service."

The key words in the above definition have been explained by the National Commission in *R.R.Goyal* v. *Chairman*, *Tamil Nadu Electricity Board*[1] as follows:–

> "Fault is a defect, imperfection, blemish or a thing wrongly done. A fault includes negligence in the ordinary exception of the term. Imperfection is incompleteness, faultiness, blemish or where the service is inchoate. Shortcoming is failure to come to a standard of performance of service or performing it defectively not,

1. 1 (1996) CPJ 143 (NC).

ripening into the set standard thus treating the service as deficient. Inadequate is not adequate or insufficient. It is lack of or absence of something essential to completeness of the service."

To succeed in a complaint against services, including supply of electricity, the complainant must establish that there was deficiency in the service provided to him. We have already seen how this expression has been interpreted by the Consumer Disputes Redressal Agencies where electric supply was disconnected by the suppliers without notice to the consumer. We may now see with the help of cases how these agencies have interpreted this term in some other areas which could be of interest to the consumers.

Complainant was served with a notice alleging loosened seal of meter – Opposite Party threatened to disconnect supply – Electricity charges levied for past without any basis – Hence complaint – Whether not following legal procedure and adopting coercive methods is deficiency in service : (yes);

J. P. Khangare v. *Executive Engineer*, *Maharashtra State Electricity Board*, II (1992) CPJ 963.

Complainant's bulbs, tube lights, stabliser and other appliances burnt due to high voltage – Complaint filed for cost of goods – District Forum held supply of excess voltage amounts to deficiency in service. Awarded costs of goods – Upheld by the State Commission in appeal;

Gujarat Electricity Board v. *Sharda Madhusudan Desai*, 1(1993) CPJ 158.

Complainant applied for an electric connection – Submitted test report on demand – Electric connection not provided within a period of one year of submission of test report – District Forum issued direction to release the connection – State Commission on appeal by both the parties confirmed the order and also awarded Rs. 10,000 as damages to the complainant – Revision – Whether directions can be issued : (yes);

Haryana State Electricity Board v. *Pirthi Singh*, National Commission, III (1993) CPJ 270.

Failure to prepare and serve bills in accordance with the billing cycle – Raising a heavy arrears bill – Raising bills without actual meter reading – Claiming arrears without details – claiming arrears over a lakh – Disconnection of electricity even before the last date of payment – Whether constitutes deficiency in service: (yes);

Delhi Electricity Supply v. *Y.N. Gupta*, National Commission, III (1993) CPJ 370.

Opposite party demanded additional amount for the slow running of meter – dispute not settled first by Electrical Inspector – Whether demand of additional amount on the ground of defective meter without prior reference to Electrical Inspector is justifiable : (No) – Whether failure to refer to Electrical Inspector before revising additional amount on the ground of defective meter, amounts to deficiency in service : (yes);

Babulal v. *M.S. Yadav*, Madhya Pradesh State Commission, II (1994) CPJ 97.

Electricity disconnected on the ground of theft and pilferage. Without any proof – F.I.R. lodged – No proof – No criminal proceedings – Disconnected without notice – Complaint allowed by the District Forum – Whether there is any deficiency in service : (yes);

C.E.S.C Ltd v. *Nand Kishore Joshi*, West Bengal State Commission, II (1994) CPJ 227.

Possession of house given by the authority concerned on 7-6-1990 – Electricity connection not provided for more than two years – Complaint – Whether amounts to deficiency in service : (yes);

Vice Chairman, HUDA v. *Kurthi Vasan*, Andhra Pradesh State Commission, II (1996) CPJ 190.

Complainant applied for electricity connection – Opposite party gave estimate of Rs.10,705 – Complainant paid the amount – Connection not released – Complaint – Whether deficiency in service : (yes);

Panchandbhai Shambubhai v. *Gujarat Electricity Board*, Gujarat State Commission, 1 (1997) CPJ 543.

Defective meter existing at the premises of the complainant not replaced for a sufficiently long time – Whether amounts to deficiency in service : (yes);

Gita Rani Chakravarti v. *Electric Supdt Bankara, West Bengal State Electricity Board*, West Bengal State Commission, 1 (1997) CPJ 450.

Meter removed for non payment of electricity charges by the previous tenant – Madhya Pradesh Electricity Board demanded payment of the whole amount of arrears from the complainant – Payment of arrears a condition precedent for supply of electric energy – M.P.E.B. has a monopoly right in distribution of electricity supply – Complainant agreed and made payment under duress – Held: Complainant entitled to be reimbursed – Deficiency and Unfair Trade Practice proved;

S.K. Dhingra v. *Madhya Pradesh Electricity Board*, Madhya Pradesh State Commission, 1 (1998) CPJ 214.

Drive to remove encroachment – Shop dismantled – Electricity meter removed – Electric connection cut off – Notice regarding one month condition precedent for cutting of electric connection – Electricity Board guilty of unilateral breach of contract – Electric connection cut off without mandatory notice – Deficiency in service;

Teekaram v. *Upyantri, M.P. Electricity Board*, M.P. State Commission, 1 (1998) CPJ 264.

Electricity meter of the complainant not working – Average bill issued – Suddenly a huge bill sent as recovery of arrears – Complaint – Opposite party contended connection used for commercial purpose – No evidence to support this contention – Whether there was deficiency in service on the part of the opposite party : (yes);

M. P. Electricity Board v. *Amitabh Kumar Jain*, M.P. State Commission, II (1998) CPJ 224.

Electricity dues paid on 10-3-1992 – Electricity disconnected on 16-3-1992 – Complaint – Whether there is deficiency in service : (yes);

M. P. Electricity Board v. *Amar Singh*, M.P. State Commission, II (1998) CPJ 52.

Complainant applied for temporary connection – Deposit made – Deposit refunded after 9 months – Complaint – Whether there is deficiency in service : (yes);

M. P. Electricity Board v. *Sudarshan*, M. P. State Commission, II (1998) CPJ 4.

Improper disconnection of electricity in contravention of the provisions of section 22 of the Indian Electricity Act, 1910 – Held deficiency in service – Complainant awarded compensation;

Additional Assistant Engineer A.P. Electricity Board v. *Saldalen Chakrapani*, A.P. State Commission, II (1998) CPJ 574.

Complainant a consumer of electricity – Reported on 9-5-1995 that glass of the window of meter was broken – On 16-8-1995, the officials of the opposite party reported theft – Raised bill of Rs.10,622 – Complaint – Whether there is deficiency in service : (yes);

Sub-Divisional Engineer Punjab State Electricity Board v. *Bhushan Kumar Gupta*, Punjab State Commission, II (1998) CPJ 95.

Electricity supply not given – Test report not submitted – Appellant body having huge staff should inform the consumer in writing what is expected of them – They cannot be permitted to get away by stating that consumer was told verbally – Lack of accountability and transparency constitute deficiency in service;

M. P. Electricity Board v. *Sanjay Kumar Pathak*, M. P. State Commission, III (1998) CPJ 189.

Petitioner approached W.B.E.B. for starting of industry – Assured of electricity supply, applied for financial loan – Loan sanctioned – Construction made – Machinery purchased – Electricity not supplied – Petitioner unable to start industry – Loan re-paid – Compensation claimed – Deficiency in service established – Compensation reduced to Rs.40,000 as against Rs. I lakh awarded by the Forum;

W. B. State Electricity Board v. *Nehrul Ali*, West Bengal State Commission, 1 (1999) CPJ 302.

Electric wire passing over the complainant's field – Wire hardly 7 to 8 feet height from grounds – Wire broke down – Buffalo grazing in the field electrocuted – Electric wire so dangerous even tractors could not pass – Not attended for three months even after writing to the Collector – Extreme example of callousness – Gross negligence on part of supervisory officers – Compensation granted;

Rajasthan Electricity Board v. *Charan Singh*, Rajasthan State Commission, 1 (1999) CPJ 162.

Electricity Billing – Two meters installed in the premises of the complainant – Meters' reading not taken for six months – Average bill sent – Complaint – Held : amounts to deficiency in service;

M. P. Electricity Board v. *Shivkant Chaubey*, M. P. State Commission, II (1998) CPJ 85.

Complainant having old tubewell connection – Some portion of his land acquired by the government for digging a canal – Had divided into two parts – No water course could be provided for the complainant's land due to high dunes and depth of the canal – Land acquisition authorities recommended separate tubewell connection – Haryana State Electricity Board failed to release necessary connection – Complainant entitled to compensation for loss of crop and mental agony;

Haryana State Electricity Board v. *Ravindra Vir Sharma*, Haryana State Commission, II (1999) CPJ 39.

Electricity Board estopped from pleading that at one premises two electric connections could not be issued – Raising demand subsequently clubbing the load of two connections illegal – Deficiency in service on the part of the Board proved;

Punjab State Electricity Board v. *Satish Kumar*, Punjab State Commission, II (1999) CPJ 359.

Excess amount charged – Refund – Bill amount increased by adding arrears and surcharge – Meter recording less consumption – Duty of Electricity Board to maintain correct electricity meter – Bill paid under threat of disconnection –Deficiency in service – Electricity Board liable to refund the excess amount charged;

Punjab State Electricity Board v. *G. M. P. Finishing Mills*, Punjab State Commission, III (1999) CPJ 76.

Complainant applied for grant of electric connection to start business of cold storage – Grant of connection delayed – Non availability of transformers not acceptable – No evidence produced on this point – Connection given after ten months of deposit – Deficiency in service on the part of Electricity Board established – Complainant awarded compensation;

New Punjab Cold Storage v. *Punjab State Electricity Board*, Punjab State Commission, III (1999) CPJ 278.

Time given for payment of electricity charges till 20-2-1998 – Electricity could not be disconnected for non-payment till then – Disconnected on 16-1-1998 – Deficiency in service – Complainant awarded compensation;

Kerala State Electricity Board v. *T. N. Rooplal*, Kerala State Commission, III (1999) CPJ 430.

High Voltage electricity supplied – Electrical equipments damaged – Contention : no possibility of higher voltage passing through single phase line, not acceptable – No evidence produced that lines in question were single phase line – Opposite party failed to regulate the supply – Deficiency in service proved – Complainant entitled to compensation;

Tamil Nadu Electricity Board v. *Appuvoo Thevar*, Tamil Nadu State Commission, I (2001) CPJ 70.

No electricity in complainant house from 2-9-1988 to 25-9-1988 – Contention that the supply was adversely affected due to heavy rains but fault was removed on the same day not acceptable – No record provided to indicate date of rectification of fault and sufficient evidence produced by the complainant in support of his contention – Deficiency in service proved – Opposite party liable to pay compensation;

Delhi Vidyut Board v. *Ram Kishore Saini*, Delhi State Commission, I (2000) CPJ 507.

Delay in installing meter – Inordinate delay of 13 months in installing meter – Contention : lease of electricity theft pending regarding complainant's flat not acceptable – Possession of the flat in question was with DDA at the relevant time of theft proved

– Undue delay in installing electric meter amounts to deficiency in service – Opposite party liable to pay compensation;

Delhi Vidyut Board v. *R. K. Bhat*, Delhi State Commission, I (2000) CPJ 545.

Connection not released – Contention : Civil suit pending and complaint not maintainable, not acceptable – Civil suit already dismissed as withdrawn – Contention : landlord opposed grant of fresh connection also not acceptable – No objection already given by the landlord for grant of fresh connection in complainant's name – Deficiency in service on the part of the opposite party proved – Complainant entitled to compensation;

Delhi Vidyut Board v. *Kamala Devi*, Delhi State Commission, I (2000) CPJ 490.

Deposited amount with the opposite party which was to be adjusted against consumption of bills for tubewell – Instead adjustment allowed through bill of domestic connection – Complainant had no domestic supply connection – Non-refunding of amount to the complainant highly arbitrary and amounts to deficiency in service – Opposite party liable to refund the amount with interest and also to pay compensation;

Sohan Singh Bullar v. *Punjab State Electricity Board*, Punjab State Commission, I (2000) CPJ 584.

Electric meters faulty – Complaints made to the opposite party – Meters not replaced – Dispute not referred to Electrical Inspector – Bill raised – There is deficiency in service – Action of opposite party not substainable in law;

Punjab State Electricity Board v. *Public Health* (PJS) Sub-Division, Punjab State Commission, I (2000) CPJ 9.

Connection disconnected for non-payment of dues during the period when electricity was used – Pole supplying electricity was damaged – Complainant not liable to pay even minimum guarantee charges for the period when no electricity was used – Disconnection without any ground amounts to deficiency in service – Opposite party had no right to charge any amount when no electricity restored due to damaged line and is liable to restore the connection without charging any amount;

UPSEB v. *Shankar Maurya*, U. P. State Commission, II (2000) CPJ 498.

Complainants purchased shops and applied for electric connection – No objection given by Delhi Development Authority to Delhi Vidyut Board – Required amount deposited – Electricity connection not sanctioned – Complaint – Opposite party held guilty of deficiency in service – Compensation of Rs.20,000 granted;

Kashyap Constructions (Pvt.) Ltd v. *Delhi Vidyut Board*, Delhi State Commission, III (2000) CPJ 440.

Amount of Rs.24,835 deposited for installation of street light – Street light not installed – Deficiency in service on the part of Electricity Board proved – Complainant entitled to refund along with interest;

U.P. State Electricity Board v. *President Nagar Panchyat*, U.P. State Commission, III (2000) CPJ 371.

Complainant applied for electric connection – Sanctioned by opposite party – Connection not provided – Complaint – District Forum directed opposite party to install a meter and awarded Rs.2,500 – Compensation – Appeal – Complainant's contention remained unrebutted – Appeal dismissed;

Delhi Vidyut Board v. *Reeta Sharma*, Delhi State Commission, III (2000) CPJ 404.

Energizing of connection delayed – Connection energized after a delay of 3 months – Complainant had to run from pillar to post to have the connection energized – Entitled to compensation – Appeal – Compensation enhanced;

J.K. Dhingra v. *Delhi Vidyut Board*, Delhi State Commission, II (2001) CPJ 29.

Complainant received inflated bills of Rs.52,239 and Rs.1,11,006 – Amount reduced to Rs. 30,366 by Bijii Adalat – Earlier bills also highly inflated established – Complainant remained without electricity for 3 years – Deficiency in service proved – Opposite party liable to pay compensation, refund security, realize amount afresh and withdraw all bills issued after disconnection – Order of District Forum upheld in appeal;

Delhi Vidyut Board v. *Krishan Lal*, Delhi State Commission, I (2001) CPJ 587.

Complainant alleged excessive electricity bills – District Forum allowed complaint – Electricity Board was directed to correct bills on basis of average consumption for one year without any surcharge or interest – State Commission upheld the order of District Forum – Revision – Whether there was ground for interference : (No);

Haryana State Electricity Board v. *Amrit Singh*, *National Commission*, I (2002) CPJ 16.

What is not "Deficiency in Service"

To avoid fruitless litigation the subscriber should know what has not been considered as deficiency in service.

Delay in providing electrical energy for the running unit of the complainant – Loss of production – Claim for damages – Complainant also responsible for delay in making payment of cost of service line charges and suppression of this fact in the complaint – Both parties equally at fault – Principle of "*imparidalicto policrest canditio defenders*" applies – No deficiency in service on the part of the opposite party;

Malaya Marnit Industries v. *Asstt. Engineer (Operation), Andhra Pradesh State Electricity Board*, Andhra Pradesh State Commission, I (2002) CPJ 128.

Electricity disconnected by landlords – Complaint filed against the Delhi Vidyut Board – No deficiency on the part of the Board;

Naresh Jaswal v. *Delhi Vidyut Board*, Delhi State Commission, III (2000) CPJ 280.

Additional connection not given – Complainant already using electricity from electric connection provided in the house – Entrance of two portions of house still common – No deficiency on the part of the opposite party in not granting additional electric connection – Instructions by the Electricity Board cannot be challenged before Fora;

Jaswinder Pal v. *Punjab State Electricity Board*, Punjab State Commission, II (2000) CPJ 46.

Excess Billing – Power shut downs, trippings and failure of supply not considered – Bills issued on the basis of average consumption – Forum ordered refund of excess amount charged – Appeal – Assessment made as per rules – Average consumption during the period of 4 months considered irrespective of lesser or excessive consumption in a particular month – No deficiency in service on the part of the opposite party – Order of Forum set aside;

T.N.E.B. Madras v. *Balamavarma Textiles Mills*, Tamil Nadu State Commission, I (2000) CPJ 284.

Inflated bills – Account of bills produced by the opposite party – Bills of minimum guarantee amount were being sent – Complainant under legal obligation to pay these bills – No payment made for three and a half years – Complainant liable to pay – No deficiency in service on the part of the opposite party;

Sarala Prakash v. *Delhi Vidyut Board*, Delhi State Commission, I (2000) CPJ 511.

Electricity Bill for arrears – Forum held dispute not referred to Electrical Inspector – Arrears could not be charged for period exceeding six months – Bill set aside – Appeal – Factum of consumption never denied – Consumer liable to pay minimum charges based on installed capacity – Order of Forum set aside;

SDO Electricity O.P. v. *Gopal Mills Store*, Chandigarh State Commission, I (1999) CPJ 169.

Complainant applied for 3 industrial electric connection – Sent only one application for 3 connections – Delay in making demand of earnest money by Electricity Board – Complaint – Whether applicant of electricity connection is consumer by deposit of earnest money : (No) – Whether there was any deficiency in service : (No);

B.J.P. Stirals v. *Tamil Nadu Electricity Board*, Tamil Nadu State Commission, I (1998) CPJ 504;

Electricity Supply to tube well not maintained – Crops damaged – District Forum granted compensation – Appeal – Complainant being not the account holder of electricity connection was not a consumer – Complaint not maintainable – No deficiency on the part of Electricity Board;

SDO Haryana State Electricity Board v. *Surinder*, Haryana State Commission, III (1998) CPJ 387.

Fluctuations in voltage of electricity – Complaint – No wilful or negligent action – Whether there is deficiency in service : (No);

Travancore Oxygen Ltd v. *Kerala State Electricity Board*, National Commission, I (1997) CPJ 17.

Complainant applied for extended electricity load – Sanctioned on 22-6-1988 – Complainant submitted report of electrical contractor on 9-7-1992 – Opposite party released connection on 21-7-1992 – Complaint – Whether there is any deficiency in service : (No);

A.Z Marbles & Chemicals Simns H.P. v. *H.P. State Electricity Board*, H.P. State Commission, II (1997) CPJ 109.

Despite compliance of all formalities, the Electricity Board has not given electricity connection to the complainant – Alleged that for want of electricity connection production in the factory could not be started – State Commission accepted the complaint and directed the Board to pay Rs.30,000 as compensation – Appeal – Whether there is deficiency in service : (No);

U.P. State Electricity Board v. *Mona Confectionery Industries*, National Commission, I (1996) CPJ 98.

Transformer burnt – Not available in store – Restored after 10–12 days – Whether amounts to deficiency in service : (No);

Haryana State Electricity Board v. *Upbhokta Kashta Niraran Samiti Reg*, Haryana State Commission, II (1996) CPJ 219.

Electricity – Whether charging of "Fixed Minimum Charges" by the Electricity Board amounts to deficiency in service : (No);

Hotel Utrav Pvt Ltd v. *Chief Engineer*, *Gujarat Electricity Board*, Gujarat State Commission, II (1996) CPJ 470.

Complainant had a tubewell with motor of 5 B.H.P – He on his own replaced it with 20 B.H.P. motor – Low voltage – Suffered loss – Complaint – Whether there is deficiency in service : (No);

Haryana State Electricity Board v. *Gurdial Singh*, Haryana State Commission, III (1996) CPJ 67.

Opposite party found unit recording of the complainant faulty in January, 1985 – Decided to assess consumption on average basis from August, 1984 to December, 1984 – Bill raised on 5-2-1993 – Whether there is deficiency in service : (No);

Maharashtra State Electricity Board v. *Swastik Industries*, National Commission, III (1996) CPJ 71.

Complainant was sanctioned electricity load to the extent of 2 KWS – On inspection found consumption ranging from 9 KWS to 12 KWS – Bill sent – Not paid – Line disconnected – Complaint – Whether deficiency in service : (No);

Charulata Mohpatra v. *Orissa State Electricity Board*, Orissa State Commission, I (1994) CPJ 102.

Complainant applied for enhancement of load – Enhanced load not sanctioned – Complaint – Whether consumer is entitled as a matter of right to a higher load than the sanctioned one – Whether refusal is deficiency in service : (No);

Imperial Melts Pvt.Ltd. v. *Haryana State Electricity Board*, Haryana State Commission, I (1994) CPJ 400.

Complainant filed a complaint as the opposite party failed to provide electric connection – District Forum allowed the complaint – State Commission confirmed the order – Revision – Whether failure to grant electric connection to a consumer who has failed to file a proper application constitutes deficiency in service : (No);

Maharashtra State Electricity Board O&M Division Wardha v. *K.L. Ramani*, National Commission, III (1994) CPJ 170.

Complainant applied for electric connection – Released after 31 months – Complaint filed – Opposite party contended transformer was not of full capacity – No reason for delay communicated to the complainant – Whether the opposite party was negligent in not giving electric connection : (No);

Ajay Kumar Aggarwal v. *Superintending Engineer, U.P. Rajya Vidyut Parishad*, U.P.State Commission, III (1994) CPJ 443.

Complainant was sanctioned 35 H.P. connection in 1989 and he deposited the cheques – Power not given – Unable to run mill – Claimed compensation – Whether there is a consumer dispute : (No);

S.R. Dal Mills v. *U.P. State Electricity Board*, National Commission, I (1993) CPJ 66.

Electricity applied for the village in 1989 – Continued for only 7 days – Pillars uprooted due to cyclone – Cultivation affected – Complaint filed – Electricity disrupted due to reasons beyond control – Whether there is deficiency in service : (No);

Srihara Chandra Dass v. *Executive Engineer, Orissa State Electricity Board, Balasore*, Orissa State Commission, I (1993) CPJ 256.

Opposite party along with police raided premises of complainant – Found theft of electricity – Opposite party registered a complaint with the police – Police disconnected electricity – Complaint filed against opposite party – Alleging deficiency in service – Whether there is deficiency in service on the part of opposite party : (No);

Shimoya Ancyl (Pvt.) Ltd. v. *Karnataka Electricity Board*, Karnataka State Commission, I (1993) CPJ 491.

Complaint filed for compensation as opposite party not supplied electricity continuously – District Forum granted compensation – Appeal – Disconnection due to power cut – No deficiency in service – Complainant not entitled to compensation;

Managing Director v. *Balmik Singh*, Madhya Pradesh State Commission, I (1993) CPJ 315.

Appeal by complainant against dismissal of his complaint about delay in giving him electric connection – Despite best efforts on the part of the respondents because of obstruction created by some other person electric lines could not be laid – Whether there is any deficiency in service on the part of respondents : (No);

Indrrabhan v. *Assistant Engineer Gramin Vidyut Shakti Samiti*, M.P. State Commission, I (1993) CPJ 598.

Negligence

To succeed in his claim, the consumer has also to prove that he suffered loss or injury due to the negligence of the other party. For, under section 14(1)(d) of the Consumer Protection Act, compensation can be granted to the consumer only if loss or injury which he may have suffered – and this is important – is attributable to the negligence of the respondent. In other words, it is negligence in the performance of a deficient service which empowers the Redressal Forums to award compensation to the complainant for loss or injury suffered by him.

Negligence, which is generally inferred, is the anti-thesis of diligence. It is, as observed by the National Commission in *R.R. Gopal* v. *Chairman, Tamil Nadu Electricity Board*:[1]

> "Absence of such care, skill and diligence in rendering the service as is expected of or required of a reasonable man. It is omitting to do something that a reasonable man would do or doing something which a reasonable man would not do. It is want of proper care or attention in rendering the service judged from the standards of performance by a reasonable man."

It also needs to be borne in mind that if loss or injury is suffered by the complainant by any reason other than the negligence of the other party, the Redressal Forums will have no jurisdiction to award compensation. In *Air India* v. *Suganda Ravi Mashelkar*[2] for example, the Gulf war disabled the Air India from carrying out the obligations of carriage and delivery of the booked cargo as the consignment could not be traced due to the war. The National Commission ruled in that case that inability to render service due to reasons beyond the control of the person required to render it cannot be said to be deficiency in service – one could add much less, negligence – as it falls within the well known exception, "Force *Merjura*". In *Consumer Unity and Trust Society, Jaipur* v. *The Chairman and Managing Director, Bank of Baroda, Calcutta*[3] damages were claimed on behalf of the depositors for failure of the bank to provide service to them during strike of their employees. The following observations of the Supreme Court in that case are pertinent :–

> "The provisions of section 14(1)(d) are attracted if the person from whom damages are claimed is found to have

1. (1996) CPJ 143 (NC).
2. 1 (1993) CPJ 63 (SC).
3. 1 (1995) CPJ (SC).

acted negligently and such negligence must result in some loss to the person claiming damages. In other words, loss or injury, if any, must flow from negligence. Mere loss or injury without negligence is not contemplated by this section. The bank has not been found to be negligent in discharge of its duties. Therefore, if any loss or damage was caused to any depositor but it was not caused due to negligence of Bank then no claim of damages under the Act was maintainable."

These examples are from other services, namely, Air Service and Banking, but the principle laid down therein is applicable to every service, including electricity. Barring such exceptional cases, action would always be there, if there is negligence in the performance of a deficient service. The burden of proving that there is apparent deficiency or negligence in the performance of service is always on the complainant as held by the Punjab State Commission in *Padma Rani* v. *Life Insurance Corporation*.[1]

1. 1994 (1) CPR 477.

12 Digest of Important Cases

Arrears – Recovery of

Defective meter – The maximum period for which a bill can be raised in respect of a defective meter is six months and no more – Section 26(6) of the Indian Electricity Act, 1910;

H. D. Shourie v. *Municipal Corporation of Delhi,* Delhi High Court, AIR 1987 Del 218 ; *Major Zorawar Singh* v. *Municipal Corporation of Delhi*, 1991 RLR 312.

The Opposite party cannot charge the amount of arrears, if any, for a period of more than six months;

Northern Indian Tiles Corporation v. *D.E.S.U.*, *Delhi State Commission*, 1(1994) CPJ 255.

Where a bill for the meter which was defective for 23 months was raised and was superadded with a surcharge penalty, the Commission observed that the Haryana State Electricity Board cannot recover the arrears of electricity charges for the defective meter from the consumer beyond the period of six months;

S.D.O. HSEB, Jind v. *Raj Kumar,* Haryana State Commission, 1(1994) CPJ 255.

An arrears bill for a period of 7 years was issued to the complainant. Despite his representation that he has been paying his electricity bills regularly his electricity was disconnected. On a complaint the District Forum held that there was laches on the part of the opposite party in not issuing the adjustment bills regularly. The State Commission upholding the decision of the District Forum held following the decision of the National Commission that recovery for more than three years was barred by limitation ;

Asstt. Accounts Officer v. *N. Timarisheshir Rao,* Andhra Pradesh State Commission, 1(1998) CPJ 463.

Where there are unpaid dues for a period of three years or more, the suppliers can stop supplying electricity under section 24 of the Indian Electricity Act till the dues are paid. The liability of the complainant to pay the dues does not stand extinguished ;

Divisional Engineer v. *R. Suraj,* Tamil Nadu State Commission, II (1996) CPJ 96.

Average basis – Billing

The electricity meter has to be maintained by the Board. The meter of the tube well run by the Gram Panchayat, Dahanu got burnt and was not replaced by the Haryana State Electricity Board. Instead a bill for Rs.3,26,485/- was sent to the Gram Panchayat which, on a representation, was reduced to Rs.1,81,701/- The bill was raised on an arbitrary basis of consumption of 5000 units per month as against an agreed basis of actual consumption. Referring to the statutory and contractual provisions applicable, the Commission allowed the complaint and set aside the demand.

How is the consumer to be billed if his newly installed meter has not recorded consumption even for one full billing month? The regulations applicable of the Karnataka Electricity Board where this peculiarly isolated case occurred did not find favour with the State Commission. Rejecting the view of the District Forum, which held that 3 months average of the consumption recorded immediately after the working meter is installed should be taken for the purpose. The Commission laid down that twelve months average should be taken to avoid the possibility of any manipulation by the consumer;

G.S. Bhagwat v. *Asstt Executive Engineer,* Karnataka State Commission, II (1994) CPJ 37.

Is it open to the Electricity Board to recover electricity charges on an average basis after a period of two years of the meter becoming non-functional? No. The Rajasthan State Commission has firmly held that any condition framed in contravention of section 26 of Indian Electricity Act is invalid ;

Rajasthan State Electricity Board v. *Kishan Chand,* Rajasthan State Commission, 1(1996) CPJ 110.

Payment for consumption of electricity was to be made on the basis of meter reading – Suddenly changed to payment on the basis of flat rate – Challenged before the District Forum –

Complaint dismissed by the Forum. The Board explained that the decision was changed because theft of electricity was being committed by the agriculturists using electricity – Setting aside the decision of the District Forum, the State Commission observed : No inspection note was prepared mentioning the commission of theft or of any other malpractice. No disconnection was made. It only shows that the opposite party wanted to get out of the agreement which it made with the complainants for being charged on the basis of meter and wanted to charge them at flat rates under colourable exercise of power. They cannot be permitted to practice fraud on their own agreement;

Nagaur Village Nalat v. *Asstt. Engineer Nagaur,* Rajasthan State Commission, III (1997) CPJ 56.

Is it open to the Electricity Board to recover electricity charges not on the basis of average consumption of preceding three or six months whichever was higher, but on the basis of succeeding period. Still the District Forum dismissed the complaint of the aggrieved party although an arrear bill for 65 months was sent to the complainant based on the consumption of the succeeding and not 54 preceding months. Setting aside the decision of the Electricity Board the State Commission observed that it was not just misconceived, it was a misadventure;

State of Rajasthan v. *M.P. Pandya*, Rajasthan State Commission, II (1997) CPJ 472 ; *Patel Kanta Lal Devaldass* v. *The Deputy Engineer, Gujarat Electricity Board*, Gujarat State Commission, III (1992) CPJ 213.

The Haryana Commission observed that a broken seal of a meter was not a conclusive proof of theft of electrical energy. The report does not bear the signatures of either the consumer or his representative nor is there any evidence that it was served on him. The whole action seems to be in violation of the rules notified by the Board itself;

H.S.E.B. v. *Krishan Dev*, Haryana State Commission, 1 (1994) CPJ 74.

If the Electricity Board discovers pilferage and, as a result, disconnects the supply, no consumer dispute arises because of this action. It will be open to the complainant to agitate the same in a civil court or before the High Court invoking Article 226, if so, advised;

Andhra Pradesh State Electricity Board v. *Uday Kumar Jaiswal*, Andhra Pradesh State Commission, III (1999) CPJ 521.

Not sending the bill for electrical consumption in accordance with the billing cycle is deficiency in service as the consumer had to pay hefty arrears which amounted to his harassment;

M. P. Electrical Board v. *Shiv Kant Dubey*, M. P. State Commission, II (1997) CPJ 472.

Meter rent is not recoverable as long as it remained inoperative;

Ram Processor Merrakat Road v. *Punjab State Electricity Board*, Punjab State Commission, 1(2001) CPJ 178.

Demand of additional amount for slow running of electrical energy is also not justified without getting the dispute settled by Electrical Inspector. Failure to refer the dispute to the Electrical Inspector is deficiency in service;

Baboo Lal v. *M.S. Yadav*, Madhya Pradesh State Commission, II (1994) CPJ 97.

Compensation

Compensation shall not be awarded if it was not claimed;

Gujarat Travels v. *Ukabhailaviji Bhat*, 1992 (1) CPR 599 (Guj SCDRC) ; *Sarvaran Steel Furniture* v. *Shabbudeen*, 1991(2) CPR 382 (TN SCDRC).

Compensation would be restricted to the amount claimed;

Tuticorin Plastic Pvt. Ltd. v. *Ebenezer*, 1993(1) CPR 338 (TN SCDRC).

Deficiency in service

The opposite party served a notice on the complainant alleging loosened seal of meter – Threatened disconnection of supply – Also levied electricity charges for the past without any basis – Complaint – Whether not following legal procedure and adopting coercive methods is deficiency in service? (yes);

J.P. Khangare v. *Executive Engineer*, *Maharashtra State Electricity Board*, II (1992) CPJ 963.

Complainant's bulbs, tube lights, stabilizer and other appliances burnt due to high voltage – Complaint filed for cost of goods – District Forum held supply of excess voltage amounts to deficiency in service – Awarded costs of goods – Upheld by the State Commission in appeal;

Gujarat Electricity Board v. *Sharda Madhusudan Desai*, 1 (1993) CPJ 158.

Complainant applied for an electric connection – Submitted test report on demand – Electric connection not provided within a period of one year of submission of test report – District Forum issued direction to release the connection – State Commission on appeal by both the parties confirmed the order and also awarded Rs.10,000/- as damages to the complainant – Revision – Whether directions can be issued? (yes);

Haryana State Electricity Board v. *Pirthi Singh*, National Commission, III (1993) CPJ 270.

Failure to prepare and serve bills in accordance with the billing cycle – Raising a heavy arrears bill – Raising bills without actual meter reading – Claiming arrears without details – Claiming arrears over one lakh – Disconnection of electricity even before the last date of payment – Whether constitutes deficiency in services? (yes);

Delhi Electricity Supply v. *Y. N. Gupta*, National Commission, III (1993) CPJ 370.

Opposite party demanded additional amount for the slow running of meter – Dispute not settled first by Electrical Inspector – Whether demand of additional amount on the ground of defective meter without prior reference to Electrical Inspector is justifiable? (No) – Whether failure to refer to Electrical Inspector before revising additional amount on the ground of defective meter, amounts to deficiency in service? (yes);

Babulal v. *M.S. Yadav*, Madhya Pradesh State Commission, II (1994) CPJ 97.

Electricity disconnected on the ground of theft and pilferage – Without any proof – F.I.R. lodged – No proof – No criminal proceedings – Disconnected without notice – Complaint allowed by the District Forum – Whether there is any deficiency in service? (yes);

C.E.S.C. Ltd v. *Nand Kishore Joshi*, West Bengal State Commission, II (1994) CPJ 227.

Possession of house given by the authority concerned on 7-6-1990 – Electricity connection not provided for more than two years – Complaint – Whether amounts to deficiency in service? (yes);

Vice Chairman, HUDA v. *Kurthi Vasan*, Andhra Pradesh State Commission, II (1996) CPJ 190.

Complainant applied for electricity connection – Opposite party gave estimate of Rs.10,705/- – Complainant paid the amount – Connection not released – Complaint – Whether deficiency in service? (yes);

Panchandbhai Shambubhai v. *Gujarat Electricity Board*, Gujarat State Commission, 1 (1997) CPJ 543.

Defective meter existing at the premises of the complainant not replaced for a sufficiently long time – Whether amounts to deficiency in service? (yes);

Gita Rani Chakravarti v. *Electric Supdt Bankara, West Bengal State Electricity Board*, West Bengal State Commission, 1 (1997) CPJ 450.

Meter removed for non-payment of electricity charges by the previous tenant – Madhya Pradesh Electricity Board demanded payment of the whole amount of arrears from the complainant – Payment of arrears a condition precedent for supply of electric energy – M.P.E.B. has a monopoly right in distribution of electricity supply – Complainant agreed and made payment under duress – Held : Complainant entitled to be reimbursed – Deficiency and Unfair Trade Practice proved;

S. K. Dhingra v. *Madhya Pradesh Electricity Board*, Madhya Pradesh State Commission, 1(1998) CPJ 214.

Drive to remove encroachment – Shop dismantled – Electricity meter removed – Electric connection cut off – Notice regarding one month condition precedent for cutting of electric connection – Electricity Board guilty of unilateral breach of contract – Electric connection cut off without mandatory notice – Deficiency in service;

Teekaram v. *Upyantri M.P. Electricity Board*, M.P. State Commission, 1(1998) CPJ 264.

Electricity meter of the complainant not working – Average bill issued – Suddenly a huge bill sent as recovery of arrears – Complaint – Opposite party contended connection used for commercial purpose – No evidence to support this contention –

Whether there was deficiency in service on the part of the opposite party? (yes);

M.P. Electricity Board v. *Amitabh Kumar Jain*, M.P. State Commission, II (1998) CPJ 224.

Electricity dues paid on 10-3-1992 – Electricity disconnected on 16-3-1992 – Complaint – Whether there is deficiency in service? (yes);

M. P. Electricity Board v. *Amar Singh*, M. P. State Commission, II (1998) CPJ 52.

Complainant applied for temporary connection – Deposit made – Deposit refunded after 9 months – Complaint – Whether there is deficiency in service? (yes);

M. P. Electricity Board v. *Sudarshan*, M. P. State Electricity Commission, II (1998) CPJ 4.

Improper disconnection of electricity in contravention of the provisions of section 22 of the Indian Electricity Act, 1910 – Held: deficiency in service – Complainant awarded compensation;

Additional Assistant Engineer, A. P. Electricity Board v. *Saldalen Chakrapani*, A.P. State Commission, II (1998) CPJ 574.

Complainant a consumer of electricity – Reported on 9-5-1995 that glass of the window of meter was broken – On 16-8-1955 the officials of the opposite party reported theft – Raised bill of Rs.10,622/- – Complaint – Whether there is deficiency in service? (yes);

Sub-Divisional Engineer, Punjab State Electricity Board v. *Bhushan Kumar Gupta*, Punjab State Commission, II (1998) CPJ 95.

Electricity Supply not given – Test report not submitted – Appellant body having huge staff should inform the consumer in writing what is expected of them – They cannot be permitted to get away by stating that consumer was told verbally – Lack of accountability and transparency constitute deficiency in service;

M. P. Electricity Board v. *Sanjay Kumar Pathak*, M. P. State Commission, III (1998) CPJ 189.

Petitioner approached W.B.E.B. for starting of industry – Assured of electricity supply, applied for financial loan – Loan sanctioned – Construction made – Machinery purchased – Electricity not supplied – Petitioner unable to start industry – Loan repaid – Compensation claimed – Deficiency in service established – Compensation reduced to Rs.40,000/- as against Rs.1 lakh awarded by the Forum;

W. B. State Electricity Board v. *Nehrul Ali*, W. B. State Commission, 1(1999) CPJ 302.

Electric wire passing over the complainant's field – Wire hardly 7 to 8 feet height from grounds – Wire broke down – buffalo grazing in the field electrocuted – Electric wire so dangerous even tractors could not pass – Not attended for three months even after writing to the Collector – Extreme example of callousness – Gross negligence on part of supervisory officers – Compensation granted;

Rajasthan Electricity Board v. *Charan Singh*, Rajasthan State Commission, 1(1999) CPJ 162.

Electricity Billing – Two meters installed in the premises of the complainant – Meter reading not taken for six months – Average bill sent – Complaint – Held : amounts to deficiency in service;

M. P. Electricity Board v. *Shivkant Chaubey*, M. P. State Commission, II (1998) CPJ 85.

Complainant having old tubewell connection – Some portion of his land acquired by the government for digging a canal – Had divided into two parts – No water course could be provided for the complainant's land due to high dunes and depth of the canal – Land acquisition authorities recommended separate tubewell connection – Haryana State Electricity Board failed to release necessary connection – Complainant entitled to compensation for loss of crop and mental agony ;

Haryana State Electricity Board v. *Ravindra Vir Sharma*, Haryana State Commission, II (1999) CPJ 39.

Electricity Board estopped from pleading that at one premises two electric connections could not be issued – Raising demand subsequently clubbing the load of two connections illegal – Deficiency in service on the part of the Board proved;

Punjab State Electricity Board v. *Satish Kumar*, Punjab State Commission, II (1999) CPJ 359.

Excess amount charged – Refund – Bill amount increased by adding arrears and surcharge – Meter recording less consumption – Duty of Electricity Board to maintain correct electricity meter –

Bill paid under threat of disconnection – Deficiency in service – Electricity Board liable to refund the excess amount charged;

Punjab State Electricity Board v. *G.M.P. Finishing Mills*, Punjab State Commission, III (1997) CPJ 76.

Complainant applied for grant of electric connection to start business of cold storage – Grant of connection delayed – Non availability of transformers not acceptable – No evidence produced on this point – Connection given after ten months of deposit – Deficiency in service on the part of Electricity Board established – Complainant awarded compensation;

New Punjab Cold Storage v. *Punjab State Electricity Board*, Punjab State Commission, III (1999) CPJ 278.

Time given for payment of electricity charges till 20-2-1998 – Electricity could not be disconnected for non-payment till then – Disconnected on 16-1-1998 – Deficiency in service – Complainant awarded compensation;

Kerala State Electricity Board v. *T.N. Rooplal*, Kerala State Commission, III (1999) CPJ 430.

High Voltage electricity supplied – Electrical equipments damaged – Contention : no possibility of higher voltage passing through single phase line, not acceptable – No evidence produced that lines in question were single phase line – Opposite party failed to regulate the supply – Deficiency in service proved – Complainant entitled to compensation;

Tamil Nadu Electricity Board v. *Appuvoo Thevar*, Tamil Nadu State Commission, 1(2001) CPJ 70.

No electricity in complainant house from 2-9-1988 to 25-9-1988 – Contention that the supply was adversely affected due to heavy rains but fault was removed on the same day not acceptable – No record provided to indicate date of rectification of fault and sufficient evidence produced by the complainant in support of his contention – Deficiency in service proved – Opposite party liable to pay compensation;

Delhi Vidyut Board v. *Ram Kishore Saini*, Delhi State Commission, 1(2000) CPJ 507.

Delay in installing meter – Inordinate delay of 13 months in installing meter – Contention case of electricity theft pending regarding complainant's flat not acceptable – Possession of the flat in question was with DDA at the relevant time of theft proved

– Undue delay in installing electric meter amounts to deficiency in service – Opposite party liable to pay compensation;

Delhi Vidyut Board v. *R.K. Bhat*, Delhi State Commission, 1(2000) CPJ 545.

Connection not released – Contention Civil suit pending and complaint not maintainable, not acceptable – Civil suit already dismissed as withdrawn – Contention landlord opposed grant of fresh connection also not acceptable – No objection already given by the landlord for grant of fresh connection in complainant's name – Deficiency in service on the part of the opposite party proved – Complainant entitled to compensation;

Delhi Vidyut Board v. *Kamala Devi*, Delhi State Commission, 1(2000) CPJ 490.

Deposited amount with the opposite party which was to be adjusted against consumption of bills for tubewell – Instead adjustment allowed through bill of domestic connection – Complainant had no domestic supply connection – Non-refunding of amount to the complainant highly arbitrary and amounts to deficiency in service – Opposite party liable to refund the amount with interest and also to pay compensation ;

Sohan Singh Bullar v. *Punjab State Electricity Board*, Punjab State Commission, 1(2000) CPJ 584.

Electric meters faulty – Complaints made to the opposite party – Meters not replaced – Dispute not referred to Electrical Inspector – Bill raised – There is deficiency in service – Action of opposite party not substainable in law;

Punjab State Electricity Board v. *Public Health* (PJS) Sub-Division, Punjab State Commission, 1(2000) CPJ 9.

Connection disconnected for non-payment of dues during the period when electricity was used – Pole supplying electricity was damaged – Complainant not liable to pay even minimum guarantee charges for the period when no electricity was used – Disconnection without any ground amounts to deficiency in service – Opposite party had no right to charge any amount when no electricity restored due to damaged line and is liable to restore the connection without charging any amount;

UPSEB v. *Shankar Maurya*, U.P.State Commission, II (2000) CPJ 498.

The complainants purchased shops and applied for electric connection – No objection given by Delhi Development Authority to Delhi Vidyut Board – Required amount deposited – Electricity connection not sanctioned – Complaint – Opposite party held guilty of deficiency in service – Compensation of Rs.20,000/- granted ;

Kashyap Constructions (Pvt) Ltd v. *Delhi Vidyut Board*, Delhi State Commission, III (2000) CPJ 440.

Amount of Rs.24,835/- deposited for installation of street light – Street light not installed – Deficiency in service on the part of Electricity Board proved – Complainant entitled to refund along with interest ;

U.P. State Electricity Board v. *President Nagar Panchyat*, U.P. State Commission, III (2000) CPJ 371.

Complainant applied for electric connection – Sanctioned by opposite party – Connection not provided – Complaint – District Forum directed opposite party to install a meter and awarded Rs.2,500/- – Compensation – Appeal – Complainant's contention remained unrebutted – Appeal dismissed;

Delhi Vidyut Board v. *Reeta Sharma*, Delhi State Commission, III (2000) CPJ 404.

Energizing of connection delayed – Connection energised after a delay of 3 months – Complainant had to run from pillar to post to have the connection energized – Entitled to compensation – Appeal – Compensation enhanced;

J.K. Dhingra v. *Delhi Vidyut Board*, Delhi State Commission, II (2001) CPJ 29.

Complainant received inflated bills of Rs.52,239/- and Rs.1,11,006/- – Amount reduced to Rs. 30,366 by Bijli Adalat – Earlier bills also highly inflated established – Complainant remained without electricity for 3 years – Deficiency in service proved – Opposite party liable to pay compensation, refund security, realize amount afresh and withdraw all bills issued after disconnection – Order of District Forum upheld in appeal ;

Delhi Vidyut Board v. *Krishan Lal*, Delhi State Commission, I (2001) CPJ 587.

Complainant alleged excessive electricity bills – District Forum allowed complaint – Electricity Board was directed to correct bills on basis of average consumption for one year without any surcharge or interest – State Commission upheld the order of District Forum – Revision – Whether there was ground for interference? (No);

Haryana State Electricity Board v. *Amrit Singh*, National Commission, I (2002) CPJ 16.

What is not "Deficiency in Service"

To avoid fruitless litigation the subscriber should know what has not been considered as deficiency in service.

Delay in providing electrical energy for the running unit of the complainant – Loss of production – Claim for damages – Complainant also responsible for delay in making payment of cost of service line charges and suppression of this fact in the complaint – Both parties equally at fault – Principle of "*imparidalicto policrest canditio defendetis*" applies – No deficiency in service on the part of the opposite party;

Malaya Marnit Industries v. *Asstt. Engineer (Operation), Andhra Pradesh State Electricity Board,* Andhra Pradesh State Commission, I (2002) CPJ 128.

Electricity disconnected by landlords – Complaint filed against the Delhi Vidyut Board – No deficiency on the part of the Board;

Naresh Jaswal v. *Delhi Vidyut Board*, Delhi State Commission, III (2000) CPJ 280.

Additional connection not given – Complainant already using electricity from electric connection provided in the house – Entrance of two portions of house still common – No deficiency on the part of the opposite party in not granting additional electric connection – Instructions by the Electricity Board cannot be challenged before Fora;

Jaswinder Pal v. *Punjab State Electricity Board*, Punjab State Commission, II (2000) CPJ 46.

Excess Billing – Power shut downs, trippings and failure of supply not considered – Bills issued on the basis of average consumption – Forum ordered refund of excess amount charged – Appeal – Assessment made as per rules – Average consumption during the period of 4 months considered irrespective of lesser or excessive consumption in a particular month – No deficiency in service on the part of the opposite party - Order of Forum set aside;

T.N.E.B. Madras v. *Balamavarma Textiles Mills*, Tamil Nadu State Commission, 1(2000) CPJ 284.

Inflated bills – Account of bills produced by the opposite party – Bills of minimum guarantee amount were being sent – Complainant under legal obligation to pay these bills – No payment made for three and a half years – Complainant liable to pay – No deficiency in service on the part of the opposite party; *Sarala Prakash* v. *Delhi Vidyut Board*, Delhi State Commission, 1(2000) CPJ 511.

Electricity Bill for arrears – Forum held : dispute not referred to Electrical Inspector – Arrears could not be charged for period exceeding six months – Bill set aside – Appeal – Factum of consumption never denied – Consumer liable to pay minimum charges based on installed capacity – Order of Forum set aside; *SDO Electricity O.P.* v. *Gopal Mills Store*, Chandigarh State Commission, I(1999) CPJ 169.

Complainant applied for 3 industrial electric connection – Sent only one application for 3 connections – Delay in making demand of earnest money by Electricity Board – Complaint – Whether applicant of electricity connection is consumer by deposit of earnest money? (No); – Whether there was any deficiency in service? (No); *B.J.P.Stirals* v. *Tamil Nadu Electricity Board*, Tamil Nadu State Commission, I (1998) CPJ 504.

Electricity supply to tubewell not maintained – Crops damaged – District Forum granted compensation – Appeal – Complainant being not the account holder of electricity connection was not a consumer – Complaint not maintainable – No deficiency on the part of Electricity Board; *SDO Haryana State Electricity Board* v. *Surinder*, Haryana State Commission, III (1998) CPJ 387.

Fluctuations in voltage of electricity – Complaint – No willful or negligent action – Whether there is deficiency in service? (No); *Travancore Oxygen Ltd.* v. *Kerala State Electricity Board*, National Commission, I (1997) CPJ 17.

Complainant applied for extended electricity load – Sanctioned on 22-6-1988 – Complainant submitted report of electrical contractor on 9-7-1992 – Opposite party released connection on 21-7-1992 – Complaint – Whether there is any deficiency in service? (No);

A.Z. Marbles & Chemicals Simns H.P. v. *H.P. State Electricity Board*, H.P. State Commission, II (1997) CPJ 109.

Despite compliance of all formalities, the Electricity Board has not given electricity connection to the complainant – Alleged that for want of electricity connection production in the factory could not be started – State Commission accepted the complaint and directed the Board to pay Rs.30,000/- as compensation – Appeal – Whether there is deficiency in service? (No);

U.P.State Electricity Board v. *Mona Confectionery Industries*, National Commission, 1 (1996) CPJ 98.

Transformer burnt – Not available in store – Restored after 10-12 days – Whether amounts to deficiency in service? (No);

Haryana State Electricity Board v. *Upbhokta Kashta Nivaran Samiti Reg.*, Haryana State Commission, II (1996) CPJ 219.

Electricity – Whether charging of "Fixed Minimum Charges" by the Electricity Board amounts to deficiency in service? (No);

Hotel Utrav Pvt. Ltd. v. *Chief Engineer, Gujarat Electricity Board*, Gujarat State Commission, II (1996) CPJ 470.

Complainant had a tubewell with motor of 5 B.H.P – He on his own replaced it with 20 B.H.P. motor – Low voltage – Suffered loss – Complaint – Whether there is deficiency in service? (No);

Haryana State Electricity Board v. *Gurdial Singh*, Haryana State Commission, III (1996) CPJ 67.

Opposite party found unit recording of the complainant faulty in January, 1985 – Decided to assess consumption on average basis from August, 1984 to December, 1984 – Bill raised on 5-2-1993 – Whether there is deficiency in service? (No);

Maharashtra State Electricity Board v. *Swastik Industries*, National Commission, III (1996) CPJ 71.

Complainant was sanctioned electricity load to the extent of 2 KWS – On inspection found consumption ranging from 9 KWS to 12 KWS – Bill sent – Not paid – Line disconnected – Complaint – Whether deficiency in service? (No);

Charulata Mohpatra v. *Orissa State Electricity Board*, Orissa State Commission, 1 (1994) CPJ 102.

Complainant applied for enhancement of load – Enhanced load not sanctioned – Complaint – Whether consumer is entitled as a matter of right to a higher load than the sanctioned one – Whether refusal is deficiency in service? (No);

Imperial Melts Pvt. Ltd. v. *Haryana State Electricity Board*, Haryana State Commission, 1(1994) CPJ 400.

Complainant filed a complaint as the opposite party failed to provide electric connection – District Forum allowed the complaint – State Commission confirmed the order – Revision – Whether failure to grant electric connection to a consumer who has failed to file a proper application constitutes deficiency in service? (No);

Maharashtra State Electricity Board O&M Division Wardha v. *K.L. Ramani*, National Commission, III (1994) CPJ 170.

Complainant applied for electric connection – Released after 31 months – Complaint filed – Opposite party contended transformer was not of full capacity – No reason for delay communicated to the complainant – Whether the opposite party was negligent in not giving electric connection? (No);

Ajay Kumar Aggarwal v. *Superintending Engineer, U.P. Rajya Vidyut Parishad*, U.P. State Commission, III (1994) CPJ 443.

Complainant was sanctioned 35 H.P. connection in 1989 and he deposited the cheques – Power not given – Unable to run mill – Claimed compensation – Whether there is a consumer dispute? (No);

S.R. Dal Mills v. *U.P. State Electricity Board*, National Commission, 1(1993) CPJ 66.

Electricity applied for the village in 1989 – Continued for only 7 days – Pillars uprooted due to cyclone – Cultivation affected – Complaint filed – Electricity disrupted due to reasons beyond control – Whether there is deficiency in service? (No);

Srihara Chandra Dass v. *Executive Engineer, Orissa State Electricity Board, Balasore*, Orissa State Commission, 1 (1993) CPJ 256.

Opposite party along with police raided premises of complainant – Found theft of electricity – Opposite party registered a complaint with the police – Police disconnected electricity – Complaint filed against opposite party – Alleging

deficiency in service – Whether there is deficiency in service on the part of opposite party? (No);
Shimoya Ancyl (Pvt.) Ltd. v. *Karnataka Electricity Board*, Karnataka State Commission, 1(1993) CPJ 491.

Complaint filed for compensation as opposite party not supplied electricity continuously – District Forum granted compensation – Appeal – Disconnection due to power cut – No deficiency in service – Complainant not entitled to compensation;
Managing Director v. *Balmik Singh*, Madhya Pradesh State Commission, 1(1993) CPJ 315.

Appeal by complainant against dismissal of his complaint about delay in giving him electric connection – Despite best efforts on the part of the respondents because of obstruction created by some other person electric lines could not be laid – Whether there is any deficiency in service on the part of respondents? (No);
Indrabhan v. *Assistant Engineer, Gramin Vidyut Shakti Samiti*, M.P. State Commission, I (1993) CPJ 598.

Disconnection

Three bills for three electric connections in the house of the complainant were delivered to him by the Delhi Electric Supply Undertaking on Sunday, the 25th March, 1990. The last date for payment was 28th March, 1990. The amount of the bills was Rs.1,06,566/- which included a sum of Rs.1,03,566/- towards arrears. The period to which the arrears related was not mentioned in the bills. On the next working day, the complainant requested the Executive Engineer for details of arrears. Instead of furnishing the requisite information, his electricity was disconnected.

On a complaint being filed, the State Commission, on facts, found that the bill preferred by D.E.S.U. were incorrect and therefore, held that it acted negligently in preparing the bills. It also held that action of the officials in disconnecting the electricity of the complainant was *malafide* on account of which he must have suffered harassment and mental torture. D.E.S.U. was not entitled to charge late fee from the complainant. It further held that the complainant was liable to pay charges for another 10,000 units which, according to D.E.S.U. remained unbilled by mistake earlier.

On further appeal, the National Commission held the following deficiencies in service to have been established :—

1. The bill for consumption of electricity was not prepared and not served in accordance with the billing cycle.
2. It was deficiency in service to have raised the bill without actual meter reading.
3. It was deficiency in service to revise the arrears bill without details of the period to which the arrears pertained.
4. It was deficiency in service to serve the bill on the consumer on Sunday.
5. It was deficiency in service to send a wrong bill to the consumer which was in five digits instead of four.
6. Charging of late fee wrongly was deficiency in service.
7. Disconnection of power supply was *malafide* and intended to harass the customer;

Y.N. Gupta v. *D.E.S.U.*, National Commission, 1 (1993) CPJ 27.

The complainant appellant was sanctioned an electric meter. He was paying his bills regularly. Two other persons were also sanctioned power supply against the separate meters. They fell into arrears. Instead of disconnecting their supply, the meters of the complainant were removed without any notice. The District Forum summarily dismissed his complaint.

The respondent Board in their reply admitted that the other two meters were sanctioned against different numbers to two different persons. The electricity connection of the complainant was disconnected being in the same premises.

Setting aside the order of the District Forum, the State Commission held that it was manifest that the Electricity Board cannot held another recipient of electricity liable for payment of arrears of another. The Commission further observed that the appellant is obviously entitled to compensation for the unwarranted action of the respondent Board and patent deficiency in the supply of electricity which they had undertaken;

Dev Raj Vinaik v. *Chairman, HSEB*, Haryana State Commission, II (1994) CPJ 566.

Disconnection with notice

The complainant received a bill for Rs.164.68 for the month it was sent. An additional amount of Rs.2,364.05 was also shown in the bill as arrears of past consumption. The complainant requested for details in respect of past consumption. The opposite party just disconnected his electric supply instead of furnishing the information asked for. The complaint filed by him was dismissed by the District Forum.

Setting aside the decision of the District Forum, the State Commission held that electric supply cannot be discontinued or disconnected if the consumer neglects to pay any charge of energy without giving him a notice of less than seven clear days. Even in the electricity bill sent to the consumer it is printed that in case it is not paid within a week of the last date of payment, the electricity connection will be disconnected. Notice under section 24 of the Electricity Act mentioning that if the consumer neglected to pay any charge of energy, has to be given of seven clear days in writing. It is only after such a clear notice of seven days is served that the electricity connection can be disconnected if the charges are not paid.

A compensation of Rs.4,000/- was awarded for wrongful disconnection of electricity supply;

Ram Rakha Vyas v. *Rajasthan State Electricity Board*, Rajasthan State Commission, 1 (1995) CPJ 136.

The plea of the complainant in assailing the action of the Electricity Board was that his supply was disconnected without giving him seven days' notice. The contention of the Board was that in the White Meter Card it was clearly mentioned that if the electricity charges are not paid within seven days from the last date of payment, the electricity will be disconnected and this amounts to seven days' clear notice.

The Commission held that disconnection in this case was in contravention of section 22 of the Indian Electricity Act. Referring to the decisions of the Supreme Court the Commission pointed out that the remedy of civil action was also available for recovering damages;

Additional Asstt. Engineer A.P. State Electricity Board v. *Saldalen Chakrapani*, A.P. State Commission, II (1998) CPJ 574.

Punjab State Electricity Board v. *Bassi Cold Storage, Khirar*, 1994 Supplement (2) SCC 124; *Punjab State Electricity Board Mahilpur* v. *Guru Nanak Cold Storage and Ice Factory, Mahilpur*, Punjab State Commission, (1996) 5 SCC 411.

Disconnection without notice – Theft

No notice of clear seven days is required when theft of electricity is discovered before disconnection as held by the National Commission in *Calcutta Electricity Supply Co. Ltd* v. *Sunita Pal*. On a surprise visit by the officials of the company, they found that the consumer was drawing electricity directly from the service controls thereby bypassing the meter which was installed for registering consumption. Her electricity was immediately disconnected. A report was also lodged with the police.

A complaint was filed in the District Forum by Smt. Sunita Pal which observed that theft of electricity was not deficiency in service. The State Commission set aside the order of the District Forum.

The National Commission held in revision that the suppliers had the power to disconnect electricity without giving a notice where it was found that the consumer had tampered with the metering equipment and the meter was being by-passed in consumption of electricity by use of artificial means which was *prima facie* evidence of theft.

Calcutta Electricity Supply Company v. *Sunita Pal*, National Commission, III (1997) CPJ 116; *M.P. Electricity Board* v. *Badhulal*, National Commission, II (1995) CPJ 132.

The Supreme Court has also held that when the Board detects that a consumer has committed any malpractice including use of devices to commit theft of electricity, it may disconnect the supply of electricity forthwith and may call upon the consumer to pay compensation for unauthorised use of electricity. Section 24, it was held does not apply to demand on detection of pilferage of electricity and disconnection without notice was justified.

The exercise of power of disconnection is in accordance with statutory powers and cannot be construed as any deficiency in service;

M.P. Electricity Board case, JT (1996) 5 SC 443.

What constitutes theft

Theft has to be proved beyond a shadow of doubt. In *S.D.O. A.E.E. City Division, Hissar* v. *Hotel Palaki*, *Hissar* for example, where theft was sought to be proved by a mere allegation that the seal of the meter was broken it was held that it was a conclusive proof of theft of electricity energy.

S.D.O. A.E.E. City Division, Hissar v. *Hotel Palaki*, Hissar, Haryana State Commission, (1992) CPJ 127.

In *Patel Kanta Lal Devaldass* v. *The Deputy Engineer, Gujarat Electricity Board*, III (1992) CPJ 213, it was observed that the Board had not produced any evidence either by way of affidavit or oral evidence to prove that the complainant was engaged in theft. It is a serious charge and one cannot jump to a conclusion merely because there is an allegation. A relatively low consumption cannot be a basis of such a charge.

A broken seal of a meter is no conclusive proof of theft of electrical energy;

Haryana State Electricity Board v. *Krishan Dev*, Haryana State Commission, 1(1994) CPJ 174.

Electrical Inspector

Whether the meter is correct or faulty not recording the actual consumption – The dispute squarely falls within the provisions of the Indian Electricity Act, 1910 – High Court right in holding that it is the Electrical Inspector who alone is empowered to decide this dispute;

Madhya Pradesh Electricity Board v. *Basantibai*, Supreme Court, AIR 1988 SC 71.

The Board is not competent – Pending the determination of this dispute by the Electrical Inspector to issue another notice threatening disconnection of supply of electricity for non-payment of supplementary bill prepared and sent by it – The Board is not even competent to send a supplementary bill;

Madhya Pradesh Electricity Board v. *Basantibai*, Supreme Court, AIR 1988 SC 71.

In *H.D.Shourie* case, the Delhi High Court has pin pointed various illegalities committed by the respondents in handling that matter. The case was never referred to the Electrical Inspector for adjudication. They took a unilateral decision and that also decision and that also without notice to the petitioner and behind his back that the meter was defective. They themselves estimated the quantity of electricity consumed which was the function of the Electrical Inspector during the period in question and that also without any notice to the petitioner. Another illegality committed by them was that the bill sent by them was in excess of six months which was contrary to the provisions of section 26(6) of the Indian Electricity Act. Thus the mandatory provisions of the aforesaid Act were not complied with;

H.D. Shourie v. *Municipal Corporation of Delhi*, Delhi High Court, AIR 1987 Del 219.

A revised bill sent for a period of 5 years is clearly illegal for even when the matter is referred to the Electrical Inspector, the revised amount can be recovered for a period of six months only;

Hamidullah Khan v. *Chairman, M.P.Electricity Board*, AIR 1983 MP 3.

Can electric connection be disconnected when the dispute is pending with the Electrical Inspector? Can the licencee stop supplying electricity under section 24(1) of the Indian Electricity Act, 1910, when the dispute is awaiting settlement by the Electrical Inspector? No;

Bharat Board and Drums Mfg Co. Ltd. v. *Bombay Municipal Corporation*, AIR 1985 Bom 415.

The respondent Electricity Board cannot prepare a revised bill and call upon the consumer to pay it – revised or supplementary by whatever name it is called. The insistence to pay such a supplementary bill is not supportable till the supply is restored by installing a correct meter. It is beyond the scope of their authority and such insistence has no foundation in law;

M.P. Electricity Board v. *Basantibai*, M.P. High Court (Indore Bench), AIR 1985 MP 72.

It has been observed that in a dispute between the consumer and electrical undertaking a reference has to be made to the Electrical Inspector. The State Commission observed that not adopting legal procedure as per rules and regulations which are required to be observed in case of disputed electric dues amounts to deficiency in service;

J.P. Khangare v. *Executive Engineer, Maharashtra State Electricity Board*, Maharashtra State Commission, II (1992) CPJ 963.

The Electricity Board is not entitled to recover any amount from the appellant on the basis that the meter was defective and was not giving correct reading unless it refers the matter to the Electrical Inspector and gets it decided through him. It is deficiency in service especially in the face of decisions against it by the High Court and the Supreme Court;

M.P. Electricity Board v. *Baboo Lal*, M.P. State Commission, II (1994) CPJ 97.

The Rajasthan State Commission struck down one of the conditions prescribed by the Board as *ultra vires* of section 26(6) of the Indian Electricity Act, 1910 and observed that in the present case it is the opposite party which was questioning the correctness of the meter and not the complainant. It is for that party to refer the matter to the Electrical Inspector. It was then for the Electrical Inspector to estimate the amount of energy supplied to the consumer. No such procedure was followed by the Board in this case. The Commission held that no such bill as aforesaid could be sent to the consumer and his electricity could not be disconnected for non-payment;

Ram Rakh Vyas v. *Rajasthan Electricity Board*, Rajasthan State Commission, I (1995) CPJ 136.

The majority law in *Gita Rani Chakraborty* v. *Electric Superintendent, Bankara*, I (1997) CPJ 450, that the meter was defective since July, 1991 to the knowledge of the respondents and they did not take any steps to replace it is a serious negligence and deficiency in service on their part appears to be more reasonable than the minority view that the complainant could have himself referred the matter to the Electrical Inspector because it is the duty of the licensee to keep the meter correct.

Where the Electricity Board issued a fresh bill for the last six months on the ground that the meter of the complainant was running slow without referring the matter to the Electrical Inspector, the Haryana State Commission held that the Board was not competent in law to issue a fresh bill without complying with the provisions of section 26(6) of the Electricity Act;

Executive Engineer, Haryana State Electricity Board v. *Madhu Sudan Gupta*, Haryana State Commission, II (1998) CPJ 24.

The Maharashtra State Commission has held that protection of section 26(6) will not be available to a consumer if the meter was not functioning but no reference was made by him to the Electrical Inspector. In support of this view the Commission has relief on *Bombay Suburban Electric Supply Ltd.* v. *The Secretary, Deepali Coop Housing Society Ltd.* that sub-section (6) of section 26 does not cast any duty on the licensee to refer any difference or dispute in respect of any matter for determination to the Electrical Inspector on behalf of the consumer. If, the Commission held, any difference or dispute was raised by the consumer, it was for him to make a reference to the Electrical Inspector for determination. When no such application was made by him, it cannot be said that the licensee was not entitled to demand the arrears due from the consumer. The Commission cited a decision of the Allahabad High Court in support of this view;

Bombay Suburban Electric Supply Ltd. v. *The Secretary, Deepali Coop Housing Society Ltd*, III (1999) CPJ 416; *R.D. Premier Ice Factory* v. *Commercial Manager, Kanpur Electricity Supply Administration*, AIR 1998 All 8.

Following the decision of the National Commission in *Y.N. Gupta* v. *D.E.S.U.*, 1 (1993) CPJ 27 (NC) and of the Supreme Court in *Balwal Spinning Mills Ltd.* v. *U.P. State Electricity Board*, AIR 1997 SC 2393 the Punjab State Commission held that the Electricity Board was required to refer the dispute of defective meter to the Electrical Inspector which was not done. The opposite party cannot assume the statutory powers and functions of the Electrical Inspector. The action of the opposite party, the Commission observed, is not sustainable in law.

Where the Electricity meter was alleged to be running slow and bills were issued to the consumer on average basis, the Punjab State Commission following the decision of the Supreme Court in *Madhya Pradesh Electricity Board* v. *Imam Bhai*, AIR 1998 SC 71 and agreeing with the decision of the Madhya Pradesh State Commission in *Baboo Lal* v. *M.S. Yadav*, II (1994) CPJ 97 and of the Karnataka High Court in *Karnataka Electricity Board* v. *Topsara*, 1 (1991) Civil Court Cases 472 held in *Punjab State Electricity Board* v. *Ram Processor*

Marakat Road, 1 (2001) CPJ 178 that opposite party could not have issued the impugned bills to the respondents in violation of section 26(6) of the Indian Electricity Act. The Commission directed the opposite party to refer the dispute to the Chief Electrical Inspector and after complying with the provisions of law recover anything due from the complainant.

Electrocution

The husband of the complainant was electrocuted in a public place. She filed a complaint claiming compensation. It was dismissed because it was held that she was not a consumer and she had even otherwise no *locus standi* to file a complaint being neither State Government nor Central Government nor even a registered voluntary organization;

Malati Devi v. *Orissa Electricity Board*, Orissa State Commission, III (1992) CPJ 123.

A cow belonging to the complainant was electrocuted by coming into contact with an electric post. The plea of the Petitioner – Complainant was that the State Electricity Board which was responsible for supply of electricity in the area shall pay compensation to make good her loss.

Referring to another decision of the Haryana State Commission, the National Commission held that the grievance put forward by the complainant did not constitute a consumer dispute as defined in the Act nor was it a case of deficiency in service on the part of the Electricity Board. The District Forum was in error in allowing compensation to the complainant;

Haryana State Electricity Board v. *Ganga Devi*, National Commission, III (1996) CPJ 182 (NC).

The electrical wire broke down on account of a severe storm the previous evening and fell into a pond. The water got electrified. Next morning a person went to the pond for fishing and died on account of electrocution. On hearing his shouts, the husband of the complainant jumped into the pond where he also died of electrocution. The widow filed a claim for compensation.

The State Commission held that she was not entitled to any compensation as the deceased was not a consumer;

West Bengal State Electricity Board v. *Champa Bai*, West Bengal State Commission, 1(2001) CPJ 51.

The complainant was carrying on cultivation and also had a farm. The electric wires passing over the fields had become so loose that they were hardly 7 or 8 feet high from the ground. Whenever there is a storm they, it was feared, could be broken and fall to the ground. Written complaints were made to the Rajasthan Electricity Board which were followed by personal representations. A letter was also written to the Collector of the District who sent it to the Executive Engineer. No action was taken to put the wires right.

On 29-6-1994 when his buffalo was grazing in the field, the wire broke down resulting in the electrocution of the buffalo. After getting the post-mortem of the buffalo, he lodged a claim before the District Forum.

The respondents filed a very casual reply stating that the complainant was not a consumer, no service was rendered to him and the Board was not liable to pay any damages to him.

The District Forum after considering the evidence produced by the complainant awarded compensation and costs to the complainant

On appeal, the State Commission observed they cannot enhance the compensation as there is no appeal before them. They passed severe strictures against the officers concerned for filing a false reply;

Rajasthan State Electricity Board v. *Charan Singh*, Rajasthan State Commission, 1(1999) CPJ 162.

Excess billing

The complainant, G.D. Khandara, was paying his bills regularly. Despite that he received three excessive bills – the last being for Rs.2393.95. According to him, he was not required to pay that bill as the electricity was not supplied to him but was supplied to the police. He paid the bill because of threat of disconnection of his own supply. The District Forum allowed his claim. The appeal filed against this order was also dismissed;

G.D. Khandash v. *Executive Engineer, Maharashtra State Electricity Board*, Maharashtra State Commission, III (1992) CPJ 555.

Electric supply of Shri Y.N. Gupta was disconnected even before the bill was due for payment. The State Commission held that action of Delhi Electricity Supply Undertaking was *mala fide*

and was taken to harass him. The correct amount of the bill was Rs.13,649/- instead of Rs.1,06,566/- claimed by the Electricity Supply Undertaking. The claim for another 10,000 units which was discovered by D.E.S.U. during the pendency of the case was also found by the National Commission to be untenable;
Y.N. Gupta v. *D.E.S.U.*, National Commission, 1(1993) CPJ 27 (NC).

The complainant had only one fan, one tubelight, and two lamps in his home. He had no other activity which may require use of electricity. He was given a bill for Rs.21,284.98 by the Gujarat Electricity Board though his average consumption came between Rs.80/- and Rs.90/- He paid Rs.69.92 for December, 1991 to March, 1992. He was a hawker and was earning his living by carrying his handcart from place to place. He did not pay the hefty bill received by him last. The District Forum dismissed his complaint.

The State Commission rejected the plea of the Board that the complainant and other did not allow the meter reader to take the actual reading by administering threat. They could seek police protection, it observed and directed that the bills should be prepared on the basis of average consumption and the rates prevailing at the relevant time should be applied and charged;
Chaman Lal Madhargi v. *Gujarat State Electricity Board*, Gujarat State Commission, II (1994) CPJ 548.

The Kerala State Commission held that the Electricity Board cannot issue a bill for excess consumption for a period prior to six months. In this case the Electricity Board had issued a bill for excess consumption for three years;
Secretary, Kerala State Electricity Board v. *N. Mani*, Kerala State Commission, III (1995) CPJ 124.

Is it open to the Electricity Board to overhaul the bill of the consumer itself after coming to know that the meter was correctly recording consumption? No. In *Daljit Singh* v. *The Punjab Electricity Board*, the electric meter installed in the industrial premises of the complainant was first checked by the S.D.O. concerned who, finding it defective charged it and then by the Flying Squad after which a bill for Rs.46,111/- was sent to him. To save his electric connection he paid this amount but later challenged the action of the Board before the District Forum. The District Forum dismissed his complaint.

Reversing the decision of the District Forum, the Punjab State Commission held that the Board could not issue arbitrarily a bill of Rs.46,111/- when the meter was earlier also found to be defective. The Board could have taken resort to section 26(6) of the Act instead of acting on its own. The action of the Board amounts to rendering deficient service to the complainant;

Daljit Singh v. *The Punjab State Electricity Board*, Punjab State Commission, III (1997) CPJ 217.

A similar view was taken by the Haryana State Commission. The Commission observed that revision or even overhauling of the bill could have been undertaken after serving a notice on the consumer and associating him with the investigation or a reference could have been made to the Electrical Inspector under section 26(6);

Suman Ice Factory v. *S.D.O. H.S.E.B*, Haryana State Commission, II (1998) CPJ 37.

If a defect is noticed in the electricity meter straightway issuing a revised bill is not contemplated by law. If the Electricity Board issues the bill arbitrarily and under threat of disconnection deficiency in rendering service would be writ large;

Punjab State Electricity Board v. *G.M.P. Finishing Mills*, Punjab State Commission, III (1997) CPJ 76.

Fluctuation

Electric equipments and fittings of nine consumers of Ballery got allegedly damaged due to sudden high voltage of electricity. On evidence the District Forum held that there was surge in voltage and awarded compensation to each of the complainants. On appeal the State Commission held that mere fluctuation in voltage did not entitle the complainants to compensation. They had to prove that they suffered loss or damage due to the negligence of the officials of the Board. They were rewarded for trading evidence on this point;

Secretary, Karnataka Electricity Board v. *Secretary, Ballery Citizens Forum*, Karnataka State Commission, (1991) CPJ 97.

V.C.R. of the complainant was damaged allegedly due to high voltage supply of electricity caused by the New Delhi Municipal Corporation or C.P.W.D. The District Forum allowed the claim of Rs.900/- against the N.D.M.C. Setting aside the order of the District Forum, the State Commission held that there was no negligence either on the part of N.D.M.C. or C.P.W.D. which was impleaded as a party by the Commission;

New Delhi Municipal Corporation (Committee) v. *S. P. Singha*, Delhi State Commission, (1991) CPJ 560.

The complainants alleged that due to irregular supply and fluctuation in voltage of electricity supplied to them by the opposite party for the past several years, their plant had to be switched off during the low voltage period resulting in production loss.

The case of the Respondent Board was that despite every effort they are unable to maintain the required voltage level due to reasons beyond their control. They pleaded that this was not due to any willful negligence attributable to them.

The Commission held that there was nothing in the complaint that the alleged voltage fluctuation was due to any willful action of the opposite party and did not find any deficiency in their service;

Travancore Oxygen Ltd. v. *Kerala State Electricity Board*, Kerala State Commission, I (1997) CPJ 17 (NC).

The District Forum Vishakhapatnam awarded an amount of Rs.2,495/- as compensation to the complainant for causing damage to his colour T.V. on account of sudden surge in the voltage of electricity. Rejecting the appeal filed by the Electricity Board, the State Commission held that when the Board undertakes to supply electrical energy at a particular voltage, the fluctuations in the voltage should be restricted to certain acceptable parameters. Unless the Board can come forward with good reasons for wide fluctuations as found factually proved, the Board would be found to be deficient in service.

Besides, if electrical energy is treated as "goods" the voltage has to be maintained at the agreed level failing which the goods supplied will not be of specified quality. On that basis also the Board will be liable;

A.P.S.E.B. v. *C. H. Appa Rao*, Andhra Pradesh State Commission, III (1998) CPJ 171.

The complainants alleged that due to surge their TV sets, fans and jet motors were damaged as a result of which they suffered loss. The District Forum awarded compensation to them. The opposite party pleaded that due to various safety devices provided by them, there was no chance of higher voltage than the one prescribed. They denied the allegation of the complainants.

Dismissing the appeal of the Board, the State Commission held that there was no oral or documentary evidence to show that the lines in question preclude the possibilities of higher voltage passing through them the burden of proving which was on the respondents under section 106 of the Indian Evidence Act; *Assistant Engineer (Urban) Tamil Nadu Electricity Board* v. *Apparwoo Thakur*, Tamil Nadu State Commission, 1 (1999) CPJ 70.

In a case in which a number of TV sets were damaged due to sudden surge in power supply, the plea taken by the Board was that it was on account of a tree falling on 3 phase - 4 phase wire system. It was purely an accident for which they cannot be held responsible. The District Forum awarded compensation. On appeal, the State Commission upheld the decision of the District Forum. It was observed that under rule 29(1) of the Indian Electricity Rules, a duty was cast on the suppliers to protect the consumer from any source which may hamper, fluctuate or cut off power supply. Rule 30(1) in particular enjoins a duty on the supplier of electricity to identify any source of danger to the installations in the premises of the consumer and take necessary steps to prevent mishap to the wires and supply lines. Tree branches crowding the power lines are a constant source of hazard which requires constant trimming to avoid any mishap; *Karnataka State Electricity Board* v. *H. S. Sita Ram*, Karnataka State Commission, 1 (2000) CPJ 508.

The complainant claimed compensation for damages to his electric equipment on account of high voltage flowing through electric lines installed in his house in Chandigarh.

The respondents denied the averments made in the complaint and took the plea that wiring in Chandigarh was insulated and the complainant was putting a concocted and false story.

A Local Commission appointed by the District Forum reported that the exposed and uninsulated main power line wires connecting power connection to the house had every chance of the two wires touching each other causing heavy sparking and possibly leading to a short circuit.

The District Forum awarded compensation to the complainant and, on appeal, the State Commission also held that negligence was writ large on the part of the Sub-Divisional Engineer;

S.D.O. Electricity (Operational) v. *R.C. Gupta*, Chandigarh State Commission, I (2001) CPJ 564.

Jurisdiction

Whether under the Consumer Protection Act the Redressal Agencies have jurisdiction to entertain a complaint relating to electricity. Yes. The complainant has a *locus standi* to file it and the Forum has a jurisdiction to entertain it. Supply of electricity is hiring of service and not sale of goods;

Haryana State Electricity Board v. *Dinesh Kumar*, Haryana State Commission, II (1991) CPJ 38.

***Monetary limit of Redressal Agencies* :**

District Forum	:	Where the compensation if any, claimed does not exceed rupees five lakhs.
State Commission	:	Where the compensation, if any, claimed exceeds rupees five lakhs but does not exceed rupees twenty lakhs.
National Commission	:	Where the compensation if any, claimed exceeds rupees twenty lakhs.

Negligence

In *Air India* v. *Suganda Ravi Mashelkar*, 1 (1993) CPJ 63 (SC), the Gulf war disabled the Air India from carrying out the obligations of carriage and delivery of the booked cargo as the consignment could not be traced due to the war. The National Commission ruled in that case that inability to render service due to reasons beyond the control of the person required to render it cannot be said to be deficiency in service – one could add much less, negligence – as it falls within the well known exception, "*Force Merjura*".

In *Consumer Unity and Trust Society, Jaipur* v. *The Chairman and Managing Director, Bank of Baroda, Calcutta*, 1 (1995) CPJ 23 damages were claimed on behalf of the depositors for failure of the Bank to provide service to them during strike of their employees. The Supreme Court in that case observed that the provisions of section 14(1)(d) are attracted if the person from whom damages are claimed is found to have acted negligently and such negligence must result in some loss to the person claiming damages. In other words, loss or injury, if any, must flow from negligence. Mere loss or injury without negligence is not contemplated by this section. The bank has not been found to be negligent in discharge of its duties. Therefore, even if any loss or damage was caused to any depositor but it was not caused due to negligence of Bank then no claim of damages under the Act was maintainable.

13 Model Forms Under The Consumer Protection Act

Notice before filing the complaint

It is not mandatory to serve a notice on the other party before filing a complaint. However, it is prudent to serve a notice. For, if the grievance is *ex facie* genuine, the other party may settle the claim out of court. This would save time and expenses of both the parties. Besides, the complainant would ordinarily be entitled to the costs of the action, if a notice is served by him and it is ignored by the other party or is rejected for reasons which are not cogent.

The notice should be sent under Registered Post, A.D.

A copy of the notice should also be sent under Postal Certificate. The reply received from the Electricity Department/Board/Undertaking, if any, should be retained and annexed, along with a copy of the notice, with the complaint.

The complainant may adopt the following format with such modification as may be necessary in the circumstance of his case.

NOTICE

To

The General Manager,

Electricity (Vidyut) Board/Undertaking

....

(here, give the address)

Subject : Electricity Meter No. ...., K.No.

Dear Sir,

I am the subscriber of Electric Connection No..........., K.No............ This meter (here state the grievance/complaint in detail).

I have brought this matter to your notice several times (give reference of earlier letters, if any, and enclose copies), but no action has been taken to redress my grievance. Due to your failure and neglect to take the requisite action, I have suffered loss/injury and unnecessary harassment for which you are liable to compensate.

(give details if possible)

I hereby call upon you to pay to me a compensation of Rs........ for the loss/injury/harassment suffered by me due to your negligence along with interest at the rate of Rs...... per annum within .... days of the receipt of this notice, failing which I shall be constraint to initiate such proceedings, civil and criminal, as advised besides filing a complaint under the Consumer Protection Act, 1986 and you will be responsible for the costs and consequences thereof which you may please note.

Address .... Signature ....

Date :

The complaint

COMPLAINT

Before the Hon'ble District Consumer Disputes Redressal Forum at (mention the place)

Or

Before the Hon'ble State Consumer Disputes Redressal Commission at (mention the place)

Or

Before the Hon'ble National Consumer Disputes Redressal Commission at New Delhi.

In Re : Complaint No. ...... of 200 (May be left blank)

XYZ S/o ...... resident of .... (here give complete address)

Or

Name and address of the firm

if the complaint is to be filed

on this behalf.

Or

Name of the Consumer Association registered under the Companies Act, 1956 or under any other law for the time being in force if the complaint is to be filed on its behalf.

Or

One or more consumers where there are numerous consumers having the same interest.

Complainant

Versus

Electricity (Vidyut) Board/Undertaking/Department

Complaint under section 11/11*/Section 21* of the Consumer Protection Act, 1986.*

Respectfully showeth :

1. In the first paragraph the complainant should introduce himself (*e.g.* the complainant is subscriber to Electricity Connection No. ..... for the last ....years)
2. In this paragraph the complainant should narrate his grievance and explain the deficiency in service rendered by the Electricity Department.
3. In paragraph 3, the complainant should mention what attempts were made by him for having his grievance redressed, *i.e.* personal visits, communications in writing, whether any notice was served, whether he approached any other Agency/Forum or Court, Civil or Criminal, the stage of the proceedings in that court and its result, if any. The reply of the Electricity Department/Undertaking/Board, if any, should also be disclosed here.
4. In this paragraph, the complainant should mention the law which is applicable in this case and which has been violated. In that case a *prima facie* case is made out against the respondents and the Forum/Redressal Agency will have no hesitation in taking cognizance.
5. In this paragraph, the complainant should give details of documents and/or witnesses he would rely upon to substantiate his claim. The documents should be attached as

Annexures and each annexure should be attested as True Copy. A list of these documents should be attached and a list of witnesses should also be filed separately.

6. In this paragraph the complainant should mention the compensation claimed from the opposite party for financial loss/injury suffered by him due to the negligence of the other party. The quantum of compensation claimed should be justified with reasons. The complainant should also pray for removal of deficiency in service (*e.g.* re-connection of electricity if it remained disconnected during the pendency of the proceedings) under the newly inserted clause (e) of section 14(1).
7. In this paragraph the complainant should state that the District Forum/State Commission has jurisdiction to entertain the complaint, the extent of amount involved being Rs......., and the cause of action having accrued at .... (here state the name of the place).
8. Here the complainant should state that the complaint has been filed within the time limit prescribed under section 24A of the Consumer Protection Act.

Or

This complaint, being barred by limitation, is accompanied by an application for condonation of delay for consideration of the Hon'ble District Forum/State Commission/National Commission as provided under section 24A.

Prayer

It is most respectfully prayed that the Hon'ble Forum/Commission may be pleased to order (here give details of relief which the complainant wants the court to grant)

Place : Complainant

Through

Dated : Counsel

Verification

I, the complainant named above, do hereby solemnly affirm and declare that the contents of the above complaint are true to the best of my knowledge and belief and no part thereof is false and that nothing material has been concealed. The Annexures are true copies of the originals.

Verified at ...... this ...... day of .... Two thousand and .....
Enclosures (Annexures I, II, III etc.)

Deponent

[**Note.—** The complainant should file an affidavit in support of the complaint. It need not be on a stamp paper but it should be attested by an Oath Commissioner]

Affidavit in support of the complaint

AFFIDAVIT

Before the Hon'ble ....

In Re : Complaint No. .... of 200...............

In the matter of ....

.... Complainant

Versus

.... Respondent(s)

Affidavit of Shri .... s/o Shri .... aged .... Years, ... Resident of .... (full address).

I, the above named deponent do hereby solemnly affirm and declare as under :-

1. That I am the complainant in the above case and I am thoroughly conversant with the facts and circumstances thereof and am competent to swear this affidavit.
2. That the facts contained in my accompanying complaint, the contents of which is not being repeated herein for brevity, may be read as part of this affidavit and are true and correct to my knowledge.

Verification

I, the above named deponent do hereby solemnly verify that the contents of the above affidavit are true and correct to my knowledge, no part of it is false and nothing material has been concealed therein. Verified this .... day of 200......... at........................

Deponent

Application for condonation of delay

Before the Hon'ble State Consumer Disputes Redressal Commission at .... or Before the Hon'ble National Consumer Disputes Redressal Commission, New Delhi.

Application for condonation of delay in Filing the Appeal/Revision Petition.

In the matter of

Name...

Full address......................

Complainant

Versus

Name ....

Full Address ....

Respondent(s)

Respectfully showeth :

1. Being aggrieved by the order dated .... of the District Forum at ..../State Commission at ....,. the appellant/revision petitioner above named has filed the accompanying appeal/revision before this Hon'ble Commission. The facts contained therein and the grounds urged may kindly be treated as part of this application for condonation of delay.
2. The appellant/revision petitioner submits that the order impugned in the appeal/revision petition is dated..... and a certified copy thereof was received, by the appellant/revision petitioner on ....
3. The appellant/revision petitioner respectfully submits that the last date for filing the appeal/revision petition in this case is........ However, in view of the following grounds there has been a delay of ...... days in filing the appeal/revision petition :–

   Grounds

   1.

   2.
4. The appellant/revision petitioner submits that the delay involved in filing the appeal/revision is not intentional or deliberate and the same, as submitted above, was due to

circumstances beyond the control of the appellant revision petitioner. The appellant/ revision petition has a very good case on merits and the balance of convenience and interest of justice are in favour of the delay condoned.

Prayer

It is, therefore, most respectfully prayed that this Hon'ble Commission may be pleased to condone the delay of .... days involving in filing this appeal/revision petition and consider the same on merits and pass such order as Hon'ble Commission may deem fit to meet the ends of justice.

Appellant/Revision Petitioner

Verification

I, ... S/o............ aged .... years, resident of .... do hereby solemnly declare and state that the facts contained in the above petition are true to the best of my knowledge and belief and no part thereof is false and nothing material has been concealed.

Verified at ....on this .... day of .... 200..

Deponent.

Form of Appeal

APPEAL

Before the Hon'ble State Consumer Disputes Redressal Commission at .... or Before the Hon'ble National Consumer Disputes Redressal Commission, New Delhi.

(Appellate Jurisdiction)

Memorandum of Appeal No................. of ....

In the matter of :

Name ....

Full Address.................................

Appellant (s)

Versus

Name ....

Full Address.................................

Respondent(s)

The humble appeal of the Appellant(s) above named most respectfully showeth :

1. This appeal is directed under section 15*/section 19* of the Consumer Protection Act, 1986 against the order of the District Forum*/State Commission* in application No. .... of .... passed on ...., received by the appellant on ....
2. This appeal is filed within the time limit provided under section 15*/section 19* of the Consumer Protection Act, 1986. This appeal, being barred by limitation, is accompanied by an application for condonation of delay for consideration by the Commission, as per rule............................ of the .... Consumer Protection Rules.
3. Brief facts of the case are stated hereunder (furnish herein the details of the case and the decision of the District Forum*/State Commission*):-
4. The grounds on which appeal is preferred are stated hereunder (the grounds should be numbered consecutively without any arguments or narrative):-
5. The appellant has not preferred any other appeal against the order impugned herein.

Prayer

It is, therefore, respectfully prayed that your Lordship may be graciously pleased to allow the appeal and set aside/modify the order of the District Forum*/State Commission* appealed against.

List of enclosures:

1. Certified copy of the order of the District Forum*/State Commission* appealed against.
2. Affidavit
3. ....
4. ....

Place : ....

Date : ....

Signature ....

(To be signed by the Appellant and Authorised Representative/Advocate).

---

*Delete whichever is not applicable.

Petition under section 27 of the Consumer Protection Act, 1986

BEFORE THE DISTRICT CONSUMER DISPUTES REDRESSAL FORUM

Sub District .... New Delhi

In RE :

Case No......... of 20... Decided on ....

IN THE MATTER OF

Shri ....

(Address)

Decree Holder/Petitioner

Versus

Delhi Vidyut Board

(Address)

Judgement Debtors/Respondent

Petition under section 27 of the Consumer Protection Act, 1988

Respectfully submits :

1. That *vide* order dated .... passed in Case No......... of .... this Hon'ble Forum was pleased to allow the complainant and direct the respondents to pay a compensation of Rs.............. along with an interest @ 18% from the date of the order til the date of payment.
2. That the opposite party filed an appeal against that order and *vide* order dated .... this Hon'ble State Commission, ... passed in Appeal No......... of

.... upheld the said order in toto/or modified to the extent or as follows :

There was a further direction to the Opposite party to comply with the said order within 30 days [if applicable].

3. That the respondents have flagrantly violated the said order dated .... of the Hon'ble State Commission [if applicable] in as much as it has not been complied with the same within the prescribed period of 30 days or even till date.

4. That the respondents have by not complying with the above order committed an offence under section 27 of the Consumer Protection Act, 1986 which is within the cognizance of this Hon'ble Forum.

5. That no previous application under this section has been filed by the complainant.

6. That the complainant petitioner/decree holder reserves the right to proceed against the respondents under the provisions of section 25 of the aforementioned Act for executing the said order/decree, if necessary.

7. That the complainant has not received any notice/stay order from the Hon'ble State/National Commission in this regard (whichever is applicable).

It is therefore, most respectfully prayed that :

(a) the respondents be summoned and tried for an offence under section 27 of the aforementioned Act and be punished accordingly.

(b) Compliance of the order dated .... passed by this Hon'ble Forum and as modified by order dated .... by the Hon'ble State Commission be affected.

(c) Costs of the present proceedings be awarded in favour of the petitioner and against the respondents.

(d) Any other appropriate order be passed in view of the facts and circumstances of the case.

Petitioner

Place :

Dated :

APPENDIX

THE CONSUMER PROTECTION ACT, 1986

INTRODUCTION

The industrial revolution and the development in the international trade and commerce has led to the vast expansion of business and trade, as a result of which a variety of consumer goods have appeared in the market to cater to the needs of the consumers and a host of services have been made available to the consumers like insurance, transport, electricity, housing, entertainment, finance and banking. A well organised sector of manufacturers and traders with better knowledge of markets has come into existence, thereby affecting the relationship between the traders and the consumers making the principle of consumer sovereignty almost inapplicable. The advertisements of goods and services in television, newspapers and magazines influence the demand for the same by the consumers though there may be manufacturing defects or imperfections or shortcomings in the quality, quantity and the purity of the goods or there may be deficiency in the services rendered. In addition, the production of the same item by many firms has led the consumers, who have little time to make a selection, to think before they can purchase the best. For the welfare of the public, the glut of adulterated and sub-standard articles in the market have to be checked. In spite of various provisions providing protection to the consumer and providing for stringent action against adulterated and sub-standard articles in the different enactments like Code of Civil Procedure, 1908, the Indian Contract Act, 1872, the Sale of Goods Act, 1930, the Indian Penal Code, 1860, the Standards of Weights and Measures Act, 1976 and the Motor Vehicles Act, 1988, very little could be achieved in the field of Consumer Protection. Though the Monopolies and Restrictive Trade Practices Act, 1969 and the Prevention of Food Adulteration Act, 1954 have provided relief to the consumers yet it became necessary to protect the consumers from the exploitation and to save them from adulterated and sub-standard goods and services and to safeguard the interests of the consumers. In order to provide for better protection of the interests of the consumer the Consumer Protection Bill, 1986 was introduced in the Lok Sabha on 5th December, 1986.

STATEMENT OF OBJECTS AND REASONS

The Consumer Protection Bill, 1986 seeks to provide for better protection of the interests of consumers and for the purpose, to make provision for the establishment of Consumer councils and other authorities for the settlement of consumer disputes and for matter connected therewith.

2. It seeks, *inter alia*, to promote and protect the rights of consumers such as—

(a) the right to be protected against marketing of goods which are hazardous to life and property;

(b) the right to be informed about the quality, quantity, potency, purity, standard and price of goods to protect the consumer against unfair trade practices;

(c) the right to be assured, wherever possible, access to an authority of goods at competitive prices;

(d) the right to be heard and to be assured that consumers interests will receive due consideration at appropriate forums;

(e) the right to seek redressal against unfair trade practices or unscrupulous exploitation of consumers; and

(f) right to consumer education.

3. These objects are sought to be promoted and protected by the Consumer Protection Council to be established at the Central and State level.

4. To provide speedy and simple redressal to consumer disputes, a quasi-judicial machinery is sought to be set up at the district, State and Central levels. These quasi-judicial bodies will observe the principles of natural justice and have been empowered to give relief of a specific nature and to award, wherever appropriate, compensation to consumers. Penalties for non-compliance of the orders given by the quasi-judicial bodies have also been provided.

5. The Bill seeks to achieve the above objects.

ACT 68 OF 1986

The Consumer Protection Bill, 1986 having been passed by both the Houses of Parliament received the assent of the President on 24th December, 1986. It came on the Statute Book as THE CONSUMER PROTECTION ACT, 1986 (68 of 1986).

LIST OF AMENDING ACTS

1. The Consumer Protection (Amendment) Act, 1991 (34 of 1991).
2. The Consumer Protection (Amendment) Act, 1993 (50 of 1993).

THE CONSUMER PROTECTION ACT, 1986

(68 of 1986)

[*24th December, 1986*]

An Act to provide for better protection of the interests of consumers and for that purpose to make provision for the establishment of consumer councils and other authorities for the settlement of consumers' disputes and for matters connected therewith.

BE it enacted by Parliament in the Thirty-seventh Year of the Republic of India as follows:—

CHAPTER I

PRELIMINARY

1. Short title, extent, commencement and application.—(1) This Act may be called the Consumer Protection Act, 1986.

(2) It extends to the whole of India except the State of Jammu and Kashmir.

(3) It shall come into force on such date[1] as the Central Government may, by notification, appoint and different dates may be appointed for different States and for different provisions of this Act.

(4) Save as otherwise expressly provided by the Central Government by notification, this Act shall apply to all goods and services.

2. Definitions.—(1) In this Act, unless the context otherwise requires,—

[2][(a) "appropriate laboratory" means a laboratory or organisation—

(i) recognised by the Central Government;

---

1. The provisions of Chapters I, II and IV of this Act have come into force in the whole of India except the State of Jammu and Kashmir on 15-4-1987: *vide* Notification No. S.O. 390 (E), dated 15th April, 1987, published in the Gazette of India, 1987, Extra., Pt. II, Sec. 3 (ii).

The provisions of Chapter III of this Act have come into force in the whole of India except the State of Jammu and Kashmir on 1-7-1987: *vide* Notification, No. S.O. 568(E), dated 10th June, 1987, published in the Gazette of India, 1987, Extra., Pt. II, Sec. 3(ii).

2. Subs. by Act 50 of 1993, sec. 2, for clause (a) (w.r.e.f. 18-6-1993).

(ii) recognised by a State Government, subject to such guidelines as may be prescribed by the Central Government in this behalf; or

(iii) any such laboratory or organisation established by or under any law for the time being in force, which is maintained, financed or aided by the Central Government or a State Government for carrying out analysis or test of any goods with a view to determining whether such goods suffer from any defect;]

[1][(aa) "branch office" means—

(i) any establishment described as a branch by the opposite party; or

(ii) any establishment carrying on either the same or substantially the same activity as that carried on by the head office of the establishment;]

(b) "complainant" means—

(i) a consumer; or

(ii) any voluntary consumer association registered under the Companies Act, 1956 (1 of 1956) or under any other law for the time being in force; or

(iii) the Central Government or any State Government, who or which makes a complaint;

[1][(iv) one or more consumers, where there are numerous consumers having the same interest;]

who or which makes a complaint;

(c) "complaint" means any allegation in writing made by a complainant that—

[2][(i) an unfair trade practice or a restrictive trade practice has been adopted by any trader;]

(ii) [3][the goods bought by him or agreed to be bought by him] suffer from one or more defects;

(iii) [4][the services hired or availed of or agreed to be hired or availed of by him] suffer from deficiency in any respect;

---

1. Ins. by Act 50 of 1993, sec. 2 (w.r.e.f. 18-6-1993).
2. Subs. by Act 50 of 1993, sec. 2, for sub-clause (i) (w.r.e.f. 18-6-1993).
3. Subs. by Act 50 of 1993, sec. 2, for "the goods mentioned in the complaint" (w.r.e.f. 18-6-1993).
4. Subs. by Act 50 of 1993, sec. 2, for "the services mentioned in the complaint" (w.r.e.f. 18-6-1993).

(iv) a trader has charged for the goods mentioned in the complaint a price in excess of the price fixed by or under any law for the time being in force or displayed on the goods or any package containing such goods;

[1][(v) goods which will be hazardous to life and safety when used, are being offered for sale to the public in contravention of the provisions of any law for the time being in force requiring traders to display information in regard to the contents, manner and effect of use of such goods,]

with a view to obtaining any relief provided by or under this Act;

(d) "consumer" means any person who—

(i) buys any goods for a consideration which has been paid or promised or partly paid and partly promised, or under any system of deferred payment and includes any user of such goods other than the person who buys such goods for consideration paid or promised or partly paid or partly promised, or under any system of deferred payment, when such use is made with the approval of such person, but does not include a person who obtains such goods for resale or for any commercial purpose; or

(ii) [2][hires or avails of] any services for a consideration which has been paid or promised or partly paid and partly promised, or under any system of deferred payment and includes any beneficiary of such services other than the person who [1][hires or avails of] the services for consideration paid or promised, or partly paid and partly promised, or under any system of deferred payment, when such services are availed of with the approval of the first mentioned person.

[3][*Explanation.*—For the purposes of sub-clause (i), "commercial purpose" does not include use by a consumer of goods bought and used by him exclusively for the purpose of earning his livelihood, by means of self-employment;]

(e) "consumer dispute" means a dispute where the person against whom a complaint has been made, denies or disputes the allegations contained in the complaint;

1. Ins. by Act 50 of 1993, sec. 2 (w.r.e.f. 18-6-1993).
2. Subs. by Act 50 of 1993, sec. 2, for "hires" (w.r.e.f. 18-6-1993).
3. Ins. by Act 50 of 1993, sec. 2 (w.r.e.f. 18-6-1993).

(f) "defect" means any fault, imperfection or shortcoming in the quality, quantity, potency, purity or standard which is required to be maintained by or under any law for the time being in force or [1][under any contract, express or implied or] as is claimed by the trader in any manner whatsoever in relation to any goods;

(g) "deficiency" means any fault, imperfection, shortcoming or inadequacy in the quality, nature and manner of performance which is required to be maintained by or under any law for the time being in force or has been undertaken to be performed by a person in pursuance of a contract or otherwise in relation to any service;

(h) "District Forum" means a Consumer Disputes Redressal Forum established under clause (a) of section 9;

(i) "goods" means goods as defined in the Sale of Goods Act, 1930 (3 of 1930);

(j) "manufacturer" means a person who—

(i) makes or manufactures any goods or parts thereof; or

(ii) does not make or manufacture any goods but assembles parts thereof made or manufactured by others and claims the end product to be goods manufactured by himself; or

(iii) puts or causes to be put his own mark on any goods made or manufactured by any other manufacturer and claims such goods to be goods made or manufactured by himself.

Explanation.—Where a manufacturer despatches any goods or part thereof to any branch office maintained by him, such branch office shall not be deemed to be the manufacturer even though the parts so despatched to it are assembled at such branch office and are sold or distributed from such branch office;

[1][(jj) "member" includes the President and a member of the National Commission or a State Commission or a District Forum, as the case may be;]

(k) "National Commission" means the National Consumer Disputes Redressal Commission established under clause (c) of section 9;

(l) "notification" means a notification published in the Official Gazette;

1. Ins. by Act 50 of 1993, sec. 2 (w.r.e.f. 18-6-1993).

(m) "person" includes,—

(i) a firm whether registered or not;

(ii) a Hindu undivided family;

(iii) a co-operative society;

(iv) every other association of persons whether registered under the Societies Registration Act, 1860 (21 of 1860) or not;

(n) "prescribed" means prescribed by rules made by the State Government, or as the case may be, by the Central Government under this Act;

[1][(nn) "restrictive trade practice" means any trade practice which requires a consumer to buy, hire or avail of any goods or, as the case may be, services as a condition precedent for buying, hiring or availing of other goods or services;]

(o) "service" means service of any description which is made available to potential users and includes the provision of facilities in connection with banking, financing insurance, transport, processing, supply of electrical or other energy, board or lodging or both, [1][housing construction,] entertainment, amusement or the purveying of news or other information, but does not include the rendering of any service free of charge or under a contract of personal service;

(p) "State Commission" means a Consumer Disputes Redressal Commission established in a State under clause (b) of section 9;

(q) "trader" in relation to any goods means a person who sells or distributes any goods for sale and includes the manufacturer thereof, and where such goods are sold or distributed in package form, includes the packer thereof;

[2][(r) "unfair trade practice" means a trade practice which, for the purpose of promoting the sale, use or supply of any goods or for the provision of any service, adopts any unfair method or unfair or deceptive practice including any of the following practices, namely:—

(1) the practice of making any statement, whether orally or in writing or by visible representation which,—

---

1. Ins. by Act 50 of 1993, sec. 2 (w.r.e.f. 18-6-1993).
2. Subs. by Act 50 of 1993, sec. 2, for clause (r) (w.r.e.f. 18-6-1993).

(i) falsely represents that the goods are of a particular standard, quality, quantity, grade, composition, style or model;

(ii) falsely represents that the services are of a particular standard, quality or grade;

(iii) falsely represents any re-built, second-hand, renovated, reconditioned or old goods as new goods;

(iv) represents that the goods or services have sponsorship, approval, performance, characteristics, accessories, uses or benefits which such goods or services do not have;

(v) represents that the seller or the supplier has a sponsorship or approval or affiliation which such seller or supplier does not have;

(vi) makes a false or misleading representation concerning the need for, or the usefulness of, any goods or services;

(vii) gives to the public any warranty or guarantee of the performance, efficacy or length of life of a product or of any goods that is not based on an adequate or proper test thereof:

Provided that where a defence is raised to the effect that such warranty or guarantee is based on adequate or proper test, the burden of proof of such defence shall lie on the person raising such defence;

(viii) makes to the public a representation in a form that purports to be—

(i) a warranty or guarantee of a product or of any goods or services; or

(ii) a promise to replace, maintain or repair an article or any part thereof or to repeat or continue a service until it has achieved a specified result,

if such purported warranty or guarantee or promise is materially misleading or if there is no reasonable prospect that such warranty, guarantee or promise will be carried out ;

(ix) materially misleads the public concerning the price at which a product or like products or goods or services, have been or are, ordinarily sold or provided, and, for this purpose, a representation as to price shall be deemed to refer to the price at which the product or goods or services has or have been sold by sellers or provided by suppliers generally in the relevant market unless it is clearly specified to be the price at which the product has been sold or services have been provided by the person by whom or on whose behalf the representation is made;

(x) gives false or misleading facts disparaging the goods, services or trade of another person.

Explanation.—For the purposes of clause (1), a statement that is—

(a) expressed on an article offered or displayed for sale, or on its wrapper or container; or

(b) expressed on anything attached to, inserted in, or accompanying, an article offered or displayed for sale, or on anything on which the article is mounted for display or sale; or

(c) contained in or on anything that is sold, sent, delivered, transmitted or in any other manner whatsoever made available to a member of the public,

shall be deemed to be a statement made to the public by, and only by, the person who had caused the statement to be so expressed, made or contained;

(2) permits the publication of any advertisement whether in any newspaper or otherwise, for the sale or supply at a bargain price, of goods or services that are not intended to be offered for sale or supply at the bargain price, or for a period that is, and in quantities that are, reasonable, having regard to the nature of the market in which the business is carried on, the nature and size of business, and the nature of the advertisement.

Explanation.—For the purpose of clause (2), "bargaining price" means—

(a) a price that is stated in any advertisement to be a bargain price, by reference to an ordinary price or otherwise, or

(b) a price that a person who reads, hears or sees the advertisement, would reasonably understand to be a bargain price having regard to the prices at which the product advertised or like products are ordinarily sold;

(3) permits—

(a) the offering of gifts, prizes or other items with the intention of not providing them as offered or creating impression that something is being given or offered free of charge when it is fully or partly covered by the amount charged in the transaction as a whole;

(b) the conduct of any contest, lottery, game of chance or skill, for the purpose of promoting, directly or indirectly, the sale, use or supply of any product or any business interest;

(4) permits the sale or supply of goods intended to be used, or are of a kind likely to be used, by consumers, knowing or having reason to believe that the goods do not comply with the standards prescribed by competent authority relating to performance, composition, contents, design, constructions, finishing or packaging as are necessary to prevent or reduce the risk of injury to the person using the goods;

(5) permits the hoarding or destruction of goods, or refuses to sell the goods or to make them available for sale or to provide any service, if such hoarding or destruction or refusal raises or tends to raise or is intended to raise, the cost of those or other similar goods or services.]

(2) Any reference in this Act to any other Act or provision thereof which is not in force in any area to which this Act applies shall be construed to have a reference to the corresponding Act or provision thereof in force in such area.

3. Act not in derogation of any other law.—The provisions of this Act shall be in addition to and not in derogation of the provisions of any other law for the time being in force.

CHAPTER II

CONSUMER PROTECTION COUNCILS

4. The Central Consumer Protection Council.—(1) The Central Government may, by notification, establish with effect from such date as it may specify in such notification, a Council to be known as the Central Consumer Protection Council (hereinafter referred to as the Central Council).

(2) The Central Council shall consist of the following members, namely:—

(a) the Minister in charge of the [1][consumer affairs] in the Central Government, who shall be its Chairman, and

(b) such number of other official or non-official members representing such interests as may be prescribed.

5. Procedure for meetings of the Central Council.—(1) The Central Council shall meet as and when necessary, but [2][at least one meeting] of the Council shall be held every year.

(2) The Central Council shall meet at such time and place as the Chairman may think fit and shall observe such procedure in regard to the transaction of its business as may be prescribed.

6. Objects of the Central Council.—The objects of the Central Council shall be to promote and protect the rights of the consumers such as,—

(a) the right to be protected against the marketing of goods [3][and services] which are hazardous to life and property;

(b) the right to be informed about the quality, quantity, potency, purity, standard and price of goods [3][or services, as the case may be] so as to protect the consumer against unfair trade practices;

(c) the right to be assured, wherever possible, access to a variety of goods [3][and services] at competitive prices;

(d) the right to be heard and to be assured that consumer's interests will receive due consideration at appropriate fora;

(e) the right to seek redressal against unfair trade practices [3][or restrictive trade practices] or unscrupulous exploitation of consumers; and

(f) the right to consumer education.

7. The State Consumer Protection Councils.—(1) The State Government may, by notification, establish with effect from such date as it may specify in such notification, a Council to be known as the Consumer Protection Council for... (hereinafter referred to as the State Council).

[4][(2) The State Council shall consist of the following members, namely:—

---

1. Subs. by Act 50 of 1993, sec. 3, for "the Department of Food and Civil Supplies" (w.r.e.f. 18-6-1993).
2. Subs. by Act 50 of 1993, sec. 4, for "not less than three meetings" (w.r.e.f. 18-6-1993).
3. Ins. by Act 50 of 1993, sec. 5 (w.r.e.f. 18-6-1993).
4. Subs. by Act 50 of 1993, sec. 6, for sub-section (2) (w.r.e.f. 18-6-1993).

(a) the Minister incharge of consumer affairs in the State Government who shall be its Chairman;

(b) such number of other official or non-official members representing such interests as may be prescribed by the State Government.

(3) The State Council shall meet as and when necessary but not less than two meetings shall be held every year.

(4) The State Council shall meet at such time and place as the Chairman may think fit and shall observe such procedure in regard to the transaction of its business as may be prescribed by the State Government.]

8. Objects of the State Council.—The objects of every State Council shall be to promote and protect within the State the rights of the consumers laid down in clauses (a) to (f) of section 6.

CHAPTER III

CONSUMER DISPUTES REDRESSAL AGENCIES

9. Establishment of Consumer Disputes Redressal Agencies.—There shall be established for the purposes of this Act, the following agencies, namely:—

(a) a Consumer Disputes Redressal Forum to be known as the "District Forum" established by the State Government [1][* * *] in each district of the State by notification:

[2][Provided that the State Government may, if it deems fit, establish more than one District Forum in a district;]

(b) a Consumer Disputes Redressal Commission to be known as the "State Commission" established by the State Government [1][* * *] in the State by notification; and

(c) a National Consumer Disputes Redressal Commission established by the Central Government by notification.

10. Composition of the District Forum.—[3][(1) Each District Forum shall consist of,—

(a) a person who is, or has been, or is qualified to be a District Judge, who shall be its President;

---

1. The words "with the prior approval of the Central Government" omitted by Act 50 of 1993, sec. 7 (w.r.e.f. 18-6-1993).

2. Ins. by Act 50 of 1993, sec. 7 (w.r.e.f. 18-6-1993).

3. Subs. by Act 50 of 1993, sec. 8, for sub-section (1) (w.r.e.f. 18-6-1993).

(b) two other members, who shall be persons of ability, integrity and standing, and have adequate knowledge or experience of, or have shown capacity in dealing with, problems relating to economics, law, commerce, accountancy, industry, public affairs or administration, one of whom shall be a woman.]

[1][(1A) Every appointment under sub-section (1) shall be made by the State Government on the recommendation of a selection committee consisting of the following, namely:—

(i) the President of the State Commission —Chairman.

(ii) Secretary, Law Department of the State —Member.

(iii) Secretary, incharge of the Department dealing with consumer affairs in the State —Member.]

(2) Every member of the District Forum shall hold office for a term of five years or up to the age of 65 years, whichever is earlier, and shall not be eligible for re-appointment:

Provided that a member may resign his office in writing under his hand-addressed to the State Government and on such resignation being accepted, his office shall become vacant and may be filled by the appointment of a person possessing any of the qualifications mentioned in sub-section (1) in relation to the category of the member who has resigned.

(3) The salary or honorarium and other allowances payable to, and the other terms and conditions of service of the members of the District Forum shall be such as may be prescribed by the State Government.

11. Jurisdiction of the District Forum.—(1) Subject to the other provisions of this Act, the District Forum shall have jurisdiction to entertain complaints where the value of the goods or services and the compensation, if any, claimed [2][does not exceed rupees five lakhs].

(2) A complaint shall be instituted in a District Forum within the local limits of whose jurisdiction,—

(a) the opposite party or each of the opposite parties, where there are more than one, at the time of the institution of the complaint, actually and voluntarily resides or [3][carries on

1. Ins. by Act 50 of 1993, sec. 8 (w.r.e.f. 18-6-1993).
2. Subs. by Act 50 of 1993, sec. 9, for "is less than rupees one lakh" (w.r.e.f. 18-6-1993).
3. Subs. by Act 50 of 1993, sec. 9, for "carries on business or" (w.r.e.f. 18-6-1993).

business or has a branch office or] personally works for gain; or

(b) any of the opposite parties, where there are more than one, at the time of the institution of the complaint, actually and voluntarily resides, or [1][carries on business or has a branch office], or personally works for gain, provided that in such case either the permission of the District Forum is given, or the opposite parties who do not reside, or [2][carry on business or have a branch office], or personally work for gain, as the case may be, acquiesce in such institution; or

(c) the cause of action, wholly or in part, arises.

[3][**12. Manner in which complaint shall be made.**—A complaint in relation to any goods sold or delivered or agreed to be sold or delivered or any service provided or agreed to be provided may be filed with a District Forum by—

(a) the consumer to whom such goods are sold or delivered or agreed to be sold or delivered or such service provided or agreed to be provided;

(b) any recognised consumer association whether the consumer to whom the goods sold or delivered or agreed to be sold or delivered or service provided or agreed to be provided is a member of such association or not;

(c) one or more consumers, where there are numerous consumers having the same interest, with the permission of the District Forum, on behalf of, or for the benefit of, all consumers so interested; or

(d) the Central or the State Government.

Explanation.—For the purpose of this section, "recognised consumer association" means any voluntary consumer association registered under the Companies Act, 1956 (1 of 1956) or any other law for the time being in force.]

13. Procedure on receipt of complaint.—(1) The District Forum shall, on receipt of a complaint, if it relates to any goods,—

(a) refer a copy of the complaint to the opposite party mentioned in the complaint directing him to give his version

1. Subs. by Act 50 of 1993, sec. 9, for "carries on business" (w.r.e.f. 18-6-1993).
2. Subs. by Act 50 of 1993, sec. 9, for "carry on business" (w.r.e.f. 18-6-1993).
3. Subs. by Act 50 of 1993, sec. 10, for section 12 (w.r.e.f. 18-6-1993).

of the case within a period of thirty days or such extended period not exceeding fifteen days as may be granted by the District Forum;

(b) where the opposite party on receipt of a complaint referred to him under clause (a) denies or disputes the allegations contained in the complaint, or omits or fails to take any action to represent his case within the time given by the District Forum, the District Forum shall proceed to settle the consumer dispute in the manner specified in clauses (c) to (g);

(c) where the complaint alleges a defect in the goods which cannot be determined without proper analysis or test of the goods, the District Forum shall obtain a sample of the goods from the complainant, seal it and authenticate it in the manner prescribed and refer the sample so sealed to the appropriate laboratory along with a direction that such laboratory make an analysis or test, whichever may be necessary, with a view to finding out whether such goods suffer from any defect alleged in the complaint or from any other defect and to report its findings thereon to the District Forum within a period of forty-five days of the receipt of the reference or within such extended period as may be granted by the District Forum;

(d) before any sample of the goods is referred to any appropriate laboratory under clause (c), the District Forum may require the complainant to deposit to the credit of the Forum such fees as may be specified, for payment to the appropriate laboratory for carrying out the necessary analysis or test in relation to the goods in question;

(e) the District Forum shall remit the amount deposited to its credit under clause (d) to the appropriate laboratory to enable it to carry out the analysis or test mentioned in clause (c) and on receipt of the report from the appropriate laboratory, the District Forum shall forward a copy of the report along with such remarks as the District Forum may feel appropriate to the opposite party;

(f) if any of the parties disputes the correctness of the findings of the appropriate laboratory, or disputes the correctness of the methods of analysis or test adopted by the appropriate laboratory, the District Forum shall require the opposite party or the complainant to submit in writing his objections in regard to the report made by the appropriate laboratory;

(g) the District Forum shall thereafter give a reasonable opportunity to the complainant as well as the opposite party of being heard as to the correctness or otherwise of the report made by the appropriate laboratory and also as to the objection made in relation thereto under clause (f) and issue an appropriate order under section 14.

(2) The District Forum shall, if the complaint received by it under section 12 relates to goods in respect of which the procedure specified in sub-section (1) cannot be followed, or if the complaint relates to any services,—

(a) refer a copy of such complaint to the opposite party directing him to give his version of the case within a period of thirty days or such extended period not exceeding fifteen days as may be granted by the District Forum;

(b) where the opposite party, on receipt of a copy of the complaint, referred to him under clause (a) denies or disputes the allegations contained in the complaint, or omits or fails to take any action to represent his case within the time given by the District Forum, the District Forum shall proceed to settle the consumer dispute,—

(i) on the basis of evidence brought to its notice by the complainant and the opposite party, where the opposite party denies or disputes the allegations contained in the complaint, or

(ii) on the basis of evidence brought to its notice by the complainant where the opposite party omits or fails to take any action to represent his case within the time given by the Forum.

(3) No proceedings complying with the procedure laid down in sub-sections (1) and (2) shall be called in question in any court on the ground that the principles of natural justice have not been complied with.

(4) For the purposes of this section, the District Forum shall have the same powers as are vested in a civil court under Code of Civil Procedure, 1908 (5 of 1908) while trying a suit in respect of the following matters, namely:—

(i) the summoning and enforcing the attendance of any defendant or witness and examining the witness on oath,

(ii) the discovery and production of any document or other material object producible as evidence,

(iii) the reception of evidence on affidavits,

(iv) the requisitioning of the report of the concerned analysis or test from the appropriate laboratory or from any other relevant source,

(v) issuing of any commission for the examination of any witness, and

(vi) any other matter which may be prescribed.

(5) Every proceeding before the District Forum shall be deemed to be a judicial proceeding within the meaning of sections 193 and 228 of the Indian Penal Code (45 of 1860), and the District Forum shall be deemed to be a civil court for the purposes of section 195, and Chapter XXVI of the Code of Criminal Procedure, 1973 (2 of 1974).

[1][(6) Where the complainant is a consumer referred to in sub-clause (iv) of clause (b) of sub-section (1) of section 2, the provisions of rule 8 of Order I of the First Schedule to the Code of Civil Procedure, 1908 (5 of 1908) shall apply subject to the modification that every reference therein to a suit or decree shall be construed as a reference to a complaint or the order of the District Forum thereon.]

14. Finding of the District Forum.—(1) If, after the proceeding conducted under section 13, the District Forum is satisfied that the goods complained against suffer from any of the defects specified in the complaint or that any of the allegations contained in the complaint about the services are proved, it shall issue an order to the opposite party directing him to [2][do] one or more of the following things, namely:—

(a) to remove the defect pointed out by the appropriate laboratory from the goods in question;

(b) to replace the goods with new goods of similar description which shall be free from any defect;

(c) to return to the complainant the price, or, as the case may be, the charges paid by the complainant;

(d) to pay such amount as may be awarded by it as compensation to the consumer for any loss or injury suffered by the consumer due to the negligence of the opposite party;

[3][(e) to remove the defects or deficiencies in the services in question;

---

1. Ins. by Act 50 of 1993, sec. 11 (w.r.e.f. 18-6-1993).
2. Subs. by Act 50 of 1993, sec. 12, for "take" (w.r.e.f. 18-6-1993).
3. Ins. by Act 50 of 1993, sec. 12 (w.r.e.f. 18-6-1993).

(f) to discontinue the unfair trade practice or the restrictive trade practice or not to repeat them;

(g) not to offer the hazardous goods for sale;

(h) to withdraw the hazardous goods from being offered for sale;

(i) to provide for adequate costs to parties.]

[1][(2) Every proceeding referred to in sub-section (1) shall be conducted by the President of the District Forum and at least one member thereof sitting together:

Provided that where the member, for any reason, is unable to conduct the proceeding till it is completed, the President and the other member shall conduct such proceeding *de novo*.

(2A) Every order made by the District Forum under sub-section (1) shall be signed by its President and the member or members who conducted the proceeding:

Provided that where the proceeding is conducted by the President and one member and they differ on any point or points, they shall state the point or points on which they differ and refer the same to the other member for hearing on such point or points and the opinion of the majority shall be the order of the District Forum.]

(3) Subject to the foregoing provisions, the procedure relating to the conduct of the meetings of the District Forum, its sittings and other matters shall be such as may be prescribed by the State Government.

15. Appeal.—Any person aggrieved by an order made by the District Forum may prefer an appeal against such order to the State Commission within a period of thirty days from the date of the order, in such form and manner as may be prescribed:

Provided that the State Commission may entertain an appeal after the expiry of the said period of thirty days if it is satisfied that there was sufficient cause for not finding it within that period.

16. Composition of the State Commission.—(1) Each State Commission shall consist of—

(a) a person who is or has been a Judge of a High Court, appointed by the State Government, who shall be its President:

[2][Provided that no appointment under this clause shall be made except after consultation with the Chief Justice of the High Court;]

---

1. Subs. by Act 34 of 1991, sec. 2, for sub-section (2) (w.r.e.f. 15-6-1991).
2. Ins. by Act 50 of 1993, sec. 13 (w.r.e.f. 18-6-1993).

(b) two other members, who shall be persons of ability, integrity and standing and have adequate knowledge or experience of, or have shown capacity in dealing with, problems relating to economics, law, commerce, accountancy, industry, public affairs or administration, one of whom shall be a woman:

[1][Provided that every appointment made under this clause shall be made by the State Government on the recommendation of a selection committee consisting of the following, namely:—

(i) President of the State Commission —Chairman.

(ii) Secretary of the Law Department of the State —Member.

(iii) Secretary, incharge of Department dealing with consumer affairs in the State —Member.]

(2) The salary or honorarium and other allowances payable to, and the other terms and conditions of service [2][* * *] of, the members of the State Commission shall be such as may be prescribed by the State Government.

[3][(3) Every member of the State Commission shall hold office for a term of five years or up to the age of sixty-seven years, whichever is earlier and shall not be eligible for re-appointment.

(4) Notwithstanding anything contained in sub-section (3), a person appointed as a President or as a member before the commencement of the Consumer Protection (Amendment) Act, 1993 (50 of 1993), shall continue to hold such office as President or member, as the case may be, till the completion of his term.]

17. Jurisdiction of the State Commission.—Subject to the other provisions of this Act, the State Commission shall have jurisdiction—

(a) to entertain—

(i) complaints where the value of the goods or services and compensation, if any, claimed exceeds rupees [4][five lakhs but does not exceed rupees twenty lakhs]; and

(ii) appeals against the orders of any District Forum within the State; and

1. Subs. by Act 50 of 1993, sec. 13, for the proviso (w.r.e.f. 18-6-1993).
2. The words "(including tenure of office)" omitted by Act 50 of 1993, sec. 13 (w.r.e.f. 18-6-1993).
3. Ins. by Act 50 of 1993, sec. 13 (w.r.e.f. 18-6-1993).
4. Subs. by Act 50 of 1993, sec. 14, for "one lakh but does not exceed rupees ten lakhs" (w.r.e.f. 18-6-1993).

(b) to call for the records and pass appropriate orders in any consumer dispute which is pending before or has been decided by any District Forum within the State, where it appears to the State Commission that such District Forum has exercised a jurisdiction not vested in it by law, or has failed to exercise a jurisdiction so vested or has acted in exercise of its jurisdiction illegally or with material irregularity.

18. Procedure applicable to State Commissions.—[1][The provisions of sections 12, 13 and 14 and the rules made thereunder] for the disposal of complaints by the District Forum shall, with such modifications as may be necessary, be applicable to the disposal of disputes by the State Commission.

[2]**[18A. Vacancy in the office of the President.**—When the office of the President of the District Forum or of the State Commission, as the case may be, is vacant or when any such President is, by reason of absence or otherwise, unable to perform the duties of his office, the duties of the office shall be performed by such person, who is qualified to be appointed as President of the District Forum or, as the case may be, of the State Commission, as the State Government may appoint for the purpose.]

19. Appeals.—Any person aggrieved by an order made by the State Commission in exercise of its powers conferred by sub-clause (i) of clause (a) of section 17 may prefer an appeal against such order to the National Commission within a period of thirty days from the date of the order in such form and manner as may be prescribed:

Provided that the National Commission may entertain an appeal after the expiry of the said period of thirty days if it is satisfied that there was sufficient cause for not filing it within that period.

20. Composition of the National Commission.—(1) The National Commission shall consist of—

(a) a person who is or has been a Judge of the Supreme Court, to be appointed by the Central Government, who shall be its President;

[3][Provided that no appointment under this clause shall be made except after consultation with the Chief Justice of India;]

---

1. Subs. by Act 50 of 1993, sec. 15, for certain words (w.r.e.f. 18-6-1993).
2. Ins. by Act 34 of 1991, sec. 3 (w.r.e.f. 15-6-1991).
3. Ins. by Act 50 of 1993, sec. 16 (w.r.e.f. 18-6-1993).

(b) four other members who shall be persons of ability, integrity and standing and have adequate knowledge or experience of, or have shown capacity in dealing with, problems relating to economics, law, commerce, accountancy, industry, public affairs or administration, one of whom shall be a woman:

[1][Provided that every appointment under this clause shall be made by the Central Government on the recommendation of a selection committee consisting of the following, namely:—

(a) a person who is a Judge of the Supreme Court, to be nominated by the Chief Justice of India —Chairman.

(b) the Secretary in the Department of Legal Affairs in the Government of India —Member.

(c) Secretary of the Department dealing with with consumer affairs in the Government of India —Member.]

(2) The salary or honorarium and other allowances payable to and the other terms and conditions of service [2][* * *] of the members of the National Commission shall be such as may be prescribed by the Central Government.

[3][(3) Every member of the National Commission shall hold office for a term of five years or up to the age of seventy years, whichever is earlier and shall not be eligible for re-appointment.

(4) Notwithstanding anything contained in sub-section (3), a person appointed as a President or as a member before the commencement of the Consumer Protection (Amendment) Act, 1993, shall continue to hold such office as President or member, as the case may be, till the completion of his term.]

21. Jurisdiction of the National Commission.—Subject to the other provisions of this Act, the National Commission shall have jurisdiction—

(a) to entertain—

(i) complaints where the value of the goods or services and compensation, if any, claimed exceeds rupees [4][twenty lakhs]; and

---

1. Ins. by Act 50 of 1993, sec. 16 (w.r.e.f. 18-6-1993).
2. The words "(including tenure of office)" omitted by Act 50 of 1993, sec. 16 (w.r.e.f. 18-6-1993).
3. Ins. by Act 50 of 1993, sec. 16 (w.r.e.f. 18-6-1993).
4. Subs. by Act 50 of 1993, sec. 17, for "ten lakhs" (w.r.e.f. 18-6-1993).

(ii) appeals against the orders of any State Commission; and

(b) to call for the records and pass appropriate orders in any consumer dispute which is pending before or has been decided by any State Commission where it appears to the National Commission that such State Commission has exercised a jurisdiction not vested in it by law, or has failed to exercise a jurisdiction so vested, or has acted in the exercise of its jurisdiction illegally or with material irregularity.

[1][**22. Power of and procedure applicable to the National Commission.**—The National Commission shall, in the disposal of any complaints or any proceedings before it, have—

(a) the powers of a civil court as specified in sub-sections (4), (5) and (6) of section 13;

(b) the power to issue an order to the opposite party directing him to do any one or more of the things referred to in clauses (a) to (i) of sub-section (1) of section 14,

and follow such procedure as may be prescribed by the Central Government.]

23. Appeal.—Any person, aggrieved by an order made by the National Commission in exercise of its powers conferred by sub-clause (i) of clause (a) of section 21, may prefer an appeal against such order to the Supreme Court within a period of thirty days from the date of the order:

Provided that the Supreme Court may entertain an appeal after the expiry of the said period of thirty days if it is satisfied that there was sufficient cause for not filing it within that period.

24. Finality of orders.—Every order of a District Forum, the State Commission or the National Commission shall, if no appeal has been preferred against such order under the provisions of this Act, be final.

[2][**24A. Limitation period.**—(1) The District Forum, the State Commission or the National Commission shall not admit a complaint unless it is filed within two years from the date on which the cause of action has arisen.

(2) Notwithstanding anything contained in sub-section (1), a complaint may be entertained after the period specified in sub-section

1. Subs. by Act 50 of 1993, sec. 18, for section 22 (w.r.e.f. 18-6-1993).
2. Ins. by Act 50 of 1993, sec. 19 (w.r.e.f. 18-6-1993).

(1), if the complainant satisfies the District Forum, the State Commission or the National Commission, as the case may be, that he had sufficient cause for not filing the complaint within such period:

Provided that no such complaint shall be entertained unless the National Commission, the State Commission or the District Forum, as the case may be, records its reasons for condoning such delay.

24B. Administrative control.—(1) The National Commission shall have administrative control over all the State Commissions in the following matters, namely:—

(i) calling for periodical return regarding the institution, disposal, pendency of cases;

(ii) issuance of instructions regarding adoption of uniform procedure in the hearing of matters, prior service of copies of documents produced by one party to the opposite parties, furnishing of English translation of judgments written in any language, speedy grant of copies of documents;

(iii) generally overseeing the functioning of the State Commissions or the District Fora to ensure that the objects and purposes of the Act are best served without in any way interfering with their *quasi-judicial* freedom.

(2) The State Commission shall have administrative control over all the District Fora within its jurisdiction in all matters referred to in sub-section (1).]

25. Enforcement of orders by the Forum, the State Commission or the National Commission.—Every order made by the District Forum, the State Commission or the National Commission may be enforced by the District Forum, the State Commission or the National Commission, as the case may be, in the same manner as if it were decree or order made by a court in a suit pending therein and it shall be lawful for the District Forum, the State Commission or the National Commission to send, in the event of its inability to execute it, such order to the court within the local limits of whose jurisdiction,—

(a) in the case of an order against a company, the registered office of the company is situated, or

(b) in the case of an order against any other person, the place where the person concerned voluntarily resides or carries on business or personally works for gain, is situated,

and thereupon, the court to which the order is so sent, shall execute the order as if it were a decree or order sent to it for execution.

[1][**26. Dismissal of frivolous or vexatious complaints.**—Where a complaint instituted before the District Forum, the State Commission or, as the case may be, the National Commission is found to be frivolous or vexatious, it shall, for reasons to be recorded in writing, dismiss the complaint and make an order that the complainant shall pay to the opposite party such cost, not exceeding ten thousand rupees, as may be specified in the order.]

27. Penalties.—Where a trader or a person against whom a complaint is made [2][or the complainant] fails or omits to comply with any order made by the District Forum, the State Commission or the National Commission, as the case may be, such trader or person [2][or complainant] shall be punishable with imprisonment for a term which shall not be less than one month but which may extend to three years, or with fine which shall not be less than two thousands rupees but which may extend to ten thousand rupees, or with both:

Provided that the District Forum, the State Commission or the National Commission, as the case may be, may, if it is satisfied that the circumstances of any case so require, impose a sentence of imprisonment or fine, or both, for a term lesser than the minimum term and the amount lesser than the minimum amount, specified in this section.

CHAPTER IV

MISCELLANEOUS

28. Protection of action taken in good faith.—No suit, prosecution or other legal proceedings shall lie against the members of the District Forum, the State Commission or the National Commission or any officer or person acting under the direction of the District Forum, the State Commission or the National Commission for executing any order made by it or in respect of anything which is in good faith done or intended to be done by such member, officer or person under this Act or under any rule or order made thereunder.

29. Power to remove difficulties.—(1) If any difficulty arises in giving effect to the provisions of this Act, the Central Government may, by order in the Official Gazette, make such provisions not inconsistent with the provisions of this Act as appear to it to be necessary or expedient for removing the difficulty:

Provided that no such order shall be made after the expiry of a period of two years from the commencement of this Act.

---

1. Subs. by Act 50 of 1993, sec. 20, for section 26 (w.r.e.f. 18-6-1993).
2. Ins. by Act 50 of 1993, sec. 21 (w.r.e.f. 18-6-1993).

(2) Every order made under this section shall, as soon as may be after it is made be laid before each House of Parliament.

[1][**29A. Vacancies or defects in appointment not to invalidate orders.**—No act or proceeding of the District Forum, the State Commission or the National Commission shall be invalid by reason only of the existence of any vacancy amongst its members or any defect in the constitution thereof.]

30. Power to make rules.—(1) The Central Government may, by notification, make rules for carrying out the provisions contained in [2][clause (a) of sub-section (1) of section 2] clause (b) of sub-section (2) of section 4, sub-section (2) of section 5, clause (vi) of sub-section (4) of section 13, section 19, sub-section (2) of section 20 and section 22 of this Act.

(2) The State Government may, by notification, make rules for carrying out the provisions contained in [2][clause (b) of sub-section (2) and sub-section (4) of section 7], sub-section (3) of section 10, clause (c) of sub-section (1) of section 13, sub-section (3) of section 14, section 15 and sub-section (2) of section 16.

31. Laying of rules.—(1) Every rule made by the Central Government under this Act shall be laid, as soon as may be after it is made, before each House of Parliament, while it is in session, for a total period of thirty days which may be comprised in one session or in two or more successive sessions, and if, before the expiry of the session immediately following the session or the successive sessions aforesaid, both Houses agree in making any modification in the rule or both Houses agree that the rule should not be made, the rule shall thereafter have effect only in such modified form or be of no effect, as the case may be; so, however, that any such modification or annulment shall be without prejudice to the validity of anything previously done under that rule.

(2) Every rule made by a State Government under this Act shall be laid as soon as may be after it is made, before the State Legislature.

---

1. Ins. by Act 34 of 1991, sec. 4 (w.e.f. 15-6-1991).
2. Ins. by Act 50 of 1993, sec. 22 (w.r.e.f. 18-6-1993).

THE INDIAN ELECTRICITY ACT, 1910

INTRODUCTION

The technology revolution has brought electricity to the forefront. To regulate the generation, supply and use of electricity, the first legislation was the Electricity Act of 1887 which provided for the protection of person and property, from injury and risks, attendant to the supply and user of electricity for lighting and other purposes. This Act was repealed and replaced by the Indian Electricity Act, 1903 (3 of 1903). Many practical, electro-technical and commercial difficulties were realised during the period of 1903 to 1909. To deal with these difficulties a Bill *viz.* the Indian Electricity Bill was introduced in the Central legislation to amend the law relating to the supply and use of electrical energy.

STATEMENT OF OBJECTS AND REASONS

When the Indian Electricity Act, 1903, was passed it was clearly recognised to be a somewhat tentative measure, and it was anticipated that amending legislation would be called for at an early date. Having regard to the experience gained in the practical working of the Act, the Government of India in 1907 came to the conclusion that the time had arrived for undertaking this amending legislation, and they referred various difficulties which had arisen in its working to a Committee on which electro-technical and commercial interests were represented.

The Act as at present framed vests its administration in Local Governments, with whom rests the power to grant licenses; but the authority or the previous sanction of the Governor-General in Council is required in regard to so many matters that the practical result has been a dual administration. In the case of cantonments and similar "places in the occupation of Government for naval or military purposes" the administration of the Act is by section 40 placed in the hands of the Governor-General in Council, but these places are situated within larger areas, in respect to which the Local Government is empowered to grant licenses, with the result that separate, and not necessarily consistent, licenses have been granted by the Governor-General in Council and the Local Government, respectively, to the same licensee for the same purpose, in one and the same place. The practical effect of the present system has been delayed, as it has hitherto been virtually impossible for a company to obtain a licence under two or three years. Delays of this nature are obviously most detrimental to the attraction of capital for the development of the resources of the country as the financial position may, and in fact frequently does, change completely between the date of the application and the granting of the license.

Under the Bill, as now drafted, the general administration of the Act, and subject to the control to the Governor-General in Council, the granting of all licenses are left in the hands of the Local Government. The rule-making power, and the delegation of the powers of the telegraph-authority to licensees, are reserved to the Governor-General in Council.

Among the more important modifications in the Bill are the following—

(i) The existing provision making licenses compulsory has been taken out, the question of supply to the public without license being otherwise dealt with. It is by no means certain that licenses are either necessary or desirable in the case of industrial companies of certain classes.

(ii) Provision is made for the grant of licenses for "bulk supply", that is to say, to meet cases where the applicant company proposes to generate energy and supply it in large quantities to distributors, who would retail it under a separate license to small consumers.

(iii) The amendment of licenses has been provided for. At present it is necessary to revoke a license and grant a fresh one in order to effect this object.

(iv) The question of compulsory purchase has been dealt with, in regard both to the splitting up of undertakings and to those cases where purchase may be impracticable. The Act provides for the modification, but not for the omission from a license, of the purchase clauses. But these clauses, conceived as they are in the interests of the local authority concerned in a small area, are entirely out of place, and in Great Britain are regularly omitted, in the case of undertakings covering large areas in which various local authorities intervene. It is proposed, therefore, to modify the provision.

(v) Many difficulties have arisen owing to the hard and fast limits of the area of supply over which a license operates, consumers just outside the boundary being debarred from participation in the benefits conferred by the public supply. A new section is proposed to deal with the matter and remove obstacles which are likely to impose quite unnecessary hardships on individuals.

(vi) It is proposed to amend the provisions of Part III of the Act so as to make them applicable to mines and binding on the Crown. As regards railways and tramways, the proviso to sub-section (1) of section 3 in Part II and the first proviso to sub-section (1) of section 31 in Part III of the Act as it stands lay down that nothing in these parts respectively relating to the supply or use of energy shall apply to any railway or tramway subject to the provisions of the Indian Railways Act, 1890. The extent to which it is proposed to modify the latter of these provisions is explained in the Notes on Clauses (clause 30) while it is proposed, as already mentioned, to repeal the former.

(vii) A slight amendment of the Land Acquisition Act, 1894, has been proposed with a view to facilitating its application to electrical works.

The examination of the provisions of the Act has brought to light many minor defects of substance or arrangement which it is desirable to correct, and the opportunity has, therefore, been taken to repeal and re-enact the Act with the necessary modification.

ACT 9 OF 1910

The Indian Electricity Bill was passed by the Legislative Council on 18th March, 1910 and it became the Indian Electricity Act, 1910 (9 of 1910) and it came into force with effect from 1st January, 1911.

LIST OF AMENDING ACTS AND ADAPTATION ORDERS

1. The Repealing and Amending Act, 1914 (10 of 1914).
2. The Devaluation Act, 1920 (38 of 1920).
3. The Indian Electricity (Amendment) Act, 1922 (1 of 1922).
4. The Indian Electricity (Amendment) Act, 1923 (4 of 1923).
5. The Repealing and Amending Act, 1925 (37 of 1925).
6. The Government of India (Adaptation of Indian Laws) Order, 1937.
7. The Indian Electricity (Amendment) Act, 1937 (10 of 1937).
8. The Arbitration Act, 1940 (10 of 1940).
9. The Repealing and Amending Act, 1940 (32 of 1940).
10. The Indian Independence (Adaptation of Central Acts and Ordinances) Order, 1948.
11. The Adaptation of (Laws) Order, 1950.
12. The Part B States (Laws) Act, 1951 (3 of 1951).
13. The Adaptation of Laws (No. 2) Order, 1956.

14. The Indian Electricity (Amendment) Act, 1959 (32 of 1959).
15. The Delegated Legislation Provisions (Amendment) Act, 1983 (20 of 1983).
16. The Indian Electricity (Amendment) Act, 1986 (31 of 1986).
17. The Electricity Laws (Amendment) Act, 1991 (50 of 1991).
18. The Electricity Laws (Amendment) Act, 1998 (22 of 1998).

THE INDIAN ELECTRICITY ACT, 1910

(9 of 1910)[1]

[18th March, 1910]

An Act to amend the law relating to the supply and use of electrical energy.

WHEREAS it is expedient to amend the law relating to the supply and use of electrical energy; It is hereby enacted as follows:—

PART I
PRELIMINARY

1. Short title, extent and commencement.—(1) This Act may be called the Indian Electricity Act, 1910.

[2][(2) It extends to the whole of India [3][except the State of Jammu and Kashmir].]

(3) It shall come into force on such date[4] as the Central Government may, by notification in the Official Gazette, direct in this behalf.

2. Definitions.—In this Act, expressions defined in the Indian Telegraph Act, 1885 (13 of 1885), [5][or in the Electricity (Supply) Act, 1948 (54 of 1948), have the meanings assigned to them in either of those Acts], and unless there is anything repugnant in the subject or context,—

---

1. The Act has been extended to—
   Goa, Daman and Diu by Regulation 12 of 1962, sec. 3 and Sch., Dadra and Nagar Haveli by Regulation 6 of 1963, sec. 2 and Sch. I, to the whole of the Union Territory of Lakshadweep by Regulation 2 of 1970, sec. 2 and Sch. This Act has been amended in U.P. by Uttar Pradesh Act 30 of 1961 and Act 14 of 1976, in Assam by Assam Act 9 of 1973, in Gujarat by Gujarat Act 3 of 1974, in Bihar by Bihar Act 15 of 1975, in M.P. by Madhya Pradesh Act 19 of 1974, in Maharashtra by Maharashtra Act 63 of 1974, in Haryana by Haryana Act 13 of 1975, in Punjab by Punjab Act 10 of 1978 and in Tamil Nadu by Tamil Nadu Act 39 of 1980.
2. Subs. by the A.O. 1950, for the original sub-section.
3. Subs. by Act 3 of 1951, sec. 3 and Sch., for "except Part B States".
4. 1st January, 1911, *see* Gazette of India, 1910, Pt. I, p. 1236.
5. Subs. by Act 32 of 1959, sec. 3, for "have the meaning assigned to them in that Act".

[1][(a) "appropriate Government" means in relation to any works or electric installations belonging to, or under the control of, the Central Government or in relation to any mines, oilfields, railways, aerodromes, telegraphs, broadcasting stations and any works of defence, the Central Government, and in any other case, the State Government;]

(b) "area of supply" means the area within which alone a licensee is for the time being authorised by his license to supply energy;

[2][(ba) "area of transmission" means the area within which a transmission licensee or any other person is for the time being authorised to transmit energy;

(bb) "Central Commission" means the Central Electricity Regulatory Commission established under sub-section (1) of section 3 of the Electricity Regulatory Commissions Act, 1998 (14 of 1998);

(bc) "Central Transmission Utility" means the utility notified by the Central Government under sub-section (1) of section 27A;]

[3][(c) "consumer" means any person who is supplied with energy by a licensee or the Government or by any other person engaged in the business of supplying energy to the public under this Act or any other law for the time being in force, and includes any person whose premises are for the time being connected for the purpose of receiving energy with the works of a licensee, the Government or such other person, as the case may be;]

(d) "daily fine" means a fine for each day on which an offence is continued after conviction therefor;

(e) "distributing main" means the portion of any main with which a service line is, or is intended to be, immediately connected;

[3][(f) "electric supply-line" means a wire, conductor or other means used for conveying, transmitting or distributing energy (whether by overhead line or underground cable), together with any casing, coating, covering, tube, pipe or insulator enclosing, surrounding or supporting the same or any part thereof, or any apparatus connected therewith for the

---

1. Subs. by Act 32 of 1959, sec. 3, for the previous clause.
2. Ins. by Act 22 of 1998, sec. 2 (w.e.f. 31-12-1998).
3. Subs. by Act 32 of 1959, sec. 3, for the former clause.

purpose of so conveying, transmitting or distributing such energy and includes any support cross-arm, stay, strut or safety device erected to set up for that purpose;]

[1][(g) "energy" means electrical energy—

(i) generated, transmitted or supplied for any purpose, or

(ii) used for any purpose except the transmission of a message;]

[2][(ga) "Government company" shall have the meaning assigned to it in section 617 of the Companies Act, 1956 (1 of 1956);

(gb) "inter-State transmission system" means, any system for the conveyance of energy by means of a main transmission line from the territory of one State to another State and includes,—

(i) the conveyance of energy across the territory of an intervening State as well as conveyance within the State which is incidental to such inter-State transmission of energy;

(ii) the transmission of energy within the territory of a State on a system built, owned, operated, maintained or controlled by a Central Transmission Utility or by any person under the suoervision and control of a Central Transmission Utility;

(gc) "intra-State transmission system" means any system for transmission of energy other than an inter-State transmission system;]

(h) "licensee" means any person licensed under Part II to supply energy;

(i) "main" means any electric supply-line through which energy is, or is intended to be, supplied [3][* * *] to the public;

[4][(ii) "overhead line" means an electric supply-line which is placed above ground and in the open air but does not include live rails of a traction system;]

(j) "prescribed" means prescribed by rules made under this Act;

(k) "public lamp" means an electric lamp used for the lighting of any street;

---

1. Subs. by Act 32 of 1959, sec. 3, for the former clause.
2. Ins. by Act 22 of 1998, sec. 2 (w.e.f. 31-12-198).
3. The words "by a licensee" omitted by Act 32 of 1959, sec. 3.
4. Ins. by Act 32 of 1959, sec. 3.

[1][(l) "service-line" means any electric supply-line through which energy is, or is intended to be, supplied [2][* * *]—

(i) to a single consumer either from a distributing main or immediately from the [3][supplier's premises], or

(ii) from a distributing main to a group of consumers on the same premises or on adjoining premises supplied from the same point of the distributing main;]

[4][(la) "State Commission" means the State Electricity Regulatory Commission established under sub-section (l) of section 17 of the Electricity Regulatory Commissions Act, 1998 (14 of 1998);

(lb) "State Electricity Board" in relation to any State means the State Electricity Board, if any, constituted for that State under section 5 of the Electricity (Supply) Act, 1948 (54 of 1948) and includes any Board which functions in that State under sections 6 and 7 of the said Act;

(lc) "State Transmission Utility" means the utility notified by the State Government under sub-section (l) of section 27B;]

(m) "street" includes any way, road, lane, square, court, alley, passage or open space, whether a thoroughfare or not, over which the public have a right of way, and also the roadway and footway over any public bridge or causeway; and

[5][(ma) "transmission license" means a license granted under Part IIA to transmit energy;

(mb) "transmission licensee" means a person who holds a transmission license;

(mc) "transmit" means conveyance of energy by means of transmission lines and the expression "transmission" shall be construed accordingly;]

[6][(n) "works" includes electric supply-line and any building, plant, machinery, apparatus and any other thing of whatever description required to supply energy to the public and to carry into effect the objects of a license or sanction granted under this Act or any other law for the time being in force.]

1. Subs. by Act 1 of 1922, sec. 2, for the original clause.
2. The words "by a licensee" omitted by Act 32 of 1959, sec. 3.
3. Subs. by Act 32 of 1959, sec. 3, for "licensee's premises".
4. Subs. by Act 22 of 1998, sec. 2 (w.e.f. 31-12-1998).
5. Ins. by Act 22 of 1998, sec. 2 (w.e.f. 31-12-1998).
6. Subs. by Act 32 of 1959, sec. 3, for the former clause.

PART II

SUPPLY OF ENERGY

Licenses

3. Grant of licenses.—(1) The State Government may, on application made in the prescribed form and on payment of the prescribed fee (if any) [1][grant after consulting the State Electricity Board, a license to any person] to supply energy in any specified area, and also to lay down or place electric supply-lines for the conveyance and transmission of energy,—

(a) where the energy to be supplied is to be generated outside such area, from a generating station situated outside such area to the boundary of such area, or

(b) where energy is to be conveyed or transmitted from any place in such area to any other place therein, across an intervening area not included therein, across such area.

(2) In respect of every such license and the grant thereof the following provisions shall have effect, namely:—

(a) any person applying for a license under this Part shall publish a notice of his application in the prescribed manner and with the prescribed particulars, and the license shall not be granted—

(i) until all objections received by the State Government with reference thereto have been considered by it:

Provided that no objection shall be so considered unless it is received before the expiration of three months from the date of the first publication of such notice as aforesaid; and

(ii) until, in the case of an application for a license for an area including the whole or any part of any cantonment [2][aerodrome,] fortress, arsenal, dockyard or camp or of any building or place in the occupation of the Government for [3][defence purposes], the State Government has ascertained that there is no objection to the grant of the license on the part of the [4][Central Government];

---

1. Subs. by Act 32 of 1959, sec. 4, for "grant to any person a license".
2. Ins. by Act 32 of 1959, sec. 4.
3. Subs. by Act 32 of 1959, sec. 4, for "naval a military purposes".
4. Subs. by Act 32 of 1959, sec. 4, for "Engineer-in-Chief, Army Headquarters, India".

(b) where an objection is received from any local authority concerned, the State Government shall, if in its opinion the objection is insufficient, record in writing and communicate to such local authority its reasons for such opinion;

(c) no application for a license under this Part shall be made by any local authority except in pursuance of a resolution passed at a meeting of such authority held after one month's previous notice of the same and of the purpose thereof has been given in the manner in which notices of meetings of such local authority are usually given;

(d) a license under this part—

(i) may prescribe such terms as to the limits within which, and the conditions under which, the supply of energy is to be compulsory or permissive, [1][* * *] and generally as to such matters as the State Government may think fit; and

(ii) save in cases in which under section 10, clause (b), the provisions of [2][sections 5 and 6], or either of them, have been declared not to apply, every such licensee shall declare whether any generating station to be used in connection with the undertaking shall or shall not form part of the undertaking for the purpose of purchase under [3][section 5 or section 6];

(e) the grant of a license under this Part for any purpose shall not in any way hinder or restrict the grant of license to another person within the same area of supply for a like purpose;

(f) the provisions contained in the Schedule shall be deemed to be incorporated with and to form part of, every license granted under this Part, save in so far as they are expressly added to, varied or excepted by the license, and shall, subject to any such additions, variations or exceptions which the State Government is hereby empowered to make, apply to the undertaking authorised by the license:

Provided that where a license is granted in accordance with the provisions of clause IX of the Schedule for the supply of energy to other licensees for distribution by them,

---

1. The words "and as to the limits if price to be charged in respect of the supply of energy" omitted by Act 32 of 1959, sec. 4.
2. Subs. by Act 32 of 1959, sec. 4, for "sections 5 and 7".
3. Subs. by Act 32 of 1959, sec. 4, for "section 5 or section 7".

then, in so far as such license relates to such supply, the provisions of clauses IV, V, VI, VII, VIII and XII of the Schedule shall not be deemed to be incorporated with the license.

[1][* * *]

4. Revocation or amendment of licenses.—(1) The State Government may, if in its opinion the public interest so requires [2][and after consulting the State Electricity Board], revoke a license in any of the following cases, namely:—

(a) where the licensee, in the opinion of the State Government, makes wilful and unreasonably prolonged default in doing anything required of him by or under this Act;

(b) where the licensee breaks any of the terms or conditions of his license the breach of which is expressly declared by such license to render it liable to revocation;

(c) where the licensee fails, within the period fixed in this behalf by his license or any longer period which the State Government may substitute therefor by order under [3][section 4A, sub-section (1)], and before exercising any of the powers conferred on him thereby in relation to the execution of works,—

(i) to show, to the satisfaction of the State Government, that he is in a position fully and efficiently to discharge the duties and obligations imposed on him by his license, or

(ii) to make the deposit or furnish the security required by his license;

(d) [4][where in the opinion of the State Government the financial position of the licensee is such that he is unable] fully and efficiently to discharge the duties and obligations imposed on him by his license;

[5][(e) where a licensee, in the opinion of the State Government, has made default in complying with any direction issued under section 22A.]

1. Sub-section (3) omitted by Act 38 of 1920, sec. 2, Sch. I, Pt. I.
2. Ins. by Act 32 of 1959, sec. 5.
3. Subs. by Act 32 of 1959, sec. 5, for "sub-section (3), clause (b)".
4. Subs. by Act 32 of 1959, sec. 5, for certain words.
5. Ins. by Act 32 of 1959, sec. 5.

[1][(2) Where in its opinion the public interest so permits, the State Government may, on the application or with the consent of the licensee, and after consulting the State Electricity Board, and the Central Government where that Government is interested, and if the licensee is not a local authority, after consulting also the local authority, if any, concerned, revoke a license as to the whole or any part of the area of supply upon such terms and conditions as it thinks fit.

(3) No license shall be revoked under sub-section (1) unless the State Government has given to the licensee not less than three months' notice, in writing stating the grounds on which it is proposed to revoke the license and has considered any cause shown by the licensee within the period of that notice, against the proposed revocation.

(4) Where the State Government might under sub-section (1) revoke a license it may instead of revoking the license permit it to remain in force subject to such further terms and conditions as it thinks fit to impose and any further terms or conditions so imposed shall be binding upon, and be observed by, the licensee, and shall be of like force and effect as if they were contained in the license.]

[2][**4A. Amendment of licenses.**—(1) Where in its opinion the public interest so permits, the State Government, on the application, of the licensee or otherwise and, after consulting the State Electricity Board, and if the licensee is not a local authority, also the local authority, if any, concerned, may make such alterations and amendments in the terms and conditions of a license, including the provisions specified in section 3, sub-section (2), clause (f), as it thinks fit:

Provided that no such alterations or amendments shall be made except with the consent of the licensee unless such consent has, in the opinion of the State Government, been unreasonably withheld.

(2) Where the licensee has made an application under sub-section (1) proposing any alterations or amendments in his license, the following provisions shall have effect, namely:—

(a) the licensee shall publish a notice of the application in the prescribed manner and with the prescribed particulars;

(b) the State Government shall not make any alterations or amendments until all objections received by it with reference to the application within three months from the date of the first publication of the notice have been considered;

1. Subs. by Act 32 of 1959, sec. 5, for sub-sections (2) and (3).

2. Ins. by Act 32 of 1959, sec. 6.

(c) in the case of an application proposing alterations or amendments in the area of supply comprising the whole or any part of any cantonment, aerodrome, fortress, arsenal, dockyard or camp or of any building or place in the occupation of the Government for defence purposes, the State Government shall not make any alterations or amendments except with the consent of the Central Government.

(3) Before making any alterations or amendments in a license otherwise than on the application of the licensee, the State Government shall publish the proposed alterations or amendments in the prescribed manner and with the prescribed particulars and consider all objections received by it with reference to the proposed alterations or amendments within three months from the date of the first publication of the notice; and where alterations or amendments have been proposed in an area of supply such as is referred to in clause (c) of sub-section (2), the State Government shall not make any alterations or amendments except with the consent of the Central Government.]

[1][**5. Provisions where license of a licensee is revoked.**— (1) Where the State Government revokes, under section 4, sub-section (1), the license of a licensee, the following provisions shall have effect, namely:—

(a) the State Government shall serve a notice of revocation upon the licensee and shall fix a date on which the revocation shall take effect; and on and with effect from that date, or on and with effect from the date, if earlier, on which the undertaking of the licensee is sold to a purchaser in pursuance of any of the succeeding clauses or is delivered to a designated purchaser in pursuance of sub-section (3) all the powers and liabilities of the licensee under this Act shall absolutely cease and determine;

(b) the State Government shall enquire from the State Electricity Board, and where the licensee is not a local authority, also from any local authority constituted for the area within which the whole of the area of supply is included, whether it is willing to purchase the undertaking;

(c) if the State Electricity Board is willing to purchase the undertaking, the State Government shall, by notice in writing require the licensee to sell, and thereupon, the licensee shall sell the undertaking to the State Electricity Board;

1. Subs. by Act 32 of 1959, sec. 7, for the former sections 5, 6 and 7.

(d) if the State Electricity Board is not willing to purchase the undertaking, the State Government shall have the option of purchasing the undertaking and if it elects to purchase, it shall by notice in writing require the licensee to sell, and thereupon the licensee shall sell the undertaking to it;

(e) if the State Electricity Board is not willing to purchase the undertaking and the State Government does not itself elect to purchase it, the State Government in any case where the local authority referred to in clause (b) is willing to purchase the undertaking shall by notice in writing require the licensee to sell, and thereupon the licensee shall sell the undertaking to that local authority;

(f) if no sale of the undertaking is effected under any of the foregoing clauses and if any other person is willing to purchase the undertaking, the State Government may by notice in writing require the licensee to sell, and thereupon the licensee shall sell the undertaking to such other person.

(2) Where an undertaking is sold under sub-section (1) the purchaser shall pay to the licensee the purchase price of the undertaking determined in accordance with the provisions of sub-sections (1) and (2) of section 7A, or as the case may be, sub-section (3) of that section.

(3) Where the State Government issues any notice under sub-section (1) requiring the licensee to sell the undertaking, it may by such notice require the licensee to deliver, and thereupon the licensee shall deliver on a date specified in the notice the undertaking to the designated purchaser pending the determination and payment of the purchase price of the undertaking:

Provided that in any such case, the purchaser shall pay to the licensee, interest at the Reserve Bank rate prevailing at the time of delivery of the undertaking *plus* one per centum, on the purchase price of the undertaking for the period from the date of delivery of the undertaking to the date of payment of the purchase price.

(4) Where before the date fixed in the notice issued under clause (a) of sub-section (1) as the date on which the revocation of the license shall take effect, no notice has been issued to the licensee requiring him to sell the undertaking or where for any reason no sale of the undertaking has been effected under that sub-section, the licensee shall have the option of disposing of all lands, buildings, works, materials and plant belonging to the undertaking in such manner as he may think fit:

Provided that if the licensee does not exercise such option within a period of six months from the aforesaid date, the State Government may forthwith cause the works of the licensee in, under, over, along, or across any street to be removed and every such street to be reinstated, and recover the cost of such removal and reinstatement from the licensee.

6. Purchase of undertakings.—(1) Where a license has been granted to any person, not being a local authority, the State Electricity Board shall,—

(a) in the case of a license granted before the commencement of the Indian Electricity (Amendment) Act, 1959 (32 of 1959), on the expiration of each such period as is specified in the license; and

(b) in the case of license granted on or after the commencement of the said Act, on the expiration of such period not exceeding [1][thirty] years and of every such subsequent period, not exceeding [1][twenty] years, as shall be specified in this behalf in the license,

have the option of purchasing the undertaking and such option shall be exercised by the State Electricity Board serving upon the licensee a notice in writing of not less than one year requiring the licensee to sell the undertaking to it at the expiry of the relevant period referred to in this sub-section.

(2) Where a State Electricity Board has not been constituted, or if constituted, does not elect to purchase the undertaking, the State Government shall have the like option to be exercised in the like manner of purchasing the undertaking.

(3) Where neither the State Electricity Board nor the State Government elects to purchase the undertaking, any local authority constituted for an area within which the whole of the area of supply is included shall have the like option to be exercised in the like manner of purchasing the undertaking.

(4) If the State Electricity Board intends to exercise the option of purchasing the undertaking under this section, it shall send an intimation in writing of such intention to the State Government at least eighteen months before the expiry of the relevant period referred to in sub-section (1) and if no such intimation as aforesaid is received by the State Government the State Electricity Board shall be deemed to have elected not to purchase the undertaking.

(5) If the State Government intends to exercise the option of purchasing the undertaking under this section, it shall send an

1. Subs. by Act 50 of 1991, sec. 2, for the words "twenty" and "ten" (w.e.f. 15-10-1991).

intimation in writing of such intention to the local authority, if any, referred to in sub-section (3) at least fifteen months before the expiry of the relevant period referred to in sub-section (1) and if no such intimation as aforesaid is received by the local authority, the State Government shall be deemed to have elected not to purchase the undertaking.

(6) Where a notice exercising the option of purchasing the undertaking has been served upon the licensee under this section, the licensee shall deliver the undertaking to the State Electricity Board, the State Government or the local authority, as the case may be, on the expiration of the relevant period referred to in sub-section (1) pending the determination and payment of the purchase price.

(7) Where an undertaking is purchased under this section, the purchaser shall pay to the licensee the purchase price determined in accordance with the provisions of sub-section (4) of section 7A.

7. Vesting of the undertaking in the purchaser.—Where an undertaking is sold under section 5 or section 6, then upon the completion of the sale or on the date on which the undertaking is delivered to the intending purchaser under sub-section (3) of section 5 or under sub-section (6) of section 6, as the case may be, whichever is earlier—

(i) the undertaking shall vest in the purchaser or the intending purchaser, as the case may be, free from any debt, mortgage or similar obligation of the licensee or attaching to the undertaking:

Provided that any such debt, mortgage or similar obligation shall attach to the purchase money in substitution for the undertaking;

(ii) the rights, powers, authorities, duties and obligations of the licensee under his license shall stand transferred to the purchaser and such purchaser shall be deemed to be the licensee:

Provided that where the undertaking is sold or delivered to a State Electricity Board or the State Government, the license shall cease to have further operation.

7A. Determination of purchase price.—(1) Where an undertaking of a licensee, not being a local authority, is sold under sub-section (1) of section 5, the purchase price of the undertaking shall be the market value of the undertaking at the time of purchase or where the undertaking has been delivered before the purchase under sub-section (3) of that section, at the time of the delivery of the undertaking and if there is any difference or dispute regarding such purchase price, the same shall be determined by arbitration.

(2) The market value of an undertaking for the purpose of sub-section (1) shall be deemed to be the value of all lands, buildings, works, materials and plant of the licensee suitable to, and used by him, for the purpose of the undertaking, other than (i) a generating station declared by the license not to form part of the undertaking for the purpose of purchase, and (ii) service-lines or other capital works or any part thereof which have been constructed at the expense of consumers, due regard being had to the nature and condition for the time being of such lands, buildings, works, materials and plant and the state of repair thereof and to the circumstance that they are in such position as to be ready for immediate working and to the suitability of the same for the purpose of the undertaking, but without any addition in respect of compulsory purchase or of goodwill or of any profits which may be or might have been made from the undertaking or of any similar consideration.

(3) Where an undertaking of a licensee, being a local authority, is sold under sub-section (1) of section 5, the purchase price of the undertaking shall be such as the State Government, having regard to the market value of the undertaking at the date of delivery of the undertaking, may determine.

(4) Where an undertaking of a licensee is purchased under section 6, the purchase price shall be the value thereof as determined in accordance with the provisions of sub-sections (1) and (2):

Provided that there shall be added to such value such percentage, if any, not exceeding twenty per centum of that value as may be specified in the license on account of compulsory purchase.]

8. Provisions where no purchase and license revoked with consent of licensee.—Where, on the expiration of any of the periods referred to [1][section 6, sub-section (1)], [1][the undertaking is not purchased by the State Electricity Board, the State Government or the local authority], and the license is, on the application or with the consent of the licensee, revoked, the licensee shall have the option of disposing of all lands, buildings, works, materials and plant belonging to the undertaking in such manner as he may think fit:

Provided that, if the licensee does not exercise such option within a period of six months, the State Government may proceed to take action as provided in [2][section 5, sub-section (4), proviso].

9. Licensee not to purchase, or associate himself with, other licensed undertaking or transfer his undertaking.—(1) The licensee shall not, at any time without the previous consent in writing

1. Subs. by Act 32 of 1959, sec. 8, for certain words.
2. Subs. by Act 32 of 1959, sec. 8, for "section 5, clause (f), proviso".

of the State Government, acquire, by purchase or otherwise, the license or the undertaking of, or associate himself so far as the business of supplying energy is concerned with any person supplying, or intending to supply, energy under any other license, and, before applying for such consent, the licensee shall give not less than one month's [1][notice of the application—

(a) to the State Electricity Board; and

(b) to every local authority both in the licensee's area of supply and also in the area in which such other person supplies, or intends to supply, energy]:

Provided that nothing in this sub-section shall be construed to require the consent of the State Government for the supply of energy by one licensee to another in accordance with the provisions of clause IX of the Schedule.

(2) The licensee shall not at any time assign his license or transfer his undertaking, on any part thereof, by sale, mortgage, lease, exchange or otherwise without the previous consent in writing of the State Government.

(3) Any agreement relating to any transaction of the nature described in sub-section (1) or sub-section (2), unless made with, or subject to, such consent as aforesaid, shall be void.

10. General power for Government to vary terms of purchase.—Notwithstanding anything in [2][sections 5, 6 and 8], the State Government may, [3][* * *] in any license to be granted under this Act,—

(a) vary the terms and conditions upon which, and the periods on the expiration of which, the licensee shall be bound to sell his undertaking, or

(b) direct that, subject to such conditions and restrictions (if any) as it may think fit to impose, the provisions of the said sections or any of them shall not apply.

11. Annual accounts of licensee.—(1) Every licensee shall, unless expressly exempted from the liability by his license, or by order in writing of the State Government, prepare and render to the State Government or to such authority as the State Government may appoint in this behalf, on or before the prescribed date in each year, an annual statement of accounts of his undertaking made up to such

1. Subs. by Act 32 of 1959, sec. 9, for certain words.
2. Subs. by Act 32 of 1959, sec. 10, for "sections 5, 7 and 8".
3. The words "with the previous sanction of the G.G. in C." omitted by Act 38 of 1920, sec. 2 and Sch. I, Pt. I.

date, in such form, and containing such particulars, as may be prescribed in this behalf.

(2) The licensee shall keep copies of such annual statement at his office and sell the same to any applicant at a price not exceeding five rupees per copy.

Works

12. Provision as to the opening and breaking up of streets, railways and tramways.—(1) Any licensee may, from time to time but subject always to the terms and conditions of his license, within the area of supply, or, when permitted by the terms of his license to lay down or place electric supply-lines without the area of supply, without that area—

(a) open and break up the soil and pavement of any street, railway or tramway;

(b) open and break up any sewer, drain or tunnel in or under any street, railway or tramway;

(c) lay down and place electric supply-lines and other works;

(d) repair, alter or remove the same; and

(e) do all other acts necessary for the due supply of energy.

(2) Nothing contained in sub-section (1) shall be deemed to authorise or empower a licensee, without the consent of the local authority or of the [1][owner or occupier] concerned, as the case may be, to lay down or place any electric supply-line, or other work in, through or against any building, or on, over or under any land not dedicated to public use whereon, whereever or whereunder any electric supply-line or work has not already been lawfully laid down or placed by such licensee:

Provided that any support of an [2][overhead line] or any stay or strut required for the sole purpose of securing in position any support of an [1][overhead line] may be fixed on any building or land or, having been so fixed, may be altered, notwithstanding the objection of owner or occupier of such building or land, if the District Magistrate or, in a Presidency-town [3][* * *], the Commissioner of Police by order in writing so directs:

Provided also, that if at any time the owner or occupier of any building or land on which any such support, stay or strut has been fixed shows sufficient cause, the District Magistrate or, in a

1. Subs. by Act 32 of 1959, sec. 11, for "owner and occupier".
2. Subs. by Act 32 of 1959, sec. 2, for "aerial line".
3. The words "or Rangoon" omitted by the A.O. 1937.

Presidency-town [1][* * *], the Commissioner of Police may by order in writing direct any such support, stay or strut to be removed or altered.

(3) When making an order under sub-section (2), the District Magistrate or the Commissioner of Police, as the case may be, shall fix the amount of compensation or of annual rent, or of both, which should in his opinion be paid by the licensee to the owner or occupier.

(4) Every order made by a District Magistrate or a Commissioner of Police under sub-section (2) shall be subject to revision by the State Government.

(5) Nothing contained in sub-section (1) shall be deemed to authorise or empower any licensee to open or break up any street not repairable by [2][the Central Government or the State Government] or a local authority, or any railway or tramway, except such streets, railways or tramways (if any), or such parts thereof, as he is specially authorised to break up by his license, without the written consent of the person by whom the street is repairable or of the person for the time being entitled to work the railway or tramway, unless with the written consent of the State Government:

Provided that the State Government shall not give any such consent as aforesaid, until the licensee has given notice by advertisement or otherwise as the State Government may direct, and within such period as the State Government may fix in this behalf, to the person above referred to, and until all representations or objections received in accordance with the notice have been considered by the State Government.

[3][(6) In this section, "occupier" of any building or land means a person in lawful occupation of that building or land.]

13. Notice of new works.—(1) Where the exercise of any of the powers of a licensee in relation to the execution of any works involves the placing of any works, in, under, over, along or across any street, part of a street, railway, tramway, canal or waterway, the following provisions shall have effect, namely:—

(a) not less than one month before commencing the execution of the works [4][* * *] the licensee shall serve upon the person responsible for the repair of the street or part of a street (hereinafter in this section referred to as "the repairing

1. The words "or Rangoon" omitted by the A.O. 1937.
2. Subs. by the A.O. 1937, for "the Government".
3. Ins. by Act 32 of 1959, sec. 11.
4. Certain words and brackets omitted by Act 32 of 1959, sec. 12.

authority") or upon the person for the time being entitled to work the railway, tramway, canal or waterway (hereinafter in this section referred to as "the owner"), as the case may be, a notice in writing describing the proposed works together with a section and plan thereof on a scale sufficiently large to show clearly the details of the proposed works, and not in any case smaller than one inch to eight feet vertically and sixteen inches to the mile horizontally, and intimating the manner in which, and the time at which, it is proposed to interfere with or alter any existing works, and shall, upon being required to do so by the repairing authority or owner, as the case may be, from time to time give such further information in relation thereto as may be desired;

(b) if the repairing authority intimates to the licensee that it disapproves of such works, section or plan, or approves thereof subject to amendment, the licensee may, within one week of receiving such intimation, appeal to the State Government, whose decision, after considering the reasons given by the repairing authority for its action, shall be final;

(c) if the repairing authority fails to give notice in writing of its approval or disapproval to the licensee within one month, it shall be deemed to have approved of the works, section and plan, and the licensee, after giving not less than forty-eight hours' notice in writing to the repairing authority, may proceed to carry out the works in accordance with the notice and the section and plan served under clause (a);

(d) if the owner disapproves of such works, section or plan, or approves thereof subject to amendment, he may, within three weeks, after the service of the notice under clause (a), serve a requisition upon the licensee demanding that any question in relation to the works or to compensation, or to the obligations of the owner to others in respect thereof, shall be determined by arbitration, and thereupon the matter shall unless settled by agreement, the determination by arbitration;

(e) where no requisition has been served by the owner upon the licensee under clause (d), within the time named, the owner shall be deemed to have approved of the works, section and plan, and in that case, or where after a requisition for arbitration the matter has been determined by arbitration, the works may, upon payment or securing of compensation, be executed according to the notice and the section and plan, subject to such modifications as may have been determined by arbitration or agreed upon between the parties.

[1][*Explanation.*—In clauses (a) to (e) the word "works" includes a service-line in, under, over, along or across a railway even if such line is immediately attached or intended to be immediately attached to a distributing main, but does not include—

(i) any other service-line so attached or intended to be so attached to a distributing main, or

(ii) works which consist of the repair, renewal or amendment of existing works of which the character or position is not to be altered;]

(f) where the works to be executed consist of the laying of any under ground service-line immediately attached, or intended to be immediately attached, to a distributing main, the licensee shall give to the repairing authority or the owner, as the case may be, not less than forty-eight hours' notice in writing of his intention to execute such works;

(g) where the works to be executed consist of the repair, renewal or amendment of existing works of which the character or position is not to be altered, the licensee shall, except in cases of emergency, give to the repairing authority, or to the owner, as the case may be, not less than forty-eight hours' notice in writing of his intention to execute such works, and, on the expiry of such notice, such works shall be commenced forthwith and shall be carried on with all reasonable despatch, and, if possible, both by day and by night until completed.

(2) Where the licensee makes default in complying with any of these provisions, he shall make full compensation for any loss or damage incurred by reason thereof, and, where any difference or dispute arises as to the amount of such compensation, the matter shall be determined by arbitration.

(3) Notwithstanding anything in this section, the licensee may, in case of emergency due to the breakdown of an underground electric supply-line, after giving notice in writing to the repairing authority or the owner, as the case may be, of his intention to do so, place an [2][overhead line] without complying with the provisions of sub-section (1):

Provided that such [2][overhead line] shall be used only until the defect in the underground electric supply-line can be made good, and in no case (unless with the written consent of the State Government)

1. Ins. by Act 32 of 1959, sec. 12.
2. Subs. by Act 32 of 1959, sec. 2, for "aerial line".

for a period exceeding six weeks, and shall be removed as soon as may be after such defect is removed.

14. Alteration of pipes or wires.—(1) Any licensee may alter the position of any pipe (not forming, in a case where the licensee is not a local authority, part of a local authority's main sewer), or of any wire under or over any place which he is authorised to open or break up, if such pipe or wire is likely to interfere with the exercise of his powers under this Act; and any person may alter position of any electric supply-lines or works of a licensee under or over any such place as aforesaid, if such electric supply-lines or works are likely to interfere with the lawful exercise of any powers vested in him.

(2) In any such case as aforesaid the following provisions shall, in the absence of an agreement to the contrary between the parties concerned, apply, namely:—

(a) not less than one month before commencing any alteration, the licensee or other person desiring to make the same (hereinafter in this section referred to as "the operator") shall serve upon the person for the time being entitled to the pipe, wire, electric supply-lines or works, as the case may be (hereinafter in this section referred to as "the owner"), a notice in writing, describing the proposed alteration, together with a section and plan thereof on a scale sufficiently large to show clearly the details of the proposed works, and not in any case smaller than one inch to eight feet vertically and sixteen inches to the mile horizontally, and intimating the time when it is to be commenced, and shall subsequently give such further information in relation thereto as the owner may desire;

(b) within fourteen days after the service of the notice, section and plan upon the owner, the owner may serve upon the operator a requisition to the effect that any question arising upon the notice, section or plan shall be determined by arbitration, and thereupon the matter shall, unless settled by agreement, be determined by arbitration;

(c) every arbitrator to whom a reference is made under clause (b), shall have regard to any duties or obligations which the owner is under, and may require the operator to execute any temporary or other works so as to avoid, as far as possible, interference therewith;

(d) where no requisition is served upon the operator under clause (b) within the time named, or where such a requisition has been served and the matter has been settled by agreement or determined by arbitration, the alteration may, upon payment or securing of any compensation accepted or determined by arbitration, be executed in accordance with the notice, section and plan and subject to such modifications as may have been determined by arbitration or agreed upon between the parties;

(e) the owner may, at any time before the operator is entitled to commence the alteration, serve upon the operator a statement in writing to the effect that he desires to execute the alteration himself and requires the operator to give such security for the repayment of any expenses as may be agreed upon or, in default of agreement, determined by arbitration;

(f) where a statement is served upon the operator under clause (e), he shall, not less than forty-eight hours before the execution of the alteration is required to be commenced, furnish such security and serve upon the owner a notice in writing intimating the time when the alteration is required to be commenced, and the manner in which it is required to be made; and thereupon the owner may proceed to execute the alteration as required by the operator;

(g) where the owner declines to comply, or does not, within the time and in the manner prescribed by a notice served upon him under clause (f), comply with the notice, the operator may himself execute the alteration;

(h) all expenses properly incurred by the owner in complying with a notice served upon him by the operator under clause (f) may be recovered by him from the operator.

(3) Where the licensee or other person desiring to make the alteration makes default in complying with any of these provisions, he shall make full compensation for any loss or damage incurred by reason thereof, and, where any difference or dispute arises as to the amount of such compensation, the matter shall be determined by arbitration.

15. Laying of electric supply-lines or other works near sewers, pipes or other electric supply-lines or works.— (1) Where—

(a) the licensee requires to dig or sink any trench for laying down any new electric supply-lines or other works, near to which any sewer, drain, water-course or work under the control of the State Government or of any local authority, or any pipe, syphon, electric supply-line or other work belonging to any duly authorised person, has been lawfully placed, or

(b) any duly authorised person requires to dig or sink any trench for laying down or constructing any new pipes or other works, near to which any electric supply-lines or works of a licensee have been lawfully placed,

the licensee or such duly authorized person, as the case may be (hereinafter in this section referred to as "the operator"), shall, unless it is otherwise agreed upon between the parties interested or in case of sudden emergency, give to the State Government or local authority or to such duly authorized person, or to the licensee, as the case may be (hereinafter in this section referred to as "the owner"), not less than forty-eight hours' notice in writing before commencing to dig or sink the trench, and the owner shall have the right to be present during the execution of the work, which shall be executed to the reasonable satisfaction of the owner.

(2) Where the operator finds it necessary to undermine, but not to alter, the position of any pipe, electric supply-line or work, he shall support it in position during the execution of the work, and before completion shall provide a suitable and proper foundation for it where so undermined.

(3) Where the operator (being the licensee) lays any electric supply-line across, or so as to be liable to touch, any pipes, lines or service-pipes, or service-lines belonging, to any duly authorized person or to any person supplying, transmitting or using energy under this Act, he shall not, except with the written consent of such person and in accordance with section 34, sub-section (1) lay his electric supply-lines so as to come into contact with any such pipes, lines or service-pipes or service-lines.

(4) Where the operator makes default in complying with any of the provisions of this section, he shall make full compensation for any loss or damage incurred by reason thereof.

(5) Where any difference or dispute arises under this section, the matter shall be determined by arbitration.

(6) Where the licensee is a local authority, the references in this section to the local authority and to sewers, drains, water-courses, or works under its control, shall not apply.

16. Streets, railways, tramways, sewers, drains or tunnels broken up to be reinstated without delay.—(1) Where any person, in exercise of any of the powers conferred by or under this Act, opens or breaks up the soil or pavement of any street, railway or tramway or any sewer, drain or tunnel, he shall—

(a) immediately cause the part opened or broken up to be fenced and guarded;

(b) before sunset cause a light or lights, sufficient for the warning of passengers, to be set up and maintained until sunrise against or near the part opened or broken up;

(c) with all reasonable speed fill in the ground and reinstate and make good the soil or pavement, or the sewer, drain or tunnel, opened or broken up, and carry away the rubbish occasioned by such openings or breaking up; and

(d) after reinstating and making good the soil or pavement, or the sewer, drain or tunnel, broken or opened up, keep the same in good repair for three months and for any further period, not exceeding nine months, during which subsidence continues.

(2) Where any person fails to comply with any of the provisions of sub-section (1), the person having the control or management of the street, railway, tramway, sewer, drain or tunnel in respect of which the default has occurred, may cause to be executed the work which the defaulter has delayed or omitted to execute, and may recover from him the expenses incurred in such execution.

(3) Where any difference or dispute arises as to the amount of the expenses incurred under sub-section (2), the matter shall be determined by arbitration.

17. Notice to telegraph authority.—(1) A licensee shall, before laying down or placing, within ten yards of any part of any telegraph-line, any electric supply-line or other works [1][not being either service-lines], or electric supply-lines for the repair, renewal or amendment of existing works of which the character or position is not to be altered, give not less than ten day's notice in writing to the telegraph-authority, specifying—

(a) the course of the works or alterations proposed,

(b) the manner in which the works are to be utilised,

(c) the amount and nature of the energy to be transmitted, and

(d) the extent to, and manner in, which (if at all) earth returns are to be used,

and the licensee shall conform with such reasonable requirements, either general or special, as may be laid down by the telegraph-authority within that period for preventing any telegraph-line from being injuriously affected by such works or alterations:

---

1. Subs. by Act 1 of 1922, sec. 4, for "not being service-line immediately attached or intended to be immediately attached to a distributing main".

Provided that, in case of emergency (which shall be stated by the licensee in writing to the telegraph-authority) arising from defects in any of the electric supply-lines or other works of the licensee, the licensee shall be required to give only such notice as may be possible after the necessity for the proposed new works or alterations has arisen.

(2) Where the works to be executed of the laying [1][or placing] of any [2][* * *] serviced-lines [3][* * *] the licensee shall, not less than forty-eight hours before commencing the work, serve upon the telegraph-authority a notice in writing of his intention to execute such works.

18. Overhead lines.—(1) Save as provided in section 13, sub-section (3), nothing in this Part shall be deemed to authorise or empower a licensee to place any [4][overhead line] along or across any street, railway, tramway, canal or waterway unless and until the State Government has communicated to him a general approval in writing of the methods of construction which he proposes to adopt:

Provided that the communication of such approval shall in no way relieve the licensee of his obligations with respect to any other consent required by or under this Act.

(2) Where any [4][overhead line] has been placed or maintained by a licensee in breach of the provisions of sub-section (1), the State Government may require the licensee forthwith to remove the same, or may cause the same to be removed, and recover from the licensee the expenses incurred in such removal.

[5][(3) Where any tree standing or laying near an [4][overhead line] or where any structure or other object which has been placed or has fallen near an [4][overhead line] subsequently to the placing of such line, interrupts or interferes with, or is likely to interrupt or interfere with, the conveyance or transmission of energy or the accessibility of any works a Magistrate of the first class or, in a presidency-town [6][* * *], [the Commissioner of Police, may, on the application of the licensee, cause the tree, structure or object to be removed or otherwise dealt with as he thinks fit.]

1. Ins. by Act 1 of 1922, sec. 4.
2. The word "underground" omitted by Act 1 of 1922, sec. 4.
3. The words "immediately attached or intended to be immediately attached to a distributing main" omitted by Act 1 of 1922, sec. 4.
4. Subs. by Act 32 of 1959, sec. 2, for "aerial line".
5. Subs. by Act 1 of 1922, sec. 5, for the original sub-section.
6. The words "or Rangoon" omitted by the A.O. 1937.

(4) When disposing of an application under sub-section (3), the Magistrate or Commissioner of Police, as the case may be, shall, in the case of any tree in existence before the placing of the [1][overhead line], award to the person interested in the tree such compensation as he thinks reasonable, and such person may recover the same from the licensee.

[2][*Explanation*.—For the purposes of this section, the expression "tree" shall be deemed to include any shrub, hedge, jungle-growth or other plant.]

19. Compensation for damage.—(1) A licensee shall, in exercise of any of the powers conferred by or under this Act, cause as little damage, detriment and inconvenience as may be, and shall make full compensation for any damage, detriment or inconvenience caused by him or by any one employed by him.

(2) Save in the case provided for in section 12, sub-section (3), where any difference or dispute arises as to the amount or the application of such compensation the matter shall be determined by arbitration.

Supply

[3][**19A. Point where supply is delivered.**—For the purposes of this Act, the point at which the supply of energy by a licensee to a consumer shall be deemed to commence shall be determined in such manner as may be prescribed.]

20. Power for licensee to enter premises and to remove fittings or other apparatus of licensee.—(1) A licensee or any person duly authorised by a licensee may, at any reasonable time, and on informing the occupier of his intention, enter any premises to which energy is or has been supplied by him, [4][of any premises or land, under, over, along, across, in or upon which the electric supply-lines or other works have been lawfully placed by him] for the purpose of—

(a) [5][inspecting, testing, repairing or altering] the electric supply lines, meters, fittings, works and apparatus for the supply of energy belonging to the licensee; or

(b) ascertaining the amount of energy supplied or the electrical quantity contained in the supply; or

1. Subs. by Act 32 of 1959, sec. 2, for "aerial line".
2. Added by Act 1 of 1922, sec. 5.
3. Ins. by Act 1 of 1922, sec. 6.
4. Ins. by Act 32 of 1959, sec. 13.
5. Subs. by Act 32 of 1959, sec. 13, for "inspecting and testing".

(c) removing where a supply of energy is no longer required, or where the licensee is authorised to take away and cut off such supply, any electric supply-lines, [1][meters,] fittings, works or apparatus belonging to the licensee.

(2) A licensee or any person authorised as aforesaid may also, in pursuance of a special order in this behalf made by [2][a Magistrate of the first class or in a presidency-town, by a Presidency Magistrate and after giving not less than twenty-four hours' notice in writing to the occupier—

(a) enter any premises or land referred to in sub-section (1) for any of the purposes mentioned therein;

(b) enter any premises to which energy is to be supplied by him, for the purpose of examining and testing the electric wires fittings, works and apparatus for the use of energy, belonging to the consumer].

[3][(3) Where a consumer refuses to allow a licensee or any person authorised as aforesaid to enter his premises [4][or land] in pursuance of the provisions of sub-section (1) or, sub-section (2), when such licensee or person has so entered, refuses to allow him to perform any act which he is authorised by those sub-sections to perform, or fails to give reasonable facilities for such entry or performance, the licensee may, after the expiry of twenty-four hours from the service of a notice in writing on the consumer, cut off the supply to the consumer for so long as such refusal or failure continues, but for no longer.]

21. Restriction on licensees controlling or interfering with use of energy.—(1) A licensee shall not be entitled to prescribe any special form of appliance for utilising energy supplied by him, or, save as provided [5][in any conditions made under sub-section (2) or] by section 23, sub-section (2), or by section 26, sub-section (7), in any way to control or interfere with the use of such energy:

Provided that no person may adopt any form of appliance, or use the energy supplied to him, so as unduly or improperly to [6][interfere with—

---

1. Ins. by Act 1 of 1922, sec. 7.
2. Subs. by Act 32 of 1959, sec. 13, for certain former words.
3. Ins. by Act 1 of 1922, sec. 7.
4. Ins. by Act 32 of 1959, sec. 13.
5. Ins. by Act 32 of 1959, sec. 14.
6. Subs. by Act 32 of 1959, sec. 14, for "interfere with the supply by the licensee of energy to any other person".

(a) the safety or efficient working of a licensee's electric supply-lines or other works; or

(b) the supply of energy by the licensee to any other person].

[1][(2) [2][* * *] A licensee may, with the previous sanction of the State Government, given after consulting [3][the State Electricity Board and also] the local authority, where the licensee is not the local authority, make conditions not inconsistent with this Act or with his license or with any rules made under this Act, to regulate his relations with persons who are or intend to become consumers, and may, with the like sanction given after the like consultation, add to or alter or amend any such conditions; and any conditions made by a licensee without such sanction shall be null and void:

Provided that any such conditions made before the 23rd day of January, 1922 shall, if sanctioned by the State Government on application made by the licensee before such date as the State Government may, by general or special order, fix in this behalf, be deemed to have been made in accordance with the provisions of this sub-section.

(3) The State Government may, after the like consultation, [4][add any new condition or cancel or amend] any condition or part of a condition previously sanctioned under sub-section (2) after giving to the licensee not less than one month's notice in writing of its intention so to do.]

[5][(4)] Where any difference or dispute arises as to whether a licensee has prescribed any appliance or controlled or interfered with the use of energy in contravention of sub-section (1), the matter shall be either referred to an [6][Electrical Inspector] and decided by him or, if the licensee or consumer so desires, determined by arbitration.

22. Obligation on licensee to supply energy.—Where energy is supplied by a licensee, every person within the area of supply shall, except in so far as is otherwise provided by the terms and conditions of the license, be entitled, on application, to a supply on the same terms as those on which any other person in the same area is entitled in similar circumstances to a corresponding supply:

---

1. Ins. by Act 1 of 1922, sec. 8.
2. The words, bracket and figure "Subject to the provisions of sub-section (1)" omitted by Act 32 of 1959, sec. 14.
3. Ins. by Act 32 of 1959, sec. 13.
4. Subs. by Act 32 of 1959, sec. 14, for "cancel".
5. Original sub-section (2) re-numbered as sub-section (4) by Act 1 of 1922, sec. 8.
6. Subs. by Act 32 of 1959, sec. 2, for "Electric Inspector".

Provided that no person shall be entitled to demand, or to continue to receive, from a licensee a supply of energy for any premises having a separate supply unless he has agreed with the licensee to pay to him such minimum annual sum as will give him a reasonable return on the capital expenditure, and will cover other standing charges incurred by him in order to meet the possible maximum demand for those premises, the sum payable to be determined in case of difference or dispute by arbitration.

[1][**22A. Powers of State Government to give direction to a licensee in regard to the supply of energy to certain class of consumers.**—(1) The State Government may, if in its opinion it is necessary in the public interest so to do, direct any licensee to supply, in preference to any other consumer, energy required by any establishment which being in the opinion of the State Government an establishment used or intended to be used for maintaining supplies and services essential to the community, is notified by that Government in the Official Gazette in this behalf.

(2) Where any direction is issued under sub-section (1) requiring a licensee to supply energy to any establishment and any difference or dispute arises as to the price or other terms and conditions relating to the supply of energy, the licensee shall not by reason only of such difference or dispute be entitled to refuse to supply energy but such difference or dispute shall be determined by arbitration.

(3) Where any agreement by a licensee, whether made before or after the commencement of the Indian Electricity (Amendment) Act, 1959, for the supply of energy with any establishment referred to in sub-section (1) expires, the licensee shall continue to supply energy to such establishment on the same terms and conditions as are specified in the agreement until he receives a notice in writing from the establishment requiring him to discontinue the supply.

(4) Notwithstanding anything contained in this Act, or in the Electricity (Supply) Act, 1948 (54 of 1948), or in his license or in any agreement entered into by him for the supply of energy, a licensee shall be bound to comply with any direction given to him under sub-section (1) and any action taken by him in pursuance of any such direction shall not be deemed to be a contravention of section 23.

22B. Power to control the distribution and consumption of energy.—(1) If the State Government is of opinion that it is necessary or expedient so to do, for maintaining the supply and securing the equitable distribution of energy, it may by order provide for regulating the supply, distribution, consumption or use thereof.

1. Ins. by Act 32 of 1959, sec. 15.

(2) Without prejudice to the generality of the powers conferred by sub-section (1) an order made thereunder may direct the licensee not to comply, except with the permission of the State Government, with—

(i) the provisions of any contract, agreement or requisition whether made before or after the commencement of the Indian Electricity (Amendment) Act, 1959, for the supply (other than the resumption of a supply) or an increase in the supply of energy to any person, or

(ii) any requisition for the resumption of supply of energy to a consumer after a period of six months, from the date of its discontinuance, or

(iii) any requisition for the resumption of supply of energy made within six months of its discontinuance, where the requisitioning consumer was not himself the consumer of the supply at the time of its discontinuance.]

23. Charges for energy to be made without undue preference.—(1) A licensee shall not, in making any agreement for the supply of energy, show under preference to any person [1][* * *].

(2) No consumer shall, except with the consent in writing of the licensee, use energy supplied to him under one method of charging in a manner for which a higher method of charging is in force.

[2][(3) In the absence of an agreement to the contrary, a licensee may charge for energy supplied by him to any consumer—

(a) by the actual amount of energy so supplied, or

(b) by the electrical quantity contained in the supply, or

(c) by such other method as may be approved by the State Government.

(4) Any charges made by a licensee under clause (c) of sub-section (3) may be based upon, and vary in accordance with, any one or more of the following considerations, namely:—

(a) the consumer's load factor, or

(b) the power factor of his load, or

(c) his total consumption of energy during any stated period, or

(d) the hours at which the supply of energy is required.]

---

1. Certain words omitted by Act 32 of 1959, sec. 16.
2. Added by Act 1 of 1922, sec. 9.

24. Discontinuance of supply to consumer neglecting to pay charge.—[1][(1)] Where any person neglects to pay any charge for energy or any [2][sum, other than a charge for energy,] due from him to a licensee in respect of the supply of energy to him, the licensee may, after giving not less than seven clear days' notice in writing to such person and without prejudice to his right to recover such charge or other sum by suit, cut off the supply and for that purpose cut or disconnect any electric supply-line or other works, being the property of the licensee, through which energy may be supplied, and may discontinue the supply until such charge or other sum, together with any expenses incurred by him in cutting off and re-connecting the supply, are paid, but no longer.

[3][(2)] [4][* * *] Where any difference or dispute [5][which by or under this Act is required to be determined by an Electrical Inspector, has been referred to the Inspector] before notice as aforesaid has been given by the licensee, the licensee shall not exercise the powers conferred by this section until the Inspector has given his decision:

[6][Provided that the prohibition contained in this sub-section shall not apply in any case in which the licensee has made a request in writing to the consumer for a deposit with the [7][Electrical Inspector] of the amount of the licensee's charges or other sums in dispute or for the deposit of the licensee's further charges for energy as they accrue, and the consumer has failed to comply with such request.]

25. Exemption of electric supply-lines or other apparatus from attachment in certain cases.—Where any electric supply-lines, meters, fittings, works or apparatus belonging to a licensee are placed in or upon any premises [8][or land], not being in the possession of the licensee, [9][* * *] such electric supply-lines, meters, fittings, works and apparatus shall not be liable to be taken in execution under any process of any Civil Court or in any proceedings in insolvency against the person in whose possession the same may be.

---

1. First paragraph of section 24 numbered as sub-section (1) of that section by Act 1 of 1922, sec. 10.
2. Subs. by Act 1 of 1922, sec. 10, for "other sum".
3. Proviso numbered as sub-section (2) by Act 1 of 1922, sec. 10.
4. The words "Provided that" omitted by Act 1 of 1922, sec. 10.
5. Subs. by Act 32 of 1959, sec. 17, for "has been referred under this Act to an Electric Inspector".
6. Added by Act 1 of 1922, sec. 10.
7. Subs. by Act 32 of 1959, sec. 2, for "Electric Inspector".
8. Ins. by Act 32 of 1959, sec. 18.
9. The words "for the purposes of supplying energy" omitted by Act 32 of 1959, sec. 18.

26. Meters.—(1) In the absence of an agreement to the contrary, the amount of energy supplied to a consumer or the electrical quantity contained in the supply shall be ascertained by means of a correct meter, and the licensee shall, if required by the consumer, cause the consumer to be supplied with such a meter:

Provided that the licensee may require the consumer to give him security for the price of a meter and enter into an agreement for the hire thereof, unless the consumer elects to purchase a meter.

(2) Where the consumer so enters into an agreement for the hire of a meter, the licensee shall keep the meter correct, and, in default of his doing so, the consumer shall, for so long as the default continues, cease to be liable to pay for the hire of the meter.

(3) Where the meter is the property of the consumer, he shall keep the meter correct and, in default of his doing so, the licensee may, after giving him seven days' notice, for so long as the default continues, cease to supply energy through the meter.

(4) The licensee or any person duly authorised by the licensee shall, at any reasonable time and on informing the consumer of his intention, have access to and be at liberty to inspect and test, and for that purpose, if he thinks fit, take off and remove, any meter referred to in sub-section (1); and, except where the meter is so hired as aforesaid, all reasonable expenses of, and incidental to, such inspecting, testing, taking off and removing shall, if the meter is found to be otherwise than correct, be recovered from the consumer; and, where any difference or dispute arises as to the amount of such reasonable expenses, the matter shall be referred to an [1][Electrical Inspector], and the decision of such Inspector shall be final:

Provided that the licensee shall not be at liberty to take off or remove any such meter if any difference or dispute of the nature described in sub-section (6) has arisen until the matter has been determined as therein provided.

(5) A consumer shall not connect any meter referred to in sub-section (1) with any electric supply-line through which energy is supplied by a licensee, or disconnect the same from any such electric supply-line [2][but he may by giving not less than forty-eight hours' notice in writing to the licensee requires the licensee to connect or disconnect such meter and on receipt of any such requisition the licensee shall comply with it within the period of the notice].

---

1. Subs. by Act 32 of 1959, sec. 2, for "Electric Inspector".
2. Subs. by Act 32 of 1959, sec. 19, for certain words.

[1][(6) Where any difference or dispute arises as to whether any meter referred to in sub-section (1) is or is not correct, the matter shall be decided, upon the application of either party, by an Electrical Inspector; and where the meter has, in the opinion of such Inspector ceased to be correct, such Inspector shall estimate the amount of the energy supplied to the consumer or the electrical quantity contained in the supply, during such time, not exceeding six months, as the meter shall not, in the opinion of such Inspector, have been correct; but save as aforesaid, the register of the meter shall, in the absence of fraud, be conclusive proof of such amount or quantity:

Provided that before either a licensee or a consumer applies to the Electrical Inspector under this sub-section, he shall give to the other party not less than seven days' notice of his intention so to do.]

(7) In addition to any meter which may be placed upon the premises of a consumer in pursuance of the provisions of sub-section (1), the licensee may place upon such premises such meter, maximum demand indicator or other apparatus as he may think fit for the purpose of ascertaining or regulating either the amount of energy supplied to the consumer, or the number of hours during which the supply is given, or the rate per unit of time at which energy is supplied to the consumer, or any other quantity or time connected with the supply:

Provided that the meter, indicator or apparatus shall not, in the absence of an agreement to the contrary be placed otherwise than between the distributing mains of the licensee and any meter referred to in sub-section (1):

Provided also that, where the charges for the supply of energy depend wholly or partly upon the reading or indication of any such meter, indicator or apparatus as aforesaid, the licensee shall, in the absence of an agreement to the contrary, keep the meter, indicator or apparatus correct; and the provisions of sub-sections (4), (5) and (6) shall in that case apply as though the meter, indicator or apparatus were a meter referred to in sub-section (1).

Explanation.—A meter shall be deemed to be "correct" if it registers the amount of energy supplied, or the electrical quantity contained in the supply, within the prescribed limits of error, and a maximum demand indicator or other apparatus referred to in sub-section (7) shall be deemed to be "correct" if it complies with such conditions as may be prescribed in the case of any such indicator or other apparatus.

---

1. Subs. by Act 32 of 1959, sec. 19, for the former sub-section.

27. Supply of energy outside area of supply.—Notwithstanding anything in this Act, the State Government may, by order in writing, and subject to such conditions and restrictions, if any, as it thinks fit to impose, authorise any licensee to supply energy to any person outside the area of supply, and to lay down or place electric supply-lines for that purpose:

Provided, first, that no such authority shall be conferred on the licensee within the area of supply of another licensee without that licensee's consent, unless the State Government considers that his consent has been unreasonably withheld:

Provided, secondly, that such authority shall not be conferred unless the person to whom the supply is to be given has entered into a specific agreement with the licensee for the taking of such supply:

Provided, thirdly, that a licensee on whom such authority has been conferred shall not be deemed to be empowered outside the area of supply to open or break up any street, or any sewer, drain or tunnel in or under any street, railway or tramway; or to interfere with any telegraph-line, without the written consent of the local authority or person by whom such street, sewer, drain or tunnel is repairable, or of the telegraph-authority, as the case may be, [1][unless the State Government, after such inquiry as it thinks fit, considers that such consent has been unreasonably withheld]:

Provided, fourthly, that, save as aforesaid, the provisions of this Act shall apply in the case of any supply authorised under this section as if the said supply were made within the area of supply.

[2][*PART IIA*

TRANSMISSION OF ENERGY

27A. Central Transmission Utility.—(1) The Central Government shall, by notification in the Official Gazette, specify any Government company as the Central Transmission Utility.

(2) The Functions of the Central Transmission Utility shall be to—

(a) undertake transmission of energy through inter-State transmission system;

(b) discharge all functions of planning and co-ordination relating to inter-State transmission system with—

(i) State Transmission Utilities;

(ii) Central Government;

---

1. Added by Act 1 of 1922, sec. 12.
2. Ins. by Act 22 of 1998, sec. 3 (w.e.f. 31-12-1998).

(iii) State Governments;

(iv) generating companies;

(v) Regional Electricity Boards;

(vi) Authority;

(vii) licensees;

(viii) transmission licensees;

(ix) any other person notified by the Central Government in this behalf.

(3) The Central Transmission Utility shall exercise supervision and control over the inter-State transmission system.

27B. State Transmission Utility.—(1) The State Government shall, by notification in the Official Gazette, specify the State Electricity Board or any Government company as the State Transmission Utility.

(2) The functions of the State Transmission Utility shall be to—

(a) undertake transmission of energy through intra-State transmission system;

(b) discharge all functions of planning and co-ordination relating to intra-State transmission system with—

(i) Central Transmission Utility;

(ii) State Governments;

(iii) generating companies;

(iv) Regional Electricity Boards;

(v) Authority;

(vi) licensees;

(vii) transmission licensees;

(viii) any other person notified by the State Government in this behalf.

(3) The State Transmission Utility shall exercise supervision and control over the intra-State transmission system.

(4) The State Transmission Utility shall comply with and ensure compliance by others in that State of the directions which the Central Transmission Utility may give from time to time in connection with the integrated grid operations and operation of the power system or otherwise in regard to matters which affect the operation of the inter-State transmission system.

27C. Grant of transmission license by the Central Government.—(1) Until the Central Commission is established, the

Central Government and thereafter the Central Commission may, subject to the provisions of sub-section (4), grant a transmission license to any person.

(2) A transmission license granted under sub-section (1) may authorise the transmission licensee to construct, maintain and operate any inter-State transmission system under the direction, control and supervision of the Central Transmission Utility.

(3) Every application under sub-section (1) shall be—

(a) subject to such terms and conditions;

(b) in such form; and

(c) accompanied by such fees,

as may be notified by the Central Government or by the Central Commission, as the case may be, in this behalf.

(4) No application shall be entertained under sub-section (1) unless the applicant has obtained the approval of the Central Transmission Utility in such manner as may be notified by the Central Government or by the Central Commission, as the case may be, in this behalf.

(5) Until the Central Commission is established, the Central Government and thereafter the Central Commission in the case of inter-State transmission system may, if it considers necessary in public interest, by order subject to such conditions, if any, as may be specified in that order, grant exemption to any person obtaining a transmission license under this section.

27D. Grant of transmission license by the State Government.—(1) Until the State Commission is established, the State Government and thereafter the State Commission may, subject to the provisions of sub-section (4), grant a transmission license to any person.

(2) A transmission license granted under sub-section (1) may authorise the transmission licensee to construct, maintain and operate any intra-State transmission system under the direction, control and supervision of the State Transmission Utility.

(3) Every application under sub-section (1) shall be—

(a) subject to such terms and conditions;

(b) in such form; and

(c) accompanied by such fees,

as may be notified by the State Government or by the State Commission, as the case may be, in this behalf.

(4) No application shall be entertained under sub-section (1) unless the applicant has obtained the approval of the State Transmission

Utility in such manner as may be notified by the State Government or by the State Commission, as the case may be, in this behalf.

(5) Until the State Commission is established, the State Government and thereafter the State Commission in the case of intra-State transmission system may, if it considers necessary in public interest, by order subject to such conditions, if any, as may be specified in that order, grant exemption to any person from obtaining a transmission license under this section.

27E. Modified application of certain sections to transmission license and transmission licensee.—The provisions of section 12 to 19 (both inclusive), section 25 and clauses XIV to XVII (both inclusive) of the Schedule shall, as far as may be, apply to a transmission licensee subject to the modification that references to "license" and "licensee" shall be construed as references to "transmission license" and "transmission licensee", respectively.

27F. Laying of certain notification and order, etc.—(1) Every notification issued and every order made by the Central Government under this Part shall be laid, as soon as may be after it is made, before each House of Parliament, while it is in session, for a total period of thirty days which may be comprised in one session or in two or more successive sessions, and if before the expiry of the session immediately following the session or the successive sessions aforesaid, both Houses agree in making any modification in the notification or order or both Houses agree that the notification or order should not be made, the notification or order shall thereafter have effect only in such modified form or be of no effect, as the case may be; so, however, that any such modification or annulment shall be without prejudice to the validity of anything previously done under that notification or order.

(2) Every notification issued by the State Government and every order made by the State Government under section 27D shall be laid, as soon as it is made or issued, before the State Legislature.]

PART III

SUPPLY, TRANSMISSION AND USE OF ENERGY BY NON-LICENSEES

28. Sanction required by non-licensees in certain cases.—[1][(1) No person, other than a licensee, shall engage in the business of supplying energy to the public except with the previous sanction of the State Government and in accordance with such conditions as the State Government may fix in this behalf, and any agreement to the contrary shall be void.

---

1. Subs. by Act 32 of 1959, sec. 20, for the former sub-section (1).

(1A) The State Government shall not give any sanction under sub-section (1)—

(a) except after consulting the State Electricity Board; and

(b) except with the consent—

(i) in any case where energy is to be supplied in any area for which a local authority is constituted, of that local authority;

(ii) in any case where energy is to be supplied in any area forming part of any cantonment, aerodrome, fortress, arsenal, dockyard or camp or of any building or place in the occupation of the Government for defence purposes, of the Central Government;

(iii) in any area falling within the area of supply of a licensee, of that licensee:

Provided that except in a case falling under sub-clause (ii), no such consent shall be necessary if the State Government is satisfied that such consent has been unreasonably withheld.]

(2) Where any difference or dispute arises as to whether any person is or is not engaging, or about to engage, in the business of supplying energy [1][to the public] within the meaning of sub-section (1), the matter shall be referred to the State Government, and the decision of the State Government thereon shall be final.

29. Power for non-licensees to break up streets.—(1) The local authority may, by order in writing, confer and impose upon any person, who has obtained the sanction of the State Government under section 28 to engage in the business of supplying energy, [2][to the public], all or any of the powers and liabilities of a licensee under sections 12 to 19, both inclusive, and the provisions of the said sections shall thereupon apply as if such person were a licensee under Part II.

(2) A local authority, not being a licensee, shall, for the purpose of lighting any street, have the powers and be subject to the liabilities respectively conferred and imposed by sections 12 to 19 (both inclusive), so far as applicable, as if it were a licensee under Part II.

(3) In cases other than those for which provision is made by sub-section (1), the person responsible for the repair of any street may, by order in writing, confer and impose upon any person who proposes to transmit energy in such street all or any of the powers

1. Ins. by Act 32 of 1959, sec. 20.

2. Ins. by Act 32 of 1959, sec. 21.

and liabilities of a licensee under sections 12 to 19 (both inclusive), in so far as the same relate to—

(a) opening or breaking up of the soil or pavement of such street, or

(b) laying down or placing electric supply-lines in, under, along or across such street, or

(c) repairing, altering or removing such electric supply-lines, and thereupon the provisions of the said sections shall, so far as aforesaid, apply to such person as if he were a licensee under Part II.

(4) If no order is made within fourteen days after the receipt of an application for the same under sub-section (1) or sub-section (3), the order so applied for shall be deemed to have been refused, and every order, and every refusal to make an order, under sub-section (1) or sub-section (3), shall be subject to revision by the State Government.

[1][**29A. Application of section 18 to over-head lines maintained by railways.**—The provisions of sub-sections (3) and (4) of section 18 and of the *Explanation* thereto shall apply in the case of any [2][overhead line] placed by any railway administration as defined [3][in clause (32) of section 2 of the Railways Act, 1989 (24 of 1989),] as if references therein to the licensee were references to the railway administration.]

30. Control of transmission and use of energy.—(1) [4][Save as otherwise exempted under this Act, no person other than Central Transmission Utility, State Transmission Utility, a transmission licensee, a licensee or a person to whom sanction is granted under section 28, duly authorised under the terms of his license or sanction, as the case may be, shall transmit or use energy at a rate exceeding two hundred and fifty watts and one hundred volts—]

(a) in any street, or

(b) in any place,—

(i) in which one hundred or more persons are likely ordinarily to be assembled, or

(ii) which is a factory within the meaning of the Factories Act, 1948 (63 of 1948) or a mine within the meaning of the Mines Act, 1952 (35 of 1952), or

1. Ins. by Act 40 of 1923, sec. 2.

2. Subs. by Act 32 of 1959, sec. 2, for "aerial line".

3. Subs. by Act 22 of 1998, sec. 4, for "in section 3 of the Indian Railways Act, 1890 (9 of 1890)" (w.e.f. 31-12-1998).

4. Subs. by Act 32 of 1959, sec. 22, for certain words and again subs. by Act 22 of 1998, sec. 5, for certain words (w.e.f. 31-12-1998).

(iii) to which the State Government, by general or special order, declares the provisions of this sub-section to apply,

without giving, before the commencement of transmission or use of energy, not less than seven days' notice in writing of his intention to the Electrical Inspector and to the District Magistrate, or in a presidency-town to the Commissioner of Police, containing particulars of the electrical installation and plant, if any, the nature and the purpose of supply, and complying with such of the provisions of Part IV, and of the rules made thereunder, as may be applicable:]

Provided that nothing in this section shall apply to energy used for the public carriage of passengers, animals or goods, on, or for the lighting or ventilation of the rolling stock of, any railway or tramway subject to the provisions of [1][the Railways Act, 1989 (24 of 1989)]:

Provided, also, that the State Government may, by general or special order and subject to such conditions and restrictions as may be specified therein, exempt from the application of this section or of any such provision or rule as aforesaid any person or class of persons using energy on premises upon or in connection with which it is generated, or using energy supplied under Part II in any place specified in clause (b).

(2) Where any difference or dispute arises as to whether a place is or is not one in which one hundred or more persons are likely ordinarily to be assembled, the matter shall be referred to the State Government, and the decision of the State Government thereon shall be final.

(3) The provisions of this section shall be binding on the Government.

PART IV

GENERAL

Protective Clauses

31. Protection of railways, aerodromes, and canals, docks, wharfs and piers.—No person shall, in the generation, transmission, supply or use of energy, in any way injure any railway, [2][aerodrome,] tramway, canal or water-way or any dock, wharf or pier vested in or controlled by a local authority, or obstruct or interfere with the traffic on any railway, [2][airway,] tramway, canal or water-way.

---

1. Subs. by Act 22 of 1998, sec. 5, for "the Indian Railways Act, 1890 (9 of 1890)" (w.e.f. 31-12-1998).
2. Ins. by Act 32 of 1959, sec. 23.

32. Protection of telegraphic, telephonic and electric signalling lines.—(1) Every person generating, transmitting, supplying or using energy (hereinafter in this section referred to as the "operator") shall take all reasonable precautions in constructing, laying down and placing his electric supply-lines and other works and in working his system, so as not injuriously to affect, whether by induction or otherwise, the working of any wire or line used for the purpose of telegraphic, telephone or electric-signalling communication, or the currents in such wire or line.

(2) Where any difference or dispute arises between the operator and the telegraph-authority as to whether the operator has constructed, laid down or placed his electric supply-lines or other works, or worked his system, in contravention of sub-section (1), or as to whether the working of any wire, line or current is or is not injuriously affected thereby, the matter shall be referred to [1][the Central Government]; and [2][the Central Government], unless [3][it] is of opinion that the wire or line has been placed in unreasonable proximity to the electric supply-lines or works of the operator after the construction of such lines or works, may direct the operator to make such alterations in, or additions to, his system as may be necessary in order to comply with the provisions of this section, and the operator shall make such alterations or additions accordingly:

Provided that nothing in this sub-section shall apply to the repair, renewal or amendment of any electric supply-line so long as the course of the electric supply-line and the amount and nature of the energy transmitted thereby are not altered.

(3) Where the operator makes default in complying with the requirements of this section, he shall make full compensation for any loss or damage incurred by reason thereof, and, where any difference or dispute arises as to the amount of such compensation, the matter shall be determined by arbitration.

Explanation.—For the purposes of this section, a telegraph-line shall be deemed to be injuriously affected if telegraphic, telephonic or electric-signalling communication by means of such line is, whether through induction or otherwise, prejudicially interfered with by an electric supply-line or work or by any use made thereof.

33. Notice of accidents and inquiries.—[4][(1) If any accident occurs in connection with the generation, transmission, supply or use

1. Ins. by Act 32 of 1959, sec. 23.
2. Subs. by the A.O. 1939, for "the Local Government".
3. Subs. by Act 38 of 1920, sec. 2, Sch. I, Pt. I, for "he".
4. Subs. by Act 32 of 1959, sec. 24, for the former sub-section.

of energy in or in connection with, any part of the electric supply-lines or other works of any person and the accident results or is likely to have resulted in loss of human or animal life or in any injury to a human being or an animal, such person shall give notice of the occurrence and of any such loss or injury actually caused by the accident, in such form and within such time as may be prescribed, to the Electrical Inspector and to such other authorities as the appropriate Government may by general or special order, direct.]

(2) [1][The appropriate Government] may, if it thinks fit, require any [2][Electrical Inspector], or any other competent person appointed by it in this behalf, to inquire and report—

(a) as to the cause of any accident affecting the safety of the public, which may have been occasioned by or in connection with, the generation, transmission, supply or use of energy, or

(b) as to the manner in, and extent to, which the provisions of this Act or of any license or rules thereunder, so far as those provisions affect the safety of any person, have been complied with.

[3][(3) Every Electrical Inspector or other person holding an inquiry under sub-section (2) shall have all the powers of a Civil Court under the Code of Civil Procedure, 1908 (5 of 1908), for the purpose of enforcing the attendance of witnesses and compelling the production of documents and material objects, and every person required by an Electrical Inspector or such other person as aforesaid to furnish any information shall be deemed to be legally bound to do so within the meaning of section 176 of the Indian Penal Code (45 of 1860).]

34. Prohibition of connection with earth and power for Government to interfere in certain cases of default.—(1) No person shall, in the generation, transmission, supply or use of energy, permit any part of his electric supply-lines to be connected with earth except so far as may be prescribed in this behalf or may be specially sanctioned by the [4][appropriate Government].

(2) If at any time it is established to the satisfaction of the [4][appropriate Government]—

(a) that any part of an electric supply-line is connected with earth contrary to the provisions of sub-section (1), or

1. Subs. by Act 32 of 1959, sec. 24, for "The State Government".
2. Subs. by Act 32 of 1959, sec. 2, for "Electric Inspector".
3. Ins. by Act 32 of 1959, sec. 24.
4. Subs. by Act 32 of 1959, sec. 25, for "State Government".

(b) that any electric supply-lines or other works for the generation, transmission, supply or use of energy are attended with danger to the public safety or to human life or injuriously affect any telegraph-line, or

(c) that any electric supply-lines or other works are defective so as not to be in accordance with the provisions of this Act or of any rule thereunder,

the [1][appropriate Government] may, by order in writing, specify the matter complained of and require the owner or user of such electric supply-lines or other works to remedy it in such manner as shall be specified in the order, and may also in like manner forbid [2][the use of, and the supply of energy to, any electric supply-line] or works until the order is complied with or for such time as is specified in the order.

Administration and Rules

35. Advisory Board.—[3][(1) The Central Government may, for the whole or any part of the territories to which this Act extends, and each State Government may, for the whole or any part of the State, by notification in the Official Gazette, constitute an Advisory Board.]

(2) Every such Board shall consist of a chairman and not less than two other members.

[4][* * *]

[5][(3)] The Central Government or the State Government, as the case may be, may [6][by general or special order published in the Official Gazette],—

[7][(a) determine the number of members of which any such Board shall be constituted and the manner in which such members shall be appointed,

[7](b)] define the duties and regulate the procedure of any such Board,

---

1. Subs. by Act 32 of 1959, sec. 25, for "State Government".
2. Subs. by Act 32 of 1959, sec. 25, for "the use of any electric supply-line".
3. Subs. by Act 3 of 1951, sec. 3 and Sch., for the former sub-section.
4. Sub-section (3) omitted by Act 1 of 1922, sec. 16.
5. Sub-section (4) re-numbered as sub-section (3) by Act 1 of 1922, sec. 16.
6. Subs. by Act 20 of 1983, sec. 2 and Sch., for certain words (w.e.f. 15.3.1984).
7. Clause (a) ins. and the original clauses (a), (b) and (c) re-lettered as (b), (c) and (d) by Act 20 of 1983, sec. 16.

[1][(c)] determine the tenure of office of the members of any such Board, and

[1][(d)] give directions as to the payment of fees to, and the travelling expenses incurred by, any member of any such Board in the performance of his duty.

[2][(4) Every order made by the State Government under sub-section (3) shall be laid, as soon as may be after it is made, before the State Legislature.

(5) Every order made by the Central Government under sub-section (3) shall be laid, as soon as may be after it is made, before each House of Parliament, while it is in session, for a total period of thirty days which may be comprised in one session or in two or more successive sessions, and if, before the expiry of the session immediately following the session or the successive sessions aforesaid, both Houses agree in making any modification in the order or both Houses agree that the order should not be made, the order shall thereafter have effect only in such modified form or be of no effect, as the case may be; so, however, that any such modification or annulment shall be without prejudice to the validity of anything previously done under that order.]

[3]**[36. Appointment of Electrical Inspector.**—(1) The appropriate Government may, by notification in the Official Gazette, appoint duly qualified persons to be Electrical Inspectors and every Electrical Inspector so appointed shall exercise the powers and perform the functions of an Electrical Inspector under this Act within such areas or in respect of such class of works and electric installations and subject to such restrictions as the appropriate Government may direct.

(2) In the absence of express provision to the contrary in this Act, or any rule made thereunder, an appeal shall lie from the decision of an Electrical Inspector to the appropriate Government or if the appropriate Government, by general or special order so directs, to an Advisory Board.]

[4]**[36A. Central Electricity Board.**—(1) A Board to be called the Central Electricity Board shall be constituted to exercise the powers conferred by section 37.

1. Clause (a) ins. and the original clauses (a), (b) and (c) re-lettered as (b), (c) and (d) by Act 20 of 1983, sec. 16.
2. Ins. by Act 20 of 1963, sec. 2 and Sch, (w.e.f. 15-3-1984).
3. Subs. by Act 32 of 1959, sec. 26, for the former section.
4. Ins. by Act 10 of 1937, sec. 3.

[1][(2) The Central Electricity Board shall consist of the following members, namely:—

(a) a chairman and five other members to be nominated by the Central Government;

(b) one member to be nominated by the Governments of each of the States, not being a Union territory, to which this Act extends;

(c) one member to be nominated by the Central Government to represent each of the Union territories of Delhi and Himachal Pradesh;

(d) one member to be nominated by the Central Government to represent the Union territories of Manipur, Tripura and the Andaman and Nicobar Islands;

(e) one member to be nominated by each of the State Electricity Boards,

(f) one member to be nominated by the Central Government to represent the Federation of Electricity Undertakings of India;

(g) one member to be nominated by the Railway Board;

(h) one member to be nominated by the Chief Inspector of Mines appointed under section 5 of the Mines Act, 1952 (35 of 1952); and

(i) one member to be nominated by the Indian Standards Institution constituted under the Indian Standards Institution (Certification Marks) Act, 1952 (36 of 1952).]

(3) Any vacancy occurring in the Board [2][* * *] shall be filled as soon as may be by a nomination made by the authority by whom the member vacating office was nominated.

(4) The Board shall have full power to regulate by bye-laws or otherwise its own procedure and the conduct of all business to be transacted by it.

(5) The powers of the Central Electricity Board may be exercised notwithstanding any vacancy in the Board.]

[3][* * *]

---

1. Subs. by Act 32 of 1959, sec. 27, for the former sub-section (2).
2. The words "otherwise than by the expiry of the term of office of the member referred to in clause (c) of sub-section (2)" omitted by the Adaptation of Laws (No. 2) Order, 1956.
3. Sub-section (6), which was ins. by the Adaptation of Laws (No. 2) Order, 1956, omitted by Act 32 of 1959, sec. 27.

[1]**36B. Certain members affected by States' re-organisation to vacate offices.**—*[Rep. by the Indian Electricity (Amendment) Act, 1959 (32 of 1959), sec. 28.]*

37. Power for Board to make rules.—(1) The [2][Central Electricity Board] may make rules, for [3][the whole or any part of the territories to which this Act extends], to regulate the generation, transmission, supply and use of energy, and, generally, to carry out the purposes and objects of this Act.

(2) In particular and without prejudice to the generality of the foregoing power, such rules may—

(a) prescribe the form of applications for licences and the payments to be made in respect thereof;

(b) regulate the publication of notices;

(c) prescribe the manner in which objections with reference to any application under Part II are to be made.

(d) provide for the preparation and submission of accounts by licensees in a specified form;

(e) provide for the securing of a regular, constant and sufficient supply of energy by licensees to consumers and for the testing at various parts of the system of the regularity and sufficiency of such supply, and for the examination of the records of such tests by consumers;

(f) provide for the protection of persons and property from injury by reason of contact with, or the proximity of, or by reason of the defective or dangerous condition of, any appliance or apparatus used in the generation, transmission, supply or use of energy;

(g) for the purposes of electric traction regulate the employment of insulated returns, or of uninsulated metallic returns of low resistance, in order to prevent fusion or injurious electrolytic action of or on metallic pipes, structures or substances, and to minimise, as far as is reasonably practicable, injurious interference with the electric wires, supply-lines and apparatus of parties other than the owners of the electric traction system, or with the currents therein, whether the earth is used as a return or not;

---

1. Section 36B was ins. by the Adaptation of Laws (No. 2) Order, 1956.
2. Subs. by Act 10 of 1937, sec. 4, for "G.G. in C."
3. Subs. by Act 3 of 1951, sec. 3 and Sch., for "the territories for the time being comprised within Part A States and Part C States or any part of such territories".

(h) provide for preventing telegraph-lines and magnetic observatories or laboratories from being injuriously affected by the generation, transmission, supply or use of energy;

(i) prescribe the qualifications to be required of [1][Electrical Inspectors];

(j) authorise any [1][Electrical Inspector] or other officer of a specified rank and class to enter, inspect, and examine any place, carriage or vessel in which he has reason to believe any appliance or apparatus used in the generation, transmission, supply or use of energy to be, and to carry out tests therein, and to prescribe the facilities to be given to such Inspectors or officers for the purposes of such examinations and tests; [2][* * *]

(k) authorise and regulate the levy of fees for any such testing or inspection and, generally, for the services of [1][Electrical Inspectors] under this Act; [3][and

(l) provide for any matter which is to be or may be prescribed.]

(3) Any rules made in pursuance of [4][clauses (e) to (j) (both inclusive)] of sub-section (2) shall be binding on the Government.

[5][(4)] In making any rule under this Act, the [6][Central Electricity Board] may direct that every breach thereof shall be punishable with fine which may extend to three hundred rupees, and in the case of a continuing breach, with a further daily fine which may extend to fifty rupees.

38. Further provisions respecting rules.—(1) The power to make rules under section 37 shall be subject to the condition of the rules being made after previous publication.

(2) The date to be specified in accordance with clause (3) of section 23 of the General Clauses Act, 1897 (10 of 1897), as that after which a draft of rules proposed to be made under section 37 will be taken into consideration shall not be less than three months from the date on which the draft of the proposed rules was published for general information.

1. Subs. by Act 32 of 1959, sec. 2, for "Electric Inspector".
2. The word "and" omitted by Act 1 of 1922, sec. 18.
3. Ins. by Act 1 of 1922, sec. 18.
4. Subs. by Act 32 of 1959, sec. 29, for "clause (f) or clause (h)".
5. Original sub-section (3) re-numbered as sub-section (4) by Act 1 of 1922, sec. 18.
6. Subs. by Act 10 of 1937, sec. 4, for "G.G. in C."

[1][(3) Every rule made under section 37 shall be published in the Gazette of India and shall be laid, as soon as may be after it is made, before each House of Parliament, while it is in section, for a total period of thirty days which may be comprised in one session or in two or more successive sessions, and if, before the expiry of the session immediately following the session or the successive sessions aforesaid, both Houses agree in making any modification in the rule or both Houses agree that the rule should not be made, the rule shall thereafter have effect only in such modified form or be of no effect, as the case may be; so however, that any such modification or annulment shall be without prejudice to the validity of anything previously done under that rule.]

Criminal Offences and Procedure

[2][**39. Theft of energy.**—Whoever dishonestly abstracts, consumes or uses any energy shall be punishable with imprisonment for a term which may extend to three years, or with fine which shall not be less than one thousand rupees, or with both: and if it is proved that any artificial means or means not authorised by the licensee exist for the abstraction, consumption or use of energy by the consumer, it shall be presumed, until the contrary is proved, that any abstraction, consumption or use of energy has been dishonestly caused by such consumer.

39A. Abetment.—Whoever abets an offence punishable under section 39 or section 44 shall, notwithstanding anything contained in section 116 of the Indian Penal Code (45 of 1860), be punished with punishment provided for the offence.]

40. Penalty for maliciously wasting energy or injuring works.—Whoever maliciously causes energy to be wasted or diverted, or, with intent to cut off the supply of energy, cuts or injures, or attempts to cut or injure, any electric supply-line or works, shall be punishable with imprisonment for a term which may extend to two years, or with fine which may extend to one thousand rupees, or with both.

41. Penalty for unauthorised supply of energy by non-licensees.—Whoever, in contravention of the provisions of section 28 engages in the business of supplying energy shall be punishable with fine which may extend to three thousand rupees, and in the case of a continuing contravention, with a daily fine which may extend to three hundred rupees.

1. Subs. by Act 20 of 1983, sec. 2 and Sch, for the former sub-section (w.e.f. 15-3-1984).
2. Subs. by Act 31 of 1986, sec. 2, for the former section 39.

[1][**41A. Penalty for unauthorised transmission of energy.**—Whoever, in contravention of the provisions of this Act or regulations or license conditions, engages in the business of transmission of energy shall be punishable with fine which may extend to three thousand rupees and in case of a continuing contravention, with a daily fine which may extend to three hundred rupees.]

[2][**42. Penalty for illegal or defective supply or for non-compliance with order.**—Whoever—

(a) being a licensee or a person who has obtained the sanction of the State Government under section 28 to engage in the business of supplying energy to the public, save as permitted under section 27 or section 51 or by his license or as the case may be, by the conditions of sanction, supplies energy or lays down or places any electric supply-line or works outside the area of supply; or

(b) being a licensee or a person who has obtained the sanction of the State Government as aforesaid, in contravention of the provisions of this Act or of the rules thereunder, or in breach of the conditions of license or of the sanction, as the case may be, and without reasonable excuse, the burden of proving which shall lie on him discontinues the supply of energy or fails to supply energy; or

(c) makes default in complying with any of the provisions of an order or of any notice or requisition issued under section 5 or section 6; or

(d) makes default in complying with any directions issued to him under section 22A; or

(e) makes default in complying with any order issued to him under section 22B or sub-section (2) of section 34,

shall be punishable with fine which may extend to one thousand rupees, and, in the case of a continuing offence or default, with a daily fine which may extend to one hundred rupees.]

43. Penalty for illegal transmission or use of energy.—Whoever, in contravention of the provisions of section 30, transmits or uses energy without giving the notice required thereby, shall be punishable with fine which may extend to five hundred rupees, and, in the case of a continuing offence, with a daily fine which may extend to fifty rupees.

---

1. Ins. by Act 22 of 1998, sec. 6 (w.e.f. 31-12-1998).
2. Subs. by Act 32 of 1959, sec. 31, for the former section.

44. Penalty for interference with meters or licensee's works and for improper use of energy.—Whoever—

(a) connects any meter referred to in section 26, sub-section (1), or any meter, indicator or apparatus referred to in section 26, sub-section (7), with any electric supply-line through which energy is supplied by a licensee, or disconnects the same from any such electric supply-line [1][* * *]; or

[2][(aa) unauthorisedly re-connects any meter referred to in sub-section (1) of section 26, or any meter, indicator or apparatus referred to in sub-section (7) of section 26, with any electric supply-line or other works, being the property of the licensee, through which energy may be supplied, when the said electric supply line or other works has or have been cut or disconnected under sub-section (1) of section 24; or]

(b) lays, or causes to be laid, or connects up any works for the purpose of communicating with any other works belonging to a licensee [3][* * *]; or

(c) maliciously injures any meter referred to in section 26, sub-section (1), or any meter, indicator or apparatus referred to in section 26, sub-section (7), or wilfully or fraudulently alters the index of any such meter, indicator or apparatus, or prevents any such meter, indicator or apparatus from duly registering; or

(d) improperly uses the energy of a licensee,

[4][shall be punishable with imprisonment for a term which may extend to three years, or with fine which may extend to five thousand rupees, or with both], and, in the case of a continuing offence, with a daily fine which may extend to [5][fifty] rupees; and [2][if it is proved that any artificial means exist] for making such connection as is referred to in clause (a) [2][or such re-connection as is referred to in clause (aa),] or such communication as is referred to in clause (b), or for causing such alteration or prevention as is referred to in clause (c), or for facilitating such improper use as is referred to in clause (d), [6][and that] the meter, indicator or apparatus is under the custody or

1. The words "without giving to the licensee forty-eight hours' notice in writing of his intention" omitted by Act 32 of 1959, sec. 32.
2. Ins. by Act 31 of 1986, sec. 3.
3. The words "without such licensee's consent" omitted by Act 32 of 1959, sec. 32.
4. Subs. by Act 31 of 1986, sec. 3, for certain words.
5. Subs. by Act 1 of 1922, sec. 19, for "thirty".
6. Subs. by Act 1 of 1922, sec. 19, for "shall, where".

control of the consumer, whether it is his property or not, [1][it shall be presumed, until the contrary is proved] [2][that such connection, re-connection, communication,] alteration, prevention or improper use, as the case may be, has been knowingly and wilfully caused by such consumer.

45. Penalty for extinguishing public lamps.—Whoever maliciously extinguishes any public lamp shall be punishable with imprisonment for a term which may extend to six months, or with fine which may extend to three hundred rupees, or with both.

46. Penalty for neglecting wasting energy or injuring works.—Whoever negligently causes energy to be wasted or diverted, or negligently breaks, throws down or damages any electric supply-line, post, pole or lamp or other apparatus connected with the supply of energy, shall be punishable with fine which may extend to two hundred rupees.

47. Penalty for offences not otherwise provided for.—Whoever, in any case not already provided for by [3][section 39, section 39A or section 40] to 46 (both inclusive), makes default in complying with any of the provisions of this Act, or with any order issued under it, or, in the case of a licensee, with any of the conditions of his license, [4][or in the case of a person who has obtained the sanction of the State Government under section 28, with any of the conditions of the sanction], shall be punishable with fine which may extend to one hundred rupees, and, in the case of a continuing default, with a daily fine which may extend to twenty rupees:

Provided that, where a person has made default complying with any of the provisions of sections 13,14,15,17 and 32, as the case may be, he shall not be so punishable if the court is of opinion that the case was one of emergency and that the offender complied with the said provisions as far as was reasonable in the circumstances.

48. Penalties not to affect other liabilities.—The penalties imposed by [3][section 39, section 39A or sections 40] to 47 (both inclusive) shall be in addition to, and not in derogation of, any liability in respect of the payment of compensation or, in the case of a licensee the revocation of his license, which the offender may have incurred.

---

1. Subs. by Act 1 of 1922, sec. 19, for "be *prima facie* evidence".
2. Subs. by Act 31 of 1986, sec. 3, for certain words.
3. Subs. by Act 31 of 1986, sec. 4, for "section 39"
4. Ins. by Act 32 of 1959, sec. 33.

49. Penalties where works belong to Government.—The provisions of [1][sections 39, 39A, 40,] 44, 45 and 46 shall, so far as they are applicable, be deemed to apply also when the acts made punishable thereunder are committed in the case of energy supplied by or of works belonging to [2][the Central Government or any State Government].

[3][**49A. Offences by companies.**—(1) If the person committing an offence under this Act is a company, every person who at the time the offence was committed was in charge of, and was responsible to the company for the conduct of the business of the company as well as the company, shall be deemed to be guilty of the offence and shall be liable to be proceeded against and punished accordingly:

Provided that nothing contained in this sub-section shall render any such person liable to any punishment, if he proves that the offence was committed without his knowledge or that he exercised all due diligence to prevent the commission of such offence.

(2) Notwithstanding anything contained in sub-section (1), where an offence under this Act has been committed with the consent or connivance of, or is attributable to any neglect on the part of, any director or manager, secretary or other officer of the company, such director, manager, secretary or other officer shall also be deemed to be guilty of that offence and shall be liable to be proceeded against and punished accordingly.

Explanation.—For the purposes of this section,—

(a) "company" means any body corporate and includes a firm or other association of individuals; and

(b) "director", in relation to a firm, means a partner in the firm.]

50. Institution of prosecutions.—No prosecution shall be instituted against any person for any offence against this Act or any rule, license or order thereunder, except at the instance of the Government [4][or a State Electricity Board] or an [5][Electrical Inspector], or of a person aggrieved by the same.

Supplementary

[6][**51. Exercise in certain cases of powers of telegraph authority.**—Notwithstanding anything contained in sections 12 to 16

1. Subs. by Act 31 of 1986, sec. 5, for "sections 39, 40".
2. Subs. by the A.O. 1948, for "any Government in British India".
3. Ins. by Act 32 of 1959, sec. 34.
4. Ins. by Act 31 of 1986, sec. 6.
5. Subs. by Act 32 of 1959, sec. 2, for "Electric Inspector".
6. Subs. by Act 22 of 1998, sec. 7 (w.e.f. 31-12-1998).

(both inclusive) and sections 18 and 19, the Central Government in the case of inter-State transmission system and the State Government in the case of intra-State transmission system, as the case may be, may, by order in writing, for placing of electric supply-lines, appliances and apparatus for the transmission of energy or for the purpose of telephonic or telegraphic communication necessary for the proper co-ordination of works, confer upon any public officer, Central Transmission Utility, State Transmission Utility, licensee, transmission licensee or any other person engaged in the business of transmission or supplying energy to the public under this Act, subject to such conditions and restrictions (if any) as the Central Government or the State Government, as the case may be, may think fit to impose, and to the provisions of the Indian Telegraph Act, 1885 (3 of 1885), any of the powers which the telegraph-authority possesses under the Act, with respect to the placing of telegraph-lines and posts for the purposes of a telegraph established or maintained by the Government or to be so establishment or maintained.]

[1][**51A. State Government to have powers and obligations of a licensee under this Act.**—Where the State Government engages in the business of supplying energy to the public, it shall have all the powers and obligations of a licensee under this Act:

Provided that nothing in sections 3 to 11 (both inclusive), section 21, sub-sections (2) and (3), sections 22 and 27 or in clauses I to V (both inclusive), clause VII and clauses IX to XII (both inclusive) of the Schedule relating to the duties and obligations of a licensee shall apply to the State Government:

Provided further that the provisions of clause VI of the Schedule shall apply to the State Government in respect of that area only where distribution mains have been laid by the State Government and the supply of energy through any of them has commenced.]

52. Arbitration.—Where any matter is, by or under this Act, directed to be determined by arbitration, the matter shall, unless it is otherwise expressly provided in the license of a licensee, be determined by such person or persons as the State Government may nominate in that behalf on the application of either party; but in all other respects the arbitration shall be subject to the provisions of the [2][* * *] [3][Arbitration and Conciliation Act, 1996 (26 of 1996)]:

---

1. Ins. by Act 32 of 1959, sec. 36.
2. The word "Indian" omitted by Act 32 of 1940, sec. 3 and Sch. II.
3. Subs. by Act 22 of 1998, sec. 8, for "Arbitration Act, 1940 (10 of 1940)" (w.e.f. 31-12-1998).

[1][Provided that where the Government or a State Electricity Board is a party to a dispute, the dispute shall be referred to two arbitrators, one to be appointed by each party to the dispute.]

53. Service of notices, orders or documents.—(1) Every notice, order or document by or under this Act required or authorised to be addressed to any person may be served by post or left,—

(a) where [2][the Central Government or the State Government] is the addressee, at the office of [3][such officer as the Central Government or the State Government, as the case may be, may designate in this behalf];

[4][* * *]

(b) where a local authority is the addressee, at the office of the local authority;

(c) where a company is the addressee, at the registered office of the company or, in the event of the registered office of the company not being in India, at the head office of the company in India;

(d) where any other person is the addressee, at the usual or last known place of abode or business of the person.

(2) Every notice, order or document by or under this Act required or authorised to be addressed to the owner or occupier of any premises shall be deemed to be properly addressed if addressed by the description of the "owner" or "occupier" of the premises (naming the premises) and may be served by delivering it or a true copy thereof, to some person on the premises, or, if there is no person on the premises to whom the same can with reasonable diligency be delivered, by affixing it on some conspicuous part of the premises.

54. Recovery of sums recoverable under certain provisions of Act.—Every sum declared to be recoverable by [5][section 5, sub-section (4)] section 14, sub-section (2), clause (b), section 16, sub-section (2), section 18, sub-section (2) or sub-section (4), or section 26, sub-section (4) and every fee liable under this Act, may be recovered, on application to a Magistrate having jurisdiction where the person liable to pay the same is for the time being resident, by

1. Added by Act 32 of 1959, sec. 37.
2. Subs. by the A.O. 1937, for "the Government".
3. Subs. by Act 1 of 1922, sec. 21, for "the Secretary in the Public Works Department".
4. Clause (aa) ins. by the A.O. 1937, omitted by the A.O. 1948.
5. Subs. by Act 32 of 1959, sec. 38, for "section 5, clause (f), section 6, sub-section (2)".

the distress and sale of any movable property belonging to such person.

55. Delegation of certain functions of State Government to Electrical Inspectors.—The State Government may, by general or special order, authorise the discharge of any of its functions under section 13 or section 18, [1][or section 34, sub-section (2)], or clause V, sub-clause (2), or clause XIII of the Schedule by an [2][Electrical inspector].

56. Protection for acts done in good faith.—[3][(1)] No suit, prosecution or other proceeding shall lie against any public officer, or any servant of a local authority, for anything done, or in good faith purporting to be done, under this Act.

[4][(2) No court shall take cognizance of an offence under this Act, by a public officer except with the sanction—

(a) in the case of a person employed in connection with the affairs of the Union, of the Central Government; and

(b) in any other case, of the State Government.]

57. Amendments of the Land Acquisition Act, 1894.—(1) In section 40, sub-section (1), clause (b), and section 41, sub-section (5), of the Land Acquisition Act, 1894 (1 of 1894), the term "work" shall be deemed to include, electrical energy supplied, or to be supplied, by means of the work to be constructed.

(2) The State Government may, if it thinks fit, on the application of any person, not being a company, desirous of obtaining any land for the purposes of his undertaking, direct that he may acquire such land under the provisions of the Land Acquisition Act, 1894 (1 of 1894), in the same manner and on the same conditions as it might be acquired if the person were a company.

58. Repeals and savings.—(1) The Indian Electricity Act, 1903 (3 of 1903), is hereby repealed:

Provided that every application for a license made and every license granted under the said Act shall be deemed to have been made and granted under this Act.

(2) Nothing in this Act shall be deemed to affect the terms of any license which was granted, or of any agreement which was made, by or with the sanction of the Government for the supply or use of electricity before the commencement of this Act.

---

1. Ins. by Act 1 of 1922, sec. 22.
2. Subs. by Act 32 of 1959, sec. 2, for "Electric Inspector".
3. Section 56 re-numbered as sub-section (1) of that section by Act 32 of 1959, sec. 39.
4. Ins. by Act 32 of 1959, sec. 39.

THE SCHEDULE

PROVISIONS TO BE DEEMED TO BE INCORPORATED WITH, AND TO FORM PART OF, EVERY LICENSE GRANTED UNDER PART II, SO FAR AS NOT ADDED TO, VARIED OR EXCEPTED BY THE LICENSE

[*See* section 3, sub-section (2), clause (f)]

Security and Accounts

I. Security for executions of work of license not being local authority.—Where the licensee is not a local authority, the following provisions as to giving security shall apply, namely:—

(a) The licensee shall, within the period fixed in that behalf by his license, or any longer period which the State Government may substitute therefor by order under [1][section 4A, sub-section (1)], of the Indian Electricity Act, 1910, before exercising any of the powers by the license conferred on him in relation to the execution of works, show, to the satisfaction of the State Government, that he is in a position fully and efficiently to discharge the duties and obligations imposed upon him by the license throughout the area of supply;

(b) The licensee shall also, within the period fixed in that behalf by his license, or any longer period which the State Government may substitute therefor by order under [1][section 4A, sub-section (1)], of the Indian Electricity Act, 1910, and before exercising any of the powers conferred on him in relation to the execution of works, deposit or secure to the satisfaction of the State Government such sum (if any) as may be fixed by the license or, if not so fixed, by the State Government;

(c) The said sum deposited or secured by the licensee under the provisions of this clause shall be repaid or released to him on the completion of the works or at such earlier date or dates and by such instalments, as may be approved by the State Government:

[2][Provided that if the works referred to in clause IV are not executed to the satisfaction of the State Government within the period specified in that clause, that Government may by order direct that the whole or any part of the sum so deposited or secured shall be forfeited to it.]

II. Audit of accounts of licensee not being local authority.—Where the licensee is not a local authority, the following provisions as to the audit of accounts shall apply, namely:—

(a) The annual statement of accounts of the undertaking shall, before being rendered under section 11 of the Indian Electricity Act, 1910, be examined and audited by such person as the State Government may appoint or approve in this behalf and the remuneration of the

1. Subs. by Act 32 of 1959, sec. 40, for "section 4, sub-section (3), clause (b)".
2. Added by Act 32 of 1959, sec. 40.

auditor shall be such as the State Government may direct, and his remuneration and all expenses incurred by him in or about the execution of the duties, to such in amount as the State Government shall approve, shall be paid by the licensee on demand;

(b) The licensee shall afford to the auditor, his clerks and assistants, access to all such books and documents relating to the undertaking as are necessary for the purposes of the audit, and shall, when required, furnish to him and them all vouchers and information [1][(including technical data and statements of energy generated and sold)] requisite for that purpose, and afford to him and them all facilities for the proper execution of his and their duty;

(c) The audit shall be made and conducted in such manner as the State Government may direct;

(d) Any report made by the auditor, or such portion thereof as the State Government may direct, shall be appended to the annual statement of accounts of the licensee, and shall thenceforth form part thereof;

(e) Notwithstanding the foregoing provisions of this clause, the State Government may, if it thinks fit, accept the examination and audit of an auditor appointed by the licensee.

III. Separate accounts.—The licensee shall unless the State Government otherwise directs, at all times keep the accounts of the [2][undertaking relating to the generation, supply or distribution of energy] distinct from the accounts kept by him of any other undertaking or business.

Compulsory Works and Supply

IV. Execution of work after commencement of license.—The licensee shall, within a period of three years after the commencement of the license, execute to the satisfaction of the State Government all such works as may be specified in the license in this behalf or, if not so specified, as the State Government may, by order in writing issued within six months of the date of the commencement of the license, direct.

V. Provisions as to laying down of further distributing mains.—(1) Where, after the expiration of two years and six months from the commencement of the license, a requisition is made by [3][two or more] owners or occupiers of premises in or upon any street or part of a street within the area of supply or by the State Government or a local authority charged with the public lighting thereof, requiring the licensee to provide distributing mains throughout such street or part thereof, the licensee shall comply within six months with the requisition, unless,—

(a) where it is made by such owners or occupiers as aforesaid, the owners or occupiers making it do not, within fourteen clear days after the service on them by the licensee of a notice in writing in

1. Ins. by Act 32 of 1959, sec. 40.
2. Subs. by Act 32 of 1959, sec. 40, for "capital employed for the purposes of the undertaking".
3. Subs. by Act 32 of 1959, sec. 40, for "six or more".

this behalf, tender to the licensee a written contract [1][in a form approved by the State Government] duly executed and with sufficient security binding themselves to take, or guaranteeing that there shall be taken, a supply of energy for not less than two years to such amount as will in the aggregate [1][assure to the licensee at the current rates charged by him, an annual revenue not exceeding fifteen per centum of the cost of the distributing mains (not including transformers and other sub-station equipment) required to comply with the requisition]; or

(b) where it is made by the State Government or a local authority, as the case may be, does not, within the like period, tender a like contract binding itself to take a supply of energy for not less than seven years for the public lamps in such street or part thereof.

[2][(2) Where any difference or dispute arises between the licensee and such owners or occupiers as to the sufficiency of the security offered under this clause, or as to the cost of the distributing mains or as to the amount of energy to be taken or guaranteed as aforesaid, the matter shall be referred to the Electrical Inspector and decided by him.]

(3) Every requisition under this clause shall be signed by the maker or makers thereof and shall be served on the licensee.

(4) Every requisition under this clause shall be in a form to be prescribed by rules under the Indian Electricity Act, 1910; and copies of the form shall be kept at the office of the licensee and supplied free of charge to any applicant.

VI. Requisition for supply to owners or occupiers in vicinity.—(1) Where, [3][after distributing mains have been laid down under the provisions of clause IV and clause V and the supply of energy through those mains or any of them has commenced,] a requisition is made by the owner or occupier of any premises situate within [4][the area of supply] requiring the licensee to supply energy for such premises, the licensee shall, within one month from the making of the requisition, [3][or within such longer period as the [5][Electrical Inspector] may allow] supply, and, save in so far as he is prevented from doing so by cyclones, floods, storms or other occurrences beyond his control, continue to supply, energy in accordance with the requisition:

Provided, first, that the licensee shall not be bound to comply with any such requisition unless and until the person making it—

(a) within fourteen days after the service on him by the licensee of a notice in writing in this behalf, tenders to the licensee a written contract, in a form approved by the State Government, duly

---

1. Subs. by Act 32 of 1959, sec. 40, for certain words.
2. Subs. by Act 32 of 1959, sec. 40, for the former sub-clause (2).
3. Ins. by Act 1 of 1922, sec. 23.
4. Subs. by Act 1 of 1922, sec. 23, for "one hundred yards from any distributing main".
5. Subs. by Act 32 of 1959, sec. 2, for "Electric Inspector"

executed and with sufficient security, binding himself to take a supply of energy for not less than two years to such amount as will [1][assure to the licensee at the current rates charged by him, an annual revenue not exceeding fifteen per centum of the cost of the service-line required to comply with the requisition], and

(b) if required by the licensee so to do, pays to the licensee the cost of so much of any service-line as may be laid down or placed for the purposes of the supply upon the property in respect of which the requisition is made, and of so much of any service-line as it may be necessary for the said purposes to lay down or place beyond one hundred feet from the licensee's distributing main, although not on that property:

Provided, secondly, that the licensee shall be entitled to discontinue such supply—

(a) if the owner or occupier of the property to which the supply is made has not already given security, or if any security given by him has become invalid or insufficient, and such owner or occupier fails to furnish security or to make up the original security to a sufficient amount, as the case may be, within seven days, after the service upon him of notice from the licensee requiring him so to do, or

(b) if the owner or occupier of the property to which the supply is made adopts any appliance, or uses the energy supplied to him by the licensee for any purposes, or deals with it in any manner, so as unduly or improperly to interfere with the efficient supply of energy to any other person by the licensee, or

(c) if the electric wires, fittings, works and apparatus in such property are not in good order and condition, and are consequently likely to affect injuriously the use of energy by the licensee, or by other persons, or

(d) if the owner or occupier makes any alterations of, or additions to, any electric wires, fittings, works or apparatus within such property as aforesaid, and does not notify the same to the licensee before the same are connected to the source of supply, with a view to their being examined and tested; [2][but the licensee shall re-connect the supply with all reasonable speed on the cessation of the act or default or both, as the case may be, which entitled him to discontinue it]:

Provided, thirdly, that the maximum rate per unit of time at which the owner or occupier shall be entitled to be supplied with energy shall not exceed what is necessary for the maximum consumption on his premises, and, where the owner or occupier has required a licensee to supply him at a specified maximum rate, he shall not be entitled to alter that maximum, except after one month's notice in writing to the licensee, and the licensee may recover from the owner or occupier any expenses incurred by him by reason of

---

1. Subs. by Act 32 of 1959, sec. 40, for certain words.
2. Added by Act 1 of 1922, sec. 23.

such alteration in respect of the service-lines by which energy is supplied to the property beyond one hundred feet from the licensee's distributing main, or in respect of any fittings or apparatus of the licensee upon that property: and

Provided, fourthly, that, [1][if any requisition is made for a supply of energy and] the licensee can prove, to the satisfaction of an [2][Electrical Inspector]—

(a) that [3][the nearest distributing main] is already loaded up to its full current-carrying capacity, or

(b) that, in case of a larger amount of current being transmitted by it, the loss of pressure will seriously affect the efficiency of the supply to other consumers in the vicinity,

the licenseme may refuse to accede to the requisition for such reasonable period, not exceeding six months, as such Inspector may think sufficient for the purpose of amending the distributing main or laying down or placing a further distributing main.

(2) Any service-line laid for the purpose of supply in pursuance of a requisition under sub-clause (1) shall, notwithstanding that a portion of it may have been paid for by the person making the requisition, be [4][maintained by the licensee who shall also have the right to use it for the supply of energy to any other person].

(3) Where any difference or dispute arises as to the amount of energy to be taken or guaranteed as aforesaid, or as to the cost of any service-line or as to the sufficiency of the security offered by any owner or occupier, [5][or as to the position of the meter board] or as to the improper use of energy, or to any alleged defect in any wires, fitting, works or apparatus, or as to the amount of the expenses incurred under the third proviso to sub-clause (1), the matter shall be referred to an [2][Electrical Inspector] and decided by him.

(4) Every requisition under this clause shall be signed by the maker or makers thereof and shall be served on the licensee.

(5) Every requisition under this clause shall be in a form to be prescribed by rules under the Indian Electricity Act, 1910; and copies of the form shall be kept at the office of the licensee and supplied free of charge to any applicant.

[6][**VII. Further provisions as to laying of service-lines.**—The licensee shall, before commencing to lay down or place a service-line in any street in which a distributing main has not already been laid down or placed,

---

1. Subs. by Act 1 of 1922, sec. 23, for "in the event of any requisition being made for a supply of energy from any distributing main of which".
2. Subs. by Act 32 of 1959, sec. 2, for "Electric Inspector".
3. Subs. by Act 1 of 1922, sec. 23, for "it".
4. Subs. by Act 32 of 1959, sec. 40, for "maintained by the licensee".
5. Ins. by Act 32 of 1959, sec. 40.
6. Subs. by Act 1 of 1922, sec. 24, for the former clause VII.

serve upon the local authority (if any) and upon the owner or occupier of all premises abutting on so much of the street as lies between the points of origin and termination of the service-line so to be laid down or placed twenty-one days' notice stating that the licensee intends to lay down or place a service-line, and intimating that, if within the said period the local authority or [1][any one or more] of such owners or occupiers require, in accordance with the provisions of the license, that a supply shall be given for any public lamps or to their premises, as the case may be, the necessary distributing main will be laid down or placed by the licensee at the same time as the service-line.]

VIII. Supply for public lamps.—(1) Where, [2][after distributing mains have been laid down under the provisions of clause IV or clause V and the supply of energy through those mains or any of them has commenced], a requisition is made by the State Government or by a local authority requiring the licensee to supply for a period of not less than seven years energy for any public lamps within the [3][area of supply], the licensee shall supply, and, save in so far as he is prevented from doing so by cyclones, floods, storms or other occurrences beyond his control, continue to supply, energy for such lamps in such quantities as the State Government or the local authority, as the case may be, may require.

[4][(1A) The State Government or, as the case may be, a local authority may require the licensee—

(a) to provide the mains and other equipments for public lamps, and

(b) to use for that purpose supports, if any, previously erected or set up by him for supply of energy.]

(2) The provisions of sub-clause (b) of the first proviso, of sub-clauses (c) and (d) of the second proviso and of the third and fourth proviso to sub-clause (1) and the provisions of sub-clauses (2) and (3) of clause VI shall, so far as may be, apply to every case in which a requisition for the supply of energy is made under this clause as if the State Government or local authority were on owner or occupier within the meaning of those provisions.

Supply by bulk-licensees

IX. Special provisions applying to supply by bulk-licensees.—(1) Where, and in so far as the licensee (hereinafter in this clause referred to as "the bulk-licensee") is authorized by his license to supply energy to other licensees for distribution by them (hereinafter in this clause referred to as "distributing-licensees"), the following provisions shall apply, namely:—

(a) any distributing licensees within the bulk-licensee's area of supply may make a requisition on the bulk-licensee, requiring him to give a supply of energy and specifying the point, and the maximum rate per unit of time, at which such supply is required, and the date upon

---

1. Subs. by Act 32 of 1959, sec. 40, for "any five or more".
2. Ins. by Act 1 of 1922, sec. 25.
3. Subs. by Act 1 of 1922, sec. 25, for "distance of one hundred yards from any distributing main".
4. Ins. by Act 32 of 1959, sec. 40.

which the supply is to commence, such date being fixed after the date of receipt of the requisition so as to allow an interval that is reasonable with regard to the locality and to the length of the electric supply-line and the amount of the plant required;

(b) such distributing-licensee shall, if required by the bulk-licensee so to do, enter into a written agreement to receive and pay for a supply of energy for a period of not less than seven years of such an amount that the payment to be made for the same at the rate of charge for the time being charged for such supply shall not be less than such an amount [1][as will assume to the bulk-licensee an annual revenue not exceeding fifteen per centum of the outlay] (excluding expenditure on generating plant then existing and any electric supply-line then laid down or placed) incurred by him in making provision for such supply;

[2][* * *]

(d) if any difference or dispute arises under this clause, it shall be determined by arbitration, and, in the event of such arbitration, the arbitrator shall have regard to the following amongst other considerations, namely:—

(i) the period for which the distributing-licensee is prepared to bind himself to take energy;

(ii) the amount of energy required and the hours during which the bulk-licensee is to supply it;

(iii) the capital expenditure incurred or to be incurred by the bulk-licensee in connection with the aforesaid supply of energy; and

(iv) the extent to which the capital expended or to be expended by the bulk-licensee in connection with such supply may become unproductive upon the discontinuance thereof.

(2) Notwithstanding anything in sub-clause (1), the bulk-licensee shall give a supply of energy to any distributing-licensee within his area of supply applying therefor, even although the distributing-licensee desires to be supplied with only a portion the energy required for distribution by him:

Provided that the distributing-licensee shall, if so required by the bulk-licensee, enter into an agreement to take such energy upon special terms (including a minimum annual sum to be paid to the bulk-licensee) to be determined, if necessary, by arbitration in the manner laid down in any clause (1)(d).

(3) The maximum price fixed by a licensee for energy supplied to a distributing-licensee shall not apply to any partial supply given under sub-clause (2).

(4) Every distributing-licensee, who is supplied with energy by a bulk-licensee and intends to discontinue to receive such supply, shall give not less than twelve months' notice in writing of such intention to the bulk-licensee:

---

1. Subs. by Act 32 of 1959, sec. 40, for "as will produce a reasonable return to the bulk-licensee on the outlay".

2. Sub-clause (c) omitted by Act 32 of 1959, sec. 40.

Provided that, where the distributing-licensee has entered into a written agreement with the bulk-licensee to receive and pay for a supply of energy for a certain period, such notice shall be given so as not to expire before the end of that period.

Charges

X. Methods of charging.—[1][* * *]

[2][(1)] [3][* * *] Where the licensee charges by any method [4][approved by the State Government in accordance with section 23, sub-section (3), clause (c), of the Indian Electricity Act, 1910], any consumer who objects to that method may, by not less than one month's notice in writing, require the licensee to charge him, at the licensee's option, either by the actual amount of energy supplied to him or by the electrical quantity contained in the supply, and thereafter the licensee shall not, except with the consent of the consumer, charge him by another method.

[5][(2)] [6][* * *] Before commencing to supply energy through any distributing main, the licensee shall give notice, by public advertisement, of the method by which he proposes to charge for energy so supplied; and, where the licensee has given such notice, he shall not be entitled to change that method of charging without giving not less than one month's notice in writing of such change to the State Government [7][to the State Electricity Board and the local authority (if any) concerned and to the Electrical Inspector], and to every consumer of energy who is supplied by him from such distributing main.

[8][(3)] [9][* * *] If the consumer is provided with a meter in pursuance of the provisions of section 26, sub-section (1), of the Indian Electricity Act, 1910, and the licensee changes the method of charging for the energy supplied by him from the distributing main, the licensee shall bear the expense of providing a new meter, or such other apparatus as may be necessary by reason of the new method of charging.

[10][* * *]

1. First part of clause X upto and including sub-clause (c) omitted by Act 1 of 1922, sec. 26.
2. First proviso numbered as sub-clause (1) by Act 1 of 1922, sec. 26.
3. The words "Provided, first, that" omitted by Act 1 of 1922, sec. 26.
4. Subs. by Act 1 of 1922, sec. 26, for "so approved by the Local Government".
5. Second proviso numbered as sub-clause (2) by Act 1 of 1922, sec. 26.
6. The words "Provided, secondly, that" omitted by Act 1 of 1922, sec. 26.
7. Subs. by Act 32 of 1959, sec. 40, for "to the local authority (if any) concerned".
8. Third proviso numbered as sub-clause (3) by Act 1 of 1922, sec. 26.
9. The words "Provided, thirdly, that", omitted by Act 1 of 1922, sec. 26.
10. Clause XI and clause XIA ins. by Act 1 of 1922, sec. 28, omitted by Act 32 of 1959, sec. 40.

XII. Charge for supply for public lamps.—The price to be charged by the licensee and to be paid to him for energy supplied for the public lamps [1][and other charges to be paid to him in connection therewith] and the mode in which those charges are to be ascertained, shall be settled by agreement between the licensee and the State Government or the local authority, as the case may be, and, where any difference or dispute arises, the matter shall be determined by arbitration.

Testing and inspection

XIII. Licensee to establish testing stations and keep instruments for testing.—The licensee shall establish at his own cost and keep in proper condition such number of testing stations, situated at such places within reasonable distance from any distributing main, as the State Government may direct for the purpose of testing the pressure or periodicity of the supply of energy in the distributing main, and shall supply and keep in proper condition thereat, and on all premises from which he supplies energy, such instruments for testing as an [2][Electrical Inspector] may approve, and shall supply energy to each testing station for the purpose of testing.

XIV. Facilities for testing.—The licensee shall afford [1][to an Electrical Inspector or other person authorised by such Inspector] all facilities for inspection and testing of his works and for the reading, testing and inspection of his instruments, and may, on each occasion of the testing of his works or the reading, testing or inspection of any instruments, be represented by an agent; who may be present, but shall not interfere with the reading, testing or inspection.

XV. Testing of works.—On the occasion of the testing of any works of the licensee by an [3][Electrical Inspector or a person authorised by him in this behalf (hereinafter referred to as the authorised person)] reasonable notice thereof shall be given to the licensee; and the testing shall be carried out at such suitable hours as, in the opinion of the [3][Electrical Inspector or the authorised person] will least interfere with the supply of energy by the licensee, and in such manner as the [3][Electrical Inspector or the authorised person] may think fit, but, except under the provisions of an order made in each case in that behalf by the State Government, the [3][Electrical Inspector or the authorised person] shall not be entitled to have access to, or interfere with, the works of the licensee at any points other than those at which the licensee himself has access to the same:

Provided that the licensee shall not be held responsible for any interruption or irregularity in the supply of energy which may be occasioned by, or required by the [3][Electrical Inspector or the authorised person] for the purpose of, any such testing as aforesaid:

Provided, also, that the testing shall not be made in regard to any particular portion of the works oftener than once in any three months, unless in

1. Ins. by Act 32 of 1959, sec. 40.
2. Subs. by Act 32 of 1959, sec. 2, for "Electric Inspector".
3. Subs. by Act 32 of 1959, sec. 40, for "Electric Inspector".

pursuance of an order made in each case in that behalf by the State Government.

Plan

XVI. Plan of area of supply to made and kept open for inspection.—(1) The licensee shall, after commencing to supply energy, forthwith cause a plan to be made of the area of supply, and shall cause to be marked thereon the alignments [1][and, in the case of underground works, the approximate depth] below the surface of all his then existing electric supply-lines, street-distributing boxes and other works, and shall once in every year cause that plan to be duly corrected so as to show the electric supply-lines, street-distributing boxes and other works for the time being in position. The licensee shall also, if so required by an [2][Electrical Inspector] cause to be made sections showing the approximate level of all his existing underground works other than service-lines.

[3][(2) Every plan shall be drawn to such scale as the State Government may require provided that no scale shall be required unless maps of the locality on that scale are for the time being available to the public.

(3) Every such section shall be drawn to horizontal and vertical scales which shall be such as the State Government may require.]

(4) Every plan and section so made or corrected, or a copy thereof, marked with the date when it was so made or corrected, shall be kept by the licensee at his principal office or place of business within the area of supply, and shall at all reasonable times be open to the inspection of all applicants, and copies thereof shall be supplied on such terms and conditions as may be prescribed by rules under the Indian Electricity Act, 1910.

(5) The licensee shall, if required by an [2][Electrical Inspector] and, where the licensee is not a local authority, by the local authority (if any) concerned, supply free of charge to such [2][Electrical Inspector] or local authority a copy of every such plan or section duly corrected so as to agree with the original kept at the principal office or place of business of the licensee.

Additional notice of certain works

XVII. Notice to Electrical Inspector.—On the day next preceding the commencement of any such works as are referred to in section 13 of the Indian Electricity Act, 1910, the licensee shall, in addition to any other notices which he may be required to give, serve upon the [2][Electrical Inspector], or such officer as the State Government may appoint in this behalf for the area of supply, a notice in writing stating that he is about to commence the works, and the nature and position of the same.

---

1. Subs. by Act 1 of 1922, sec. 29, for "and the approximate height above or depth".
2. Subs. by Act 32 of 1959, sec. 2, for "Electric Inspector".
3. Subs. by Act 1 of 1922, sec. 29, for the original sub-clauses (2) and (3).

THE ELECTRICITY (SUPPLY) ACT, 1948

INTRODUCTION

To provide for the co-ordinated development of electricity in India there was a need of a specific legislation and to meet this, on the broad lines of the Electricity (Supply) Act, 1926, in force in the United Kingdom, the Electricity (Supply) Bill, 1948 was introduced in the Central legislature as a specific legislation to facilitate the establishment of regional co-ordination in the development of electricity transcending the geographical limits of local bodies.

STATEMENT OF OBJECTS AND REASONS

The co-ordinated development of electricity in India on a regional basis is a matter of increasingly urgent importance for post-war reconstruction and development. The absence of co-ordinated system, in which generation is concentrated in the most efficient units and bulk supply of energy centralised under the direction and control of one authority is one of the factors that impedes the healthy and economical growth of electrical development in this country. Besides, it is becoming more and more apparent that if the benefits of electricity are to be extended to semi-urban and rural areas in the most efficient and economical manner consistent with the needs of an entire region, the area of development must transcend the geographical limits of a Municipality, a Cantonment Board or a Notified Area Committee, as the case may be. It has, therefore, become necessary that the appropriate Governments should be vested with the necessary legislative powers to link together under one control electrical development in contiguous areas by the establishment of what is generally known as the "Grid-System". In the circumstances of this country such a system need not necessarily involve inter-connection throughout the length and breadth of a Province; regional co-ordination inclusive of some measure of inter-connection may be all that is needed. An essential pre-requisite is, however, the acquisition of necessary legislative power not only to facilitate the establishment of this system in newly licensed areas but also to control the operations of existing licensees so as to secure fully co-ordinated development.

Government feel that it is not possible to legislate for this purpose within the framework of the Indian Electricity Act, 1910, which was conceived for a very different purpose. In their view what is needed is specific legislation on the broad lines of the Electricity (Supply) Act, 1926, in force in the United Kingdom, which will enable Provincial

Governments to set up suitable organisations to work out "Grid Schemes" within the territorial limits of the Provinces. Although executive power under the proposed Bill will necessarily vest in the Provinces, two considerations indicate the necessity for Central legislation,—

(i) the need for uniformity in the organisation and development of the "Grid System", and

(ii) the necessity for the constitution of semi-autonomous bodies like Electricity Boards to administer the "Grid Systems". In the view of Government it is bodies like these which are likely to be the most suitable organisations for working the "Grid Systems" on quasi-commercial lines. Such Boards cannot, however, be set up by Provincial Governments under the existing Constitutional Act as they would be in the nature of trading corporations within the meaning of Entry 33 of the Federal Legislative List.

ACT 54 OF 1948

The Electricity (Supply) Bill, 1948 was passed by the Central Legislature and received its assent on 10th September, 1948. It came on the Statute Book as THE ELECTRICITY (SUPPLY) ACT, 1948 (54 of 1948).

LIST OF AMENDING ACTS AND ADAPTATION ORDER

1. The Electricity (Supply) Amendment Act, 1949 (57 of 1949).
2. The Adaptation of Laws Order, 1950.
3. The Part B State (Laws) Act, 1951 (3 of 1951).
4. The Electricity (Supply) Amendment Act, 1956 (101 of 1956).
5. The Indian Electricity (Amendment) Act, 1959 (32 of 1959).
6. The Electricity (Supply) Amendment Act, 1962 (44 of 1962).
7. The Electricity (Supply) Amendment Act, 1966 (30 of 1966).
8. The Electricity (Supply) Amendment Act, 1976 (115 of 1976).
9. The Electricity (Supply) Amendment Act, 1978 (23 of 1978).
10. The Electricity (Supply) Amendment Act, 1983 (16 of 1983).
11. The Delegated Legislation Provisions (Amendment) Act, 1983 (20 of 1983).
12. The Electricity (Supply) Amendment Act, 1984 (48 of 1984).
13. The Repealing and Amending Act, 1988 (19 of 1988).
14. The Electricity Laws (Amendment) Act, 1991 (50 of 1991).
15. The Electricity Laws (Amendment) Act, 1998 (22 of 1998).

THE ELECTRICITY (SUPPLY) ACT, 1948

(54 of 1948)[1]

[10th September, 1948]

An Act to provide for the rationalisation of the production and supply of electricity, and generally for taking measures conducive to [2][electrical development].

WHEREAS it is expedient to provide for the rationalisation of the production and supply of electricity, for taking measures conducive to [2][electrical development] and for all matters incidental thereto;

It is hereby enacted as follows:—

CHAPTER I

INTRODUCTORY

1. Short title, extent and commencement.—(1) This Act may be called the Electricity (Supply) Act, 1948.

(2) It extends to the whole of India [3][except the State of Jammu and Kashmir].

[4][(3) This section and sections 2, 3, 4, 4A, 4B, 4C, 15A, 18A, 26A, 28 to 34 (both inclusive), sub-section (2) of section 39, section 42, sub-section (3) of section 43 and sections 57, 57A, 57B, 58, 75A, 76, 77, 77A, 77B, 77C, 82 and 83 and the provisions of the [5][Sixth Schedule] shall come into force at once.]

(4) The remaining provisions of this Act shall come into force in a State on such date, not later than two years from the coming into force of the sections, Schedule and Table mentioned in sub-section (3), as the State Government may, by notification in the Official Gazette, appoint:

---

1. For Statement of Objects and Reasons, *see* Gazette of India, 1947, Pt. V, p. 514, and for Report of Select Committee, *see* Gazette of India, 1948, pp. 201-203.

   The Act has been extended to Dadra and Nagar Haveli by Reg. 6 of 1963, sec. 2 and Sch. 1 (w.e.f. 1-7-1965).

2. Subs. by the A.O. 1950, for "the electrical development of the Provinces of India".
3. Subs. by Act 3 of 1951, sec. 3 and Sch., for "except Part B States".
4. Subs. by Act 101 of 1956, sec. 2 (w.e.f. 30-12-1956) and again subs. by Act 115 of 1976, sec. 2, for sub-section (3) (w.r.e.f. 8-10-1976).
5. Subs. by Act 23 of 1978, sec. 2, for "Sixth and Seventh Schedules" (w.e.f. 3-6-1978).

Provided that the Central Government may as respects any State extend the said period of two years and in such event the remaining provisions of the Act shall come into force in that State on such date, not later than the extended period, as the State Government may, by notification in the Official Gazette, appoint.

[1][(5) Notwithstanding anything contained in sub-section (4),—

(a) where any provision of this Act, to which sub-section (4) applies, is in force in any State immediately before the commencement of the Electricity (Supply) Amendment Act, 1978 (23 of 1978), that provision as amended by the Electricity (Supply) Amendment Act, 1978 (23 of 1978), shall on and from such commencement, be in force in that State;

(b) the provisions of this Act, to which sub-section (4) applies, which are not in force in any State on the commencement of the Electricity (Supply) Amendment Act, 1978 (23 of 1978), shall come into force in that State on such date as the State Government may, with the concurrence of the Central Government, by notification in the Official Gazette, appoint.]

2. Interpretation.—In this Act, unless there is anything repugnant in the subject or context,—

(1) "Authority" means the Central Electricity Authority constituted under section 3;

(2) "Board" means a State Electricity Board constituted under section 5;

(3) "bulk-licensee" means a licensee who is authorized by his license to supply electricity to other licensees for distribution by them;

[2][(3A) "competent government" means the Central Government in respect of a Generating Company wholly or partly owned by it and in all other cases the Government of the State in which the generating station of a Generating Company is located or proposed to be located;]

(4) "controlled station" means a generating station designated in a scheme sanctioned under Chapter V as a controlled station;

1. Ins. by Act 23 of 1978, sec. 2 (w.e.f. 3-6-1978).

2. Ins. by Act 50 of 1991, sec. 3 (w.e.f. 15-10-1991).

[1][(4A) "Generating Company" means a company registered under the Companies Act 1956 (1 of 1956) and which has among its objects the establishment operation and maintenance of generating stations;]

(5) "generating station" or "station" means any station for generating electricity, including any building and plant [2][(with step-up transformer, switch-gear, cables or other appurtenant equipment, if any)] used for that purpose and the site thereof, a site intended to be used for a generating station, and any buildings used for housing the operating staff of a generating station, and where electricity is generated by water-power, includes penstocks, head and tail works, main and regulating reservoirs, dams and other hydraulic works, but does not in any case include any sub-station [3][* * *];

(6) "licensee" means a person licensed under Part II of the Indian Electricity Act, 1910 (9 of 1910) to supply energy or a person who has obtained sanction under section 28 of that Act to engage in the business of supplying energy [4][but, the provisions of section 26, or 26A of this Act notwithstanding, does not include the Board or a Generating Company];

(7) "main transmission lines" means all height pressure cables and over-head lines (not being an essential part of the distribution system of a licensee) transmitting electricity from a generating station to another generating station or to a sub-station, together with any step-up and step-down transformers, switch-gear and other works necessary to and used for the control of such cables or overhead lines, and such buildings or part thereof as may be required to accommodate such transformers, switch-gear and other works and the operating staff thereof;

[5][(8) "maximum demand" in relation to any period shall, unless otherwise provided in any general or special order of the

---

1. Clause (4A) ins. by Act 115 of 1976 sec. 2 (w.r.e.f. 8-10-1976) and subs. by Act 50 of 1991, sec. 3 (w.e.f. 15-10-1991).
2. Ins. by Act 115 of 1976, sec. 3 (w.r.e.f. 8-10-1976).
3. The words "for transforming, converting or distributing electricity" omitted by Act 115 of 1976, sec. 3 (w.r.e.f. 8-10-1976).
4. Subs. by Act 115 of 1976, sec. 3, for "but, the provisions of section 26 of this Act notwithstanding does not include the Board" (w.r.e.f. 8-10-1976).
5. Subs. by Act 101 of 1956, sec. 3, for clause (8) (w.e.f. 30-12-1956).

State Government, mean twice the largest number of kilowatt-hours or kilo-volt-ampere-hours supplied and taken during any consecutive thirty minutes in that period;]

[1][(8A) "power system" means all aspects of generation, transmission, distribution and supply of energy; and includes the following or any combination thereof—

(a) generating stations;

(b) transmission or main transmission lines;

(c) sub-stations;

(d) tie-lines;

(e) load despatch activities;

(f) mains or distribution mains;

(g) electric supply-lines;

(h) overhead lines;

(i) service lines;

(j) works;]

(9) "prescribed" means prescribed by rules [2][made under this Act];

[3][(9A) "Regional Electricity Board" means a Board constituted by resolution of the Central Government for a specified region for facilitating the integrated operation of the power systems in that region;

(9B) "Regional Load Despatch Centre" means the Centre so designated for a specified region where the operation of the power system in that region and the integration of the power system with other regions and areas (within the territory of India or outside) are co-ordinated;]

[4][(9C) "State Load Despatch Centre", in relation to a State, means the Centre so designated where the operation of the power system in that State and integration of such State power system with other power system are co-ordinated;]

(10) "regulations" means regulations made by the Board under section 79;

---

1. Clause (8A) ins. by Act 115 of 1976, sec. 3 (w.r.e.f. 8-10-1976) and subs. by Act 22 of 1998, sec. 9 (w.e.f. 31-12-1998).
2. Subs. by Act 115 of 1976, sec. 3, for "made under section 78" (w.r.e.f. 8-10-1976).
3. Clauses (9A) and (9B) ins. by Act 50 of 1991, sec. 3 (w.e.f. 15-10-1991) and subs. by Act 22 of 1998, sec. 9 (w.e.f. 31-12-1998).
4. Clause (9C) ins. by Act 22 of 1998, sec. 9 (w.e.f. 31-12-1998).

(11) "Reserve Bank" means the Reserve Bank of India;

[1][(11A) "sub-station" means a station for transforming or converting electricity for the transmission or distribution thereof and includes transformers, convertors, switch-gear, capacitors, synchronous condensors, structures, cables and other appurtenant equipments and any buildings used for that purpose and the site thereof, a site intended to be used for any such purpose and any buildings used for housing the staff of the sub-station;

(11B) "tie-line" means a line for the transfer of electricity between two, power systems together with switch-gear and other works necessary to, and used for, the control of such line;]

[2][(12) "transmission lines" means all works mentioned in sub-section (7) used wholly or partially for the purposes of distribution or transmission of energy;]

(13) "year" means, in relation to the Board [1][or a Generating Company], the year commencing on the 1st day of April;

(14) "year of account" means, in relation to a licensee, his financial year;

(15) other expressions have the meanings respectively assigned to them in the Indian Electricity Act, 1910 (9 of 1910).

CHAPTER II
THE CENTRAL ELECTRICITY AUTHORITY

3. Constitution of the Central Electricity Authority.—(1) The Central Government shall constitute a body called the Central Electricity Authority generally to exercise such functions and perform such duties under the Act and in such manner as the Central Government may prescribe or direct, and in particular to—

(i) develop a sound, adequate and uniform national power policy, [3][formulate short-term and perspective plans for power development and co-ordinate the activities of the planning agencies] in relation to the control and utilisation of national power resources;

(ii) act as arbitrators in matters arising between the State Government or the Board and a licensee or other person as provided in this Act;

1. Ins. by Act 115 of 1976, sec. 3 (w.r.e.f. 8-10-1976).
2. Subs. by Act 22 of 1998, sec. 9 (w.e.f. 31-12-1998).
3. Subs. by Act 115 of 1976, sec. 4, for "and particularly to co-ordinate the activities of the planning agencies" (w.r.e.f. 8-10-1976).

[1][(iii) collect and record the data concerning the generation, distribution and utilisation of power and carry out studies relating to cost, efficiency, losses, benefits and such like matters;]

(iv) make public from time to time information secured under this Act and to provide for the publication of reports and investigations;

[2][(v) advise any State Government, Board, Generating Company or other agency engaged in the generation or supply of electricity on such matters as will enable such Government, Board, Generating Company or agency to operate and maintain the power system under its ownership or control in an improved manner and, where necessary, in co-ordination with any other Government, Board, Generating Company or other agency owning or having the control of another power system;

(vi) promote and assist in the timely completion of schemes sanctioned under Chapter V;

(vii) make arrangements for advancing the skill of persons in the generation and supply of electricity;

(viii) carry out, or make arrangements for, any investigation for the purpose of generating or transmitting electricity;

(ix) promote research in matters affecting the generation, transmission and supply of electricity;

(x) advise the Central Government on any matter on which its advice is sought or make recommendation to that Government on any matter if, in the opinion of the Authority, the recommendation would help in improving the generation, distribution and utilisation of electricity; and

(xi) discharge such other functions as may be entrusted to it by or under any other law.]

(2) The Authority shall consist of [3][not more than fourteen members of whom not more than eight shall be full-time members] appointed by the Central Government [4][* * *].

---

1. Subs. by Act 115 of 1976, sec. 4, for clause (iii) (w.r.e.f. 8-10-1976).
2. Ins. by Act 115 of 1976, sec. 4 (w.r.e.f. 8-10-1976).
3. Subs. by Act 115 of 1976, sec. 4, for "not more than six members" (w.r.e.f. 8-10-1976).
4. The words "of whom at least three shall be full-time members" omitted by Act 57 of 1949, sec. 3.

[1][(2A) A full-time member shall be a person who has experience of, and has shown capacity in,—

(a) design, construction, operation and maintenance of generating stations;

(b) transmission and supply of electricity;

(c) applied research in the field of electricity;

(d) applied economics; or

(e) industrial, commercial or financial matters.]

(3) The Central Government shall appoint [2][one of the full-time members] to be the Chairman of the Authority.

(4) All the members of the Authority shall hold office during the pleasure of the Central Government.

[1][(4A) The Chairman of the Authority and the other full-time members shall receive such salaries and allowances as may be determined by the Central Government and the other members shall receive such allowances and fees for attending the meetings of the Authority, as the Central Government may prescribe.

(4B) The other terms and conditions of service of the members of the Authority [including, subject to the provisions of sub-section (4), their terms of office] shall be such as the Central Government may prescribe.]

(5) No full-time member of the Authority shall [3][have any share or interest for his own benefit, whether in his own name or otherwise,] in any company or other body corporate or an association of persons (whether incorporated or not), or a firm engaged in the business of supplying electrical energy or [4][fuel, in whatever form, for the generation of electricity or in the manufacture of electrical equipment].

(6) The Authority may appoint a Secretary and such other officers and [5][employees] as it considers necessary for the performance of its functions under this Act on such terms as to salary, remuneration,

1. Ins. by Act 115 of 1976, sec. 4 (w.r.e.f. 8-10-1976).
2. Subs. by Act 115 of 1976, sec. 4, for "one of the members" (w.r.e.f. 8-10-1976).
3. Subs. by Act 115 of 1976, sec. 4, for "be directly or indirectly concerned or interested in or have any share or interest" (w.r.e.f. 8-10-1976).
4. Subs. by Act 115 of 1976, sec. 4, for "fuel, solid or liquid, for the generation of electricity" (w.r.e.f. 8-10-1976).
5. Subs. by Act 23 of 1978, sec. 3 for "servants" (w.e.f. 3-6-1978).

fee, allowance, pension, leave and gratuity, as the Authority may, in consultation with the Central Government, fix:

Provided that the appointment of the Secretary shall be subject to the approval of the Central Government.

[1][(7) The Chairman of the Authority may, by order, appoint any two or more members of the Authority to act on behalf of the Authority in relation to any matter referred to in clause (ii) of sub-section (1).

(8) No act or proceeding of the Authority shall be invalid merely on the ground of the existence of any vacancy in, or any defect in the constitution of, the Authority.]

4. Power to require accounts, statistics and returns.—It shall be the duty of each [2][State Electricity Board, Generating Company,] State Government Electricity Department or other licensee or person supplying electricity for public or private purposes, or generating electricity for its or his own use [3][or consuming electricity] to furnish to the Authority such accounts, statistics, [4][returns or other information] relating to the generation supply and use of electricity as it may require and at such times and in such form and manner as it may direct.

[5][**4A. Directions by Central Government to the Authority.**—(1) In the discharge of its functions, the Authority shall be guided by such directions in matters of policy involving public interest as the Central Government may give to it in writing.

(2) If any question arises as to whether any such direction relates to a matter of policy involving public interest, the decision of the Central Government thereon shall be final.

4B. Power of Central Government to make rules.—(1) The Central Government may, by notification in the Official Gazette, make rules for carrying out the purposes of this Chapter.

(2) In particular and without prejudice to the generality of the foregoing powers, such rules may provide for all or any of the following matters, namely:—

---

1. Subs. by Act 115 of 1976, sec. 4, for sub-section (7) (w.r.e.f. 8-10-1976).
2. Subs. by Act 115 of 1976, sec. 5, for "State Electricity Board" (w.r.e.f. 8-10-1976).
3. Ins. by Act 115 of 1976, sec. 5 (w.r.e.f. 8-10-1976).
4. Subs. by Act 115 of 1976, sec. 5, for "and returns" (w.r.e.f. 8-10-1976).
5. Sections 4A, 4B and 4C ins. by Act 115 of 1976 sec. 6 (w.r.e.f. 8-10-1976).

(a) the functions and duties of the Authority and the manner in which such functions and duties shall be exercised and performed, under sub-section (1) of section 3;

(b) the terms and conditions of service of the Chairman and other members of the Authority (including the allowances and fees payable to members, but not including the salaries and allowances payable to the Chairman and other full-time members, of the Authority) under sub-section (4A) and sub-section (4B) of section 3;

(c) any other matter which is required to be, or may be, prescribed by the Central Government.

(3) Every rule made by the Central Government under this Chapter shall be laid, as soon as may be after it is made, before each House of Parliament while it is in session for a total period of thirty days which may be comprised in one session or in two or more successive sessions, and if, before the expiry of the session immediately following the session or the successive sessions aforesaid, both Houses agree in making any modification in the rule or both Houses agree that the rule should not be made, the rule shall thereafter have effect only in such modified form or be of no effect, as the case may be; so, however, that any such modification or annulment shall be without prejudice to the validity of anything previously done under that rule.

4C. Power of Authority to make regulations.—[1][(1)] The Authority may [2][by notification in the Official Gazette,] make regulations, not inconsistent with the provisions of this Act and the rules made by the Central Government thereunder, to provide for all or any of the following matters, namely:—

(a) summoning and holding of meetings of the Authority, the times and places at which such meetings shall be held, the conduct of business thereat and the number of members required to constitute a quorum;

(b) any other matter arising out of the functions of the Authority under this Act for which it is necessary or expedient to make regulations.]

[2][(2) The Central Government shall cause every regulation made under this section to be laid, as soon as after it is made, before each House of Parliament, while it is in session, for a total period of thirty days which may be comprised in one session or in two or more

1. Section 4C re-numbered as sub-section (1) thereof by Act 20 of 1983, sec. 2 and Sch. (w.e.f. 15-3-1984).

2. Ins. by Act 20 of 1983, sec. 2 and Sch. (w.e.f. 15-3-1984).

successive sessions, and if, before the expiry of the session immediately following the session or the successive sessions aforesaid, both Houses agree in making any modification in the regulation, or both Houses agree that the regulation should not be made, the regulation shall thereafter have effect only in such modified form or be of no effect, as the case may be; so, however, that any such modification or annulment shall be without prejudice to the validity of anything previously done under that regulation.]

CHAPTER III

[1][STATE ELECTRICITY BOARDS, GENERATING COMPANIES, STATE ELECTRICITY CONSULTATIVE COUNCILS AND LOCAL ADVISORY COMMITTEES]

5. Constitution and composition of State Electricity Boards.—(1) The State Government shall, as soon as may be after the issue of the notification under sub-section (4) of section 1, constitute by notification in the Official Gazette a State Electricity Board under such name as shall be specified in the notification.

(2) The Board shall consist of not less than three and not more than seven members appointed by the State Government.

[2][* * *]

[3][(4) Of the members—

(a) one shall be a person who has experience of, and has shown capacity in, commercial matters and administration;

(b) one shall be an electrical engineer with wide experience; and

(c) one shall be a person who has experience of accounting and financial matters in a public utility undertaking, preferably an electricity supply undertaking.]

(5) One of the members possessing any of the qualifications specified in sub-section (4) shall be appointed by the State Government to be the Chairman of the Board.

(6) A person shall be disqualified from being appointed or being a member of the Board if he is [4][* * *] a member of [5][Parliament] or of any State Legislature or any local authority.

---

1. Subs. by Act 115 of 1976, sec. 7, for "STATE ELECTRICITY BOARDS" (w.r.e.f. 8-10-1976).
2. Sub-section (3) omitted by Act 57 of 1949, sec. 4.
3. Subs. by Act 101 of 1956, sec. 4, for sub-section (4) (w.e.f. 30-12-1956).
4. The words ", or within the twelve months last preceding was," omitted by Act 30 of 1966, sec. 2 (w.e.f. 16-9-1966).
5. Subs. by the A.O. 1950, for "the Central".

(7) No act done by the Board shall be called in question on the ground only of the existence of any vacancy in, or any defect in the constitution of, the Board.

6. Inter-State agreement to extend Board's jurisdiction to another State.—(1) Subject to the provisions of this section, the Government of any State may, after it has issued a notification under sub-section (4) of section 1, in lieu of constituting a Board under section 5 enter into an agreement with the Government of a contiguous State to provide that the Board constituted for the latter State shall exercise the functions of a Board under this Act in the former State.

(2) Subject to such modifications (being of a character not affecting the general operation of the agreement) of the terms of the agreement as may from time to time be agreed upon by the State Government concerned, an agreement entered into under this section shall be for a period of not less than twenty-five years but may be determined earlier by mutual consent.

(3) An agreement under this section may—

(a) make such financial arrangements between the participating State Governments as may be necessary for the purposes of the agreement;

(b) provide for consultation between the participating State Governments either generally or with reference to particular matters arising under this Act;

(c) generally make such incidental, supplementary or ancillary provisions, not inconsistent with this Act, as may be deemed necessary or expedient for giving effect to the agreement.

7. Effect of inter-State agreement.—Where an agreement is entered into under section 6, the participating State Governments shall, by notification in the Official Gazette, declare a date on which the agreement shall come into force, and on and after that date—

(a) the Board constituted for the one State shall have all the powers and duties of a Board under this Act in respect of both States as if they constituted a single State;

[1][(b) reference in this Act to—

(i) the State,

(ii) the State Electricity Consultative Council, and

(iii) the State Legislature,

---

1. Subs. by Act 30 of 1966, sec. 3, for clause (b) (w.e.f. 16-9-1966).

shall, unless the context otherwise requires, be construed as references respectively to—

(A) both States,

(B) where more than one State Electricity Consultative Council has been constituted under section 16, to all such Councils, and

(C) the Legislatures of both States;]

(c) the provisions of section 60 in relation to the assumption by the Board of the rights and liabilities of the State Government arising before the first constitution of the Board shall apply to the assumption by the Board of the rights and liabilities of the Government of the State to which the exercise of its functions under this Act is extended under the agreement, as if in that section for the words "before the first constitution of the Board" there were substituted the words and figure "before the date on which the agreement under section 6 came into force".

[1][**8. Term of office and conditions for re-appointment of members of the Board.**—The Chairman and other members of the Board shall hold office for such period, and shall be eligible for re-appointment under such conditions, as may be prescribed.]

9. Members not to hold interest in certain concerns.—(1) A member of the Board shall, prior to his appointment, give to the State Government intimation of, and shall, before taking charge of his office, sell or divest himself of, any interest which he may have for his own benefit whether in his own name or otherwise, in any firm or company carrying on the business of supplying electricity or any fuel for the generation of electricity, or of the manufacture, sale or hire of machinery, plant, equipment, apparatus or fittings for the generation, transmission, distribution or use of electricity, or any interest in the managing agency or shares or securities of any such company; and it shall not be lawful for a member of the Board, so long as he holds office, to acquire or purchase any such interest in any such firm or company and if he, under any will or by succession or gift becomes entitled for his own benefit to any such interest, he shall sell the same within three months after becoming so entitled thereto; and he shall also, within three months, sever any connection he may have and cease to have any interest, direct or indirect, in any such concern.

(2) Nothing contained in sub-section (1) shall prevent a member from acquiring or holding any share or interest in any firm or company other than a firm or company mentioned in sub-section (1):

1. Subs. by Act 57 of 1949, sec. 5, for section 8.

Provided that if the Board has entered into, or is about to enter into any contract or agreement with any such firm or company in which a member holds any share or interest, he shall disclose the fact and nature of such interest and he shall not be entitled to vote on any decision of the Board relating to such contract or agreement.

(3) A disclosure referred to in the proviso to sub-section (2) shall forthwith be recorded in the minutes of the Board and communicated to the State Government and the State Government may thereupon give such directions as it may deem proper.

10. Removal or suspension of members.—[1][(1)] The State Government may suspend from office for such period as it thinks fit or remove from office any member of the Board who—

(a) is found to be a lunatic or becomes of unsound mind; or

(b) is adjudged insolvent; or

(c) fails to comply with the provisions of section 9; or

(d) becomes or seeks to become a member of [2][Parliament] or any State Legislature or any local authority; or

[3][(e) in the opinion of the State Government—

(i) has refused to act; or

(ii) has become incapable of acting; or

(iii) has so abused his position as a member as to render his continuance on the Board detrimental to the interests of the general public; or

(iv) is otherwise unfit to continue as a member; or]

(f) is convicted of an offence involving moral turpitude.

[4][(2) The State Government may suspend any member pending an inquiry against him.

(3) No order of removal shall be made under this section unless the member concerned has been given an opportunity to submit his explanation to the State Government, and when such order is passed, the seat of the member removed shall become vacant and another member may be appointed under section 5 to fill up the vacancy.

(4) A member who has been removed shall not be eligible for re-appointment as member or in any other capacity to the Board.

---

1. Section 10 re-numbered as sub-section (1) thereof by Act 101 of 1956, sec. 5 (w.e.f. 30-12-1956).
2. Subs. by the A.O. 1950, for "the Central".
3. Subs. by Act 101 of 1956, sec. 5, for clause (e) (w.e.f. 30-12-1956).
4. Ins. by Act 101 of 1956, sec. 5 (w.e.f. 30-12-1956).

(5) If the Board fails to carry out its functions, or refuses or fails to follow the directions issued by the State Government under this Act, the State Government may remove the Chairman and the members of the Board and appoint a Chairman and members in their places.]

[1][**10A. Power of State Government to declare certain transactions void.**—(1) The State Government may declare void any transaction in connection with which a member has been removed under sub-clause (iii) of clause (e) of sub-section (1) of section 10 after considering the report on the facts of the case made to it by a District Judge nominated by it in this behalf.

(2) A District Judge nominated under sub-section (1) shall, before making his report under that sub-section to the State Government in relation to any transaction, give all parties interested in the transaction a reasonable opportunity of being heard.

(3) Where a transaction is declared void under this section, it shall not be enforceable by any party to the transaction but the provisions of section 65 of the Indian Contract Act, 1872, shall, so far as may be, apply to such transaction as they apply to an agreement which is discovered to be void or a contract which becomes void.

(4) The decision of the State Government declaring any transaction void under this section shall be final and shall not be called in question in any court.]

11. Temporary absence of members.—If the Chairman or any other member of the Board is by infirmity or otherwise rendered temporarily incapable of carrying out his duties or is absent on leave or otherwise in circumstances not involving the vacation of this appointment, the State Government may appoint another person to officiate for him and carry out his functions under this Act or any rule or regulation made thereunder.

12. Incorporation of Board.—The Board shall be a body corporate by the name notified under sub-section (1) of section 5, having perpetual succession and a common seal, with power to acquire and hold property both movable and immovable, and shall by the said name sue and be sued.

[2][**12A. Board may have capital structure.**—(1) The State Government may, if it consider expedient so to do, by notification in the Official Gazette, direct that the Board shall, with effect from such date as may be specified in the notification, be a body corporate with

1. Ins. by Act 101 of 1956, sec. 6 (w.e.f. 30-12-1956).

2. Ins. by Act 23 of 1978, sec. 4 (w.e.f. 3-6-1978).

such capital, not exceeding ten crores of rupees, as the State Government may specify from time to time.

(2) The State Government may, from time to time, with the approval of the State Legislature, increase the maximum limit of the capital referred to in sub-section (1) to such extent as that Government may deem fit, so, however, that the increased maximum limit of capital aforesaid shall not exceed the amount representing the aggregate of the outstanding loans of the Board.

(3) Such capital may be provided by the State Government, from time to time, after due appropriation made by the State Legislature by law for the purpose and subject to such terms and conditions as may be determined by that Government.]

13. Authentication of orders and other instruments of the Board.—All orders and decisions of the Board shall be authenticated by the signature of the Chairman or any other member authorized by the Board in this behalf, and all other instruments issued by the Board shall be authenticated by the signature of such member or officer of the Board as may in like manner be authorized in this behalf.

14. Meetings of the Board.—(1) The Board shall hold ordinary meetings at such intervals as may be provided in the regulations; and a meeting may be convened by the Chairman at any other time for the transaction of urgent business.

(2) The number of members necessary to constitute a quorum at a meeting shall be such as may be provided in the regulations.

15. Appointment of staff.—The Board may appoint a Secretary and such other officers and [1][employees] as may be required to enable the Board to carry out its functions under this Act:

[2][Provided that the appointment of the Secretary shall be subject to the approval of the State Government.]

[3][**15A.** [4][* * *] **Objects, jurisdiction, etc., of Generating Companies.**—[5][* * *]

[6][(2) The objects of a Generating Company shall include—

1. Subs. by Act 23 of 1978, sec. 5, for "servants" (w.e.f. 3-6-1978).
2. Ins. by Act 101 of 1956, sec. 7 (w.e.f. 30-12-1956).
3. Ins. by Act 115 of 1976, sec. 8 (w.r.e.f. 8-10-1976).
4. The word "Formation," omitted by Act 50 of 1991, sec. 4 (w.e.f. 15-10-1991).
5. Sub-section (1) omitted by Act 50 of 1991, sec. 4 (w.e.f. 15-10-1991).
6. Subs. by Act 50 of 1991, sec. 4, for sub-sections (2) and (3) (w.e.f. 15-10-1991).

(a) establishment, operation and maintenance of generating stations and tie-lines, sub-stations and main transmission lines connected therewith;

(b) operation and maintenance of such generating stations, tie-lines, sub-stations and main transmission lines as assigned to it by the competent government or governments.

(3) The Generating Company shall carry on its activities within such areas as the competent government or governments, as the case may be, may, from time to time, specify in this behalf.]

[1][***]

(5) A full-time member of the Board of Directors of a Generating Company shall be a person who has experience of, and has shown capacity in,—

(a) design, construction, operation and maintenance of generating stations;

(b) transmission and supply of electricity;

(c) applied economics;

(d) organising workers;

(e) industrial, commercial or financial matters; or

(f) administration in a Government Department or other establishment.

[1][***]

[1][***]

16. State Electricity Consultative Council.—(1) The State Government shall constitute a [2][State Electricity Consultative Council] for the State, and in cases to which sections 6 and 7 apply, the State Governments concerned shall constitute such one or more [2][State Electricity Consultative Council] or Councils and for such areas as they may by agreement determine.

(2) The [2][State Electricity Consultative Council] shall consist of [3][the members of the Board and, if there are any Generating Company or Generating Companies operating in the State, one representative of the Generating Company or each of the Generating

---

1. Sub-sections (4), (6) and (7) omitted by Act 50 of 1991, sec. 4 (w.e.f. 15-10-1991).

2. Subs. by Act 101 of 1956, sec. 8, for "State Electricity Council" (w.e.f. 30-12-1956).

3. Subs. by Act 115 of 1976, sec. 9, for "the members of the Board" (w.r.e.f. 8-10-1976).

Companies, to be nominated by the Generating Company concerned,] and such other persons being not less than [1][eight] and not more than fifteen as the State Government or the State Governments concerned may appoint after consultation with such representatives or bodies representative of the following interests as the State Government or the State Governments concerned thinks or think fit, that is to say, local self-government, electricity supply industry, commerce, industry, transport, agriculture, [2][labour employed in the electricity supply industry and consumers of electricity], but so that there shall be at least one member representing each such interest in the Council.

(3) The Chairman of the Board shall be *ex officio* Chairman of the [3][State Electricity Consultative Council].

(4) The [3][State Electricity Consultative Council] shall meet at least once in every three months.

(5) The functions of the [3][State Electricity Consultative Council] shall be as follows:—

(i) to advise [4][the Board and the Generating Company or Generating Companies, if any, operating in the State] on major questions of the policy and major schemes;

(ii) to review the progress and the work of [2][the Board and the Generating Company or Generating Companies, if any, operating in the State] from time to time;

(iii) to consider such other matters as [2][the Board or the Generating Company or Generating Companies, if any, operating in the State] may place before it; and

(iv) to consider such matters as the State Government may by rules prescribe.

[5][(6) The Board shall place before the State Electricity Consultative Council the annual financial statement and supplementary statement, if any, and shall take into consideration any comments made on such statement in the said Council before submitting the same to the State Government under section 61.]

1. Subs. by Act 30 of 1966, sec. 4, for "seven" (w.e.f. 16-9-1966).
2. Subs. by Act 101 of 1956, sec. 8, for "and labour employed in the electricity supply industry" (w.e.f. 30-12-1956).
3. Subs. by Act 101 of 1956, sec. 8, for "State Electricity Council" (w.e.f. 30-12-1956).
4. Subs. by Act 115 of 1976, sec. 9, for "the Board" (w.r.e.f. 8-10-1976).
5. Subs. by Act 30 of 1966, sec. 4, for sub-section (6) (w.e.f. 16-9-1966).

17. Local Advisory Committee.—(1) The State Government may from time to time constitute for such areas as it may determine Local Advisory Committees, consisting of such number of persons as it may think fit in each case and on such terms and conditions as may be prescribed.

(2) The Board may if it thinks fit consult the Local Advisory Committees concerned on any business coming before it, and shall so do in respect of such business as the State Government may by general or special order in this behalf specify or when required by the regulations so to do.

(3) The Chairman of the Board or such other member of the Board as he may nominate in this behalf shall be *ex officio* Chairman of a Local Advisory Committee.

(4) Local Advisory Committees shall meet at such intervals as may be prescribed, and for the transaction of urgent business on such other occasions as the Chairman of the Board may require.

(5) The number of members necessary to constitute a quorum at a meeting of a Local Advisory Committee shall be such as the State Government when constituting the Committee may specify.

CHAPTER IV

POWERS AND DUTIES OF [1][STATE ELECTRICITY BOARDS AND GENERATING COMPANIES]

[2][**18. General duties of the Board.**—Subject to the provisions of this Act, the Board shall be charged with the following general duties, namely:—

(a) to arrange, in co-ordination with the Generating Company or Generating Companies, if any, operating in the State, for the supply of electricity that may be required within the State and for the transmission and distribution of the same in the most efficient and economical manner with particular reference to those areas which are not for the time being supplied or adequately supplied with electricity;

(b) to supply electricity as soon as practicable to a licensee or other person requiring such supply if the Board is competent under this Act so to do;

(c) to exercise such control in relation to the generation, distribution and utilisation of electricity within the State as is provided for by or under this Act;

---

1. Subs. by Act 115 of 1976, sec. 10 for "STATE ELECTRICITY BOARDS" (w.r.e.f. 8-10-1976).

2. Subs. by Act 115 of 1976, sec. 11, for section 18 (w.r.e.f. 8-10-1976).

(d) to collect data on the demand for, and the use of, electricity and to formulate perspective plans in co-ordination with the Generating Company or Generating Companies, if any, operating in the State, for the generation, transmission and supply of electricity within the State;

(e) to prepare and carry out schemes for transmission, distribution and generally for promoting the use of electricity within the State; and

(f) to operate the generating stations under its control in co-ordination with the Generating Company or Generating Companies, if any, operating in the State and with the Government or any other Board or agency having control over a power system.]

[1][**18A. Duties of Generating Company.**—(1) Subject to the provisions of this Act, a Generating Company shall be charged with the following duties, namely:—

(a) to establish, operate and maintain such generating stations and tie-lines, sub-stations and main transmission lines connected therewith, as may be required to be established by the [2][competent government or governments] in relation to the Generating Company;

(b) to operate and maintain in the most efficient and economical manner the generating stations, tie-lines, sub-stations and main transmission lines, assigned to it by the [2][competent government or governments] in co-ordination with the Board or Boards, as the case may be, and the Government or agency having control over the power system, if any, connected therewith; and

(c) to carry out, subject to the provisions of section 21, detailed investigations and prepare schemes, in co-ordination with the Board or Boards, as the case may be, for establishing generating stations and tie-lines, sub-stations and transmission lines connected therewith, in such manner as may be specified by the Authority.

(2) Without prejudice to the generality of its duties under section 18, the Board shall, until a Generating Company begins to operate in any State, perform the duties of a Generating Company under this section in that State.]

---

1. Ins. by Act 115 of 1976, sec. 11 (w.r.e.f. 8-10-1976).
2. Subs. by Act 50 of 1991, sec. 5, for "promoting government or promoting governments" (w.e.f. 15-10-1991).

19. Powers of the Board to supply electricity.—(1) The Board may, subject to the provisions of this Act, supply electricity to any licensee or person requiring such supply in any area in which a scheme sanctioned under Chapter V is in force:

Provided that the Board shall not—

(a) supply electricity for any purpose directly to any licensee for use in any part of the area of supply of a bulk-licensee without the consent of the bulk-licensee, unless the licensee to be supplied has an absolute right of veto on any right of the bulk-licensee to supply electricity for such purpose in the said part of such area, or unless the bulk-licensee is unable or unwilling to supply electricity for such purpose in the said part of such area on reasonable terms and conditions and within a reasonable time, or

(b) supply electricity for any purpose to any person, not being a licensee for use in any part of the area of supply of a licensee without the consent of the licensee, unless—

(i) the actual effective capacity of the licensee's generating station computed in accordance with paragraph IX of the First Schedule at the time when such supply was required was less than twice the maximum demand asked for by any such person; or

(ii) the maximum demand of the licensee, being a distributing licensee and taking a supply of energy in bulk is, at the time of the request, less than twice the maximum demand asked for by any such person; or

(iii) the licensee is unable or unwilling to supply electricity for such purpose in the said part of such area on reasonable terms and conditions and within a reasonable time.

(2) After the Board has declared its intention to supply electricity for any purpose in any area for which purpose and in which area it is under this section competent to supply electricity, no licensee shall, the provisions of his licence notwithstanding, at any time be entitled without the consent of the Board to supply electricity of that purpose in that area.

(3) For the purposes of sub-section (1) "absolute right of veto" means an unqualified right vested in a licensee by virtue of any law, licence or other instrument whereby a bulk-licensee is prevented from supplying electricity in any specified area without the consent of the licensee in whom the right of veto vests.

(4) If any question arises under sub-section (1) as to the reasonableness of the terms or conditions or time therein mentioned, it shall be determined [1][by arbitration] as provided in section 76.

20. Power to Board to engage in certain undertakings.—(1) The Board may, in accordance with any regulations made in this behalf, manufacture, purchase, sell or let on hire on the execution of a hire-purchase agreement or otherwise, any electric machinery, control-gear, fittings wires or apparatus for lighting, heating, cooling, or motive power or for any other purpose for which electricity can or may be used, or any industrial or agricultural machinery operated by electricity, any may instal, connect, repair, maintain or remove such fittings, wires, apparatus, machinery or control-gear and in respect thereof demand and take such remuneration or rents and charges and make such terms and conditions as it deems fit.

(2) The Board may maintain shops and show-rooms for the display, sale or hire of fittings, wires, apparatus and machinery as aforesaid, conduct displays, exhibitions and demonstrations thereof, and generally do all things, including advertising, incidental to the sale and hire of such fittings, wires, apparatus and machinery and to the promotion and encouragement of the use of electricity.

(3) The Board shall show separately in its accounts moneys received and expended by it in connection with any undertakings in which it engages under this section.

[2][**20A. Leasing out, etc., of generating stations.**—The State Government may, in respect of any generating station owned by it (including transmission lines and other works connected therewith) make arrangements with the Board or a Generating Company for its operation and maintenance on such terms and conditions as may be agreed upon between the State Government and the Board or the Generating Company, as the case may be.]

21. Powers of Board in relation to water-power.—[3][The Board or a Generating Company may], with the previous approval of the State Government, take such measures as [4][in the opinion of the Board or the Generating Company, as the case may be,] are calculated to advance the development of water-power in the State,

1. Ins. by Act 30 of 1966, sec. 5 (w.e.f. 16-9-1966).
2. Section 20A ins. by Act 44 of 1962, sec. 2 (w.e.f. 28-11-1962) and subs. by Act 115 of 1976, sec. 12, (w.r.e.f. 8-10-1976).
3. Subs. by Act 115 of 1976, sec. 13, for "The Board may" (w.r.e.f. 8-10-1976).
4. Subs. by Act 115 of 1976, sec. 13, for "in the opinion of the Board" (w.r.e.f. 8-10-1976).

and may organise and carry out power and hydrometric survey work and cause to be made such maps, plans, sections and estimates as are necessary for any of the said purposes [1][and in such manner as the Authority may, from time to time, specify]:

Provided that where any such measures relate to a source of water-power already operated upon by a licensee under a licence, the Board shall give the licensee notice of such measure and an opportunity to be heard on any representations he may desire to make in that behalf and may consider such representation.

22. Power to Board to conduct investigations.—Subject so far as the provisions of this section relate to water-power to the previous approval of the State Government, the Board may at its own expense conduct such investigations, experiments and trials as it thinks fit for the improvement of the methods of transmission, distribution and supply of electricity or of the utilisation of fuel, water-power or other means of generating electricity, and may establish and maintain laboratories for the testing and standardisation of electrical instruments and equipment.

23. Loans by Board to licensees.—(1) Subject to any regulations made in this behalf, the Board may grant loans or advances to any licensee for the purposes of his undertaking on such terms as the Board thinks proper.

(2) The Board in the discharge of its functions may call upon a licensee to expand his undertaking and offer to advance to him a loan on such terms and conditions as it may deem proper for such expansion, and if the licensee refuses, fails or neglects to accept the loan from the Board on the terms and conditions offered or to raise a loan from other sources or to employ his own funds [2][* * *] for purposes of such expansion and to carry out such expansion, the Board may, after giving the licensee six months' notice is writing, purchase his undertaking.

24. Power to Board to contribute to certain associations.—The Board may, subject to any regulations made in this behalf,—

(1) pay such subscriptions as it thinks fit to any association for the promotion of the common interests of persons engaged in the generation, distribution and supply of electricity and the members of which consist mainly of such persons;

(2) contribute such sums as it thinks fit to the funds of any recognised society the object of which is to foster the

1. Ins. by Act 115 of 1976, sec. 13 (w.r.e.f. 8-10-1976).
2. The words "on terms similar to the terms offered by the Board" omitted by Act 101 of 1956, sec. 9 (w.e.f. 30-12-1956).

development and use of electricity or promotion of knowledge and research in respect of electricity or electrical appliances.

25. Consulting engineers.—The Board may, subject to such conditions as may be prescribed, from time to time appoint qualified persons to be consulting engineers to the Board and pay them such remuneration as it thinks proper.

26. Board to have powers and obligations of licensee under Act 9 of 1910.—Subject to the provisions of this Act, the Board shall, in respect of the whole State, have all the powers and obligations of a licensee under the Indian Electricity Act, 1910, and this Act shall be deemed to be the licence of the Board for the purposes of that Act:

Provided that nothing in sections 3 to 11, sub-sections (2) and (3) of section 21 and [1][section 22, sub-section (2) of section 22A and sections 23 and 27] of that Act or in [2][clauses 1 to V, clause VII and clauses IX to XII] of the Schedule to that Act relating to the duties and obligations of a licensee shall apply to the Board:

[3][Provided further that the provisions of clause VI of the Schedule to that Act shall apply to the Board in respect of that area only where distribution mains have been laid by the Board and the supply of energy through any of them has commenced.]

[4][**26A. Applicability of the provisions of Act 9 of 1910 to Generating Company.**—(1) Notwithstanding anything contained in sub-section (2), nothing in the Indian Electricity Act, 1910, shall be deemed to require a Generating Company to take out a licence under that Act, or to obtain sanction of the State Government for the purpose of carrying on any of its activities.

(2) Subject to the provisions of this Act, sections 12 to 19 (both inclusive) of the Indian Electricity Act, 1910 (9 of 1910) and clauses XIV to XVII (both inclusive) of the Schedule thereto, shall, as far as may be, apply in relation to a Generating Company as they apply in relation to a licensee under that Act (hereafter in this section referred to as the licensee) and in particular a Generating Company may, in connection with the performance of its duties, exercise—

1. Subs. by Act 32 of 1959, sec. 41, for "sections 22, 23 and 27" (w.e.f. 5-9-1959).
2. Subs. by Act 101 of 1956, sec. 10, for "clauses I to XII" (w.e.f. 30-12-1956).
3. Ins. by Act 101 of 1956, sec. 10 (w.e.f. 30-12-1956).
4. Ins. by Act 115 of 1976, sec. 14 (w.r.e.f. 8-10-1976).

(a) all or any of the powers conferred on a licensee by sub-section (1) of section 12 of the Indian Electricity Act, 1910, as if—

(i) the reference therein to licensee were a reference to the Generating Company;

(ii) the reference to the terms and conditions of licence were a reference to the provisions of this Act and to the articles of association of the Generating Company; and

(iii) the reference to the area of supply were a reference to the area specified under sub-section (3) of section 15A in relation to the Generating Company;

(b) all or any of the powers conferred on a licensee by sub-section (1) of section 14 of the Indian Electricity Act, 1910 (9 of 1910), as if—

(i) the references therein to licensee were references to the Generating Company, and

(ii) the Generating Company had the powers of a licensee under the said Act.

(3) The provisions of section 30 of the Indian Electricity Act, 1910 (9 of 1910) shall not apply to the transmission or use of energy by a Generating Company.

(4) For the removal of doubts, it is hereby declared that sections 31 to 34 (both inclusive) of the Indian Electricity Act, 1910 (9 of 1910), shall apply to a Generating Company.]

27. Other functions of the Board.—[1][The Board or a Generating Company] shall have such further powers and duties as are provided in this Act.

CHAPTER V

[2][THE WORKS AND TRADING PROCEDURE OF THE BOARD AND THE GENERATING COMPANY]

[3][**28. Preparation and sanctioning of scheme.**—(1) For the efficient performance of its duties under this Act, the Board or a Generating Company, as the case may be, may prepare one or more schemes, relating to the establishment or acquisition of generating

1. Subs. by Act 115 of 1976, sec. 15, for "The Board" (w.r.e.f. 8-10-1976).

2. Subs. by Act 115 of 1976, sec. 16, for the former heading (w.r.e.f. 8-10-1976).

3. Subs. by Act 115 of 1976, sec. 17, for section 28 (w.r.e.f. 8-10-1976).

stations, tie-lines, sub-stations or transmission lines, as are referred to in clause (e) of section 18 or clause (c) of sub-section (1) of section 18A, as the case may be.

(2) The Board or, as the case may be, the Generating Company which has prepared a scheme may, sanction such scheme either generally or in respect of any part of the area specified in the scheme and where a scheme has been sanctioned in respect of any part of the area, such scheme may subsequently be sanctioned in respect of any other part of that area:

Provided that where the scheme is of the nature referred to in sub-section (1) of section 29, the scheme shall not be sanctioned (generally or for part of an area) by the Board or the Generating Company except with the previous concurrence of the Authority.

[1][(2A) The Board or, as the case may be, the Generating Company shall, as soon as may be after it has sanctioned any scheme which is not of the nature referred to in section 29, forward the scheme to the Authority and, if required by the Authority so to do, supply to the Authority any information incidental or supplementary to the scheme within such period as may be specified by the Authority.]

(3) Every scheme sanctioned under this section shall be published in the Official Gazette and in such local newspapers as the Board or, as the case may be, the Generating Company may consider necessary.]

[2][29. Submission of schemes for concurrence of Authority, etc.—[3][(1) Every scheme estimated to involve a capital expenditure exceeding such sum, as may be fixed by the Central Government, from time to time, by notification in the Official Gazette, shall, as soon as may be after it is prepared, be submitted to the Authority for its concurrence.]

(2) Before finalisation of any scheme of the nature referred to in sub-section (1) and the submission thereof to the Authority for concurrence, the Board or, as the case may be, the Generating Company shall cause such scheme, which among other things shall contain the estimates of the capital expenditure involved, salient features thereof and the benefits that may accrue therefrom, to be published in the Official Gazette of the State concerned and in such local newspapers as the Board or the Generating Company may

---

1. Ins. by Act 48 of 1984, sec. 2 (w.e.f. 1-10-984).
2. Section 29 subs. by Act 30 of 1966, sec. 6 (w.e.f. 16-9-1966) and again subs. by Act 115 of 1976, sec. 17 (w.r.e.f. 8-10-1976).
3. Subs. by Act 50 of 1991, sec. 6, for sub-section (1) (w.e.f. 15-10-1991).

consider necessary along with a notice of the date, not being less than two months after the date of such publication, before which licensees and other persons interested may make representations on such scheme.

(3) The Board or, as the case may be, the Generating Company may, after considering the representations, if any, that may have been received by it and after making such inquiries as it thinks fit, modify the scheme and the scheme so finally prepared (with or without modifications) shall be submitted by it to the Authority along with the representations.

(4) A copy of the scheme finally prepared by the Board or, as the case may be, the Generating Company under sub-section (3) shall be forwarded to the State Government or State Governments concerned:

Provided that where the scheme has been prepared by a Generating Company in relation to which the Central Government is the [1][competent government or one of the competent governments], a copy of the scheme finally prepared shall be forwarded also to the Central Government.

(5) The Authority may give such directions as to the form and contents of a scheme and the procedure to be followed in, and any other matter relating to, the preparation, submission and approval of such scheme, as it may think fit.

(6) In respect of any scheme submitted to the Authority for its concurrence under sub-section (1), the Board or, as the case may be, the Generating Company shall, if required by the Authority so to do, supply any information incidental or supplementary to the scheme within such period, being not less than one month, as may be specified by the Authority.]

30. Matters to be considered by the Authority.— [2][The Authority shall, before concurring in any scheme submitted to it under sub-section (1) of section 29, have particular regard to, whether or not in its opinion—].

(a) any river-works proposed [3][* * *] will prejudice the prospects for the best ultimate development of the river or its tributaries for power-generation, consistent with the

---

1. Subs. by Act 50 of 1991, sec. 6, for "promoting government or one of the promoting governments" (w.e.f. 15-10-1991).
2. Subs. by Act 115 of 1976, sec. 18, for the original paragraph (w.r.e.f. 8-10-1976).
3. The words "by the Board" omitted by Act 115 of 1976, sec. 18 (w.r.e.f. 8-10-1976).

requirements of irrigation, navigation and flood-control, and for this purpose the Authority [1][shall satisfy itself, after consultation with the State Government, the Central Government, or such other agencies as it may deem appropriate,] that an adequate study has been made of the optimum location of dams and other river-works;

(b) the proposed scheme will prejudice the proper combination of hydro-electric and thermo-electric power necessary to secure the greatest possible economic output of electric power;

(c) the proposed main transmission lines will be reasonably suitable for regional requirements;

(d) the scheme provides reasonable allowances for expenditure on capital and revenue account;

(e) the estimates of prospective supplies of electricity and revenue therefrom contained in the scheme are reasonable;

[2][(f) in the case of a scheme in respect of thermal power generation, the location of the generating station is best suited to the region, taking into account the optimum utilisation of fuel resources, the distance of load centre, transportation facilities, water availability and environmental considerations;

(g) the scheme conforms to any other technical, economic or other criteria laid down by the Authority in accordance with the national power policy evolved by it in pursuance of the provisions contained in clause (i) of sub-section (1) of section 3 [3][and such other directions as may be given by the Central Government].]

[4][**31. Concurrence of Authority to scheme submitted to it by Board or Generating Company.**—(1) Where a scheme is submitted to the Authority under sub-section (1) of section 29, the Authority may, having regard to the matters referred to in section 30, either concur in the scheme without modification or require the Board or, as the case may be, the Generating Company to modify the scheme in such manner as the Authority specifies in the requisition so as to

1. Subs. by Act 115 of 1976, sec. 18, for "shall satisfy itself" (w.r.e.f. 8-10-1976).
2. Ins. by Act 115 of 1976, sec. 18 (w.r.e.f. 8-10-1976).
3. Added by Act 50 of 1991, sec. 7 (w.e.f. 15-10-1991).
4. Subs. by Act 115 of 1976, sec. 19, for sections 31, 32 and 33 (w.r.e.f. 8-10-1976).

ensure that the scheme conforms to the national power policy evolved by the Authority in pursuance of the provisions contained in clause (i) of sub-section (1) of section 3 and in either case the Authority shall also communicate its decision to the State Government or State Governments concerned:

Provided that where the scheme was submitted for concurrence by a Generating Company in relation to which the Central Government is the [1][competent government or one of the competent governments], the decision shall be communicated also to that Government.

(2) Where under sub-section (1) the Authority requires that a scheme may be modified, the Board or, as the case may be, the Generating Company may prepare a revised scheme in accordance with such requisition and submit it to the Authority for concurrence and thereupon the Authority shall, if satisfied that the revised scheme complies with the requisition, concur in the same.

32. Power to alter or extend schemes.—The Board or, as the case may be, the Generating Company may, from time to time, alter or extend a scheme by a supplementary scheme prepared in the manner specified in section 31:

Provided that any alterations or extensions of a scheme which are, in the opinion of the Board or, as the case may be, the Generating Company, minor in character may be made without preparing a supplementary scheme:

Provided further that where any alteration or extension of the nature referred to in the first proviso is made in respect of a scheme concurred in by the Authority, details of such alteration or extension shall be intimated to the Authority as soon as may be after such alteration or extension is made.

33. Provisions applicable to scheme prepared by State Government.—The provisions of sections 28 to 32 (both inclusive) shall, so far as may be, apply also in relation to a scheme prepared by a State Government for the generation, transmission or distribution of electricity.]

34. Controlled stations.—[2][(1)] Where a generating station situate within an area for which a scheme is in force has been designated in the scheme as a controlled station, the relations

1. Subs. by Act 50 of 1991, sec. 8, for "the promoting government or one of the promoting governments" (w.e.f. 15-10-1991).

2. Section 34 re-numbered as sub-section (1) thereof by Act 115 of 1976, sec. 20 (w.r.e.f. 8-10-1976).

between the Board and the licensee owning the station shall, subject to any arrangements agreed under section 47, be regulated by the provisions of the First Schedule.

[1][(2) Notwithstanding anything contained in this Act or any scheme made thereunder, no generating station owned by a Generating Company shall be designated as a controlled station.]

35. Supply by the Board to licensees owning generating stations.—The Board may at any time declare to a licensee owning a generating station, other than a controlled station, situate within an area for which a scheme is in force that it is ready to make a supply of electricity available to the licensee for the purposes of his undertaking, and thereupon, but without prejudice to the provisions of section 47, the provisions of the Second Schedule shall apply in respect of the relations between the Board and the said licensee.

36. Power to Board to close down generating stations.—The Board may at any time declare to a licensee owning a generating station situate within an area for which a scheme is in force that the station shall be permanently closed down, and thereupon but without prejudice to the provisions of section 47, where the station is a controlled station the provisions of Part III of the First Schedule, or in other cases the provisions of the Third Schedule, shall apply in respect of the relations between the Board and the said licensee with reference to the station to be closed down.

37. Purchase of generating stations or undertakings or main transmission lines by the Board.—(1) Where under the First or Third Schedule any generating station or undertaking is to be purchased by the Board, or where a sanctioned scheme provides for the purchase by the Board of a main transmission line belonging to any licensee,—

(a) the generating station or undertaking from such date of purchase as may be fixed under the appropriate Schedule, or the main transmission line from such date of purchase as the Board shall, by notice in writing given not less than one month before the said date, intimate to the licensee, shall vest in the Board free, save as provided in sub-section (2), from any debt, mortgage, lien or other similar obligation of the licensee or attaching to the station or undertaking or line, as the case may be, and any such debt, mortgage, lien or obligation shall, save as aforesaid, attach to the purchase-money in substitution of the station or undertaking or line:

1. Ins. by Act 115 of 1976, sec. 20 (w.r.e.f. 8-10-1976).

Provided that notwithstanding any agreement to the contrary the licensee shall pay and the mortgagee, chargee, lien-holder or obligee shall accept the whole or part of the purchase-money as the case may be in full or part satisfaction of the debt according as the amount of the purchase-money is more or less than the amount of his debt;

(b) without prejudice to the provisions of section 47, the Board shall pay, or tender payment of, the price to be determined in accordance with the Fourth Schedule as soon as the amount thereof has been determined, together with interest on such amount from the date of purchase to the date of payment or tender of payment as aforesaid at the rate of one *per centum* over the average of the Reserve Bank rates between the said dates;

(c) the receipt of the licensee shall notwithstanding anything in any other law, be a full and sufficient discharge to the Board for the payment due in respect of the purchase.

(2) Where a generating station or undertaking or main transmission line purchased by the Board under this Act is in course of construction, extension or repair at the date of purchase, the rights and liabilities of the former owner thereof under any contract for such construction, extension or repair shall be deemed to have been transferred to the Board, except such rights or liabilities acquired or incurred after the date of receipt of the notice of purchase without the prior sanction of the Board.

(3) Notwithstanding anything contained elsewhere in this Act,—

(i) where any generating station purchased by the Board under this Act contains any plant or apparatus which, while the station was in operation, were used jointly for the purposes of generation and transmission or distribution or wholly for the purposes of transmission or distribution, then unless otherwise agreed between the Board and the licensee, such plant or apparatus shall not be purchased by the Board but shall remain the property of the licensee;

(ii) where under the provisions of section 28 a scheme provides for the purchase of any main transmission line belonging to any licensee the Board shall not exercise the powers of acquisition thereby afforded without the prior consent of the licensee, which consent shall not be unreasonably withheld.

38. Provision of new generating stations.—*[Rep. by the Electricity (Supply) Amendment Act, 1976 (115 of 1976), sec. 21 (w.r.e.f. 8-10-1976).]*

39. Operation of Board's generating stations.—[1][(1)] Where the Board itself establishes a new generating station or acquires a generating station otherwise than for the purpose of closing it down, it shall operate the station itself, but the Board may with the sanction of the State Government make arrangements with any licensee or other person for its operation, if in the opinion of the Board it is desirable so to do.

[2][(2) Where a Generating Company has been established having its activities wholly or partly in a State, the State Government may direct the Board to make over any generating station established or acquired by the Board to the Generating Company subject to such terms and conditions as may be specified in the direction and the Board shall comply with such direction:

Provided that where the Central Government is the [3][competent government or one of the competent governments] in relation to the Generating Company, no direction shall be made by any State Government under this sub-section without the concurrence of the Central Government.]

[4][(3) For the purposes of this section, no direction shall be issued to a Generating Company wholly or partly owned by the Central Government unless and until the prior concurrence of that Government is obtained.]

40. Provision regarding connections with main transmission lines purchased by the Board.—Where the Board has purchased a main transmission line and by reason of the user thereof by the Board any alteration or replacement of switch-gear or other apparatus of any licensee connected with the line becomes necessary, the Board may in its discretion itself carry out such alteration or replacement at its own cost or defray the reasonable expenses incurred by the licensee in effecting such alteration or replacement; and any question whether such alteration or replacement is necessary or whether the expenses incurred in connection therewith are reasonable shall in default of agreement be determined [5][by arbitration] as provided under section 76.

---

1. Section 39 re-numbered as sub-section (1) thereof by Act 115 of 1976, sec. 22 (w.r.e.f. 8-10-1976).
2. Ins. by Act 115 of 1976, sec. 22 (w.r.e.f. 8-10-1976).
3. Subs. by Act 50 of 1991, sec. 9, "promoting government or one of the promoting governments" (w.e.f. 15-10-1991).
4. Ins. by Act 50 of 1991, sec. 9 (w.e.f. 15-10-1991).
5. Ins. by Act 30 of 1966, sec. 10 (w.e.f. 16-9-1966).

[1][**41. Use of transmission lines.**—(1) Until the Central Commission is established, the Central Government and thereafter the Central Commission in the case of inter-State transmission system and until the State Commission is established, the State Government and thereafter the State Commission in the case of intra-State transmission system may determine the charges payable to the Central Transmission Utility or State Transmission Utility as the case may be, for the use of transmission system by a Board, its successor entity, generating company, licensee or any other person.

(2) The Central Transmission Utility or State Transmission Utility, as the case may be, may enter into an agreement with any transmission licensee for the exclusive use of the transmission system constructed, maintained and operated by the transmission licensee.

(3) Where the Central Transmission Utility or the State Transmission Utility, as the case may be, considers it necessary to use for any purpose any transmission system or transmission line or main transmission line of a generating company or a licensee, it shall have the power to use such lines to the extent to which the capacity thereof is surplus to the requirements of the generating company or the licensee on payment of charges calculated in accordance with the provisions of the Fifth Schedule.]

42. Powers to Board for placing wires, poles, etc.—[2][(1)] Notwithstanding anything contained in sections 12 to 16 and 18 and 19 of the Indian Electricity Act, 1910 (9 of 1910) but without prejudice to the requirements of section 17 of that Act where provision in such behalf is made in a sanctioned scheme, the Board shall have, for the placing of any wires, poles, wall-brackets, stays apparatus and appliances for the transmission and distribution of electricity, or for the transmission of telegraphic or telephonic communications necessary for the proper co-ordination of the works of the Board, all the powers which the telegraph authority possesses under Part III of the Indian Telegraph Act, 1885 (13 of 1885) with regard to a telegraph established or maintained by the Government or to be so established or maintained:

Provided that where a sanctioned scheme does not make such provision as aforesaid, all the provisions of sections 12 to 19 of the first-mentioned Act shall apply to the works of the Board.

[3][(2) A Generating Company may, for the placing of wires, poles, wall brackets, stays apparatus and appliances for the transmission of

1. Subs. by Act 22 of 1998, sec. 10, for section 41 (w.e.f. 31-12-1998).
2. Section 42 re-numbered as sub-section (1) thereof by Act 115 of 1976, sec. 24 (w.r.e.f. 8-10-1976).
3. Ins. by Act 115 of 1976, sec. 24 (w.r.e.f. 8-10-1976).

electricity, or for the transmission of telegraphic or telephonic communications necessary for the proper co-ordination of the works of the Generating Company, exercise all or any of the powers which the Board may exercise under sub-section (1) and subject to the conditions referred to therein.]

43. Power to Board to enter into arrangements for purchase or sale of electricity under certain conditions.—(1) The Board may enter into arrangements with any person producing electricity within the State for the purchase by the Board on such terms as may be agreed, of any surplus electricity which that person may be able to dispose of.

(2) Where a sanctioned scheme so provides, the Board may, on such terms as may be agreed upon, enter into arrangements with any Government or person for the purchase or sale of electricity to be generated or used outside the State:

Provided that the Board may not enter into such arrangements with any such Government or person without the consent of the State Government, or into arrangements with any such person without the consent of the Government of the State within which the electricity is to be generated or used.

[1][* * *]

[2][**43A. Terms, conditions and tariff for sale of electricity by Generating Company.**—(1) A Generating Company may enter into a contract for the sale of electricity generated by it—

(a) with the Board constituted for the State or any of the States in which a generating station owned or operated by the company is located;

(b) with the Board constituted for any other State in which it is carrying on its activities in pursuance of sub-section (3) of section 15A; and

(c) with any other person with consent of the competent government or governments.

[3][(2) The tariff for the sale of electricity by a Generating Company to the Board shall be determined in accordance with the norms regarding operation and the Plant Load Factor as may be laid down by the Authority and in accordance with the rates of depreciation and reasonable return and such other factors as may be determined, from

1. Sub-section (3) ins. by Act 115 of 1976, sec. 25 (w.r.e.f. 8-10-1976) and omitted by Act 50 of 1991, sec. 10 (w.e.f. 15-10-1991).

2. Ins. by Act 50 of 1991, sec. 11 (w.e.f. 15-10-1991).

3. Sub-section (2) omitted by Act 14 of 1998, sec. 51.

time to time, by the Central Government, by notification in the Official Gazette:

Provided that the terms, conditions and tariff for such sale shall, in respect of a Generating Company, wholly or partly owned by the Central Government, be such as may be determined by the Central Government and in respect of a Generating Company wholly or partly owned by one or more State Governments be such as may be determined, from time to time, by the government or governments concerned.]]

44. Restriction on establishment of new generating stations or major additions or replacement of plant in generating stations.—(1) Notwithstanding anything contained in any other law for the time being in force or in any licence, but subject to the provisions of this Act, it shall not be lawful for a licensee, or any other person, not being the Central Government or any Corporation created by [1][a Central Act] [2][or any Generating Company], except with the previous consent in writing of the Board, to establish or acquire a new generating station or to extend or replace any major unit of plant or works pertaining to the generation of electricity in a generating station:

Provided that such consent shall not, except in relation to a controlled station, be withheld unless within three months from the date of receipt of an applicatior —

(a) for consent to the establishment or acquisition of a new generating station, the Board—

(i) gives to the applicant being a licensee an undertaking that it is competent to, and will, within twenty-four months from the said date, afford to him a supply of electricity sufficient for his requirements pursuant to his application; or

(ii) shows to the applicant that the electricity required by him pursuant to his application could be more economically obtained within a reasonable time from another appropriate source;

(b) for consent to the extension of any major unit of plant or works as aforesaid, the Board—

(i) gives to the applicant being a licensee an undertaking that within twenty-four months from the said date either

1. Subs. by the A.O. 1950, for "legislation enacted by the Central Legislature".
2. Ins. by Act 115 of 1976, sec. 26 (w.r.e.f. 8-10-1976).

the station to which the application pertains will become a controlled station in terms of section 34, or the Board will make a declaration to the applicant in terms of section 35 offering him a supply of electricity sufficient for his requirements pursuant to his application, or the Board will make a declaration to him in terms of section 36; or

(ii) shows to the applicant that the electricity required by him pursuant to his application could be more economically obtained within a reasonable time from another appropriate source or by other appropriate means;

(c) for consent to the replacement of any major unit of plant or works, the Board—

(i) gives to the applicant being a licensee an undertaking that within eighteen months from the said date either the station to which the application pertains will become a controlled station in terms of section 34 or the Board will make a declaration to him in terms of section 36; or

(ii) shows to the applicant that the electricity required by him pursuant to his application could be more economically obtained within a reasonable time from another appropriate source or by other appropriate means.

(2) There shall be stated in every application under this section such particulars as the Board may reasonably require of the station plant or works, as the case may be, in respect of which it is made, and where consent is given thereto, in acting in pursuance of such consent, the applicant shall not, without the further consent of the Board, make any material variation in the particulars so stated.

[1][(2A) The Board shall, before giving consent under sub-section (1), to the establishment or acquisition of a new generating station or to the extension or replacement of any major unit of plant or works, consult the Authority, in cases where the capacity of the new generating station or, as the case may be, the additional capacity proposed to be created by the extension or replacement exceeds twenty-five thousand kilowatts.]

(3) Any difference or dispute arising out of the provisions of this section shall be referred to the arbitration of the Authority.

1. Ins. by Act 115 of 1976, sec. 26 (w.r.e.f. 8-10-1976).

45. Power to Board to enter upon and shut down generating stations in certain circumstances.—(1) If any licensee fails to close down his generating station pursuant to a declaration of the Board under section 36, or if any person establishes or acquires a new generating station or extends or replaces any plant or works in any generating station in contravention of section 44, the Board may authorise any of its officers to enter upon the premises of such station and shut down the station or the plant or works, as the case may be, in respect of which the failure or contravention has occurred.

(2) Any expenses incurred by the Board under this section shall be recoverable by it from the licensee or person concurred as an arrear of land revenue, and for such purpose the Board shall be deemed to be a public officer within the meaning of section 5 of the Revenue Recovery Act, 1890 (1 of 1890).

(3) Any difference or dispute arising out of the provisions of this section shall be referred to the arbitration of the Authority.

46. The Grid Tariff.—(1) A tariff to be known as the Grid Tariff shall, in accordance with any regulations made in this behalf, be fixed from time to time by the Board in respect of each area for which a scheme is in force, and tariffs fixed under this section may, if the Board thinks fit, differ for different areas.

(2) Without prejudice to the provisions of section 47, the Grid Tariff shall apply to sales of electricity by the Board to licensees where so required under any of the First, Second and Third Schedules, and shall, subject as hereinafter provided, also be applicable to sale of electricity by the Board to licensees in other cases:

Provided that if in any such other case it appears to the Board that, having regard to the extent of the supply required, the transmission expenses involved in affording the supply are higher than those allowed in fixing the Grid Tariff, the Board may make such additional charges as it considers appropriate.

(3) The Grid Tariff shall be so framed as to include as part of the charge, and show separately a fixed kilowatt charges component and a running charges component:

Provided that if in respect of any area the electricity to be sold by the Board is wholly or substantially derived from hydro-electric sources, the running charges component may be omitted.

(4) The fixed kilowatt charges component in the Grid Tariff may be framed so as to vary with the magnitude of maximum demand.

(5) Where only a portion of a licensee's maximum demand for the purposes of his undertaking is chargeable at the Grid Tariff the price payable for that portion shall not be greater than the average price

which would have been payable had the whole of the said maximum demand of the licensee been chargeable at the Grid Tariff.

(6) The Grid Tariff may contain provisions for—

(a) adjustment of price having regard to the power factor of supply taken or the cost of fuel or both;

(b) a minimum charge related to a past or prospective demand of a licensee on the Board.

(7) The Grid Tariff may contain such other terms and conditions, not inconsistent with this Act and the regulations, as the Board thinks fit.

47. Power to Board to make alternative arrangements with licensees.—Notwithstanding anything contained in sections 34 to 37 and sub-section (2) of section 46 but subject to any regulations made in this behalf, the Board may make such arrangements as may be mutually agreed with any licensee whose area of supply is situate within an area for which a scheme is in force, in regard to the purchase or sale of electricity and the price thereof, or the purchase, operation or control of any generating station or main transmission line:

Provided that in making any such arrangement the Board shall not show undue preference to any licensee.

48. Power to licensee to carry out arrangements under this Act.—Where under any provision of this Act the Board is authorised or required to enter into arrangements with any licensee for any purpose, then notwithstanding anything contained in any law or in any licence, memorandum of association or other instrument regulating the constitution or powers of the licensee, it shall be lawful for the licensee to enter into and carry out any such arrangements.

[1][**49. Provision for the sale of electricity by the Board to persons other than licensees.**—(1) Subject to the provisions of this Act and of regulations, if any made in this behalf, the Board may supply electricity to any person not being a licensee upon such terms and conditions as the Board thinks fit and may for the purposes of such supply frame uniform tariffs.

(2) In fixing the uniform tariffs, the Board shall have regard to all or any of the following factors, namely:—

(a) the nature of the supply and the purposes for which it is required;

1. Subs. by Act 30 of 1966, sec. 11, for section 49 (w.e.f. 16-9-1966).

(b) the co-ordinated development of the supply and distribution of electricity within the State in the most efficient and economical manner, with particular reference to such development in areas not for the time being served or adequately served by the licensee;

(c) the simplification and standardisation of methods and rates of charges for such supplies;

(d) the extension and cheapening of supplies of electricity to sparsely developed areas.

(3) Nothing in the foregoing provisions of this section shall derogate from the power of the Board, if it considers it necessary or expedient to fix different tariffs for the supply of electricity to any person not being a licensee, having regard to the geographical position of any area, the nature of the supply and purpose for which supply is required and any other relevant factors.

(4) In fixing the tariff and terms and conditions for the supply of electricity, the Board shall not show undue preference to any person.]

50. Board not to supply electricity in certain circumstances.—Nothing contained in sections 34, 35 and 36 shall apply in any case where under section 19, it is not permissible for the Board to supply electricity directly to a licensee owning a generating station; and nothing in sections 46, 47 and 49 shall empower the Board to supply electricity directly to any licensee or person to whom it is not otherwise entitled so to supply electricity.

51. Provisional payments.—Where the price to be paid for electricity by or to the Board under this Act cannot be finally ascertained until after the end of a year of account, the amount to be paid shall be ascertained as soon as practicable thereafter, but the party from whom the payment is due shall make to the other monthly payments on account of the net amounts due in accordance with estimates made for the purpose, subject to adjustment as soon after the end of the year of account as the actual liability can be ascertained.

52. Lower limit of power factor in supply by Board.—Unless otherwise agreed between the Board and the licensee, no supply of electricity taken by a licensee from the Board under this Act shall be taken at an average power factor below 0.85 during the period of maximum demand of the licensee in any month, and in the event of the average power factor as aforesaid being lower than 0.85, the licensee shall within a reasonable time take such measures, the cost of which shall not be borne by the Board, as may be necessary to raise it to a value not lower than 0.85.

53. Provision of accommodation and right of way.—(1) Where the Board for the purposes of any arrangements which it has made with any licensee under this Act requires accommodation on, in, under or over the premises of the licensee for any works or apparatus to be provided by the Board, the licensee shall, if suitable and sufficient accommodation exists, grant such accommodation free of cost to the Board, or if such accommodation does not exist, it shall be provided upon such terms and conditions as may be agreed between the Board and the licensee.

(2) The Board and any licensee shall each have a right of access at all times to his own property on, in, over and under the property of the other.

54. Power to Board to connect meters, etc., to apparatus of licensees.—The Board shall have power to connect with the apparatus of any licensee any such correct meters, switch-gear and other equipment as may be necessary to enable it to carry out the provisions of this Act, and such meters, switch-gear and other equipment shall, unless otherwise agreed, be provided and maintained by the Board at its own cost.

[1][**55. Compliance of directions of the Regional Electricity Board, etc., by licensees or generating companies.**—(1) Until otherwise specified by the Central Government, the Central Transmission Utility shall operate the Regional Load Despatch Centres and the State Transmission Utility shall operate the State Load Despatch Centres.

(2) The Regional Load Despatch Centre shall be the apex body to ensure integrated operation of the power system in the concerned region.

(3) The Regional Load Despatch Centre may give such directions and exercise such supervision and control as may be required for ensuring integrated grid operations and for achieving the maximum economy and efficiency in the operation of the power system in the region under its control.

(4) Subject to the provisions of sub-section (3), the State Load Despatch Centre in a State may give such directions and exercise such supervision and control as may be required for ensuring the integrated grid operations and for achieving the maximum economy and efficiency in the operation of the power system in that State.

(5) Every licensee, transmission licensee, Board, generating company, generating stations, sub-stations and any other person

1. Subs. by Act 50 of 1991, sec. 12 (w.e.f. 15-10-1991) and again subs. by Act 22 of 1998, sec. 11 (w.e.f. 31-12-1998).

connected with the operation of the power system shall comply with the directions issued by the Load Despatch Centres under sub-sections (3) and (4).

(6) All directions issued by the Regional Load Despatch Centres to any transmission licensee of State transmission lines or any other licensee of the State or generating company (other than those connected to inter-State transmission system) or sub-station in the State shall be issued through the State Load Despatch Centre and the State Load Despatch Centres shall ensure that such directions are duly complied by the transmission licensee or licensee or generating company or sub-station.

(7) Subject to the above provisions of this section, the Regional Electricity Board in the region from time to time may mutually agree on matters concerning the smooth operation of the integrated grid and economy and efficiency in the operation of the power system in that region and every licensee, transmission licensee and others involved in the operation of the power system shall comply with the decision of the Regional Electricity Board.

(8) The Regional Load Despatch Centre or the State Load Despatch Centre, as the case may be, shall enforce the decision of the Regional Electricity Boards.

(9) Subject to regulations made under the Electricity Regulatory Commissions Act, 1998 (14 of 1998) by the Central Commission, in the case of Regional Load Despatch Centres or the State Commission in the case of State Load Despatch Centres, any dispute with reference to the operation of the power system including grid operation and as to whether any directions issued under sub-section (3) or sub-section (4) is reasonable or not, shall be referred to the Authority for decision:

Provided that pending the decision of the Authority, the directions of the Regional Load Despatch Centres or the State Load Despatch Centres, as the case may be, shall be complied with.

(10) Until the Central Commission is established, the Central Government and thereafter the Central Commission in the case of Regional Load Despatch Centre and until the State Commission is established, the State Government and thereafter the State Commission in the case of the State Load Despatch Centre of that State, may, by notification, specify the fees and charges to be paid to the Regional Load Despatch Centres and the State Load Despatch Centres, as the case may be, for undertaking the load despatch functions entrusted by the Central Government or by the State Government, as the case may be.

(11) The provision of sub-section (3) of section 4B shall apply in relation to any notification issued by the Central Government or the Central Commission as the case may be under sub-section (10), as they apply in relation to the rules made by that Government under Chapter II.]

56. Leases of generating stations.—No licensee shall except with the previous approval in writing of the Board and subject to any conditions which the Board may think fit to impose, enter into any arrangement whereby any generating station is to be let or held on lease by him, and any such arrangement entered into in contravention of this sub-section shall be void and of no effect.

[1][**57. Licensee's charges to consumers.**—The provisions of the Sixth Schedule [2][* * *] shall be deemed to be incorporated in the licence of every licensee, not being a local authority—

(a) in the case of a licence granted before the commencement of this Act, from the date of the commencement of the licensee's next succeeding year of account; and

(b) in the case of a licence granted after the commencement of this Act, from the date of the commencement of supply,

and as from the said date, the licensee shall comply with the provisions of [3][the said Schedule] accordingly, and any provisions of the Indian Electricity Act, 1910 (9 of 1910), and the licence granted to him thereunder and of any other law, agreement or instrument applicable to the licensee shall, in relation to the licensee, be void and of no effect in so far as they are inconsistent with the provisions of section 57A and [3][the said Schedule].]

[4][**57A. Rating committees.**—(1) Where the provisions of the Sixth Schedule [5][* * *] are under section 57 deemed to be incorporated in the licence of any licensee, the following provisions shall have effect in relation to the said licensee, namely:—

(a) the Board or where no Board is constituted under this Act, the State Government—

(i) may, if satisfied, that the licensee has failed to comply with any of the provisions of the Sixth Schedule; and

1. Subs. by Act 101 of 1956, sec. 14, for section 57 (w.e.f. 30-12-1956).
2. The words "and the Seventh Schedule" omitted by Act 23 of 1978, sec. 6 (w.e.f. 3-6-1978).
3. Subs. by Act 23 of 1978, sec. 6, for "the said Schedules" (w.e.f. 3-6-1978).
4. Ins. by Act 101 of 1956, sec. 14 (w.e.f. 30-12-1956).
5. The words "and the Seventh Schedule" omitted by Act 23 of 1978, sec. 7 (w.e.f. 3-6-1978).

(ii) shall, when so requested by the licensee in writing, constitute a rating committee to examine the licensee's charges for the supply of electricity and to make recommendations in that behalf to the State Government:

Provided that where it is proposed to constitute a rating committee under this section on account of the failure of the licensee to comply with any provisions of the Sixth Schedule, such committee shall not be constituted unless the licensee has been given a notice in writing of thirty clear days (which period, if the circumstances so warrant may be extended from time to time) to show cause against the action proposed to be taken:

Provided further that no such rating committee shall be constituted if the alleged failure of the licensee to comply with any provisions of the Sixth Schedule raises any dispute or difference as to the interpretation of the said provisions or any matter arising therefrom and such difference or dispute has been referred by the licensee to the arbitration of the Authority under paragraph XVI of that Schedule before the notice referred to in the preceding proviso was given or is so referred within the period of the said notice:

Provided further that no rating committee shall be constituted in respect of a licensee within three years from the date on which such a committee has reported in respect of that licensee, unless the State Government declares that in its opinion circumstances have arisen rendering the orders passed on the recommendations of the previous rating committee unfair to the licensee or any of his consumers;

(b) a rating committee under clause (a) shall,—

(i) where such committee is to be constituted under sub-clause (i) of that clause, be constituted not later than three months after the expiry of the notice referred to in the first proviso to that clause;

(ii) where such committee is to be constituted at the request of the licensee be constituted within three months of the date of such request;

(c) a rating committee shall, after giving the licensee a reasonable opportunity of being heard and after taking into consideration the efficiency of operation and management and the potentialities of his undertaking, report to the State Government within three months from the date of its constitution, making recommendations with reasons therefor, regarding the charges for electricity which the licensee may make to any class or classes of consumers so, however, that the recommendations are not likely to prevent the licensee from earning clear profit sufficient when taken with the sums available in the Tariffs and Dividends Control Reserve to afford him a reasonable return as defined in the Sixth Schedule during his next succeeding three years of account:

Provided that the State Government may, if it so deems necessary, extend the said period of three months by a further period not exceeding three months within which the report of the rating committee may be submitted to it;

(d) within one month after the receipt of the report under clause (c), the State Government shall cause the report to be published in the Official Gazette, and may at the same time make an order in accordance therewith fixing the licensee's charges of the supply of electricity with effect from such date, not earlier that two months or later than three months, after the date of publication of the report as may be specified in the order and the licensee shall forthwith give effect to such order;

(e) the charges for the supply of electricity fixed under clause (d) shall be in operation for such period not exceeding three years as the State Government may specify in the order:

Provided that nothing in this clause shall be deemed to prevent a licensee from deducting at any time any charges so fixed.

(2) Where a Board is constituted under this Act, the rating committee shall consist of three members as follows:—

(i) one member shall be nominated by the State Government who shall be a person who is or has been a judicial officer not below the rank of a District Judge;

(ii) one member shall be a member of the Board having experience of accounting and financial matters; and

(iii) one member shall be a representative co-opted jointly by the two members referred to in clauses (i) and (ii) from an association of licensees of which the licensee concerned is or is eligible to be a member and if there is no such association, from such Chamber of Commerce or similar body as the State Government may direct.

(3) Where no Board is constituted under this Act the rating committee shall consist of five members of whom three members shall be nominated by the State Government, one member shall be nominated by the licensee and one member shall be nominated by the association referred to in sub-section (2) or if there is no such association, by such Chamber of Commerce or similar body as the State Government may direct.

(4) Of the three members to be nominated by the State Government under sub-section (3), one shall be a person who is or has been a judicial officer not below the rank of a District Judge, one shall be a registered accountant within the meaning of the Chartered Accountants Act, 1949 (38 of 1949), having at least ten years' experience and one shall be a person with administrative experience.

(5) The Judicial member of a rating committee shall be its chairman.

(6) A rating committee may act notwithstanding that one of its members is absent.

(7) The expenditure incurred in connection with a rating committee as certified by it shall be payable—

(a) where the rating committee was constituted at the request of a licensee, or where the rating committee has held that the licensee has failed to comply with any of the provisions of the Sixth Schedule, by the licensee from that part of the clear profit to which the licensee is entitled under that Schedule;

(b) in any other case, by the Board or the State Government, as the case may be.

(8) Where a licensee makes default in paying any amount which he is liable to pay under sub-section (7), such amount may, on application to a civil court having jurisdiction, be recovered from the licensee by the distress and sale of any movable property of the licensee.]

[1][**57B. Power of rating committee to call for information etc.**—A rating committee constituted under section 57A may, for the purpose of discharging its functions, by notice in writing, require the licensee to give such information, or to furnish such accounts and other documents in his possession or power, as may be specified in the notice.]

58. Power to direct amortization and tariffs policies of licensees being local authorities.—The Board or where no Board

1. Ins. by Act 101 of 1956, sec. 14 (w.e.f. 30-12-1956).

is constituted under this Act, the State Government shall have power to direct the amortization and tariffs policies of any licensee, being a local authority, with respect to his licensed undertaking in such manner as the Board or the State Government, as the case may be, after giving the local authority a reasonable opportunity of being heard, considers expedient for the purposes of the Act; and the licensee, being a local authority, the provisions of any other law or of any rules made or directions given thereunder notwithstanding, shall give effect to any such directions of the Board or the State Government, as the case may be:

[1][Provided that the Board shall not issue any directions under this section except after obtaining the prior approval of the State Government.]

CHAPTER VI

THE BOARD'S FINANCE, ACCOUNTS AND AUDIT

[2][**59. General principles for Board's finance.**—(1) The Board shall, after taking credit for any subvention from the State Government under section 63, carry on its operations under this Act and adjust its tariffs so as to ensure that the total revenues in any year of account shall after meeting all expenses properly chargeable to revenues, including operating, maintenance and management expenses, taxes (if any) or income and profits, depreciation and interest payable on all debentures, bonds and loans, [3][leave such surplus as is not less than three per cent, or such higher precentage, as the State Government may, by notification in the Official Gazette, specify in this behalf, of the value of the fixed assets of the Board in service at the beginning of such year.

Explanation.—For the purposes of this sub-section, "value of the fixed assets of the Board in service at the beginning of the year" means the original cost of such fixed assets as reduced by the aggregate of the cumulative depreciation in respect of such assets calculated in accordance with the provisions of this Act and consumers' contributions for service lines.]

(2) In specifying [4][any higher percentage] under sub-section (1), the State Government shall have due regard to the availability of amounts accrued by way of depreciation and the liability for loan amortization and leave—

1. Ins. by Act 101 of 1956, sec. 15 (w.e.f. 30-12-1956).
2. Subs. by Act 23 of 1978, sec. 8, for section 59 (w.e.f. 3-6-1978).
3. Subs. by Act 16 of 1983, sec. 2, for "leave such surplus, as the State Government may, from time to time, specify" (w.e.f. 1-4-1985).
4. Subs. by Act 16 of 1983, sec. 2, for "the surplus" (w.e.f. 1-4-1985).

(a) a reasonable sum to contribute towards the cost of capital works; and

(b) where in respect of the Board, a notification has been issued under sub-section (1) of section 12A, a reasonable sum by way of return of the capital provided by the State Government under sub-section (3) of that section and the amount of the loans (if any) converted by the State Government into capital under sub-section (1) of section 66A.]

60. Board to assume obligations of State Government in respect of matters to which this Act applies.—(1) All debts and obligations incurred, all contracts entered into and all matters and things engaged to be done by, with or for the State Government for any of the purposes of this Act before the first constitution of the Board shall be deemed to have been incurred, entered into or engaged to be done by, with or for the Board; and all suits or other legal proceedings instituted or which might but for the issue of the notification under sub-section (4) of section 1 have been instituted by or against the State Government may be continued or instituted by or against the Board.

[1][(lA) All schemes sanctioned by the State Government and transferred to the Board shall, for the purposes of this Act, be deemed to have been sanctioned by the Board.]

(2) All expenditure which the State Government may, not later than [2][one year] after the first constitution of the Board, declare to have been incurred [3][* * *] on capital account in connection with the purposes of this Act shall be deemed to be a loan advanced to the Board under section 64 on the date of the said declaration, and all the assets acquired by such expenditure shall thereupon vest in the Board.

[4][**60A. Period of limitation extended in certain cases.**—When the right to recover any amount due to the State Government for or in connection with the consumption of electricity is vested in the Board and the period of limitation to enforce such right has expired before the constitution of the Board, or within three years of its constitution, then, notwithstanding anything contained in the Indian Limitation Act, 1908 (9 of 1908) or any other law for the time being

1. Ins. by Act 101 of 1956, sec. 16 (w.e.f. 30-12-1956).
2. Subs. by Act 23 of 1978, sec. 9, for "two months" (w.e.f. 3-6-1978).
3. The words "before the issue of the notification under sub-section (4) of section 1" omitted by Act 23 of 1978, sec. 9 (w.e.f. 3-6-1978).
4. Ins. by Act 30 of 1966, sec. 12 (w.e.f. 16-9-1966).

in force relating to limitation of action, the Board may institute a suit for the recovery of such amount,—

(i) where it has been constituted before the commencement of the Electricity (Supply) Amendment Act, 1966 (30 of 1966) within three years of such commencement; and

(ii) where it has been constituted after such commencement, within three years of its constitution.]

61. Annual financial statement.—(1) In February of each year the Board shall submit to the State Government a statement in the prescribed form of the estimated capital and revenue receipts and expenditure for the ensuing year.

(2) The said statement shall include a statement of the salaries of [1][members and officers and other employees] of the Board and of such other particulars as may be prescribed.

(3) The State Government shall as soon as may be after the receipt of the said statement cause it to be laid on the table of the [2][House], or as the case may be, [3][Houses] of the State Legislature; and the said statement shall be open to discussion therein, but shall not be subject to vote.

(4) The Board shall take into consideration any comments made on the said statement in the State Legislature.

(5) The Board may at any time during the year in respect of which a statement under sub-section (1) has been submitted, submit to the State Government a supplementary statement, and all the provisions of this section shall apply to such statement as they apply to the statement under the said sub-section.

62. Restriction on unbudgeted expenditure.—(1) Save where in the opinion of the Board circumstances of extreme urgency have arisen, no sum exceeding [4][seventy-five thousand] rupees on account of recurring expenditure or exceeding [5][three lakhs] of rupees on account of non-recurring expenditure shall be expended by the Board in any year of account unless such sum has been included in a statement submitted under sub-section (1) or sub-section (5) of section 61.

---

1. Subs. by Act 23 of 1978, sec. 10, for "members, officers and servants" (w.e.f. 3-6-1978).
2. Subs. by the A.O. 1950, for "Chamber".
3. Subs. by the A.O. 1950, for "Chambers".
4. Subs. by Act 30 of 1966, sec. 13, for "twenty-five thousand" (w.e.f. 16-9-1966).
5. Subs. by Act 30 of 1966, sec. 13, for "one lakh" (w.e.f. 16-9-1966).

(2) Where any such sum is expended under circumstances of extreme urgency [1][, it shall be expended in accordance with the regulations made by the Board with the previous approval of the State Government and] a report thereon indicating the source from which it is proposed to meet the expenditure shall be made as soon as practicable to the State Government.

63. Subventions to the Board.—The State Government may, with the approval of the State Legislature from time to time make subventions to the Board for the purposes of this Act on such terms and conditions as the State Government may determine.

64. Loans to the Board.—The State Government may, from time to time, advance loans to the Board on such terms and conditions, not inconsistent with the provisions of this Act, as the State Government may determine.

65. Power of Board to borrow.—(1) The Board may, from time to time, with the previous sanction of the State Government and subject to the provisions of this Act and to such conditions as may be prescribed in this behalf, borrow any sum required for the purposes of this Act.

(2) Rules made by the State Government for the purposes of this section may empower the Board to borrow by the [2][issue of debentures or bonds] or otherwise and to make arrangements with bankers, and may apply to the Board with such modifications as may be necessary to be consistent with this Act the provisions of the Local Authorities Loans Act, 1914 (9 of 1914) and the rules made thereunder as if the Board were a local authority.

(3) The maximum amount which the Board may at any time have on loan under sub-section (1) shall be ten crores of rupees, unless the State Government, with the approval of the State Legislative Assembly, fixes a higher maximum amount.

(4) [3][Debentures or bonds issued] by the Board under this section shall be issued, transferred, dealt with the redeemed in such manner as may be prescribed.

66. Guarantee of loans.—The State Government may guarantee in such manner as it thinks fit the payment of the principal and interest of any loan proposed to be raised by the Board or of either the principal or the interest:

---

1. Ins. by Act 23 of 1978, sec. 11 (w.e.f. 3-6-1978).
2. Subs. by Act 23 of 1978, sec. 12, for "issue of bonds or stock" (w.e.f. 3-6-1978).
3. Subs. by Act 23 of 1978, sec. 12, for "stock issued" (w.e.f. 3-6-1978).

Provided that the State Government shall, so long as any such guarantees are in force, lay before the [1][House] or, as the case may be, [2][Houses] of the State Legislature in every year during the budget session a statement of the guarantees, if any, given during the current financial year of the State and an up-to-date account of the total sums, if any, which have been paid out of State revenues by reason of any such guarantees or paid into State revenues towards repayment of any money so paid out.

[3][**66A. Conversion of amount of loans into capital.**—(1) Notwithstanding anything contained in section 12A, where any loan has been obtained from the State Government by a Board, in respect of which Board a notification has been made under sub-section (1) of that section, or any loan is deemed to be advanced to such Board by the State Government under sub-section (2) of section 60, the State Government may, if in its opinion it is necessary in the public interest so to do, by order, direct that the amount of such loan or any part thereof shall be converted into capital provided to the Board on such terms and conditions as appear to that Government to be reasonable in the circumstances of the case, even if the terms of such loan do not include a term providing for an option for such conversion.

(2) In determining the terms and conditions of such conversion, the State Government shall have due regard to the following circumstances, that is to say, the financial position of the Board, the terms of the loan, the rate of interest payable on the loan, the capital of the Board, its loan liabilities and its reserves.

(3) Notwithstanding anything contained in this Act, where the State Government has, by an order made under sub-section (1), directed that any loan or any part thereof shall be converted into capital, and such order has the effect of increasing the capital of the Board, the capital of the Board shall stand increased by the amount by which the conversion increases the capital of the Board in excess of the capital specified under sub-section (1) of section 12A:

Provided that the amount of the loan so converted together with the capital provided under sub-section (3) of section 12A shall not exceed the amount representing the aggregate of the outstanding loans of the Board after such conversion.]

[4][**67. Priority of liabilities of the Board.**—The Board shall distribute the surplus referred to in sub-section (1) of section 59 to the extent available in a particular year in the following order, namely:—

1. Subs. by the A.O. 1950, for "Chamber".
2. Subs. by the A.O. 1950, for "Chambers".
3. Ins. by Act 23 of 1978, sec. 13 (w.e.f. 3-6-1978).
4. Section 67 subs. by Act 23 of 1978, sec. 14 (w.e.f. 3-6-1978) and again subs. by Act 16 of 1983, sec. 3 (w.e.f. 1-4-1985).

(i) repayment of principal of any loan raised (including redemption of debentures of bonds issued) under section 65 which becomes due for payment in the year or which became due for payment in any previous year and has remained unpaid;

(ii) repayment of principal of any loan advanced to the Board by the State Government under section 64 which becomes due for payment in the year or which became due for payment in any previous year and has remained unpaid;

(iii) payment for purposes specified in sub-section (2) of section 59 in such manner as the Board may decide.]

[1][**67A. Interest on loans advanced by State Government to be paid only after other expenses.**—Any interest which is payable on loans advanced under section 64 or deemed to have been advanced under section 60 to the Board by the State Government and which is charged to revenues in any year may be paid only out of the balance of the revenues, if any, of that year which is left after meeting all the other expenses referred to in sub-section (1) of section 59 and so much of such interest as is not paid in any year by reason of the provisions of this section shall be deemed to be deferred liability and shall be discharged in accordance with the provisions of this section in the subsequent year or years, as the case may be.]

[2][**68. Charging of depreciation by Board.**—(1) [3][* * *] The Board shall provide each year for depreciation such sum calculated in accordance with such principles as the Central Government may, after consultation with the Authority, by notification in the Official Gazette, lay down from time to time.

[4][* * *]

(3) The provisions of this section shall apply to the charging of depreciation for the year in which the Electricity (Supply) Amendment Act, 1978 (23 of 1978), comes into force.]

[5][**69. Accounts and audit.**—(1) The Board shall cause proper accounts and other records in relation thereto to be kept, including

---

1. Ins. by Act 16 of 1983, sec. 4 (w.e.f. 1-4-1985).
2. Section 68 subs. by Act 101 of 1956, sec. 18 (w.e.f. 30-12-1956) again subs. by Act 30 of 1966, sec. 15 (w.e.f. 16-9-1966) and again subs. by Act 23 of 1978, sec. 15 (w.e.f. 3-6-1978).
3. The words "Subject to the provisions of section 67," omitted by Act 16 of 1983, sec. 5 (w.e.f 1-4-1985).
4. Sub-section (2) omitted by Act 16 of 1983, sec. 5 (w.e.f. 1-4-1985).
5. Subs. by Act 101 of 1956, sec. 18, for section 69 (w.e.f. 30-12-1956).

a proper system of internal check and prepare an annual statement of accounts, including the profit and loss account and the balance-sheet in such form [1][as the Central Government may, by notification in the Official Gazette, prescribe by rules made in this behalf in consultation with the Comptroller and Auditor-General of India and State Governments].

(2) The accounts of the Board shall be audited by the Comptroller and Auditor-General of India or by such person as he may authorize in this behalf and any expenditure incurred by him in connection with such audit shall be payable by the Board to the Comptroller and Auditor-General of India.

(3) The Comptroller and Auditor-General of India and any person authorized by him in connection with the audit of the accounts of the Board shall have the same rights, privileges and authority in connection with such audit as the Comptroller and Auditor-General of India has in connection with the audit of Government accounts and in particular shall have the right to demand the production of books, accounts, connected vouchers and other documents and papers, and to inspect any of the offices of the Board.

(4) The accounts of the Board as certified by the Comptroller and Auditor-General of India or any other person authorized by him in this behalf together with the audit report thereon shall be [2][forwarded to the Authority and to the State Government within six months of the close of the year to which the accounts and audit report relate] and that Government may issue such instructions to the Board in respect thereof as it deems fit and the Board shall comply with such instructions.

(5) The State Government shall—

(a) cause the accounts of the Board together with the audit report thereon forwarded to it under sub-section (4) to be laid annually before the State Legislature; and

(b) cause the accounts of the Board to be published in the prescribed manner and make available copies thereof on sale at a reasonable price.]

[3][(6) The provisions of sub-section (3) of section 4B shall apply in relation to any rules made by the Central Government under sub-section (1) as they apply in relation to rules made by that Government under Chapter II.]

---

1. Subs. by Act 16 of 1983, sec. 6, for certain words (w.e.f. 1-4-1985).
2. Subs. by Act 23 of 1978, sec. 16, for "forwarded annually to the State Government" (w.e.f. 3-6-1978).
3. Ins. by Act 16 of 1983, sec. 6 (w.e.f. 1-4-1985).

CHAPTER VII

MISCELLANEOUS

70. Effect of other laws.—(1) No provision of the Indian Electricity Act, 1910 (9 of 1910), or of any rules made thereunder or of any instrument having effect by virtue of such law or rule shall, so far as it is inconsistent with any of the provisions of this Act, have any effect:

Provided that nothing in this Act shall be deemed to prevent the State Government from granting, after consultation with the Board, a licence not inconsistent with the provisions of the Indian Electricity Act, 1910 (9 of 1910), to any person in respect of such area and on such terms and conditions as the State Government may think fit.

(2) Save as otherwise provided in this Act, the provisions of this Act shall be in addition to, and not in derogation of, the Indian Electricity Act, 1910 (9 of 1910).

71. Rights and options to purchase under Act 9 of 1910 to vest in Board.—*[Rep. by the Indian Electricity (Amendment) Act, 1959 (32 of 1959), sec. 41 (w.e.f. 5-9-1959).]*

72. Water-power concessions to be granted only to [1][the Board or a Generating Company].—The State Government shall not grant any concession for the development or use of water-power for any electrical purpose to any person other than [1][the Board or a Generating Company], unless the State Government is of opinion that it is not expedient for the Board [2][or the Generating Company so to develop] or use the water-power concerned.

73. Co-ordination between the Board's schemes and multi-purpose schemes.—Where a multi-purpose scheme for the development of any river in any region is in operation, [3][the Board and the Generating Company shall co-ordinate their activities] with the activities of the persons responsible for such scheme in so far as they are inter-related.

74. Powers of entry.—Any [4][officer or other employee] [5][of the Board or of a Generating Company] generally or specially [6][authorised

---

1. Subs. by Act 115 of 1976, sec. 27, for "the Board" (w.r.e.f 8-10-1976).
2. Subs. by Act 115 of 1976, sec. 27, for "or that the Board is unable so to develop" (w.r.e.f. 8-10-1976).
3. Subs. by Act 115 of 1976, sec. 28, for "the Board shall co-ordinate its activities" (w.r.e.f. 8-10-1976).
4. Subs. by Act 23 of 1978, sec. 17, for "officer or servant" (w.e.f. 3-6-1978).
5. Subs. by Act 115 of 1976, sec. 29, for "servant of the Board" (w.r.e.f. 8-10-1976).
6. Subs. by Act 115 of 1976, sec. 29, for "authorised by the Board" (w.r.e.f. 8-10-1976).

by the Board or by the Generating Company, as the case may be,] in this behalf may at any reasonable time after giving the owner or occupier reasonable notice enter upon any land or premises and there do such things as may be reasonably necessary for the purposes of lawfully using any transmission lines or main transmission lines or of making any survey, examination or investigation preliminary or incidental to the exercise of powers or the performance of [1][duties by the Board or by the Generating Company, as the case may be,] under this Act.

75. Annual reports, statistics and returns.—[2][* * *]

[3][[4][(1)][5][* * *] The Board shall, as soon as may be after the end of each financial year, prepare and submit to the State Government [6][before such date and] in such form as may be prescribed a report giving an account of its activities during the previous financial year and the report shall also give an account of the activities, if any, which are likely to be undertaken by the Board in the next financial year; and the State Government shall cause every such report to be laid before the State Legislature as soon as may be after it is received by the State Government.]

(2) The Board shall furnish to the State Government at such times and in such form and manner as may be prescribed or as the State Government may direct, such statistics and returns and such particulars in regard to any proposed or existing scheme as the State Government may from time to time require.

(3) The Board may at any time by notice in writing require any licensee [7][or person or agency] supplying electricity for public or private purposes or generating electricity for his own use to furnish it with such information and accounts relating to such supply or generation and in such form and manner as the notice may specify:

---

1. Subs. by Act 115 of 1976, sec. 29, for "duties by the Board" (w.r.e.f. 8-10-1976).
2. Sub-section (1) omitted by Act 30 of 1966, sec. 16 (w.e.f. 16-9-1966).
3. Sub-section (1A) ins. by Act 101 of 1956, sec. 19 (w.e.f. 30-12-1956).
4. Sub-section (1A) re-numbered as sub-section (1) by Act 30 of 1966, sec. 16 (w.e.f. 16-9-1966).
5. The words " Without prejudice to the provisions of sub-section (1)" omitted by Act 30 of 1966, sec. 16 (w.e.f. 16-9-1966).
6. Ins. by Act 30 of 1966, sec. 16 (w.e.f. 16-9-1966).
7. Subs. by Act 115 of 1976, sec. 30, for "or person" (w.r.e.f. 8-10-1976).

[1][Provided that nothing in this sub-section shall be deemed to empower the Board to require a Generating Company to furnish it with any information or accounts.]

[2][75A. Annual reports and accounts of Generating Company.—[3][* * *]

(2) A Generating Company shall, as soon as may be after the end of each year, prepare a report giving an account of its activities during the previous year and shall, within six months from the date of closure of the year, forward to the [4][competent] government, or where there are more than one [4][competent] government, to all such [4][competent] governments, the report together with a statement of accounts, in such form and containing such particulars as may be specified by the government or the governments, as the case may be, a copy of the balance-sheet and profit and loss account and the auditor's report, in relation to the accounts of the year aforesaid.

[5][(3) For the purpose of preparing the statement of accounts referred to in sub-section (2), the depreciation to be provided every year shall be calculated at such rate as may be specified by the Central Government, by notification in the Official Gazette, in accordance with the provisions of section 43A.]

[6][* * *]

(4) The provisions of [7][sub-section] (2) shall be in addition to and not interrogation of the provisions contained in the Companies Act, 1956 (1 of 1956), in relation to reports, statement of accounts and other documents required to be prepared or kept or submitted by a company within the meaning of section 3 of that Act.]

76. Arbitration.—[8][* * *]

---

1. Ins. by Act 115 of 1976, sec. 30 (w.r.e.f. 8-10-1976).
2. Ins. by Act 115 of 1976, sec. 31 (w.r.e.f. 8-10-1976).
3. Sub-section (1) omitted by Act 50 of 1991, sec. 13 (w.e.f. 15-10-1991).
4. Subs. by Act 50 of 1991, sec. 13, for "promoting" (w.e.f. 15-10-1991).
5. Subs. by Act 50 of 1991, sec. 13, for sub-section (3) (w.e.f. 15-10-1991).
6. Sub-section (3A) ins. by Act 23 of 1978, sec. 18 (w.e.f. 3-6-1978) and omitted by Act 50 of 1991, sec. 13 (w.e.f. 15-10-1991).
7. Subs. by Act 50 of 1991, sec. 13, for "sub-section (1) and" (w.e.f. 15-10-1991).
8. Sub-section (1) omitted by Act 30 of 1966, sec. 17 (w.e.f. 16-9-1966).

(2) Where any question or matter is, by this Act, required to be referred to arbitration, it shall be so referred—

(a) in cases where the Act so provides, to the Authority and on such reference the Authority shall be deemed to have been duly appointed as Arbitrators, and the award of the Authority shall be final and conclusive; or

(b) in other cases, to two arbitrators, one to be appointed by each party to the dispute.

(3) Subject to the provisions of this section, the provisions of the [1][Arbitration and Conciliation Act, 1996 (26 of 1996)] shall apply to arbitrations under this Act.

[2][(3A) Where any question or matter is referred to the Authority for arbitration under this section, the Authority may, having regard to the circumstances of each case, charge such arbitration fee as it may deem reasonable.]

[3][(3B) All fees and charges due to the Authority in respect of any arbitration and award and all costs and charges for filing the award incurred by the Authority may, if they are not paid by the person from whom they are due within a period of one month from the date of a notice given to him by the Authority in this behalf, be recovered from him in the same manner as an arrear of land revenue.]

(4) The arbitrators shall in making their award have regard to the provisions of this Act and any rules and regulations made thereunder relevant to the reference.

(5) The arbitrators may, if they think it expedient so to do, call in the aid of one or more qualified assessors and hear the reference wholly or partially with the aid of such assessors.

(6) The provisions of sub-sections (4) and (5) shall apply to the umpire, if he enters on the reference, as they apply to the arbitrators.

[4][**77. Penalties.**—If any licensee or other person, not being the Board, fails without reasonable excuse to comply with, or give effect to, any direction, order or requirement made under any of the following provisions, namely:—

(a) section 4; or

(b) section 55; or

---

1. Subs. by Act 22 of 1998, sec. 12, for "Arbitration Act, 1940 (10 of 1940)" (w.e.f. 31-12-1998).
2. Ins. by Act 101 of 1956, sec. 20 (w.e.f. 30-12-1956) and subs. by Act 22 of 1998, sec. 12 (w.e.f. 31-12-1998).
3. Sub-section (3B) ins. by Act 101 of 1956, sec. 20 (w.e.f. 30-12-1956).
4. Subs. by Act 101 of 1956, sec. 21, for section 77 (w.e.f. 30-12-1956).

(c) clause (d) of sub-section (1) of section 57A; or

(d) section 57B; or

(e) section 58; or

(f) sub-section (3) of section 75,

he shall be punishable with fine which may extend to five hundred rupees, and in the case of a continuing offence with a further fine which may extend to fifty rupees for each day after the first during which the offence continues.

77A. Source from which fines may be paid.—All fines payable by a licensee under this Act or under any other law for the time being in force in respect of any offence committed by the licensee, shall be payable by him from that part of the clear profit to which he is entitled under the Sixth Schedule.

77B. Offences by companies.—(1) If the person committing an offence under this Act is a company, every person who at the time the offence was committed was in charge of, and was responsible to, the company for the conduct of the business of the company as well as the company, shall be deemed to be guilty of the offence and shall be liable to be proceeded against and punished accordingly:

Provided that nothing contained in this sub-section shall render any such person liable to any punishment, if he proves that the offence was committed without his knowledge or that he exercised all due diligence to prevent the commission of such offence.

(2) Notwithstanding anything contained in sub-section (1), where an offence under this Act has been committed with the consent or connivance of, or is attributable to any neglect on the part of, any director or manager, secretary or other officer of the company, such director, manager, secretary or other officer shall also be deemed to be guilty of that offence and shall be liable to be proceeded against and punished accordingly.

Explanation.—For the purposes of this section,—

(a) "company" means any body corporate and includes a firm or other association of individuals; and

(b) "director" in relation to a firm means a partner in the firm.

77C. Cognizance of offences.—No Court shall take cognizance of an offence under section 77, except on the complaint of,—

(a) in the case of an offence relating to section 4, by an officer of the Authority authorized in that behalf by the Authority;

(b) in the case of any other offence,—

(i) where a Board is constituted, by an officer of the Board authorized by the Board in that behalf;

(ii) where no Board is constituted, by an officer of the State Government authorised by the State Government in that behalf.]

78. Power to make rules.—(1) The State Government may after previous publication, by notification in the Official Gazette make rules to give effect to the provisions of this Act.

(2) In particular, and without prejudice to the generality of the foregoing power, such rules may provide for—

[1][(a) [2][the powers of the Chairman and the term of office] of the Chairman and other members of the Board, the conditions under which they shall be eligible for re-appointment and their remuneration, allowances and other conditions of service;]

(b) the terms and conditions of appointment of members of [3][State Electricity Consultative Councils] and Local Advisory Committees, the convening of meetings of such Councils and Committees, and the conduct of business thereat;

(c) the form in which the annual financial statement and supplementary statements under section 61 shall be prepared by the Board, and the particulars to be included therein;

(d) the conditions subject to which the Board may borrow under section 65;

(e) the manner in which stock issued by the Board shall be issued, transferred, dealt with and redeemed;

(f) the manner in which the accounts of the Board shall be published under section 69;

(g) the form in which and the date by which the annual report of the Board shall be submitted under section 75, and the form and manner of furnishing statistics and returns by the Board under that section;

(h) the business of the Board upon which the local Advisory Committees concerned shall be consulted.

---

1. Subs. by Act 57 of 1949, sec. 6, for clause (a).
2. Subs. by Act 101 of 1956, sec. 22, for "the term of office" (w.e.f. 30-12-1956).
3. Subs. by Act 101 of 1956, sec. 22, for "State Electricity Councils" (w.e.f. 30-12-1956).

[1][**78A. Directions by the State Government.**—(1) In the discharge of its functions, the Board shall be guided by such directions on questions of policy as may be given to it by the State Government.

(2) If any dispute arises between the Board and the State Government as to whether a question is or is not a question of policy, it shall be referred to the Authority whose decision thereon shall be final.]

79. Power to make regulations.—[2][The Board may by notification in the Official Gazette, make regulations] not inconsistent with this Act and the rules made thereunder to provide for all or any of the following matters, namely:—

(a) the administration of the funds and other property of the Board, and the maintenance of its accounts;

(b) the summoning and holding of meetings of the Board, the times and places at which such meetings shall be held, the conduct of business thereat and the number of members necessary to constitute a quorum;

(c) the duties of [3][officers and other employees] of the Board, and their salaries, allowances and other conditions of service;

(d) all matters necessary or expedient for regulating the operations of the Board under section 20;

(e) the making of advances to licensees by the Board under section 23 and the manner of repayment of such advances;

(f) the making of contributions by the Board under section 24;

(g) the procedure to be followed by the Board in inviting, considering and accepting tenders;

(h) principles governing the fixing of Grid Tariffs;

(i) principles governing the making of arrangements with licensees under section 47;

(j) principles governing the supply of electricity by the Board to persons other than licensees under section 49;

---

1. Ins. by Act 101 of 1956, sec. 23 (w.e.f. 30-12-1956).
2. Subs. by Act 20 of 1983, sec. 2 and Sch., for "The Board may make regulations" (w.e.f. 15-3-1984).
3. Subs. by Act 23 of 1978, sec. 19, for "officers and servants" (w.e.f. 3-6-1978).

[1][(jj) expending sum not included in statement submitted under sub-section (1) or sub-section (5) of section 61, under sub-section (2) of section 62;]

(k) any other matter arising out of the Board's functions under this Act for which it is necessary or expedient to make regulations:

Provided that regulations under clauses (a) [2][, (d) and (jj)] shall be made only with the previous approval of the State Government and regulations under clauses (h) and (i) shall be made with the concurrence of the Authority.

[3][**79A. Laying of notification before the State Legislature.**—Every notification issued under section 55 by the State Government, or the State Commission, as the case may be, every rule made by that Government under section 78 and every regulation made by the Board under section 79, shall be laid, as soon as may be, before the State Legislature.]

80. Provision relating to income-tax and super-tax.—(1) For the purposes of the Indian Income-tax Act, 1922 (11 of 1922), the Board shall be deemed to be a company within the meaning of that Act and shall be liable to income-tax and super-tax accordingly on its income, profits and gains.

(2) The State Government shall not be entitled to any refund of any such taxes paid by the Board.

81. Members, officers and servants of the Board to be public servants.—All [4][members and officers and other employees] of the Board shall be deemed, when acting or purporting to act in pursuance of any of the provisions of this Act, to be public servants within the meaning of section 21 of the Indian Penal Code (45 of 1860).

82. Protection to persons acting under this Act.—No suit, prosecution or other legal proceeding shall lie against [5][any [6][member or officer or other employee] of the Board] for anything which is in good faith done or intended to be done under this Act.

---

1. Ins. by Act 23 of 1978, sec. 19 (w.e.f. 3-6-1978).
2. Subs. by Act 23 of 1978, sec. 19, for "and (d)" (w.e.f. 3-6-1978).
3. Section 79A ins. by Act 20 of 1983, sec. 2 and Sch. (w.e.f. 15-3-1984) and subs. by Act 22 of 1998, sec. 13 (w.e.f. 31-12-1998).
4. Subs. by Act 23 of 1978, sec. 20, for "member, officers or servants" (w.e.f. 3-6-1978).
5. Subs. by Act 30 of 1966, sec 18, for "any person" (w.e.f. 16-9-1966).
6. Subs. by Act 23 of 1978, sec. 20, for "member, officer or servant" (w.e.f. 3-6-1978).

83. Saving of application of Act.—Nothing in this Act shall be deemed to apply to a licensee on which a notice under section 5 or section 7 of the Indian Electricity Act, 1910 (9 of 1910) has been served prior to the coming into force of the sections, Schedule and Table mentioned in sub-section (3) of section 1.

THE FIRST SCHEDULE

(*See* sections 34 and 36)

ARRANGEMENTS IN RESPECT OF CONTROLLED STATIONS

PART I

Assumption of control

I. (1) The Board shall by notice in writing to the licensee fix a date (hereafter in this Schedule referred to as the date of control), being the first day of a year of account of the licensee, and from such date the licensee shall, except where prevented by causes beyond his control, be under obligation—

(a) subject to such directions as the Board may from time to time give him, to keep the station at all times in good and substantial repair and condition and ready for use, together with adequate staff for operating, maintaining and controlling the station, and not to make any substantial alterations or renewals in, or remove any essential or substantial part of, the station without the consent in writing of the Board;

(b) to operate the station so as to generate such quantity of electricity with such units of plant at such rates of output and at such times, or to cease to generate electricity during such periods, as the Board may direct;

(c) to carry out as soon as may be practicable such reasonable extensions, alterations or renewals of the station or any part thereof as the Board may from time to time direct;

(d) to supply to the Board all the electricity generated at the station.

(2) To enable a licensee to comply with any direction under sub-paragraph (1) requiring extension of the station or any part thereof for purposes of the Board, the Board may, if it considers it expedient and practicable so to do, offer to advance to him a loan upon such terms and conditions as it may deem proper and the licensee [1][may accept the loan from the Board on the terms and conditions offered or may raise a loan from other sources or employ his own funds for the purpose of such extension]:

Provided that notwithstanding anything contained in any law or in any mortgage, charge or instrument executed by the licensee, the loan so advanced by the Board and the interest thereon shall be a first charge on the extension and subject to any prior encumbrance shall also be charged on the

1. Subs. by Act 101 of 1956, sec. 24, for certain words (w.e.f. 30-12-1956).

undertaking and all the revenues of the licensee and no such loan shall be amortized in any way by the licensee:

Provided further that if at the date of purchase of the station under this Act or of the licensee's undertaking under the Indian Electricity Act, 1910 (9 of 1910), the said principal or any part thereof remains unpaid though due for redemption or is not on that date due for redemption, then any sum payable by the purchaser as a percentage on account of compulsory purchase under this Act or the said Act shall be reduced by an amount which bears the same proportion to that sum as the amount of the said principal or part thereof remaining unpaid or not being due for redemption as aforesaid bears to the total of the ordinary, preference and debenture capital of the licensee and the loans advanced by the Board under this sub-paragraph.

Explanation.—In the sub-paragraph, the expressions "ordinary capital", "preference capital" and "debenture capital" have the meanings respectively assigned to them in the Sixth Schedule.

II. From the date of control the Board shall, except where prevented by causes beyond its control, be under obligation to supply to the licensee, and the licensee shall be under obligation to take from the Board, the whole of the electricity required by the licensee for the purposes of his undertaking except such quantity of electricity as the licensee may from the time being be entitled under paragraph III to purchase from a source other than the Board or as he may be generating in another station, not being a controlled station.

III. Unless otherwise agreed between the Board and the licensee, the licensee shall not, where he has received a notice under paragraph I, purchase after the date of control any quantity of electricity from a source other than the Board:

Provided that where on the date of the receipt of such notice the licensee is bound under any contract to purchase any quantity of electricity from some other source, he may, for a period not exceeding two years after the date of control or for such further period, if any, as the Board may allow, continue to purchase electricity under the said contract from such other source.

IV. The Board shall pay to the licensee, whether or not any electricity is generated at the station, the costs ascertained in accordance with the provisions of the Eighth Schedule.

V. The price to be paid by the licensee for electricity supplied by the Board shall be determined in the manner provided in the appropriate Part of this Schedule.

VI. The points at which electricity to be supplied under this Schedule shall be delivered by the Board and the licensee respectively shall, unless otherwise agreed between the Board and the licensee, be at the generating station, and the pressure of the supplies shall be such as the Board and the licensee may agree.

VII. Where any licensee owns more than one controlled station—

(a) such of the several controlled stations as are inter-connected shall, for the purposes of this Schedule, be deemed to comprise a single controlled station, and, unless the subject or context otherwise requires, the provisions of this Schedule shall be construed as if the word "combined" had been inserted before the word "station" or the words "generating station" wherever they occur;

(b) the electricity supplied at the several controlled stations by the licensee to the Board, or by the Board to the licensee, shall each respectively be treated as single supplies;

(c) in the application of clause (a) of paragraph XII, the costs of production at each of the several controlled stations shall be separately ascertained, and in the application of clause (c) of the said paragraph—

(i) the sums ascertained in accordance with clause (a) of paragraph I of the Eighth Schedule in respect of each of the several controlled stations shall be separately allocated between fixed costs and running costs, and

(ii) the sum of the several fixed costs and the sum of the several running costs shall be the fixed costs and the running costs respectively of the combined station;

(d) in directing the operation of the combined station under clause (b) of sub-paragraph (1) of paragraph I the Board shall have regard to the nature and capacity of the licensee's transmission system inter-connecting the several controlled stations and to the requirements of the licensee at each of those stations.

VIII. In the event of the licensee failing, except where prevented by causes beyond his control, to perform or continue to perform any obligation imposed upon him under this Part, the Board may give notice to him in writing that on the first day of the licensee's next succeeding year of account the generating station will be purchased by the Board, and on such day the Board shall purchase the station at a price determined in accordance with the Fourth Schedule, and thereafter—

(a) all the provisions of this Schedule except paragraph II and this paragraph shall, in relation to the licensee, cease to have effect;

(b) the Board shall supply the licensee with the electricity required by him under paragraph II at such price and on such conditions as the Board may determine.

PART II

Price to be paid for electricity supplied by the Board under Part I

IX. There shall be agreed between the Board and the licensee in respect of each month of the licensee's year of account—

(a) the maximum capacity of the station, that is to say, the maximum capacity (expressed in kilowatts available for supply to feeders) of such plant and works appertaining to the generation of electricity at the station as were available for reliable and regular commercial operation on the first day of the month, including the capacity of such plant and works as were temporarily out of commission;

(b) the number and size of units of plant and works, forming part of the aforesaid plant and works, which ought properly to be deemed to be standby if the station were not a controlled station;

(c) the standby capacity of the station, that is to say, the number of kilowatts (expressed in kilowatts available for supply to feeders) by which the maximum capacity of the station would be reduced if the standby plant and works referred to in clause (b) were to be left out of account;

(d) the actual effective capacity of the station, that is to say, the number of kilowatts by which the maximum capacity exceeds the standby capacity.

X. (1) The licensee shall be entitled to purchase from the station in each month at a price determined under paragraph XIII a number of kilowatts not exceeding the scheduled effective capacity of the station on the first day of that month as determined in sub-paragraph (2).

(2) The scheduled effective capacity of the station shall be agreed between the Board and the licensee in respect of each month of the year of account, and shall be computed in the same manner as the actual effective capacity under paragraph IX, except that there shall be left out of account such units of plant and works, if any, forming part of the plant and works referred to in clause (a) of the said paragraph, as the licensee declares to be surplus to his requirements for the time being:

Provided that the licensee shall not declare to be surplus to his requirements any such units of plant and works as were installed or were on order at the date of control or which were included in any previous computation of the scheduled effective capacity:

Provided further that if as a result of the licensee declaring as surplus to his requirements any units of plants or works, the scheduled effective capacity is in respect of any month computed to be less than the maximum demand of the licensee on the station for the purposes of his own undertaking, then such units of plant or works and all further additional units of plant or works shall thereafter always be deemed to be surplus to the requirements of the licensee as aforesaid unless the Board decides otherwise.

XI. Of the kilowatt-hours purchased by the licensee from the Board in each month, a number kilowatt-hours not exceeding the number which bears the same proportion to the total number purchased as the scheduled effective capacity for the month bears to the maximum demand of the licensee on the Board in that month shall be purchased at a price determined under paragraph XIII; the balance being purchased at a price determined under paragraph XIV:

Provided that if the station is a hydro-electric station or if any unit of a combined station is a hydro-electric unit, the number of kilowatt-hours which the licensee shall be entitled to purchase as aforesaid shall be reduced by such amount, if any, as may be agreed between the Board and the licensee, having regard to the number of kilowatt-hours actually supplied in the month from such hydro-electric station or unit.

XII. As soon as practicable after the end of a year of account—

(a) there shall be ascertained in respect of that year the cost of production at the station in accordance with the provisions of the Eighth Schedule;

(b) there shall be deducted from the total sum ascertained in respect of that year under clauses (b), (c), (d), (e) and (f) of paragraph I of the Eighth Schedule, such proportion of the charges referred to in the said clauses as are wholly attributable to so much of the plant and works, if any, as has been declared by the licensee under sub-paragraph (2) of paragraph X to be surplus to his requirements, and the balance remaining after such deduction shall for the purposes of this Schedule be referred to as the scheduled overhead charges:

Provided that in assessing the said proportion regard shall be had to the period during which any such plant or works were declared to be surplus as aforesaid;

(c) there shall be allocated between fixed costs and running costs in accordance with the provisions of the Ninth Schedule the sum ascertained in respect of that year under clause (a) of paragraph I of the Eighth Schedule, and the amount of running costs divided by the number of kilowatt-hours supplied from the station in that year shall for the purposes of this Schedule be referred to as the running charges component;

(d) there shall be ascertained in respect of that year an amount (in this Schedule referred to as the scheduled fixed works costs) calculated from the expression

“$\frac{A}{2} + \frac{A}{2} \times \frac{B}{C}$” Where—

A=the amount of fixed costs ascertained in respect of that year under clause (c);

B=the sum of the scheduled effective capacities for each month of that year;

C=the sum of the actual effective capacities for each month of that year.

XIII. The licensee shall pay to the Board in respect of each month of the year of account for the electricity purchased under paragraphs X and XI—

(a) in respect of kilowatts, an amount equal to one-twelfth of the sum of the scheduled overhead charges and the scheduled fixed works costs;

(b) in respect of kilowatt-hours a sum found by multiplying the number of kilowatt-hours supplied by the running charges component:

Provided that if in any year of account the station for any reason ceases to generate electricity for one thousand hours or more, then for the purposes of ascertaining the running charges component and the scheduled fixed works costs under clauses (c) and (d) respectively of paragraph XII—

(i) the said clause (c) shall be construed as if there were substituted for the words “that year” in both places where they occur, the words “the most recent year of account in which the station did not cease to generate electricity for one thousand hours or more” and as if to the said clause the following proviso were added, namely:—

"Provided that so much of the said sum as is represented by the cost of fuel shall be adjusted to take account of the cost which would have been incurred had that fuel been consumed at the average prices prevailing in the actual year of account.";

(ii) in evaluating the expression contained in the said clause (d), the letter C shall be deemed to be equal to the sum of the actual effective capacities for each month of the most recent year of account in which the station did not cease to generate electricity for one thousand hours or more:

Provided further that if in any year of account there exist in the station any units of plant or works which have been declared by the licensee under sub-paragraph (2) of paragraph X to be surplus to his requirements in that year, there shall be added to the running charges component in respect of that year the amount, if any, by which that part of the said component attributable to the cost of fuel is less than ninety *per centum* of the corresponding part of the running charges component in respect of the year of account immediately preceding that in which the earliest installed of the said units of plant or works first came into commercial operation in the station, and in ascertaining the corresponding part as aforesaid, the fuel consumed shall be deemed to be of the same average quality and to be consumed at the same average cost per ton as the fuel consumed in the year of account:

Provided further that if in respect of any month of the year of account any units of plant or works previously declared by the licensee as aforesaid to be surplus to his requirements are for the first time take into account in assessing the scheduled effective capacity for that month, then in addition to the payment referred to in clause (a) the licensee shall pay to the Board a sum equal to any sums previously paid by the Board to the licensee on revenue account (in respect of any period prior to the date on which the said units of plant or works came into commission) by way of interest, depreciation, testing and turning-up expenses attributable to the said units of plant or works; and the sum to be paid as aforesaid shall become due in one or more instalments and at such time or times as the Board may direct.

XIV. The price payable by the licensee to the Board for all electricity supplied by the Board to him in excess of the quantities referred to in paragraphs X and XI shall be the Grid Tariff.

XV. The licensee shall have the right at any time, on giving to the Board prior notice in writing expiring at the end of any year of account, to purchase from the Board at the Grid Tariff the whole of the electricity supplied to him by the Board thereafter:

Provided that the Board in those circumstances may make it a condition that the licensee shall, until the date on which the scheduled effective capacity of the station becomes nil, pay to the Board in respect of each month in addition to the Grid Tariff one-twelfth of such proportion as the Board may fix of the annual charges by way of interest and depreciation which would have been payable to the Board in respect of the year of account had the said notice not been given:

Provided further that in assessing the scheduled effective capacity for the purposes of the first proviso all units of plant or works which may have been under this Schedule declared or deemed to be surplus to the requirements of the licensee at the date of the expiration of the said notice and all additional units of plant or works shall after that date always be deemed to be surplus to the requirements of the licensee:

Provided further that after the expiration of the said notice the licensee shall not be entitled any time to purchase electricity from the Board at the price ascertained under paragraph XIII.

PART III

Permanent closing down of a controlled station

XVI. The Board may give the licensee not less than six months' notice in writing expiring at the end of any year of account that from the first day of next succeeding year of account it will not again direct the licensee to generate any electricity in the station, and upon that date (hereinafter in this Schedule referred to as the date of closing down) the station shall be permanently closed down.

XVII. From the date of closing down paragraphs I, IV and VIII shall, in relation to the stations, cease to have effect, and on receipt of the notice under paragraph XVI the licensee shall have the option (to be exercised by a date not later than three months prior to the date of closing down) either—

(a) (i) to sell the station at any time after the date of closing down, and

(ii) to purchase the electricity supplied to him by the Board at the Grid Tariff, or

(b) (i) to require the Board to purchase the station or at the option of the licensee the undertaking of the licensee at the date of closing down at a price determined under the Fourth Schedule, and

(ii) to purchase the electricity supplied to him by the Board in accordance with the provisions of Part II as modified by paragraph XVIII:

Provided that where the station cannot be severed from the distributing system of the licensee or where the severance of the station from the distributing system of the licensee is likely to affect prejudicially the interests of the licensee, the licensee shall be entitled to demand that the Board shall purchase his entire undertaking and on such demand being made the Board shall purchase the entire undertaking of the licensee.

Any question arising under the proviso to this paragraph shall be referred to arbitration under section 76.

XVIII. Where licensee exercises his option under paragraph XVII in terms of clause (b) thereof, the Board shall comply with the requirement to purchase the station under sub-clause (i) of that clause, and in applying the provisions of Part II to the purchase by the licensee of electricity supplied to him by the Board,—

(a) the station shall, notwithstanding that it has been permanently closed down, be deemed to remain a controlled station in operation but to be such a station which has ceased to generate electricity for one thousand hours or more during each year of account;

(b) clause (a) of paragraph IX shall be construed as if the following were substituted therefor, namely:—

"(a) the maximum capacity of the station, that is to say, the maximum capacity (expressed in kilowatts available for supply to feeders) of such plant and works appertaining to the generation of electricity at the date of closing down as would have been available for reliable and regular commercial operation on the first day of each month had the station not been closed down under Part III and had no replacement of any major item of such plant or works been carried out;";

(c) clause (a) of paragraph XII shall be construed as if the following were substituted therefor, namely:—

"(a) there shall be ascertained in respect of the year of account such annual charges by way of interest and depreciation attributable to the assets purchased by the Board under Part III as would have resulted from the application of clauses (e) and (f) of paragraph I of the Eighth Schedule and had those assets remained in the ownership of the licensee;";

(d) clause (b) of paragraph XII shall be construed as if the reference therein to clauses (b), (c) and (d) of paragraph I of the Eighth Schedule were omitted;

(e) there shall be added to the sum payable by the licensee to the Board under clause (a) of paragraph XIII in each month of the year of account a sum equal to one-twelfth of the amount calculated from the expression,

$$\text{“}\frac{A \times B}{C}\text{”} \quad \text{Where—}$$

A=that part of the scheduled overhead charges payable by the licensee to the Board in respect of the most recent year of account during which the station did not cease to generate electricity for one thousand hours or more, which relates to the items referred to in clauses (b), (c) and (d) of paragraph I of the Eighth Schedule;

B=the sum of the scheduled effective capacities for each month of the year of account;

C=the sum of the scheduled effective capacities for each month of the most recent year of account as aforesaid.

PART IV

Purchase by Board of controlled station not to be closed down

XIX. Where in respect of any month notified by the Board (and hereinafter in this Schedule referred to as the relevant month), the scheduled effective capacity of the station is computed under paragraph X to be less than one-half of the actual effective capacity of the station, the Board may give to the licensee six month's notice in writing that on the first day of the year of account next following the date of expiration of such notice the station will be purchased by the Board.

XX. Notwithstanding anything contained in paragraph X, in computing the scheduled effective capacity for purposes of paragraph XIX there shall be left out of account all such units of plant and works as would not reasonably have been required by the licensee for purposes other than supply to the Board had the station not been a controlled station.

XXI. Where a notice under paragraph XIX has been served by the Board on the licensee, the Board shall purchase the station or where a severance of the station from the distributing system of the licensee is not possible or is likely to affect prejudicially the interest of the licensee and the licensee so requires the entire undertaking of the licensee at the date specified in the notice and at a price determined under the Fourth Schedule.

XXII. From the date of purchase of the station or at the option of the licensee the undertaking of the licensee under paragraph XXI the provisions of paragraphs I, IV and VIII shall, in relation to the station, cease to have effect, and the licensee shall be required to purchase the electricity supplied to him by the Board in accordance with the provisions of Part II as modified by paragraph XXIII.

XXIII. In applying the provisions of Part II to the purchase by a licensee whose station has been purchased under this Part of electricity supplied to him by the Board,—

(a) the station shall, notwithstanding that it has been purchased by the Board, be deemed to remain a controlled station;

(b) clause (a) of paragraph XII shall be construed as if the reference therein to the provisions of the Eighth Schedule excluded a reference to clauses (b), (c) and (d) of paragraph I of that Schedule, and as if the following proviso were added to the said clause (a), namely:—

> "Provided that the annual charges to be included in accordance with clauses (e) and (f) of paragraph I of the said Schedule shall be such as would have resulted had the assets purchased by the Board under Part IV remained in the ownership of the licensee";

(c) clause (b) of paragraph XII shall be construed as if the reference therein to clauses (b), (c) and (d) of paragraph I of the Eighth Schedule were omitted;

(d) there shall be added to the sum payable by the licensee to the Board under clause (a) of paragraph XIII in each month of the year of account a sum equal to one twelfth of the amount calculated from the expression,

$$\text{“}\frac{A \times B}{C}\text{”} \quad \text{Where—}$$

A=that part of the scheduled overhead charges payable by the licensee to the Board in respect of the last year of account in which the station was in the ownership of the licensee, which relates to the items referred to in clauses (b), (c) and (d) of paragraph I of the Eighth Schedule;

B=the sum of the scheduled effective capacities for each month of the year of account;

C=the sum of the scheduled effective capacities for each month of the said last year of account.

THE SECOND SCHEDULE

(*See* section 35)

SUPPLY BY BOARD TO LICENSEES OWNING STATIONS OTHER THAN CONTROLLED STATIONS

I. Before the end of each year the Board shall declare to the licensee in respect of each of the two next succeeding years the maximum number of kilowatts which it will make available for the purpose of the licensee's undertaking.

II. Where the Board and the licensee agree that the number of kilowatts declared under paragraph I will be inadequate to meet the requirements of the licensee having regard to the capacity of the licensee's generating plant, the Board shall not refuse its consent under section 44, the provisions of that section notwithstanding, to the installation by the licensee of such generating plant as he may reasonably require for the purposes of his undertaking, unless the Board is able appropriately to amend its declaration within a reasonable time.

III. The licensee shall be entitled to demand from the Board, and the Board shall, except where prevented by causes beyond its control, be under obligation to supply to the licensee, a maximum number of kilowatts in each year not exceeding, without the consent of the Board, the maximum number of kilowatts declared under this Schedule in respect of that year.

IV. The point at which the electricity to be supplied under this Schedule shall be delivered to the licensee shall, unless otherwise agreed between the Board and the licensee, be at the licensee's generating station, and the pressure of supply shall be such as may be agreed between the Board and the licensee.

V. The Board shall bear the whole of the cost of the service apparatus required for making the supply under this Schedule available to the licensee.

VI. The price to be paid by the licensee to the Board in respect of each year for electricity supplied under this Schedule shall be the Grid Tariff.

THE THIRD SCHEDULE

(*See* section 36)

CLOSING DOWN OF GENERATING STATIONS OTHER THAN CONTROLLED STATIONS

I. Where the Board proposes under section 36 permanently to close down a generating station other than a controlled station, it shall give the licensee owning the station not less than six months, notice in writing expiring at the end of any year of account that from the first day of the next succeeding year of account (hereafter in this Schedule referred to as the date of closing down) the station shall be permanently closed down.

II. From the date of closing down the Board shall be under obligation to supply to the licensee, except where prevented by causes beyond its control, and the licensee shall be under obligation to take from the Board, the whole of the electricity required by the licensee for the purposes of his undertaking, except such quantity of electricity as the licensee may for the time being be entitled under paragraph III to purchase from a source other than the Board or as he may be generating in another station, not being a controlled station.

III. Unless otherwise agreed between the Board and the licensee, the licensee shall not, where he has received a notice under paragraph I, purchase after the date of closing down any quantity of electricity from a source other than the Board:

Provided that where on the date of the receipt of such notice the licensee is bound under any contract to purchase any quantity of electricity from some other source, he may, for a period not exceeding two years after the date of closing down or for such further period, if any, as the Board may allow, continue to purchase electricity under the said contract from such other source.

IV. (1) The point at which electricity to be supplied by the Board shall be delivered to the licensee shall, unless otherwise agreed between the Board and the licensee, be at the licensee's generating station, and the pressure of supply shall be such as may be agreed between the Board and the licensee.

(2) The Board shall bear the whole of the cost of the service apparatus required for making the supply available to the licensee.

V. The licensee shall have the option, to be exercised by a date not later than three months prior to the date of closing down, either—

(a) (i) to sell the station at any time after the date of closing down, and

(ii) to purchase the whole of the electricity supplied to him by the Board at the Grid Tariff, or

(b) (i) to require the Board to purchase the station [1][or the entire undertaking] at the date of closing down at a price determined under the Fourth Schedule, and

(ii) to purchase the whole of the electricity supplied to him by the Board on the terms hereafter set out in this Schedule.

VI. Where a licensee exercises his option under paragraph V in terms of clause (b) thereof, the Board shall comply with the requirement to purchase under sub-clause (i) of that clause, and the following provisions of this Schedule shall apply.

VII. As soon as practicable after the licensee has exercised his option as aforesaid, there shall be ascertained and agreed between him and the Board the following quantities in respect of each year of account subsequent to the date of closing down, namely:—

(a) The maximum capacity of the station, that is to say, the maximum capacity (expressed in kilowatts available for supply to feeders) of such plant and works appertaining to the generation of electricity at the date of closing down as would have been available for reliable

---

1. Ins. by Act 101 of 1956, sec. 25 (w.e.f. 30-12-1956).

and regular commercial operation on the first day of the year of account, had the station not been closed down under this Schedule and had no replacement of any major item of such plant or works been carried out subsequent to the date of closing down.

(b) The number and size of units of plant and works, forming part of the aforesaid plant and works, which would have represented reasonable standby in the station.

(c) The standby capacity of the station, that is to say, the number of kilowatts (expressed in kilowatts available for supply to feeders) by which the maximum capacity of the station would be reduced if the standby plant and works referred to in clause (b) were to be left out of account.

(d) The agreed effective capacity of the station, that is to say, the number of kilowatts by which the maximum capacity exceeds the standby capacity.

VIII. As soon as practicable after the date of closing down there shall be ascertained in agreement between the Board and the licensee in respect of each of the three consecutive years of account immediately preceding the date of closing down (hereafter in this Schedule referred to as the basic years)—

(a) the sums expended by the licensee and wholly attributable to the generation of electricity under the following heads, namely:—

(i) fuel;

(ii) less oil, water and stores consumed;

(iii) salaries and wages and any contribution by the licensee for pensions, provident fund, superannuation and insurance of officers and servants;

(iv) repairs and maintenance, and renewals not chargeable to capital account;

(v) management, rents, rates and taxes (including super-tax payable by the licensee as a company, but excluding other taxes on profits), insurance of plant and general establishment charges;

(vi) any other expense on revenue account;

(b) the actual effective capacity of the station on the first day of each such year agreed in accordance with the principles set out in paragraph IX of the First Schedule.

IX. As soon as practicable after the beginning of each year of account there shall be ascertained in respect of that year such annual charges by way of interest and depreciation attributable to the assets purchased by the Board under this Schedule as would have resulted from the application of clauses (e) and (f) of paragraph I of the Eighth Schedule, had those assets remained in the ownership of the licensee.

X. The licensee shall be entitled to purchase from the Board in each year of account at a price determined under paragraph XI—

(a) a number of kilowatts not exceeding the agreed effective capacity ascertained in respect of that year under paragraph VII, and

(b) a number of kilowatt-hours not exceeding the number of kilowatt-hours which bears the same proportion to the total number of kilowatt-hours required by the licensee in that year for the purposes of his undertaking as the agreed effective capacity ascertained in respect of that year bears to the total maximum demand of the licensee in that year for the said purposes.

XI. The price payable by the licensee in respect of each year of account for the quantity of electricity specified in paragraph X shall be—

(a) in respect of kilowatts, a fixed charge equal to the sum of—

(i) an amount calculated from the expression,

$$\text{“}\frac{A}{2} + \frac{A}{2} \times \frac{B}{C}\text{”};$$

(ii) an amount calculated from the expression

$$\text{“}\frac{B \times D}{C}\text{”};$$

(iii) the annual charges by way of interest and depreciation ascertained in respect of the year of account under paragraph IX, where—

A=one-third of the total costs during the basic years under heads (ii), (iii), (iv) and (vi) set out in clause (a) of paragraph VIII;

B=the agreed effective capacity for the year of account;

C=one-third of the sum of the actual effective capacities [ascertained under clause (b) of paragraph VIII] for each of the basic years;

D=one-third of the total costs during the basic year under head (v) set out in clause (a) of paragraph VIII;

(b) in respect of kilowatt-hours, a running charge per kilowatt-hour ascertained—

(i) by multiplying the total number of tons of fuel consumed in the station in the basic years by the estimate agreed between the Board and the licensee of the cost per ton which would have been incurred in delivering the handling the same quantity of fuel of equivalent calorific value to the furnaces in the station during the year of account, had the station remained in the ownership of the licensee, and

(ii) by dividing the total cost so found by the total number of units sent out from the station in the basic years.

XII. The price payable by the licensee for all electricity supplied to him by the Board in excess of the quantity specified in paragraph X shall be the Grid Tariff.

XIII. The licensee shall have the right at any time on giving the Board prior notice in writing expiring at the end of a year of account of purchase at the Grid Tariff the whole of the electricity supplied to him by the Board:

Provided that the Board in those circumstances may make it a condition that the licensee shall, until the date on which the agreed effective capacity of the station becomes nil, pay to the Board in each year of account in addition to the Grid Tariff a sum equal to such proportion as the Board may fix of the annual charges by way of interest and depreciation ascertained in respect of the year under paragraph IX:

Provided further that after the expiration of the said notice, the licensee shall not be entitled at any time to purchase electricity from the Board at the price ascertained under paragraph XI.

THE FOURTH SCHEDULE

(*See* sections 23 and 37 and First and Third Schedules)

PRICE FOR UNDERTAKINGS, GENERATING STATIONS AND MAIN TRANSMISSION LINES PURCHASED BY THE BOARD

I. For the purposes of this Schedule—

(a) "date of vesting" means the date on which the undertaking, generating station, main transmission line or asset forming part of such station or line, as the case may be, vests in the Board;

(b) "original cost" of an asset means the amount of expenses certified or determined under paragraph II to have been properly incurred on and incidental to the provision of the asset for the purposes of the undertaking, generating station or main transmission line, as the case may be;

[1][* * *]

II. The price to be paid for any undertaking, generating station or main transmission line as the case may be purchased by the Board under this Act shall be such sum as may be certified by an auditor appointed by the State Government in this behalf to have been the amount properly incurred on and incidental to the establishment of the undertaking, station or main transmission line, as the case may be, less depreciation thereon [2][calculated in accordance with the provisions of paragraph VI of the Sixth Schedule]:

Provided that there shall be added to such sum as aforesaid on account of such purchase of the generating station or main transmission line such reasonable compensation as may be determined by the Board having due regard to the fact that a portion of the undertaking is to be acquired:

Provided further that if the Board or the licensee is dissatisfied with the sum so certified, the matter shall, in default of agreement between them, be determined [3][by arbitration] as provided in section 76.

1. Clause (c) omitted by Act 23 of 1978, sec. 22 (w.e.f. 3-6-1978).
2. Subs. by Act 23 of 978, sec. 22, for "on the scale set out in paragraph III" (w.e.f. 3-6-1978).
3. Ins. by Act 30 of 1966, sec. 19 (w.e.f. 16-9-1966).

[1][* * *]

IV. The auditor appointed under paragraph II shall be a person qualified under the provisions of [2]section 144 of the Indian Companies Act, 1913 (7 of 1913), to act as an auditor of companies.

V. The auditor's cost under this Schedule shall be shared equally by the Board and the licensee concerned.

THE FIFTH SCHEDULE

(*See* section 41)

CHARGES FOR USE [3][BY BOARD OR GENERATING COMPANY] OF TRANSMISSION LINES AND MAIN TRANSMISSION LINES

1. The following charges and allowances shall be made in respect of a year of account for the use by [4][the Board or the Generating Company] of main transmission lines or transmission lines (hereafter in this Schedule referred to as lines), namely:—

(a) the actual cost of maintenance of the lines, including renewals thereof not chargeable to capital account;

(b) sums paid in respect of the lines for insurance and as rents, rates and taxes [5][(including all taxes payable on income and profits)];

(c) the proportion of management and general establishment charges properly attributable to the lines;

(d) any other expenses on revenue account properly attributable to the lines;

(e) [6][interest on the depreciated cost of the lines shown in the books of the undertaking and properly attributable to the lines (whether defrayed out of capital or revenue) and interest on such working capital as is properly attributable to the lines]:

Provided that for the purpose of ascertaining the principal on which interest is payable within the meaning of this clause, there shall be left out of account any part of principal interest on which is charged to capital;

---

1. Paragraph III omitted by Act 23 of 1978, sec. 22 (w.e.f. 3-6-1978).
2. *See* sections 224 and 226 of the Companies Act, 1956 (1 of 1956).
3. Subs. by Act 115 of 1976, sec. 32, for "BY BOARD" (w.r.e.f. 8-10-1976).
4. Subs. by Act 115 of 1976, sec. 32, for "the Board" (w.r.e.f. 8-10-1976).
5. Subs. by Act 101 of 1956, sec. 26, for "(including super-tax payable by the licensee as a company, but excluding other taxes on profits)" (w.e.f. 30-12-1956).
6. Subs. by Act 101 of 1956, sec. 26, for certain words (w.e.f. 30-12-1956).

(f) an allowance for depreciation of an amount determined in respect of the lines in accordance with the provisions of paragraph VI of the Sixth Schedule.

II. If the lines are used partly by [1][the Board or the Generating Company] and partly by the licensee owning them, or if the arrangement for their use comes into force or determines otherwise than at the beginning or end of a year of account, the charges and allowances referred to in paragraph I shall be the proper proportion thereof having regard to the use made of the lines by [1][the Board or the Generating Company] and the period of such use during the year and with the addition of the cost of such additional transmission losses as may have been incurred by the licensee as a result of the Board's user of the lines.

[2][**III.** For the purposes of clause (e) of paragraph I,—

(i) "depreciated cost of the lines" means original cost thereof as determined in accordance with the provisions of sub-paragraph (6) of paragraph XVII of the Sixth Schedule less the amount written off or set aside on account of depreciation on fixed assets and the amount written off in respect of intangible assets thereof in the books of the undertaking before or after the commencement of this Act;

(ii) the rate of interest shall be,—

(a) where the licensee owning the lines in a local authority, the average rate payable on the money raised by that authority for the purpose of constructing the lines;

(b) in any other case, the Reserve Bank rate ruling at the beginning of the year referred to in paragraph I *plus* two *per centum*.]

THE SIXTH SCHEDULE

[3][*See* sections 57 and 57A]

FINANCIAL PRINCIPLES AND THEIR APPLICATION

I. [4][Notwithstanding anything contained in the Indian Electricity Act, 1910 (9 of 1910) [5][[except sub-section (2) of section 22A]], and the provisions in the licence of a licensee, the licensee shall so adjust his [6][charges] for the sale of electricity whether by enhancing or reducing them that his clear profit in any year of account shall not, as far as possible, exceed the amount of reasonable return:]

1. Subs. by Act 115 of 1976, sec. 32, for "the Board" (w.r.e.f. 8-10-1976).
2. Subs. by Act 30 of 1966, sec. 20, for paragraph III (w.r.e.f. 1-4-1966).
3. Subs. by Act 101 of 1956, sec. 27, for "(*See* section 57)" (w.e.f. 30-12-1956).
4. Subs. by Act 101 of 1956, sec. 27, for certain words (w.e.f. 30-12-1956).
5. Ins. by Act 32 of 1959, sec. 41 (w.e.f. 5-9-1959).
6. Subs. by Act 30 of 1966, sec. 21, for "rates" (w.e.f. 1-4-1966).

[1][Provided that such [2][charges] shall not be enhanced more than once in any year of account:

Provided further that the licensee shall not be deemed to have failed so to adjust his [2][charges] if the clear profit in any year of account has not exceeded the amount of reasonable return by [3][twenty] *per centum* of the amount of reasonable return:

Provided further that the licensee shall not enhance the [2][charges] for the supply of electricity until after the expiry of a notice in writing of not less than sixty clear days of his intention to so enhance the [2][charges], given by him to the State Government and to the Board:

Provided further that if the [2][charges] of supply fixed in pursuance of the recommendations of a rating committee constituted under section 57A are lower than those notified by the licensee under and in accordance with the preceding proviso, the licensee shall refund to the consumers the excess amount recovered by him for them:]

[4][Provided also that nothing in this Schedule shall be deemed to prevent a licensee from levying with the previous approval of the State Government, minimum charges for supply of electricity for any purpose.]

[4]**[IA.** The notice referred to in the third proviso to paragraph I shall be accompanied by such financial and technical data in support of the proposed enhancement of charges as the State Government may, by general or special order, specify.]

II. (1) If the clear profit of a licensee in any year of account is in excess of the amount of reasonable return, one-third of such excess, not exceeding [5][five per cent.] of the amount of reasonable return, shall be at the disposal of the undertaking. Of the balance of the excess, one-half shall be appropriated to a reserve which shall be called the Tariffs and Dividends Control Reserve and the remaining half shall either be distributed in the form of a proportional rebate on the amounts collected from the sale of electricity and meter rentals or carried forward in the accounts of the licensee for distribution to the consumers in future, in such manner as the State Government may direct.

(2) The Tariffs and Dividends Control Reserve shall be available for disposal by the licensee only to the extent by which the clear profit is less than the reasonable return in any year of account.

(3) On the purchase of the undertaking under the terms of its licence any balance remaining in the Tariffs and Dividends Control Reserve shall be handed over to the purchaser and maintained as such Tariffs and Dividends Control Reserve:

---

1. Subs. by Act 101 of 1956, sec. 27, for the proviso (w.e.f. 1-4-1957).
2. Subs. by Act 30 of 1966, sec. 21, for "rates" (w.e.f. 1-4-1966).
3. Subs. by Act 30 of 1966, sec. 21, for "fifteen" (w.e.f. 1-4-1966).
4. Ins. by Act 30 of 1966, sec. 21 (w.e.f. 1-4-1966).
5. Subs. by Act 101 of 1956, sec. 27, for "7.5 per cent." (w.e.f. 1-4-1957).

[1][Provided that where the undertaking is purchased by the Board or the State Government, the amount of the Reserve may be deducted from the price payable to the licensee.]

[2][(4) On the purchase of the undertaking after the expiry, or on the revocation, of its licence or otherwise, all amounts of rebate lying undistributed to the consumers on the date of such purchase, shall be handed over to the purchaser who, in turn, shall enter the same in his books of account, under the heading Consumers' Rebate Reserve and any amount lying undistributed in that Reserve shall be carried forward for distribution to the consumer concerned:

Provided that the share of money in the Consumers' Rebate Reserve payable to the consumers who are not traceable or who have ceased to be consumers in relation to that undertaking, may be utilised in the development works of the purchaser.]

III. There shall be created from existing reserves or from the revenues of the undertaking a reserve to be called "Contingencies Reserve".

IV. (1) The licensee shall appropriate to Contingencies Reserve from the revenues of each year of account a sum not less than one-quarter of one *per centum* and not more than one-half of one *per centum* to the original cost of fixed assets, provided that if the said reserve exceeds, or would by such appropriation, be caused to exceed, five *per centum* of the original cost of fixed assets, no appropriation shall be made which would have the effect of increasing the reserve beyond the said maximum.

[3][(2) The sums appropriated to the Contingencies Reserve shall be invested in securities authorised under the Indian Trusts Act, 1882 (2 of 1882) and such investment shall be made within a period of six months of the close of the year of account in which such appropriation is made.]

V. [4][(1)] The Contingencies Reserve shall not be drawn upon during the currency of the licence except to meet such charges as the State Government may approve as being—

(a) expenses or loss of profits arising out of accidents, strikes or circumstances which the management could not have prevented;

(b) expenses on replacement or removal of plant or works other than expenses requisite for normal maintenance or renewal;

(c) compensation payable under any law for the time being in force and for which no other provision is made.

[5][(2) On the purchase of the undertaking, the Contingencies Reserve, after deduction of the amounts drawn under sub-paragraph (1), shall be handed over to the purchaser and maintained as such Contingencies Reserve:

---

1. Added by Act 30 of 1966, sec. 21 (w.e.f. 1-4-1966).
2. Ins. by Act 115 of 1976, sec. 33 (w.r.e.f. 8-10-1976).
3. Subs. by Act 30 of 1966, sec. 21, for sub-paragraph (2) (w.e.f. 1-4-1966).
4. Paragraph V re-numbered as sub-paragraph (1) thereof by Act 101 of 1956, sec. 27 (w.e.f. 1-4-1957).
5. Sub-paragraph (2) ins. by Act 101 of 1956, sec. 27 (w.e.f. 1-4-1957) and subs. by Act 30 of 1966, sec. 21 (w.e.f. 1-4-1966).

Provided that where the undertaking is purchased by the Board or the State Government, the amount of the Reserve computed as above shall, after further deduction of the amount of compensation, if any, payable to the employees of the outgoing licensee under any law for the time being in force, be handed over to the Board or the State Government, as the case may be.]

[1][**VA.** (1) There shall be created a reserve to be called the Development Reserve to which shall be appropriated in respect of each accounting year a sum equal to the amount of income-tax and super-tax calculated at rates applicable during the assessment year for which the accounting year of the licensee is the previous year, on the [2][amount of investment allowance] to which the licensee is entitled for the accounting year [3][under section 32A of the Income-tax Act, 1961 (43 of 1961)]:

Provided that if in any accounting year, the clear profit [excluding the special appropriation to be made under item (va) of clause (c) of sub-paragraph (2) of paragraph XVII] together with the accumulations, if any, in the Tariffs and Dividends Control Reserve less the sum calculated as aforesaid falls short of the reasonable return, the sum to be appropriated to the Development Reserve in respect of such account year shall be reduced by the amount of the shortfall.

(2) Any sum to be appropriated towards the Development Reserve in respect of any accounting year under sub-paragraph (1), may be appropriated in annual instalments spread over a period not exceeding five years from the commencement of that accounting year.

(3) The Development Reserve shall be available only for investment in the business of electricity supply of the undertaking.

(4) On the purchase of the undertaking, the Development Reserve shall be handed over to the purchaser and maintained as such Development Reserve:]

[4][Provided that where the undertaking is purchased by the Board or the State Government, the amount of the Reserve [5][(whether such amount is in the form of cash or other assets)] may be deducted from the price payable to the licensee.]

[6][**VI.** (a) The licensee shall provide each year for depreciation such sum calculated in accordance with such principles as the Central Government may, after consultation with the Authority, by notification in the Official Gazette, lay down from time to time.

---

1. Ins. by Act 101 of 1956, sec. 27 (w.e.f. 1-4-1957).
2. Subs. by Act 23 of 1978, sec. 23, for "amount of development rebate" (w.e.f. 3-6-1978).
3. Subs. by Act 23 of 1978, sec. 23, for "under clause (vib) of sub-section (2) of section 10 of the Indian Income-tax Act, 1922 (11 of 1922)." (w.e.f. 3-6-1978).
4. Added by Act 30 of 1966, sec. 21 (w.e.f. 1-4-1966).
5. Ins. by Act 23 of 1978, sec. 23 (w.e.f. 3-6-1978).
6. Subs. by Act 23 of 1978, sec. 23, for paragraphs VI, VII, VIII, IX, X and XI (w.e.f. 3-6-1978).

(b) Where in any particular year depreciation cannot be adjusted against revenues, the same may be carried over to subsequent years.

(c) The provisions of this paragraph shall apply to the charging of depreciation for the year in which the Electricity (Supply) Amendment Act, 1978 (23 of 1978), comes into force.]

XII. Where contributions are made by consumers towards the cost of construction of service lines constructed after the date on which this Act comes into force only the net cost of such service lines after deducting such contributions shall be included in the cost of fixed assets for the purposes of arriving at the capital base:

Provided that for the purposes of depreciation under paragraph VI, the total original cost of construction of the service lines shall be taken into account.

XIII. (1) Subject to the provisions of sub-paragraph (2) the ordinary remuneration of a managing agent excluding the office allowance mentioned in sub-paragraph (3) but including purchasing commission, if any, shall be based on a percentage of net profits [1][as determined in accordance with the provisions of section 349 of the Companies Act, 1956 (1 of 1956)], and shall not exceed—

(a) in respect of the first Rs. 5 lakh of such net profits—10 per cent.; and

(b) in respect of all net profits in excess of Rs. 5 lakh—7 per cent.

(2) The amount paid to a managing agent shall be subject to a minimum payment on account of ordinary remuneration not exceeding two rupees per annum for each complete thousand rupees of paid up share and debenture capital, provide that for purposes of computing the minimum payment should the share and debenture capital be less than rupees five lakh it shall be taken as rupees five lakh and should the said capital be greater than rupees one crore it shall be taken as rupees one crore.

(3) An office allowance drawn by a managing agent which shall include the salaries and wages of all persons employed in the office of the managing agent, but not the salaries of the engineering staff employed for purposes of the undertaking, shall be a percentage of the operating expenditure and the expenditure during the year of account on capital works. The office allowance so drawn shall not exceed—

(a) In respect of the first Rs. 1 lakh of operating expenditure—8 per cent.

In respect of the next Rs. 2 lakh of operating expenditure—5 per cent.

In respect of the next Rs. 7 lakh of operating expenditure—2.5 per cent.

In respect of all operating expenditure in excess of Rs. 10 lakh—1.5 per cent.; and

---

1. Subs. by Act 101 of 1956, sec. 27, for "as defined in section 87C (3) of the Indian Companies Act, 1913 (7 of 1913)" (w.e.f. 1-4-1957).

(b) In respect of the first Rs. 1 lakh of capital expenditure incurred during the year of account—4 per cent.

In respect of the next Rs. 2 lakh of capital expenditure incurred during the year of account— 3 per cent.

In respect of the next Rs. 7 lakh of capital expenditure incurred during the year of account—1.5 per cent.

In respect of all capital expenditure in excess of Rs. 10 lakh incurred during the year of account—1 per cent.

Operating expenditure for the purposes of sub-paragraph (3) (a) above shall mean the sum of the items of expenditure as defined in sub-paragraph (2) (b) of paragraph XVII with the omission of those under clauses (i), (iv), (ix) and (x) thereof.

[1][*Explanation*.—For the purposes of this paragraph, the expression "managing agent" shall include every person, by whatever name called, who is in charge of the management of the whole, or substantially the whole, of the undertaking and where more persons than one are placed in charge of the management of the whole, or substantially the whole, of the undertaking, the total remuneration payable to all such persons shall not in the aggregate exceed the limits specified in this paragraph.]

XIV. The Board of Directors of an undertaking shall not contain more than ten directors.

XV. (1) Where at any time within three years before the next option of purchase under the licence arises, the licensee proposes to make any capital expenditure which exceeds [2][in any year of account,] twenty-five thousand rupees or two *per centum* of the capital base, whichever is more, in respect of which any amount would in the event of purchase under the option be payable by the purchaser to the license, the licensee shall, before giving effect to such proposal, apply to the Board or where no Board is constituted, the State Government for its concurrence.

(2) If the Board or the State Government, as the case may be, does not within one month from the receipt of such application, consent to such expenditure, the licensee may refer the matter to the arbitration of the Authority.

XVI. Any dispute or difference as to the interpretation or any matter arising out of the provisions of this Schedule shall be referred to the arbitration of the Authority:

[1][Provided that where a rating committee has been constituted under section 57A, no such dispute or difference shall be referred to the arbitration of the Authority during the period between the date of the constitution of such committee and the date of the order of the State Government made on the recommendations of the committee.]

1. Added by Act 101 of 1956, sec. 27 (w.e.f. 1-4-1957).
2. Ins. by Act 30 of 1966, sec. 21 (w.e.f. 1-4-1966).

Definitions

XVII. For the purposes of this Schedule—

(1) "capital base" means the sum of—

[1][(a) the original cost of fixed assets available for use and necessary for the purpose of the undertaking subject to the provisions of paragraph XII in respect of service lines, and the excess amount referred to in the proviso to sub-paragraph (2) of paragraph VII in respect of any fixed assets which has ceased to be available for use;]

(b) the cost of intangible assets [2][including expenses on account of new capital issue];

(c) the original cost of works in progress;

[3][(d) the amount of investments compulsorily made under paragraph IV of this Schedule together with the amount of such investments made after the commencement of this Act from contributions towards depreciation as in the opinion of the Authority could not be utilised for the purpose of the business of electricity supply of the undertaking;]

(e) an amount on account of working capital equal to the sum of—

(i) one-twelfth of the sum of the book cost of stores, materials and supplies including fuel on hand at the end of each month of the year of account;

(ii) one-twelfth of the sum of [4][cash and bank balances (whether credit or debit)] and call and short-term deposits at the end of each month of the year of account, not exceeding in the aggregate an amount equal to one-quarter of the expenditure under sub-paragraph (2) (b) of this paragraph excluding [5][sub-clauses (i), (iv), (iva), (ivb) and (x)];

less—

(i) the amounts written of or set aside on account of depreciation of fixed assets and amounts written off

1. Subs. by Act 101 of 1956, sec. 27, for clause (a) (w.e.f. 1-4-1957).
2. Ins. by Act 30 of 1966, sec. 21 (w.e.f. 1-4-1966).
3. Subs. by Act 101 of 1956, sec. 27, for clause (d) (w.e.f. 1-4-1957).
4. Subs. by Act 30 of 1966, sec. 21, for "cash and bank balances" (w.e.f. 1-4-1966).
5. Subs. by 30 of 1966, sec. 21, for "clauses (i), (iv) and (x)" (w.e.f. 1-4-1966).

in respect of intangible assets in the books of the undertaking before or after the commencement of this Act; [1][* * *]

(ii) the amount of any loans advanced by the Board [2][* * *];

[3][(iia) the amount of any loans borrowed from organisations or institutions approved by the State Government;

(iib) the amount of any debentures issued by the licensee;]

[4][(iii) the amounts deposited in cash with the licensee by consumers by way of security;]

[5][(iv) the amount standing to the credit of the Tariffs and Dividends Control Reserve [6][at the beginning of the year of account];]

[7][(v) the amount standing to the credit of the Development Reserve at the close of the year of account;]

[5][(vi) the amount carried forward [8][at the beginning of the year of account] in the accounts of the licensee for distribution to the consumers under paragraph II.]

(2) "clear profit" means—

the difference between the amount of income and the sum of expenditure *plus* specific appropriations made up in each case as follows:—

(a) income derived from—

(i) gross receipts from sale of energy, less discounts applicable thereby;

(ii) rental of meters and other apparatus hired to consumers;

(iii) sale and repair of lamps and apparatus;

---

1. The word "and" omitted by Act 101 of 1956, sec. 27 (w.e.f. 1-4-1957).
2. The words "under the provisions of sub-paragraph (2) of paragraph I of the First Schedule" omitted by 101 of 1956, sec. 27, (w.e.f. 1-4-1957).
3. Ins. by Act 30 of 1966, sec. 21 (w.e.f. 1-4-1966).
4. Sub-clause (iii) ins. by Act 101 of 1956, sec. 27 (w.e.f. 1-4-1959) and subs. by Act 31 of 1966, sec. 21 (w.e.f. 1-4-1966).
5. Ins. by Act 101 of 1956, sec. 27 (w.e.f. 1-4-1957).
6. Ins. by Act 30 of 1966, sec. 21 (w.e.f. 1-4-1966).
7. Sub-clause (v) ins. by Act 101 of 1956, sec. 27 (w.e.f. 1-4-1957) and subs. by Act 30 of 1966, sec. 21 (w.e.f. 1-4-1966).

(iv) rents, less outgoings not otherwise provided for;

(v) transfer fees;

(vi) investments, fixed and call deposits, and bank balances;

(vii) other general receipts accountable in the assessment of Indian income-tax and arising from the ancillary or incidental to the business of electricity supply;

(b) [1][expenditure properly incurred on]—

(i) generation and purchase of energy;

(ii) distribution and sale of energy;

(iii) rents, rates and taxes, other than all taxes on income and profits;

(iv) interest on loans advanced by the Board [2][* * *];

[3][(iva) interest on loans borrowed from organisations or institutions approved by the State Government;

(ivb) interest on debentures issued by the licensee;]

(v) interest on security deposits;

(vi) legal charges;

(vii) bad debts;

(viii) auditors' fees;

(ix) management including managing agents' remuneration as provided for in para XII;

(x) depreciation, computed as [4][hereinbefore] set out;

(xi) other expenses [5][(excluding interest on debentures and loans)], admissible under the law for the time being in force in the assessment of Indian Income-tax and arising from ancillary or incidental to the business of electricity supply;

[6][(xii) contributions to provident fund, staff pension and gratuity computed under any law for the time being in force or any such scheme as is approved by the State Government;

(xiia) expenses on apprentice and other training schemes;]

[5][(xiii) bonus paid to the employees of the undertaking—

---

1. Subs. by Act 101 of 1956, sec. 27, for "expenditure incurred on" (w.e.f. 1-4-1957).
2. The words "under sub-paragraph (2) of paragraph I of the First Schedule" omitted by Act 101 of 1956, sec. 27 (w.e.f. 1-4-1957).
3. Ins. by Act 30 of 1966, sec. 21 (w.e.f. 1-4-1966).
4. Subs. by Act 101 of 1956, sec. 27, for "hereinafter" (w.e.f. 1-4-1957).
5. Ins. by Act 101 of 1956, sec. 27 (w.e.f. 1-4-1957).
6. Subs. by Act 30 of 1966, sec. 21, for sub-clause (xii) (w.e.f. 1-4-1966).

(a) where any dispute regarding such bonus has been referred to any tribunal or other authority under any law for the time being in force relating to industrial or labour disputes, in accordance with the decision of such tribunal or authority;

(b) in any other case, with the approval of the State Government;]

(c) special appropriations sufficient to cover—

(i) previous losses (that is to say excess of expenditure over income) which have arisen from the business of electricity supply to the extent in any year [1][permitted by the State Government];

(ii) all taxes on income and profits;

(iii) instalments of written down amounts in respect of intangible assets and new capital issue expenses to the extent in any year actually appropriated for the purpose in the book of the undertaking:

Provided that the amounts so appropriated shall not exceed the amount found by dividing the written down cost of such assets by the number of complete years remaining before the next option of purchase under the licence arises;

(iv) contributions to the Contingency Reserve, computed as [2][hereinbefore] sort out;

(v) contributions towards arrears of depreciation;

[3][(va) contributions to the Development Reserve referred to in paragraph VA;]

[4][(vb) debt redemption obligation of the private licensees which may be done on a year to year basis, taking into account the requirement of debt redemption and resource generation through depreciation, retained surplus,]

(vi) other special appropriations permitted by the State Government.

(3) "debenture capital" means—

capital raised against debentures or other instruments creating a charge or lien on the assets of the undertaking.

---

1. Subs. by Act 101 of 1956, sec. 27, for "actually appropriated for the purpose in the books of the undertaking" (w.e.f. 1-4-1957).
2. Subs. by Act 101 of 1956, sec. 27, for "hereinafter" (w.e.f. 1-4-1957).
3. Ins. by Act 101 of 1956, sec. 27 (w.e.f. 1-4-1957).
4. Ins. by Act 50 of 1991, sec. 14 (w.e.f. 15-10-1991).

(4) "intangible assets" means—

underwriter's commission and such preliminary and promotional expenditure shown as a debit in the capital account of the undertaking, as has fairly arisen in promoting the business of electricity supply excluding any amount paid on account of goodwill.

(5) "ordinary capital" means—

in the case of a company, the amount of ordinary capital paid up and attributable to the undertaking of the licensee;

in other cases the net amount standing to the credit of the proprietor or proprietor's account or accounts whether in capital, personal or any other account howsoever called and property attributable to the business of electricity supply.

(6) "original cost" means in respect of any asset the sum of—

(a) the cost of the asset to the licensee, including the cost of delivery and all charges properly incurred in erecting and bringing the asset into beneficial use,

[1][(b) interest charges on capital expenditure incurred during the period between the date of grant of the licence and the date when the undertaking commences supply, from borrowed money and properly attributable to the assets as actually accrued up to the date of such supply, as well as interest incurred on outlays for subsequent expansions,]

(c) a proper addition on account of supervision not exceeding fifteen *per centum* of the cost referred to in sub-paragraph (a),

so, however, that the original cost of any asset shall not in any case exceed the original cost attributed thereto in the books of the undertaking.

(7) "Preference Capital" means—

the amount of paid up capital attributable to the undertaking of the licensee, issued on such preferred terms as are sufficient to qualify it for such description.

[2][* * *]

(9) "Reasonable return" means—

in respect of any year of account, the sum of the following:—

(a) the amount found by applying the standard rate to the capital base at the end of that year,

[3][(b) the income derived from investments other than those included in the capital base under the provisions of clause (d) of sub-paragraph (1);]

---

1. Subs. by Act 50 of 1991, sec. 14, for clause (b) (w.e.f. 15-10-1991).
2. Clause (8) omitted by Act 23 of 1978, sec. 23 (w.e.f. 3-6-1978).
3. Subs. by Act 101 of 1956, sec. 27 for clause (b) (w.e.f. 1-4-1957).

(c) an amount equal to one-half of one *per centum* on any loans advanced by the Board [1][* * *];

[2][(c-1) an amount equal to one-half of one *per centum* on the amounts borrowed from organisations or institutions approved by the State Government;

(c-2) an amount equal to one-half of one *per centum* on the amounts realised by the issue of debentures;]

[3][(d) an amount equal to one-half of one *per centum* on the accumulations in the Development Reserve created under paragraph VA of this Schedule;]

[4][(e) such other amount as may be allowed by the Central Government, having regard to the prevailing tax structure in the country.]

[5][(10) "standard rate" in respect of any year of account means—

(a) in relation to that part of the capital base for that year of account which is equivalent to the capital base as on the 31st day of March, 1955, seven *per centum* per annum;

(b) in relation to the remaining [6][capital base for that year, the Reserve Bank rate ruling at the beginning of that year plus—

(i) two *per centum* for investment made up to the date of the commencement of the Electricity Laws (Amendment) Act, 1991; and

(ii) five *per centum* for investments made thereafter:]

Provided that the Central Government may, by notification in the Official Gazette, and with effect from such date as may be specified therein, increase or decrease the standard rate specified in clause (b), if, after consultation with the Authority, that Government considers it necessary so to do to ensure that any rise or fall in the Reserve Bank rate does not affect the reasonable return in any subsequent year of account in relation to that part of the capital base which is equivalent to the capital base as computed on the last date of the previous year of account.]

---

1. The words "under sub-paragraph (2) of paragraph I of the First Schedule" omitted by Act 101 of 1956, sec. 27 (w.e.f 1-4-1957).
2. Ins. by Act 30 of 1966, sec. 21 (w.e.f. 1-4-1966).
3. Ins. by Act 101 of 1956, sec. 27 (w.e.f. 1-4-1957).
4. Ins. by Act 30 of 1966, sec. 21 (w.e.f. 1-4-1966).
5. Sub-paragraph (10) subs. by Act 101 of 1956, sec. 27 (1-4-1957) and again subs. by Act 30 of 1966, sec. 21 (w.e.f. 1-4-1966).
6. Subs. by Act 50 of 1991, sec. 14, for certain words (w.e.f. 15-10-1991).

(11) "Written down cost" means—

original cost less the amounts set aside or written off on account of depreciation in the books of the undertaking.

THE SEVENTH SCHEDULE

[Omitted by the Electricity Supply (Amendment) Act, 1978, (23 of 1978), sec. 24 (w.e.f. 3-6-1978).*]*

THE EIGHTH SCHEDULE

(*See* the First and Third Schedules)

DETERMINATION OF COST OF PRODUCTION OF ELECTRICITY AT GENERATING STATIONS

I. For the purposes of the First and Third Schedules, the cost of production of electricity at a generating station shall be ascertained by calculating and taking into account the following costs, charges and allowances in respect of the year of account, namely:—

(a) sums expended for fuel, oil, water and stores consumed, for salaries and wages, and any contribution by the licensee for pensions, provident fund, superannuation and insurance of [1][officers and other employees], for repairs and maintenance and for renewals not chargeable to capital account;

(b) sums paid in respect of the station for insurance and as rents, rates and taxes [2][(including all taxes payable on income and profits)];

(c) the proportion of management and general establishment charges properly attributable to the station;

(d) any other expenses on revenue account properly attributable to the station;

(e) [3][interest on the depreciated cost of the station shown in the books of the undertaking and properly attributable to the station (whether defrayed out of capital or revenue) and interest on working capital properly attributable to the station and the production of electricity therein]:

Provided that for the purpose of ascertaining the principal on which interest is payable within the meaning of this clause, there shall be left out of account any part of principal on which interest is payable out of capital;

(f) an allowance for depreciation of an amount determined in respect of the station in accordance with the provisions of paragraph VI of the Sixth Schedule.

---

1. Subs. by Act 23 of 1978, sec. 25, for "officer and servants" (w.e.f. 3-6-1978).
2. Subs. by Act 101 of 1956, sec. 29, for "(including super-tax payable by the licensee as company but excluding other taxes on profits)" (w.e.f. 30-12-1956).
3. Subs. by Act 101 of 1956, sec. 29, for certain words (w.e.f. 30-12-1956).

II. [1][For the purposes of clause (e) of paragraph I—

(i) "depreciated cost of the station" means original cost thereof as determined in accordance with the provisions of sub-paragraph (6) of paragraph XVII of the Sixth Schedule *less* the amount written off or set aside on account of depreciation on fixed assets and the amount written off in respect of intangible assets thereof in the books of the undertaking before or after the commencement of this Act;

(ii) the rate of interest shall be,—]

(a) on such part of the principal on which interest is payable within the meaning of the said clause as has been advanced on loan by the Board under paragraph I of the First Schedule, the actual rate charged by the Board *plus* one-half of one *per centum* per annum on the loan in the year of account;

(b) on the balance of the said principal—

(i) where the licensee owning the station is a local authority, the average rate payable in the year of account on the money raised by that authority for the purposes of the station;

(ii) in any other case, [2][the Reserve Bank rate ruling at the beginning of that year *plus* two *per centum*].

THE NINTH SCHEDULE

(*See* the First Schedule)

ALLOCATION OF COSTS OF PRODUCTION AT GENERATING STATIONS

I. For the purposes of this Schedule—

(a) the average load factor of a station shall be expressed as a percentage, and shall be ascertained by multiplying the number of kilowatt-hours supplied from the station during the year of account by 100, and dividing the product so obtained by the product of the average monthly maximum demand multiplied by the number of hours during which the station was in commission in the year of account;

(b) the average monthly maximum demand shall be the arithmetical average of the monthly maximum demands on the station in those calendar months during which the station was in commission in the year of account;

(c) a station shall be deemed to be in commission when the whole or any portion of the plant in the station is generating electricity or is in readiness to generate electricity upon demand;

(d) "cost of fuel" means the sums expended for fuel consumed *plus* the cost of any transport, handling, preparation or treatment incurred in

1. Subs. by Act 30 of 1966, sec. 22, for certain words (w.e.f 1-4-1966).
2. Subs. by Act 101 of 1956, sec. 29, for "5 *per centum* per annum" (w.e.f. 30-12-1956).

connection with the delivery of fuel to the boiler hoppers, furnaces or engines and in connection with the disposal of the products or residues of combustion, *plus* the proportion of salaries and wages and any contributions made by the owner of the station for pensions, provident fund, superannuation and insurance of officers and servants properly attributable to such delivery or disposal, *less* any sums received from the sale of any products or residues of combustion;

(e) "cost of oil, water and stores" means the sums expended for oil, water and stores consumed;

(f) "cost of repairs, maintenance and renewals" means the sums expended for repairs and maintenance and for renewals not chargeable to capital account, together with the proportion of salaries and wages and any contributions made by the owner of the station for pensions, provident fund, superannuation and insurance of [1][officers and other employees] properly attributable to repairs, maintenance and renewals;

(g) "salaries and wages" means the sums expended for salaries and wages and any contributions made by the owner of the station for pensions, provident fund, superannuation and insurance of officers and servants, *less* the proportion of such sums properly attributable to the cost of fuel under clause (d) and to the cost of repairs, maintenance and renewals under clause (f).

II. Of the cost of production of electricity at a generating station ascertained in accordance with the Eighth Schedule, the following costs, charges and allowances in respect of the year of account shall be allocated as "fixed costs", namely:—

(a) of the costs, charges and allowances set out in clause (a) of paragraph I of the said Schedule, portions calculated from the appropriate formulae set out in paragraph III;

(b) the whole of the costs, charges and allowances set out in the remaining clauses of paragraph I of the said Schedule.

III. The portion of the following costs, charges and allowances to be allocated as fixed costs shall be ascertained from the formula hereinafter set out against each, namely:—

(a) cost of fuel $\dfrac{100}{100+12.8L}$;

(b) cost of oil, water and stores $\dfrac{100}{100+9.66L}$;

(c) salaries and wages $\dfrac{100}{100+0.38L}$;

---

1. Subs. by Act 23 of 1978, sec. 25, for "officers and servants" (w.e.f. 3-6-1978).

(d) cost of repairs, maintenance and renewals $\dfrac{100}{100+0.0001NL}$;

Where—

[1][L=the percentage average load factor of the station;]

N=the number of hours during which the station was in commission in the year of account.

IV. The amount of the difference between the costs of production at a generating station ascertained in accordance with the Eighth Schedule and the fixed costs in respect of the year of account determined in accordance with this Schedule shall be allocated as "running costs".

V. The foregoing provisions of this Schedule shall not apply in any case where it is agreed between the Board and the owner of the station that the circumstances or conditions of operation in the station, whether temporary or continuing, are such that the said provisions ought not reasonably to be applied; and in such case the allocation between fixed costs and running costs shall be made in such manner as the Board and the said owner may agree.

---

1. Subs. by Act 30 of 1966, sec. 23, for "L = the average load factor of the station" (w.e.f. 16-9-1966).

THE ELECTRICITY REGULATORY COMMISSIONS ACT, 1998

INTRODUCTION

The rapidly growing demand for energy brought about by economic liberalisation has created numerous problems. To over come these problems and other issues facing the power sector the Government of India organised two Conferences of Chief Ministers to discuss the whole gamut of issues in the power-sector and the outcome of these meetings was the adoption of the Common Minimum National Action Plan for power. Under the Common Minimum National Action Plan. It was considered necessary to create a regulatory Commission as a step to arrest deteriorating conditions of the State Electricity Boards and to make plans for the future developments. The Ministry of Power assigned the task of studying the restructuring needs of the regulatory system to Administrative Staff College of India at Hyderabad. The Administrative Staff College of India strongly recommended the creation of independent Electricity Commissions both at the Centre and the States. To give effect to the aforesaid recommendations, The Electricity Regulatory Commissions Bill, 1997 was introduced in the Lok Sabha on 14th August, 1997. Due to the dissolution of the Lok Sabha the Bill could not be passed. Since it was considered essential to ensure speedy establishment of the Regulatory Commissions and as the Parliament was not in session, the President promulgated the Electricity Commissions Ordinance, 1998 on 25th April, 1998. To replace the said Ordinance by an Act of Parliament the Electricity Regulatory Commissions Bill was introduced in the Parliament.

STATEMENT OF OBJECTS AND REASONS

India's power sector is beset by problems that impede its capacity to respond to the rapidly growing demand for energy brought about by economic liberalisation. Despite the stated desire for reform and the initial measures that have been implemented, serious problems persist. As the problems of the Power Sector deepen, reform becomes increasingly difficult underscoring the need to act decisively and without delay. It is essential that the Government implement significant reforms by focussing on the fundamental issues facing the power sector, namely the lack of rational retail tariffs, the high level of cross-subsidies, poor planning and operation, inadequate capacity, the neglect of the consumer, the limited involvement of private sector skills and resources and the absence of an independent regulatory authority. Considering the paramount importance of restructuring the power sector, Government of India organised two Conferences of Chief Ministers to discuss the whole gamut of issues in the power sector and the outcome of these meetings was the adoption of the Common Minimum National Action Plan for Power (CMNPP).

2. The CMNPP recognised that the gap between demand and supply of power is widening and acknowledged that the financial position of State Electricity Boards is fast deteriorating and the future development in the power sector cannot be sustained without viable State Electricity Boards and improvement of their operational performance. The CMNPP identified creation of regulatory Commission as a step in this direction and specifically provided for establishment of the Central Electricity Regulatory Commission (CERC) and State Electricity Regulatory Commissions (SERCs). After the finalisation of the national agenda contained in CMNPP, the Ministry of Power assigned the task of studying the restructuring needs of the regulatory system to Administrative Staff College of India (ASCI), Hyderabad. The ASCI report strongly recommended the creation of independent Electricity Regulatory Commissions both at the Centre and the States.

3. To give effect to the aforesaid proposals, the Electricity Regulatory Commissions Bill, 1997 was introduced in the Lok Sabha on 14th August, 1997. However it could not be passed due to the dissolution of the Eleventh Lok Sabha. This has resulted in delay in establishing the Regulatory Commissions leading to confusion and misgivings in various sections about the commitment of the Government to the reforms and restructuring of the power sector. Needless to say, this has also slowed down the flow of public and private investment in power sector. Since it was considered necessary to ensure the speedy establishment of the Regulatory Commissions and as Parliament was not in session, the President promulgated the Electricity Regulatory Commissions Ordinance, 1998 on the 25th day of April, 1998.

4. The salient features of the said Ordinance are as follows:—

(a) It provides for the establishment of a Central Electricity Regulatory Commission at the Central level and State Electricity Commissions at the State levels;

(b) the main functions of CERC are—

(i) to regulate the tariff of generating companies owned or controlled by the Central Government;

(ii) to regulate inter-State transmission including tariff of the transmission utilities;

(iii) to regulate inter-State sale of power;

(iv) to aid and advise the Central Government in the formulation of tariff policy;

(c) the main functions of the SERC, to start with, shall be—

(i) to determine the tariff for electricity, wholesale, bulk, grid and retail;

(ii) to determine the tariff payable for use of the transmission facilities;

(iii) to regulate power purchase and procurement process of the transmission utilities, etc.

(iv) subsequently, as and when each State Government notifies, other regulatory functions could also be assigned to SERCs;

(d) it also aims at improving the financial health of the State Electricity Boards (SEBs) which are loosing heavily on account of irrational tariffs and lack of budgetary support from the State Governments as a result of which, the SEBs have become incapable of even proper maintenance, leave alone purposive investment. Further the lack of creditworthiness of SEBs has been a deterrent in attracting investment both from the public and private sectors. Hence, it is made mandatory for State Commissions to fix tariff in a manner that none of the consumers or class of consumers shall be charged less than fifty per cent. of the average cost of supply, it enables the State Governments to exercise the option of providing subsidies to weaker sections on condition that the State Governments through a subsidy compensate the SEBs. As regards the agriculture sector, it provides that if the State Commission considers it necessary it may allow the consumers in the agricultural sector to be charged less than fifty per cent. for a maximum period of three years from the date of commencement of the Ordinance. It also empowers the State Government to reduce the tariff further but in that case it shall compensate the SEBs or its successor utility, the difference between the tariff fixed by the State Commission and the tariff proposed by the State Government by providing budgetary allocations. Therefore, it enables the State Governments to fix any tariff for agriculture and other sectors provided it gives subsidy to State Electricity Boards to meet the loss.

5. The Bill seeks to replace the said Ordinance.

ACT 14 OF 1998

The Electricity Regulatory Commissions Bill having been passed by both the Houses of Parliament received the assent of the President on 2nd July, 1998 and it came on the Statute Book as THE ELECTRICITY REGULATORY COMMISSIONS ACT, 1998 (14 of 1998).

AMENDING ACT

The Electricity Regulatory Commissions (Amendment) Act, 2001 (21 of 2001).

THE ELECTRICITY REGULATORY COMMISSIONS ACT, 1998

(14 of 1998)

[*2nd July, 1998*]

An Act to provide for the establishment of a Central Electricity Regulatory Commission and State Electricity Regulatory Commissions, rationalization of electricity tariff, transparent policies regarding subsidies, promotion of efficient and environmentally benign policies and for matters connected therewith or incidental thereto.

Be it enacted by Parliament in the Forty-ninth Year of the Republic of India as follows:—

CHAPTER I

PRELIMINARY

1. Short title, extent and commencement.—(1) This Act may be called the Electricity Regulatory Commissions Act, 1998.

(2) It extends to the whole of India except the State of Jammu and Kashmir.

(3) It shall be deemed to have come into force on the 25th day of April, 1998.

2. Definitions.—In this Act, unless the context otherwise requires,—

(a) "Central Commission" means the Central Electricity Regulatory Commission established under sub-section (1) of section 3;

(b) "Chairperson" means the Chairperson of the Commission;

(c) "Commission" means the Central Commission [1][or the State Commission or the Joint Electricity Regulatory Commission], as the case may be;

(d) "High Court" means—

(i) the High Court within the jurisdiction of which the aggrieved party ordinarily resides or carries on business or personally works for gain; and

(ii) where the Central Government is the aggrieved party, the High Court within the jurisdiction of which the

1. Subs. by Act 21 of 2001, sec. 2, for "or the State Commission".

respondent, or in a case where there are more than one respondent, any of the respondents ordinarily resides or carries on business or personally works for gain;

(e) "inter-State transmission" includes—

(i) the conveyance of energy by means of a main transmission line from the territory of one State to the territory of another State;

(ii) the conveyance of energy across the territory of an intervening State as well as conveyance within the State which is incidental to such inter-State transmission of energy;

(iii) the transmission of energy within the territory on a system built, owned, operated, maintained or controlled by a central transmission utility or by any person under the supervision and control of a central transmission utility;

[1][(ea) "Joint Electricity Regulatory Commission" means the Joint Electricity Regulatory Commission constituted under section 21A;]

(f) "licensee" means a person licensed under Part II of the Indian Electricity Act, 1910 (9 of 1910) to supply energy or a person who has obtained sanction under section 28 of that Act to engage in the business of supplying energy (but does not include the Board or a Generating company);

(g) "Member" means the Member of the Commission and includes the Chairperson but does not include a Member, *ex officio*;

(h) "prescribed" means prescribed by rules made under this Act;

(i) "regulations" means regulations made under this Act;

(j) "State Commission" means the State Electricity Regulatory Commission established under sub-section (1) of section 17;

(k) "transmission utility" means any generating company, board, licensee or other person engaged in the transmission of energy;

(l) "utility" means any person or entity engaged in the generation, transmission, sale, distribution or supply, as the case may be, of energy;

(m) words and expressions used and not defined in this Act but defined in the Electricity (Supply) Act, 1948 (54 of 1948) or

---

1. Ins. by Act 21 of 2001, sec. 2.

the Indian Electricity Act, 1910 (9 of 1910) shall have the meanings respectively assigned to them in those Acts.

CHAPTER II

CENTRAL ELECTRICITY REGULATORY COMMISSION

3. Establishment and incorporation of Central Commission.—(1) The Central Government shall, within three months from the date of the commencement of this Act by notification in the Official Gazette, establish a body to be known as the Central Electricity Regulatory Commission to exercise the powers conferred on, and the functions assigned to it under this Act.

(2) The Central Commission shall be a body corporate by the name aforesaid, having perpetual succession and a common seal with power to acquire, hold and dispose of property, both movable and immovable, and to contract and shall, by the said name, sue or be sued.

(3) The head office of the Central Commission shall be at such place as the Central Government may, by notification in the Official Gazette, specify.

(4) The Central Commission shall consist of the following Members, namely:—

(a) a Chairperson and three other Members;

(b) the Chairman of the Central Electricity Authority appointed under sub-section (3) of section 3 of the Electricity (Supply) Act, 1948 (54 of 1948) who shall be the Member, *ex officio*.

(5) The Chairperson and the other Members of the Central Commission shall be appointed by the Central Government on the recommendation of the Selection Committee referred to in section 5:

Provided that nothing contained in this sub-section shall apply to the appointment of a person as the Chairperson, where such person is or has been a Judge of the Supreme Court or the Chief Justice of a High Court.

4. Qualification for appointment of Chairperson and other Members of Central Commission.—(1) The Chairperson and the Members of the Central Commission shall be persons having adequate knowledge, experience or shown capacity in dealing with problems relating to engineering, law, economics, commerce, finance or management and shall be appointed in the following manner, namely:—

(a) one person having qualification and experience in the field of engineering with specialisation in generation, transmission or distribution of electricity;

(b) one person having qualification and experience in the field of finance; and

(c) two persons having qualification and experience in the field of economics, commerce, law or management:

Provided that not more than one Member shall be appointed under the same category under clause (c).

(2) Notwithstanding anything contained in sub-section (1), the Central Government may appoint any person as the Chairperson from amongst persons who is or has been a Judge of the Supreme Court or the Chief Justice of a High Court:

Provided that no appointment under this sub-section shall be made except after consultation with the Chief Justice of India.

(3) The Chairperson or any other Member of the Central Commission shall not hold any other office.

(4) The Chairperson shall be the Chief Executive of the Central Commission.

5. Constitution of Selection Committee to recommend Members.—(1) The Central Government shall, for the purpose of sub-section (5) of section 3, constitute a Selection Committee consisting of—

(a) Member of the Planning Commission incharge of the energy sector —Chairperson;

(b) Secretary-in-charge of the Ministry of the Central Government dealing with the Department of Legal Affairs —Member;

(c) Chairman of the Public Enterprises Selection Board —Member;

(d) a person to be nominated by the Central Government in accordance with sub-section (2) —Member;

(e) a person to be nominated by the Central Government in accordance with sub-section (3) —Member;

(f) Secretary-in-charge of the Ministry of the Central Government dealing with Power —Member.

(2) For the purposes of clause (d) of sub-section (1), the Central Government shall nominate from amongst persons holding the post or Chairman of Managing Director, by whatever name called, of any public financial institution specified in section 4A of the Companies Act, 1956 (1 of 1956).

(3) For the purposes of clause (e) of sub-section (1), the Central Government shall nominate from amongst persons holding the post of Director or the head of the institution, by whatever name called, of any research, technical or management institution notified by the Central Government in the Official Gazette for this purpose.

(4) Secretary-in-charge of the Ministry of the Central Government dealing with Power shall be the Convenor of the Selection Committee.

(5) The Central Government shall, within one month from the date of occurrence of any vacancy by reason of death, resignation or removal of the Chairperson or a Member and six months before the superannuation or end of tenure of any Chairperson or Member, make a reference to the Selection Committee for filling up of the vacancy.

(6) The Selection Committee shall finalise the selection of the Chairperson and Members within one month from the date on which the reference is made to it.

(7) The Selection Committee shall recommend a panel of two names for every vacancy referred to it.

(8) Before recommending any person for appointment as a Chairperson or other Member of the Central Commission, the Selection Committee shall satisfy itself that such person does not have any financial or other interest which is likely to affect prejudicially his functions as a Member.

(9) No appointment of the Chairperson or other Member shall be invalid merely by reason of any vacancy in the Selection Committee.

6. Term of office, salary and allowances and other conditions of service of Chairperson and Members.—(1) The Chairperson or other Member shall hold office as such for a term of five years from the date on which he enters upon his office, but shall not be eligible for re-appointment:

Provided that no Chairperson or other Member shall hold office as such after he has attained,—

(a) in the case of the Chairperson, the age of sixty-five years; and

(b) in the case of any other Member, the age of sixty-two years.

(2) The salary and allowances payable to, and the other terms and conditions of service of, the Chairperson and other Members shall be such as may be prescribed.

(3) The salary, allowances and other conditions of service of the Chairperson and other Members shall not be varied to their disadvantage after appointment.

(4) The Chairperson and every Member shall, before entering upon his office, make and subscribe to an oath of office and of secrecy in such form and in such manner and before such authority as may be prescribed.

(5) Notwithstanding anything contained in sub-section (1), the Chairperson or any Member may—

(a) relinquish his office by giving in writing to the President notice of not less than three months; or

(b) be removed from his office in accordance with the provisions of section 7.

(6) The Chairperson or any Member ceasing to hold office as such shall—

(a) be ineligible for further employment under the Central Government or any State Government for a period of two years from the date he ceases to hold such office;

(b) not accept any commercial employment for a period of two years from the date he ceases to hold such office; and

(c) not represent any person before the Central Commission or a State Commission in any manner.

Explanation.—For the purposes of this sub-section,—

(i) "employment under the Central Government or the State Government" includes employment under any local or other authority within the territory of India or under the control of the Central Government or State Government or under any corporation or society owned or controlled by the Government.

(ii) "commercial employment" means employment in any capacity under, or agency of, a person engaged in trading, commercial, industrial or financial business in the electricity industry and includes also a director of a company or partner of a firm and it also includes setting up practice either independently or as partner of a firm or as an adviser or a consultant.

7. Removal of Members.—(1) Subject to the provisions of sub-section (3), any Member of the Central Commission shall only be removed from his office by order of the President on the ground of proved misbehaviour after the Supreme Court, on reference being made to it by the President, has, on an inquiry, held in accordance with the procedure prescribed in this behalf by the Supreme Court, reported that the Member, ought on any such ground to be removed.

(2) The President may suspend any Member of the Central Commission in respect of whom a reference has been made to the Supreme Court under sub-section (1) until the President has passed an order on receipt of the report of the Supreme Court.

(3) Notwithstanding anything contained in sub-section (1), the President may by order remove from office the Chairperson or any other Member, if the Chairperson or such other Member, as the case may be,—

(a) has been adjudged an insolvent; or

(b) has been convicted of an offence which, in the opinion of the Central Government, involves moral turpitude; or

(c) has become physically or mentally incapable of acting as a Member; or

(d) has acquired such financial or other interest as is likely to affect prejudicially his functions as a Member; or

(e) has so abused his position as to render his continuance in office prejudicial to the public interest.

(4) Notwithstanding anything contained in sub-section (3), no Member shall be removed from his office on the ground specified in clause (d) or clause (e) of that sub-section unless the Supreme Court, on a reference being made to it in this behalf by the President, has, on an inquiry, held by it in accordance with such procedure as prescribed in this behalf by the Supreme Court, reported that the Member ought on such ground or grounds to be removed.

8. Officers of Central Commission and other staff.—(1) The Central Commission may appoint a Secretary to exercise and perform under the control of the Chairperson such powers and duties as may be specified by regulations made by the Central Commission.

(2) The Central Commission may, with the approval of the Central Government, determine the number, nature and categories of other officers and employees required to assist the Central Commission in the discharge of its functions.

(3) The salaries and allowances payable to, and other conditions of service of, the Secretary, officers and other employees shall be such as may be determined with the approval of the Central Government, by regulations.

(4) The Central Commission may appoint consultants required to assist the Central Commission in the discharge of its functions on the terms and conditions as may be determined by regulations made by the Central Commission.

9. Proceedings of Central Commission.—(1) The Central Commission shall meet at the head office or any of its offices at such time as the Chairperson may direct, and shall observe such rules of procedure in regard to the transaction of business at its meetings (including the quorum at its meetings) as may be determined by regulations.

(2) The Chairperson or, if he is unable to attend a meeting of the Central Commission, any other Member nominated by the Chairperson in this behalf and, in the absence of such nomination or where there is no Chairperson, any Member chosen by the Members present from among themselves, shall preside at the meeting.

(3) All questions which come up before any meeting of the Central Commission shall be decided by a majority of votes of the Members (including the Member, *ex officio*) present and voting, and in the event of an equality of votes, the Chairperson or the person presiding shall have the right to exercise a second or casting vote.

(4) Save as otherwise provided in sub-section (3), every Member shall have one vote.

(5) All orders and decisions of the Central Commission shall be authenticated by the Secretary or any other officer of the Central Commission duly authorised by the Chairperson in this behalf.

10. Vacancies, etc. not to invalidate proceedings of Central Commission.—No act or proceedings of the Central Commission shall be questioned or shall be invalidated merely on the ground of existence of any vacancy or defect in the constitution of the Central Commission.

11. Expenses of Central Commission to be charged upon Consolidated Fund of India.—The expenses of the Central Commission including all salaries and allowances payable to, or in respect of, the Chairperson and the Member of the Central Commission shall be charged upto the Consolidated Fund of India.

12. Powers of Central Commission.—The Central Commission, shall, for the purposes of any inquiry or proceedings under this Act have the powers as are vested in a civil court under the Code of Civil Procedure, 1908 (5 of 1908), in respect of the following matters, namely:—

(a) the summoning and enforcing the attendance of any witness and examining him on oath;

(b) the discovery and production of any document or other material object producible as evidence;

(c) the reception of evidence on affidavits;

(d) the requisition of any public record;

(e) the issue of commission for examination of witnesses;

(f) review its decisions, directions and orders;

(g) any other matter which may be prescribed.

CHAPTER III

POWERS AND FUNCTIONS OF THE CENTRAL COMMISSION

13. Functions of Central Commission.—The Central Commission shall discharge all or any of the following functions, namely:—

(a) to regulate the tariff of generating companies owned or controlled by the Central Government;

(b) to regulate the tariff of generating companies, other than those owned or controlled by the Central Government specified in clause (a), if such generating companies enter into or otherwise have a composite scheme for generation and sale of electricity in more than one State;

(c) to regulate the inter-State transmission of energy including tariff of the transmission utilities;

(d) to promote competition, efficiency and economy in the activities of the electricity industry;

(e) to aid and advise the Central Government in the formulation of tariff policy which shall be—

(i) fair to the consumers; and

(ii) facilitate mobilisation of adequate resources for the power sector;

(f) to associate with the environmental regulatory agencies to develop appropriate policies and procedures for environmental regulation of the power sector;

(g) to frame guidelines in matters relating to electricity tariff;

(h) to arbitrate or adjudicate upon disputes involving generating companies or transmission utilities in regard to matters connected with clauses (a) to (c) above;

(i) to aid and advise the Central Government on any other matter referred to the Central Commission by that Government.

14. Central Advisory Committee.—(1) The Central Commission may, by notification, establish with effect from such date as it may specify in such notification, a Committee to be known as the Central Advisory Committee.

(2) The Central Advisory Committee shall consist of not more than thirty-one members to represent the interests of commerce, industry, transport, agriculture, labour, consumers, non-governmental organisations and academic and research bodies in the energy sector.

(3) The Chairperson and Members of the Central Commission shall be the *ex officio* Chairperson and *ex officio* Members of the Central Advisory Committee.

15. Objects of Central Advisory Committee.—The objects of the Central Advisory Committee shall be to advise the Central Commission on,—

(i) major questions of policy;

(ii) matters relating to quality, continuity and extent of service provided by the licensees;

(iii) compliance by the licensees with the conditions and requirements of their licence;

(iv) protection of consumer interest; and

(v) energy supply and overall standards of performance by utilities.

16. Appeal to High Court in certain cases.—(1) Any person aggrieved by any decision or order of the Central Commission may file an appeal to the High Court.

(2) Except as aforesaid, no appeal or revision shall lie to any court from any decision or order of the Central Commission.

(3) Every appeal under this section shall be preferred within sixty days from the date of communication of the decision or order of the Central Commission to the person aggrieved by the said decision or order:

Provided that the High Court may entertain an appeal after the expiry of the said period of sixty days if it is satisfied that the aggrieved person had sufficient cause for not preferring the appeal within the period of sixty days.

CHAPTER IV

STATE ELECTRICITY REGULATORY COMMISSION

17. Establishment and incorporation of State Commission.—(1) The State Government may, if it deems fit, by notification in the Official Gazette, establish, for the purposes of this Act, a Commission for the State to be known as the (name of the State) Electricity Regulatory Commission.

(2) The State Commission shall be a body corporate by the name aforesaid, having perpetual succession and a common seal, with

power to acquire, hold and dispose of property, both movable and immovable, and to contract and shall, by the said name, sue or be sued.

(3) The head office of the State Commission shall be at such place as the State Government may, by notification in the Official Gazette, specify.

(4) The State Commission shall consist of not more than three Members including the Chairperson.

(5) The Chairperson and the Members of the State Commission shall be persons of ability, integrity and standing who have adequate knowledge of, and have shown capacity in dealing with problems relating to engineering, finance, commerce, economics, law or management.

(6) The Chairperson and the Members of the State Commission shall be appointed by the State Government on the recommendation of a Selection Committee referred to in section 18.

(7) Notwithstanding anything contained in sub-section (5) or sub-section (6), the State Government may appoint any person as the Chairperson from amongst persons who is or has been a Judge of a High Court:

Provided that no appointment under this sub-section shall be made except after consultation with the Chief Justice of that High Court.

(8) The Chairperson shall be the Chief Executive of the State Commission.

(9) The Chairperson or any other Member of the State Commission shall not hold any other office.

18. Constitution of Selection Committee by State Government.—(1) The State Government shall, for the purposes of selecting the Members of the State Electricity Commission, constitute a Selection Committee consisting of—

(a) a person who has been a Judge of the High Court —Chairperson;

(b) the Chief Secretary of the concerned State —Member;

(c) the Chairperson or a Member of the Central Electricity Authority —Member:

Provided that nothing contained in this clause shall apply to the appointment of a person as the Chairperson who is or has been a Judge of the High Court.

(2) No appointment of a Member shall be invalid merely by reason of any vacancy in the Selection Committee.

(3) The State Government shall, within one month from the date of occurrence of any vacancy by reason of death, resignation or removal and six months before the superannuation or end of tenure of any Chairperson or a Member, make a reference to the Selection Committee for filling up of the vacancy.

(4) The Selection Committee shall finalise the selection of the Member, within one month from the date on which the reference is made to it.

(5) The Selection Committee shall recommend a panel of two names for every vacancy referred to it.

(6) Before recommending any person for appointment as a Member, the Selection Committee shall satisfy itself that such person does not have any financial or other interest which is likely to affect prejudicially his functions as a Member.

19. Term of office, salary and allowances and other conditions of service of Chairperson and Members.—(1) The Chairperson or other Member shall hold office as such for a term of five years from the date on which he enters upon his office, but shall not be eligible for reappointment:

Provided that no Chairperson or other Member shall hold office as such after he has attained,—

(a) in the case of the Chairperson, the age of sixty-five years; and

(b) in the case of any other Member, the age of sixty-two years.

(2) The salary and allowances payable to, and the other terms and conditions of service of, the Members of the State Commission shall be such as may be prescribed by the State Government.

(3) The salary, allowances and other conditions of service of the Members, shall not be varied to their disadvantage after appointment.

(4) Every Member of the State Commission shall, before entering upon his office, make and subscribe to an oath of office and of secrecy in such form and in such manner and before such authority as may be prescribed.

(5) Notwithstanding anything contained in sub-section (1) or sub-section (2), a Member may—

(a) relinquish his office by giving in writing to the Governor notice of not less than three months; or

(b) be removed from his office in accordance with the provisions of section 20.

(6) Any Member ceasing to hold office as such shall—

(a) be ineligible for further employment under the Central Government or any State Government for a period of two years from the date he ceases to hold such office;

(b) not accept any commercial employment for a period of two years from the date he ceases to hold such office; and

(c) not represent any person before the Central Commission or State Commission in any manner.

Explanation.—For the purposes of this sub-section,—

(i) "employment under the Central Government or under the State Government" includes employment under any local or other authority within the territory of India or under the control of the Central Government or a State Government or under any corporation or society owned or controlled by the Government.

(ii) "commercial employment" means employment in any capacity under, or agency of, a person engaged in trading, commercial, industrial or financial business in the electricity industry and includes also a director of a company or partner of a firm and it also includes setting up practice either independently or as partner of a firm or as an adviser or a consultant.

20. Removal of Members.—(1) Subject to the provisions of sub-section (3), any Member of the State Commission shall only be removed from his office by order of the Governor on the ground of proved misbehaviour after the High Court, on reference being made to it by the Governor, has, on inquiry, held in accordance with the procedure prescribed in that behalf by the High Court, reported that the Member, ought on any such ground to be removed.

(2) The Governor may suspend any member of the State Commission in respect of whom a reference has been made to the High Court under sub-section (1) until the Governor has passed orders on the receipt of the report of the High Court on such reference.

(3) Notwithstanding anything contained in sub-section (1), the Governor may by order remove from office, the Member if he—

(a) has been adjudged an insolvent; or

(b) has been convicted of an offence which, in the opinion of the State Government, involves moral turpitude; or

(c) has become physically or mentally incapable of acting as a Member; or

(d) has acquired such financial or other interest as is likely to affect prejudicially his functions as a Member; or

(e) has so abused his position as to render his continuance in office prejudicial to the public interest.

(4) Notwithstanding anything contained in sub-section (3), no Member shall be removed from his office on the ground specified in clause (d) or clause (e) of that sub-section unless the High Court on a reference being made to it in this behalf by the Governor, has, on an inquiry, held by it in accordance with such procedure as prescribed in this behalf by the High Court, reported that the Member ought on such ground or grounds to be removed.

21. Officers of State Commission and other staff.—(1) The State Commission may appoint a Secretary to exercise and perform under the control of the Chairperson such duties and powers as may be specified by regulations made by the State Commission.

(2) The State Commission may, with the approval of the State Government, determine the number, nature and categories of other officers and employees required to assist the State Commission in the discharge of its functions.

(3) The salaries and allowances payable to, and other conditions of service of, the Secretary, officers and other employees shall be such as may be determined by regulations with the approval of the State Government.

(4) The State Commission may appoint consultants required to assist the State Commission in the discharge of its functions on the terms and conditions as may be determined by regulations by the State Commission.

[1][*CHAPTER IVA*

JOINT ELECTRICITY REGULATORY COMMISSION

21A. Constitution of Joint State Commission.—(1) Notwithstanding anything contained in this Act, an agreement may be entered into—

(a) by two or more State Governments,

(b) by the Central Government (in respect of one or more Union territories) and one or more State Governments,

to be in force for such period and to be subject to renewal for such further period, if any, as may be specified in the agreement to provide for the constitution of a Joint Electricity Regulatory Commission,—

(i) in a case referred to in clause (a), for all the participating States; and

1. Ins. by Act 21 of 2001, sec. 3.

(ii) in a case referred in clause (b), for the participating Union territory or Union territories and the State or States.

(2) The Joint Electricity Regulatory Commission shall consist of one Member from each of the participating States and Union territories and the Chairperson shall be appointed from amongst the Members by consensus, failing which by rotation.

(3) An agreement under sub-section (l) shall contain provisions as to the name of the Joint Electricity Regulatory Commission, the manner in which the participating States may be associated in the selection of the Chairperson and Members of the Joint Electricity Regulatory Commission, manner of appointment of Chairperson and Members by consensus, failing which by rotation, places at which the Commission shall sit, apportionment among the participating States of the expenditure in connection with the Joint Electricity Regulatory Commission and may also contain such other supplemental, incidental and consequential provisions not inconsistent with this Act as may be deemed necessary or expedient for giving effect to the agreement.

21B. Special provision relating to giving of directions.—Notwithstanding anything contained in this Act, where any Joint Electricity Regulatory Commission is constituted under section 21A,—

(a) the Government of the State for which the Joint Electricity Regulatory Commission is constituted shall be competent to give any direction under this Act only in cases where such direction relates to a matter within the exclusive territorial jurisdiction of the State;

(b) the Central Government alone shall be competent to give any direction under this Act where such direction relates to a matter within the territorial jurisdiction of two or more States or pertains to a Union territory if the participating Governments fail to reach an agreement or the participating States or majority of them request the Central Government to issue such directions.]

CHAPTER V

POWERS AND FUNCTIONS OF STATE COMMISSION

22. Functions of State Commission.—(1) Subject to the provisions of Chapter III, the State Commission shall discharge the following functions, namely:—

(a) to determine the tariff for electricity, wholesale, bulk, grid or retail, as the case may be, in the manner provided in section 29;

(b) to determine the tariff payable for the use of the transmission facilities in the manner provided in section 29;

(c) to regulate power purchase and procurement process of the transmission utilities and distribution utilities including the price at which the power shall be procured from the generating companies, generating stations or from other sources for transmission, sale, distribution and supply in the State;

(d) to promote competition, efficiency and economy in the activities of the electricity industry to achieve the objects and purposes of this Act.

(2) Subject to the provisions of Chapter III and without prejudice to the provisions of sub-section (1), the State Government may, by notification in the Official Gazette, confer any of the following functions upon the State Commission, namely:—

(a) to regulate the investment approval for generation, transmission, distribution and supply of electricity to the entities operating within the State;

(b) to aid and advise the State Government, in matters concerning electricity generation, transmission, distribution and supply in the State;

(c) to regulate the operation of the power system within the State;

(d) to issue licences for transmission, bulk supply, distribution or supply of electricity and determine the conditions to be included in the licences;

(e) to regulate the working of the licensees and other persons authorised or permitted to engage in the electricity industry in the State and to promote their working in an efficient, economical and equitable manner;

(f) to require licensees to formulate perspective plans and schemes in co-ordination with others for the promotion of generation, transmission, distribution, supply and utilisation of electricity, quality of service and to devise proper power purchase and procurement process;

(g) to set standards for the electricity industry in the State including standards relating to quality, continuity and reliability of service;

(h) to promote competitiveness and make avenues for participation of private sector in the electricity industry in the State, and also to ensure a fair deal to the customers;

(i) to lay down and enforce safety standards;

(j) to aid and advise the State Government in the formulation of the State power policy;

(k) to collect and record information concerning the generation, transmission, distribution and utilisation of electricity;

(l) to collect and publish data and forecasts on the demand for, and use of, electricity in the State and to require the licences to collect and publish such data;

(m) to regulate the assets, properties and interest in properties concerning or related to the electricity industry in the State including the conditions governing entry into, and exit from, the electricity industry in the such manner as to safeguard the public interest;

(n) to adjudicate upon the disputes and differences between the licensees and utilities and to refer the matter for arbitration;

(o) to co-ordinate with environmental regulatory agencies and to evolve policies and procedures for appropriate environmental regulation of the electricity sector and utilities in the State; and

(p) to aid and advise the State Government on any other matter referred to the State Commission by such Government.

(3) The State Commission shall exercise its functions in conformity with the national power plan.

23. Application of certain provisions relating to Central Commission to State Commissions.—The provisions of sections 9, 10 and 12 shall apply to a State Commission and shall have effect, subject to the following modifications, namely:—

(a) references to "Central Commission" shall be construed as references to "State Commission";

(b) in sub-section (3) of section 9, the brackets and words "(including the Member *ex officio*)" shall be omitted.

24. State Advisory Committee.—(1) The State Commission may, by notification, establish with effect from such date as it may specify in such notification, a Committee to be known as the State Advisory Committee.

(2) The State Advisory Committee shall consist of not more than twenty-one members to represent the interests of commerce, industry, transport, agriculture, labour, consumers, non-governmental organisations and academic and research bodies in the energy sector.

(3) The Chairperson and the Members of the State Commission shall be *ex officio* Chairperson and *ex officio* Members of the State Advisory Committee.

25. Objects of State Advisory Committee.—The objects of the State Advisory Committee shall be to advise the Commission on—

(i) major questions of policy;

(ii) matters relating to quality, continuity and extent of service provided by the licensees;

(iii) compliance by licensees with the conditions and requirements of their licence;

(iv) protection of consumer interest; and

(v) energy supply and overall standards of performance by utilities.

26. Representation before State Commission.—The State Commission shall authorise any person as it deems fit to represent the interest of the consumers in all the proceedings before it.

27. Appeal to High Court in certain cases.—(1) Any person aggrieved by any decision or order of the State Commission may file an appeal to the High Court.

(2) Except as aforesaid, no appeal or revision shall lie to any court from any decision or order of the State Commission.

(3) Every appeal under this section shall be preferred within sixty days from the date of communication of the decision or order of the State Commission to the person aggrieved by the said decision or order:

Provided that the High Court may entertain an appeal after the expiry of the said period of sixty days if it is satisfied that the aggrieved person had sufficient cause for not preferring the appeal within the said period of sixty days.

CHAPTER VI

ENERGY TARIFF

28. Determination of tariff by Central Commission.—The Central Commission shall determine by regulations the terms and conditions for fixation of tariff under clauses (a), (b) and (c) of section 13, and in doing so, shall be guided by the following, namely:—

(a) the generating companies and transmission entities shall adopt such principles in order that they may earn an adequate return and at the same time that they do not exploit their dominant position in the generation, sale of electricity or in the inter-State transmission of electricity;

(b) the factors which would encourage efficiency, economical use of the resources, good performance, optimum investments and other matters which the Central Commission considers appropriate;

(c) national power plans formulated by the Central Government; and

(d) such financial principles and their applications contained in Schedule VI to the Electricity (Supply) Act, 1948 (54 of 1948) as the Commission considers appropriate.

29. Determination of tariff by State Commission.—(1) Notwithstanding anything contained in any other law, the tariff for intra-State transmission of electricity and the tariff for supply of electricity, grid, wholesale, bulk or retail, as the case may be, in a State (hereinafter referred to as the tariff), shall be subject to the provisions of this Act and the tariff shall be determined by the State Commission of that State in accordance with the provisions of this Act:

[1][Provided that in States or Union territories where Joint Electricity Regulatory Commission has been constituted, such Joint Electricity Regulatory Commission shall determine different tariff for each of the participating States or Union territories.]

(2) The State Commission shall determine by regulations the terms and conditions for the fixation to tariff, and in doing so, shall be guided by the following, namely:—

(a) the principles and their applications provided in sections 46, 57 and 57A of the Electricity (Supply) Act, 1948 (54 of 1948) and the Sixth Schedule thereto;

(b) in the case of the Board or its successor entities, the principles under section 59 of the Electricity (Supply) Act, 1948 (54 of 1948);

(c) that the tariff progressively reflects the cost of supply of electricity at an adequate and improving level of efficiency;

(d) the factors which would encourage efficiency, economical use of the resources, good performance, optimum investments, and other matters which the State Commission considers appropriate for the purpose of this Act;

(e) the interests of the consumers are safeguarded and at the same time, the consumers pay for the use of electricity in a reasonable manner based on the average cost of supply of energy;

(f) the electricity generation, transmission, distribution and supply are conducted on commercial principles;

1. Ins. by Act 21 of 2001, sec. 4.

(g) national power plans formulated by the Central Government.

(3) The State Commission, while determining the tariff under this Act, shall not show undue preference to any consumer of electricity, but may differentiate according to the consumer's load factor, power factor, total consumption of energy during any specified period or the time at which the supply is required or the geographical position of any area, the nature of supply and the purpose for which the supply is required.

(4) The holder of each licence and other persons including the Board or its successor body authorised to transmit, sell, distribute or supply electricity wholesale, bulk or retail, in the State shall observe the methodologies and procedures specified by the State Commission from time to time in calculating the expected revenue from charges which he is permitted to recover and in determining tariffs to collect those revenues.

(5) If the State Government requires the grant of any subsidy to any consumer or class of consumers in the tariff determined by the State Commission under this section, the State Government shall pay the amount to compensate the person affected by the grant of subsidy in the manner the State Commission may direct, as a condition for the licence or any other person concerned to implement the subsidy provided for by the State Government.

(6) Notwithstanding anything contained in sections 57A and 57B of the Electricity (Supply) Act, 1948 (54 of 1948) no rating committee shall be constituted after the date of commencement of this Act and the Commission shall secure that the licensees comply with the provisions of their licence regarding the charges for the sale of electricity both wholesale and retail and for connections and use of their assets or systems in accordance with the provisions of this Act.

30. Reasons for deviation by Commissions.—Where the Commissions depart from factors specified in clauses (a) to (d) of section 28 and clauses (a) to (f) of sub-section (2) of section 29, they shall record the reasons for such departure in writing.

CHAPTER VII

ACCOUNTS, AUDIT AND REPORTS

31. Budget of Central Commission.—The Central Commission shall prepare, in such form and at such time in each financial year as may be prescribed, its budget for the next financial year, showing the estimated receipts and expenditure of the Central Commission and forward the same to the Central Government.

32. Accounts and audit of Central Commission.—(1) The Central Commission shall maintain proper accounts and other relevant records and prepare an annual statement of accounts in such form as may be prescribed by the Central Government in consultation with the Comptroller and Auditor-General of India.

(2) The accounts of the Central Commission shall be audited by the Comptroller and Auditor-General at such intervals as may be specified by him and any expenditure incurred in connection with such audit shall be payable by the Central Commission to the Comptroller and Auditor-General.

(3) The Comptroller and Auditor-General and any person appointed by him in connection with the audit of the accounts of the Central Commission under this Act shall have the same rights and privileges and authority in connection with such audit as the Comptroller and Auditor-General generally has in connection with the audit of Government accounts and, in particular, shall have the right to demand the production of books, accounts, connected vouchers and other documents and papers and to inspect any of the offices of the Central Commission.

(4) The accounts of the Central Commission, as certified by the Comptroller and Auditor-General or any other person appointed by him in this behalf, together with the audit report thereon shall be forwarded annually to the Central Government by the Central Commission and the Central Government shall cause the audit report to be laid, as soon as may be after it is received, before each House of Parliament.

33. Budget of State Commission.—The State Commissions shall prepare, in such form and at such time in each financial year as may be prescribed, its budget for the next financial year, showing the estimated receipts and expenditure of the State Commission and forward the same to the State Government.

34. Accounts and audit of State Commission.—(1) The State Commission shall maintain proper accounts and other relevant records and prepare and annual statement of accounts in such form as may be prescribed by the State Government in consultation with the Comptroller and Auditor-General of India.

(2) The accounts of the State Commission shall be audited by the Comptroller and Auditor-General at such intervals as may be specified by him and any expenditure incurred in connection with such audit shall be payable by the State Commission to the Comptroller and Auditor-General.

(3) The Comptroller and Auditor-General and any person appointed by him in connection with the audit of the accounts of the

State Commission under this Act shall have the same rights and privileges and authority in connection with such audit as the Comptroller and Auditor-General generally has in connection with the audit of Government accounts and, in particular, shall have the right to demand the production of books, accounts, connected vouchers and other documents and papers and to inspect any of the offices of the State Commission.

(4) The accounts of the State Commission, as certified by the Comptroller and Auditor-General or any other person appointed by him in this behalf, together with the audit report thereon shall be forwarded annually to the State Government by the State Commission and the State Government shall cause the audit report to be laid, as soon as may be after it is received, before the State Legislature.

35. Annual report of Central Commission.—(1) The Central Commission shall prepare once every year, in such form and at such time as may be prescribed, an annual report giving a summary of its activities during the previous year and copies of the report shall be forwarded to the Central Government.

(2) A copy of the report received under sub-section (1) shall be laid, as soon as may be after it is received, before each House of Parliament.

36. Annual report of State Commission.— (1) The State Commission shall prepare once every year in such form and at such time as may be prescribed, an annual report giving a summary of its activities during the previous year and copies of the report shall be forwarded to the State Government.

(2) A copy of the report received under sub-section (l) shall be laid, as soon as may be after it is received, before the State Legislature.

CHAPTER VIII
MISCELLANEOUS

37. Transparency in Commissions.—The Commissions shall ensure transparency while exercising their powers and discharging their functions.

38. Directions by Central Government.—(1) In the discharge of its functions, the Central Commission shall be guided by such directions in matters of policy involving public interest as the Central Government may give to it in writing.

(2) If any question arises as to whether any such direction relates to a matter of policy involving public interest, the decision of the Central Government thereon shall be final.

39. Directions by State Government.—(1) In the discharge of its functions, the State Commission shall be guided by such directions in matters of policy involving public interest as the State Government may give to it in writing.

(2) If any question arises as to whether any such direction relates to a matter of policy involving public interest, the decision of the State Government thereon shall be final.

40. Members, officers and employees of Central Commission to be public servants.—The Chairperson, Members, officers and other employees of the Commissions shall be deemed, when acting or purporting to act in pursuance of any of the provisions of this Act, to be public servants within the meaning of section 21 of the Indian Penal Code (45 of 1860).

41. Special provision relating to the Orissa Electricity Reform Act, 1995 or Haryana State Electricity Reform Act, 1997.—The provisions of this Act in so far as they relate to the State Commission shall not apply to the Commissions established under the Orissa Electricity Reform Act, 1995 or the Haryana State Electricity Reform Act, 1997.

42. Proceedings before Commission.—All proceedings before the Commission shall be deemed to be judicial proceedings within the meaning of sections 193 and 228 of the Indian Penal Code (45 of 1860) and the Commission shall be deemed to be a civil court for the purposes of sections 345 and 346 of the Code of Criminal Procedure, 1973 (2 of 1974).

43. Protection of action taken in good faith.—No suit, prosecution or other legal proceedings shall lie against the Central or State Government or the Central or State Commission or any officer of Central or State Government or any Members, officer or other employees of the Central or State Commission for anything which is in good faith done or intended to be done under this Act or the rules or regulations made thereunder.

44. Punishment for non-compliance of orders or directions under the Act.—Whoever fails to comply with any order or direction given under this Act, within such time as may be specified in the said order or direction or contravenes, or attempts to contravene or abets the contravention of any of the provisions of this Act or any rules or regulations made thereunder shall be punishable with imprisonment for a term which may extend to three months or with fine, which may extend to rupees one lakh or, with both in respect of each offence and in the case of a continuing failure, with an additional fine which may extend to rupees four thousand for every day during which the failure continues after conviction of the first such offence.

45. Punishment for non-compliance of directions given by a Commission.—(1) In case any complaint is filed before the Commission by any person or if the Commission is satisfied that any person has contravened any directions issued by the Commission under this Act, rules or regulations made thereunder, the Commission may after giving such person an opportunity of being heard in the matter, by order in writing, direct that, without prejudice to any other penalty to which he may be liable under this Act, such person shall pay, by way of penalty, which shall not exceed rupees one lakh for each contravention and in case of a continuing failure with an additional penalty which may extend to rupees six thousand for every day during which the failure continues after contravention of the first such direction.

(2) Any amount payable under this section, if not paid, may be recovered as if it were an arrear of land revenue.

46. Power of seizure.— The Commission or any other officer, not below the rank of a Gazetted Officer, specially authorised in this behalf by the Commission may enter any building or place where the Commission has reasons to believe that any document relating to the subject matter of the inquiry may be found, and may seize any such document or take extracts or copies therefrom subject to the provisions of section 100 of the Code of Criminal Procedure 1973 (2 of 1974), in so far as it may be applicable.

47. Offences by companies.—(1) Where an offence under this Act has been committed by a company, every person who at the time, the offence was committed was in charge of, and was responsible to the company for the conduct of the business of the company, as well as the company, shall be deemed to be guilty of the offence and shall be liable to be proceeded against and punished accordingly:

Provided that nothing contained in this sub-section shall render any such person liable to any punishment provided in this Act if he proves that the offence was committed without his knowledge or that he has exercised all due diligence to prevent the commission of such offence.

(2) Nothwithstanding anything contained in sub-section (1), where an offence under this Act has been committed by a company and it is proved that the offence has been committed with the consent or connivance of, or is attributable to any neglect on the part of any director, manager, secretary or other officer of the company, such director, manager, secretary or other officer shall also be deemed to be guilty of the offence and shall be liable to be proceeded against and punished accordingly.

Explanation.—For the purposes of this section,—

(a) "company" means any body corporate and includes a firm or other association of individuals; and

(b) "director", in relation to a firm, means a partner in the firm.

48. Cognizance of offences.—No court shall take cognizance of an offence punishable under this Act except upon a complaint, in writing, made by the Commission or by any other officer duly authorised by the Commission for this purpose.

49. Inconsistency in laws.—Nothing contained in this Act or any rule or regulation made thereunder or any instrument having effect by virtue of this Act, rule or regulation shall have effect in so far as it is inconsistent with any other provisions of the Consumer Protection Act, 1986 (68 of 1986) or the Atomic Energy Act, 1962 (33 of 1962).

50. Delegation.—The Central or the State Commission may, by general or special order in writing, delegate to any Members, officer of the Central or the State Commission or any other person subject to such conditions, if any, as may be specified in the order, such of its powers and functions under this Act (except the power to settle disputes under Chapters III and V and the power to make regulations under section 55 or section 58) as it may deem necessary.

51. Amendment of Act 54 of 1948.—With effect from such date as the Central Government may, by notification, in the Official Gazette appoint, sub-section (2) of section 43A of the Electricity (Supply) Act, 1948 shall be omitted:

Provided that different dates may be appointed for different States.

52. Overriding effect.—Save as otherwise provided in section 49, the provisions of this Act shall have effect notwithstanding anything inconsistent therewith contained in any enactment other than this Act.

53. Power to give directions.—The Central Government may give directions to a State Government as to the carrying out into execution of this Act in the State.

54. Power of Central Government to make rules.—(1) The Central Government may, by notification in the Official Gazette, make rules for carrying out the purposes of this Act.

(2) In particular and without prejudice to the generality of the foregoing power, such rules may provide for all or any of the following matters, namely:—

(a) the salary and allowances payable to and the other conditions of service of the Chairperson and Members under sub-section (2) of section 6;

(b) the form and the manner in which and the authority before whom oath of office and secrecy should be subscribed under sub-section (4) of section 6;

(c) the form in which and the time at which, the Central Commission shall prepare its budget under section 31;

(d) the form in which annual statement of accounts to be prepared by the Central Commission under sub-section (1) of section 32;

(e) the form and the time within which annual report should be filed under sub-section (1) of section 35;

(f) any other matter which is to be, or may be, prescribed, or in respect of which provision is to be made, by rules.

55. Power of Central Commission to make regulations.—(1) The Central Commission may, by notification in the Official Gazette, make regulations consistent with this Act and the rules generally to carry out the purposes of this Act.

(2) In particular and without prejudice to the generality of the foregoing power, such regulations may provide for all or any of the following matters, namely:—

(a) the powers and duties of the Secretary under sub-section (1) of section 8;

(b) the salaries, allowances and other conditions of service of the Secretary, officers and other employees under sub-section (3) of section 8;

(c) the terms and conditions of the consultants appointed under sub-section (4) of section 8;

(d) the rules of procedure to be observed by the Central Commission under sub-section (1) of section 9;

(e) the manner in which charges for energy may be determined under section 28.

56. Rules and regulations to be laid before Parliament.—Every rule made by the Central Government and every regulation made by the Central Commission under this Act shall be laid, as soon as may be after it is made, before each House of Parliament, while it is in session, for a total period of thirty days which may be comprised in one session or in two or more successive sessions, and if, before the expiry of the session immediately following the session or the successive sessions aforesaid, both Houses agree in making any modification in the rule or regulation or both Houses agree that the rule or regulation should not be made, the rule or regulation shall thereafter have effect only in such modified form or be of no effect, as the case may be; so, however, that any such modification or annulment shall be without prejudice to the validity of anything previously done under that rule or regulation.

57. Power of State Government to make rules.—(1) The State Government may, by notification in the Official Gazette, make rules to carry out the provisions of this Act.

(2) In particular and without prejudice to the generality of the foregoing power, such rules may provide for all or any of the following matters, namely:—

(a) the salary, allowances and other conditions of service of the Members under sub-section (2) of section 19;

(b) the form and the manner in which and the authority before whom the oath of office and secrecy should be subscribed under sub-section (4) of section 19;

(c) the form in which and the time at which, the State Commission shall prepare its budget under section 33;

(d) the form in which annual statement of accounts to be prepared by the State Commission under sub-section (1) of section 34;

(e) the form and the time within which annual report shall be furnished under sub-section (1) of section 36;

(f) any other matter which is to be, or may be, prescribed or in respect of which provision is to be made by rules.

58. Power of State Commission to make regulations.—(1) The State Commission may, by notification in the Official Gazette, make regulations consistent with this Act and the rules made thereunder to carry out the purposes of this Act.

(2) In particular and without prejudice to the generality of the foregoing power, such regulations may provide for all or any of the following matters, namely:—

(a) the duties and powers of the Secretary under sub-section (1) of section 21;

(b) the salary, allowances and other conditions of service of the Secretary, officers and other employees under sub-section (3) of section 21;

(c) the terms and conditions of consultants appointed under sub-section (4) of section 21;

(d) the manner in which charges for energy may be determined under sub-section (2) of section 29;

(e) any other matter which is to be, or may be, specified.

59. Rules and regulations to be laid before State Legislature.—Every rule made by the State Government and every regulation made by the State Commission under this Act shall be laid, as soon as may be after it is made, before each House of the State Legislature where it consists of two Houses, or where such Legislature consists of one House, before that House

60. Power to remove difficulties.—(1) If any difficulty arises in giving effect to the provisions of this Act, the Central Government may, by order, published in the Official Gazette, make such provisions not inconsistent with the provisions of this Act as may appear to be necessary for removing the difficulty:

Provided that no order shall be made under this section after the expiry of two years from the date of commencement of this Act.

(2) Every order made under this section shall be laid, as soon as may be after it is made, before each House of Parliament.

61. Repeal and Saving.—(1) The Electricity Regulatory Commissions Ordinance, 1998 (Ord. 14 of 1998) is hereby repealed.

(2) Notwithstanding such repeal, anything done or any action taken under the said Ordinance shall be deemed to have been done or taken under the corresponding provisions of this Act.

SUBJECT INDEX